# RECONSTRUCTION IN NORTH CAROLINA

BY

JOSEPH G. DE ROULHAC HAMILTON

STUDIES IN HISTORY, ECONOMICS AND PUBLIC LAW

EDITED BY THE FACULTY OF POLITICAL SCIENCE
OF COLUMBIA UNIVERSITY

Volume LVIII]                    [Whole Number 141

# RECONSTRUCTION IN NORTH CAROLINA

BY

JOSEPH G. DE ROULHAC HAMILTON

*The Black Heritage Library Collection*

 BOOKS FOR LIBRARIES PRESS
FREEPORT, NEW YORK
1971

First Published 1914
Reprinted 1971

INTERNATIONAL STANDARD BOOK NUMBER:
0-8369-8899-X


LIBRARY OF CONGRESS CATALOG CARD NUMBER:
73-173607


PRINTED IN THE UNITED STATES OF AMERICA
BY
NEW WORLD BOOK MANUFACTURING CO., INC.
HALLANDALE, FLORIDA 33009

To

THE MEMORY OF

DANIEL HEYWARD HAMILTON

1838–1908

THIS VOLUME IS REVERENTLY AND
AFFECTIONATELY DEDICATED

# PREFACE

THE following study was commenced by the author, in 1902, as a doctoral dissertation in Columbia University, and in 1906, for that purpose, the first six chapters were privately printed, but in a somewhat different form from that in which they now appear, the chief changes having been made on account of the discovery of new material relating to the period covered. Since that time, the investigation has been steadily continued in order to cover the entire period until the close of Reconstruction in 1876. During that interval, one chapter has been published in the *Sewanee Review,* and one chapter and part of another in the *South Atlantic Quarterly,* and these are included through the courtesy of the editors of those publications.

The author has sought throughout the work to divest himself of any prejudice in his treatment of a period which, while it closed before his birth, has been the cause of so much later bitterness, prejudice, and sectional misunderstanding. He has held no thesis, but has sought only to present the truth, and, in the main, to relate rather than interpret. In his search for material one great obstacle has been found, namely, the marked disinclination of many of the actors in the period to discuss at all the matters therein involved. This will explain why so much of the material bearing on many disputed questions appears to be derived from one side. One or two Republicans of the period, however, have been of incalculable assistance.

To the many who have aided him in his investigations, the author desires to return his hearty thanks. In particu-

lar, he wishes to mention his indebtedness to Mrs. William
H. Bagley and Mrs. E. E. Moffitt for the use of the correspondence of their father, Governor Jonathan Worth;
to Major William A. Graham and Major John W. Graham for a similar favor in regard to the papers of their
father, Governor William A. Graham, and for much valuable information; to Hon. Josephus Daniels for the use of
his files of the *Sentinel* and for many courtesies; to Captain S. A. Ashe, the late Colonel A. K. McClure, Governor
Thomas J. Jarvis, Hon. Jacob A. Long, Dr. Kemp P.
Battle, the late Hon. Richard H. Battle, the late Hon. C. L.
Harris, and Hon. John Nichols for much valuable material
and many helpful suggestions. To his friends, Professors
James W. Garner and Walter L. Fleming who blazed the
trail which he has followed, he owes a debt not to be expressed in words. To his friend and colleague, Professor
N. W. Walker, who has done him infinite service by a critical reading of the proof, he renders his sincere thanks. To
his wife, who has been of constant and invaluable assistance to him in writing the book, in preparing the manuscript for the printer, and in reading the proof, he makes
his grateful acknowledgments. Above all, the author
wishes to pay a tribute of gratitude and affection to his
friend and inspired teacher, Professor William A. Dunning, of Columbia University, without whose constant guidance, encouragement, and cordial assistance, the book would
never have been written.

Chapel Hill, North Carolina,
    January 25, 1914.

# CONTENTS

PAGE

## CHAPTER V

### MILITARY GOVERNMENT UNDER THE RECONSTRUCTION ACTS

## CHAPTER VI

### THE CONVENTION OF 1868 AND ITS WORK

## CHAPTER VII

### THE FREEDMEN'S BUREAU

## CHAPTER VIII

### THE UNION LEAGUE

## CHAPTER IX

### THE REPUBLICAN RÉGIME

## CHAPTER X

### THE REPUBLICAN RÉGIME (CONTINUED)

# CONTENTS

## CHAPTER XVII

### THE OVERTHROW OF RECONSTRUCTION

# CHAPTER ONE

## SECESSION AND WAR IN NORTH CAROLINA

### I. DISUNION SENTIMENT PRIOR TO 1860

NORTH CAROLINA after November 21, 1789, the day on which it adopted the Constitution of the United States, was, while closely allied by association, blood, and interest with the Southern States, strongly attached to the Union. Stirred as the State was at times by sectional feeling, and acting always in the interest of the slave States when the sectional issue was drawn, the deep love for the Union in all classes of the people prevented any great spread of disunion sentiment until long after most of the Southern States looked upon secession as by no means a remote possibility.

When nullification was proposed in South Carolina it was repudiated utterly in North Carolina. Anti-nullification meetings were held in almost every county in the State, and resolutions passed denouncing nullification and the tariff in the same terms and professing attachment to the Union. In the General Assembly of 1830, Jonathan Worth, the member from Randolph, introduced into the House resolutions declaring that, while the tariff laws were unequal and unjust, the right of nullification was not recognized by that body. They provoked a sharp debate, but were adopted by a large majority.[1] The legislature of 1832, by large majorities in each house, passed resolutions proclaiming the

---

[1] *House Journal*, Dec. 31, 1830.

unalterable attachment of the State to the Federal Union and declaring the theory of nullification subversive of the Constitution and tending to a dissolution of the Union.[1]

The fact that slavery was less profitable here than in the states farther south may have accounted in some measure for the absence of disunion feeling. With North Carolina, as with Virginia and Tennessee, slavery was not of first economic importance. The large slaveholders formed a comparatively small part of its white population. The non-slaveholders, on the other hand, formed a large class to whom, unconscious of it though they were, slavery was a terrible burden. Moreover, by 1860, there were in the State 30,000 free negroes.[2] Until 1835, this last class was endowed with the franchise under the same conditions as the white citizens. The amendment to the constitution which deprived free blacks of the right to vote passed the convention of 1835 by only a small majority,[3] and was sharply criticised in that body and by the people. It was strongly opposed by Judge Gaston, Governor Swain, and other leaders of the convention. They were, however, willing that certain qualifications should be required. But for the excitement caused by the then recent Southampton trouble in Virginia, it is hardly probable that the privileges of the free negroes would have been limited at all at that time.

But the great bond which held North Carolina to the Union was the Whig party. In its ranks were men of all classes, and from its ranks came the leaders of political thought in the State from the time of the foundation of the party. Men of political wisdom, of strength, depth, and patriotism guided the party, and through it, controlled

---

[1] *Resolutions,* 1832, p. 1; *Journals,* Dec. 25, 1832, and Jan. 7, 1833.
[2] *Census of 1860.*
[3] *Journal of the Convention of 1835,* p. 74.

the State. But the tendency of the party was conservative, and conservatism finally lost its hold on the people. In 1850, largely through the influence of William W. Holden, the editor of the *Standard,* the Democratic organ, the Whig party was defeated and a new class of men assumed control—men of apparently equal ability, but of less depth; of equal patriotism, but in a narrower sense; all of high character, but politicians, in the main, instead of statesmen.

The decisive battle was fought on the ever-popular issue of abolition of privilege. The Democrats proposed free or manhood suffrage, and the conservative Whigs, while at heart opposed to the change, dared not show very active opposition. Under the existing constitution, a freehold qualification of fifty acres of land was necessary for voting for state senators. This put power in the hands of the landed class and was consequently opposed by the masses. Through the unpopularity of this provision, David S. Reid was elected governor, on the issue of its abolition. This was the first Democratic victory since 1834.

The credit for the victory may be given largely to Holden. He had much to do with choosing the issue and he directed the campaign. This man, at that time a power in the State and destined to be a prominent figure in its history for the two following decades, was born in Orange county in 1818. His early education was received as assistant in the office of the *Hillsboro Recorder.* From its editor, Dennis Heartt, he derived his politics and was an enthusiastic Whig. In 1837, he went to Raleigh, where he studied law and was admitted to the bar. He also became an associate on the *Star,* a Whig paper edited by Thomas Loring. His ability was soon recognized, and in 1843, through the influence of James B. Shepherd, he was offered the editorship of the *Standard,* a Democratic paper formerly edited by Philo White. He at once accepted, making the first of his numer-

ous political changes of heart. While self-interest undoubtedly led, in great part, to his change of party, all his ideas
were in accord with the doctrines which he now adopted.
His paper speedily became the most ably edited in the State,
and his influence grew accordingly.

He was an intense admirer of Calhoun and endorsed his
theories repeatedly and vehemently. In the decade from
1850 to 1860, Holden was the strongest as well as the ablest
advocate in North Carolina of the right of secession, being
far in advance of his party in the State, and in full sympathy with the secession party in South Carolina.

In 1850, he took advanced ground on the subject, although the occasion for action, in his opinion, had not
arisen.[1] Governor Reid's message to the legislature in January, 1851, contained, also, a decided threat. But the legislature was not in accord with them on this point. The question was discussed as a purely abstract one, and resolutions
extremely conservative in tone were adopted, while the
series presented as a minority report by the committee,
which declared the right existent, were rejected.[2] The question appeared again in the campaign of 1851. Alfred Dock-

---

[1] The following is part of one of his editorials at the time: "We
have heard the idea recently expressed that a State has no right to
secede from the Union—that there is no help from oppression except by
revolution; in other words, that the States are the creatures and de-
pendents of the Federal Government and, of course, subject to its physical coercion. Such an assumption, we humbly submit, is unsupported
by any testimony derived from the Constitution itself or from any
single circumstance attending its foundation or adoption. It is, moreover, at war with all regular ideas of free republican government and
the undoubted independence of the States, as that independence has
been displayed in their separate organizations since 1787. We hold
that as no State could originally have been forced into the Union, none
can be forced in or rather prevented from going out."—*Standard*, Dec.
4, 1850.

[2] *Legislative Docs.*, 1850-1, vol. ii, pp. 246, 261.

ery was a Whig candidate for Congress in a district composed largely of counties on the South Carolina line, and made his campaign on the question of secession, stating as his position that, if South Carolina should secede, he would vote men and money " to whip her back into the Union," and would do the same if his own State were in question.[1] He was elected with a majority of over a thousand votes. His district was usually a strongly contested one, the Whigs and Democrats being about equal in number. Edward Stanly, expressing the same sentiments, was elected in an eastern district in the same year.[2] The *Standard,* although the organ of the Democratic party, was, as thus appears, far in advance of party sentiment, or at least, more outspoken. In this same campaign it said, " It is sufficient for us to say that whenever the Constitution is palpably violated by Congress . . . or whenever that body fails to carry out the plain provisions of that instrument when required to protect Southern rights, the Union is dissolved, and that by a sectional majority." [3]

Much the same sentiments were expressed during the presidential campaign of 1856. Just before the election, a meeting of the Southern governors was called at Raleigh for deliberation as to the course to be pursued in the event of Fremont's election. Only Governor Wise of Virginia and Governor Adams of South Carolina came, and consequently the meeting was unimportant. An informal consultation was held at the Governor's Mansion, and several prominent men of Raleigh were invited to be present, including W. W. Holden, M. A. Bledsoe, and L. O'B. Branch. This may be said to have been the first secession meeting held in the State. But Governor Bragg's position was most conservative and in sharp contrast to that assumed by Gov-

---

[1] *Standard,* July 2, 1851.       [2] *Ibid.,* Aug. 20, 1851.
[3] *Ibid.,* Jan. 15, 1851.

ernor Wise. The outcome of the election prevented any direct result of the meeting.

Holden had been an earnest and faithful worker for his party for many years and had been rewarded by no office of importance. He was intensely ambitious and desired a more definite reward than his influence, although that gave him power even, politically speaking, " to kill and make alive." Feeling that he deserved it, in 1858, he was a candidate before his party for the nomination for governor. In spite of a determined secret opposition to him, he secured a large number of delegates and relied largely upon the uninstructed delegations. When the convention met in Charlotte, one delegate, holding a large number of proxies, although instructed for him, voted against the adoption of the two-thirds rule, and defeated it. This secured the nomination of Judge John W. Ellis, of Rowan. Holden's humble origin, and, to a lesser extent, his agrarian tendencies were responsible for his defeat. He acquiesced in the result, but with ill-concealed bitterness. With justice, he felt wronged, but visited his anger upon his innocent opponent, whom he accused of using "means that would be considered unfair by a New York politician." [1] At this point began a change of sentiment in Holden which divided him from his party. This was hastened by the failure of the legislature at its next session to elect him to the United States Senate.[2]

The State as a whole was comparatively free from discussion of secession during most of the decade, and when the subject was mentioned, it was generally only as an abstract question. But two events were to bring a change. In 1857, Hinton Rowan Helper, a native of North Carolina,

---

[1] *Standard*, Nov. 24, 1860.

[2] Thomas Bragg was elected over David S. Reid and Holden.

published *The Impending Crisis.* Its attacks upon slavery
aroused a storm of denunciation throughout the State and
the whole South. To own a copy of the book amounted
almost to political death and threatened social ostracism.
The other event, it is needless to say, was John Brown's
raid. This stirred the State deeply. Secessionists had now
a forcible argument to prove the designs of the Northern
people, and the secession movement may here be said to
begin. Sympathy with Virginia was expressed in many
ways. Military organizations from every part of the State
tendered their services, but Governor Wise refused all.[1]

In December, the Council of State met and passed resolutions approving the course pursued by Governor Wise, extending sympathy to Virginia, and assuring him of the support of North Carolina in all efforts to maintain the vital
interests of the slaveholding States, which could never be
surrendered without dishonor. President Buchanan was
thanked for his prompt aid. The following resolutions containing a decided threat were also passed:

That the union of the States can only be perpetuated so long
as it continues to be a union of equals.

We are devoted to it and would behold its dissolution with
profound regret; yet, if we cannot hold our slave property,
and at the same time enjoy repose and tranquility in the Union,
we will be constrained, in justice to ourselves and to our posterity, to establish new forms and to establish new guards for
our security and well being; relying for success in so doing
in the righteousness of our cause and on the support of that
Providence who so signally guided and secured our ancestors
in times of danger.

That, while declaring our sincere devotion to the Union
according to the Constitution as it was established by our forefathers, and while we are ready to uphold and maintain it as

[1] *Standard*, Nov. 23, 1859.

a Union of equals, we are not unmindful of the fact that the disturbers of our peace have received and are receiving the active sympathy and the substantial support of large portions of the people of the non-slaveholding States; and that it behooves the people of the non-slaveholding States, if they would restore domestic tranquility and perpetuate the Union, to rouse themselves from the condition of indifference and lethargy which seems to prevail among them, and to take such action and adopt such measures as may be necessary to prevent a continuance of assaults upon the people of the South, and may assure our people that they are still faithful as Confederate Sta'es to the common Union which still unites us.

The governor was advised to encourage the organization of volunteer military companies and to apply to the President for arms, to take measures to prevent the distribution through the mails of incendiary matter from the North, and to require justices of the peace to subject canvassers from the North to a severe scrutiny, and to require bond for good behavior when it was thought necessary.[1]

The press of the State was equally outspoken regarding the possible and even probable consequences of the attack upon a Southern State, which was considered an attack upon the entire South. Even the *Register,* the intensely conservative organ of the Whig party, began to advocate the industrial independence of the South with a view to possible political independence.[2] As usual, the *Standard* was the most extreme. It said, " After Seward's Rochester speech, after the Harper's Ferry outrage and after Helper's book, endorsed as it is by the leaders of Black Republicanism, the people of the South will not submit to Black Republican rule. They will sunder the bonds in 1860, in 1864, in 1868, or in 1872, before they will do it. We mean pre-

---

[1] *Council of State Records,* 1859; *Standard,* Dec. 10, 1859.

[2] Issues of Nov. 30, and Dec. 21, 1859.

cisely what we say, and ninety-nine hundredths of those who may read this article agree with us." [1]

Meetings were held at various places in the State and resolutions passed, all breathing the same spirit of defiance to the North. One of these meetings, held in Chatham County, sent a committee to request Governor Ellis to call a special session of the legislature to place the State in an attitude of full military defence. Governor Ellis declined, however, with the statement that there was no necessity for any such action.[2] Requests for arms for new military organizations kept pouring in and Governor Ellis applied twice to the Secretary of War to furnish them. Secretary Floyd responded that North Carolina already had her quota and, if the ten thousand rifles desired were furnished, it would be an advance of six years, and this he declined to make.[3]

All the winter following, the State was kept in a condition of excitement and unrest by numerous arrests and trials of persons for peddling abolition tracts and books, and for preaching abolitionist sentiments to the negroes. Several were tarred and feathered instead of being delivered into the hands of the law. The most noted trial of an abolitionist was that of the Rev. Daniel Worth, in Guilford County. He was a native of North Carolina, of Quaker origin, who had lived for many years in Indiana and had become a monomaniac on the subject of slavery. He was sentenced to be imprisoned for one year, and appealed to the Supreme Court. While his appeal was pending he escaped to New York and did not return.[4]

---

[1] Issue of Dec. 14, 1859.          [2] *Standard*, Jan. 18, 1860.
[3] *Register*, Jan. 11, 1860.

[4] Hamilton, ed., *The Correspondence of Jonathan Worth*, i, pp. 110, 115. The court was authorized to add a public whipping to this punishment. When asked why as a minister he did not obey the law, he said: "I have no respect for North Carolina laws, for they are enacted by adulterers, drunkards, and gamblers."—*Standard*, Dec. 21, 1859.

In one year secession sentiment had grown more than in all the preceding ones, and a secession party, small but active, had come into existence.

## 2. THE CAMPAIGN OF 1860

The state Democratic convention met in Raleigh in March and unanimously re-nominated Governor Ellis. The platform protested against the alteration of any national compromise and announced that interference with the constitutional rights of the States would not be tolerated. But, on the whole, the sentiment of the delegates, as expressed in the platform and in the speeches in the convention, was conservative and entirely favorable to the Union.[1]

The opposition party had already nominated John Pool on a platform demanding the *ad valorem* taxation of slave property. He was hardly the candidate that would have been expected, as he had voted against *ad valorem* taxation in the preceding legislature; but his personal position was no more surprising than that of his supporters, for a party made up of old Whigs would hardly have been expected to advocate *ad valorem* taxation. The platform laid the blame for all the national troubles on the Democracy, and, with more than usual vigor, declared its doctrines dangerous and its success a menace to the welfare of the nation.[2]

A vigorous campaign opened at once, conducted largely, at first, on internal matters. In the discussion of these the advantage was clearly with Pool, but national questions soon interfered in behalf of Governor Ellis.

When the Democratic national convention met in Charleston, nineteen delegates were present from North Carolina. Prominent among these were W. W. Avery, who was chairman of the committee on resolutions, W. W.

[1] *Standard,* March 14, 1860.
[2] *Register,* Feb. 30, 1860.

Holden, W. S. Ashe, and Bedford Brown. The details of the convention are familiar. When the minority report of the committee on resolutions was substituted for that of the majority, W. S. Ashe addressed the convention, saying, that if the platform was forced upon the South, he would be forced to withdraw. Bedford Brown also spoke, warning the convention that if the second resolution was adopted, the fate of the Democratic party was sealed.[1] W. W. Holden also appeared before the convention, addressing it on the danger of secession.[2] But when the withdrawal of the Southern delegates took place, those from North Carolina refused to go. It is not doubtful that, if they had wavered, the delegations from Virginia, Tennessee, Maryland, and Kentucky would also have withdrawn.[3]

When the balloting began for the presidential nomination, North Carolina voted as a unit thirteen times for R. M. T. Hunter, twelve times for Lane, and six times for D. S. Dickinson. Then, until the balloting ceased, her vote was cast for Lane and Douglas, the latter receiving one vote.[4] The press of the State and the people in general approved the action of the delegates. In only one instance were they criticised for not withdrawing with the other Southern delegations.[5]

Holden returned from Charleston with a changed view of secession. What policy he would pursue, however, seemed doubtful. Still bitter against the Republicans, he announced in the first issue of his paper, after his return,

[1] *Charleston Mercury*, quoted in *Standard*, May 9, 1860.
[2] *Memoirs of W. W. Holden*, p. 13.
[3] *Standard*, May 16, 1860.
[4] *Ibid.*, May 9, 1860. R. P. Dick voted for Douglas.
[5] The *Charlotte Bulletin* claimed that they should have gone with the Cotton States.

that he was " for the Constitution and the Union, and against all who would trample on the one or dissolve the other." [1] But a month later, he again declared that secession should follow the election of a Republican President. [2]

When the Baltimore convention met, all the delegation from North Carolina withdrew except R. P. Dick, W. W. Holden, and J. W. B. Watson. The two last-named refused to vote, but Dick voted for Douglas. For some time Holden was doubtful as to whom he would support, but finally announced that he would favor the Breckinridge ticket, with the understanding that the electors would vote for Douglas, if by doing so they could defeat Lincoln. R. P. Dick, however, called a meeting of those favoring Douglas, and a full electoral ticket was chosen. Douglas was present and addressed the meeting. But the Douglas ticket played no part in the campaign and received less than three thousand votes. The contest was between Breckinridge and Bell and resulted in a victory for the former in spite of the vigorous campaign made by the Whigs. The Democratic state ticket was

---

[1] *Standard*, May 9, 1860.

[2] The editorial is in part as follows: " But it is said that the Supreme Court may be in the future an unsafe tribunal for the South; that the Black Republicans will obtain control of it and turn its decisions against the slaveholding States. That may be so. At present it is certainly a safe tribunal for the South. It may be changed and no doubt will be, if the Black Republicans should obtain possession of the government. But what of that? Must we wait until this change is made? Shall we permit Lincoln to pervert the whole power of the Government, and in addition to turn the Supreme Court against us? We are for meeting the enemy at the threshold—for vanquishing him or being vanquished long before his law, his adjudications against us are made. If the people of the South are true to themselves they will never be troubled by the decisions of Black Republican judges. But if they submit to the inauguration and rule of Black Republicans, they will bind themselves to submit to the decisions of an abolition court."— *Standard*, June 2, 1860.

elected by a majority of over six thousand votes.[1] In the General Assembly the Democrats had a working majority in both houses.

### 3. THE SECESSION MOVEMENT

The result of the election had scarcely been announced when the question of secession became the leading topic of the time. The election of Lincoln was not regarded in North Carolina as a sufficient cause of withdrawal from the Union, but the action of the other Southern States forced a consideration of the matter. During the campaign little had been said on the subject. No public speaker had advocated secession and many had denied the existence of the right.[2] But the secession party was only quiet for a time. A secession meeting was held in Cleveland County early in November, and a largely-attended meeting in Wilmington on November 19 inaugurated a campaign conducted by means of similar meetings.[3] By the first of January secession meetings had been held in more than thirty counties, and this number was more than doubled by the following April. In opposition to these, Union meetings were held in fewer counties, it is true, but in greater number.[4]

The battle commenced when the General Assembly met. All the members seemed conscious of the gravity of the situation and of the importance of the work ahead of them.[5] The elements favorable to secession were well organized,

---

[1] The total vote cast was 112,586.

[2] Letter from Gov. Ellis to Gov. Gist, Oct. 19, 1860.

[3] *Wilmington Journal*, Nov. 20, 1860.

[4] An example of intense Union sentiment was in Rowan County, where nine large Union meetings were held during December and January.

[5] *Memoir of A. S. Merrimon*, p. 61.

and this fact later prevented some of the Union men from voting with them on the question of a convention. The body, as a whole, was able and conservative, but still there was a tendency on the part of some of the Union men to be factious, and some of the secessionists were illiberal.

The governor's message was a clear statement of the conditions which the legislature had to face. He suggested an invitation to the Southern States to hold a conference through delegates, the calling of a convention of the people,[1] and a thorough re-organization of the militia. It was evident from the tone of the message that Governor Ellis had little hope of a peaceful settlement of the sectional differences.

A joint committee on federal relations was appointed and reported early in December, recommending that a convention limited in power should be called. A minority report dissented both in regard to the possibility of a limited convention and the necessity for calling one at that time. Bills providing for calling a convention had already been introduced, but the bill reported by the committee was substituted for them. The debate which now followed was long and heated. Discussion was not confined to the legislature. The question was argued all over the State, and the press entered into the discussion in even a more vigorous way than the legislature. At this time its sentiment was overwhelmingly for the Union.[2] The course of events, however, was having an effect upon it as well as upon the people and the legislature. When a convention was first

[1] Governor Ellis had been in consultation with Thomas Bragg, Thomas L. Clingman, W. W. Avery, R. R. Bridgers, John F. Hoke, and R. O. Burton, the last four members of the legislature which was to meet in a few days. All but Bragg favored a convention. Ellis: *Diary*, Nov. 17, 1860, *et seq.*

[2] At this time only the *Charlotte Bulletin, Goldsboro Rough Notes, Wilmington Journal*, and the Raleigh *State Journal* favored secession.

proposed it seemed very doubtful if one could be called, but, as time passed, the idea grew in favor. Many of the strongest advocates of the Union commenced to support it, trusting that the Union sentiment in the State would keep the secessionists from obtaining control of it.[1] The secession element was increased by the influence of the secession of the various Cotton States and the appearance in Raleigh of representatives from several of them. Jacob Thompson, of Mississippi, S. Hall, of Georgia, and I. W. Garrott and R. H. Smith, of Alabama, were received by the legislature as commissioners from their States. All were natives of North Carolina. The members of Congress from the State also took part in the discussion. The address of the Southern members of Congress was signed by Ruffin and Craige. The two senators and four of the representatives wrote requesting the legislature to call a convention, and it was known that two others favored it.[2]

Another thing added to the excitement and uneasiness of the people. There were at this time four United States army posts in the State—the Fayetteville arsenal and Forts Johnston, Caswell, and Macon. At the request of the mayor and citizens of Fayetteville, who feared an insurrection, and against the advice of the officer in command, troops had been sent there early in November.[3] At each of the other posts an ordnance sergeant was in charge. Early in January a committee from Wilmington visited Governor Ellis and begged him to seize Forts Johnston and Caswell. He refused to entertain the proposition, and on the morn-

---

[1] A letter from Z. B. Vance, dated Jan. 9, 1861, shows this feeling. He felt that better terms could be obtained if the State were in convention.

[2] Senators Bragg and Clingman, Representatives Branch, Craige, Winslow, and Ruffin. Vance and Smith were known to favor it.

[3] *Off. Rec.*, no. 1, pp. 480-4.

ing of the tenth Fort Johnston was captured by citizens of
Wilmington, organized as a committee of safety under
the name of " Cape Fear Minute Men " and under the command of John J. Hedrick. That afternoon, accompanied
by S. D. Thruston, captain of the " Smithville Guards,"
and a number of citizens of Smithville, they captured Fort
Caswell. This latter was a most important fort, as it commanded the mouth of the Cape Fear river. The next day,
Governor Ellis, hearing unofficially of the seizure, telegraphed Warren Winslow in Washington to ascertain if
the administration intended to garrison the forts in North
Carolina.[1] He also sent orders to Thruston to evacuate
the forts at once. The order was complied with and the
two forts were restored to the officers in charge. Governor
Ellis was of the opinion that the seizure had been made by
the militia under orders. Later information showed the
error of this. He at once reported the matter to the President and asked if the forts were to be garrisoned. Secretary Holt replied thanking him for his prompt action, and
declaring that there was, at that time, no intention of placing garrisons in the forts as they were considered entirely
safe in " law-abiding " North Carolina; but that, if a disposition was shown to attack them, they would be protected.[2]

These events all had their effect, and on January 30 both
houses of the General Assembly agreed upon a bill providing for submitting to the people the question of a convention, limited in its powers to Federal relations, and for
the election of delegates at the same time. If called, no
action of the convention was to become valid until ratified
by the people. The bill was most strongly supported by W.

---

[1] *North Carolina Regimental History*, vol. i, p. 26.
[2] *Off. Rec.*, no. 1, pp. 484-5.

W. Avery and V. C. Barringer in the Senate, and Samuel Person in the House, while the opposition was led by Bedford Brown and R. S. Donnell in the Senate and House, respectively. In the Senate, Jonathan Worth, Alfred Dockery, Josiah Turner, L. Q. Sharpe, and David Outlaw contested every step made by the secessionists and gave them infinite trouble. But the movement was gaining a headway which rendered ineffectual all opposition.[1] The legislature, after passing the convention bill, went further. An appropriation of $300,000 was made to purchase arms, and a military commission was chosen to advise the governor on the subject.[2] A new militia law was passed, making all white males between eighteen and forty-five years of age liable to service. A volunteer corps of ten thousand men was provided for, and the governor was authorized to enroll twenty thousand more to serve, in case of invasion, at the pleasure of the commander-in-chief.[3] Commissioners were elected to represent the State near the Confederate Government, and at the Peace Conference in Washington. On the former commission were ex-Governor David L. Swain, president of the State University, M. W. Ransom, and John L. Bridgers, while ex-Chief Justice Thomas Ruffin, ex-Governor David S. Reid, ex-Governor John M. Morehead, D. M. Barringer, and George Davis composed the latter. In both, Union men were in the majority.

[1] Gov. Ellis, in a private letter to I. W. Garrott, of Alabama, said that North Carolina would much sooner join an organized government than secede without one being already formed, but that the State could take no part in its organization. "But," said he, "rely upon it, the Southern Rights men in North Carolina will never desert you. We have submissionists here; but the great heart of the people is right. You may count on us, for we will be with you soon."

[2] D. H. Hill and C. C. Tew, the superintendents of the two military schools in the State, were appointed commissioners. *Laws,* 1860-1, chap. xxvii.

[3] *Laws,* 1860-1, chap. xxiv.

The commissioners to Montgomery attended the sessions of the Confederate Congress, but declined to take any part in their deliberations. The delegation to Washington, soon after the Peace Conference met, came to the conclusion that there was no hope of peace. Barringer, Reid, and Davis voted against the Conference's proposition with the exception of the third and fourth sections. Ruffin and Morehead, while not satisfied, were unwilling to reject anything that might prevent the war on honorable terms, and voted for the entire proposition. This recommended a number of amendments to the Constitution, the substance of which was as follows: By the first, slavery was to be prohibited in the territories north of latitude 36 degrees and 30 minutes. South of that line the institution was to remain as it was at the time, and no law could be passed abridging the right of a citizen to take a slave thither. The status of new States was to be determined by their constitutions. The second provided that no further acquisition of territory should be made without the consent of a majority of the senators from both the free States and the slave States. The third declared that no amendment to the Constitution should be made interfering with slavery in the States, nor should Congress prohibit it in the District of Columbia, nor interfere with the domestic slave trade between slave States, nor tax slaves at a higher rate than land. The slave trade in the District of Columbia was abolished, but Congress was prohibited from assuming any power to prevent slaves from being taken into the District and then brought away. The fourth provided that the Constitution should not be so construed as to prevent any of the States from aiding in the arrest and delivery of fugitive slaves. The fifth prohibited forever the foreign slave trade. The sixth provided that the amendments to the Constitution so proposed should not be abolished or changed without the consent of all the

States. Finally, the seventh provided for payment by the United States for all slaves released by violence from federal officials, or whose re-capture should be prevented by violence. All these amendments were included in one proposed article. It was adopted with nothing like unanimity among the delegates to the conference and was doomed to failure before it ever reached Congress.[1]

Up to the time of the meeting of the Peace Conference there had been great hopes in the State that by it all the vexing questions between the sections would be settled and peace restored.[2] But the hope was all in vain.[3] On their return to North Carolina the commissioners announced that all hope of peace was gone. Judge Ruffin, who had gone to the conference as a violent Union man, made a speech in Hillsboro consisting of only three words, " Fight! Fight! Fight! " Nothing' illustrates more clearly the change of sentiment which was taking place. The same thing is noticeable in the newspapers. With the exception of the *Standard,* all began to advise military preparations. This was defended by all of them as a necessity. One of them said, " The extremists of both sides have left nothing for us but secession." [4] And gradually most of them began to advocate what they had so persistently fought.

[1] The voting in the conference was by States and consequently the vote of the majority of any delegation prevailed for the vote of its State.

[2] Report of S. Hall to Georgia Convention. *Journal,* p. 330. Mr. Hall said that the great obstacle "to the immediate co-operation of North Carolina with the Confederate States is the belief entertained by a large number of citizens that the Peace Conference will compose the dissensions between the sections."

[3] The attitude of many people in the State may be seen in Governor Ellis' statement that he would rather see the Chicago platform in the Constitution than the plan of the conference.

[4] New Bern *Progress,* Jan. 18, 1861.

The vote on the question of a convention and the election of delegates were held February 28. The issue of the campaign had been made " Union or Disunion," and notwithstanding the fact that many of the leaders of the Union party desired a convention as the best means of settlement, and that the act providing for it had only been passed through their support, the call was defeated. The people still hoped for peace and were afraid of a convention. The majority against it was small—651 votes out of a total of 93,995—but a majority of the delegates chosen were Union men. Representatives of three views as to the course to be pursued were found among the delegates. There were 52 " submissionists," as the secessionists called them, 22 " conditional submissionists," and 46 " Southern Rights " men.

The strongest advocate of the Union could not think that this was a final decision of the question. It was only a gain in time, a success for those advocating a " Watch and Wait " policy,[1] and it gave them only a momentary advantage. The secession party had the advantage of being coherent, in marked contrast to their opponents, and were more enthusiastic in their cause. Lincoln's inaugural did not satisfy the people as a whole, nor could they be reached by the new administration. He offered John A. Gilmer a place in his cabinet but the latter refused it. Seward wished a place offered to William A. Graham but did not succeed in influencing Lincoln in the matter.[2] In the east, beginning in Wilmington, a strong and united movement now commenced. " States Rights " meetings were held in various places and delegates chosen to a state meeting to be held in Goldsboro in March. This movement spread to other parts of the State, and when the meeting was held on

---

[1] This was the watchword of the *Standard*

[2] *Diary of Gideon Welles*, ii, p. 390.

the twenty-second about a thousand persons were present, representing twenty-five counties. Weldon N. Edwards, of Warren, was called to the chair. Formal organization of a party resulted, and plans were made for a campaign extending all over the State. Franklin J. Moses, of South Carolina, who had been appointed by his State as a commissioner to the defeated convention, was present and addressed the meeting. Edmund Ruffin, of Virginia, came over from Charleston to attend, and made a vigorous secession speech. Determination and energy marked the whole meeting. After providing for another meeting in Charlotte on May 20, they adjourned, confident of success.[1] Later events rendered the adjourned meeting unnecessary, and the call was withdrawn. A vigorous campaign was carried on for the next three weeks, and apparently with results.

Then the agony of doubt ended. Sumter fell, and the President's call for troops followed. Governor Ellis was notified by the Secretary of War that a call had been made on him for two regiments for immediate service. The governor at once replied:

RALEIGH, April 15.

To the Secretary of War:

Your dispatch is received, and if genuine (which its extraordinary character leads me to doubt), I have to say in reply that I regard a levy of troops for the purpose of subjugating the States of the South, as in violation of the Constitution and a usurpation of power.

I can be no party to this wicked violation of the laws of the country, and to this war upon the liberties of a free people. You can get no troops from North Carolina.

JOHN W. ELLIS,
*Governor of North Carolina.*[2]

---

[1] *Wilmington Journal*, March 27, 1861.

[2] *Executive Correspondence*, Ellis, p. 394.

Two days later he summoned the legislature to meet in extra session. Immediately upon the call for troops he had ordered the seizure of the forts. Fort Macon had already been taken without orders. Those on the Cape Fear were captured by the Wilmington Light Infantry,[1] and the Fayetteville arsenal was occupied, without resistance being made, by Warren Winslow with a force of militia.[2]

L. P. Walker, the Confederate Secretary of War, at once asked Governor Ellis to send a regiment to Virginia and this was promised within a few days.[3] The governor at once called for 30,000 volunteers, and a camp of instruction was established at Raleigh.[4] These acts placed North Carolina in the same category with the other Southern States, and consequently President Lincoln on April 27 declared its ports blockaded.[5]

The Union newspapers had now given up the fight, the *Register* saying, " It is the part of prudence and of common sense to look at things as they are and not as we would wish them to be. We believe that Abraham Lincoln is about to wage a war of coercion against these States. We believe that in this war the remaining slaveholding States will be involved, and we shall be found on the side of the section in which we were born and bred and in which live our kindred, connections and friends. If this makes us secessionists, then let us be so called." [6] The *Standard,* also, acknowledged the necessity for war but was very lukewarm at first. Later, it became exceedingly warlike in tone.[7]

---

[1] *Off. Rec.*, no. 1, pp. 476-8.

[2] *Ibid.*, p. 479.

[3] *Ibid.*, pp. 486-7.

[4] *Governor's message*, extra session of 1861.

[5] McPherson, *History of the Rebellion*, p. 149.

[6] Issue of April 17, 1861.

[7] Until the call for troops, the position of the newspapers of the

The Council of State met on April 23 and passed resolutions approving the action of Governor Ellis in taking
possession of the forts, and ratifying, by their approval, his
reply to Secretary Cameron.  They requested him to call
out troops not to exceed 5,000 to drill and be prepared for
public defence in any emergency.[1]

The General Assembly met on May 1.  The governor's
message gave an account of his actions and advised the calling of a convention with full powers, as the people were
known to have but one opinion as to the course to be pursued.  In less than two hours the House passed, unanimously, a bill calling an unlimited convention.[2]  In the
Senate, the House bill was immediately passed.  Jonathan
Worth, L. Q. Sharpe, and Josiah Turner voted nay.  They
based their opposition on the short time given for a canvass, and the fact that the action of the convention would
not be submitted to the people.[3]  The same day Governor
Ellis issued a proclamation, calling an election for delegates

State on the question of secession was as follows: For secession, Ra-
leigh State Journal, Wilmington Journal, Fayetteville Carolinian, Mur-
freesboro Citizen, Elizabeth City Pioneer, Asheville News, Salisbury
Banner, Charlotte Bulletin, Charlotte Democrat, Goldsboro Tribune,
Goldsboro Rough Notes, Shelby Eagle, Warrenton News, Washington
Times, Tarboro Mercury, Winston Western Sentinel, Wilson Ledger,
Tarboro Southerner, and Hillsboro Plaindealer, all Democratic; the
Wilmington Herald, Albermarle Southron, Charlotte Whig, Milton
Chronicle, Western Carolinian, all Whig, and the New Bern Progress,
Concord Flag, Raleigh Leisure Hour, all independent.  Against seces-
sion, the Raleigh Standard and Raleigh Banner, Democratic, and the
following Whig papers: Raleigh Register, Fayetteville Observer, Salis-
bury Watchman, Greensboro Patriot, Iredell Express, Washington
Dispatch, Kinston Advocate, Hendersonville Times, Salem Press, Ashe
Spectator, Wadesboro Argus, and the Hillsboro Recorder.  After the
call for troops, all were for war.

[1] Records of the Council of State, p. 81.

[2] P. T. Henry voted affirmatively with a protest.

[3] State Journal, May 8, 1861.

to be held May 17, and calling the convention to meet May 20th.

Before the convention bill was passed, the governor was authorized to send troops to Virginia, without limit as to number. The legislature then turned its attention to war preparations. Franklin J. Moses was again present and was given the freedom of the floor.[1] A vote of thanks to Governor Ellis for his promptness in preparing for war was passed, receiving only two negative votes.[2] Acts were passed making it unlawful to administer the oath to support the Constitution of the United States; providing for the manufacture of arms at the Fayetteville arsenal and appropriating $200,000 for the purpose; authorizing the governor to appoint a commissioner near the government of the Confederate States;[3] authorizing the governor to enroll 10,-000 state troops; declaring North Carolina free from liability for the federal debt incurred after March 4, 1861; authorizing the governor to accept 20,000 twelve-months' volunteers and to arm and equip them and to offer a bounty of $10 to each; authorizing the governor to commission with equal rank officers of the army and navy of the United States, who resigned to enter the service of the State; appropriating $5,000,000 for public defence; defining and providing for the punishment of treason against the State; and providing for a stay in the execution of judgments in civil suits.[4]

Before the legislature met, it had been suggested that it should pass a declaration of secession and submit it to the

---

[1] *Journal of the General Assembly*, May 1, 1861.

[2] Josiah Turner and Alfred Dockery in the Senate voted against this resolution.

[3] Thomas L. Clingman was appointed commissioner and visited the Confederate Congress.

[4] These acts are to be found in the *Laws*, First Extra Session, 1861.

people as a constitutional amendment. This, however, was very generally opposed.[1] But in the Senate Josiah Turner introduced a declaration of independence from the United States. It was, of course, an effort to bring the proceedings of the majority into ridicule, and was not considered.

The campaign for the convention was devoid of any particular interest. The issue was no longer " Union or Disunion," nor a discussion as to the right and propriety of secession, but simply should North Carolina go with the North or with the South.[2] On this the result was assured, and not a person in the State advocated anything but separation. The cause of the South was regarded as the cause of North Carolina.[3] Quite a number of the old Union men, not caring to take part in the act of separation, declined to be candidates for the convention, but they advocated a vigorous preparation for war, and war itself, if the existing conditions should continue.

### 4. SECESSION AND WAR

The convention assembled in Raleigh on May 20, a day then generally celebrated in North Carolina as the anniversary of the Mecklenburg Declaration of Independence. The delegates now, regardless of their opinion on the right of secession, were resolved on separation. The only issue was how it should take place.

The body, as assembled, was probably the ablest and most distinguished in the history of the State. The reason for this is simple. The gravity of the situation made the people forget party and elect their most trusted men regard-

---

[1] *Western Democrat*, April 30, 1861.

[2] *Ibid*, April 22, 1861.

[3] This feeling is particularly noticeable in the speeches and letters of men of the type of W. A. Graham, George E. Badger, and Jonathan Worth.

less of differences in political opinion, and so the best men
of both parties were chosen. In many counties a delegate
was chosen from each party. The lights of the old Whig
party, obscured by uninterrupted Democratic success, again
appeared in political position. In fact, the Whigs were in
the majority in the convention. And of the Democrats, the
majority had been opposed to secession before the call for
troops.

Probably the most influential of the leaders in the convention were George E. Badger, Thomas Ruffin, William A.
Graham, and Weldon N. Edwards. Among the other
prominent men were Asa Biggs, David S. Reid, William
Johnston, Warren Winslow, Bedford Brown, W. W. Holden, Kenneth Rayner, R. P. Dick, Burton Craige, George
Howard, and John A. Gilmer.[1]  Five members of the convention, Edwards, Biggs, Rayner, E. T. Brodnax, and W.
F. Leak, had also been delegates in 1835.

---

[1] An idea of the prominence of the group above named can be gained
from the positions they had filled. George E. Badger had been a member of the House of Commons, Superior Court judge, United States
Senator, and Secretary of the Navy. He was nominated for the United
States Supreme Court, but failed of confirmation. Thomas Ruffin had
been member and speaker of the Commons, Superior Court judge,
President of the State Bank, Chief Justice of the Supreme Court, and a
member of the Peace Conference. W. A. Graham had been member and
speaker of the Commons, State Senator, United States Senator, Governor, and Secretary of the Navy. He was the Whig candidate for Vice-
President in 1852. Weldon N. Edwards had been a member of Congress, State Senator, and for many terms Speaker, a member of the
Convention of 1835. Asa Biggs had been a member of the Commons
and Senate, and a member of the convention of 1835, member of Congress, United States Senator, and United States District judge. David S.
Reid had been State Senator, member of Congress, Governor, and United
States Senator. William Johnson was prominent as a railroad president
and business man. He received every vote in Mecklenburg County as
a delegate. Warren Winslow had been speaker of the Senate, Governor *ex officio*, and a member of Congress. Bedford Brown had been
a member of the Commons, Speaker of the Senate, and United States

The convention organized by the election of president. Weldon N. Edwards and William A. Graham were placed in nomination. The election was, in a sense, a test of the strength of the two elements composing the convention, which may be called for convenience the secessionists and the revolutionists. The former won, and Edwards was elected by a vote of 65 to his opponent's 48. As soon as he had taken the chair George E. Badger presented a paper for consideration. It was not read at the time but postponed until complete organization should be effected. After this had been completed the president read a communication from F. J. Moses, commissioner from South Carolina to present her ordinance and to invite the coöperation of North Carolina. He was received by the convention and made a most insolent and patronizing speech, welcoming the prospects which he saw for North Carolina's joining in the cause of the South.[1]

Judge Badger's paper was then read to the convention. It was an elaborate review of the condition of the country and the causes which made separation necessary, and it provided for separation by means of revolution, without any mention of secession in the applied meaning of the word.[2]

Senator. W. W. Holden had been a member of the Commons. Kenneth Rayner had been a member of the convention of 1835, member of the Commons and of the Senate, and member of Congress. R. P. Dick had been United States District Attorney. Burton Craige had been a member of the Commons and of Congress. George Howard had been prominent as an editor and was a Superior Court judge. John A. Gilmer had been State Senator and member of Congress. He was the Whig candidate for Governor in 1854, but was defeated. He declined the Treasury portfolio in President Lincoln's cabinet.

[1] *State Journal*, May 22, 1861.

[2] The following is a summary of the Badger ordinance: The preamble asserts—

1. That Lincoln and Hamlin were chosen by a sectional party, hostile to Southern institutions.

2. That North Carolina, though aggrieved thereby, declined to join

Burton Craige then offered as a substitute an ordinance

the States first seceding, but being ardently attached to the Union, remained therein, hoping that what was threatening might be removed and guarantees for the security of her rights be given, in the meantime exerting her influence for the accomplishment of these ends.

3. While indulging this hope President Lincoln called on the States for troops to invade the seceding States, in order to subject them to military authority; that there was no act of Congress authorizing such call, and that such act, if passed, would be unconstitutional.

4. The call was answered with enthusiasm throughout the non-slaveholding States.

5. It is evident from the tone of the press of those States and the avowal of their public men, that their "government and people intend to wage a cruel war against the seceded States, to destroy utterly the fairest portion of their continent, and to reduce its inhabitants to absolute subjection and abject slavery."

6. President Lincoln, without shadow of rightful authority, has declared the ports of North Carolina as well as all the other Atlantic and Gulf States, under blockade, thus seeking to cut off her trade with all parts of the world.

7. The whole conduct and words of said Lincoln have been false, disingenuous and treacherous.

8. That he is governing by military rule alone, increasing army and navy without authority, and setting aside constitutional and legal restraints.

9. His "unconstitutional, illegal and oppressive acts," his "wicked and diabolical purposes," and his "position of usurper and military dictator" were sustained by the non-slaveholding States.

Therefore this convention, in the name and with the sovereign power of the people of North Carolina declare—

1st. All connection of government between this State and the United States, dissolved and abrogated, and this State to be a free, sovereign, and independent State, owing no subordination, obedience, support or other duty to them, their constitution, or authorities.

2nd. That "this State has full power to levy war, conclude peace, contract alliances, and do all other acts and things which independent States may of right do."

3rd. "Appealing to the Supreme Governor of the world for the justice of our cause, and beseeching Him for His gracious help and blessing, we will to the uttermost of our power, and to the last extremity, maintain, defend, and uphold this declaration."

This summary is taken from Dr. K. P. Battle's monograph, *Legislation of the Convention of 1861.*

which had been prepared by Judah P. Benjamin and which he introduced at the request of Governor Ellis.[1] It was as follows:

An ordinance dissolving the union between the State of North Carolina and the other States united with her under the compact of government entitled "The Constitution of the United States."

*We, the people of the State of North Carolina, in convention assembled, do declare and ordain, and it is hereby declared and ordained,* that the ordinance adopted by the State of North Carolina in the convention of 1789, whereby the Constitution of the United States was ratified and adopted, and also all acts and parts of acts of the General Assembly, ratifying and adopting amendments to the said Constitution, are hereby repealed, rescinded, and abrogated.

*We do further declare and ordain* that the union now subsisting between the State of North Carolina and the other States, under the title of "The United States of America," is hereby dissolved, and that the State of North Carolina is in full possession and exercise of all those rights of sovereignty which belong and appertain to a free and independent State.[2]

An attempt to have the convention sit with closed doors failed. Judge Ruffin then introduced a resolution declaring it the sentiment of the convention that the State should sever its connection with the United States and join the Confederacy, and referring the whole question of the means which should be employed to a committee which should be instructed to consider the matter and report a suitable ordi-

---

[1] The ordinance, which was prepared by Judah P. Benjamin, was brought to Raleigh from Montgomery by James Hines, a North Carolinian, and delivered to Gov. Ellis, who asked Burton Craige, the member from his county, to introduce it.

[2] *Convention Journal*, p. 13.

nance.[1] The minority in the convention, with possibly a very few exceptions, were as thoroughly convinced as the majority that separation was necessary, and under existing circumstances, desirable. But they were not prepared, except as a last resort, to give their assent to the doctrine of secession, the right of which had been utterly denied by many of them. They believed that the time had fully come for revolution, and their contention was that the convention ought to ignore any question of secession and pass an ordinance which would not be a constitutional, but simply a revolutionary act. But the majority of the convention were secessionists now, whatever their belief had been in the past, and they would not hear of the plan, nor would they submit to any delay. Badger's ordinance was stricken out by a vote of 72 to 40. He at once left the hall and went home.[2] Judge Ruffin, still hoping to alter the Craige ordinance, moved to amend it so that it would be a simple declaration of the dissolution of the union existing between North Carolina and the other States. Kenneth Rayner said that it made little difference to him personally what kind of ordinance was adopted, but that he thought something was due the secessionists and South Carolina. This was the opinion of the majority, for the resolution was defeated.[3] The Craige ordinance was then passed receiving the vote of every delegate present, one hundred and fifteen in all. William A. Graham, as he voted, said that in so doing, he waived all further question of the right of secession. Judge Ruffin, for most of his life probably the staunchest believer

[1] *State Journal*, May 22, 1861.

[2] A member of Judge Badger's family relates that after his return home, he was seated at the dinner table when the ringing of the Capitol bell announced secession. Judge Badger raised his hand and said, " The death knell of slavery."

[3] The vote on Judge Ruffin's resolution was 49 yeas to 66 nays.

in and supporter of the Union in the convention, said that if a halter were about his neck he would still vote aye.[1]

The announcement of the vote was received with great applause on the floor and in the galleries, and the bell on the Capitol was the signal for a roar of salutes which followed from the military companies in the Capitol Square and all over Raleigh. When quiet was restored the convention, on motion of W. F. Leak, cheered South Carolina vigorously.[2]

An ordinance was then introduced ratifying the Constitution of the Provisional Government of the Confederate States and signifying North Carolina's willingness to join the Confederacy. An attempt to submit the ordinance to the people for ratification failed, the unanimous vote of the convention being its only ratification. A resolution ratifying the permanent Constitution of the Confederacy was referred to a committee and the convention adjourned for the day. Its action excited the wildest enthusiasm throughout the State. Secession had been an assured fact, but no one had dreamed of its receiving a unanimous vote.[3]

The following day, when Judge Badger returned to the convention, he asked leave to have his name recorded as voting for the secession ordinance, saying, at the same time, that he objected to the wording of the ordinance, and utterly repudiated any belief in the right of secession.[4] That night, in the presence of a large and enthusiastic body of spec-

---

[1] *State Journal*, May 22, 1861.

[2] *Ibid.*, May 22, 1861.

[3] Holden said four years later that he voted for the secession ordinance only because, if he had not, he would have been hung in the Capitol Square by order of Gov. Ellis, or forced to leave the State. Apart from anything else to the contrary, the fact that no demonstration hostile or discourteous to Badger was made, proves the falsity of his belief.

[4] *State Journal*, May 29, 1861.

tators, the enrolled ordinance of secession was signed by one hundred and twenty delegates, the full membership of the convention.  Holden is reported to have held up the pen with which he signed and said that he would hand it down to his children as their proudest heritage.[1]  The first act was completed, the reversal of which was only to be accomplished by four long years of war with its attendant bitterness, sorrow, privation, and misery of every sort. But at the time no thought of this was present.  There was sincere regret at separation from the Union which had been cherished to the last; but rejoicing at freedom from conditions which had long been irksome and martial excitement were dominant, and, casting regret behind, all now turned their attention to preparation for the war.  Regarding this, there seems to have been little doubt in the public mind of the ultimate success of the South, but very few deceived themselves with the belief that the contest would be a campaign simply of one summer.

Copies of the ordinance of secession and the ratifying ordinance were sent to President Davis by the convention, and on May 27 North Carolina was proclaimed a member of the Confederacy.  On June 6, an ordinance was passed, ratifying the permanent Constitution of the Confederate States. This ordinance was not formally ratified until June 19.  The convention was much criticised for its delay in ratification. Under the lead of W. A. Graham, assisted by R. P. Dick and Kenneth Rayner, a strong fight was made against immediate action.  Graham preferred that the State should act alone in her sovereign capacity, and not join any confederacy at that time.  Judge Ruffin and Judge Badger favored immediate ratification.  The discussion at times

---

[1] This has often been denied, but has repeatedly been vouched for by those present.

became somewhat heated, particularly between Graham and Badger. Party spirit too became apparent.[1] An ordinance declaring the right of secession for cause was introduced and debated but never finally acted on.[2] In the meantime the convention had begun the transfer to the Confederacy of the forts and arsenals within the borders of the State.

During the first session the convention passed in all thirty-five ordinances. These were of more or less importance, but it seems that the convention after the first day spent time in discussion far out of proportion to the amount of legislation accomplished. This was in part due to the large number of lawyers and political leaders in the body. Besides the ordinances already mentioned its work included acts defining treason against the State,[3] postponing the next session of the legislature from June 25 to August 15,[4] relieving volunteers from the payment of poll tax,[5] securing to the citizens of the State in the military service of the State or the Confederacy the right to vote,[6] and appropriating the sum of $3,200,000 to meet the demands on the treasury for the next two years.[7]

The convention elected a full delegation to the Provisional Congress of the Confederacy. The "old Union men" held a caucus, presided over by W. A. Graham, and

[1] Speaking of party spirit, Judge Ruffin said, "Let us no longer talk of being secessionists now or Union men now, for we are all secessionists from Northern tyranny and Union men for the Southern Confederacy."

[2] *Journal*, p. 74.

[3] *Ordinances*, p. 7.

[4] *Ibid.*, p. 7. This caused much dissatisfaction, as did a proposition to dissolve the General Assembly.

[5] *Ibid.*, p. 35.

[6] *Ibid.*, pp. 40-1.

[7] *Ibid.*, pp. 42-6.

nominated candidates,[1] but the independent vote decided the election, and the delegates were chosen from both of the old parties.[2] After this the convention adjourned on June 28 to meet the following November, unless sooner called by its president.[3]

In the meantime the State was making every effort in preparation for the war. Volunteering was still going on with no sign of any decrease. It is not the purpose of this study to enter into military history. But a more accurate view of internal conditions can be obtained if it be mentioned that by August, 1862, the State had furnished to the military service of the Confederacy 64,636 volunteers. By November, 1864, 21,608 had been added to this number. Before the end of the war, it furnished also 21,343 conscripts, 9,893 reserves, 3,203 state troops, 3,117 detailed men, and 3,100 serving in regiments from other States, making a total of over 126,000. Besides this, several thousand home guards were in service. This was nearly one-sixth of the Confederate army.[4] Her military population was 115,369. North Carolina also furnished to the Union army 3,146 white and 5,035 colored soldiers. But of the latter 1,781, enlisted in 1864, were credited to several Northern States to fill out their quota for the draft.[5] Of the

[1] Battle, *Legislation of the Convention of 1861*, p. 126.

[2] The delegates were as follows: For the State-at-large, George Davis and W. W. Avery. For the districts, W. N. H. Smith, Thomas Ruffin (of Wayne), Thomas D. McDowell, Abram Venable, John M. Morehead, R. C. Puryear, Burton Craige, and A. T. Davidson. Avery, Ruffin, Craige, Venable, and McDowell were Democrats and original secessionists. The rest of the delegates were Whigs. Davis had favored secession since the close of the Peace Conference.

[3] A committee, consisting of W. A. Graham, Thomas Ruffin, J. W. Osborne, and Asa Biggs, was empowered to summon it in the event of the death of the president.

[4] *North Carolina Regimental History*, vol. v, p. 1.

[5] *Off. Rec.*, no. 126, pp. 116 *et seq.*

higher officers in the military service of the Confederacy, the State had two lieutenant generals,[1] seven major generals,[2] and twenty-six brigadier generals.[3]

Governor Ellis died in July in Virginia where he was trying to recuperate after the severe strain of the preceding months. He was succeeded by Henry T. Clark, speaker of the Senate.

The General Assembly met in August. It spent most of the session arguing against the assumption of power by the convention. An attempt was made to submit to the people the question as to whether the convention should meet again. This, naturally, was unsuccessful. Adjournment came in September, after a session of more than a month.

The early battles of the war produced intense enthusiasm, often out of proportion to their importance. The fight at Bethel, for example, was hailed as a great victory and caused more rejoicing than some of the later successes of infinitely greater importance. But hardships soon began. By the autumn of 1861 prices were rising and speculation in the necessaries of life commencing. And there also

[1] T. H. Holmes and D. H. Hill. General Hill's nomination was never sent to the Senate for confirmation.

[2] W. H. C. Whiting (killed), Robert Ransom, William D. Pender (killed), Robert F. Hoke, S. D. Ramseur (killed), J. F. Gilmer, and Bryan Grimes.

[3] R. C. Gatlin, L. O'B. Branch (killed), J. J. Pettigrew (killed), George B. Anderson (killed), J. G. Martin, T. L. Clingman, Junius Daniel (killed), James H. Lane, John R. Cooke, R. B. Vance, A. M. Scales, M. W. Ransom, L. S. Baker, W. W. Kirkland, R. D. Johnston, James B. Gordon (killed), W. R. Cox (temporary), T. F. Toon (temporary), W. G. Lewis (temporary), Rufus Barringer, John D. Barry (temporary), A. C. Godwin (killed), William McRae, C. Leventhorpe, Gabriel Rains, and W. P. Roberts. Generals Hill, Cooke, and Whiting were not natives of the State. Generals Bragg, Leonidas Polk, Lucius Polk, Wilcox, Zollicoffer, L. A. Armistead, Loring, and McCullough were natives of North Carolina, but were appointed from other States.

appeared a bitter party spirit, which, at this time, above all others, should have been absent. Party feeling, always intense in the State, had never been more so than in the period which now followed.

### 3. WAR POLITICS AND THE PEACE MOVEMENT

Party spirit slept, or more properly, appeared to sleep, only a short time after May 20.[1] Reference has already been made to the caucus held by the " Union men " during the first session of the convention. This was held at Holden's residence, and the *Standard* was the recognized organ of the faction, which was soon to assume a party name. Holden's attacks upon Governor Ellis ceased for a short time after secession, but were soon renewed with increased bitterness. His paper, from being very lukewarm towards the Confederacy, had become, by this time, apparently, a strong supporter of it and was most violent against the North. But in the state administration it found no good. Governor Ellis's military appointments were sharply criticised, and this led to a newspaper war that lasted to the close of actual hostilities, and in fact, during the whole period of Reconstruction, with one short truce. The hatreds aroused at this time materially influenced the history of the State for the next ten years. Bitterness, however, was by no means confined to Holden or those who acted with him. He was hated by the Democrats, who felt that he had deserted them, and distrusted by as many Whigs for the same reason.

The opposition to the war party was quiet at first, but grew steadily. By a combination with the friends of William T. Dortch, the opposition secured his election to the

[1] Jonathan Worth, in a letter to James B. Troy, May 21, 1861, said there was only a feigned alliance between the two parties. Hamilton, ed., *The Correspondence of Jonathan Worth,* i, p. 150.

Confederate Senate. The reason assigned for defeating W. W. Avery, who had been delegate for the State at large to the Provisional Congress, was that the views of Dortch regarding secession had been more moderate.[1] The first open division along party lines was in the presidential election in November, 1861. The *Standard* published an electoral ticket which failed to meet with the approval of the *State Journal,* and the latter at once published an opposition ticket containing, however, five of the names which were on the original ticket.[2] The *Journal's* ticket was successful, and this was regarded by the war party as a vote of confidence. The cleavage was more evident when the convention re-assembled in the winter. Early in the session a resolution was unanimously passed declaring their belief in the justice of the war and in the patriotism and integrity of the state and Confederate administrations. But little else in its proceedings showed unanimity.

Probably the most important question of the session was regarding an ordinance to define and punish sedition, which was introduced by Judge Biggs, and which, among other things,[3] provided for a test oath to be administered to all

---

[1] *Standard*, September 18, 1861.

[2] It is interesting to notice that during the war there was no state political convention. The nearest approach to it was a peace meeting in the Tenth Congressional District in 1864, which nominated George W. Logan for the Confederate Congress. All other nominations were made by or through the newspapers.

[3] The ordinance also declared any of the following offences to be a misdemeanor and, as such, punishable: (a) Attempting to convey information to the enemy. (b) Publishing and deliberately speaking against the public defence. (c) Maliciously and advisedly endeavoring to excite the people to resist the government of the State or of the Confederate States. (d) Persuading the people to return to a dependence on the government of the United States. (e) Knowingly spreading false and dispiriting news. (f) Maliciously or advisedly terrifying and discouraging the people from enlisting into the service of the State

males in the State except the volunteers. The penalty for refusal to take it was exile from the State. Naturally it met with great opposition. This was led in the convention by William A. Graham and R. P. Dick. The former's speech in opposition to it was probably the main cause of its failure. He placed particular stress on the injustice to the Quakers. The latter argued that it would lead to the belief that North Carolina was a nest of traitors, a theory which was disproved by the large number of volunteers that had gone to the front, and that the spirit of the thing was contrary to the principles and ideas of the State.[1] The ordinance was tabled indefinitely by a large vote in December, and an attempt made the following February to consider it without the test oath, was defeated by a vote of 41 to 37.[2] The matter was brought up again at the last session with the same result. The proposed ordinance was never popular in the State, and was regarded with horror by many.[3]

During the session resolutions were introduced, declaring against party spirit, but they were never allowed to come to a vote, as the friends of the administration saw in them a veiled attack upon President Davis, Governor Ellis, and Governor Clark, and succeeded in having them tabled. Many other things were considered by the convention, and, remembering the difficulties experienced in the past in secur-

---

or Confederate States. (g) Stirring up or exciting tumults, disorders, or insurrections in the State. (h) Disposing the people to favor the enemy. (i) Opposing or endeavoring to prevent the measures carried on in support of the freedom and independence of the Confederate States. This summary is taken from Battle, *Legislation of the Convention of 1861.*

[1] *Standard,* Dec. 18, 1861.

[2] The *State Journal* said this was a strict party vote.

[3] Battle, *Legislation of the Convention of 1861,* p. 124. The vote on tabling it was 47 to 43. *Journal,* p. 64.

ing amendment and revision of the constitution, it discussed
and laid plans for quite a number of important constitutional changes. These were never finally adopted by this
convention. Various matters, however, occupied its attention, and a fourth session was held in April, 1862. It adjourned in May, subject to the call of the president, and if
no call was made by November, 1862, this adjournment
was to become *sine die.*

By the time of its last session, the convention had become unpopular with the people generally. It accomplished
little that they felt could not have been done by the General
Assembly, and they were anxious for its adjournment. The
original secessionists in the convention were in part responsible for this feeling, for they were in the minority and consequently desired adjournment in order that the legislature,
in which they had a majority, might control the State.[1]

An effort was made before the convention adjourned to
influence it to declare the office of governor vacant and to
elect a successor to Governor Clark. As Holden was promi-
nently connected with this enterprise, it was commonly supposed that he desired the office.[2] The plan failed, but the
convention provided for an election for governor and ordered that he should assume the duties of the office in September, instead of the following January.[3] Immediately
the campaign began. The *State Journal* proposed that a
convention should be held and its nominee elected without
a contest. The press, with the exception of the *Standard,*
favored this idea, but when it was seen that a contest was
inevitable, the Charlotte *Democrat* nominated William
Johnston. He was, although a Whig, representative of the

[1] *Journal,* p. 130.
[2] *Western Sentinel,* Jan. 31, 1862.
[3] *Ordinances,* 2d sess., p. 7.

secession party, and it was felt that his business training
and his executive ability as shown in his career as a railroad president, and, since the beginning of the war, as commissary general of the State, would render him suitable for
the position.

Meanwhile the "Conservatives," as they now called themselves, were casting about for a candidate. William A. Graham was their first choice, but he declined to allow the use
of his name. Through the influence of A. S. Merrimon, the
*Fayetteville Observer* nominated Zebulon B. Vance, of
Buncombe, at the time colonel of the 26th North Carolina
regiment. He had been a Whig member of the Thirty-sixth
Congress and had opposed secession until the call for troops,
when he became a secessionist.[1] He then volunteered and
rose rapidly to the rank of colonel. In the fall of 1861 he
declined to be a candidate for Congress on the ground that
there was greater need of fighting men,[2] and even now he
was very doubtful as to the wisdom of allowing his name
to be used, but finally consented.[3]

A large part of the press opposed a personal canvass in
1862, but the *Standard* said, " Honest men do not fear a
public discussion, but only the venal and corrupt," [4] and
urged that one should be held. But apart from Vance's
speeches in the army, the candidates took little part in it.
The campaign was one of extreme heat and bitterness, especially among the newspapers.[5] There was no real issue

---

[1] Vance said he was speaking for the Union with his arm raised
when the news came of the President's call for troops and his arm fell
to the side of a secessionist. *Speech to Andrew Post, G. A. R.*

[2] Dowd, *Life of Vance*, p. 68.

[3] His letter of acceptance is in the Fayetteville *Observer* of June 18,
1862.

[4] Quoted in *Western Sentinel* of April 18, 1862.

[5] In the campaign the *Standard, Fayetteville Observer, Hillsboro*

regarding the war, for both parties claimed to have the same objects in view. It was really a campaign fought on the personality of the leaders. This was frankly the case so far as the Conservatives were concerned. But the original secessionists or " Confederate " party, saw, or appeared to see, in the success of the Conservatives, a complete surrender to the North. They adopted as a platform the resolutions of confidence passed by the convention, and placed a summary of them upon their ticket which was as follows:

## NORTH CAROLINA CONF. TICKET.

......

### ITS PRINCIPLES:

An unremitting prosecution of the war; the war to the last extremity; complete independence; eternal separation from the North; no abridgement of Southern territory; no alteration of Southern boundaries; no compromise with enemies, traitors, or tories.

JEFF. DAVIS, OUR ARMY, AND THE SOUTH.

......

### FOR GOVERNOR :
## WILLIAM JOHNSTON,
### OF MECKLENBURG.

It was not remarkable that the designs of the Conservatives were a cause of suspicion to their opponents. Nor is it probable that they were mistaken in their opinion of the objects of Holden. He was outspoken now in his opinion of the war, and said, " All those who, with South Carolina, preferred to break up the government, and who have not repented for so doing, will vote for Colonel Johnston." [1]

*Recorder, Greensboro Patriot,* Wadesboro *Argus, Franklin Carolinian,* Hendersonville *Times,* Salem *Press,* and Salisbury *Watchman* favored Vance, while the *Wilmington Journal, Raleigh Register, State Journal,* Winston *Sentinel,* Concord *Flag,* Statesville *Express, Shelby Eagle, Asheville News, Western Democrat, Charlotte Bulletin,* and Charlotte *Whig,* were for Johnston.

[1] *Standard,* June 21, 1862.

But both Holden and his opponents were mistaken regarding the character and purpose of most of his associates.

During the campaign a number of things, apart from the political questions involved, contributed to aid the Conservative cause. Since the beginning of the war there had been much dissatisfaction in the State at the attitude of Virginia towards North Carolina. There was a feeling also that it was due largely to Virginia influence that more North Carolina officers were not rewarded for their services by promotion. The *Standard,* as a ground for attack on the Confederate government, commented frequently on this. Just at this time the Richmond *Enquirer* commenced a series of attacks on the State. It is needless to say that the most was made of them for campaign material. Another material advantage was gained when Judge Badger made public a letter he had written to John S. Ely, of New York, and transmitted through Edward Stanly, who had lately been appointed military governor of North Carolina. This defended the action of the former Union men of the State and declared that they were all true to the Confederacy and would never consent to a reunion with the North. This had effect in allaying the fears of many who were in doubt as to the loyalty of the leading Conservatives.

The " Confederates " tried to offset this by quotations from the Northern papers, which were just now devoting much attention to North Carolina, and declaring that the election of Vance would be a Union victory.[1] The *New*

---

[1] The *Philadelphia Inquirer* of June 18, 1862, commenting on the editorials of the *Standard,* said, " But here it comes out square and full, and in defiance of the Rebel powers, plants itself beside the old and honored Union. Who can doubt that a State where such words are boldly uttered at a hundred miles distance from our armies, is ready to return, is even now returning, from her prodigal and ruinous career?" After the election it said, " The issue in North Carolina was squarely secession against anti-secession. * * * The result is a Union victory."

*Era,* published in Washington, N. C., which was now occupied by the Federal troops, issued an appeal to all Union men to vote for Vance and the other Conservative candidates.[1]  But the people could not be convinced that Vance was untrue, and an overwhelming victory was the result of the election.  Out of a total vote of 74,871 he received a majority of 33,975.  Johnston carried only twelve counties.  Out of the army vote of 11,683, not distributed by counties, Vance's majority was 3,691.  Never before had there been such a majority in a North Carolina election.

Governor Vance, in his inaugural, outlined his policy and brought comfort to those of his opponents who had believed that he favored a return to the Union.  Speaking of secession, he said, " It was not a whim or sudden freak, but the deliberate judgment of our people.  Any other course would have involved the deepest degradation, the vilest dishonor, and the direst calamity.  We also accepted with the act all its inevitable consequences, a long and bloody war. . . . To prosecute this war with success is quite as much for our people as for our soldiers to do.  One of the most vital elements of our success is harmony.  On this great issue of existence itself let there, I pray you, be no dissenting voice in our borders."  To the surprise of many he pledged the enforcement of the conscript law.  The speech throughout was a plea, and at the same time a pledge, for the untiring prosecution of the war.  It met with hearty

[1] The *Register* answered the appeal of the *New Era* as follows: " Voters of North Carolina!  Do you doubt now the end and aim of Conservatism?  Do you doubt that the Conservatives of the Department of North Carolina (Stanly's Department) and the Conservatives of the rest of the State are united by the common tie of reconstruction.  Will you not see the gulf that is yawning at your feet and crush out a party that would force you into a Union with those who are waging against you the most brutal war that the malice of the devil ever instigated?"

approval all over the State, the most cordial feeling being expressed by his political opponents, and all question of his position regarding the war was at an end.

It is not likely that at this time many people in the State meditated a return to the Union. It is certain that there was a small number who were planning for such a thing whenever a suitable opportunity arose. But extreme dissatisfaction was present in many quarters and from various causes. The lack of an adequate coast defence, from the beginning of the war, was a ground of attack upon the Confederate government.[1] The establishment of the military prison at Salisbury caused much dissatisfaction, particularly in its neighborhood. This increased as the war progressed and many North Carolinians were imprisoned there.[2] Disloyalty appeared in the eastern counties at the time of Federal occupation, and there was more or less of it throughout the war. As the year 1862 advanced cases elsewhere became more frequent. The assertion was constantly made that extreme disloyalty existed in Davidson,[3] Forsyth, Randolph, and Guilford counties. In Forsyth it was, at first, only a feeling in favor of peace, lacking leaders to make it a definite movement. In the campaign of 1862 one of the candidates for the legislature declared in favor of a compromise with the North and a reconstruction of the old Union.[4] The great Quaker element in these coun-

---

[1] The *Wilmington Journal* even called for the southeastern counties to unite with South Carolina, as the State disregarded their necessity. September 25, 1862.

[2] Clark to Seddon, January 5, 1862.

[3] As early as July, 1861, Gov. Clark was notified of treasonable utterances and actions in Davidson, but was powerless to do more than appeal to the people to assist him by their influence. *Executive Correspondence*, Clark, p. 57.

[4] His speeches were quoted in the *Western Sentinel* of July, 1862.

ties was largely responsible for the opposition to the war, and although from it was furnished a considerable number of volunteers, the discouraging of volunteering and quiet resistance to conscription were so frequent that Governor Clark was compelled to issue a proclamation against them.[1] Deserters, also, began to come to these counties in such numbers as to excite attention. In March, a company was ordered for duty in Chatham for the purpose of arresting them. The state administration was practically powerless, for the criminal code made no provision for the offence, and the military code was almost useless in North Carolina.[2] At the election of 1862 troops had to be sent to Wilkes and Yadkin to prevent the deserters from interfering at the polls.

In the extreme West, matters had assumed a still more serious aspect. General E. Kirby Smith was forced to send a detachment of troops to Madison County. He wrote Governor Clark that the whole population of Laurel Valley was hostile to the Confederacy and that all the males were under arms. Skirmishing was kept up the whole time the troops were in the valley.[3] Application was made to the War Department by the State for a military court for western North Carolina for the sole purpose of trying deserters,[4] but no attention was paid to the request. Governor Vance, soon after his inauguration, asked that troops might be sent there, and suggested that they should be from other States that the temptation to desert might be less. In the autumn many of the deserters crossed over into Tennessee, and many formed organizations there for their defence.[5]

[1] *Executive Correspondence*, Clark, p. 301.
[2] Message to the Council of State, February, 1862.
[3] *Off. Rec.*, no. 10, p. 629.
[4] *Ibid.*, no. 128, p. 674.
[5] *Ibid.*, no. 23, p. 940.

In the spring of 1862 another cause of discontent was
the appointment of W. S. Ashe by the Confederate government to procure arms in the State.  He advertised that he
was authorized to purchase arms, and if necessary, impress
them.  Governor Clark at once issued a proclamation to the
people, declaring that there was no legal authority to direct
the seizure of arms, and asking them to sell to the State
whatever arms they had.  He also wrote to Ashe and told
him that no seizure of arms would be permitted.[1]

The new General Assembly had a decided Conservative
majority, and at once proceeded to oust the secretary of
state and treasurer and replace them with Conservatives.[2]
This was the beginning of the execution of the plan which
Holden had mapped out.  Every Conservative member
who exercised his own judgment in voting and so gave "aid
and comfort" to the "Destructives," as he called the "Confederates," was condemned as guilty of bad faith.[3]  In
further pursuance of the policy William A. Graham was
elected to the Confederate Senate to succeed George Davis.
The adjutant general of the State, J. G. Martin, held also
the rank of brigadier general in the Confederate service;
and because of this his office was declared vacant, and a
successor chosen.[4]  The attorney general shared the same
fate.[5]

The usual resolutions declaring the separation from the
Union final and endorsing President Davis and Governor
Vance were passed.[6]  The North Carolina delegation in the

---

[1] *Executive Correspondence,* Clark, p. 301.

[2] J. H. P. Russ was elected secretary of state and Jonathan Worth,
treasurer.

[3] *Standard,* December 3, 1862.

[4] Daniel G. Fowle became adjutant general.

[5] Sion H. Rogers succeeded W. A. Jenkins as attorney general.

[6] *Laws,* 1862-3, p. 43.

Confederate Congress were requested to urge the repeal of the " twenty-negro " clause of the military exemption act as unnecessary and in violation of the Bill of Rights and the spirit of North Carolina institutions.[1] A protest was made against the policy of burning cotton in the eastern part of the State.[2]

A great deal of unfriendly criticism had been aroused a short time before by the arrest as a spy, by order of the Confederate authorities, of Rev. J. R. Graves, a minister of Orange County.[3] His chief offences had been an unwise conversation while on his way South through the federal lines, and a letter predicting a long war, which gave some slight information to the enemy. He was carried to Richmond and imprisoned. The General Assembly now directed the governor to demand his release. Upon his demand, Secretary Seddon gave an account of the causes of his arrest, justifying it on the ground of necessity, but disavowing the responsibility for removing Graves from the State. No evidence was found against him and he was released.[4] Acts of this kind produced intense indignation in the State and fed the growing discontent with the Confederate government and its policy. Governor Vance in his message informed the legislature that there were many citizens of the State confined at Salisbury for political offences, and asked that steps be taken to preserve the rights of the people. He was accordingly instructed to inquire into the causes of the arrest of the political prisoners,[5] and relief was granted by

---

[1] *Laws*, 1862-3, p. 49.

[2] General French had lately ordered all cotton east of the Wilmington and Weldon railroad to be burned to prevent its capture by the enemy.

[3] *Off. Rec.*, no. 118, pp. 98-100, 794-5.

[4] *Governor's message*, 1862.

[5] *Laws*, 1862-3, chap. xlvi.

an act providing that the writ of *habeas corpus* should be issued, directed when necessary to the sheriff of the county where the arrest took place, by whom it should be executed.[1]

A bill was introduced providing for the enlistment of ten regiments of volunteers between the ages of eighteen and forty-five years of age, not liable to conscription. The bill was introduced by Judge Person. But it was so amended as to omit the provision of non-liability to conscription, and an effort to insert a preamble stating that no conflict should occur with the laws of the Confederacy was unsuccessful. It was clearly the purpose of the Conservatives to prevent the execution of the conscript law, and this excited so much opposition that the bill was defeated in the Senate after passing the House. Immediately afterwards, as an answer to criticism from Virginia, a resolution was passed, vindicating the loyalty of the State and of the General Assembly. Seven " Confederate " members of the Senate and thirteen of the House voted against it on the ground that it endorsed the " Ten Regiment Bill." [2]

The whole tendency of the majority in the legislature as expressed in their acts and resolutions was to oppose all further centralization of power by the Confederate government, and in so doing, oppose that government in other respects. W. W. Holden, although not a member, was the dominating influence in this policy.

Immediately after the adjournment of the legislature a meeting was held by the members who favored a vigorous prosecution of the war together with citizens who cared to join them. An address to the people was issued, condemning the action of those who were opposing the war, and a central committee and a committee of correspondence were ap-

---

[1] *Laws,* 1862-3, p. 76.

[2] *Journal,* 1862-3, pp. 31, 190.

pointed. Prominent in this movement were ex-Governor Bragg, who had lately resigned from President Davis's cabinet and was in a sense a representative of the Confederate government in the State, Kenneth Rayner, D. M. Barringer, ex-Governor Reid, W. W. Avery, and Weldon N. Edwards.[1]

The period between the adjournment of the legislature in February and its assembling in extra session on June 30 at Governor Vance's call to consider financial matters, was without events of importance. It was marked, however, by a growing aversion to the conscript law and by constant appeals to the judiciary for writs of *habeas corpus* to obtain the release of those conscripted. Governor Vance, in May,[2] ordered the militia officers not to arrest persons who had been discharged under the writ, and to resist such arrests by any persons not authorized by a court having jurisdiction. At the same time the increase of desertions caused him to issue a proclamation urging all those absent from their commands to return at once.[3] He issued a third proclamation asking for volunteers to enable him to comply with the President's call for seven thousand men for six months service in the State. He also referred the matter to the legislature when it met.

The session lasted only a week. In this time laws were passed providing for the enrolment of a force of militia and for the punishment of those assisting and encouraging desertion. The governor was authorized to use the militia to enforce the conscript laws.[4] Governor Vance visited the body while in secret session and urged the drafting of mag-

---

[1] *Register*, February 18, 1863.
[2] Proclamation of May 11, 1863.
[3] *Register*, May 16, 1863.
[4] *Laws*, Extra Session, 1863.

istrates and secured the adoption of the exemption bill of the Confederate Congress.[1]

Up to this time the peace sentiment had been expressed only individually. It reached the public, as a general thing, only through the editorial columns of the *Standard* and the *Progress*[2] and such papers as quoted them in opposition to their policy. But a change now took place. Major Bradford, a Virginian, was appointed to collect the Confederate tithes in North Carolina. The ill feeling existing at the time on account of North Carolina's troops being placed under officers from other States was intense, and the discontent at other acts of the government has been noticed. This was well known at Richmond, and the appointment was regarded in the State as showing a total disregard for the wishes of the people. Criticism was so severe and the people were so aroused that Governor Vance finally requested the withdrawal of Bradford and the appointment of a North Carolinian. This was done, but a pretext had already been given for action by the discontented element. Early in July the *Standard* called upon the people to assemble and express their opinion on the state of the country.[3] This was followed a week later by an editorial which expressed the feeling behind the movement, " Peace! When shall we have peace? " It then quoted with approval from the *Progress* as follows: " We favor peace because we believe that peace now would save slavery, while we very much fear that a prolongation of the war will obliterate the last vestige of it." [4]

---

[1] *Off. Rec.*, no. 128, p. 619.

[2] The *Progress* had been published in New Bern until federal occupation of the place. It was now conducted in Raleigh and was strongly opposed to the Confederate government. It had formerly been a strong secession paper.

[3] Issue of July 8, 1863.          [4] *Standard*, July 17, 1863.

During the last week in July two meetings were held in Wake County. One demanded any peace that would give equality with the North. The other requested President Davis to suspend hostilities and call a convention of the States.[1] Both denounced the Confederate administration and endorsed Holden. Surry followed a few days later demanding " The Constitution as it is and the Union as it was." [2] In close succession there followed meetings all over the State. The proceedings of sixty, held in about thirty counties were published.[3] A large meeting was also held for the Tenth Congressional District. There is such a similarity in the resolutions passed that it is evident that they originated from the same source. Holden denied this and said that the meetings and resolutions were purely spontaneous.[4] But the evidence proves the contrary. During the preceding January a meeting had been held in the 14th North Carolina Regiment to protest against the proposed " Ten Regiment Bill." Holden then threatened that if such meetings were held in the army he would start them at home for the people to " express their opinion on the state of the country." [5] President Davis had been warned before the movement began that a series of such meetings was to be held and that many feared that there was to be open resistance to the Confederacy. It was also intimated that the plan was to excite the people and co-operate with the enemy.[6] He informed Governor Vance of this, who replied that there was no reconstruction party in North

[1] *Standard*, July 29, 1863.
[2] *Ibid.*, Aug. 12, 1863.
[3] Holden said that over one hundred were held.
[4] *Standard*, Aug. 12, 1863.
[5] *Ibid.*, Jan. 14, 1863.
[6] *Off. Rec.*, no. 108, p. 739.

Carolina and that it would be unwise to take any steps against Holden. The governor acknowledged, however, the existence in the State of widespread bad feeling and dissatisfaction with the Confederate government.[1]   Holden was evidently feeling the pulse of the State with a view to decided action for the Union. He had, a short while before, written Andrew Johnson, then military governor of Tennessee, that the people of North Carolina were true to the Union and would seize the first opportunity to free themselves from the Confederacy.[2]   General J. G. Foster also heard from some private source that such a plan was on foot.[3]

The publication of the proceedings of these meetings aroused a storm of abuse, particularly in the army. Over thirty regiments passed resolutions denouncing Holden and the meetings. A convention composed of delegates from every North Carolina regiment met at Orange Court House, Virginia, and issued a protest, declaring false the claim of the *Standard* that the troops approved its action.[4]   In a few counties opposition meetings were held, and the grand jury of Surry, where the demand for peace had been most outspoken, at the ensuing court, requested that all such meetings should cease, as they were disloyal and dangerous.[5] Holden was burnt in effigy in several places, and the feeling against him was more bitter than it had ever been. Every paper in the State, with the single exception of the *Progress,* condemned him. William A. Graham and E. J. Hale both sought to dissuade him from his course but with-

---

[1] *Off. Rec.,* no. 108, p. 740.

[2] *Ibid.,* no. 50, p. 183.          [3] *Ibid.,* no. 45, p. 751.

[4] *Wilmington Journal,* August 20, 1863. Holden claimed afterwards that the delegates were all officers and that the privates were in sympathy with him. But many of the delegates were privates.

[5] *Western Sentinel,* Oct. 1, 1863.

out success.[1] Secure in the belief that he would not be harmed, he calmly watched the storm and said, " Let the people speak; it is refreshing to hear them."

Meanwhile Governor Vance, who, while anxious for peace, had opposed the meetings as dangerous until overtures came from the North,[2] issued a proclamation urging the people to desist. General R. F. Hoke's brigade was ordered into the State about this time, and it was supposed that it was there to be on hand in case of any outbreak. So the meetings ceased. But Holden, and for that matter many others, felt that he had the masses with him. The army, however, was still hostile.[3] So he contented himself with keeping the *Standard* full of communications that would keep the subject of peace before the people,[4] and that would excite hostility to the Confederate government. He attempted to identify the movement with the one in Georgia, ignoring the fact that the latter demanded Confederate action, while he favored action by the State. The reports of the meetings which reached the North led there to the belief that North Carolina was about to withdraw from the Confederacy.[5]

[1] Holden to Vance, Sept. 9, 1863.

[2] *Standard*, July 29, 1863.

[3] Jonathan Worth to J. M. Worth, August, 1863.

[4] Lewis Hanes commenced a series of ably written articles against secession and the war, signed "Davidson". Dr. J. T. Leach also contributed a series of letters bitterly attacking the Confederate administration.

[5] Edward Everett, in his speech at Gettysburg in 1864, said: "The heart of the people North and South is for the Union. Indications, too plain to be mistaken, announce the fact . . . . In North Carolina the fatal chain at length is broken. At Raleigh the lips of honest and brave men are unsealed, and an independent press is unlimbering its artillery. The weary masses are yearning to see the dear old flag floating again upon the Capitol, and they sigh for the return of peace, prosperity, and happiness which they enjoyed under a government whose power they felt only by its blessings."

The meetings and discussions had one effect: they caused desertions from the army in considerable numbers.[1] The matter now became alarming. The deserters congregated in the mountains where it was almost impossible to reach them and plundered and murdered at their own will. They made overtures to Governor Vance to enlist them for service in the State, but it was never allowed by the war department.[2] The home guard was utterly unable to cope with them, and in many places they were assisted and encouraged by the inhabitants, who were actuated either by sympathy or fear.[3] Nor were they only in the mountains. In Wilkes County five hundred of them were in a military organization under arms, and there were large numbers in Randolph, Catawba, Yadkin, and Iredell, not to mention other localities where they were not so numerous.[4] A decided growth of Union sentiment was noticeable after Gettysburg and the fall of Vicksburg.[5]

The feeling aroused by the peace meetings was not long left without an outlet. In September a portion of Benning's Georgia brigade [6] spent a night in Raleigh. A number of the soldiers went to Holden's residence, but he eluded them and went to the Governor's Mansion and took refuge there until Governor Vance returned. After failing to find Holden the soldiers went to the *Standard* office and sacked it, throwing the type into the street. The press, however,

---

[1] *Off. Rec.*, no. 49, p. 660; *Carolina Watchman*, March 21, 1864.

[2] *Off. Rec.*, no. 128, p. 674.

[3] *Ibid.*, no. 49, p. 676.

[4] *Ibid.*, no. 128, pp. 783-5.

[5] *Ibid.*, no. 35, p. 950.

[6] The Georgia troops claimed afterwards that the soldiers of the 48th N. C. regiment were engaged in the riot, and *The Spirit of the Age* said the same thing.

was not injured. Governor Vance, who was sent for, came and urged the mob to disperse without further violence. The next morning, in retaliation, a mob composed of citizens of Raleigh, led by Mark Williams, a strong Union man, sacked the office and utterly destroyed the property of the *State Journal*. Governor Vance again interfered to prevent further trouble. But for his preventive measures the *Progress* would have been destroyed the following night.[1] He at once complained to the President, but, beyond an investigation resulting in no evidence, nothing was done. For some time troops were not allowed to pass through the city for fear of the consequences, but even this prohibition did not last long.

The fall elections showed that although the peace feeling was strong in the State its voting strength was less than that of the Conservatives in 1862. The new delegation to the Confederate Congress had five of the *Standard's* candidates. But in nearly every instance they were elected by a plurality vote over several candidates. A total vote of 30,641 was cast, and a majority of 2,834 was against the Holden candidates. This, from the number of elements entering into the contest, is slight evidence in itself, but it marks a difference.[2] The successful candidates representing the peace feeling were James T. Leach, Josiah Turner, George W. Logan,[3] Samuel Christian, and J. G. Ramsey.

So generally was the sentiment for peace diffused among the people, though no longer expressed in resolutions, that Governor Vance finally wrote to the President that the dis-

---

[1] *Fayetteville Observer*, September, 1863. The *State Journal* never resumed publication. The *Standard* resumed in about a month.

[2] *Western Sentinel*, January 28, 1864.

[3] George W. Logan was nominated by the peace meeting for the tenth district. *Standard*, October 14, 1863.

content in the State could only be removed by an attempt at negotiations with the enemy.[1]  The President replied that it was impossible on account of the refusal of the Washington authorities.  At the same time he expressed his distrust of any movement like that in North Carolina, and warned Governor Vance against delaying action too long in efforts at conciliation.[2]

The General Assembly met in November.  Little legislation of importance resulted.  The governor was directed to use the militia for arresting conscripts and deserters only in their own or adjacent counties.[3]  The salaries of the state officers were increased to keep up to some extent with the depreciation of the currency.

Early in 1864 the Attorney General of the Confederacy resigned and was succeeded by George Davis, whose term in the Confederate Senate had not expired.  W. A. Graham had already been elected to succeed him, and Governor Vance asked him to fill out the unexpired term.  He refused, as did David L. Swain, who was later offered the appointment.  Judge Edwin G. Reade finally accepted as a favor to Governor Vance.[4]

During the winter Governor Vance visited the Army of Northern Virginia, and a general review was held in his honor.[5]  He was there several days and spoke to the North Carolina troops frequently, urging and encouraging them to renewed efforts.[6]

---

[1] *Off. Rec.*, no. 108, p. 807.

[2] *Ibid.*, pp. 809-10.

[3] *Laws*, 1863, chap. xviii.

[4] *Executive Correspondence*, Vance, vol. ii, p. 64 *et seq.*

[5] This seems to have been the only instance of the kind during the war.

[6] General Lee said Vance's visit to the army in its results was equivalent to a re-enforcement of 50,000 men.  Dowd, *Life of Vance*, p. 125.

In North Carolina talk of the necessity of a convention was beginning to be heard. Resolutions demanding the call of one were prepared by Holden and J. T. Leach and introduced by the latter at a peace meeting held in Johnston County.[1] Holden then decided that another series of meetings should be held. Governor Vance, while regretting the division which now came definitely between Holden and himself, refused to coöperate in the movement for a convention, and even thought of declining to be a candidate for re-election.[2] Another series of thirty or more peace meetings was now held and their proceedings published. All were hostile to the Confederate government and nearly all demanded a convention. It is noticeable that Governor Vance was endorsed by nearly all of them. Holden, evidently, still hoped to control him, but Vance finally told him that all his pledges had been for a vigorous prosecution of the war and that his policy had been outlined in his inaugural address.[3]

The Richmond authorities were kept informed of the

[1] The important part of the resolutions is as follows:

"Whereas, the alarming and fearful tendency of the Confederate Government towards a military despotism by the enactment of unjust and oppressive laws, to citizens is just cause of complaint.

Resolved, That North Carolina, as a sovereign and independent State, has a right to consult the present good and future happiness of her citizens, and when she is forced to choose between a military despotism and her State sovereignty, for the good of the people, she will choose the latter by a convention of her citizens." *Standard*, January 12, 1864.

[2] Spencer, *Last Ninety Days of the War in North Carolina*, pp. 124 *et seq.*

[3] Holden and Dr. Leach asserted later that Governor Vance had approved of the Johnston County resolutions. This was, on the face of it, false. In the summer B. F. Moore and Holden sought to gain Vance's support and he declared that sooner than withdraw the North Carolina troops he would let his arm fall from its socket. Moore to Holden, July 20, 1866.

condition of feeling in the State,[1] and if matters had assumed a more serious aspect, would probably have interfered.   Governor Vance, too, entered into a correspondence with President Davis which became decidedly unpleasant in tone as it progressed.   The President was warned that if the writ of *habeas corpus* should be suspended and arrests made in the State,[2] there would be resistance, particularly if these arrests appeared unconstitutional.   Governor Vance advised as little use of military power as possible, and said that if there were no military interference he had no fear of the appeal to the ballot box, as good and true men were working against any call of a convention and would do so while the civil law remained intact, and he did not believe the required majority for calling a convention could be obtained.   He accused President Davis of proscribing " old Union men " and gave that as one reason for the discontent with the Confederate administration.[3]   In his reply the President denied the charge, but acknowledged that he suspected that a nest of traitors were conspiring at home, and hinted at arbitrary measures, promising that if they were necessary due regard would be paid to civil rights.[4]   Governor Vance again wrote renewing the charge, but denying any personal feeling.[5]   The President made an explanation, and after declaring that Governor Vance had overstepped

[1] *Off. Rec.*, no. 129, p. 88.

[2] B. F. Moore told Holden in 1865 that only W. T. Dortch's efforts had prevented President Davis from ordering his (Holden's) arrest and that of R. S. Donnell.

[3] President Davis sent this letter to George Davis, endorsed as follows: " For consideration and advice.   The assertions are discourteous and untrue.   The rhetoric is after the manner of the *Standard*. Neither my acts nor my words can justify the slander that I have regarded North Carolinians with distrust or withheld due promotion to any of her gallant soldiers. J. D." *Off. Rec.*, no. 108, pp. 218-20.

[4] *Ibid.*, pp. 824-7.                         [5] *Ibid.*, pp. 830-3.

the bounds of propriety, requested that the correspondence might cease.[1] At the request of the North Carolina members of Congress, Governor Vance published the correspondence in June, omitting the portions of the President's letters that he thought would do harm.

On February 24 the *Standard* announced the passage of the act of Congress suspending the writ of *habeas corpus,* and, in the same issue, Holden announced that the publication of the paper would be suspended indefinitely. The latter was a surprise to the public, but the reason is evident. On March 3, he issued an extra edition and announced himself as a candidate for governor. Reversing his opinion of 1862,[2] he requested that there might not be any canvass, as it would cause useless disturbance and excitement. He declared himself a Conservative " after the straitest sect." The announcement caused no surprise, for it had been generally predicted that he would be a candidate. The campaign was thus begun five months before the election.

The *Standard* resumed publication in May, and active work was commenced in behalf of Holden's candidacy. The opposition, at first, caused consternation among the friends of Governor Vance, as many of them did not appreciate his power. Holden relied mainly on the masses from whom he had sprung and whom he had hitherto led. But Governor Vance, also, was pre-eminently a man of the people, and his efforts to relieve suffering of every kind, and his steadfast determination to preserve civil liberty, had endeared him to thousands. His care of the soldiers, the fact that he had been a soldier himself, and his efforts for a vigorous prosecution of the war made friends for him among those who had opposed him most bitterly only two

[1] *Off. Rec.*, no. 108, pp. 844-6.
[2] *Cf. supra.*, p. 40.

years before, and who were still intensely hostile to Holden.
But it was a battle of giants.  Holden was an old and experienced political leader and had always been able to interpret public sentiment.  And he had usually been on the
popular side.  But he now failed to realize how much he
had helped to create and mould the peace sentiment, and,
believing that it originated with the people, he thought their
minds could not be turned from it.  His editorials were as
vigorous as ever, and were even more widely read than
ever,[1] but a new power had risen against him—the oratory
of Vance.  Nothing more stirring or effective was ever
known in the politics of North Carolina.  The people
flocked to hear him, and his speeches, particularly those at
Fayetteville, Raleigh, and Wilkesboro, attracted great attention.  From this time, regardless of past affiliations, but
with no change in his policy, Governor Vance was allied
with the war party.  His platform, terse and vigorous, in-
dicates this:

The supremacy of the civil over military law.

A speedy repeal of the act suspending the writ of *habeas
corpus.*

A quiet submission to all laws, good or bad, while they remain on the statute books.

No reconstruction or submission, but perpetual independence.

An unbroken front to the common enemy; but timely and
repeated negotiations for peace by the proper authorities.

No separate State action through a convention, no counter
revolution, no combined resistance to the government.

Opposition to despotism in every form and the preservation
of our republican institutions in all their purity.[2]

---

[1] The circulation of the *Standard* was increasing very rapidly at this
time.  Holden would send it when desired, regardless of payment
for it.

[2] Raleigh *Conservative*, May 4, 1864.  This paper was regarded
as the organ of the state administration.

After he perceived that his power with the mass of the people was departing, Holden attempted to win the support of prominent political leaders and men of property. But here his past record, by contrast with that of his opponent, was sufficient to blight his aspirations. The old leaders had been willing to make use of him, but they neither respected nor trusted him, and so declined to follow him. R. P. Dick, Thomas Settle, and Alfred Dockery [1] were the only men of prominence in the State who supported him.

Holden had great difficulty in justifying his change of opinion regarding Governor Vance. Consistency, however, was never one of Holden's virtues and he usually laid no claim to it. But, in this case, he assumed that a change had taken place in the governor's actions and declared that he had "made his bed with the Destructives" and was entirely controlled by a clique composed of Thomas Bragg, H. K. Burgwyn, and George Little, and, consequently, although he had been elected as a peace candidate, was eager for war. Accordingly Holden declared the issue now to be simply war or peace. [2]

During the campaign the legislature met for a session of two weeks. The governor, in his message, took ground against the suspension of the writ of *habeas corpus* and advised them to lay down what they considered a fair basis for peace, warning them against efforts that might be made to treat with the State individually. The only law of im-

[1] Alfred Dockery said he would support Holden as a peace man, but that he had no confidence in him. *Fayetteville Observer*, July 25, 1864.

[2] Holden headed his editorial sheet with the following: " The Two Ways: Fight it Out. *Zebulon B. Vance, Governor of North Carolina.* ' Wisdom's ways are ways of pleasantness, and all her paths are *Peace.*' *Solomon, Son of David, King of Israel.*" *Standard*, April 6, 1864.

portance passed was one to secure the benefit of the writ of *habeas corpus* and to prevent the transportation of citizens by violence beyond the limits of the State.[1]  Resolutions were adopted declaring it the duty of the Confederate government, after some signal success, to treat for peace on the basis of independence.  A vote of confidence in the President was passed, and he was declared with the Senate to have the sole treaty-making power.[2]  Governor Vance was also endorsed, only five votes in both houses being cast against the resolution.[3]  Resolutions protesting against the suspension of the *habeas corpus* and declaring that North Carolina did not consent to it, against the Conscript Act, and against the restrictions on importations imposed by the Secretary of the Treasury, were also passed.  A resolution declaring the exemption of state officers from military service was passed as a protest against the change made by the Confederate Congress.  The people were urged to cooperate and bring about harmony by abandoning all party feuds.[4]

During the session four members of the House [5] made statements that they had heard Holden say that it was the plan of his party for the legislature to call a convention to take the State out of the Confederacy.  R. P. Dick and his other supporters had denied any such thought or purpose, claiming that the only object of a convention was to begin negotiations with other Southern States and to make valid

[1] *Laws*, 1863-4, chap. ii.

[2] The first article passed the House 62 to 19, and the second 79 to 0. The vote in the Senate was not recorded.

[3] The Vance and Davis resolutions were at first joined, but the friends of the former wanted a better vote and separated them. *Standard*, June 1, 1864.

[4] *Resolutions*, 1863-4.

[5] Horton, Hampton, Gentry, and Welborn.

any acts of Congress which might be unconstitutional.[1] About the same time Dr. Leach, who, after Holden, was the most active member of the peace party, introduced in Congress a set of peace resolutions. They were not considered at all, being immediately tabled, though every member from North Carolina, except B. S. Gaither and R. R. Bridgers, voted against their being so disposed of.[2]

Meanwhile, the gubernatorial campaign dragged on without interesting developments until July, when great excitement was caused by the discovery of the existence of a secret and treasonable political society, known as " The Heroes of America." [3] Its object was to protect those who favored a return to the Union and to increase their number as much as possible. There were three degrees,[4] and the initiated had numerous signs and signals by which they might recognize one another. The usual name given them and used also by themselves was " Red Strings," derived from the badge of the society, which was to be worn in the lapel of the coat. The idea was suggested by a well-known Scriptural story.[5] The extension of the society had been largely carried on by ministers and other non-combatants. The revelation of its existence and purpose was made by a minister in Caswell County.[6] He had joined, ignorant of its nature, and when he saw its designs, he made the whole thing public. The society was widespread and in constant

[1] R. P. Dick in Greensboro *Patriot*, February 18, 1864.

[2] *Conservative*, June 1, 1864.

[3] The *Conservative* of July 6, 1864, first called attention to the existence of the society. Most of the confessions were made to the editor of the paper.

[4] A full account of this society with the ritual of the three degrees is to be found in an article by the author in the *Publications of the Southern History Association*, Jan., 1907.

[5] Joshua, ii, 18.

[6] Rev. Orrin Churchill.

communication with the North.   J. L. Johnson, of Forsyth County, went to Washington during the war and initiated President Lincoln, Benjamin S. Hedrick, and Commissioner Barrett.[1]   It was, naturally, ardent in its support of Holden, and orders were issued to members to vote for him as aiding their cause and as a member.[2]   One confession led to another, and within two weeks a very large number announced their withdrawal from membership.   Holden ridiculed the idea of its existence, but the dread it produced probably lost him many votes.   He was accused of being in the pay of the North,[3] and this was believed by many.

The election in the army came first, and Governor Vance received a very large majority—13,209 out of 15,033 votes cast.   Evidently the " Red Strings " had only a small army membership.[4]   The election in the State followed, and Holden carried only two counties—Randolph and Johnston. Out of a total vote of 72,561 Governor Vance had a majority of 43,579.   Holden made accusations of fraud and intimidation, but did not press the matter, recognizing that, even if his charges were well founded, which was a matter of doubt, there was little possibility of securing redress.[5] He issued an address to the people, declaring himself a friend of the state and Confederate governments and de-

[1] *Sen. Report*, no. 1, p. 227, 42 Cong. 2d sess.

[2] This information was gathered from the various confessions made at the time and published, and from the statements made to the writer by living members of the society.

[3] *Greensboro Patriot*, July 21, 1864.

[4] The *Greensboro Patriot* said that many votes were lost to Holden by no provision being made for ballot boxes in the woods, where most of his military supporters were hiding.

[5] A careful examination of the records and the newspapers and conversations with participants in the election have failed to show the existence of fraud. Without question, voting for Holden subjected one to violent unpopularity.

sirous of a vigorous prosecution of the war, at the same time favoring every effort for peace on honorable terms.[1]

Governor Vance called the Council of State into session early in October. He then expected the end of the war to come in the last days of 1864. He urged prompt assistance to General Lee, and suggested that there were many state officers that might well be put into service. He also mentioned that he had called a meeting of the governors of the States east of the Mississippi, in Augusta, Georgia, to agree upon some uniform plan of action. He asked for authority to call a special session of the legislature immediately after this meeting, but the Council unanimously refused to grant it.[2]

The meeting of the governors was held with no particular results of importance, except that the possibility of any separate state action was made more remote than ever. Resolutions were passed calling for a vigorous prosecution of the war,[3] and after some discussion the meeting adjourned.

In the State the autumn was gloomy, with no outlook for any brighter future. Depression was everywhere, for much of the energy of the people was exhausted. Such a large proportion of the citizens were in the military service that a lifeless condition at home followed. The conscript law, in spite of its unpopularity, had been more thoroughly enforced than in any other State.[4] In the mountains, deserters from the State, and also from South Carolina, Georgia, and Tennessee had assembled, and in some localities had driven away the inhabitants who were in sympathy with the Confederacy. Federal officers were seen among them, and in

---

[1] *Standard*, August 17, 1864.

[2] *Council of State Records*, pp. 161-2.

[3] *Off. Rec.*, no. 89, pp. 1149-50.

[4] President Davis's speech at Greensboro, October, 1864.

the early part of the year, in accordance with a suggestion of General Sherman,[1] a regiment was raised by George W. Kirk, who commanded it.[2]

The governor's message to the legislature recommended that the age limit for military service be raised to fifty-five years, and that more power be given to him as commander-in-chief. Both these recommendations were adopted in part.[3] The governor was authorized to ship $200,000 worth of cotton and tobacco to be applied to the necessities of the North Carolina prisoners at the North. Resolutions were adopted protesting against arming the slaves and against any legislation by Congress regarding the writ of *habeas corpus*; but on the other hand, it was formally declared to be the purpose of the State to continue the war vigorously. In secret session four commissioners were appointed to visit Richmond and confer with the President upon the condition of the country.[4] As a result of a combination to defeat the Holden candidate, Thomas S. Ashe was elected over Edwin G. Reade to succeed W. T. Dortch in the Confederate Senate.

Although the war party, since the election, was again in the ascendant, the opposition was not silenced altogether. During the session of the legislature John Pool introduced in the Senate a series of peace resolutions which provided for commissioners to meet those from other States and to act upon instructions from the President. These were referred to a committee, from which two reports were made. That of the majority favored the adoption of the resolu-

[1] *Off. Rec.*, no. 77, pp. 233-4.

[2] *Ibid.*, no. 89, pp. 1251-4; no. 59, p. 741.

[3] *Laws*, 1864-5, chap. xx.

[4] Raleigh *Confederate*, February 15, 1865. This paper was the successor of the *State Journal* as the organ of the Confederate administration.

tions. The minority opposed adoption, declaring that the State, while it remained a member of the Confederacy, could not form such an agreement with the other States as was proposed by the resolutions. A sharp debate followed, resulting in the tabling of the resolutions.[1] In the House a resolution introduced by L. Q. Sharpe, declaring the right of individual state action, met a similar fate.[2] A bill for calling a convention was also introduced but never acted on.

In Congress the majority of the North Carolina members were constantly urging that the President should make propositions for peace. In December Dr. Leach introduced in the House of Representatives resolutions declaring that secession had taken place in an unguarded moment and without deliberation, and that when the United States should recognize the reserved rights of the States, the Confederacy should treat for peace on any terms that the commissioners of both might agree upon. On a motion to reject, all present voted in the affirmative except six of the North Carolina members.[3] Three of these immediately asked leave to change their vote, as they had only voted that way out of consideration for a colleague.[4] Later in the session the resolutions were introduced and considered in secret session.[5]

The fall of Fort Fisher and the consequent capture of Wilmington convinced many that there was no need of any further movement toward peace, for it would come without aid in North Carolina. Some talk of a convention again

[1] The vote on tabling was 24 to 20.

[2] McPherson, *History of the Rebellion*, p. 619. The vote was 52 to 50.

[3] T. C. Fuller, J. M. Leach, J. T. Leach, J. G. Ramsey, G. W. Logan, and Josiah Turner.

[4] Fuller, Ramsey, and J. M. Leach.

[5] *Conservative*. February 1, 1865.

began, but without any effect. Governor Vance still addressed the people urging unity of action, and public meetings were held in various counties, pledging support to the Confederacy.[1]

After the failure of the Hampton Roads conference William A. Graham, who was at the time president *pro tempore* of the Confederate Senate, and who had been instrumental in bringing about the conference, was one of the committee which interviewed the President regarding it. Afterwards he gave notice in the Senate that he would introduce a resolution to open negotiations with the United States, but for some reason, probably perceiving its uselessness, he never did so.

The most of the people at home, with all hope of the success of the Confederate cause gone, waited for the end to come with no thought of the constitutional and political questions which were therein involved.

### 6. FINANCIAL AND ECONOMIC CONDITIONS IN WAR

When the ordinance of secession was passed the total bonded indebtedness of the State was $11,119,500. The annual interest on this sum amounted to $667,170. There was also an endorsement of railroad bonds to the amount of $150,000.[2] The greater part of the debt had been contracted for internal improvements, and all of it had been made since 1849, the last of the bonds maturing in 1890. Before January, 1866, $364,000 would fall due. During the early years of the war more bonds were issued for internal improvements, amounting to $1,619,000.[3] Of this

---

[1] Such meetings were held in Wayne, Chatham, Wake, Granville, Cabarrus, Halifax, Mecklenburg, Gaston, Rowan, and Davidson counties.

[2] The bonds were endorsed for the Wilmington & Weldon R. R.

[3] This was for the benefit of the Chatham R. R., Western R. R., Western North Carolina R. R., and the Wilmington, Charlotte and Rutherford R. R.

amount $420,000 was issued under acts passed before May 20, 1861. To offset this indebtedness the State held bonds and stocks of corporations[1] to the value of $9,297,664.88.

Before the meeting of the convention the legislature authorized three issues of treasury notes, amounting to $2,000,000, and three issues to the banks of six per cent bonds to the amount of $2,250,000. The issues of notes and bonds were to alternate. Banks were relieved of specie payment while the State owed this debt[2] At the second extra session of the legislature issues of $800,000, in notes of small denominations, and $1,000,000 in large were authorized. The treasurer was forbidden to receive in payment of public dues the bills or notes of any bank that should refuse to receive treasury notes as currency. Holders of notes were allowed to exchange them at any time for six per cent bonds.[3] In December, 1862, issues of $1,500,000, in bills of small denominations, and $3,000,000 in large were provided for, redeemable January, 1866, and fundable only in twenty-year bonds, bearing interest at six per cent.[4] In July, 1863, Confederate notes, without regard to the date of issue, were made payable for taxes, and the treasurer and other state officers were directed to fund such notes in seven per cent Confederate bonds.[5] In December the treasurer was directed, in case of a deficit, to sell six per cent thirty-year bonds not to exceed $2,000,000, and also to issue $400,000 in small notes.[6] The following May an ad-

---

[1] Bonds were held of the Western R. R., Wilmington, Charlotte and Rutherford R. R., and the Atlantic and N. C. R. R. Stocks were held of the Western, Atlantic & N. C. R. R., Raleigh and Gaston R. R. and North Carolina R. R., and in the Albemarle and Chesapeake canal.

[2] *Laws*, first extra session, 1861, chap. iv.

[3] *Ibid.*, second extra session, 1861, chap. xviii.

[4] *Ibid.*, 1862-3, chap. xxix.   [5] *Ibid.*, Ex. Sess., 1863, chap. xii.

[6] *Ibid.*, Adjourned Sess., 1863, chap. xxvi.

ditional issue of notes to the amount of $3,000,000 was provided for.[1] In December, 1864, it was enacted that all future treasury notes, including those re-issued, should be payable in 1876.[2] At the same session the treasurer was directed to pay the debt of the State, becoming due in 1865, in bonds.[3]

The convention, in the meantime, had authorized the issue after March, 1862, of $3,200,000 in notes, redeemable in 1866, subject to a change of date by the General Assembly. Included in the same act was provision for a loan, not to exceed $3,000,000, including the amount already borrowed from the banks, and the issue therefor of bonds bearing interest at six per cent payable in twelve months and redeemable at such a time and on such terms as the treasurer might see fit to impose. Banks which had loaned their *pro rata* share, and whose charter forbade the issue of notes of small denominations, were authorized to make such issues. Specie payment should not be required as long as the debt remained unpaid.[4] In December an issue of $3,000,000 in notes was provided for, bearing six per cent interest and payable in 1865. These were receivable at any time for debts due the State at the treasury. They were also fundable in thirty-year six per cent bonds. None were to be re-issued, but new ones issued in their place not to exceed the original amount.[5] The interest-bearing feature was later repealed.[6] In February, 1862, provision was made for funding any of the treasury notes issued under ordinance of convention, in eight per cent twenty-year bonds, or in six per cent thirty-year bonds. The notes so funded could be re-issued. The treasurer was also author-

[1] *Laws*, Adjourned Sess., 1864, chap. xviii.

[2] *Ibid.*, 1864-5, chap. xxiii.          [3] *Ibid.*, 1864-5, chap. ii.

[4] *Ordinances*, no. 34.                  [5] *Ibid.*, second session, no. 16.

[6] *Ibid.*, third session, no. 2.

ized if necessary to issue further $2,500,000 in notes, payable in 1866. [1]

In the war period, thus, a total of $20,400,000 in treasury notes was authorized, and of this $8,507,847.50 were issued, $3,261,511.25 being withdrawn later, leaving in circulation at the close of the war $5,246,336.25. Bonds were issued to the amount of $13,121,500. [2] After deducting the unsold bonds in England, those redeemed, and those in the sinking fund, the balance was $9,119,000. Unpaid interest and similar items made the total war debt, including treasury notes and internal improvement bonds, $16,596,485.61. But corporation bonds amounting to $6,800,000 were held as a partial offset to this. [3]

In addition to the state debt individual counties owed a sum estimated in 1864 at $20,000,000. [4] This debt had been contracted by the county courts, chiefly to provide for the destitute families of soldiers. Their acts were legalized by the legislature in 1861 [5]

The financial legislation of the period is thus seen to be complex, not because it was part of an elaborate financial scheme, but from its numerous contradictions, its multiplicity of acts, and its slip-shod methods. But at the same time it must be remembered that it was not the work of trained financiers but of unskilled men who were suddenly compelled to make bricks without straw. The fact that two separate bodies were enacting financial legislation at the same time was also, in part, a cause of lack of method. One thing can be said of it—it bears eloquent witness to the confidence felt in the state officers.

[1] *Ordinances,* third session, no. 35.

[2] Treasurer's *Report,* January 19, 1866.

[3] These bonds were of the city of Raleigh and the R. & G. R. R.

[4] *Standard,* June 28, 1864. Schwab, *Confederate States of America, 1861-1865,* p. 307.

[5] Act of May 11, 1861.

The banks of the State suspended specie payments in November, 1860. Resumption, as has been seen, was delayed until the state debt should be paid. In May, 1861, the banks agreed to lend the State twenty per cent of their capital stock. This proportion, in most cases, was largely increased later.[1] Bank-note extension never went so far in North Carolina as in the other Southern States,[2] and consequently depreciation was less. But Confederate currency fell in value to such an extent that the legislature in 1863, attempting to raise it, passed a resolution pledging that the State would resist any attempt to repudiate it.[3] Naturally, with such an immense volume of currency, depreciation began soon in the State's notes as well. This continued until the end of the war.[4] At the beginning of the war the

---

[1] Schwab, *Confederate States of America*, p. 128.

[2] *Ibid.*, p. 131.

[3] *Resolutions*, called session 1863, p. 19.

[4] After the war a table of depreciation was adopted. While it is necessarily imperfect, it gives some idea of the progress of depreciation. It was,

| Months. | 1861. | 1862. | 1863. | 1864. | 1865. |
|---|---|---|---|---|---|
| January, | ...... | $1.20 | $3.00 | $21.00 | $50.00 |
| February, | ...... | 1.30 | 3.00 | 21.00 | 50.00 |
| March, | ...... | 1.50 | 4.00 | 23.00 | 60.00 |
| April, | ...... | 1.50 | 5.00 | 20.00 | 100.00 |
| May, | ...... | 1.50 | 5.50 | 19.00 | ...... |
| June, | ...... | 1.50 | 6.50 | 18.00 | ...... |
| July, | ...... | 1.50 | 9.00 | 21.00 | ...... |
| August, | ...... | 1.50 | 14.00 | 23.00 | ...... |
| September, | ...... | 2.00 | 14.00 | 25.00 | ...... |
| October, | ...... | 2.00 | 14.00 | 26.00 | ...... |
| November, | $1.10 | 2.50 | 15.00 | 30.00 | ...... |
| December, | 1.15 | 2.50 | 20.00 | ...... | ...... |
| Dec. 1st to 10th | ...... | ...... | ...... | 35.00 | ...... |
| Dec. 10th to 20th, | ...... | ...... | ...... | 42.00 | ...... |
| Dec. 20th to 30th, | ...... | ...... | ...... | 49.00 | ...... |

This table is found in *Laws*, 1866, chap. xxxix.

banks had more than a million dollars in specie,[1] and at the close they still had $800,000.[2]

The State assumed the Confederate tax and levied a special tax to pay it. This was never fully collected. The payment to the Confederate government was in excess of what was due and the State was later reimbursed. The Confederacy also paid it about $8,000,000 for supplies for the army. The state expenditures for military purposes to November, 1864, were nearly twenty millions.

The military stores were obtained, for the most part, from Europe by means of blockade-runners. In 1862, General J. G. Martin suggested that the State should purchase and operate a vessel of its own. In spite of opposition[3] the plan was adopted and the vessel was purchased for $190,000 and paid for with cotton without drawing on the treasury. The " Ad-Vance," as the vessel was named, was an English vessel, built for passenger service and described by Governor Vance as " long-legged." It could carry eight hundred bales of cotton and a double supply of coal. Thus it was able to bring from Bermuda enough Welsh coal for the return voyage. Eleven successful trips were made. After the fifth trip Governor Vance sold a half-interest for $130,000, with which he redeemed state bonds. The vessel was finally lost through the act of the captain of the Confederate cruiser, " Tallahassee." Being short of coal, he took from the " Ad-Vance " her extra supply. This obliged her to make her outward trip with North Carolina coal, which reduced her speed, left a trail of smoke, and

---

[1] *Report of Finance Committee,* 1861.

[2] Governor Worth's message, 1865.

[3] B. F. Moore opposed it as unconstitutional. Holden also opposed it for political reasons.

thus made her fall a victim to the Federal blockaders.[1]  The
State also had an interest in the " Hansa " and the " Don."
Their use, however, was abandoned on account of the ex-
cessive charge made by the Confederate government, one-
half of each cargo being seized.  Through the use of these
vessels an immense amount of valuable stores was imported.  No entirely accurate figures can be obtained as to
the amount, but Governor Vance said in 1885 [2] that he had
distributed large quantities of machinery, 60,000 pairs of
hand wool cards, 10,000 scythes, 200 barrels of bluestone
for fertilizing wheat, 250,000 pairs of shoes, 50,000
blankets, cloth for 250,000 uniforms, 12,000 overcoats,
2,000 Enfield rifles with 100 rounds of ammunition each,
100,000 pounds of bacon, 500 sacks of coffee, $50,000
worth of medicines at gold prices, and an immense supply
of minor stores.  Through this means the North Carolina
troops were clothed.

The state taxes were increased several times during the
war.  The tax on real estate in 1861 was one-fifth of one
per cent, and in 1863 it was two-fifths of one per cent, and
in 1864 was one per cent.  The revenue, consequently, more
than doubled in amount, but in specie value fell one-third
in 1862 and one-half in 1863.[3]  The revenue acts show a
decided extension.  That of 1862 included a graduated inheritance tax on all amounts exceeding $100, and also an
income tax. [4]  Of all the taxes, the Confederate tax in kind
bore most heavily and was, consequently, the most unpopular.  To it North Carolina was one of the largest con-
tributors.  No accurate record can be found of the entire

---

[1] Governor's message, 1864.

[2] Speech at Baltimore.  A more accurate and detailed account is in
the *Confederate* of June 28, 1864.

[3] Schwab, *Confederate States of America*, p. 303.

[4] *Laws*, 1862-3, chap. lvii.

amount of produce collected. By June, 1864, 3,000,000 pounds of bacon, 75,000 tons of hay and fodder, 770,000 bushels of wheat, besides other produce valued at $150,000 had been collected.[1] For the other Confederate taxes, the State paid, by 1864, $10,000,000.

During the years immediately preceding the war, many of the newspapers and a few of the leading men had advocated taking steps towards the commercial independence of the South. But the plan went no further than suggestion before hostilities commenced. In 1860, the manufacturing interests of the State were of but slight importance. There were 39 cotton factories, all of them small. Of the seven woollen mills, only two, at Rock Island and Salem, were of any importance. Iron was worked to a small extent, but the total capital invested was only $200,000, and this was distributed among more than thirty plants. Of every kind there were only 3,689 manufacturing establishments in the State, and out of a population of 992,622, only 14,217 were employed in these factories.[2] It is true that home manufacture supplied many of the domestic needs, but this was of small aid in solving the economic problems which the war imposed.

The State was even without an adequate source for a supply of salt, and this early occupied the attention of the convention. An ordinance was passed, providing for the election of a commissioner to manufacture salt and sell it to the people at cost price.[3] A later ordinance gave the commissioner power to purchase land for salt works, and if necessary, seize it under the right of eminent domain.[4] The same act exempted from military service all persons under

[1] Schwab, *Confederate States of America*, p. 297.
[2] The figures were obtained from the census of 1860.
[3] *Ordinances*, second session, no. 8.   [4] *Ibid.*, third session, no. 18.

contract to make salt. This remained in force until 1864, when General Whiting broke up the salt works and conscripted the employees.[1] In 1862, the governor was directed to employ in the works Quakers who could not pay the exemption fee of $100.[2] Dr. John M. Worth was appointed commissioner. He was later succeeded by D. G. Worth. The first works were at Morehead City and were captured by the enemy before they were well in operation. Works were then located near Wilmington, and were producing 250 bushels per day when yellow fever broke out. The industry was later resumed and carried on, with some interruptions, until the capture of Wilmington. The works were raided by the federal troops in 1864, but with little damage. During the year, 66,100 bushels of salt were made and sold at $7.75 per bushel, when the market price at Wilmington was $19. Before the end of the year, the price was raised to $13, the market price rising to $25. By March, 1865, the market price in Raleigh was $70. The works were entirely self-supporting and paid back the original outlay. The State was also interested in the works at Saltville, Virginia. In addition to the state works, it was estimated that private individuals made about 2,500 bushels a day. Most of this was carried to other States for speculation.[3] The value of the salt works cannot be fully realized unless the conditions existing in the army and in some of the other States where no provision for a supply was made, are remembered.

The danger of speculation was another thing which early attracted attention. Prices of the necessaries of life began to rise during the first year of the war and soon reached a speculative point. The *Standard* was particularly and

---

[1] Hamilton, ed., *The Correspondence of Jonathan Worth*, i, pp. 321-49.
[2] *Ordinances*, fourth session, p. 164.
[3] Governor's message, 1864. *Report of Salt Commissioner*, 1864.

justly abusive of the speculators and promised to keep a "Roll of Dishonor" for publication at the close of the war.[1] To lessen the evil, Governor Clark, acting under the advice of the Council of State, proclaimed an embargo upon the exportation of certain supplies from the State, except for the use of the state or Confederate governments.[2] An extension of this was made a few weeks later.[3] The convention, at its second session, made speculation in the necessaries of life a misdemeanor.[4] This was evidently inoperative for some reason, and the legislature at various times during the war considered the matter. One law was enacted prohibiting the practice,[5] but it seems to have been utterly futile. Governor Vance had recommended its passage and at the same time placed an embargo on the necessaries of life for thirty days.[6]

Prices rose steadily as the war progressed.[7] A board of

---

[1] *Standard*, October 2, November 20, 1861, *et seq.*

[2] *Register*, September 25, 1861.  [3] *Ibid.*, October 9, 1861.

[4] *Ordinances*, second session, p. 75.  [5] *Laws*, 1862-3, chap. lvi.

[6] *Off. Rec.*, no. 128, p. 214.

[7] The following table, gathered from the Raleigh market reports, gives a good idea of the rise of prices on various articles:

| Article. | Price, Sept. 15, 1862. | June 8, 1863. | Aug. 29, 1864. | March 27, 1865. |
|---|---|---|---|---|
| Bacon, per pound, | $0.33 | $1.00 | $5.50 | $7.50 |
| Beef, per pound, | .12 | .50 | 2.50 | 3.00 |
| Corn, per bushel, | 1.10 | 5.50 | 20.00 | 30.00 |
| Meal, per bushel, | 1.25 | 5.50 | 20.00 | 30.00 |
| Coffee, per pound, | 2.50 | None | 15.00 | 40.00 |
| Eggs, per dozen, | .30 | 1.75 | 1.40 | 5.00 |
| Fowls, each, | .40 | 1.50 | 3.00 | 6.00 |
| Lard, per pound, | .30 | 1.00 | 5.50 | 7.50 |
| Molasses, per gallon, | 3.00 | 10.00 | 25.00 | 25.00 |
| Potatoes, per bushel, | 1.00 | 4.00 | 7.00 | 30.00 |
| Sweet potatoes, per bushel, | 1.50 | 5.00 | 6.00 | 35.00 |
| Wheat, per bushel, | 3.00 | 8.00 | 25.00 | 50.00 |
| Flour, per barrel, | 18.00 | 35.00 | 125.00 | 500.00 |
| Pork, per pound, | ...... | 1.60 | 4.00 | 5.50 |
| Sugar, per pound, | .75 | 1.60 | 12.00 | 30.00 |
| Brandy or whiskey, per gal., | 5.00 | 20.00 | 40.00 | 100.00 |

appraisement was appointed to value articles for purchase by the government, but their prices were far below the market. Every two months a new schedule of prices was published for the information of the people.

Many families had every male member in the army and no other means of support but their labor. The pay of a private, or for that matter, of an officer, in the Confederate army, was not sufficient for the support of one person, and consequently widespread distress soon appeared. In and around Raleigh, everyone could get a living by working in the factories and hospitals. But this only affected a small part of the population. Early in his administration, Governor Vance saw the condition which would arise, and took immediate steps to prevent suffering so far as possible. He asked Weldon N. Edwards to assemble the convention to consider what plan should be adopted to relieve distress, but this request was refused.

At the governor's recommendation, the legislature authorized him to purchase and store provisions to sell to the poor at cost.[1] A large quantity was purchased in the fall of 1862, but only a small part was needed, as the crops were unusually good.[2] But the value of the plan was seen in the later years of the war, when the crops were smaller and food more scarce. One great cause of the distress in the State was the lack of facilities for transportation. This often kept supplies from being sent where they were most needed. There were portions of the State where the amount of suffering was very slight. The few records that remain of the tithe collection, show that in many places the crops were good and food abundant. But impressment and foraging by detachments of Confederate troops, and the

---

[1] *Laws*, 1862-3, chap. xv.

[2] Governor's message, November, 1863.

foraging and destruction by the enemy, in the eastern and western portions of the State, led to the loss of a great part. Governor Vance sent frequent and bitter complaints to Secretary Seddon. In one of his letters, he said: "If God Almighty had yet in store another plague for the Egyptians, worse than all others, I am sure it must have been a regiment or so of half-armed, half-disciplined Confederate cavalry."[1] Another cause of just complaint was the bringing of large numbers of worn-out horses to the western part of the State to recuperate. There, they were turned loose, and in the absence of fences caused immense damage to the growing crops. Complaints to Richmond, however, brought no redress and no cessation of the nuisance.[2]

A great cause of suffering was the lack of drugs. Such as were used were mostly of home manufacture. The "Ad-Vance" brought in large quantities, but nearly all were sent to the front or used in the military hospitals in the State. Sickness, as might be expected, was very frequent. Smallpox existed in many neighborhoods and the lesser epidemics were everywhere. In 1862, Wilmington was visited by a virulent type of yellow fever which in two months caused 441 deaths. The total number of cases was 1,505. New Bern also had a sharp epidemic of yellow fever, but it was during federal occupation and no statistics are available.

In May, 1861, the legislature passed a stay law. This was declared unconstitutional by the Supreme Court, and was repealed in September and another passed. This prevented executions' being issued in civil suits. In 1863, the provisions of the statute of limitations were extended for

---

[1] Vance to Seddon, December 1, 1863.
[2] *Laws*, second session, 1861, chap. xi.

civil matters by omitting the period from May 20 to the end of the war.

By 1865, the State was, in an economic sense, almost prostrate.[1] The end of the war thus averted much suffering that would have followed had hostilities continued longer.

[1] The following extract from *The Last Ninety Days of the War* gives an excellent idea of the condition of the portion of the population that had been wealthy before the war: "In North Carolina families of the highest respectability and refinement lived for months on corn bread, sorghum, and peas. Meat was seldom on the table, tea and coffee never; dried apples and peaches were a luxury. Children went barefoot through the winter, and ladies made their own shoes and wove their own homespuns; carpets were cut into blankets, and window curtains and sheets were torn up for hospital use; soldiers' socks were knit day and night, while for home service, clothes were turned twice and patches were patched again."

# CHAPTER TWO

## Beginnings of Reconstruction During the War

No sooner had the federal troops gained a foothold in the State than efforts were made to gather together such of the people as favored the cause of the Union and such as were dissatisfied with the Confederacy, by means of the establishment of a new state government around which they might rally. Two such attempts were made, both of which were unsuccessful. In the first instance, the movement professed to originate within the State. Although it was sponsored by the federal military forces, it was designed to form a civil government. The second was avowedly military and had its origin in an order from the President of the United States.

### I. THE HATTERAS CONVENTION AND GOVERNMENT.

The fall of Fort Hatteras and the capture of Hatteras Inlet by the federal fleet and forces under General B. F. Butler in 1861, gave an opportunity for the first enterprise. Certain persons who were disloyal to the state government began a movement, avowedly intended to restore the State to the Union, but really designed, as the sequel indicated, chiefly to promote their own interests.

The population of Hyde and Washington counties was sparse and was almost entirely unprotected from the invading forces. Practically all of the male population who were in sympathy with the Confederacy, were in the army. Those at home were Unionists in feeling, partly through genuine dislike of the war and a desire to avoid military service for the Confederacy, and partly also by fear of the federal forces, at whose mercy they were placed on account of the lack of any adequate coast defence.

Almost immediately after the capture of the Inlet, Colonel Rush C. Hawkins of the Ninth New York Volunteers was approached by some of the inhabitants who had taken flight at the approach of the federal fleet, and asked to grant them permission to return to their homes, as they had taken no part against the United States and had no desire to do so. At his suggestion, about thirty took the oath of allegiance and promised to keep the commander of the federal forces informed of the movements of the Confederates. In return they were promised protection. Within a week, two hundred and fifty persons had taken the oath under similar conditions. They declared that secret meetings were being held in all the counties bordering on Pamlico Sound and that fear alone prevented the people from openly avowing their Union sentiments.[1] Colonel Hawkins, in his report, suggested the possibility of a convention of the State's being called by the people under the protection of the federal forces, through which, he thought, a third of the State would be at once restored to the Union. In order to forward a movement of this kind, as fast as the inhabitants took the oath they were sent across the sound to act as spies and to test opinion there. Their reports led him to believe that it would be productive of good results to enlist North Carolina volunteers for service in the State. He suggested that, as a pledge of

[1] *Off. Rec.*, no. 4, p. 608.

good intentions, the government should pay for the property which had been plundered and destroyed by federal troops, not amounting in all, he thought, to more than $5,000, and also provide the inhabitants with food and clothing.[1] He was greatly hindered in his progress toward pacification by the depredations of the 20th New York Regiment and threatened their commanding officer, Colonel Weber, with the use of artillery against them if a stop was not put to it.[2]

Acting upon his suggestions, President Lincoln in September wrote General Scott, requesting him to frame an order for recruiting North Carolina volunteers at Fort Hatteras. He left it to General Scott to decide about the officers, but said Secretary Seward thought his nephew, Clarence Seward, "would be willing to go and play colonel and assist in raising the force."[3] In accordance with this, the acceptance of North Carolina volunteers, not to exceed one regiment, was authorized. On September 17, Colonel Hawkins, in order to clear the minds of the people of prejudice against the federal forces, issued a proclamation, addressed to the people of North Carolina, declaring as the purpose of the invasion the relief of the loyal people of the State from "rebels and traitors," and calling upon the people to return to their allegiance to the United States.[4] He scattered copies of this proclamation through all the country along Pamlico Sound and sent them to various inland towns. Almost immediately, the state authorities became aware of it, but Governor Clark, while alarmed at the reports which reached him, was unable to do anything which would remedy matters. Judge Biggs, of

[1] *Off. Rec.*, no. 4, pp. 608-9.    [2] *Ibid.*, p. 610.
[3] *Ibid.*, p. 613.    [4] *Ibid.*, pp. 658-9.

the Confederate District Court, wrote General R. C. Gatlin, who commanded the Confederate forces in the East, that he was doubtful if a majority of the population of Washington County could be depended on, in case of invasion, and that while few were openly disloyal, the sentiment in Tyrrell and Beaufort was such as to cause grave uneasiness.[1] This was the condition of affairs when the self-constituted leaders of Union sentiment in eastern North Carolina began the movement which, it was hoped, would result in the restoration of the State to the Union.

These leaders were Charles Henry Foster and Marble Nash Taylor. Comparatively little is known of either of them. Taylor was a Methodist minister, a native of the "Pan-Handle" of Virginia, who was with the Confederate troops at Hatteras. He joined the federal forces before the capture and was accused, whether falsely or not, of giving to them information which contributed to the ease with which victory was obtainéd. In a letter to a brother-in-law in Cumberland County, where he himself had formerly lived, he said that he had been compelled by the force of circumstances to side with the Union.[2]

Charles Henry Foster was a native of Maine and a graduate of Bowdoin College. He had first come South in the employ of some land company, and in 1860 was editor of a Breckinridge newspaper in Murfreesboro.[3] He was, apparently, in favor of secession, but after the fall of Sumter, his attitude made the people suspicious, and he was expelled from the town by a public meeting

[1] *Off. Rec.*, no. 4, p. 671.
[2] *Western Democrat*, October 1, 1861.
[3] New Bern *Progress*, December 12, 1861

of the citizens. He appealed to Governor Ellis for permission to remain in the State and, through the efforts of friends, the vote was rescinded. He had in the meantime declared his good intentions.[1] But in November he had succeeded in reaching New York, and in company with Taylor attended a large meeting at which George Bancroft presided, which was held for the assistance and encouragement of the proposed new administration in North Carolina.[2] The plan of action was largely mapped out there and the state department was notified of their intentions by Foster, who stated that all the North Carolinians in New York, who were loyal to the Union, favored the plan and that it was hoped and expected that it would largely increase the Union sentiment in the State. He also said that six counties would be represented in the convention, which had already been called, and that while the Unionists of the western part of the State had desired that the movement should begin there, they had agreed to the plan as formed and would ratify all the acts of the new administration. No change in the laws and constitution of the State, as they were in April, 1861, was intended. The proposed government would have authority with a majority of the freemen of the State, and when " rebel intimidation " was disposed of, it would be recognized by 60,000 men, since all the great mining, railroad, and other business interests of the State were committed to the plan.[3]

The so-called convention of the people met, November 18, at Hatteras. The minutes of the meeting name

---

[1] *Register*, May 21, 1862. He stated in a letter that his oath as a Knight of the Golden Circle would prevent his taking sides against the South.

[2] New York *Tribune*, November 8, 1861.

[3] *Off. Rec.* no. 122, pp. 630-1.

forty-five counties as represented. Only six or eight persons, however, composed the convention, Taylor and Foster holding what they called proxies for the rest of the counties named. These so-called proxies were authorized by no meetings of citizens, but merely by individuals, who, in most instances, lived in other States.[1]

An ordinance proclaimed Taylor provisional governor, and another declared the ordinance of secession null and void and instructed the governor to issue a call for an election of members of Congress.[2] He took the oath of office before a justice of the peace, and two days later issued the proclamation. The election was held and Foster received all the votes cast. He, accordingly, presented himself in Washington, as a member from either the first or the second district. The matter was referred to a committee, which reported unfavorably, and in December a resolution was passed declaring him not entitled to a seat from either of the districts named.[3] He was not discouraged and another similar election was held January 16, at which he again received all the votes. A large number of memorials requesting his admission were sent to Congress, and, in the meantime, for some reason, possibly because he feared his case was weak, another election was held January 30, with the same result. Later, he claimed that this was a postponement

---

[1] The following is one of the proxies:

"Lima, N. Y., November 15, 1861.

Dear Sir:—I address you this line to request you to represent the Union men of Onslow County, North Carolina, in the State convention to organize a provincial government, having once been a resident of the county and knowing something of the feeling there existing.

Rev. M. N. Taylor.             I am, respectively,

J. W. BAILEY."

[2] *House Mis. Docs.*, no. 2, 37 Cong., 2 sess.

[3] *Ibid.*, no. 15, 37 Cong., 2 sess.

from the sixteenth. Taylor, as a private citizen, then petitioned Congress to order an election, and Foster requested the same thing.

The voting in all the elections was in Hyde County only. The memorials ratifying his election were, in several cases, signed in only one or two handwritings, and when he appeared before the committee on elections, he could give only a very inadequate explanation of the fact, but claimed that he had been rightfully, if not legally, elected. He made no claim for the existence, *de facto* or *de jure*, of the Hatteras government, but urged that the Union men of North Carolina should be recognized by Congress. He was forced to acknowledge that only about four hundred citizens of the district had expressed their approval of his claim, although its voting population was over nine thousand. The chief basis for his claim was the precedent set by the admission of Maynard and Clements from Tennessee, who had been elected in somewhat the same way.[1] His claim was so poorly supported and his statements so contradictory that the resolution declaring him not entitled to a seat passed with no opposition. An attempt made to compensate him as a contestant failed.

And so ended the first attempt at reconstruction.[2]

## 2. THE ADMINISTRATION OF EDWARD STANLY.

The second attempt at reconstruction was begun May 19, 1862, when President Lincoln, as commander-in-chief of the army, at the suggestion of Reverdy Johnson, appointed Edward Stanly military governor of North

---

[1] *House Reports*, no. 118, 37 Cong., 2 sess.

[2] Taylor became a newspaper correspondent. Foster was later captain of a company of colored troops and was dismissed from the service through General Butler's efforts. In 1868, he was defeated for the convention.

Carolina, with the rank of brigadier-general.[1] Unlike all the other nominations of this kind, this was never sent to the Senate for confirmation.[2] He was empowered to perform all the duties of governor, and to appoint officers, institute courts, and suspend the writ of *habeas corpus*, during the pleasure of the President, or until a civil government should be organized.[3]

A general belief prevailed in the North that there was so strong a Union sentiment in North Carolina that, with a capable leader, the State could soon be reclaimed for the Union. So far as devotion to the Union was concerned, Edward Stanly was a most suitable choice to "foster Union sentiment."[4] He was born in North Carolina in 1808 and had attained great prominence there. He had been three times a member of the House of Commons and twice had been speaker. He had also been a representative in Congress, where he had been very influential. In addition, he had served one term as attorney general of the State. He had removed to California in 1853, and in 1857, although a believer in slavery and a slaveholder himself, had been nominated by the Republicans there for governor, but had been defeated. He was a man of high and uncontrolled temper and was noted for his bitter denunciation of political opponents. He made many warm friends, but as many equally bitter enemies, and was consequently ill adapted for a conciliatory mission. The fact that he was a native only made his task more difficult.

---

[1] President Lincoln, without success, urged Stanly to take the rank of major-general. New Bern *Republic-Courier*, Jan. 3, 1873.

[2] *House Reports*, no. 7 (testimony), p. 885, 40 Cong., 1 sess.

[3] *Off. Rec.*, no. 9, p. 396.

[4] So expressed by Hon. John S. Ely of New York, in a letter to Stanly.

The day after his appointment, Secretary Stanton notified him of his duties and ordered General Burnside to co-operate with him and furnish any military assistance that might be necessary.[1]  Governor Stanly arrived in New Bern, May 26.  General Burnside was at first, seemingly, doubtful of their relations,[2] but later was thoroughly in sympathy with his policy.[3]  No sooner had he reached North Carolina than Stanly, in seeking to conciliate the people and to execute the state laws, made himself an object of dislike and suspicion to the element in Congress and at the North to whom the chief purpose of the war was the abolition of slavery with all its concomitants.  An enthusiastic gentleman from New England had established a school for negro children in New Bern.  Concerning this, Stanly announced that while he approved of kindness to the destitute, black or white, he had been sent there to restore the old order of things and, consequently, could not give his approval to the school, as it would injure the Union cause.  He consented that such religious instruction might be given as was thought best.  Apart from this, he said that the laws of North Carolina forbade the teaching of slaves to read and write, and he could not expect success in his undertaking, if, at the start, he encouraged violation of the law.  Consequently, he demanded the closing of the school.  In respect to fugitive slaves, also, Stanly took like ground.  Slaves were constantly leaving their masters and coming into the Union lines, and in many instances they were taken away by the soldiers and notified that they were free.  Whenever the owners would take the oath of allegiance to the United States, Stanly had the slaves restored to them.[4]  He also threatened with

---

[1] *Off. Rec.*, no. 9, p. 397.  
[2] *Ibid.*, p. 403.  
[3] *Ibid.*, p. 394.  
[4] *Ibid.*, p. 400.

confiscation the owners of vessels who carried off slaves.[1]

H. H. Helper, a brother of Hinton Rowan Helper, who held a civil position in New Bern, wrote a letter to Stanly offering some advice as to how he should execute the duties of his office. Stanly resented it and ordered Helper to leave New Bern. He at once went North, in company with Vincent Colyer, the gentleman whose school had been closed, and furnished the newspapers with a highly-colored account of Stanly's official actions. This led to sharp criticism of the governor and to the accusation that he was in sympathy with the South. On June 3 the House of Representatives passed a resolution asking the President to furnish information as to the powers conferred upon Stanly by his appointment, whether he had interfered to prevent the education of children, black or white, and if so, by what authority. If by the authority of the government, for what purpose were such instructions given? Similar resolutions were also passed in the Senate.[2] Secretary Stanton referred the matter to Stanly, who at once replied outlining his policy and asking for instructions. The following points on which he desired information show the difficulties he had to meet almost daily:

When slaves are taken violently from loyal owners by armed men and negroes, what protection can be given for the future? When persons connected with the army cause slaves to leave their masters, can the latter, if loyal, have permission and protection to prevail on them to return? Will authority be given to prevent the removal of slave property by vessel without the consent of the owners? If the military governor

---

[1] Correspondence of *New York Herald* of May 31st, 1862.

[2] *Sen. Journal*, pp. 553, 566.

should interfere with actions that are in violation of long-established laws of the State, and persons connected with the army should make inflammatory appeals to a crowd composed of several hundred negroes, exhorting them to violence and bloodshed, what action should he take to prevent its recurrence? When slaves of loyal owners are employed by the United States authorities, can any steps be taken to secure a part of their earnings for their owners?[1]

It is apparent that there was a decided difference of opinion between the governor and the officers commanding in North Carolina, for in April, General Parke had notified citizens of Beaufort, who had appealed to him to prevent slaves from coming into his lines, that he would not use force to aid owners in their recovery, but would only allow them to use persuasion.[2] General Burnside had also adopted the policy, almost necessarily, it is true, of never returning any escaped slaves to their owners.[3] In addition to these difficulties, Stanly was beginning to discover that a difference had arisen between himself and those with whom he had been intimately associated in the past and that Union sentiment was at a minimum in North Carolina. Even in New Bern, occupied as it was by federal troops, very little appeared.[4] This change of sentiment, since the time when he lived in North Carolina before, had not been comprehended by him when he came back to the State, and seemed inexplicable.

In the hope of arousing some feeling he visited the various towns in which he was well known, and which were now occupied by the Union forces, and made speeches.[5] But he accomplished little for the Union

[1] *Off. Rec.*, no. 9, pp. 401–2.  [2] *Ibid.*, no. 9, p. 382.
[3] *Ibid.*, p. 390.  [4] *Ibid.*, p. 409.
[5] *Western Sentinel*, June 27, 1862.

cause, for he was generally regarded with hatred and suspicion as a traitor to his State, and this kept from him the support of all men of character and influence. For a time the federal officers in the State thought he would be of great benefit to the Union cause, but this feeling disappeared when his policy was clearly seen. [1]

The policy of the state government and of the Confederate officers was to ignore Stanly's pretensions to the office of governor and to communicate officially only with General Burnside. [2]   In the fall of 1862 Stanly wrote to Governor Vance and asked for an interview with him or with any citizens of the State that he might select. He said that he felt sure that North Carolina was in the quarrel only through a misunderstanding, and he wished to confer in regard to measures that might lead to an honorable peace; that he was authorized to negotiate an exchange of political prisoners and wished this interview with its object to be perfectly open. Governor Vance declined the proposal [3] on the ground that he was without authority from the Confederate government to treat for peace and that separate state action was not to be thought of. [4]   A correspondence with General D. H. Hill and General S. G. French did not lead to any more hope of reconciliation, but, if possible, rendered it more unlikely, since Stanly provoked indignation by the violence of his language.

[1] *Off. Rec.*, no. 9, p. 397.

[2] *Executive Correspondence*, Clark, p. 337.

[3] Holden said in 1867 that, on his advice, Governor Vance would have consented to treat with Stanly for peace, but was prevented by W. A. Graham.  As the statement was made in a political attack upon the latter, it is not worthy of credit. *Standard*, January 16, 1867.

[4] The correspondence will be found in *Off. Rec.*, no. 123, pp. 845–9. Governor Vance ignored Stanly's military title, and Stanly himself wrote as a private citizen.

He was greatly handicapped in his peaceful efforts by the operations of the Union troops in the eastern part of the State. His argument, that they were a " glorious army of noble patriots," lost its significance in view of their constant plundering and burning, and his protests against this were without avail. General Burnside, when he first landed in the State, had forbidden all unnecessary injury to the property or persons of the inhabitants,[1] but when General Foster assumed command no attention was paid to this order.[2] Stanly's last official act was a protest against the conduct of the troops in Hyde County.[3] The condition of the "loyal" population was thus pitiful. Cut off from Confederate protection, partly by circumstances and still more by their own acts, their "loyalty" insured them no immunity from outrage and violence at the hands of the federal troops.

In December Stanly ordered an election to be held for a member of Congress from the second district. Jennings Pigott, a native of the State who had been a resident of Washington City for many years, and had only returned as Stanly's private secretary, was chosen. Charles H. Foster contested the election, but neither was seated.[4]

In the meantime, Stanly had become convinced of the hopelessness of his mission. More than that, he was utterly out of sympathy with the policy of the adminis-

---

[1] *Off. Rec.*, no. 9, p. 359.

[2] General Foster's course was very different from that of most of the Union officers of high rank in the State. In 1863, he gave his approval to a plan for beginning a general slave insurrection. *Off. Rec.*, no. 26, pp. 1068-9.

[3] *Ibid.*, p. 182.

[4] *Contested Elections*, p. 462. *House Mis. Docs.*, 39 Cong., 2 sess. *Globe*, pp. 1209-12.

tration in regard to the slaves. He protested against the enlisting and drilling of them on the ground that subordinate military officers were unfit to decide when their condition was suitable in the meaning of the President's proclamation, and because it created a danger of a servile war.[1] Finally, January 15, 1863, he sent his resignation to the President, giving at the same time the reason for his action. He stated that he had assured the people of the State that the administration was only trying to restore the Union and would secure the rights of the people. But since the emancipation proclamation, any further assurance of the kind was impossible. Regarding the proclamation he said, "It is enough to say I fear it will do infinite mischief. It crushes all hope of making peace by any conciliatory measures. It will fill the hearts of Union men with despair and strengthen the hands of the detestable traitors whose mad ambition has spread desolation and sorrow over our country. To the negroes themselves it will bring the most direful calamities." He reviewed his course as military governor and said concerning this, "That I have offended some is probable; but they were those whose schemes of plunder I defeated—whose oppressions of the innocent and helpless I resisted—whose purposes seemed to have been to join or follow the troops and to encourage and participate in the most shameful pillaging and robbery that ever disgraced an army in any civilized land."[2]

[1] *Off. Rec.*, no. 26, p. 525.

[2] *House Report*, no. 7 (testimony), pp. 331–2. Stanly's letter to Senator Sumner was even more caustic. In part he said, "Had the war in North Carolina been conducted by soldiers who were Christians and gentlemen, the State would long ago have rebelled against rebellion. But instead of that, what was done? Thousands and thousands of dollars' worth of property were conveyed North. Libraries, pianos, carpets, mirrors, family portraits, everything in short, that

His resignation was accepted in March, and he returned to California. No successor was appointed. In the State it was thought that Daniel R. Goodloe, a North Carolina abolitionist, would be appointed, but the position probably seemed to the President a very useless one. In 1864 Stanly wrote the President that he had been asked to return to the State and that when he was needed in his private capacity he was ready to go.[1] But no occasion for his services ever arose.

The second attempt at reconstruction had ended as disastrously as the first, so far as the progress of Union sentiment was concerned.[2] It remained for the military forces of the United States to begin the final and ultimately successful attempt when all resistance in the State to the authority of the United States was at an end.

### 3. THE DOWNFALL OF THE STATE GOVERNMENT.

The fall of Richmond and the steady advance of the federal army on the state capital showed that the end of the struggle was at hand. It was clear that no effective opposition to Sherman's advance could be made, and preparations were begun to save what little remained unhurt in the State, particularly the property of the State.

could be removed, was stolen by men abusing flagitious slaveholders and preaching liberty, justice, and civilization. I was informed that one regiment of abolitionists had conveyed North more than $40,000 worth of property. They literally robbed the cradle and the grave. Family burying vaults were broken open for robbery; and in one instance (the fact was published in a Boston paper and admitted to me by an officer of high position in the army), a vault was entered, a metallic coffin removed, and the remains cast out that those of a dead soldier might be put in the place." *Sentinel*, Jan. 26, 1870.

[1] Governor Stanly, after his return to California, opposed the radical policy of Congress, and in 1867, canvassed the State against the Republican candidate for governor. He died in 1872.

[2] Stanly was of infinite service to the people of New Bern as a protector against injury.

Ex-Governor Swain, from his retirement at Chapel Hill, entered into correspondence with Senator Graham and Governor Vance. Perceiving the impossibility of a meeting of the legislature in time to be of service, he suggested that Governor Vance should hold a conference with the former governors of the State as to the best course to follow.[1] Graham had been convinced ever since his return from Richmond, at the close of the session of Congress, that the Confederate cause was hopeless and also that, as long as supplies for the army could be obtained by the administration, the war would be continued. Consequently he thought it the duty of the state administration to attempt to make as good terms as possible with the federal forces. In any event he thought it best that the legislature should be in session and ready to act when it should be necessary. He accordingly advised Governor Vance to this effect. Then, in conference with Swain, he worked out a complete plan of action: the General Assembly should be summoned and should pass resolutions expressing a desire for peace and inviting the other Southern States to join the movement; commissioners should be elected to treat with the United States and report to a convention which should at once be called, and in the meantime a commission should treat with General Sherman for a suspension of hostilities.

Senator Graham had warned Governor Vance that the North Carolina members of the Confederate House of Representatives, or most of them, were ready to call the legislature by advertisement. But the governor was still doubtful of the wisdom of the proposed plan. He did finally summon the Council of State, but only a bare

---

[1] Of these, Swain, Graham, Morehead, Manly, Reid, Bragg, and Clark were still living.

quorum were present, and the vote on the question submitted to them resulted in a tie. The governor then refused to issue the summons to the legislature. But when the plan matured by Graham and Swain was laid before him by the latter and when it became evident that General Sherman would occupy the capital in a few days, he yielded, and after consulting General Johnston, decided to send for Graham and discuss the question of treating with the enemy. The conference was held and a letter to General Sherman prepared, asking for an interview regarding the suspension of hostilities.[1] General Johnston in the meantime had retired westward; but before he left Raleigh he advised Governor Vance to make the best terms possible.[2] Ex-Governor Bragg, B. F. Moore, and Kenneth Rayner were consulted and agreed to the plan. General Hardee was present at the conference and gave Graham and Swain, who agreed to act as commissioners, a safe-conduct through the lines.[3]

In Raleigh there was great excitement but very little disorder. The inhabitants were busy concealing valuables in hope that these might escape the usual fate of movable property along the line of march of Sherman's army. A large number of houses in Fayetteville had been burned and it was greatly feared that Raleigh would not escape. The legislature, at its last session, had authorized the removal of all the state records, and cases had been made for that purpose. The Council of State, at a meeting in March, decided that the governor and treasurer or one of them should take the records away if it became necessary. They were now placed in the care of Treasurer Worth and carried to Company Shops, a

[1] *Off. Rec.*, no. 100, p. 178.
[2] Dowd, *Life of Vance*, p. 483.
[3] Spencer, *Last Ninety Days of the War*, pp. 142-4.

small place in Alamance County.  At the same time an immense quantity of supplies belonging to the State was distributed along the line of the North Carolina Railroad between Raleigh and Salisbury.  Governor Vance remained in Raleigh to hear the result of the conference with Sherman, in doubt whether to continue there or to retreat with the army as he was urged to do.

The same day General Archer Anderson notified President Davis that commissioners were going to Sherman with proposals for peace, and ordered General Hampton not to allow them to pass.  Governor Vance also notified President Davis of the fact.  General Johnston then directed General Hampton to arrest the members of the deputation, and to allow no communication with the enemy, except by flag of truce.   In the meantime the commissioners, accompanied by three members of the governor's staff, [1] had left Raleigh to meet General Sherman who was about fourteen miles distant.  When they had gone some distance from Raleigh they were stopped by General Hampton, who was unwilling to pass them but could not refuse to obey General Hardee's order.  Consequently, after some delay, he passed them and sent a courier to General Sherman with communications from himself and from the commissioners.  They had hardly started when the order came from General Johnston for them to return to Raleigh.  They were again stopped and turned back, but on the way to Raleigh the train was captured by General Atkins and the commissioners carried to General Kilpatrick's headquarters.  There they received the first news of Lee's surrender.  From there they were sent to General Sherman, who treated them with every courtesy and with whom they remained until

[1] These were Surgeon-General Warren, Colonel Burr, and Major Devereux.

the next day. [1] He requested them to inform the governor that, in accordance with his instructions from the President, he wished the state officers to continue in the performance of their duties until he could communicate with President Lincoln. [2] He also replied to Governor Vance's letter stating that it was impossible to give him an interview at the time, but enclosed a safe-conduct for himself and such state officers as would remain in Raleigh. [3]

When the commissioners, on their return, reached Raleigh, they found that Governor Vance, who in the meantime had decided to remain in Raleigh, had again, under military pressure, changed his mind and had gone to Hillsboro with General Hoke, who passed through Raleigh that day.[4] Before his departure, he had authorized the mayor to surrender the city, and had written a letter to General Sherman asking his protection for the capital and the state property.

The next day the city was surrendered by a committee of citizens, and the keys of the Capitol were delivered by David L. Swain to an officer of the Union army.[5]

Another safe-conduct was then sent to Governor Vance, but he declined to return before seeing President Davis, who had summoned him to Greensboro. General Breckinridge invited him to be present at the conference with General Sherman, but for some reason he was ex-

[1] Spencer, *Last Ninety Days of the War*, pp. 145–55.

[2] Sherman's *Memoirs*, vol. ii, pp. 327, 345.

[3] *Off. Rec.*, no. 100, pp. 178–9.

[4] Only with great difficulty did Governor Vance decide what course to pursue. Worth entreated him to remain and surrender the Capitol himself, but the influence and insistence of the Confederate officers probably caused his decision to retreat.

[5] Spencer, *Last Ninety Days of the War*, p. 162.

cluded and went on to Greensboro. There he begged permission of the Confederate authorities to accept General Sherman's offer of protection for the state property which was in great danger at the Shops, and to send it back to Raleigh in the care of Jonathan Worth. This General Breckinridge refused to allow. From Greensboro, Governor Vance followed President Davis to Charlotte, where they had a conference. Davis intimated that he wished Vance to accompany him in the retreat, but General Breckinridge interfered, advising him to return to his position and its duties.[1] This he resolved to do, and accordingly sent Worth to Raleigh with a letter to General Sherman in which he volunteered to return, summon the legislature, and recommend its calling a convention.[2] But General Sherman had left Raleigh, and General Schofield, although he and General Sherman had shortly before approved a petition asking Governor Vance to return and call a special session of the legislature,[3] refusing to see him, instructed Worth to bring the records to Raleigh.

Negotiations had been going on in the meantime between Johnston and Sherman in regard to the terms of surrender. During the progress of the negotiations Governor Vance suggested to the former that if they were successful he should turn over the army stores to North Carolina in part payment of the debt owed to the State by the Confederate government. He stated as an additional reason for doing so that the soldiers in Johnston's army had taken possession of much of the state property. General Johnston declined to accede to the

---

[1] Dowd, *Life of Vance*, p. 486.
[2] Letter from Jonathan Worth to the *Sentinel*, October 28, 1865.
[3] Warren to Vance, Aug. 27, 1865.

request and denied that his soldiers had been guilty of plundering the State.[1] When the terms of surrender had been agreed upon and General Schofield came to Greensboro, Governor Vance asked his protection for the state property and offered to surrender himself, but General Schofield, in accordance with his instructions, refused to receive his surrender and advised him to go home.[2] Governor Vance then requested that William A. Graham, John A. Gilmer, and Bedford Brown might go to Washington. By the President's order this was refused.[3] Governor Vance then went home and remained there until May 14, when he was arrested by the President's order, carried to Washington, and confined in Old Capitol Prison.[4] Just before going home he issued an address to the people urging them to abstain from violence of any kind and pledging himself to do all he could to restore the civil authority.[5]

The capture of Raleigh on April 13 was accompanied by very little disorder. Private property, in most instances, was respected, though this was by no means always the case.[6] The offices and property of the *Confederate* and *Conservative* newspapers were immediately destroyed. A few days later General Sherman ordered the *Progress* to suspend publication for criticism of some act of his. Later he allowed its publication to be re-commenced. When the news of President Lincoln's

[1] *Off. Rec.*, no. 111, pp. 419–420.    [2] *Ibid.*, no. 100, pp. 426.

[3] *Ibid.*, pp. 395, 404, 432.

[4] He was arrested by General Kilpatrick, who, according to Vance, improved the opportunity of stealing two spoons. Most of the furniture was then taken, and Mrs. Vance, who was ill, was left on the floor. *Sentinel*, Nov. 1, 1870.

[5] *Standard*, May 3, 1865.

[6] Spencer, *Last Ninety Days of the War*, pp. 174 *et seq.*

assassination came, there was great fear in Raleigh that revenge would be taken by the soldiers upon the town, a fear that was shared by the officers.[1]   The guards were doubled, and every precaution taken, and no violence followed.

There was a great deal of destitution in the town, and this was relieved, in part, by the action of the military authorities in furnishing rations to those in want.   The place was crowded with negroes who had followed the army or come in from the adjoining country, and these were entirely supported by the rations issued.   The policy was adopted of making them return to their homes whenever possible, but this was attended with great difficulty.   Similar conditions, as regards both races, existed in the other towns of the State.   In Wilmington there was probably greater destitution.

General Sherman was anxious to make use of the existing state government for the purpose of re-organization, but the authorities at Washington prevented him.   His wish was well known, and members of the legislature appealed to him to allow them to meet in Raleigh and arrange for holding a session.   Of course this request was refused.[2]

Early in May, General Schofield succeeded him in command of the State.   The disturbances arising from the end of the war and the disbanding of the armies were great, and his efforts to bring quiet at first met with

---

[1] Gen. F. P. Blair, who was staying at the residence of Dr. R. B. Haywood, a classmate at the University of North Carolina, gave him a suit of his own uniform, telling him it might be necessary for him to become a Union general instead of a Confederate surgeon. It is a matter of tradition in Raleigh that General Logan saved the city from being burned by stopping the soldiers who were coming in from Morrisville for the purpose.

[2] *Off. Rec.*, no. 100, pp. 254, 272.

very little success. Proclamations were issued announcing the definitive cessation of hostilities and, in order to remove all doubt, the freedom of the slaves.[1] The taking of the oath of allegiance was hastened by making it a prerequisite for the practice of a profession or for engaging in any business. Nor could marriage licenses be issued until the oath had been taken by both parties.[2] The towns were soon quiet, but the country was not. Nor were the inhabitants altogether to blame; for the federal troops did not soon shake off the habits formed during the war, and even after the proclamation of the final cessation of hostilities, the plundering and wanton destruction of property continued, often accompanied by outrage and violence.[3] This, however, was the exception, and not the rule. The disbanded Confederate soldiers, particularly the cavalry, foraged to some extent as they went home. But their opportunities were not so great and sympathy with them, naturally, was greater.

To put an end to this condition of affairs, General Schofield began the organization of a police force for each county,[4] detailing General J. D. Cox for the work in the western part of the State, General Terry for the central, and Generals Hawley and Palmer for the eastern. They were instructed to have bodies of troops visit all portions of the State and arrest marauders.[5] General Schofield also had the oath of allegiance administered to certain magistrates of known Union sympathies and left them in the exercise of their functions.[6] Prompt justice

[1] *General Orders*, nos. 31 and 32.   [2] *Ibid.*, no. 52.
[3] *Off. Rec.*, no. 100, p. 330 *et seq. Last Ninety Days of the War*, p. 43 *et seq.*
[4] *Off. Rec.*, no. 100, pp. 460, 522 *et seq.*
[5] *General Orders*, no. 35.
[6] *Off. Rec.*, no. 100, p. 610 *et seq.*

was meted out to offenders, in and out of the army, whenever it was possible,[1] and whenever the troops showed disorganization they were mustered out.[2] Every effort was used to have the restrictions on trade removed, for the commander felt that peace would be more quickly restored when destitution, resulting from the abnormal conditions, was relieved, and the people were employed in their usual occupations. He also opposed the rulings of the treasury department in regard to trade.[3]

The delay in making known the policy of the United States government regarding re-organization of the civil government of the State was considered very unfortunate by General Schofield, since he was convinced that the people were well disposed and were ready to make and accept any necessary changes.[4] For the re-organization, he desired the appointment of a military governor who should declare in force the constitution of the State as it existed previous to secession, and appoint officers to serve until the work was completed. An enrolment should then be made of all citizens qualified to vote by state law, after administration of the amnesty oath. A convention should be called and its action submitted to the people. He was anxious to be selected as military governor for North Carolina, provided some such plan as this was adopted, but if negro suffrage was to be included he preferred to have no part in it.[5] General Halleck recommended him for the position, but later withdrew his endorsement on the ground that he could not recommend anyone who had advised Sherman to make the terms which had been proposed with

[1] *Off. Rec.*, no. 100, p. 470.
[3] *Ibid.*, p. 593.
[5] *Ibid.*, pp. 461-3.
[2] *Ibid.*, p. 609.
[4] *Ibid.*, pp. 405, 411.

Johnston.[1] General Schofield's measures for pacifica-
tion and conciliation, meanwhile, were meeting with
such success that when he applied for leave, early in
June, he said that the presence of troops in the State
seemed almost unnecessary.[2] His conduct of affairs met
with the hearty approval of his superiors,[3] and, in every
way, he deserved and received the cordial gratitude of
the people of the State.

[1] *Off. Rec.*, no. 100, pp. 434, 454.       [2] *Ibid.*, p. 513.
[3] *Ibid.*, p. 586.

# CHAPTER THREE

## PRESIDENTIAL RECONSTRUCTION

### I. THE PROVISIONAL GOVERNMENT

ON May 9, 1865, the President summoned W. W. Holden to Washington for a conference. He was detained and did not reach there until the eighteenth. In the meantime D. L. Swain, B. F. Moore, and William Eaton had also been summoned.[1] In company with John H. Wheeler the latter were received by the President, who showed them the proclamation which had already been prepared containing the plan for the restoration of North Carolina. Moore at once objected and urged its unconstitutionality. He desired the President to allow the legislature to meet and to call a convention. General Sherman had promised transportation for the members on the military lines in the State, and it could be accomplished very quickly. The President took the ground that the body had no legal status, and asked further what he could do if, after recognition by him, it should refuse to conform to the terms deemed necessary. Moore assured him that there was " no one of that body who might not be led back into the Union with a silken thread." In the discussion he grew very caustic, particularly so in stating his objection to the appointment of the governor by the President and the calling of a

---

[1] *Off. Rec.*, no. 100, p. 489.

convention without the intervention of the legislature. The President was very good-natured, but was unchangeable in his opinion and plan.

The day after their interview with the President, they returned to the White House at his invitation and found another party from North Carolina present. It was made up of those whom Holden had brought with him.[1] The President laid before them the amnesty proclamation and the North Carolina proclamation, leaving blank in the latter the name of the provisional governor, saying that he would appoint the person they should nominate. Moore, Eaton, and Swain declined to take any part in the proceedings and left the room, as did the President, Swain having seen Holden first and urged him not to accept the appointment.[2] Holden's name was then inserted by those remaining, and the President, on his return, expressed himself as much gratified at their choice and duly made the appointment.[3]

It is an interesting speculation as to who would have been appointed by President Lincoln. The North Carolina proclamation had been prepared the day of his assassination,[4] and it is, at least, likely that he had some one in mind for the position. It is hardly likely that it

[1] The members of the party, besides Holden, were R. P. Dick, Willie Jones, W. R. Richardson, J. H. P. Russ, W. S. Mason, Rev. Thos. Skinner, and Dr. R. J. Powell. The latter was a native of the State, holding a position in the Patent Office.

[2] *Memoirs of W. W. Holden*, p. 47.

[3] The account of the interviews with the President is in Wheeler's *Reminiscences*, p. 60 *et seq*. It is interesting to know that among the candidates for provisional governor was George W. Kirk, already notorious for his part in the border warfare in the West, and destined to become again famous, or rather infamous, in the Reconstruction history of the State. Spencer, *Last Ninety Days of the War*, p. 229.

[4] McCulloch, *Men and Measures of Half a Century*, p. 378.

would have been Holden.[1] His appointment was the
one that President Johnson would have been expected
to make, for there was much to make him appear to the
President the most suitable man for the position. Between Johnson and Holden there was the bond of like
social origin and like political opinions in the past, and
this fact, coupled with their old friendship and communication during the war, makes it probable that Holden
was the choice of the President and that his nomination
by the committee was only a matter of form. At any
rate, it was certain that the members of the delegation,
selected with three exceptions by Holden, would choose
him.

President Johnson formally began his policy of reconstruction on May 29 by issuing a proclamation granting
general amnesty and pardon to those who had been
engaged in rebellion against the authority of the United
States. This restored rights of property except in slaves
and except when legal proceedings for confiscation had
been instituted. An oath was provided to be taken by
all accepting the benefits of the proclamation. It was
as follows:

I . . . do solemnly swear, (or affirm), in the presence of
Almighty God, that I will henceforth faithfully support, protect and defend the Constitution of the United States and the
Union of the States thereunder; and that I will in like manner
abide by and faithfully support all laws and proclamations
which have been made during the existing rebellion with
reference to the emancipation of slaves. So help me God.

---

[1] The late D. F. Caldwell, of Guilford, stated that he had authoritative information that President Lincoln had considered his name and
that of Jonathan Worth, and had finally decided upon the latter for the
position. The author has been unable to find any other evidence sub-
stantiating this or, in fact, any contradicting it.

Fourteen classes of persons were excepted from the benefits of this proclamation. These included the executive and diplomatic officers of the Confederacy, those who left the service of the United States to aid the Confederacy, the governors of the States in insurrection, all military and naval officers in the Confederate service whose rank was above that of colonel and lieutenant, respectively, and all who voluntarily took part in the war whose taxable property exceeded in value $20,000. Any person belonging to an excepted class could make application to the President for a special pardon, and a promise of liberal executive clemency was extended. The Secretary of State was directed to establish rules for the administration of the oath.

The same day the President issued another proclamation appointing William W. Holden provisional governor of North Carolina. This was the first of a series of similar proclamations for all the Southern States. It was based upon the war power of the President as commander-in-chief. It gave the provisional governor so appointed power to prescribe the necessary rules for calling and assembling a convention whose delegates should be chosen by the portion of the population that was loyal to the United States at that time when it should be called. This convention was given authority to exercise all powers necessary to restore the State to her constitutional relations with the United States government, and present such a republican form of government as would entitle the State to the guarantee of the United States against invasion, insurrections, and domestic violence. It was directed to prescribe qualifications for electors and for holders of office. The proclamation itself prescribed as qualifications for electors and delegates to the convention that they should have taken the amnesty oath as provided in the President's proclamation, and that they should be voters qualified by the state constitution in force previous to May 20, 1861. All persons in the military and naval service were directed to aid the provisional governor and enjoined from hindering and discouraging the loyal people from organizing a state government. The Secretary of State was directed to put in force in the State the laws of the United States, the administration of which belonged to his department. The Secretary of the Treasury was instructed to nominate officials and put in execution the revenue laws. The Postmaster General was directed to establish post-offices and post routes and to put the postal laws in execution. The District judge was directed to hold courts within the State, and the Attorney General was instructed to enforce, through the proper officers, the administration of justice in all matters within the jurisdiction of the federal courts, and to libel and bring to judgment, confiscation, and sale all property subject to confiscation. The heads of the departments of the navy and interior were given instructions similar to the others.

Secretary Seward formally notified Governor Holden of his appointment the same day the proclamation was issued. For some reason he was not required to take the "iron-clad" oath as were the other provisional governors. The appointment was announced to the State through the *Standard* a week later, and, at the same time, Holden retired from the nominal editorial control of the paper.

As might be imagined, the appointment was not received in the State with unmixed gratification. It had been the hope of the majority that some man might be chosen who was without the bitter enmity of so large a proportion of the people. But after it was a settled fact there seems to have been a general disposition to give Holden a fair chance, both from a desire to support the President and from policy. But though the feeling against him was hidden, it was no less intense.

On June 12 Governor Holden issued a proclamation which had first been submitted to the President for approval. After a summary of the President's North Carolina proclamation the governor outlined his policy. He stated that a call would soon be issued for a convention of the people, which would provide for the election of a governor and legislature; that the latter would elect two United States senators, and a general election would also be held for members of Congress. He announced that, in conformity with the rules established by Secretary Seward, he would appoint justices of the peace to administer the amnesty oath, and through subordinates hold the election for delegates to the convention. These justices would be further authorized to hold county courts and appoint sheriffs and clerks. Other necessary officers would be appointed by the provisional governor to serve until the meeting of the convention. He invited the loyal people of the State to assist him by taking an interest in public affairs, by discouraging disloyal sentiment, and by electing to office friends of the United States government. He devoted some space to violent abuse of the Confederate government, congratulating the people on their deliverance from it. The latter part of the proclamation contained good and kindly advice to the colored people of the State, with a promise of assistance from the government and the people wherever it was deserved. He closed with a declaration of "charity for all, with malice towards none."

Beginning soon after the close of hostilities, a series of Union meetings were held in the State. Of these there were two distinct types. In one class, which was numerically the smaller, there was manifested an inclination to win favor at the North by violent abuse of the Confederacy and its leaders, oblivious, apparently, to the fact that, four years before, many, if not the majority, of those who prompted this policy had been enthusiastic members of the "last man and last dollar" party. The majority of the meetings, however, passed resolutions simply acknowledging that the war had been a failure, expressing gratification at the return of peace, and declaring a desire to return to full allegiance to the United States.

Governor Holden moved very slowly and carefully in carrying out the work of re-organization. This was made necessary by the duties of his position which, at the time, were enormously increased by the thousands of applications for pardon and by the necessity of appointing magistrates and other officers. The delay in calling a convention caused extreme dissatisfaction in the State, and criticism which was hardly just, followed.

The governor's action regarding pardons admitted of and caused better-founded criticism. He recommended the pardon of a large number of original secessionists and war men, and advised the suspension of the pardon of such men as William A. Graham, John A. Gilmer, Josiah Turner,[1] John M. Morehead, and many others who had striven against secession and for the Union until hostilities had actually commenced. This, naturally, gave great offense to the latter class and their friends. No other adequate reason than personal preju-

---

[1] Holden recommended the suspension of Turner's pardon on the ground that his petition was a bill of indictment against the Democratic party.

dice can be found for this action.[1]  In spite of his recommendation to the contrary, a pardon was granted to ex-Governor Bragg.[2]  Ex-Governor Clark made application for pardon and was told by Governor Holden that he would oppose its being granted, as he would under no circumstances recommend or approve Vance's pardon, and if he should make any discrimination it would give Vance's friends ground for attacking him. The application was never forwarded to Washington, and was found in the office by Governor Worth during the following winter.[3]  In other ways, not calculated to win friends, Governor Holden used the power he had in the matter of pardons.[4]

To assist him in communicating with the President, Governor Holden appointed Dr. R. J. Powell agent of the State in Washington.  Through him the President was informed of the governor's opinion of the vari-

---

[1] In his *Memoirs*, written many years afterwards, Governor Holden said it was to protect the President from pardoning too many prominent "rebels," and because he thought Graham and Turner were not sufficiently in sympathy with him.

[2] *Trinity College Historical Papers*, Series III, pp. 103–5.

[3] *Executive Correspondence*, Worth, vol. i, pp. 234–5.

[4] The following correspondence gives an example of this:

"Weldon, N. C., Sept. 18, 1865.
To Mr. Hanes,
    Secretary to Governor Holden.
Why have I not been pardoned as well as John B. Odom, J. W. Newsom, Samuel Calvert, and others?        THOS. I. PERSON."

"Raleigh, September 18, 1865.
To Thos. I. Person, Weldon, N. C.
Sir:—Your despatch received.  The governor instructs me to say that Mr. Odom's pardon has not been received but will be received in time for him to take his seat in the convention.  Also that the pardon of those who may take part against Mr. Odom and Dr. Barrow for the convention in Northampton will be delayed.        L. HANES.
                    Private Secretary."

ous petitioners apart from his formal endorsement. All
the applications were referred by the President to the
Attorney General for investigation.[1]  On several occasions
pardons were issued without the approval of Governor
Holden.  George Mordecai and Dr. W. J. Hawkins, both
prominent in Raleigh in a business way, went to Washington and were unable to find any trace of their applications for pardon in Attorney General Speed's office.
At his suggestion they filed new ones which the President signed.  Governor Holden had advised suspension
of pardon in their case, and he at once complained to
the President, who declined to revoke their pardons, but
notified him through Dr. Powell that he might tax them
for their pardon as he saw fit.[2]  Governor Holden, however, took no action of the kind, but wrote that he was
losing ground because pardons were granted for personal reasons when those recommended by him were not
acted on.[3]  By June 27, 1866, pardons had been issued
to citizens of North Carolina to the number of 1912
Of these, 1450 bore the recommendation of Governor
Holden and 419 of Governor Worth.  Most of the latter
were made before Governor Worth took office.  It is
impossible to ascertain how large a number of persons
belonged to the classes excepted by the President's
proclamation.  Over two thousand applications for pardon were forwarded to Washington, but there were
many in the excepted classes who did not apply.  Of the
pardons issued, 815 were granted to Confederate post-
masters, many of whom had been United States postmas-

[1] *Record of the Provisional Governor*, p. 123.

[2] Dr. Powell wrote Gov. Holden that they had been obtained by a
pardon broker who was a cousin of the Attorney General.

[3] *Executive Correspondence*, Provisional Governor, p. 61.

ters prior to 1861; 510 came under the thirteenth exception, that is, were worth more than $20,000. The remainder of the pardons, in the main, were granted to Confederate army officers above the rank of colonel, tax assessors, mail contractors and carriers, members of the legislature, and a variety of minor officers. A few who had held high office received pardons, and the circumstances under which some were granted are interesting. John A. Gilmer was recommended by a number of his former colleagues in the 36th Congress and by several army officers stationed in North Carolina, including General J. D. Cox. J. C. Washington, who had been a member of the secession convention, was recommended by Attorney General Speed on condition that he should arrange with the freedmen on his land in a manner satisfactory to the Freedmen's Bureau. William A. Graham's pardon was granted, in spite of Governor Holden's request to the contrary, on the recommendation of thirty-eight members of the state Senate and forty-three members of the House.[1]

By the end of July Governor Holden had appointed over three thousand magistrates. He had also appointed mayors and commissioners for the towns.[2] His effort was to fill all these places with Union men. In one instance he declared the action of a county court null and void because the county officers appointed by it had in the past been disloyal to the United States. He ordered a new election of officers, appointing at the same time new magistrates, until there was a working majority of those of whose opinions he could be certain.[3] In ano-

[1] *House Ex. Docs.*, no. 32, 40 Cong., 1 sess.

[2] *Executive Correspondence*, Provisional Governor, p. 20.

[3] *Record of the Provisional Governor*, p. 139.

th<br>r case he revoked the commissions of certain Magistrates against whom objections were raised.  In the same period appointments were made of directors and proxies for the various corporations in which the State had an interest, and of judges and solicitors of the state courts.  In almost every instance the appointees had originally been Whigs.  R. P. Dick was the only Democrat chosen to a high position.  He had been appointed a federal judge by the President soon after the establishment of the provisional government, but could not take the oath required by law, [1] and after two months' waiting for the repeal of the law, resigned and was made a provisional judge.  George W. Brooks was then appointed and qualified.

About this time [2] charges were made at the North that Union men were ignored in the appointments to office made by the provisional governors.  The animus of these reports is easy to perceive and was recognized at the time.  Ground for them regarding North Carolina was given by the *Progress*, which for a time represented the State as entirely disloyal, and also by the correspondence to the Northern newspapers.  The latter painted such a lurid picture of the conditions in the State that suspicion was aroused as to its source.  An examination made by Dr. Powell showed that the matter was never telegraphed from North Carolina as was claimed, but was probably written in Washington. [3]  In many instances allusions were made to persons as prominent in the State who were unknown there.  The President, while not crediting the reports, notified Governor Holden that they were

[1] Act of March 2, 1862.
[2] August, 1865.
[3] *Executive Correspondence*, Provisional Governor, pp. 40–42.

being circulated.[1] Governor Holden was thus attacked at once on both sides, for in the State, in addition to the matter of pardons, many of his appointments were criticised. It certainly cannot be said with justice that he was favorable to the former secession element, unless to those who had changed during the war. In public and in private he insisted that they must be content to follow, not lead, in the work of re-organization. His enforcement of the directions contained in the proclamations and orders of the President seems to have been careful and, on the whole, impartial. He refused to allow the unpardoned stockholders of the railroads to take part in the meetings and gave notice that, when a majority of the stock was controlled by such persons, the State would take charge of the corporation's affairs until they had been pardoned.[2] This is a fair type of his action when questions of the kind had to be settled by him.

Throughout this period the governor was giving attention to all the various details of state government, multiplied by the war and the prostration of the people resulting therefrom. Leaving out all question of motive or of action in certain individual cases, his work was well done. He was less proscriptive than might have been expected or, in fact, than was expected when he was appointed, in view of the events of the preceding five years, and he showed consideration for the feelings of his opponents by asking for Vance's release on parole on account of the illness of his wife, and by various other acts to which his kindly nature impelled him.

Finally, on August 8, he issued a proclamation ordering the election of delegates to a convention to meet

---

[1] *Sen. Docs.*, no. 26, p. 223, 39 Cong., 1 sess.
[2] *Executive Correspondence*, Provisional Governor, p. 73.

October 2. Justices of the peace in every county were directed to administer the amnesty oath and to provide for holding the election in accordance with law. By his delay in ordering the election he had made it possible for many to vote who, otherwise, would have been disqualified for lack of pardon.

There was very little discussion during the campaign of any issues. The questions of secession and slavery were regarded as definitely settled and only the matter of the war debt remained. It was generally thought that the convention ought not to act upon this at all during the first session, and, beyond some little discussion of the matter in the newspapers, little was said regarding it. The *Standard* published during the campaign, under the heading "Union Landmarks," the following as its policy: "The prompt non-recognition of debts contracted by the State in aid of the rebellion; but an equally prompt determination to pay every cent of the State debt contracted previously to the war." But less than a month later it declared that by non-recognition it meant that the convention should leave the question untouched.[1]

The quiet in politics, which had settled over the State at the close of hostilities, now began to be broken by disagreements between the *Standard* and the *Sentinel*. The latter was a paper established shortly before in Raleigh and edited by William E. Pell, a former assistant of Holden. It soon began to represent the anti-Holden element which was beginning to appear, and, in fact, was in part responsible for its appearance. It endorsed the administration of Governor Holden until after the meet-

---

[1] *Standard*, August, 25, 1865. The editorial columns of this paper must be regarded as expressing the views of Governor Holden, as he controlled it actually, if not in name.

ing of the convention, but at times criticised his actions. This was regarded by the *Standard* as amounting to treason and disloyalty to the United States, and it at once made charges that an attempt was being made to revive Confederate issues.

The question of the eligibility of unpardoned persons to seats in the convention was the cause of some discussion. William A. Graham was the choice of Orange County but declined to be a candidate because he had not been pardoned, stating at the same time that he believed that he was eligible. Governor Holden appealed to the President for a decision in the matter and was sustained in his opinion that no person who was unpardoned, and so not a voter, could qualify as a delegate. The President also informed him that any unpardoned person, elected to the convention, would be immediately pardoned upon his recommendation.[1]

The administration of the amnesty oath and preparations for the election were carried on quietly with little question of any kind being raised. Occasionally there were complaints that partiality was being shown. In Rutherford County about forty persons were not allowed to take the oath because they were " original war men." They went to Morganton and took it before the military authorities there, but were not allowed to vote at the election in Rutherford.[2]

The election was held peaceably in every part of the State except at Concord, the county seat of Cabarrus. General Ruger had given orders that on election day no soldier should visit the polls or even leave camp, unless summoned by the civil authorities,[3] and in no instance

---

[1] *Sen. Docs.*, no. 26, p. 223, 39 Cong., 1 sess.

[2] *Executive Correspondence*, Provisional Governor, p. 96.

[3] *Standard*, September 16, 1865.

were they required.   The trouble at Concord was caused
by the attempt of a party of intoxicated negroes to vote.
A Union veteran, who lived in the town, fired a pistol
into the crowd of freedmen and precipitated a sharp
little fight, which, however, had no serious results.[1]

Many persons who were regularly qualified, refused to
take any part in the election on the ground that, in
every case, the candidates were dictated.   This refusal
to endorse what was felt to be the dictation of the provisional governor showed what might be the attitude of
the State towards him in the fall elections after the convention should have completed the work required of it
and adjourned, leaving the government to be carried on
directly by the people.

Governor Holden was much gratified at the general
result of the election, but greatly chagrined at the defeat
of Dr. Leach and Chief Justice Pearson.   He assured
the President that the ultra-Union men or "straitest
sect" would control in everything.   Eleven persons who
had not been pardoned were elected, but on the governor's recommendation they received pardons in time to
take their seats.[2]

## 2. THE CONVENTION OF 1865

The convention thus secured by Governor Holden, in
accordance with the President's directions, met in
Raleigh on the appointed day (October 2) and organized
by unanimously electing Judge Edwin G. Reade president.[3]   Among its members were few who had originally favored secession and none who were very prom-

[1] *Standard*, September 28, 1865.

[2] *Sen. Docs.*, no. 26, 39 Cong., 1 sess.

[3] An informal ballot had already been held.   Nathaniel Boyden received the second largest number of votes in this.

inently connected with the secession party. Most of them were old Whigs who, while opposed to secession, had submitted to the will of the majority. With these were many members of the peace party during the war. The delegates were unanimous in their desire to restore the State to normal relations with the federal government, and this was constantly shown as the session progressed.

As a whole, probably, the body was composed of less able men than the convention of 1861, but it was by no means lacking in ability. Three of its members had also been delegates to the convention of 1835.[1] Twelve had been members of the secession convention.[2] Two had been in the Confederate Congress,[3] and two had been Union rangers. A majority were middle-aged, very few being either very young or very old.[4] The most prominent member and probably the ablest was B. F. Moore' of Wake. His record as a Union sympathizer was unbroken, although he was unable to take the "iron-clad'-oath, having been a member of the Board of Claims elected by the convention of 1861. Thomas Settle, Judge George Howard, William Eaton, Nathaniel Boyden, Edward Conigland, D. D. Ferebee, Judge M. E. Manly, and Bedford Brown all took a prominent part in the debates and were the leaders of the convention.

Edwin G. Reade, the president, had long been a prominent lawyer in the State. He had served one term in Congress, and while there, in 1856, was the only mem-

---

[1] These were Faison, Dockery, and Gilliam.

[2] These were John Berry, Bedford Brown, R. P. Dick, George Howard, Giles Mebane, R. L. Patterson, R. S. Donnell, A. H. Joyce, E. J. Warren, D. H. Starbuck, and W. A. Smith.

[3] E. G. Reade and G. W. Logan.

[4] *Sentinel*, November 11, 1865.

ber from the South who voted to censure Keitt for his part in the assault upon Sumner. In 1861 he was elected a delegate to the convention which the people rejected, but refused to be a candidate for the later one, as he was opposed to secession. He was for a short time a Confederate senator, and in 1863 was elected a judge of the Superior Court. Governor Holden appointed him a provisional justice of the Supreme Court. He was a most suitable choice for presiding officer and proved a very able one. When he took the chair he made a very eloquent address closing as follows:

Fellow Citizens, we are going home. Let painful reflections upon our late separation and pleasant memories of our early union quicken our footsteps toward the old mansion, that we may grasp hard again the hand of friendship which stands at the door, and sheltered by the old homestead which was built upon a rock and has weathered the storm, enjoy together the long, bright future which awaits us.

The governor's message was brief. He reviewed the President's position in regard to the reconstruction of the Southern States, praising its breadth and liberality, and congratulating the members on the favorable conditions under which they met.[1] He alluded to the questions of secession and slavery but made no mention of the disposition of the war debt.

The first subject of discussion by the convention was the abrogation of the ordinance of secession. So far as the end to be obtained was concerned, the convention was a unit. Regarding the means, a decided difference was noticeable. On the third day, Jones of Rowan introduced an ordinance repealing the ordinance of seces-

[1] *Journal*, p. 11.

sion, with a declaration that the convention in no sense endorsed the theory of secession, but wished simply to repeal the ordinance out of consideration for the feelings of their fellow citizens who had believed in it, and from a desire for cordial reconciliation. The same day Nathaniel Boyden from the committee on the subject reported the following ordinance:

*Be it ordained by the delegates of the good people of the State of North Carolina in convention assembled, and it is hereby declared and ordained* that the ordinance of the convention of the State of North Carolina, ratified on the 21st day of November, 1789, which adopted the Constitution of the United States, and also all acts and parts of acts of the General Assemlby ratifying and adopting amendments to the said Constitution, are now and at all times since the adoption and ratification thereof have been in full force and effect, notwithstanding the supposed ordinance of the 20th of May, 1861, declaring that the same be repealed, rescinded and abrogated, and the said supposed ordinance is now and hath been at all times, null and void.

Jones's ordinance was then tabled indefinitely without discussion. The following day Dennis D. Ferebee offered a substitute, differing in form from the draft reported by the committee, and, in fact, embodying a compromise between this and the one proposed by Jones. A sharp debate then followed. The opposition to the committee's draft was led by Judge Howard. He prefaced his speech with the declaration that he had voted heartily for secession, but, convinced that it was a failure, he was ready to do all in his power to effect a restoration; that so far as the United States was concerned the ordinance of secession had always been null and void; but to the people of the State it was the charter under which they had acted and carried on a *de facto* government for four years, and he would not wrong them by taking it away. During the period of the war, the State, sustaining its action by arms, was to all intents independent, with all the machinery of government in the full exercise of its functions. If the ordinance of secession had no effect, all acts in the period following were null and void. He denied that the military power, while sustaining a theoretical independence of the State, had succeeded in making independence actual for any period, and held that consequently opposition to the ordinance under discussion did not mean hostility to a restoration of the Union. Others opposed the proposed ordinance on the ground that it was a reflection on the convention of 1861, and because the convention was by nature a legislative body and not a judicial one.[1]

B. F. Moore, who drew the committee's ordinance, said his main reason for favoring it was that through it the right of citizenship in the United States would be retained, and not otherwise. He did not believe that declaring the ordinance of secession null and void would permanently invalidate all acts done during the war, but said that the convention could make them valid by an additional ordinance.[2] A great deal of feeling was shown in the debate by several of those favoring the committee's ordinance. Judge Warren, who voted for the ordinance of secession in 1861, declared that the object of the substitute was to "hoodwink" the convention into an endorsement of secession.[3] Samuel F. Phillips voiced the sentiment of a large number when he said that, as the convention of 1861 had expressed an opinion

---

[1] Andrews, *The South Since the War*, pp. 144, 151.
[2] *Ibid.*, pp. 150–1.          [3] *Ibid.*, p. 151.

one way, a body of equal rank should register a counter opinion, and, as the functions of a convention of the people in its sovereign capacity were both legislative and judicial, it could either repeal or declare null and void the acts of a former body. As secession was a creature of the mind, and could not, in consequence, be affected by the success or failure of an army, it was necessary to declare against it.[1]

The substitute was rejected by a vote of ninety-four to twenty.[2] The original was then put upon its second reading and passed with nine still voting in the negative.[3] A few moments later, after some discussion as to whether another reading was necessary, it passed its third reading. Several delegates, including Judge Howard and McKay, voted against it, and a still larger number, including Judge Manly and Ferebee, declined to vote.[4] Secession, already dead in North Carolina for some time past, was legally pronounced never to have had life.

On October 5, Thomas Settle reported an ordinance forever prohibiting slavery in the State. A few of the members attempted to have the cause of its abolition inserted as a preamble, but the plan failed and, two days

[1] Andrews, *The South Since the War*, p. 147.

[2] The following voted nay: Alexander, Allen, Brown, Conigland, Eaton, Faison, Ferebee, Hanrahan, Howard, Jarvis, Joyner, Kennedy, Manly, McKay, McIver, Mebane, Murphy, Ward, Winborne, and Wright.

[3] These were Allen, Faison, Ferebee, Howard, Joyner, Manly, McKay, Murphy, and Ward.

[4] Judge Howard relates that Judge Manly and Ferebee were about to leave the hall before the vote, but stayed with him. Settle was standing in the aisle and suggested a third reading. He turned to Judge Howard and said, "Howard, let it be unanimous. You have already voted." Judge Howard replied with emphasis, "I'll see you damned first."

later, the ordinance was passed unanimously.[1]   It was then provided that both ordinances should be submitted separately to the people at the next election.[2]   An amendment was offered to this providing that the people should vote on the question in the words " Secession" or " No Secession " and " Slavery" or " No Slavery." This was purely for political purposes and was resented by those who had opposed the anti-secession ordinance.   Judge Howard, in opposing the amendment, attacked bitterly those who never spoke or acted for the Union until the Confederacy fell and then became proscriptive and vindictive.[3]  This was aimed at several of the members of the convention and was applicable to many more.[4]

The two great objects of the convention were thus accomplished.  There still remained other matters of importance, mainly internal in their nature.  These were settled in the next few days by the passage of various ordinances.  The election of state and county officers and also of a General Assembly and members of Congress was provided for.[5]  To remove doubts as to the validity of official acts after May 20, 1861, all laws consistent with the state and federal constitutions were declared in full force.  Judicial proceedings were also held valid and contracts declared binding.  In relation to the latter, it was made the duty of the General Assembly to provide a scale of depreciation of the currency from the

---

[1] *Journal*, p. 28.

[2] *Ordinances*, p. 46.

[3] *Sentinel*, October 25, 1865.

[4] Sidney Andrews, in his *South Since the War*, p. 136, declares that he found in the convention much hatred of secession and secessionists, but that it was from political feeling and not from love of the Union.

[5] *Ordinances*, p. 42.

first issue until the end of the war, and all contracts were to be deemed solvable on that basis, unless evidence was produced of a contrary intention at the time the contract was made. All acts of civil and military officers of the State or of the Confederate States, in accordance with law, were declared valid, and such officers were relieved of any penalty for their actions. The acts of the provisional governor and his agents were made valid, and it was provided that all offices created by him should become vacant at the close of the next session of the General Assembly.[1] Offices whose incumbents had taken the oath of allegiance to the Confederate States were declared vacant.[2] This produced some debate, as, by a decision of the Supreme Court of North Carolina, it had been held that the holder of an office had a right of property therein.[3] But it was argued that a convention was bound only by the Constitution of the United States, and the ruling of the Supreme Court of the United States on the question differed from that of the state court.[4]

The State was divided into seven congressional districts in preparation for the coming election. Provision was made for the organization of a military police in every county, if it should be thought necessary by the sheriff and magistrates. The necessity for this action was strongly urged by Ferebee and Alfred Dockery, who stated that the white people were unarmed and in a constant state of uneasiness at the presence of many strange negroes, the majority of whom were armed.[5] Some doubt was expressed as to the wisdom of attempting

[1] *Ordinances*, p. 58.     [2] *Ibid.*, p. 63.
[3] *Hoke v. Henderson*, 15 N. C., 1.
[4] *Butler v. Pennsylvania*, 10 Howard, 402.
[5] *Annual Cyclopædia*, 1865, p. 627.

such a thing while the State was under martial law.  It was stated, however, that General Ruger was heartily in favor of it, and attention was called to the President's approval of Governor Sharkey's establishment of a militia in Mississippi.  This removed all opposition and secured the unanimous passage of the ordinance.  The President was requested to withdraw all colored troops from the State as unnecessary and dangerous.[1]  He was also requested to proclaim speedily a general amnesty,[2] and to proclaim that the people of North Carolina were restored to their rights and privileges under the Constitution and in the Union.[3]  Congress was requested to repeal the "iron-clad" oath.[4]  Provision was made for revenue in 1866 by the passage of an ordinance providing for an extensive system of taxation.[5]  Governor Holden was requested to confer with General Ruger and secure to the people the broken-down horses and mules which had been left by the federal troops in exchange for those taken away.[6]  In order to define the status of the freedmen, the governor was instructed to appoint a commission of three persons to prepare and report to the next General Assembly a system of laws relating to the freedmen, and to indicate what laws then in force should be repealed.[7]

The only matter of importance remaining, upon which the convention was likely to take any action, was the state debt.  As has been seen,[8] it had not been the subject of much discussion during the period preceding the meeting of the convention.  When the convention met, a committee was appointed to consider the subject.

[1] *Ordinances*, p. 69.      [2] *Ibid.*, p. 67.      [3] *Ibid.*, p. 74.
[4] *Ibid.*, p. 70.      [5] *Ibid.*, p. 48.      [6] *Ibid.*, p. 74.
[7] *Ibid.*, p. 73.      [8] *Cf. supra*, p. 118.

On October 10, P. H. Winston from the committee reported that they had been able to discover no difference of opinion on the question of the old debt, all agreeing that it should be paid. But in view of the fact that there was a great diversity of opinion regarding the debt incurred since May 20, 1861, and, since the information in the hands of the committee as to the purpose of a large part of it was very meagre, they recommended an adjourned session and that no action should be taken at the time.[1] Settle at once introduced a resolution prohibiting the assumption of the war debt. He said that, while there had been little or no discussion of the matter before the election, he believed the minds of the people were made up and that they wanted the thing settled finally. He was strongly opposed by D. F. Caldwell and Edward Conigland, who represented the element favoring the payment of the entire debt. A combination of this element with the members who preferred longer discussion and a delay until the adjourned session resulted in the tabling of Settle's resolution.[2] This action was in part due to a letter from Dr. Powell, the state agent, to Governor Holden, in which an account was given of separate conversations with every member of the cabinet. Secretary Stanton declined to discuss the subject, but all the rest agreed that the convention ought not to take any action, at the time, in regard to the debt. This letter was circulated and read by the majority of the members of the convention.[3]

The matter seemed settled and, so far as can be judged from the press, the people approved. But a surprise was in store for the State and the convention, though

<hr>

[1] *Standard*, Oct. 11, 1865.    [2] October 13, 1865.
[3] Jonathan Worth to the editor of the *Sentinel*, Oct. 30, 1865.

not for certain individuals.  Governor Holden, who had apparently favored the tabling of Settle's resolution, either changed his mind or became aware that his views were not in accord with those of the President.  So he telegraphed the latter as follows:

RALEIGH, October 17, 1865.

SIR: Contrary to my expectation, the convention has involved itself in a bitter discussion of the State debt made in aid of the rebellion.  A continuance of this discussion will greatly excite the people and retard the work of reconstruction.  Our people are believed to be against assuming the debt by a large majority.  Is it not advisable that our Convention, like that of Alabama, should positively ignore this debt now and forever?  Please answer at once.

W. W. HOLDEN.[1]

So far as this implied that the bitter discussion had occupied the formal proceedings of the convention, it was untrue.  The whole matter had been tabled on the thirteenth with no prospect of further action being taken during the session.  The discussion had never been bitter and had been very brief.  The next day Governor Holden sent to the convention the President's reply:

WASHINGTON CITY, October 18, 1865.

W. W. HOLDEN, *Provisional Governor:*

Every dollar of the State debt, created to aid the rebellion against the United States, should be repudiated, finally and forever.  The great mass of the people should not be taxed to pay a debt to aid in carrying on a rebellion which they, in fact, if left to themselves, were opposed to.  Let those who have given their means for the obligations of the State, look to that power they tried to establish in violation of law, Constitution, and the will of the people.  They must meet their

[1] *Sentinel*, March 23, 1866.  Quoted from *Senate Documents*.

fate. It is their misfortune and they cannot be recognized by the people of any State professing themselves loyal to the government of the United States in the Union.

I repeat, that the loyal people of North Carolina should be exonerated from the payment of every dollar of indebtedness created to aid in carrying on the rebellion. I trust and hope that the people of North Carolina will wash their hands of everything that partakes in the slightest degree of the rebellion which has been so recently crushed by the strong arm of the government in carrying out the obligations imposed by the Constitution of the Union.     ANDREW JOHNSON,

*President United States.*[1]

This telegram changed the sentiment of the convention. D. F. Caldwell said his opinion was changed by the knowledge of the President's desire, and that he favored immediate repudiation. B. F. Moore, who had taken little part in the debate before, now became vehement in his opposition to immediate action. He opposed any acceptance of dictation from the President and criticised him sharply for sending the message. George W. Brooks made a long and rather bitter speech, favoring repudiation on the ground that, as the object of the debt had been "the persecution of loyal persons," they should not be forced to bear the burden.[2] Eugene Grissom, a close friend of Governor Holden, then moved an amendment to Settle's resolution, providing for submitting the matter to the people. This was passed,[3] but later reconsidered and rejected, the convention deciding not to put the burden of decision on the people. Settle's resolution was then passed.[4] A protest against its passage was made by William Eaton, who was joined in it by ten others. The ordinance imposed

---

[1] *Executive Correspondence*, Provisional Governor, p. 83.

[2] *Sentinel*, Oct. 20, 1865.     [3] *Journal*, p. 90.     [4] *Ibid.*, p. 92.

upon the General Assembly the duty of providing, as soon as practicable, for the payment of the state debt not incurred in aid of the war. It further declared all debts and obligations created in direct or indirect aid of the rebellion void, and removed from the General Assembly all power to provide for their payment.[1] President Johnson was notified of the convention's action by Governor Holden in the following letter:

RALEIGH, October 20, 1865.

*The President of the United States :*

SIR:—The convention has adjourned. It has promptly repudiated every dollar of the rebel debt and bound all future legislatures not to pay any of it. Your telegram had a most happy effect. The Worth faction is working hard, but will be defeated by a large majority. Turner and other contumacious leaders ought to be handled at the proper time. Please pardon no leading man unless you hear from me.

W. W. HOLDEN.

After passing a resolution of thanks to President Johnson and Governor Holden for their endeavors toward a restoration of the State to its rights in the Union, the convention adjourned until May 24, 1866.

The action of Governor Holden and the President was resented deeply in the State. This feeling was independent, in many cases, of opinion regarding repudiation. The *Sentinel* voiced it as follows: "One of the last acts of the convention, and certainly the most humiliating act ever performed by a body claiming to be the embodiment of the sovereignty of the people of a State, and ever put upon record, was the passage of the ordinance repudiating for all time the war debt of the State."[2]

The ordinances and resolutions passed by the conven-

---

[1] *Ordinances*, p. 66.          [2] *Sentinel*, Oct. 26, 1865.

tion were carried to Washington by a committee headed by Judge Reade and submitted to the President for his approval.[1]

### 3. THE CAMPAIGN AND ELECTION OF 1865

On October 14, a letter, signed by fifty-three members of the convention, was sent to Governor Holden, requesting him to be a candidate for governor at the approaching election. He replied in a somewhat fulsome manner, accepting the nomination but declaring that he had not sought it. He entered into a criticism of party spirit, declaring that faction was the bane of the country. He said that as provisional governor he had known no party, but for the future, he was a member of the National Union Party with Andrew Johnson at its head.

It was recognized generally that he had endeavored during the whole period of his incumbency of the office of provisional governor to build up a machine in his own interest,[2] but many of his political associates were content to follow his lead and nominate him. Many, however, revolted and refused to give him their support. Lewis Hanes, his private secretary, who had been a staunch ally in the peace movement during the war, was among these. Defining his position, he said: " I believe that in everything he [Governor Holden] did, he kept constantly in view no object but his own political advancement." [3]

The announcement of Governor Holden's candidacy was not made until October 18, when the correspondence

---

[1] *Sentinel*, Nov. 18, 1865. The *Sentinel* was strongly in favor of paying the debt.

[2] Testimony of Rev. Hope Bain, *Reports of Committees*, part 2, p. 206, 39 Cong., 1 sess.

[3] *Old North State* quoted in *Standard*, July 18, 1866.

with the members of the convention was published.  In
the meantime, sixty-seven members of the convention,
who had declined to join in the request that Governor
Holden should be a candidate, looked about for some one
on whom the opposition could join.  The name of
Jonathan Worth, suggested during the summer, now
recurred.[1]  He had won golden opinions for his skill-
ful management of the business affairs of the State,
and his past record made him eminently suitable as
a candidate.  Many of those who had joined in the
call on Governor Holden favored Worth, but had been
induced to sign by the representation that he would not
be a candidate.  Others were known to have signed only
because they were under such obligations to Governor
Holden for their pardons and for various political favors
that they felt bound to support him.[2]  Under such circumstances, Worth was urged to allow the use of his
name and finally, with great reluctance, consented.
Many of his friends, including John Pool and Lewis
Thompson, believed that there was no hope of his election,
and he, himself, was very doubtful at first.  Others
thought it unwise to oppose Holden.  Worth, however,
was convinced that Holden was not a suitable candidate
on account of the dislike he inspired in so many of the
people, and soon felt fairly confident of success.  His
candidacy was announced before Governor Holden's, and
he had the advantage, if there was any, of being the first
in the field.  He at once resigned his place as provisional
treasurer, expressing his willingness, if Governor Holden

[1] William A. Graham, Josiah Turner, P. H. Winston, and C. C.
Clark were prominent in the movement which resulted in Worth's
nomination.  In spite of their efforts, Worth for a week refused to
consider it.

[2] Hamilton, ed., *The Correspondence of Jonathan Worth*, i, p. 433.

should so desire, to continue in the performance of its duties until the election.[1] The resignation, however, was accepted, and Dr. William Sloan, of Gaston, was appointed to succeed him.

About the same time candidates for Congress were announced. Twenty-three aspirants for the seven seats appeared. The active work of the campaign was carried on by them, for neither of the gubernatorial candidates took part in the canvass. The usual newspaper battle commenced, and the general line of party division begun at this time, has continued ever since. Political peace, or even a semblance of it, was to be absent for at least twenty years. Worth was at once attacked by the *Standard*, first with ridicule,[2] and then, as the growth of opinion in his favor became more evident, with violent abuse. He was attacked because, in 1861, he had opposed the "stay law." Josiah Turner, who was a candidate for Congress, although as yet unpardoned, had for years been closely associated with Worth and was included in the attacks. The two were accused of being the representatives of a faction of "place hunters,"[3] and not only of being the candidates of the "Confederate" party, but even of having been original secessionists. In proof of the accusation, the declaration of independence, which Turner had introduced in the Senate in 1861,[4] and for which Worth and every Union man in that body had voted in order to provoke the secession-

[1] Worth to Holden, Oct. 18, 1865.

[2] The *Standard* said the nomination was a "bait composed of old secession hooks dressed up in the feathers of a few Union geese."

[3] Among these were included Thomas Bragg, Judge Manly, P. H. Winston, Judge Howard, T. L. Clingman, Abram Venable, and D. D. Ferebee. *Standard*, Oct. 24, 1865.

[4] *Cf. supra*, p. 25.

ists, was brought forward and urged as conclusive evidence.[1] The prospects of the State for readmission to the Union, it was declared, would be entirely destroyed if Worth should be elected, and the issue was defined as, " W. W. Holden and Go Back to the Union, or Jonathan Worth and Stay Out of the Union. Or, in other words, Holden and live again under Washington's government, or Jonathan Worth and perish."[2] This gave Worth much uneasiness and he appealed to friends in Washington to try to find means to efface the impression which was being created by the friends of Holden that the President preferred the latter's election.[3] Worth's position regarding the war debt was criticised, regardless of the fact that, almost until the adjournment of the convention, Governor Holden held a similar opinion. It was stated that, in the event of Worth's election, the convention would reassemble and, in defiance of the expressed wish of the President, assume the entire war debt of the State and crush the people under the burden of an immense taxation, besides bringing the State into conflict with the authorities of the United States, and having martial law under negro troops prolonged indefinitely.[4] Governor Holden's record was enlarged upon, particular emphasis being laid on his hostility to the Confederate government and his part in the peace movement.

---

[1] *Standard*, Oct. 24, 1865.          [2] *Ibid.*, Oct. 21, 1865.

[3] Worth to B. S. Hedrick, Oct. 21, 1865. Hamilton, ed., *The Correspondence of Jonathan Worth*, i, p. 472. Hedrick had been a professor at the University of North Carolina and had been forced to leave on account of his being in favor of Fremont in 1856. This was largely through the influence of Holden, and Hedrick, in consequence, had no good feeling for him.

[4] *Standard*, Oct. 21, 23, and 24, 1865.

It is not doubtful that many of these arguments had a boomerang effect. The people in general, while uncertain what they wished regarding the final disposition of the war debt, were at least certain that they wanted the matter considered from every standpoint. The President's action in forcing repudiation was resented, and the burden of this fell upon Governor Holden because, after acquiescing in the policy of postponement of the question, he had brought the matter to the notice of the President and was, to that extent, responsible for repudiation. As regards Governor Holden's record, it was a delicate matter, and bringing it up showed a lack of political sagacity. It cannot be doubted that, at this time, North Carolina was honestly desirous of a return to the Union, where peace could be found. The purpose to remain loyal to the Union in the future is equally certain. The utter failure of secession was recognized, and fewer mourned it than might have been expected. But there was little or no change of opinion on the question of the right involved. It could hardly be expected that such a change would occur, but it was demanded in the State by the " straitest sect " element, and in the North by the radicals. It would have been a wonderful thing, in view of his past record, if Holden had had the love, respect, or confidence of the people of North Carolina in 1865, even if his record since the war had been left out of account. The great marvel was that the feeling against him remained quiet as long as it did. Only the course of the *Standard* was necessary to arouse it and insure his defeat.

The opposition to him was, to an extent, based on his past record, and his numerous changes of political affiliation were once more brought up against him. But the main fight was made on his action as provisional governor and the claim that his election was a prerequisite for the return of the State to its normal place in the Union. As the campaign progressed, the *Standard* and the *Progress* began to charge that all opposition to Governor Holden was an evidence of disloyalty. This course of action was sharply criticised by the rest of the state press, even by the papers supporting Governor Holden. The *Charlotte Times,* which supported Worth, said, "Vote for Holden and be loyal, and vote against him and be a traitor. That is the English of it. And if that is to be the test, then we are a traitor and glory in the treason. As a provisional governor, we have not aught to say against him, but as a politician, we are against him, and if chance should throw us on the same side with him, it would make us question the correctness of our view." [1]  Still another cause of opposition, brought forward by the *Sentinel,* was the necessity of bringing out a full vote as an assurance of the loyalty of the people of the State, and as a sign of their acceptance of the terms of reconstruction; and it was thought that, if Governor Holden should run alone, it would be regarded by the people as dictated from Washington and they would not care to vote. [2]  This was a weak reason, and yet the condition stated was actual, as is shown by the election for delegates to the convention, when a great many failed to vote from the very belief mentioned here.

Governor Holden had the support of a more influential and representative class of men than in 1864. John Pool, R. S. Donnell, Bedford Brown, and Thomas Settle signed the request that he should be a candidate. B. F. Moore, desiring that no party division should occur, was

[1] Quoted in the *Sentinel,* Nov. 22, 1865.
[2] *Ibid.,* Oct. 19, 1865.

in favor of his election, "if he continues to exercise the office as heretofore and if his programme of principles and measures should not be very objectionable." [1] Many others of the same type would have supported him but for the violence and the proscriptive tendency of the *Standard*.

The number of congressional candidates was lessened by the withdrawal of several before election day. In the campaign, no mention seems to have been made of the two ordinances submitted to the people. In fact, they were not regarded as issues, and, besides, all issues had been merged into the one of Holden. His suitability, politically and personally, was the one question to be decided.

The election was held November 9. Its result was a victory for Worth, who received a majority of 5,937 out of a total vote of nearly 60,000, and carried fifty-four of the eighty-nine counties in the State. A much smaller vote was cast on the two ordinances, which were both ratified. [2] The congressional elections were regarded by both sides as comparatively unimportant. All who were elected had originally opposed secession, and all but two had been Whigs. Two had been members of the Confederate Congress, and only one of the seven could take

---

[1] B. F. Moore to T. R. Caldwell, Oct. 14, 1865. Illustrative of Moore's foresight, the following is interesting: "A division, placing the Unionists on one side and the secessionists on the other, will lead to a breach made wider and deeper every day, until the extremest partizan on either side will become the most powerful man of his party, and the most dangerous to the quiet and prosperity of the State. With such tools as these, we shall be sure to dig up negro suffrage and worship it as many did the cotton bag."

[2] The vote on the ratification of the anti-secession ordinance was: for, 20,870; against, 1,983. Anti-slavery ordinance: for, 19,039; against, 3,970.

the "iron-clad" oath required for admission to a seat in Congress.[1]   Of the defeated candidates, only one could take the oath.

Before the election, President Johnson told Judge Reade that the provisional government would not terminate at once.   Two days after the election, Governor Holden was notified by Secretary Seward to continue in the exercise of his duties until relieved by directions from the President.

Many things in the campaign tended to create the impression in the North that the result of the election was a victory of those who were still hostile to the United States, and who hoped that, in a different way than by arms, the results of the war might be changed.   This impression was largely caused by the course of the *Standard* and the *Progress*, but they met with assistance from other sources.   The result of the congressional elections, for instance, was not calculated to assist the State to its original place in the Union.   The election of an unpardoned person, as in the case of Turner, created a bad impression.   In fact the wisdom of electing any of the delegation, except, possibly, A. H. Jones, who could take the oath, is doubtful, if it was hoped that they would be admitted to their seats.   They were all men who favored the Union and who represented the opinions and feelings of the State, but it was fairly certain that none would be recognized when Congress met. The opinion of the President on the result is best seen in the following communication to Governor Holden :

[1] The successful candidates were: J. R. Stubbs, C. C. Clark, T. C. Fuller, Josiah Turner, Bedford Brown, S. H. Walkup, and A. H. Jones. The last mentioned could take the oath.

WASHINGTON, November 27, 1865.

Accept my thanks for the noble and efficient manner in which you have discharged your duty as Provisional Governor. You will be sustained by the government.

The results of the recent elections in North Carolina have greatly damaged the prospects of the State in the restoration of its governmental relations. Should the action and spirit of the legislature be in the same direction, it will greatly increase the mischief already done and might be fatal.

It is hoped that the action and spirit manifested by the legislature will be so directed as rather to repair than to increase the difficulties under which the State has already placed itself.

ANDREW JOHNSON,
*President of the United States.*

The period between the election and the meeting of the General Assembly was devoid of events of interest. So long as something was to be gained from loyalty by the element of which the *Progress* was representative, the State had been declared to be loyal. But when the result of the election was known, that paper asserted that " universal loyalty may come with the next generation, but we who live in this will never see it."[1] The *Standard* said that the provisional governor was hindered in his work and that it was the " unmistakable work of unpardoned violent traitors."[2] The latter also dilated much upon the lack of wisdom shown in electing men to Congress who could not take the oath, forgetful of the fact that it had endorsed the candidacy of five who were unable to do so.

After the receipt of the President's letter requesting him to continue in the exercise of the duties of his office, Governor Holden seems to have thought that the provisional government would be continued until Congress

[1] *Progress*, Nov. 14, 1865.  [2] *Standard*, Nov. 17, 1865.

had recognized the new state government by admitting the members from North Carolina. The people were anxious in regard to it, and there was a general desire for some assurance from the President as to his intentions.

#### 4. THE RETURN TO CIVIL GOVERNMENT.

The General Assembly met on November 27.[1] In the Senate, Thomas Settle was chosen speaker over Dennis D. Ferebee. This would indicate a majority of the supporters of Holden. As speaker of the House, Samuel F. Phillips was chosen unanimously.

The governor's message laid special stress on the importance of immediately ratifying the Thirteenth Amendment. The House had already taken up the matter and passed a ratifying resolution with only four negative votes. An attempt was made to amend by adding a clause stating that any legislation by Congress upon the political status or civil relations of the freedmen would be unconstitutional and in opposition to the policy of the President, as expressed in his proclamations. This was defeated by a large vote.[2] In the Senate the opposition to the amendment was strongly shown. John M. Morehead voiced this in declaring his objection to the clause giving Congress the power of enforcement. Through it, he thought, Congress was given unlimited power of legislation, and a State would be powerless to resist. The result of its adoption would be legislation giving the freedmen the privilege of bearing arms, giving testimony, intermarriage with the whites, and the elective

---

[1] Six members of the Senate and eight of the House were also members of the convention. No information can be obtained of the former political affiliations of the majority of the members.

[2] *House Journal*, 1865, p. 26.

franchise. He denied any desire to impede its passage, but declined to vote for it.[1] Ferebee made an elaborate protest against its passage, which was spread upon the journal. His objections were based upon the same grounds as Morehead's, and also on the fact that the Southern States were not free agents, advantage being taken of their condition to force their consent to what they would otherwise reject. Three other senators united with him in the protest.[2] The resolution passed without further opposition. The blow at the rights of the States was perceived, but just at this time there was apparently very little inclination to discuss the constitutional question of States' rights. Its interest for the time had waned. After ratification, the subject was referred to a committee, which reported a resolution declaring that the amendment was ratified, with the understanding that the power of Congress to legislate on the subject of the freedmen was in no way enlarged.[3] This passed at the end of the session and, of course, was inoperative, amounting simply to a protest.

The publication in the *Standard* of the President's criticism of the State's action led to the passage of resolutions declaring that the people of the State had accepted in good faith the terms of the President and had complied with the conditions imposed; that they were loyal to the government of the United States and were ready to make any concessions, not inconsistent with their honor and safety, for a restoration of harmony. A declaration of confidence in the President and of thanks for his liberal policy was added.[4]

[1] His speech is quoted in the *Sentinel*, Dec. 2, 1865.
[2] *Senate Journal*, 1865, pp. 153-5.
[3] *Ibid.*, 1865, p. 84.  [4] *Resolutions*, 1865, p. 10.

The greater part of the session was spent in filling the
various offices declared vacant by the convention. Two
United States senators were elected, William A. Graham
and John Pool. The former, who had not been pardoned,
received the unanimous vote of Orange County for the
state Senate, but did not make any effort to take his seat.
A large number of the members of both houses then
petitioned the President to pardon him. The day he was
elected United States senator,[1] the pardon was signed,
but it was not sent to him, nor was he notified of the fact
for some time. Governor Holden, who, a short time before, had again advised against his pardon, notified the
President of his election, adding a characteristic expression of doubt whether a Northern member of Congress could with propriety consent to sit with one who
had been a member of the Confederate Congress.[2] The
short term was offered to Holden privately, but he refused
to accept it.[3] Thomas L. Clingman, who had been elected
in 1861, claimed the seat and went to Washington with
the intention of presenting himself as the member, but
a committee, appointed by the state Senate to investigate
the matter, declared that he had no claim to the seat,
and Pool was elected. The legislature also elected a full
set of judges. In the Supreme Court, two of the old
members were re-elected, and Judge Reade replaced
Judge Manly. Five of the provisional Superior Court
judges and several of the solicitors, appointed by Governor Holden, were elected permanently. Nearly all the
officers chosen had been formerly members of the Whig
party.[4]

[1] Only fourteen votes in both houses were cast against Graham.

[2] *Sen. Docs.*, no. 26, p. 228, 39 Cong., I sess.

[3] *Sentinel*, Dec. 15, 1865.

[4] The state officers were as follows: Governor, Jonathan Worth;

No disposition was shown to take up general legislative matters. The members felt that there was no assurance that any act would be regarded as valid, and considered it wise to await the outcome of the attempt of the representatives-elect to take their seats in Congress. Consequently, after filling the vacant state offices and administering the oath of office to Worth, with a provision that he should enter upon the duties of the office at the termination of the provisional government, the legislature adjourned until February, 1866, without taking any action regarding the freedmen or other matters of importance.

Governor Holden kept the President informed of the actions of the legislature, everything being presented in its worst light. He also made a strong effort to induce the President to set aside the election and retain him as provisional governor.[1] The President would not consent to this, and finally, on December 23, sent, through Secretary Seward, the following dispatch to Governor Holden :

DEPARTMENT OF STATE,
WASHINGTON, December 23, 1865.

*To His Excellency*, W. W. HOLDEN, *Provisional Governor of the State of North Carolina, Raleigh, North Carolina:*

SIR :—The time has arrived when, in the judgment of the President of the United States, the care and conduct of the

---

Secretary of State, R. W. Best; Treasurer, K. P. Battle; Comptroller, Curtis H. Brogden; Attorney General, S. H. Rogers; Justices of the Supreme Court, R. M. Pearson, W. H. Battle, E. G. Reade; Judges of the Superior Court, D. A. Barnes, E. J. Warren, D. G. Fowle, R. B. Gilliam, R. P. Buxton, Anderson Mitchell, W. M. Shipp, A. S. Merrimon; Solicitors, M. L. Eure, W. T. Faircloth, S. H. Rogers, Thomas Settle, Neill McKay, L. Q. Sharpe, W. P. Bynum, David Coleman.

[1] R. S. Hedrick to Jonathan Worth, July 8, 1866. Hamilton, ed., *The Correspondence of Jonathan Worth*, ii, p. 675.

proper affairs of the State of North Carolina may be remitted
to the constitutional authorities chosen by the people thereof,
without danger to the peace and safety of the United States.

By direction of the President, therefore, you are relieved
from the trust hitherto reposed in you as provisional governor
of North Carolina. Whenever the governor-elect shall have
accepted and become qualified to discharge the duties of the
executive office you will transfer the papers and property of
the State, now in your custody, to his excellency, the governor-elect.

It gives me especial pleasure to convey to you the President's acknowledgement of the fidelity, the loyalty and the
discretion which has marked your administration.

You will please give me a reply specifying the day on
which this communication is received.

I have the honor to be your excellency's most obedient servant,

WILLIAM H. SEWARD.[1]

He also notified Governor Worth of the termination
of the provisional government and offered him the co-
operation of the United States government in all his
efforts towards an early restoration of the State. Governor Worth replied, on December 28, that he had that
day assumed the duties of his office, and assured the President of his hearty desire to establish harmonious relations between the state and federal governments.[2]

As has been noted,[3] the convention passed an ordinance providing that all offices filled by the provisional
governor should become vacant at the close of the provisional government. The legislature made no provision
for new justices of the peace, and, in consequence, the

[1] *Executive Correspondence*, Worth, vol. i, p. 3.
[2] *Ibid.*, pp. 2–4.
[3] *Cf. supra*, p. 127; also *Ordinances*, p. 59.

newly-elected county officers were unable to qualify. The machinery of county government was stopped, and with it, the execution of state law by the civil power. The unimportance of the minor civil officers at this time prevented this condition of affairs from being harmful to the general welfare of the people, but it was one of the anomalies which this period so frequently presented. Governor Worth, by the advice of the Council of State, at once summoned the legislature to meet in extra session to remedy the defect. The session opened January 18, and acts were promptly passed authorizing the provisional officers to administer the oaths of office to their successors and to the magistrates elected by the legislature at the extra session.[1] The acts of the *de facto* sheriffs until March 1, 1866, were legalized;[2] and all other officers were authorized to hold over until the qualification of their successors.[3]

Other questions then engaged the attention of the legislature. The legislation regarding the freedmen occupied some time. The law of evidence was changed in criminal suits so as to admit the testimony of an accused person, which up to this time was incompetent.[4] A resolution was introduced into the House requesting the President to proclaim a general amnesty. Immediately a substitute was offered which, after reciting the supposed hardships endured by Union men, declared that no office should be held by an original secessionist or "latter-day war man," and requesting the President to declare all offices so held vacant. To avoid discussion of this, the original resolution was dropped. The session lasted until the middle of March, most of the time being spent on private legislation.

[1] *Laws*, 1866, chap. iv.
[3] *Ibid.*, chap. xxxvi.
[2] *Ibid.*, chap. vi.
[4] *Ibid.*, chap. lxiv.

# CHAPTER FOUR

## Political and Social Conditions Under the Restored Government

### I. THE FREEDMEN

EVEN before the termination of hostilities, the Negro question arose in North Carolina, but at first the problem was necessarily one for the military authorities solely. The first question requiring solution was regarding the disposition of the great numbers of freedmen who had assembled in various places, particularly in New Bern and Wilmington. When Sherman reached Fayetteville, about 8,000 Negroes were with the army. The burden was too great, and he sent them to Wilmington, where a great number had already congregated.[1] When it was decided, on account of expense, the danger of disease, and other causes, to disperse them as much as possible, General Hawley settled part of those in Wilmington on Smith's Island, at the mouth of the Cape Fear, and part near Fort Anderson, at Old Brunswick.[2] They were supplied with food and encouraged to begin planting crops.

General Schofield, in his proclamation announcing emancipation, advised the freedmen not to congregate in the towns but to seek employment under their former masters.[3] He was fearful of the result of the delay in settling the question of their status and disposal, believing that they

---

[1] *Off. Rec.*, no. 99, p. 978.  [2] *Ibid.*, no. 100, pp. 39, 80.
[3] *Ibid.*, p. 331.

148

would become a " huge white elephant " on the hands of the government.[1]  On May 15, he published a set of regulations for their government.  Parents were declared to have control of their children and, at the same time, the obligations of their former masters to take care of the children became theirs.  Orphans and the aged and infirm, if they had no near relations, were still to remain in the care of their former masters, who were forbidden to turn them away.  The question of wages was left to be decided by employers and employees; but the latter were warned to expect only moderate wages or a fair share of the crops.  District commanders were directed to appoint superintendents to take charge of matters relating to the freedmen.[2]  Provision was also made for the registration of marriages between the freedmen.  When the provisional government was established no ruling was made on the subject, but freedmen were advised to go through the same formalities as the whites, and clerks were directed to issue licenses to them.[3]  General Schofield's regulations were fair and, where they had any effect, worked for good.  The care and support of the aged negroes, without the assistance of the younger ones, was often a great burden upon the former masters, but one that was borne generally with no thought of complaint.

During the spring and early summer of 1865, outside influences were brought to bear upon the freedmen and a petition was circulated among them which asked the President, in his work of re-organization, to give them equal rights with the whites.[4]  A series of meetings was held in

---

[1] *Off. Rec.*, no. 100, p. 405.

[2] *Ibid.*, p. 503.

[3] *Executive Correspondence*, Provisional Governor, p. 93.

[4] North Carolina correspondence of the *New York Herald*, May 15, 1865.

various towns to choose delegates to a general meeting to be held later. Prominent in the proceedings of these meetings were negroes from the North who had come down to begin a movement among their race for equal rights and privileges. Several of these newcomers were natives who had escaped to the North and had received some education. The general meeting was held in Raleigh in September. The whole affair was under the control of J. W. Hood, a colored minister from Connecticut, and James H. Harris, a native who had been educated in Ohio. The latter had unusual ability as a speaker and was exceedingly shrewd. A. H. Galloway, a native, but recently from the North, and Isham Sweat, of Fayetteville, were also prominent. This group was again to become prominent in 1868. The tendency of the convention was towards a demand for equal political rights, including the suffrage, but, through the influence of Harris and Galloway, a set of resolutions addressed to the state convention, which was about to assemble, was adopted. These asked in moderate and well-chosen language that the race might have protection and an opportunity for education. They also asked that discrimination before the law might be abolished. No reference was made to the suffrage.[1] Before adjournment the convention resolved itself into an Equal Rights League, which at once began to work for the abolition of all distinctions on account of race and color and established a newspaper in Raleigh in aid of the cause.[2]

The question of Negro suffrage was already under discussion. In July, Alfred M. Waddell, a prominent citizen of Wilmington, the ante-bellum editor of the *Herald* and later a lieutenant-colonel in the Confederate service, in a

---

[1] *Standard*, Oct. 2 and 3, 1865.
[2] *Ibid.*, Jan. 2, 1866.

speech to the colored people of Wilmington, denounced taxation without representation and advocated a future extension of the suffrage to those of the negroes that were qualified for the privilege.[1]  In September, the *Sentinel* said it was opposed to Negro suffrage but was willing to open its pages to a discussion of the matter.  A series of articles favoring it appeared, written by Victor C. Barringer, but unsigned.  He took strong ground for granting the suffrage to the negroes, if only as a matter of policy, since the North would soon be united on the subject and it would be well to forestall the Radicals and grant qualified suffrage.[2]  His views were probably absorbed from his brother, General Rufus Barringer, who, while a prisoner at Fort Delaware, had come to the conclusion from his conversation with the Northern officers that nothing less than negro suffrage would be accepted by the North.[3]

The noticeable fact about the discussion of the question was that it caused no excitement or strong feeling.  Opposition was expressed, but calmly, and enfranchisement was discussed as a possibility, though an objectionable one.  David L. Swain said that if the freehold qualifications for voting for state senators should be restored he would favor restricted colored suffrage for the House of Commons.[4]  In all the arguments the bitterness shown a year later was lacking.  But it is true that few believed that there was any possibility of the imposition of Negro suffrage upon the South and there was no objection to a discussion where freedom of action was possible.  Foremost in opposition to any extension of the suffrage was the *Standard*.  Among

---

[1] *Sentinel*, Aug. 8, 1865.

[2] *Ibid.*, Sept. 1 and 11, 1865.

[3] *Ibid.*, Feb. 7, 1866.

[4] *Executive Correspondence*, Worth, vol. i, p. 265.

its so-called " Union Landmarks," before mentioned,[1] was " The right of the States to determine the question of suffrage for themselves. Unqualified opposition to what is called negro suffrage." [2] The discussion was without any good effect and possibly made a calm discussion later a matter of difficulty.

As has been mentioned, the position of the free Negroes in North Carolina previous to the war was different from that in most of the other Southern States. The same was true after general emancipation had taken place. By a decision rendered by Judge Gaston in 1838 [3] the inhabitants of the State were declared to form two classes, citizens and aliens. Slaves, from their condition, belonged to the latter class, but free persons of color formed part of the former class. By emancipation, therefore, citizenship was immediately conferred upon some 300,000 persons who had hitherto been " aliens through the disability of slavery." Free Negroes hitherto had been, like other citizens, entitled to the privilege of the writ of *habeas corpus,* to trial by jury, to own property, even in slaves,[4] to prosecute and defend suits in courts of justice, and, as incident to this, to make affidavits for a continuance and to prove by their own oaths, even against white persons, accounts for labor to the amount of $60.[5] But the free Negroes had been accustomed to the exercise of their liberties and were limited in number. When the end of the war brought general emancipation, the fear naturally arose that the freedmen, newly endowed with citizenship, would be unprepared for its rights without

---

[1] *Cf. supra,* p. 118.

[2] *Standard,* Aug. 5, 1865.

[3] State *v.* Manuel, 20 N. C., 20.

[4] In 1861 free negroes were forbidden thereafter to own slaves.

[5] Graham to Holderby, Feb. 6, 1866. Published in the *Sentinel.*

special limitations. The question thus arose as to what changes would have to be made to enable this new class of citizens to enter upon their rights, and, at the same time, their duties, without disturbance and injury to the body politic. To decide this question, the convention had authorized a commission to be appointed by the provisional governor, and Governor Holden had appointed B. F. Moore, W. S. Mason, and R. S. Donnell, who at once began their work.

They presented their report to the General Assembly in January, 1866. It was an able and elaborate discussion of the whole subject with a proposed scheme of legislation, based on the recognized citizenship of the freedmen. They advised the repeal of all laws which affected specially the colored race, and the re-enacting of such as were necessary. The main bill which they recommended, and which was passed with a few minor changes, defined as persons of color negroes and their issue to the fourth generation, even when one parent was white in each generation.[1] They were declared entitled to the same rights and privileges and subject to the same disabilities as free persons of color prior to general emancipation. They were also declared entitled to the same privileges as white persons in suits and proceedings at law and in equity. The law of apprenticeship was altered so as to apply to both races alike, with the one exception, that in the case of the negroes, former owners had a preference over all other persons. The marriage of former slaves was made valid, and provision was made for registration. Marriage between white and colored persons was forbidden, and a penalty provided for issuing licenses in such cases or for performing the ceremony. All contracts, where

[1] Indians were included in the bill as first presented, but were omitted later.

one or more of the parties was colored, for property of the value of ten dollars or more, were void, unless put in writing, signed by the parties, and witnessed by a white person who could read and write.  Persons of color were declared competent witnesses in all cases at law or in equity where the rights or property of persons of color were involved, and also in pleas of the State where the offence was alleged to have been committed against a person of color.  In other cases their testimony was admissible by consent.  This was not to go into effect until jurisdiction in affairs relating to the freedmen should be left to the state courts.[1]  All criminal laws were changed so as to apply alike to both races, and the punishment was made the same except in the case of an assault with the intent to commit rape upon a white woman. When the assault was commited by a person of color it was a capital offence; otherwise it was an aggravated assault and punishable under the common law by fine and imprisonment.[2]  A special court of wardens for the colored poor was authorized for each county.

The scheme, even with its amendments, met with considerable opposition in both houses and in the State generally.  The press, however, almost unanimously favored it. The *Standard* was silent on the subject, and the editor was hostile to the proposed legislation.  It was charged that he attempted to defeat the plan in the hope that the State might again be put under a provisional government.[3]  Many persons in the State seemed unconvinced that citizenship had already been conferred upon the negroes and that any deprivation of their rights would be an injustice.  When

---

[1] This provision was first inserted in the House.

[2] The report will be found in the *Legislative Documents* for 1865-6 and in the newspapers of January, 1866.

[3] *Sentinel*, March 14, 1866.

the November election took place, it is hardly doubtful that a majority in the State was opposed to giving negroes the right to testify. Their testimony had not been admissible against white persons for many years, if ever, but since 1821, slaves had been permitted to testify against free negroes.[1] When the report of the commission was presented the chief fight was made on the portion relating to testimony, and the debate lasted four days. Two grounds for the passage of this part of the bill had been stated by the commission: first, that the helpless and unprotected condition of the colored race demanded it; and second, that the admission of their testimony was necessary to secure to colored people their property rights. Other reasons were advanced in the debate—the well-known desire of the President for its passage, the hope that full jurisdiction would be given the state courts in cases relating to the freedmen, and that the Freedmen's Bureau would be withdrawn. The general unreliability of negro testimony was fully recognized, but it was thought better to admit all than to deny any, and at times defeat justice. And it was believed that it would be a means of education in telling the truth. In opposition, it was urged that it was a step towards negro suffrage, and in any case would arouse hopes in the negroes that would be of no benefit to them. Finally the bill obtained in the House of Commons a majority of one vote. In the Senate it failed to pass its second reading, but on reconsideration it obtained a majority of eight. Many of the members had changed their opinion during the debate, but were pledged to their constituents to vote against negro testimony. This accounts in part for the small majorities obtained.[2]

---

[1] It is said that this law was enacted to humble the free negroes.

[2] *Sentinel*, March 5, 1866.

The commission recommended and obtained the passage of acts providing punishment for pursuing live stock with the intention of stealing,[1] for seditious language, insurrection and rebellion, and for vagrancy. The vagrancy act was a substitute for two statutes already existing which made a distinction between the races. Acts were also passed to prevent wilful trespass on lands and stealing from them, to prevent the enticing of servants from fulfilment of contracts or the harboring of servants who had already broken a contract, and to secure to agricultural laborers their pay in kind. A system of work-houses was provided for, to be used in the punishment of minor offences. All these laws operated equally upon both races, and the whole " code," if it could be so called, was characterized by justice and moderation.

The slight discrimination shown, however, was sufficient to cause objection by the officers of the Freedmen's Bureau, and, in consequence of their refusal to surrender jurisdiction, Governor Worth recommended to the convention which met in May that it should make alterations satisfactory to the Bureau.[2] This was done by making penalties the same for both races in all cases and abolishing all discriminations before the law.[3] The act was, however, only legislative, and did not bind the further action of any general assembly.

The social and economic condition of the freedmen during 1865 and 1866 was one that might well excite pity. Their first instinct upon emancipation had naturally been to move about and put their freedom to a test. This test was frequently made by a change of name, residence, em-

---

[1] This was made necessary by the increase of theft of live stock, particularly of hogs.

[2] *Journal*, p. 5.                    [3] *Ordinances*, p. 8.

ployment, and wife. Town life, with its excitement, furnished an almost irresistible attraction, and only the presence of troops was necessary to render it completely so. Freedom, in their minds, meant freedom not only from slavery but from work, with a continuation of their former freedom from responsibility. Refusal to work resulted naturally in want of the necessaries of life, and sickness and destitution were general in the towns. In the country matters were somewhat better. There the demoralization of those that remained was not so great and support was more easily obtained either by labor or dishonesty. Crime increased greatly as time went by. The proceedings of the provost marshal's court in Raleigh show somewhat the extent of petty offences. Serious offences of all sorts were turned over to the Freedmen's Bureau, but larceny, disorder, and similar transgressions were usually punished by hanging the convicted parties by their thumbs to the lamp posts in the streets. The newspapers, in almost every issue, had accounts of violence and crime committed by freedmen, and, in most cases, these went unpunished. The Bureau agents, either from intention or inability, accomplished little to remedy the condition of affairs. In many instances it was impossible for the farmers to keep the smaller live stock with any degree of security, and even horses and cattle were frequently stolen. The large number of wandering Negroes increased the difficulty of bringing the offenders to justice.

## 2. CONFLICT OF THE CIVIL AND MILITARY POWERS

At the beginning of the provisional government there was, naturally, no question of the distinction between the civil and military powers. In a sense, the provisional governor was more a military than a civil officer. His appointment and authority were based on the war power of the

President, and the object of his appointment was to restore a civil government.  This was a work that would necessarily take time, and to the military forces was confided the duty of at least preserving order.  At the close of the war North Carolina formed a distinct military department.  At first General Schofield was in command, but he was succeeded by General Thomas H. Ruger.  The latter divided the department into five districts, each with a general commanding.[1]  In June, 1866, the State was included with South Carolina in the Department of the South and placed under General Daniel E. Sickles.[2]  North Carolina formed a separate command under General J. C. Robinson, who was also an assistant commissioner of the Freedmen's Bureau.  This arrangement continued until the establishment of the military government.

The first difference which arose was in regard to the county police force.  While General Schofield was in command, he had a definite agreement with the provisional governor, by which the whole matter was left to the various county courts.[3]  Acting in accordance with this agreement, Governor Holden gave the justices of several counties permission to establish such a force.  But General Ruger, who in the meantime had succeeded General Schofield, refused to recognize the agreement or to allow the forces thus organized to act.[4]

The next matter of which Governor Holden complained was in regard to the colored troops stationed in the State.

[1] They were as follows: New Bern, Gen. C. J. Paine; Wilmington, Gen. J. W. Ames; Raleigh, General A. Ames; Greensboro, Gen. S. P. Carter; and West North Carolina, Gen. T. T. Heath, with headquarters at Morganton. *Off. Rec.*, no. 100, p. 675.

[2] *General Orders*, no. 32; May 19, 1866.

[3] *Executive Correspondence*, Provisional Governor, p. 77.

[4] *Ibid.*, pp. 70, 77.

The first complaint to Governor Holden came from Wilmington. The town had a negro garrison, and with its large negro population was in a state of great alarm. Alfred M. Waddell wrote the governor early in June that outrages by the troops were of daily occurrence and that the effect of the presence of the colored troops on the negro population was very dangerous. Arrests were constantly made without any cause, and in one instance the soldiers were instructed, if the person arrested said or did anything, to run him through. There was little or no redress, as unusual latitude was given the colored troops.[1] In July the mayor and commissioners wrote describing the conduct of the negroes and the apprehension felt by the white people of an insurrection. The negroes had demanded that they should have some of the city offices and had made threats when they were refused. The governor replied that the citizens had acted rightly in refusing to appoint the negroes to office, as the right to hold office depended on the right of suffrage. He also assured them that if the negroes attempted by force to gain control of public affairs or avenge grievances suffered at the hands of the whites, they would be visited with swift punishment; but if obedient to the laws, they would be protected. He also wrote General Ruger and appealed to him to take steps in the matter, suggesting that the police guard of New Hanover County should be armed and that the city authorities should have a reserve of arms at their disposal. In September, orders were issued to muster out all the negro troops from the North that were in the State, but a considerable number were left.[2] Wherever they were stationed there was genuine alarm among the inhabitants. A report in Raleigh in 1866 that a com-

[1] *Executive Correspondence*, Provisional Governor, p. 35.
[2] *Off. Rec.*, no. 126, p. 108.

pany was to be ordered there caused intense uneasiness.[1] In the case of Elizabeth City and Edenton, all alarm was unfounded, as the soldiers behaved very well.[2] But in Beaufort, a party of them from Fort Macon committed a brutal rape and were also guilty of attempting the same crime a second time. They were arrested in the town and the garrison of Fort Macon threatened to turn its guns upon the town if they were not surrendered.[3] The condition of affairs there was so bad that General Ruger forbade any soldier to leave the fort except under a white officer.[4] Near Wilmington, Thomas Pickett was murdered and his two daughters dangerously wounded by three soldiers from the negro garrison at Fort Fisher in company with a negro from Wilmington.[5] In Kinston, a citizen was beaten by the soldiers, and, upon Governor Holden's complaint to General Ruger, the garrison was removed.[6] Soon afterwards the governor notified General Ruger that a car of muskets and ammunition had been side-tracked at Auburn, and while left unguarded had been opened by the freedmen and its contents distributed. The possessors of the arms then became the terror of the community.[7] Complaints of colored troops were also sent in from New Bern, Windsor, and other eastern towns.[8] General Ruger and General Cox both showed a disposition to do everything in their power to prevent any trouble, the latter issuing special orders on the subject.[9] In September, 1866, the last remaining regi-

---

[1] *Sentinel*, Aug. 18, 1865.    [2] *Ibid.*, Sept. 25, 1865.

[3] *Standard*, Jan. 5, 1866.

[4] *Executive Correspondence*, Worth, vol. i, p. 38.

[5] *Sentinel*, Jan. 18, 1865.

[6] *Executive Correspondence*, Provisional Governor, p. 81.

[7] *Ibid.*, p. 82.    [8] *Ibid.*, pp. 78-9.

[9] *Ibid.*, p. 8.

ment of negro volunteers was mustered out, and that cause of discontent disappeared.[1]

The white troops as a general thing, after the confusion incident to the surrender was over, behaved well. In Asheville, however, they were so disorderly and undisciplined that great efforts were made by the citizens to have them withdrawn.[2]

The chief cause of friction between the civil and the military authorities was, however, as might be supposed, concerning the administration of justice. Governor Holden, as has been seen, appointed a full number of provisional judges, and when the civil government went into operation the office in every district was filled by election. A number of the provisional judges decided that they had no jurisdiction in cases of offences committed prior to May 29, 1865, and the rest assented to this opinion,[3] but it only applied to the provisional judges and in no way bound those elected by the General Assembly.

The question of conflicting jurisdictions first arose in July, 1865. In June, a white man in Chatham County killed a freedman. Governor Holden had not then appointed any judges and therefore turned the prisoner over to General Cox, who at once ordered him to be held by the provost marshal until the civil courts should be open. In July, when Governor Holden requested that the prisoner should be delivered to the civil authorities for trial, General Ames refused on the ground that in view of the facts of the case a military trial was necessary.[4] The same month the question again arose over three citizens of Person County who

---

[1] *House Ex. Docs.* no. 1, p. 299, 40 Cong., 1 sess.

[2] Vance to Worth, Feb. 6, 1866.

[3] The opinion is in the *Standard*, Dec. 15, 1865.

[4] *Executive Correspondence*, Provisional Governor, pp. 8, 20, 23.

were arrested for an assault upon a freedman and carried
to Raleigh for trial by a military commission.  Governor
Holden at once called the attention of General Ruger to
the re-organization of the civil government of the county,
and requested that the prisoners might be remanded there
for a civil trial.  General Ruger refused on the ground that
the military authorities had a clear jurisdiction in all cases
relating to the preservation of order, and consequently did
not have to wait for the call of the civil power or to obey
the writ of *habeas corpus*.  He declared that violence
toward the freedmen was not uncommon in the State, but
that he knew of no instance where the provisional magistrates had taken official notice of such cases.  He further
said that he was informed by the agents of the Bureau that
hostility to the freedmen was succeeding apathy, and that
consequently no dependence could be put on grand juries, so
the only remedy for offences against the blacks was prompt
trial by a military commission.  He also objected to the
procedure of the civil courts as clumsy and productive of
delay.[1]  Governor Holden maintained that the proclamation of the President gave the civil power exclusive jurisdiction and showed the utter impossibility of concurrent
jurisdiction.  He defended the State against the charge
of hostility to the freedmen, suggesting that the Bureau
commissioners had probably heard only one side of the
question.[2]  But General Ruger was not to be convinced and
closed the discussion, declaring that martial law existed at
the surrender, and in his opinion existed still, except where
modified by the President.  He expressed his confidence in
the honesty of the courts, but declared that they were without power to prevent violence.[3]

---

[1] *Executive Correspondence*, Provisional Governor, pp. 27-32.

[2] *Ibid.*, pp. 31-6.                    [3] *Ibid.*, p. 37.

Governor Holden referred the whole matter to the President, who did not interfere in behalf of the State. The governor in the meantime made every effort to conform to the wishes of General Ruger. Courts of Oyer and Terminer were ordered to be held in various parts of the State, and this removed ground for the charge that justice was delayed. Finally Governor Holden reached a definite agreement with General Ruger as to military and civil jurisdiction. All cases of misdemeanor or violation of law in which white persons alone were concerned were placed within the jurisdiction of the courts of Oyer and Terminer constituted by the governor, while all cases in which freedmen were concerned were declared to be under military jurisdiction.[1] Later the judges of the courts of Oyer and Terminer were given power to bind over to court or to bind to keep the peace, and even to lodge in jail accused persons, regardless of color. The trial of such cases as concerned freedmen was, however, still by military commissions.[2] General Meade approved the arrangement, assuring Governor Holden that whenever the laws of the State and the practice of the courts left no doubt that the freedmen would receive justice, the use of military commissions would cease.[3]

The conflict of the two jurisdictions was carried to its ultimate issue in the trial of Major John H. Gee, of Florida, by a military commission for violation of the laws of war in his treatment of federal prisoners at Salisbury. A short review of the case will be interesting, as it was the most important one tried by a military commission in North Carolina. The commission assembled in Raleigh on February 21, 1866. Major Gee, through counsel, claimed that

[1] *Sentinel*, Sept. 19, 1865.

[2] *Record of the Provisional Governor*, pp. 143-4.

[3] *Executive Correspondence*, Provisional Governor, p. 74.

under the terms of the Sherman-Johnston agreement he, as a paroled prisoner, was not liable to trial. The commission, however, claimed jurisdiction, and the trial followed. Major Gee then pleaded his acceptance of the terms of amnesty as laid down in the President's proclamation, but the commission decided that he was debarred under the sixth exception.[1] The trial lasted over eighty days, though only fifty-five of these were actually consumed in the proceedings of the court. More than a hundred witnesses were examined. At the close of the examination of the witnesses for the prosecution, the defence entered a plea that the jurisdiction of the commission had been removed by the President's proclamation declaring that the insurrection had ceased,[2] and moved that the case should be referred to the civil authorities. The commission, after hearing the matter argued by counsel, refused to assent to the motion and ordered a continuance of the trial. Colonel Holland, counsel for Major Gee, then sued out a writ of *habeas corpus* directed to General Ruger and returnable to Judge Fowle. General Ruger refused to produce Major Gee on the ground that he held him under the President's order. Colonel Holland then moved that an attachment be issued against General Ruger. Judge Fowle announced as his opinion that, under the President's proclamation, the prisoner was entitled to civil trial. But he postponed his decision for two weeks. The day before the time specified for rendering the decision, President Johnson notified the governor that his proclamation was not intended to operate in the case of a military commission already instituted, and that General Ruger had been instructed to allow the trial to proceed, but to report all proceedings to the war department for revision.

[1] This excepted those who had violated the laws of war.

[2] Proclamation of April 2, 1866.

The next day,[1] Judge Fowle rendered a formal decision declaring that, by virtue of the official declaration of the President the insurrection was at an end, Major Gee was entitled to the privileges of the writ of *habeas corpus,* and consequently that General Ruger's return was insufficient. He then issued an attachment against the general, with instructions to the sheriff not to serve it if the writ should be obeyed. General Ruger of course declined to obey the writ or to submit to arrest. The matter was then referred to the governor, and thus came to an end.[2] The result of the trial was the acquittal of Major Gee.

The most important of the military trials in which the accused were citizens of North Carolina occurred in 1867, when William J. Tolar, Duncan G. McRae, Thomas Powers, Samuel Phillips, and David Watkins, all of Cumberland, were accused of the murder of a negro named Archie Beebe when he was about to be tried for an attempt at rape. The purpose of the deed was to prevent the appearance of the woman concerned in court and the negro was shot while in the custody of the sheriff of the county. A dense crowd was present and it was impossible to discover who had fired the fatal shot. McRae and Phillips were soon discharged for lack of any evidence against them but the other three were convicted after a trial that lasted with some intermissions for more than three months. The evidence was very conflicting but the general impression at the time was that one of the three had fired the shot. Major General Robert Avery was judge advocate and Colonel J. V. Bomford, president of the commission. The defendants had a very strong array of counsel and the case was contested at every

---

[1] April 28, 1866.

[2] The account of this case has been gathered from the files of the *Sentinel* and *Standard* for 1866.

step. Public sympathy was much on the side of the accused, as was usually the case when the trial was before a military commission, and, as soon as conviction resulted, appeals were made to the President for pardon. A year later all three were pardoned.

Another case that attracted much attention was that of Mrs. Isham Ball of Warren County, in February, 1866, for the murder of a freedman. The testimony showed beyond doubt that he had entered upon her premises after being forbidden to do so, and was advancing upon her in a most threatening way when she fired the shot which killed him. The commission, however, found her guilty of manslaughter, and sentenced her to three years' imprisonment. General Ruger reduced it to one, and a later appeal to the President resulted in her pardon. No attempt was made to procure a civil trial for her.

These were the chief instances of disputed jurisdiction and of trial by military commission. But they are merely examples chosen from the great number in the period extending from July, 1865, until the establishment of military government in name as well as in fact in 1867.

In the fall of 1865, Captain W. H. Doherty, an assistant quartermaster at New Bern, petitioned General Ruger to order a military commission to investigate the hanging of twenty North Carolina Union volunteers in March, 1864, by General George E. Pickett and General R. F. Hoke, "merely because of their devotion to the Union cause." A board of inquiry was accordingly constituted and recommended that the officers composing the court-martial that ordered the executions referred to, General Pickett, General Hoke, Colonel Baker, and others unnamed, should be tried and punished for violation of the laws of war. The testimony taken by the board showed that those executed had all been deserters, but the board claimed that it was only from the state service, and that consequently the court-martial had no authority. The judge advocate general, J. Holt, to whom the case was referred, decided that no personal charge could be sustained, as those executed had been deserters. Another court of inquiry was constituted in January, 1866, but was able to obtain no incriminating evidence. In the meantime General Holt had changed his opinion in regard to the possiblity of punishment, and recommended General Pickett's arrest and trial.[1] General Pickett and General Hoke, however, had already appealed to General Grant, and this, in connection with the impossibility of securing a conviction, led to the dropping of the whole matter.

Injudicious expressions of opinion by newspaper editors resulted on several occasions in the application of military law. The publisher of the Goldsboro *News* was arrested, and the publication of his paper suspended on account of a criticism of some women who had come from the North to teach in colored schools.[2] He was released without punishment. Benjamin Robinson, one of the editors of the Fayetteville *Observer,* was arrested in December, 1865, for so-called seditious language, and was brought to Raleigh. Later he was released on parole.[3] But the most noted of such cases was that of Robert P. Waring, editor of the Charlotte *Times.* He was arrested in December, 1865, and after several weeks' confinement was tried on the charge of " publishing and circulating disloyal and seditious writings within a district under martial law," the writing referred to being calculated and intended, it was alleged, to produce hostility to the government of the United States.

[1] *House Ex. Docs.*, no. 98, 39 Cong., 1 Sess.
[2] *Standard*, Jan. 11, 1866.
[3] *Ibid.*, Dec. 18. 1865.

It was an editorial declaring the South to be under a despotism.[1]    To the charge above-mentioned, so far as concerned the act, he pleaded guilty.    The intention alleged he denied.    He was ably defended, but the result was a foregone conclusion and he was found guilty and fined $300.[2]

The only other important case of interference by the military authorities in criminal proceedings was in December, 1866, when corporal punishment was forbidden except in the case of apprenticed minors.    The same order forbade the enforcement of the vagrancy laws when any distinction was made on account of race.[3]    As regards corporal punishment, the State had no prison, and for many years punishment by whipping had been administered to the criminals of both races.    The prejudice against it originated with the negroes and the Freedmen's Bureau agents, who alike re-

[1] The editorial was as follows: "We are still without Washington news, and look forward to the report of the committee on credentials with some interest, though without hope of receiving justice.    The South is now under a more grinding despotism than has heretofore found a place upon the face of the earth.    Raised under a form of government, as expounded by the early fathers of the republic, when to say ' I am an American citizen ' was to be equal to a king, we feel our serfdom more painfully by reflecting upon what we have lost.    We have fallen from our high estate, and now there is ' none so poor as to do us reverence.'    Other nations, suffering under the iron heel of lawless tyranny, can console themselves with the reflection that their condition is no worse than that of their predecessors.    Not so with the proud Southron.    He once roamed his field a free man, and sat under his own vine and fig tree, and none dared make him afraid.    He was the equal if not the superior of the mercenary race which now dominates over him."

[2] This was not his first experience of the military power of the United States, for, in 1861, when he returned to New York, after resigning the consulship at St. Thomas, he was arrested and confined for some time for raising his hat to a Confederate flag.    Dowd, *Prominent North Carolinians*, p. 73.

[3] *General Orders*, no. 15.

garded it, when applied to the former, as a remnant of slavery. For months before the order forbidding it was issued, there had been constant interference by the Bureau in the execution of the sentences of the courts. The cruelty of the punishment could hardly have been the cause of its abolition, for, as has been noticed, hanging by the thumbs was the usual punishment administered by the provost marshal's courts in Raleigh.[1] Governor Worth appealed to the President, and in company with Thomas Ruffin, David L. Swain, and Nathaniel Boyden went to Washington to see him, but no change in the order was made. In any case, it would have been too late, as the military government was established by Congress soon afterwards.

In numerous other ways military authority was exercised. Interference in civil suits, while not so frequent as in criminal cases, was not unknown. An instance of this occurred in Raleigh in February, 1866. Two men from the North rented a hotel property in the town. The owner, after some time, unable to collect the rent, sued for the amount. Finding that the lessees were about to leave town, he had them arrested, but General Ruger, who had refused to interfere in the suit on account of lack of jurisdiction, now forced the sheriff to release them because there was no judge to summon the plaintiff to show the cause of their arrest. The defendants, soon after their release, left the State without settling their indebtedness. General Ruger claimed that he had not intended to prevent recovery by the plaintiff, but only to delay arrest until a judge should be present in the town.[2]

Several times interference occurred in the collection of

---

[1] Proceedings of the Provost Marshal's court, published in the *Standard* during 1865.

[2] *Executive Correspondence*, Worth, vol. i, pp. 44-6.

taxes. The convention of 1865 levied a tax on all mercantile business for that year. In Wilmington, in January, 1866, General Cook, who was then in command, issued an order restraining the sheriff of New Hanover from collecting the tax from firms trading under a federal license. This ruling, however, was revoked by General Ruger.[1] In 1866, General J. C. Robinson interfered in the collection of a poll tax in Cumberland and Columbus counties, ordering the sheriffs to refund all collected above one dollar, as the State had only levied that amount. He was probably ignorant of the fact that the law had a provision for increasing the amount according to the necessities of each county.[2]

Such was the part played by the army in North Carolina in civil affairs during the period of Presidential Reconstruction. Enough has been shown of the workings of the state government to make it clear that while. by degrees, much was left to the state authorities, the government was practically military in that the state government performed its functions only through the acquiescence of the military commanders. These commanders, in general, showed themselves to be considerate and animated by a desire for peace and harmony. But they were naturally inclined to disregard points of law which were of importance to a civilian, and when their minds were made up to any course it was practically useless to advance any arguments in opposition. While their interference in civil affairs was deeply resented and sharply, if uselessly, opposed in the State, the officers generally were personally popular in the various communities in which they were stationed.

---

[1] *Executive Correspondence,* Worth, vol. i, pp. 36-7.

[2] *Ibid.,* pp. 208-9.

## 3. STATE POLITICS IN 1866

At the close of the provisional government, Holden, embittered by his defeat and disappointed in his plan to continue in office, resumed the editorship of the *Standard*. He still had the ear of the President and felt that through this fact he might succeed in the end. But abuse of the Radical policy at Washington became less and less frequent in Holden's paper, and at the same time less violent; and by the summer of 1866, it had ceased entirely. His quiet opposition to the admission of negro testimony showed what was in his mind. No thinking person, aware of the condition of public sentiment at the North, doubted that a refusal to make this concession, demanded alike by justice and policy, would solidify the Radicals in Congress against any recognition of the existing state government, and it is also very clear that Holden did not desire the recognition by Congress of those who had defeated him. He was accused of this by the *Sentinel* in March and thereafter.[1]

Early in the year, the *Standard* said that if the laudation of Vance in the state press should continue and should be accompanied by disparagement of Holden, an appeal would be made to the President to cause Vance to be again confined in prison, and with Jefferson Davis to be tried for treason.[2] In March, Holden said editorially that, while he had in the past favored universal amnesty, he was compelled by the course of the secessionists to demand that the law should be allowed to take its course.[3] Four days thereafter war was formally declared upon his opponents in the following words: " We know that the true Unionists are depressed at the prospects before them, and feel that they have a right to look to Washington for sympathy and for

---

[1] *Sentinel*, March 20, 1866.       [2] *Standard*, Jan. 17, 1866.
[3] *Ibid.*, March 2, 1866.

such practicable aid as will enable them to put the enemies of the Union where they ought to be—under their feet. And we now give notice that we have commenced this warfare on traitors, not without having counted the cost, and we intend to continue it until they are driven from every office of importance in the State. Nothing shall divert us from our purpose." [1] The challenge was accepted, and the *Sentinel* became as violent as the *Standard.* The course of the *Sentinel* was regarded with distaste and apprehension by Governor Worth and his friends, who believed that but for Pell's violence Holden would be politically dead,[2] but their appeals to the former were without effect.

When the convention assembled in adjourned session in May, opposition had developed to its taking any action in regard to the state constitution. This opposition had a twofold basis. A large number of lawyers opposed any action on the ground that the convention had been called for special purposes which it had accomplished at its first session, and that it should therefore adjourn *sine die.* Still others desired its dissolution because a large number of its members were adherents of Holden. They based their arguments upon the same reasons as the former class, but a difference is readily seen. As soon as the convention met, resolutions for adjournment were introduced, declaring that it had no authority from the people, and consequently that any alteration of the fundamental law of the State, further than was required by existing conditions, would be revolutionary and dangerous. Without debate the resolutions were defeated by a vote of 61 to 30. Samuel F. Phillips at once attempted to secure the passage of a resolution directing a committee to prepare an ordinance calling for a con-

[1] *Standard,* March 6, 1866.

[2] Hamilton, ed., *The Correspondence of Jonathan Worth,* pp. 779-83.

vention of the people to meet in 1871 to amend the constitution, and providing for the adjournment of the existing
body. He argued that, as the chief matter of discussion was
the question of a new basis of representation, it would be
better to wait until the census of 1870 was taken. His resolution, however, was tabled and never acted upon.

Up to this time representation in the State had been based
upon federal population. This worked an injustice upon
the west and had been the cause of a long contest prior
to the war. All efforts to secure a change had failed
hitherto, but a new movement now began and was favored
by the " straitest sect " element, as it would greatly increase
the power of the west where their chief strength lay, and
might give the control of the legislature into their hands.

An attempt was made to pass a resolution providing for
sending a commission to Washington to confer with the
President and members of Congress in regard to what
would be necessary to secure the restoration of the State to
her position in the Union. But the resolution contained
an indirect endorsement of the congressional policy, and,
although the wording was changed, it failed.

The convention remained in session until late in June.
Most of the time was spent in reconstructing the constitution. The draft as proposed to the convention embodied
most of the old document, with certain additions and amendments. Its arrangement was the work of B. F. Moore, who
was the most experienced and learned lawyer in the body.
Throughout the debates he was its strongest defender, and
to him was largely due its adoption by the convention. It
was provided that the new instrument should be submitted to
the people for ratification.[1] The date of the state election was
changed to October to allow the new constitution, if ratified,

[1] *Journal*, June 25, 1866.

to go into effect. This was a shrewd political move by the " straitest sect," who thought that by this they would gain control of the legislature on account of the change of the basis of representation. The influence of this element was much more apparent in the convention than in the General Assembly, but it was not great enough to overcome the conservative forces. The whole session was marked by a series of compromises; so, if the advantage remained with any particular faction, it cannot be distinguished. The constitution, as a whole, was not a matter on which the two factions divided. On its final adoption the vote was 63 to 30.

As submitted to the people, the constitution was a more compact instrument than the original, for all the various amendments made from time to time were incorporated in their proper places. The only important change in the Bill of Rights was the addition of clauses prohibiting slavery, prohibiting the quartering of troops upon citizens except under certain laws, and providing that the courts should always be open to every person. The basis of representation for the House of Commons was changed to white population. The office of lieutenant governor was established. No one could hold the office of governor or of lieutenant governor unless he had been a citizen of the United States for twenty years, a resident of the State for five years immediately preceding the election, be thirty years of age, and possessed of land in fee to the value of $2,000. Senators were required to be thirty years of age and to possess three hundred acres of land in fee or a freehold of not less value than $1,000.[1] Members of the House of Commons were required to have a freehold of one hundred acres, or to the value of $300. Five years' residence previous to election was required for members of both houses. None but white

[1] Formerly it was required that a senator should own three hundred acres.

persons were eligible as voters or office-holders.[1] All persons on taking office were required to take, besides their official oath, one to support the state constitution, in so far as it was not inconsistent with that of the United States. It provided that no amendment should be made to the constitution except by a convention.[2] Magistrates were thereafter to be chosen by the people for a term of six years.

In addition to being more compact, the constitution was clearer and fuller than the existing one. In fact, only one great fault could be found with it, and that defect defeated it. As soon as it was submitted to the people an exceedingly able discussion on the question of ratification began. All the opposition of importance was based on the question of the validity of the action of the convention. Judge Ruffin and Judge Manly were probably the most distinguished of its opponents. The former was opposed to the white basis of representation, but his chief argument was against the authority of the convention. He said that it had no more authority in law than any voluntary assemblage of persons, and advised the rejection of the constitution on this ground.[3] This involved a doubt of the validity of the convention's actions at its first session, and also raised a question as to the status of the governments of the various Southern States. Thaddeus Stevens later quoted him as an authority on his own position regarding them.[4]

[1] The term "white" meant one having less than one-sixteenth of negro blood.

[2] Before this the constitution could be amended by the concurrent votes of successive legislatures, ratified by the people.

[3] *Sentinel*, July 28, 1866. This letter written to Edward Conigland was not published over Ruffin's name, but was recognized.

[4] Stevens said: "I quote Judge Ruffin, one of the ablest and fairest of secessionists. The Chief Justice is right. Not a rebel State has this day a lawful government." Speech at Bedford, Pa., Sept. 4, 1866. *Standard*, Sept. 19, 1866.

Judge Manly objected to the constitution itself, and also claimed that, while the convention had a valid existence and authority for the purposes mentioned by the President in his proclamation, it had none for any further action.[1] William A. Graham was also opposed to its ratification.

As might be imagined, B. F. Moore was the strongest defender of the constitution, or rather of the authority of the convention. Unfortunately, his main argument, a discussion of the war power of the President, and an exceedingly able one, did not appear until after the constitution had been rejected. It was written in reply to the argument of Judge Ruffin, and while not showing, possibly, as great a respect for and knowledge of constitutional law as that of the former chief justice, it indicated a clearer perception of the changed conditions brought about by the war.[2] Governor Worth also favored ratification.[3] Holden was a champion of the constitution and said that its rejection would be the worst blow that the President's policy had received. The *Sentinel* also favored ratification, but without enthusiasm.

The vote on the question was taken on August 2, and resulted in the rejection of the constitution by a majority of 1,982 out of a total vote of 41,122.

During the period in which occurred the events just related, there were other matters of interest to the State. In April, Holden came out in favor of allowing Congress to act without opposition.[4] A little later he declared that while he had favored the President's plan of restoration it had been rendered useless by the traitors who had obtained

---

[1] *Standard*, Aug. 1, 1866.

[2] *Ibid.*, Sept. 12, 1866.

[3] Winston to Worth, Sept. 5, 1866. Hamilton, ed., *The Correspondence of Jonathan Worth*, ii, p. 763.

[4] *Standard*, April 25, 1866.

office, and, as it was necessary for the State to get back into the Union and for the control of affairs to be restored to loyal men, he would advocate the adoption of the proposed Fourteenth or Howard Amendment to the Constitution of the United States.[1] About this time, to the delight of his opponents, Holden was nominated by the President as minister to San Salvador. It is not improbable that the nomination was made to quiet him and to get him out of the way. He went to Washington to press the matter, but was unable to convince the Senate of his suitability and the nomination was rejected. It was thought at the time that he desired confirmation only that he might decline the position, but still be aided politically.[2]

In May, Governor Worth was nominated for re-election by a meeting in Randolph County, and a month later he announced himself as a candidate. He was much stronger in the State than he had been at the preceding election, and in consequence there was no attempt to run Holden. But if not a candidate, Holden was at least in entire control of the opposition to Governor Worth. He settled upon General M. W. Ransom, of Northampton, as the most suitable person to oppose Governor Worth, and used every effort to induce him to consent to become a candidate; but the general declined on the ground that he was opposed to any contest.[3] James M. Leach and General W. R. Cox were then mentioned by the opposition, but the leaders, meeting with no encouragement, either from them or from the people, dropped their names. It then became the idea of most of the opposition to try to elect the lieutenant-governor and not to attempt to elect the governor. This plan met with

---

[1] *Standard,* June 6 and 13, 1866.

[2] Hedrick to Worth, June 20, 1866.

[3] *Standard,* Aug. 1, 1866. Also Hamilton, ed., *The Correspondence of Jonathan Worth,* ii, p. 764.

favor among men like John Pool and Lewis Thompson, who were pledged to support Worth but were in sympathy with the Radicals.[1] The plan probably failed to meet with the approval of Holden. For the nomination for lieutenant-governor, Thomas Settle was informally chosen by the opposition; while to oppose him Pell, in spite of the opposition of the Worth leaders, insisted upon pressing the claims of Dennis D. Ferebee. The rejection of the constitution necessitated a change in these plans. The white basis of representation was at once declared by Holden to be the issue of the campaign, and George W. Logan, of Rutherford, who had been a member of the Confederate Congress, was settled upon as a candidate for governor. P. T. Henry was a second choice.[2] But both were soon dropped, probably at their own request. The position of a candidate against Governor Worth at this juncture was not one to be sought by anyone with political ambitions.

During the summer, the friends of the national administration called a convention of the supporters of the President and his policy to meet in Philadelphia on August 14. By this means it was hoped that a consolidation of the Administration Republicans and the Democrats might be brought about. The call met with a hearty response in North Carolina, but very little hope was entertained there that good results would follow from it. However, a full delegation attended, composed almost entirely of the adherents of Governor Worth.[3] The movement was strongly

---

[1] P. H. Winston to Worth, Sept. 5, 1866.          [2] *Ibid.*

[3] R. C. Puryear, George Davis, formerly Attorney-General of the Confederate States, William A. Graham, and Judge George Howard were delegates from the State at large. From the congressional districts the delegations were as follows: 1st, W. N. H. Smith, H. A. Gilliam; 2nd, M. E. Manly, William A. Wright; 3d, Thomas S. Ashe, Arch. McLean; 4th, A. H. Arrington, Vacancy; 5th, Jno. A. Gilmer, Thos. Ruffin, Jr.; 6th, Joseph H. Wilson, Nathaniel Boyden; 7th, M. Patton and S. F. Patterson.

opposed by Holden who said that the delegates who had been chosen would not be admitted. The convention met and issued a dignified and able address to the country. The opponents of the President's policy ridiculed the proceedings with considerable effect, and it is doubtful if much good was accomplished. Of the North Carolina delegation, John A. Gilmer was one of the vice-presidents of the convention and William A. Graham was on the committee on resolutions.

Two weeks later, another convention met in the same city. This was called by Southern Unionists who wished an opportunity to explain their sentiments and position to the country. Among the signers of the call were Daniel R. Goodloe and Byron Laflin, from North Carolina. The former was about to return to the State after an absence of many years. The latter, a Northern man, had come with the Union army and had settled in Pitt County. He was a native of Massachusetts and was the first of this class of new residents to enter politics in North Carolina. The delegation from North Carolina to the convention, besides these, was composed of five Northern men and two natives of the State.[1] The personnel of the delegation is enough to show that it was in no sense representative of the State

---

[1] The delegates were A. W. Tourgee, a native of Ohio, who had come to Guilford County after service in the Union army; Rev. Hope Bain, a Northern minister, who had settled in Goldsboro before the war; G. O. Glavis, a former Union chaplain and Bureau agent, lately convicted of dishonesty by a military commission; Rev. James Sinclair, a native of Scotland, educated in Pennsylvania, who had lived in the State before 1861, had been a Confederate lieutenant-colonel, and after being accused of treason, had become a Union chaplain and later a Bureau agent; H. K. Furniss, a Northern man, of whom little is known; J. W. Wynne, a native, and A. H. Jones, a native, who had been elected to Congress immediately after the war, but had not been admitted.

as a whole.  At the same time that this convention met, delegates from most of the Northern States met in Philadelphia to receive the Southern delegates, organizing themselves into a convention for the purpose.  The " Loyalists " remained in session for five days and adopted an address denouncing the President and his policy and demanding the adoption of the proposed Fourteenth Amendment as an absolute necessity in the South.  Of the North Carolina delegates, the most prominent were A. W. Tourgee and Daniel R. Goodloe.  The former took a very prominent part in all the proceedings of the convention but particularly in the debate which took place on negro suffrage.  Tourgee advocated it strongly with the usual argument that it was necessary to protect not only the freedmen, but also all Union men.[1]  Goodloe was opposed to the convention's taking any definite ground on the subject.

While this convention was holding its meetings, Holden denied that there was any difference between the plans of the President and of Congress.[2]  The same day the *Standard,* acting upon the suggestion of a mass meeting in New Bern as expressed in its resolution, contained a call for a " loyal Union " convention to meet in Raleigh two weeks later.  The New Bern meeting was presided over by Charles R. Thomas, but the resolutions were the work of the Northern settlers in the town.  Resolutions of a similar nature, except that they demanded negro suffrage, had been passed

---

[1] Tourgee said at the same time that he had been lately informed " by a Quaker " that the bodies of fifteen negroes had been dragged out of one pond in Guilford County.  He also said that 1,200 Union soldiers, who had settled in the State, had been forced to sacrifice their property and leave the State to save their lives.  *Executive Correspondence*, Worth, vol. ii, p. 2.

[2] *Standard*, Sept. 5, 1866.

in August by a meeting in Guilford which was controlled by A. W. Tourgee and G. W. Welker.[1]

The convention thus called met on September 20. It passed resolutions favoring the proposed Fourteenth Amendment to the Constitution of the United States, censuring Governor Worth's administration, and declaring that only the unmistakably loyal ought to hold office in North Carolina, and then nominated Alfred Dockery for governor. Holden addressed the body and outlined the reasons why the conditions of Congress should be accepted. He still, however, declared against negro suffrage.[2] A regular organization was begun, and here, for the first time since the war, there was a definite division into parties. The party formed now was the germ of the Republican party in North Carolina.

Dockery declined to be a candidate, but expressed himself as favorable to the Howard Amendment, in preference to risking the action of the next Congress. He also favored placing certain disabilities in the State and the retirement of those who could not take the " iron-clad " oath.[3] Holden, fearing the consequence to his organization if there should be no opposition, advised the people to vote for Dockery, regardless of his refusal to run.

The campaign, if it can be so called, was devoid of interest. Governor Worth was re-elected, receiving a majority of 23,496 out of a total vote of 44,994. Dockery carried nine counties—among them Randolph, the home of Governor Worth. Richmond County, Dockery's home, was carried by Governor Worth.

---

[1] G. W. Welker was a minister and a native of Pennsylvania who had lived in North Carolina many years.

[2] *Standard*, Sept. 26, 1866.

[3] *Ibid.*, Oct. 3, 1866.

Every effort was now made by the Radicals to paint as dark a picture as possible of the condition of affairs in the State. Petitions in great numbers, from various parts of the State, were sent to the President asking that protection from " rebel persecution " might be given the signers. In the case of one petition, from Camden County, a copy was sent to Governor Worth. The petitioners claimed that persecution was carried on by means of indictments for acts performed during the war in aid of the Union cause. An investigation was at once made by Judge Brooks, of the United States District Court, who discovered that only two of the fifty-six named had been indicted, and that the offence in those cases was retailing liquor without a license.[1] Several attempts had been made to indict others for acts committed during the war, but no court would recognize the matter. In the west, where there was more ill feeling on account of the greater division in sentiment and the fact that the war had there been, in reality, civil war, it is not unlikely that cases of persecution occurred, but they were private. Careful investigations were made repeatedly by Judge Merrimon and other judges of the state courts into the truth of the charges without their being substantiated. The fact of the matter is that every criminal, against whom the state courts had an indictment, became at once, in his own eyes at least, a Union patriot, suffering for his devotion to his country, and this view was taken, apparently, by the opposition party in the State.

The General Assembly, like its predecessor, was composed largely of old Whigs. Judge Manly was elected speaker of the Senate, and R. Y. McAden speaker of the House of Commons. Governor Worth, in his message, earnestly urged the rejection of the Fourteenth Amend-

[1] *Executive Correspondence*, Worth, vol. i, pp. 108-9.

ment as dangerous and degrading. He reviewed the condition of the State and suggested much necessary legislation.

Judge Manly was elected to the United States Senate to succeed John Pool who, although he had voted for Worth in the last election, was suspected of favoring the radical policy, and had become exceedingly unpopular since his plea, at the time he sought admission to the United States Senate, that during the war he had sought and obtained election as a state senator only that he might embarrass the Confederate government. Soon after his defeat, Holden went on to Washington to join him there, declaring, before his departure, his opposition to the proposed amendment as not sufficiently stringent against traitors.[1]

Soon after the legislature assembled, a joint committee of both houses was constituted to report on the proposed amendment. Its report, signed by twelve members, with only one member dissenting, was made within a few days. The committee stated that a number of radical changes in the fundamental law were proposed with no opportunity of accepting one or more without ratifying all, and in strong terms expressed their disapproval of such a plan of amendment, which, they declared, was without precedent in the history of the country. They opposed the amendment, also, as submitted in an unconstitutional manner, no representatives from eleven Southern States having taken part in its passage, after the same States had been recognized as parts of the Union; by Congress in the resolutions of July, 1861, declaring the object of the war and in acts apportioning taxation, assigning to the said States, their respective number of representatives, readjusting the federal judicial circuits, and accepting as valid the assent of Virginia to the division of the State; by the Judiciary in the hearing and decision

---

[1] *Standard*, Dec. 5, 1866.

of cases carried up from their courts; and by the Executive in approval of the acts of Congress before mentioned. The submission of the amendment was also advanced as an act of recognition. The committee took the ground that if the votes of the Southern States were necessary to a valid ratification of the amendment, they were equally necessary on the question of submitting it to the States. Another ground of disapproval was the fact that the resolution containing the proposition to amend the Constitution had never been submitted to the President for his approval. The committee disclaimed any spirit of captiousness or the advocacy of merely sectional interests, recognizing, however, that the proposed amendment was designed to operate mainly upon the Southern States and was proposed only for that reason, but declared that the cause of free constitutional government was at stake, and that too great precautions could not be employed. The various sections of the amendment were then taken up separately.

The main criticism of the first section was regarding the lack of any definition of the " privileges and immunities " of citizens of the United States. The committee declared that the language of the section left the matter in too great doubt, for it might mean the privileges enjoyed in the past, or any others that the federal government might thereafter declare to belong to citizens. In such a case, the right of a State to regulate its internal affairs would be destroyed.

In the second section, the committee claimed that the old right of the individual States to regulate the suffrage was impaired and the whole matter left in doubt, with an implication in favor of the power of the federal government in the matter. The committee claimed that this clause, in conjunction with the final one giving Congress power to enforce the article by appropriate legislation, was a dangerous innovation, in that it would authorize the federal government to " come in as an intermeddler between a State and the citizens of a State in almost all conceivable cases, to supervise and interfere with the ordinary administration of justice in the state courts, and to provide tribunals—as had to some extent been already done in the Civil Rights Bill—to which an unsuccessful litigant or a criminal convicted in the courts of the State can make complaints that justice and the equal protection of the laws have been denied him, and however groundless may be his complaint, can obtain a rehearing of his case." This, it was urged, was calculated to bring the state courts into contempt and ultimately to transfer the administration of civil and criminal justice to the federal courts. The same section was also opposed on account of the imposition of a penalty for any restriction of the suffrage, and the attempt thereby to bring about universal suffrage. The change in the basis of representation from population to voters was objected to for its own sake, as inconsistent with the theory of the political system which had always prevailed in the United States.

The third section was opposed on account of the fact that it was directed against the South, and because thereby the majority of the mature men of the State, the committee thought, would be disqualified from holding office, and the whole state government would be overthrown. The committee stated further, as their opinion, that the people of North Carolina would prefer to commit their interests to Congress as then composed, than to intrust them to a class of men, no more loyal in most instances than those disqualified, whose only hope of political advancement lay in the banning of better men. The power of Congress to remove disabilities was declared to be an interference with the pardoning power of the President, and was also opposed as placing too great a political power in the hands of Congress by which it might control elections in the States, and even the state governments.

The fourth section was declared useless on account of the intention of the people to pay the federal debt and their determination that the Confederate debt should not be paid. So in regard to compensation for the slaves, the committee thought it injustice, but declared that the people of the South had never expected to be paid for them.

The final section was opposed as opening too wide a door to congressional interference, with the consequent centralization of power in the federal government.

The committee also asked what guarantees North Carolina had, in the event that its people should yield up their honest convictions of duty in the hope of restoration and ratify the amendment, that such restoration would take place. They expressed the opinion that ratification would not have any effect of the kind. As to the probability that more unwelcome and humiliating terms would be demanded, the committee, while asserting their belief that such would not be the case, declared, nevertheless, that if it were to be so, the State ought not to humiliate itself in the beginning by yielding to intimidation, and ratifying a measure of which it disapproved. Consequently, with but one dissenting voice, the committee recommended the rejection of the amendment.[1]

The report of the committee embodied the objections which had already been raised in the State and represented fairly the opinion of a majority of the people. Consequently when it reached the Senate it was adopted with only two

[1] J. M. Leach, H. T. Clark, H. M. Waugh, J. J. Davis, Thomas S. Kenan, J. H. P. Russ, Arch. McLean, Phillip Hodnett, J. M. Perry, J. Morehead, Jr., D. A. Covington, and W. D. Jones signed the report. P. A. Wilson favored the ratification of the amendment.

dissenting votes. When the rejection resolution came upon its passage, C. L. Harris, of Rutherford County, attempted to secure the substitution of a ratifying resolution. This was defeated, receiving only the vote of Harris. The resolution rejecting the amendment also received only his negative vote. Six other members had promised to vote with him, but failed him when the time came. In the House of Commons, fifteen votes were cast against adopting the report, but only ten on the final passage of the rejecting resolution.

C. L. Harris and D. A. Jenkins at once went to Washington to join W. W. Holden and John Pool in the conference going on there with the radical leaders. On December 13, the same day the amendment was rejected, Thaddeus Stevens had introduced in the House of Representatives, at the request of the North Carolinians, a bill providing for the reconstruction of North Carolina, which had been prepared by James F. Taylor, John Pool, and W. W. Holden, and approved by the North Carolina radicals.[1] This bill, after rehearsing the facts of secession, war, and Presidential Reconstruction, and calling attention to the duty of Congress to preserve a republican form of government in all the States, and in the " district " named, provided that, on May 20, 1867, a convention of the loyal citizens of the "district formerly comprising the State of North Carolina" should meet in Raleigh and prepare a constitution which should be afterwards submitted to Congress for approval. All male citizens of North Carolina who could read or

---

[1] *Standard*, Dec. 26, 1866. A large part of the material for the bill .was furnished to Stevens by W. W. Holden. The North Carolinians who were back of the plan were Lewis Thompson, John Pool, D. M. Carter, Eugene Grissom, Tod R. Caldwell, R. M. Henry, Thomas Settle, R. P. Dick, G. W. Logan, Alfred Dockery, O. H. Dockery, C. J. Cowles, J. T. Leach, D. A. Barnes, Charles R. Thomas, J. F. Taylor, D. A. Jenkins, and C. L. Harris.

write, or who owned real estate to the value of one hundred dollars, could vote. No person who formerly had the right to vote could be disqualified. No person could have a seat in the convention or hold any office under the new constitution without taking an oath that at all times, after March 4, 1864, he would have complied with the terms of the President's proclamation of December 8, 1863, providing for the restoration of the seceded States, had it been possible, and that, after that date he was opposed to the rebellion and Confederacy and gave no aid thereto, but desired the success of the Union. It was placed within the discretion of officers administering the oath to refuse to do so, when doubt existed in their minds as to the truth of the applicant's declarations. The existing state government was to cease at the pleasure of the convention. The provisions of the act were to be executed by the officials of the United States. The bill was referred, and no report upon it was ever made. But Stevens later introduced the oath as an amendment to a general reconstruction bill, previously introduced. In this latter bill, the oath was a prerequisite for voting.[1] This met with entire approval from Holden, for he had already decided that the original was too lenient and, in fact, he recommended some such change as was made.[2]

The House of Commons took notice of the charges that were constantly made that Union men were being persecuted in the courts. James Blythe, a member, who made the charge on the floor of the House, was examined by a committee and testified that there was no use of the courts for persecution. He said that by persecution was meant abuse of those who favored the Howard Amendment as being in

[1] *Globe*, 39 Cong., 2 sess., p. 250.
[2] *Standard*, Dec. 25, 1866.

favor of negro suffrage. C. L. Harris, although a member of the Senate, was also examined and gave similar evidence. The committee's report, that justice was administered in the courts of the State, was unanimously adopted.[1] Holden tried to create the impression that the legislature was taking testimony in order to begin prosecutions for treason against the State.[2] Harris proved that this was incorrect, but it furnished material for numerous appeals to Congress to rescue the Union men of the State from " rebel persecution for their unswerving loyalty." That the majority in both houses of the legislature would have favored, if practicable, the punishment of those who were attempting to overthrow the existing state government is undoubted, and it was frankly acknowledged on the floor of the House of Commons.[3] To put a stop to the complaints of persecution in the courts and to go on record against anything of the kind, the legislature passed an amnesty act, applying to both Union and Confederate soldiers. This act was soon put into effect.[4]

A commission at Washington was authorized for the purpose of looking after state claims, or anything that might seem necessary to the governor. Accordingly Governor Worth appointed as the commission Nathaniel Boyden, Bedford Brown, P. H. Winston, J. M. Leach, A. S. Merrimon, and Lewis Hanes. John A. Gilmer, Thomas Ruffin, and D. L. Swain were also offered appointments, but declined. The commission went to Washington and, for part of the time, in company with Governor Worth, investigated the condition of affairs. At first hopeful, they finally

---

[1] *Journal*, p. 215.

[2] *Standard*, Dec. 19, 1866.

[3] *Journal* and debates, Dec. 18, 1866.

[4] State *v*. Blalock, 61 N. C., 242.

saw what would be the end of the struggle with Congress, and, after conferring with Governor Orr, of South Carolina, ex-Governor Parsons, of Alabama, Governor Marvin, of Florida, Judge J. T. James, of Arkansas, and some of the members of Congress, suggested a plan of compromise. This was an amendment to the Constitution of the United States, designed to replace the Howard Amendment. It added a section declaring the Union perpetual, dropped the section imposing disabilities, and, while retaining the connection of apportionment of representation and suffrage, limited the power of the States to impose property and intelligence qualifications. A part of the compromise plan was an amendment to the state constitution. This extended the franchise in accordance with the other amendment.[1]

The scheme was received with no enthusiasm and, after being introduced in the legislature, as a substitute for a resolution proposing a national convention, was withdrawn. It would, however, in all probability, have been passed, but for the feeling that further humiliation would be required and that it was useless to attempt to do anything but save self-respect.[2] A bill calling a convention of the people was then passed, but without the required majority.[3] The resolution proposing a national convention also passed both houses, only the extreme radicals voting against it. The proceedings of the session were marked by extreme bitterness, the debates being stormy, with evidence of the most intense party feeling. The radical element, while in a minority, was strong enough to give trouble to the conservatives. But all their efforts failed to produce any action approving the plans of Congress.

[1] The details of this plan are discussed in the *American Historical Review* of October, 1913.

[2] Governor Worth to Governor Orr, Feb. 27, 1867.

[3] *Journal*, pp. 387-93; March 1, 1867.

In the meantime, the various changes in position of the " straitest sect " or " Loyal Union " party, as they now called themselves, had finally brought them all to the extreme position of the Northern radicals. On December 26, 1866, Holden wrote the Albany *Evening Journal,* taking strong ground for negro suffrage and saying, in conclusion, " The rebel leaders, who are controlling these States, are totally regardless of political duty, and totally bent on mischief. You must govern them, or they will at last again govern you." [1] And on January 1, 1867, at a meeting of the negroes in the African church in Raleigh, he declared himself in favor of unqualified negro suffrage, and introduced a resolution requesting Congress to reorganize the state government on the basis of " loyal white and black suffrage." [2] For the future, or as long as he was in political life,[3] he promoted negro suffrage as violently as he had opposed it in the past. He at once commenced the preparation of petitions to Congress praying that negro suffrage might be established, and circulated them among both black and white.

Beginning now, with the new year, there followed a campaign based, as similar ones before, on the supposed alarming conditions in the State. The life and property of all Union men were declared to be in extreme danger, unless Congress should interfere at once in their behalf. Those conducting the campaign hinted at severe measures, and Holden said that he regretted that the property of about five hundred. persons in each State had not been confiscated, and that eight or ten of the leaders in each State had not been executed.[4] Later he said that confiscation was a pos-

---

[1] Quoted in the *Wilmington Journal,* Jan. 7, 1867.
[2] *Sentinel,* Jan. 3, 1867. *Standard,* Jan. 9, 1867.
[3] In later years he changed his opinion again.
[4] *Standard,* Jan. 9, 1867.

sibility, and even a probability. Already many of his followers were demanding it in the hope that they would profit
thereby.[1]

The whole State was excited and uneasy. Doubt as to
the outcome of the struggle between the President and Congress had almost entirely disappeared, and the only question was how far Congress would go in the destruction of
the institutions of the Southern States. In the west, A. H.
Jones was leading in an effort to secure from Congress the
division of the State, so that the Union men of that section
could protect themselves from the " rebels " of the east. In
this turmoil and excitement, the news came of the passage
of the Reconstruction Act and the establishment of the military government.

### 4. ECONOMIC AND FINANCIAL PROBLEMS

Before taking up the consequences of these extreme
measures, it is important to trace the general course of
economic and social transformation during the period of
the presidential régime.

Secretary Seward, in his letter notifying Governor Holden of his appointment, stated that his salary and the other
expenses of the provisional government would be paid out
of the contingent fund of the War Department. This was
due to the fact that the provisional government was dependent on the military power of the President. It was well for
the State that it was so, for financial conditions were de-
plorable and the people were at the time unable to bear a
tax that would pay the running expenses of the state government. The expenses of the convention were, of course,
met by the State. Immediately before the close of hos-

---

[1] *Standard*, Jan. 16, 1867. The previous autumn Holden said confiscation would be the result of a failure to ratify the Fourteenth
Amendment.

tilities the State owned a very large quantity of cotton and rosin. Secretary Seward, on July 8, informed Governor Holden that the State could take possession of this property and use it for the necessary expenses of government. But a large part of it had been taken by the troops after the close of hostilities and turned over to the agent of the Treasury Department, and Secretary McCulloch had directed that it should be shipped North. But after he had been informed of the financial condition of the State, he consented that the " ungathered debris " might be collected and used by the State, and he accordingly directed his agents not to be too inquisitorial in their work.[1]

Jonathan Worth took charge of its collection and found a considerable amount. The rosin was particularly valuable, for it was still in beds and untouched. Comparatively little cotton was secured, for most of what was left by the government agents was stolen by individuals from the State or from the North. Redress was impossible for lack of testimony against the persons suspected. The records of collection have been lost, but the sale of the rosin and cotton so gathered brought about $150,000. Of this amount, after the expenses of the convention and many other demands upon the State had been paid, there remained $40,000.

Even after collection, losses were frequent. An agent was sent to Georgia to collect state cotton, and at great expense got together seventy bales. It was hauled to the depot and while awaiting shipment, it was seized by a Treasury agent, and the Department declined to return it. Elsewhere in Georgia, 421 bales were seized by the government with the same result.[2] And when property was safely in the

[1] *House Reports*, 40 Cong., 1 sess. McCulloch's testimony in impeachment investigation.

[2] The United States later refunded the price of these two lots amounting to nearly $50,000. *House Reports*, no. 7, 45 Cong., 3 sess.

possession of the State, a close watch was necessary. Soon after Governor Worth went into office, he discovered that Dr. Sloan, who had succeeded him as provisional treasurer, had instructed the firm of Swepson, Mendenhall & Co., of New York, who were selling the state cotton, to sell all on hand to A. J. Jones, a member of the state Senate, for 33 cents per pound. The market price on the day the instructions were given was 47½ cents. No money passed at the transaction, for the cotton was at once sold at the market price and the net amount of $2,224.44 paid to Jones. Governor Worth investigated the matter at once and Jones refunded the amount, declaring that he had decided to do so before the investigation was commenced.[1] The State also owned property of considerable value in England, but from various causes, including fraud, nothing was ever realized from it.

Every bank in the State, after the repudiation of the war debt, was forced into liquidation. The Bank of North Carolina, the most important in the State, compromised with its creditors at about 36 per cent. The Bank of Cape Fear paid only 25 per cent. Later some of the creditors, who had refused to compromise, recovered the full value of their notes. All the banks were in better condition than might have been expected, but the tax on notes prevented any attempt at reorganization from being made. Owing to the lack of capital, new banks came very slowly. Three national banks, at Charlotte, Raleigh, and Fayetteville, were established during the period of Presidential Reconstruction.

All these things had their effect upon the condition of the people at large. This was already serious enough. The country, wherever it had been touched by the invading

---

[1] *Legislative Docs.*, 1865-66, no. 13. A. J. Jones later became notorious as one of the most unblushing of the thieves that infested the State during Reconstruction.

armies, was stripped of everything of value that could be carried away and had attracted the notice of the soldiers. This was particularly the case along the line of Sherman's march. Horses and cattle had been taken away and some killed from pure wantonness.[1] A considerable shrinkage is noticeable in the number in the State as compared with 1860. The following table gives the figures:[2]

|  | 1860. | 1866. | 1868. |
|---|---|---|---|
| No. of horses | 150,661 | 99,436 | 98,441 |
| No. of mules | 51,388 | 32,560 | 32,885 |
| No. of milch cattle | 228,623 | 203,555 | 205,590 |
| No. of oxen, *etc.* | 465,187 | 292,921 | 287,062 |
| No. of sheep | 546,749 | 339,259 | 325,684 |
| No. of swine | 883,214 | 1,160,816 | 975,085 |
| Value live stock | $31,130,805 | $22,946,758 | $20,052,456 |

The decrease in numbers and value shown in 1868, when the report was more accurate, forces the conclusion that the figures for 1866 were the result of an over-estimate.

The troops in their march through the State left worn-out horses and took good ones wherever found. The worn-out stock had scarcely become of value to those holding it, when orders were issued by the quartermaster general for its collection and sale.[1] Numerous protests were at once made. In December, 1865, Secretary McCulloch had ordered that such horses and mules should not be taken, but this latter order superseded that, and all horses that were branded with either the United States or Confederate marks were seized. The best terms obtainable were that wherever possible they should be sold in the counties where they were taken. Great hardship was produced by this seizure

---

[1] *Last Ninety Days of the War*, p. 43.

[2] These estimates are gathered from the reports of the Department of Agriculture.

[3] *Executive Correspondence*, Worth, vol. i, p. 11.

of stock, particularly as, at the time, the direct tax of 1861 was being collected, and the people had been drained of all ready money. The total amount of the tax collected before July, 1866, when an act was passed suspending further collection for two years, was $394,847.63. The quota of the State was $576,194.66.[1]

Beginning in 1862, the United States levied a heavy tax on cotton which rose as high as two and one-half cents a pound. This was collected from the seceded States at the close of the war, North Carolina paying for this tax $1,959,704.87.

Crops in large areas had been destroyed by the horses which had been turned out to rest and fatten. Fences were gone and often stables and other farm buildings, and even, in some cases, the dwellings, were destroyed. The last case, however, was the exception. Vehicles of every description had almost disappeared. The path of the main army was comparatively limited, but foraging parties, during and immediately after the war, penetrated to almost every portion of the State. The treasury agents followed, and by June, 1865, had collected, abandoned, or captured private property which sold for nearly $80,000. During the remainder of the year, $14,000 was added.[2] The total receipts for captured cotton amounted to $428,071.31.

To alleviate the distress which followed inevitably from the conditions outlined, a great deal was done by the Union army and the Freedmen's Bureau. Rations were issued to the white people as well as to the negroes, and in this way many families were literally kept from starvation. Large sums of money were received from the North in 1866 and

---

[1] *Report of the Secretary of the Treasury,* 1866, p. 62.

[2] *Ibid.,* 1865. By January, 1865, property, excluding cotton, worth $201,164.42 had been seized.

1867, and grain and provisions as well. Fortunately the crops in 1865, which had been planted before the end of the war, were unusually good. The fruit crop, particularly, was immense. The crops of the next two years were poor. In fact, in 1867, the cotton crop was a complete failure and the food crops much smaller than in the preceding year. The estimated value of the corn, wheat, rye, oats, barley, buckwheat, potatoes, tobacco, and hay in the State in 1866 was $45,551,450. The next year it was $38,332,716.

The large loss in the male population consequent upon the war, and the great number of disabled, naturally accounted for a falling off in production. But when, in addition, it is considered that the status of the chief laboring class had been entirely changed, and that the majority of that class were making their freedom evident to themselves by abstaining as much as possible from labor, it is not wonderful that, apart from bad seasons, the crops should have been poor. The whole matter of labor was very much unsettled from the nature of the great changes that had taken place, and the disturbance was increased by the constant interference of the Freedmen's Bureau in the contracts and arrangements made, as well as by its general influence in creating dissatisfaction among the negroes.

The actual conditions regarding labor are very difficult to ascertain, owing to the chaotic situation in the State. In 1865, it was difficult in North Carolina, and indeed all over the South, to obtain laborers, on account of the belief held by the negroes that land would be given them by the United States Government.[1] However, when Christmas passed and the new year began without any gifts, this belief was largely abandoned and necessity compelled those who were

---

[1] General Grant thought this belief had been started by the **Bureau** agents. See his report to the President in 1865.

waiting for " forty acres and a mule " to find employment.[1]
The contracts made in 1865 were very vague, but the disposition of the land owners to treat their employees fairly
led to a gradual increase in the number made.  But long-
time contracts were discouraged by the Bureau agents and
were unpopular on account of the suspicion the negroes felt
at their condition and, in many instances, on account of distrust of their former owners.  Indeed, in very many cases,
the negroes left their old masters and hired themselves to
others, at times on plantations immediately adjoining.  This
was in part due to a desire to have some visible evidence of
freedom.

The contract system, in general, worked badly on account
of the tendency of the negroes to stop work, often when
they were most needed.  Many farmers found it more profitable to hire only for a short period and pay wages.  The
average rate was about $10 per month for men and $6 for
women.  The tendency of wages during the period was
downward, and in 1867 the average was lower.[2]  The majority of the people, however, had no ready money to pay
wages, and the system of working " on shares," in spite of
its many disadvantages, of necessity, resulted.  The usual
plan was for the farmer to furnish the stock, feed, and im-
plements and the tenant to furnish the labor.  The crop was
divided between them, the proportion each received varying
according to the nature of the crop and the section of the
State.  The share the tenant received varied from one-
fourth to one-half.  As examples of the working of the
system, the following seem fair :

[1] Report of Asst. Commissioner, *Sen. Ex. Docs.*, no. 27, p. 17, 39
Cong., 1 sess.

[2] *Report, Dept. of Agriculture,* 1867, *Report, Freedmen's Bureau,*
1866. *Sen. Ex. Docs.*, no. 6, p. 104, 39 Cong., 2 sess.

In Stanly County, a farmer in 1860 had kept six male hands, two women, and several children on a plantation of 160 acres. With the help of six horses, he made an average crop of twenty bales of cotton, 150 barrels of corn, 50 bushels of rye, besides roots, hay, and garden vegetables. In 1866, he divided his farm into three lots, the land being of the same quality in each. The first he put in charge of the most intelligent of his former slaves with his wife and four children, old enough to work. The owner supplied two mules, feed, and all the tools required. Apart from the expenses of his family, there was no charge on the tenant. The second lot was given to two good married hands and supplied as the first. The third was given to the son of the owner, who hired a colored man for a share of the crop. The rent in each case was one-half the crop. Each tenant was left to his own judgment in the choice of the crop to be planted. The result was that the crops produced by the freedmen were small, less than 40 barrels of corn, 60 bushels of wheat, 100 bushels of oats, and four bales of cotton between them. They had gone so far into debt for provisions that only a little corn and wheat was left as their share, with no money to begin another crop. The owner's son made as much as both the freedmen together and his crop was regarded as below the average. But another side is seen in another case in the same county. Two families of colored people, composed of six men, two women, and four children, undertook to plant a farm of 125 acres. In spite of the bad season, they raised 100 barrels of corn, 200 bushels of wheat, 100 bushels of oats, 25 bushels of peas, 75 bushels of potatoes, and about 4,000 pounds of ginned cotton. The value of the crop was $1,800, and they received a half.[1] It is safe to say, however, that the efforts of the

---

[1] *Report of Dept. of Agriculture*, 1867.

freedmen, unless under white direction, for the most part resulted in failure and disaster. In consequence of the war and these conditions, real estate between 1860 and 1867 had greatly decreased in value.[1]

Just as the repudiation of the war debt wrecked the banks, it destroyed many private fortunes and reduced thousands from comfort to extreme poverty. Business was at a standstill for lack of money, and the people were utterly unable to meet their obligations. A complicated " stay law " was passed by the convention of 1866.[2] This did not go far enough, and the legislature passed another, which was declared unconstitutional by the courts.[3] As regards the debts due by individuals to creditors in the North, some had been collected under the Confederate sequestration act. When the creditors entered their claims, the debtors pleaded their forced payments to the Confederacy as a release. The question was argued before the United States Circuit Court in session at Raleigh, and Chief Justice Chase held that the payment was no discharge of the debt.[4] War contracts also caused dispute, but the Supreme Court of the State held that they were valid.[5]

To promote a general economic improvement, efforts were made to induce immigration from the Northern States. In the fall of 1865, hostile feeling was fast dying out and the people seemed genuinely anxious for Northern people to come into the State. But when it looked most favorable for an influx of new population, the campaign of misrepre-

---

[1] *Report Department of Agriculture*, 1867.

[2] *Ordinances*, 1866, p. 31.

[3] This was a decision in the Superior Court. It never reached the Supreme Court.

[4] Shortridge *v.* Macon, 1 Abbot U. S., 58.

[5] Phillips *v.* Hooker, 62 N. C., 193.

sentation for political purposes began, and deterred many from coming. Probably the great cause of their failure to come was the presence of the negro. The experience of those who did come was not such as to strengthen them in the belief that they could profitably engage in agriculture with the existing conditions of labor. Whatever was the cause, too few came to have any appreciable effect as agents in the economic rehabilitation of the State. Few as they were, however, their political influence, in the period which followed, was great enough to delay improvement for many years.

### 5. TRANSPORTATION AND THE MAILS

At the beginning of the war there were about 890 miles of railroad in the State. During the war the construction of a military road from Greensboro to Danville added about 50 miles to this. The most important of the systems in operation were the North Carolina, Raleigh and Gaston, the Atlantic and North Carolina, and the Wilmington and Weldon. The State owned a large interest in each of the three first mentioned. All these roads were seized by the United States army and used as military lines. Largely to this is due the fact that the roads were in condition for immediate operation at the close of hostilities; for during this period of military occupation, an extensive work of repair and improvement was kept up on all the roads. They were all under the control of the Department of Military Railroads, which had been created for the management and operation of the captured roads in the South. Some idea of what was done in North Carolina can be gathered from the following tables: [1]

[1] *Off. Rec.*, no. 126, p. 968.

| Name. | From | To | Length in Miles. |
|---|---|---|---|
| Atlantic and North Carolina, | Morehead City | Goldsboro, | 95. |
| Wilmington and Weldon, | Wilmington | Goldsboro, | 85. |
| North Carolina, | Goldsboro | Hillsboro, [1] | 89. |
| Raleigh and Gaston, | Raleigh | Cedar Creek, | 25. |
| | | Total, | 294. |

| Name. | Track Laid. Miles. | Bridges Built. Linear Feet. | Cost of bridges, track and maintenance of way. |
|---|---|---|---|
| Atlantic and North Carolina, | 22.46 | 1288 | $597,041.30 |
| Wilmington and Weldon, | .46 | 879 | 110,243.05 |
| North Carolina, | 7.62 | 564 | 243,266.36 |
| Raleigh and Gaston, | .15 | 532 | 13,565.32 |
| Total, | 30.69 | 3263 | $964,116.03 |

Other expenses for labor, rolling stock, and the like, brought the amount expended during the period to $2,596,-660.05, a small amount compared to that spent in some of the other military departments.

In spite of this, the condition of the roads was not good, for the rebuilt bridges and track were only temporary. The North Carolina road had well-equipped shops and was probably in better condition than any of the others. It suffered less damage from the two armies and also received less in the way of repairs. The road ran from Goldsboro to Charlotte, a distance of 228 miles. At the close of the war it had twenty-one engines, all in good condition, and had lost only one since 1860, but the rest of its rolling stock had become scanty in amount and poor in condition. Four engines had been bought from the Confederate government, but the Baltimore and Ohio road claimed them and the engines

---

[1] The road from Raleigh to Hillsboro, forty miles in length, was restored at once, leaving forty-nine miles under military control, the portion from Hillsboro to Charlotte never having been seized.

were delivered to it by the United States. The road-bed was in fair condition, but seven bridges had been lost by fire in 1865, two having been burned by incendiaries, three by the Confederate, and two by the Union army. The warehouses, tanks, and stations at Salisbury and High Point were burned by Stoneman, the station and warehouses at Raleigh by retreating Confederate soldiers the day Sherman occupied the town, and the warehouse at Goldsboro accidentally by Union soldiers. The estimated cost of repairing this damage was $75,000.

The road was restored to the company in October. Reorganization had already taken place under the provisional government. The financial condition of the company was at first thought to be very good, but investigation showed that this was an error. The Confederacy had owed the road $1,379,941, of which $600,000 had been paid in old metal—brass and iron—and a further reduction had been made by the transfer of a part interest in the Navy Department's machine shops at Charlotte. The State also owed the road a large debt, which could be met by repaying the dividends received from the state's interest in the road. From securities of a nominal value of $351,535, only $14,-324 could be realized. It owed, in addition to its current accounts and capital stock, about $350,000.

Great dependence was put by this road in a large amount of cotton, over eight hundred bales, which had been purchased in 1863 and stored in South Carolina. In 1866, a committee of investigation reported that a large part of it had been lost or stolen. The same committee, after looking into the management of the sinking fund, reported a case of fraud practiced there, resulting in great loss to the road. In July, 1864, the road had $58,000 in North Carolina ante-war bonds, "old sixes" as they were called. In the latter part of the year, George W. Swepson, now entering upon the financial operations which during the next few years were to do so much towards the financial ruin of the State, contracted to exchange new state bonds for the old, at the rate of two for one, to the amount of $25,000. Later he contracted for the remainder at the same rate. On January 12, 1865, the directors ordered that no more of the old bonds should be disposed of, except for the bonds of the corporation. Notwithstanding the fact that Swepson had not attempted in any way to carry out his part of the contract, which was verbal, the commissioners of the sinking fund allowed him to deliver the new bonds after General Johnston's surrender had made them practically worthless. He bought them by this exchange at three per cent of their face value.[1]

The United States, after March, 1862, controlled half of the Atlantic and North Carolina road, including its shops and offices at New Bern. After April, 1865, the whole road was thus controlled. After the corporation was reorganized in the summer of 1865, the president, Charles R. Thomas, applied for the restoration of the road, at the same time presenting a bill for $319,500 for its use, and serving notice that after September 15, $50,000 per month would be charged. But as more than $175,000 had been spent for material and labor, the government refused to pay anything. The road was not surrendered until the immense stores at Morehead and Beaufort had been moved over it. This work was completed in October and the road was then delivered to the corporation. At the same time it bought rolling stock and materials from the government amounting to over $50,000 in value.

The Wilmington and Weldon road was restored in Au-

---

[1] Report of the legislative committee on N. C. R. R. *Report of N. C. R. R. for 1867*. The information regarding the railroads not otherwise annotated, is from their annual reports.

gust. Property to the amount of $50,000 was bought from the government.

The Raleigh and Gaston road was restored early in May. Its finances were in better condition, probably, than those of any other road in the State.

The Western North Carolina Railroad was never controlled and operated by the military forces, but it suffered from raiders, so far as track and equipment were concerned. The greatest loss it sustained was at Salisbury, where all the buildings and shops had been destroyed by Stoneman. The road was unfinished and steps were at once taken to continue the work of construction westward. Bonds were issued by the State in 1866 to the amount of $500,000 for the benefit of the road, and stock was taken in payment. This was insufficient and the State was again appealed to. This, however, belongs to a later period.

All the roads suffered in 1866 and 1867 from the impoverished condition of the people. The poor crops made the freight traffic very light. This was only temporary, and the recovery of the roads was steady for some years. It was interrupted by events in the State in the period which now followed. The connection of the roads with politics was a great disadvantage as every change of administration brought a change of the officers, the State controlling a majority of stock in several of the most important of the roads.

Closely connected with the railroads was the matter of the mails. The United States mail service ceased in North Carolina in May, 1861. Many of the persons employed by the Post-office Department entered that of the Confederacy. Most of the funds belonging to the government were turned over to the Confederacy. The total amount was $37,-770.42.[1] The larger part of this was collected when the war

---

[1] Of this $12,391.38 was due from the seven presidential offices in the State: Chapel Hill, Fayetteville, Goldsboro, Greensboro, New Bern, Raleigh, and Wilmington. *Report of the Postmaster-General, 1865.*

closed. [1] Immediately after the organization of the provisional government, the Postmaster General, in obedience to the directions of the President's proclamation of May 29, notified Governor Holden that he was ready to reorganize the mail service as soon as arrangements could be made with the railroads. By November, fourteen routes were in operation, supplying the service to a large part of the State. But there was constant trouble with the railroads on account of the small sum paid for transportation, and the uncertain and poor service of the roads made the mail facilities exceedingly bad. The difficulty of securing persons to fill the offices under the requirements of the law also delayed a return to good service. It was several years before an adequate system was established.

[1] *Report of the Postmaster General, 1866.*

# CHAPTER FIVE

## MILITARY GOVERNMENT UNDER THE RECONSTRUCTION ACTS

### I. THE RECONSTRUCTION ACTS

THE experiment, if it be so called, of restoration on the plan laid down by the President, lacked, from the standpoint of the individual States concerned, but one thing to be successful. Within these States the various departments of goverment, when free from outside interference, exercised their normal functions apparently in the manner prescribed by law and custom. But the relations of these States to the United States were abnormal by reason of the refusal of Congress to receive their representatives. Recognition of the existing state governments by the legislative branch of the general government was utterly lacking.

There were many things which, united, caused the existence of this condition of affairs. Congress, before the close of hostilities, had clearly shown and expressed the opinion that the matter of the reconstruction of the seceded States was a question the solution of which properly belonged to Congress. The reason of this, beyond jealousy for the prerogatives of the legislative branch of the government, encroached upon by the executive branch during the war, was largely the difference which appeared between the view of the results of the war held by the majority of the members and that held by the President, particularly as related to the status of the seceded States and the treatment of the freedmen. This difference increased after the death of President Lincoln and the succession of President Johnson. A combination of sentimentalism and of solicitude for the future welfare of the Republican party caused the radical element of that party to demand that the suffrage should be extended to the lately emancipated slaves. This demand formed a basis of opposition to the President. [1] At first the many differences of opinion in the party and a desire to avoid an open rupture with the President made a policy of waiting advisable, if not actually necessary. In this period of delay a consolidation of opinion took place which enabled the radicals to cope with the President successfully when the occasion arose.

In pursuance of this policy of delay, a resolution was passed providing for a joint committee of both houses on the condition of the States lately in insurrection. The committee was chosen, and to it were referred all matters relating to the States in question. [2] When, at the opening of Congress, the delegations from the Southern States presented themselves, as has been seen, no action was taken at first, and finally a resolution, introduced by Thaddeus Stevens, was passed by both houses, forbidding the admission of members from any of the eleven Southern States until Congress should formally have declared such a State entitled to representation. [3] During the period which elapsed before the reconstruc-

[1] Dunning, *Essays on Civil War and Reconstruction*, p. 80.

[2] The membership of the committee was as follows: Majority, Senators Fessenden, Grimes, Harris, Howard, and Williams, and Representatives Stevens, Washburne, Morrill, Bingham, Conkling, Boutwell, and Blow. Minority, Senator Johnson, and Representatives Grider and Rogers.

[3] This resolution passed the House February 20, 1866, and the Senate March 2, 1866.

tion committee reported finally, many individual bills were reported by it and considered in Congress. Through this discussion the policy of Congress was finally outlined and developed. In the meantime, an investigation was being made by the committee of the condition of affairs in the South.

Investigations into the conditions existing in the Southern States had already been made. General Grant, with the approval of the President and the Secretary of War, in November, 1865, visited Virginia, the Carolinas, and Georgia. His report was altogether favorable to the President's policy, both as to conditions and to the feeling existing among the people towards the general government. The two questions which had hitherto divided the two sections—slavery and the right of secession—he thought were regarded as finally settled by arms, and the people were ready to accept the decision in good faith. War had left such a condition that military occupation was necessary for the time to preserve order; but the mere presence of a military force, however small, was sufficient for the purpose. Colored troops should be entirely withdrawn, as they were provocative of trouble. He, expressed the belief that the people were anxious to return to self-government in the Union, and were ready to do what the government required of them, provided it was not humilating. He criticised the administration of the Freedmen's Bureau, bearing witness at the same time to the good accomplished by it.[1]

Two other commissioners, Carl Schurz, a major-general in the volunteer service, and Benjamin C. Truman, a civilian, also came south at different times. Neither of them came to North Carolina, and it is suffi-

[1] *Sen. Docs.*, no. 2, p. 106, 39 Cong., I sess.

cient to say of their reports that Schurz was more gloomy regarding conditions than General Grant had been, and his report consequently was more to the taste of the radicals,[1] while Truman, on the other hand, found everything most encouraging for a perfect restoration of peace and order.[2] President Johnson sent the two former reports to the Senate with a message reviewing the conditions in the South. All was without effect, for the message and the report of General Grant were regarded, as Senator Sumner expressed it, as "whitewashing,"[3] and they did not contain the sort of information desired by the radicals. To obtain the desired indictment of the presidential policy and of the South an investigation of their own was made. Sub-committees of the reconstruction committee were appointed to take evidence from the different States. The sub-committee for North Carolina and also for Virginia, South Carolina, and Georgia was composed of Conkling, Howard, and Blow. The testimony for North Carolina, however, was all taken by Senator Howard. He remained in Washington and summoned such witnesses as he desired. In March, William A. Graham wrote to Senator Fessenden and asked that, as a claimant for a seat and as a representative of North Carolina, he might be present at the investigations of the committee and be allowed to cross-examine the witnesses and produce evidence. Fessenden responded that the first two parts of the request could not be granted, but that the committee would be glad to examine any witnesses he might suggest. Graham was much disturbed because, so far as he could discover, only one witness from North Carolina had been examined

---

[1] *Sen. Doc.*, no. 2, pp. 1–106, 39 Cong., 1 sess.    [2] *Ibid.*, no. 43.

[3] *Annual Cyclopædia*, 1866, p. 187.

and he was not a native, but an officer of the army and an agent of the Freedmen's Bureau. It later appeared that there were several more who had been examined. Possibly the protest had some effect in causing the examination of additional witnesses.

In all, twelve witnesses were examined by the committee for North Carolina.[1] Of these only one was a native of the State.[2] Two had lived in the State prior to 1860, both ministers of the gospel and agents of the Bureau.[3] Eight were or had been officers in the Union army, and of these, six were connected with the Bureau.[4] The other witness was a newspaper editor who had been a war correspondent of the *New York Herald* until the capture of Wilmington.[5] Most of the testimony, as might be expected, painted a dark picture of conditions. Most of the witnesses agreed that the freedmen were hated by the whites, and without the protection of troops would again be enslaved; that there was a secret but intense hostility to the United States government; that without protection Northern men and all Unionists would be unsafe in the State;[6] and that Northern people

[1] The testimony will be found in *House Report* no. 30, part 2, 39 Cong., 1 sess.

[2] Bedford Brown.

[3] Rev. James Sinclair and Rev. Hope Bain. The former had been a lieutenant-colonel in the Confederate service, but on account of disgraceful conduct at the battle of New Bern was dropped by his regiment at re-organization in 1862. He informed the committee that he had given up his commission because he would not take part against the United States.

[4] Lieut. G. O. Sanderson, Col. E. Whittlesey, Capt. H. A. Cooke, Col. D. A. Clapp, Col. J. A. Campbell, Col. W. H. H. Beadle, Maj. H. C. Lawrence, and J. W. Alvord.

[5] Thomas M. Cook.

[6] Col. Whittlesey and Maj. Lawrence dissented from this and stated that there was no danger of violence.

were disliked, and as a rule not received socially.   What value this latter fact, true as it undoubtedly was, had as evidence regarding political conditions would be hard to say.   One witness complained that no approach to equality was allowed the freedmen;[1] another thought that every Southern man was opposed to granting the negroes equal rights in the courts, and that there was a prejudice in the courts against the holding of property in land by a negro.[2]   A majority of those questioned about the matter thought the people favored the repudiation of the war debt of the State,[3] and most of them noted, apparently with surprise, that men who had distinguished themselves as Confederate soldiers were very popular with the people.   Major Lawrence, formerly an agent of the Freedmen's Bureau and an Illinois Republican, dissented entirely from the unfavorable testimony given by the other witnesses.   He expressed the belief and offered proof that Northern men in the State were entirely safe, quoting General Abbott,[4] who said, "Tell them (the committee) that a Northern man is just as safe anywhere in the State of North Carolina as he is anywhere in the North.   I do not say that a man cannot come here and act so without sense and discretion that he will get into difficulty with the people; he can do that anywhere.   But a man who comes here and attends to his own business and does not take some pains to make himself odious, I think, is as safe here as anywhere

[1] Testimony of G. O. Sanderson, p. 173.

[2] Testimony of W. H. H. Beadle, p. 265.

[3] Testimony of Sinclair, Brown, Whittlesey, Cook, and Lawrence; for the other view see Cooke and Campbell.

[4] A Northern man who had settled in Wilmington.

else."[1] Major Lawrence thought that the people generally had accepted the results of the war and were prepared to show it by their acts, including full protection to the freedmen.[2]

The testimony so far has been analyzed merely to show its general character. It probably had no effect upon the opinion of the committee or upon the final result of their work. Nor is it likely that any such effect was intended. The object of the appointment of the committee had been, largely, to gain time while plans of legislation might be formed, independently of the result of any investigation such as was thus conducted. The mass of the testimony collected was to be used later as a justification and defence of the plan of reconstruction formulated and proposed, and also to secure the support of the North by means of the effect it would have upon the minds of the people.

The committee made its report in June, 1866. The majority report declared that the seceded States at the close of hostilities had been in a state of complete anarchy, without governments or the power to frame them except by permission of the victors. The plan of res-

---

[1] Testimony, p. 290.

[2] *Ibid.*, p. 289. Major Lawrence's examination was suggested to the committee by Hon. Reverdy Johnson at the instance of Hon. Robert S. Hale, of New York. Probably his arraignment of the Freedmen's Bureau, an extract of which is here given, was the cause. Major Lawrence said, "I confess that I am tired out and half worn out with the annoyances of my position and need rest; and am so far from having any sympathy with the views that seem to prevail in Congress that I am unwilling to be a humble instrument in carrying them out. * * * I felt ashamed for myself as an American and for my government when, a few days ago, Judge Buxton, of the Supreme [*sic*] Court of this State called at my office to inquire as to the extent of jurisdiction he would be permitted to exercise in a term he was about to hold." *Globe*, pp. 1483-4, 39 Cong., 1 sess.

toration adopted by the President was approved as a temporary military expedient for preserving order. The President's recommendation to Congress that these States should be admitted to representation was declared to have been based on incomplete evidence. When he made it, he had not withdrawn the military forces or restored the privilege of the writ of *habeas corpus*, and he still exercised over the people of these States military power and jurisdiction. Moreover, the report alleged, in all the seceded States, except perhaps Arkansas and Tennessee, the elections for state officers and members of Congress "had resulted almost universally in the defeat of candidates who had been true to the Union, and in the election of notorious and unpardoned rebels who could not take the prescribed oath and made no secret of their hostility to the government and people of the United States."

From the evidence which it had secured, the committee was convinced that devotion to the Confederacy and its leaders was still existent, and republican government endangered by a "spirit of oligarchy" based on slavery. The final opinion of the committee was that the States lately in rebellion had become, through war, disorganized communities; that Congress could not be expected to recognize as valid the election of representatives from these communities, nor would it be justified in admitting the respective communities to participation in government "without first providing such constitutional or other guarantees as will tend to secure the civil rights of all citizens of the republic; a just apportionment of representation; protection against claims founded in rebellion and crime; a temporary restoration of the right of suffrage to those who have not actively participated in the efforts to destroy the Union and overthrow the government, and the exclusion from positions of public trust of at least a portion of those whose crimes have proved them to be enemies of the Union and unworthy of public confidence." [1]

The minority members of the committee presented a report dissenting from the conclusions drawn by the majority, and attacking the constitutionality of their theory and of the legislation proposed.

This legislation was embodied in a resolution which, after modification, became the Fourteenth Amendment to the Constitution of the United States, [2] a bill providing that whenever this proposed amendment should become a part of the Constitution, and any State lately in insurrection should ratify it and modify its own constitution in conformity therewith, its senators and representatives

---

[1] Many statements of fact and inference in the majority report were conspicuously untrue so far as concerned North Carolina. For example, that "the elections which were held for State officers and members of Congress had resulted, almost universally, in the defeat of candidates who had been true to the Union, and in the election of notorious and unpardoned rebels, men who could not take the prescribed oath of office, and who made no secret of their hostility to the government and people of the United States." Again, "It appears quite clear that the anti-slavery amendments, both to the State and Federal Constitutions, were adopted with reluctance by the bodies which did adopt them." And again: "The witnesses examined as to the willingness of the people of the South to contribute under existing laws to the payment of the national debt, prove that the taxes levied by the United States will be paid only on compulsion and with great reluctance, while there prevails to a considerable extent, an expectation that compensation will be made for slaves emancipated and property destroyed during the war." The first part of this last extract was without doubt true, but there was no basis for the latter part.

[2] The chief modification was in the third section where the original provided that, until July 4, 1870, all persons who had voluntarily adhered to the late insurrection, giving it aid and comfort, should be deprived of the right to vote for members of Congress and electors for President.

might be admitted, if duly qualified, after taking the required oath ; and a bill declaring ineligible to office under the United States all persons in the classes excepted by the President's amnesty proclamation of May 29, 1865, except those under the thirteenth exception.[1]  The two bills never passed.

The fate of the Fourteenth Amendment, when submitted to the North Carolina legislature, has been noticed.[2]  It met with rejection in all the other Southern States except Tennessee.  When Congress met in December, 1866, enough of the Southern States had rejected the amendment to show the prevailing opinion in the South, and consequently the question at once arose as to what policy should be adopted.  The uncertainty in regard to this became less as the remaining Southern States in turn rejected the amendment.  Consequently, in February, 1867, it became a determined fact that the state governments, as organized by the President, should be superseded by others organized under military authority; that the political leaders of the Southern States should be disqualified from taking part in the reorganization of the governments; and that the right of suffrage should be extended to the negro by national legislation, in utter defiance of the constitutional right of the individual States in the matter.  In pursuance of this determination, the act of March 2, 1867, "to provide for a more efficient government of the rebel States," was passed.  It was vetoed by the President, but was passed over the veto on the same day.  Declaring in the preamble that no legal state governments or adequate protection for life or property existed in the

[1] This class was composed of those who owned $20,000.

[2] *Cf. supra*, p. 187.

ten "rebel" States,[1] the act provided that these States should be divided into five military districts, each under an officer of the army of not lower rank than brigadier general, and made subject to the military authority of the United States. North Carolina and South Carolina formed the second district. The commander of each district was required to protect all persons in their rights and to suppress insurrection, disorder, and violence. In the punishment of offenders, he was authorized to allow the civil tribunals to take jurisdiction, or if he deemed it necessary, to organize military commissions for the purpose. All interference with such tribunals by the state authorities was declared void and of no effect. It was further provided that the people of any of the said States should be entitled to representation whenever they should have framed and ratified a constitution in conformity with the Constitution of the United States. This constitution must be framed by a convention elected by the male citizens of the State, regardless of race, color, or previous condition, with the exception of those disfranchised for participation in rebellion or for felony. Those persons on whom disabilities would be imposed by the proposed Fourteenth Amendment were disqualified from holding a seat in the convention and from voting for delegates. The constitution thus framed, and containing the provision that all persons whom the act of Congress made electors should retain the electoral franchise, must then be approved by Congress. Whenever representatives should be admitted, the portion of the act establishing military governments would become inoperative so far as concerned the State in question. Until the completion of this reconstruction, the existing

[1] Tennessee was not included in the provisions of this act, as its representatives had been admitted.

civil governments were declared provisional and liable at
any time to modification or abolition.[1]

On March 23, a supplementary act was passed. The
original act left the whole matter of the initiation of reconstruction very indefinite. The supplementary act
provided that the district commanders should cause a
registration to be made of all male citizens who could
take a required oath as to their qualifications as electors.
The election of delegates to a convention should then
be held by the commanders. For the sake of giving at
least an appearance of following the will of the people,
the act provided that the question of holding a convention should be submitted to them at the same time.
Unless a majority of the registered voters took part in
the election and a majority in favor of holding the convention resulted, no convention should be held. Provision was made for boards of election composed only of
those who could take the " iron-clad " oath. Finally, it
was provided that a majority of those registered must
take part in the voting on the ratification of the constitution in order to make it valid.[2] This act was also
vetoed by President Johnson and promptly repassed by
the required majorities.

In July, Congress met again. In the meantime Attorney-General Stanbery had sent to the President an
interpretation of the act, which closely restricted the
power of the military commanders. At once another
supplementary act was passed, as an authoritative interpretation of the former acts. It gave the commanders
full power to make any removals from office that they
might see fit, and authorized the boards of registration

[1] *Laws*, 40 Cong., 1 sess., chap. vi.
[2] *Laws*, 39 Cong., 2 sess., chap. cliii.

to go behind the oath of an applicant for registration whenever it seemed to them necessary. District commanders, the boards of registration, and all officers acting under either were relieved from the necessity of acting in accordance with the opinion of any civil officer of the United States. The executive and judicial officers referred to in the imposition of disabilities [1] were declared to include the holders of all civil offices created by law for the administration of justice or for the administration of any general law of a State. An extension of time for registration was authorized, and also a revision of the lists of registered voters before the election. [2] This act, as was now the customary thing, had to be passed over the President's veto.

Such was the most important legislation enacted for the restoration of the South. Questions of precedent and of constitutional law were alike disregarded in their passage, and justification found for all. A discussion of their constitutionality, however, is not a part of this study. It is sufficient to say that the laws were effective.

Within the State, as has been seen, the debates in Congress on reconstruction had caused the greatest excitement and anxiety. In January, Governor Worth appealed to the Council of State for instructions as to the course he should pursue in the event of the passage of a reconstruction bill. He himself at that time favored resistence to such an extent as would bring the question before the Supreme Court of the United States. The Council agreed with him and authorized him to secure the best legal talent as counsel for the State in his attempt to bring the matter before the court. [3] Acting on

---

[1] *Constitution of the United States*, Amendments, Art. XIV.

[2] *Laws*, 40 Cong., 2 sess., chap. xxviii.

[3] *Council of State Records*, pp. 193–5.

the advice of Thomas Ruffin and William A. Graham, Governor Worth consulted Hon. Benjamin R. Curtis, a former justice of the Supreme Court of the United States, at this time a practicing lawyer in Massachusetts. He agreed with Judge Ruffin that it would be practically impossible to get a test case before the court. Judge Ruffin also advised that the State should not become a party to any attempt of the kind.[1]

Accordingly in March, after the first reconstruction act had gone into effect, Governor Worth asked the Council if he should take any steps in the matter. He had come to the conclusion that it was useless and impossible to make any attempt without the authority from the General Assembly, and thought correctly that it would be impossible for that body to assemble. He advised that the people should be urged to register, and, after sending as good men as possible to the convention, to ratify or reject the constitution as they saw fit. The Council agreed with this view and passed a resolution containing the suggestion just mentioned.[2] With the governor, and in fact with all the State, they doubted the value of any application to the Supreme Court, feeling that, even were the case considered and decided in favor of the State, the decision would not be respected by Congress. Governor Worth had been in correspondence with several of the Southern governors, and now notified them that North Carolina would take no part in their attempt to secure justice through a judicial decision.

[1] *Executive Correspondence*, Worth, vol. i, pp. 395–400.
[2] *Council of State Records*, pp. 200–04.

## 2. MILITARY GOVERNMENT UNDER GENERAL SICKLES [1]

The first reconstruction act was declared in force in North Carolina by General Robinson. General Daniel E. Sickles, however, was assigned to the command of the second district, with headquarters at Columbia, South Carolina.[2] He was not unknown in the State, for he had been in command of the department of which North Carolina formed a part, and had been rather popular than otherwise. Consequently his assignment was received with as much satisfaction as could be expected under the circumstances. As a matter of fact, opposition to the enforcement of the reconstruction act was apparently dead. It had been violent until the passage of the act, and then there seemed to be a general acquiescence if not agreement. But it was only resignation. No one can believe that anything approaching a majority of the white people of the State favored the destruction of the existing state government. But power to resist was lacking, and apathy succeeded protestation. The *Sentinel* expressed the feeling, saying, " In a political sense we suppose the integrity of the glorious old State of North Carolina has been blotted out of existence. * * * Well, so be it; we submit. The sword is a mighty convincer, and if such be its decision we accept it with all the logical consequences present and prospective." The supplementary act was really received with joy by the conservative element.[3] This feeling was caused by the effect it had upon the plans of the radicals

---

[1] The orders and correspondence not otherwise referred to will be found in *Sen. Ex. Docs.*, no. 14, *Correspondence Relative to Reconstruction*, 40 Cong., 1 sess.

[2] This was later changed to Charleston.

[3] The term "conservative" is used merely in contradistinction to "radical." It had not yet become a party title.

in the State. Immediately after the passage of the first reconstruction act, the "loyal" members of the legislature, which was then in session, acting under the influence of Holden, issued a call for a meeting of "loyal" citizens to devise a plan for calling a convention of the people. The primary meeting was held and a committee appointed to devise and carry out a plan for organization.[1] By comparison with what this meant, military government seemed to the conservatives far preferable.

General Sickles, soon after he took command, issued an order declaring the civil government of the State provisional, but continuing it with directions that it should be obeyed. He requested the coöperation and assistance of all officers and citizens. He indicated that, in general, jurisdiction in criminal cases would be left to the civil courts. Particular cases might be referred by his order to military commissions.[2] His idea and intention were, evidently, to cause as little change in the state government as possible. Consequently, he conferred frequently with Governor Worth, who had been in Washington with him before he assumed command of the district, and who went to Charleston in April at General Sickles' invitation for a consultation with him and with Governor Orr, of South Carolina.[3] General Sickles frequently took his advice, particularly regarding the appointment of provisional officers. For convenience in the military government, the State was immediately divided into eleven military posts.[4] The post commanders

---

[1] The plan included a threat of confiscation of the property of all those who should refuse to join in the petition for a convention.

[2] *General Orders*, no. 1.

[3] Sickles to Grant, April 18, 1867.

[4] Morganton, Salisbury, Charlotte, Greensboro, Raleigh, Fayetteville, Goldsboro, Wilmington, Plymouth, New Bern, and Fort Macon.

were instructed to supervise the action of the various civil officers, and also to give notice to headquarters of elections of any nature that were to be held within the limits of their posts, and, if necessary, suggest removals.

In April, General Sickles, in response to a demand for something of the kind in South Carolina, to stay executions for debt, issued his well-known "General Order, No. 10." After rehearsing the conditions which made action necessary, it prohibited imprisonment for debt unless accompanied by fraud. Judgments and executions on causes of action arising after December 19, 1860, and prior to May 15, 1865, were ordered not to be enforced then or thereafter. On causes arising prior to that time, execution was stayed for twelve months. Judgments on actions subsequent to May 15, 1865, might be enforced. Proceedings for recovery of money in payment for the purchase of slaves were suspended. Wages for labor were made a lien on crops. A homestead exemption of $500 was provided. The requirement of bail in cases *ex contractu* was forbidden but allowed in cases *ex delicto*. The carrying of concealed weapons was forbidden, and when injury resulted from a concealed weapon, it was to be regarded as evidence of an intent to commit murder. Corporal punishment for crime was forbidden.

The order was issued with reference to conditions in South Carolina. Its injustice in several particulars as regarded North Carolina, is manifest. In ordering the stay of legal proceedings, the fact that North Carolina did not secede until May 20, 1861, instead of on December 19, 1860, was entirely ignored. It was stated at the time, how correctly is uncertain, that most of the cases in which a stay was ordered in North Carolina had arisen in the interval named. The interference with the punishment of criminals worked an injustice to the State;

for there was no state prison, and it was a heavy tax on the counties to keep criminals idle in jails, but as the order forbidding corporal punishment was construed by the military authorities to forbid the use of ball and chain, convicts could not be worked on the roads.[1] To remedy this condition of affairs Governor Worth and General Sickles later began to perfect a plan for the establishment of a penitentiary. General Sickles designated as a committee to consider the plan, Governor Worth, Treasurer K. P. Battle, and M. L. Wiggins and J. C. Harper, chairmen, respectively, of the finance committees of the Senate and House of Commons.[2] It was hoped that the legislature would be allowed to meet and complete the plan, but General Sickles forbade the session. Owing to the removal of General Sickles from command, the matter was left for the attention of the new state government.

The order for a general registration was published in May and provided that it should begin in the latter part of July. At once the work of organizing the boards of registration for the one hundred and seventy registration districts began.[3] To the great disgust of the radicals, the *Standard* already protesting against "any agency whatever by Governor Worth in the work of reconstruction,"[4] the governor was consulted in the appointment of members of the boards and asked to recommend suitable persons from each county.[5] He accordingly sent recommendations for every county except

[1] *Executive Correspondence*, Worth, vol. i, p. 542.

[2] *Ibid.*, pp. 547, 560.

[3] McPherson, *Political Manual for 1868*, p. 315.

[4] Issue of April 27, 1867.

[5] *Executive Correspondence*, Worth, vol. i, p. 441.

Polk and Wilson.[1] It was necessary to find men who could take the oath, and, as very few native whites could do so, and as he wished to avoid the appointment of negroes, he endeavored to find as many former Union soldiers as possible. A few colored men were recommended by the governor, but very few applied, and he refused to recommend any member of the Union League.[2] For the general board on rules and regulations one of his nominations was accepted. For the other place a colored minister from the North was selected by General Sickles.[3] General Nelson A. Miles, who commanded the post of Raleigh and was also assistant commissioner of the Freedmen's Bureau, had already issued a circular to the agents of the Bureau instructing them to select one colored and two white men from each election district to be registrars and inspectors of elections. He decided that one of the white men must be a native of the State and the other an army officer or Bureau agent.[4] All preparations were made for beginning the enrolment of the voters, but General Sickles, thinking it best to wait until Congress should decide who could vote, and with his usual regard for the welfare of the people, wishing the "crop laid by" before the distractions incident to registration should begin,[5] postponed indefinitely the beginning of registration. But by August 1, the order was issued with an elaborate set of rules and regulations. Under these, post commanders were given power of supervision in their districts, and authority to preserve

---

[1] *Executive Correspondence*, Worth, vol. i, p. 421.

[2] *Ibid.*, p. 485.

[3] H. H. Helper and G. W. Brodie were the persons in question.

[4] *Standard*, May 1, 1867.

[5] Sickles to Trumbull. Quoted in *Register*, July 11, 1867.

order; provision was made for the recovery of damages by persons injured while attempting to vote or deprived of employment on account of their registration; and registrars were directed, regardless of any challenge, to examine the right of every applicant to register. The lists when completed should be exposed for five days and then revised.[1] After the removal of General Sickles, a circular of instructions prepared by him was also published.[2]

General Sickles failed to exercise his power of removal to any great extent. When Attorney General Stanbery gave a construction to the reconstruction acts which deprived district commanders of the right of removal, General Sickles at once wrote the adjutant general that, without the power of removing civil officers, it was "not practicable to afford adequate security to person and property." He also said, "Without military control I believe reconstruction would be impossible. Anarchy would rule—ruin to all interests would follow." He also informed General Grant that, up to June 17, 1867, not more than twelve removals had been made in the Carolinas, and that those were for misconduct. Very few were made by him later. Policemen in Wilmington in several instances were removed,[3] and town commissioners in Wilson, Newport, and Fayetteville. The mayor in the last-named place was also removed. Successors were appointed in these instances, and also when the term of office of the municipal officers of New Bern expired; and the realm of politics was left and trustees appointed for the New Bern Academy, which was par-

[1] *General Orders.* no. 65, *Sen. Docs.*, no. 341, p. 50, 40 Cong., 2 sess.
[2] *Ibid.*, p. 58.
[3] *Correspondence Relative to Reconstruction*, pp. 48–80.

tially controlled by the town.[1] A town election was suspended in Tarboro until the reconstruction acts could go into effect.[2] All appointments were in accordance with an agreement made with Governor Worth, at the conference in Charleston, that no municipal elections should be held until after the meeting of the convention. All officers ordinarily elected by the people were to be appointed by the commander, and those ordinarily chosen by the legislature were to be appointed by the governor.[3]

Throughout the administration of General Sickles there was a marked tendency towards an exceedingly strict supervision from headquarters of the actions of civil officers. All officers empowered to make arrests were required to report to the provost marshals and to act under their orders.[4] Orders were constantly issued in reference to various subjects that had attracted General Sickles' notice. For instance, in one order, among other things the distillation of grain was forbidden, very properly, in view of the destitution in the district; license to sell liquor was confined to inns; discrimination in public conveyances of any kind on account of race was forbidden; any qualified voter under the reconstruction acts was declared eligible to hold office, and the remedy by distress for unpaid rent was abolished.[5]

Interference in the affairs of the courts was more general than before and had a greater effect in the State, probably, than the rest of the commander's official actions. The first instance of this was in the matter of juries. In

---

[1] *Correspondence Relative to Reconstruction*, p. 79.

[2] *Ibid.*, p. 75.

[3] *Annual Cyclopædia*, 1867, p. 692.

[4] *General Orders*, no. 34.

[5] *General Orders*, no. 32.

May, General Sickles declared in "General Order, No. 32," that all citizens who had been assessed for taxes and had paid them were qualified to serve as jurors, and the proper civil officers were ordered to revise the jury lists in accordance with the order. According to his interpretation, the payment of poll tax was sufficient qualification.[1] The requisite in the State hitherto had been a freehold.[2] When Chief Justice Chase held the United States Circuit Court in Raleigh in June, he ordered that the jury list should contain "all persons, regardless of race or color, otherwise qualified." This, although it admitted negroes, in other respects followed North Carolina law and precedent.[3] Governor Worth asked General Sickles to suspend his jury order until October, when it could be ascertained who had paid taxes. Accordingly the order was suspended in the North Carolina courts till the October terms.[4] Judge Barnes in June adjourned Edgecombe Superior Court because negroes had not been summoned in accordance with General Sickles' order.[5] A still more important judicial action was at Martin Superior Court in August, when Judge Fowle rendered a decision that colored freeholders under the laws of North Carolina, without regard to military orders, were qualified as jurors. Their exclusion, prior to 1865, he held, was a natural and unavoidable result of slavery, and the abolition of slavery in 1865 made all negroes, otherwise qualified, eligible.[6]

[1] *Executive Correspondence*, Worth, vol. i, p. 576.

[2] Judge Fowle's decision in Martin Superior Court, *Register*, August 30, 1867.

[3] Wilmington *Journal*, June 22, 1867.

[4] *Annual Cyclopædia*, 1867, p. 548.

[5] Wilmington *Journal*, June 21, 1867.

[6] The decision is quoted in full in the *Register*, August 30, 1867.

Interference with the action of the courts was also frequent. In one instance the interference was at the request of the governor. A conviction of burglary had, in accordance with state law, been followed by the imposition of the death sentence. The case was one in which Governor Worth wished to lessen the severity of the sentence, but under the law he had power only to pardon. At his request General Sickles commuted the sentence to ten years' imprisonment.[1]

Probably the most remarkable case was that of Henderson Cooper, a freedman. He had been convicted of rape, on proof beyond any shadow of doubt, in March, 1865, in Granville county, and had afterwards confessed his guilt. He had been sentenced to be hanged, but having escaped to Virginia, had gone to Washington, where he had been arrested and returned to the custody of the State in the fall of 1866. Later the sentence was about to be carried into effect by order of court, when General Sickles, at the representation of Colonel Bomford, the commanding officer of the post of Raleigh, declared the sentence null and void. Colonel Bomford was ordered to investigate the charges against the prisoner, and a court of inquiry was accordingly instituted. Neither the victim of the assault, the original witnesses, nor the court officers at his trial were summoned. The court of inquiry reported, without presenting any testimony to substantiate it, and contrary to fact, that the character of the prosecutrix was bad. It further stated that at the time the assault was committed "the woman's husband was engaged in overseeing slaves; he was at that time, in fact, in the rebel army." The conclusion of the court was that "a crime has been committed which, although not

[1] *Correspondence Relative to Reconstruction*, p. 76.

meriting so severe a penalty as that of death, should receive some punishment." A military commission was then ordered. The State asked to have counsel present but was refused. The commission found the prisoner guilty and sentenced him to be hanged. Just at this point General Canby replaced General Sickles and held that the action of the state court and that of the military commission were alike void, and directed that the prisoner should be remanded to the civil authorities for trial on a new indictment. This was virtually an order of release, for the prisoner could have pleaded a former indictment and conviction and the judge would have been compelled to charge the jury to acquit." [1]  But while the prisoner was confined in Granville jail, it caught fire and he was burned to death.[2]  It was reported at the time that he himself set the building on fire in an effort to escape. But there is strong ground for the belief that it was fired from outside with the object of his destruction.

Another interesting case was in Buncombe County, where a freedman, after a trial which was acknowledged to be fair by his own counsel, was convicted of an assault. The solicitor was a Republican, so it could not have been political persecution. The convict was bound out for costs, but an agent of the Freedmen's Bureau at once insisted upon his release, stating that "things were not going on right" in that part of the State as regarded the colored people. He was sustained by the officer commanding the post, who released the prisoner by military force and made an entry on the court records forbidding further proceedings in the case.[3]

Provost courts were established at various points to

[1] *Executive Correspondence*, Worth, vol. ii, pp. 5-15.
[2] *Ibid.*, pp. 111-116.                    [3] *Ibid.*, vol. i, pp. 554-7.

have jurisdiction in small cases. The members of these courts were not always chosen with the care which their importance demanded.[1] These, also, in several instances claimed jurisdiction in matters that were before the state courts.

These are examples of numerous similar cases. As interference became more frequent, the position of the state judges became increasingly difficult. They were sworn to execute the laws of the State, and the military orders often conflicted with the law. Judge Merrimon, unwilling to hold the office under the existing conditions, resigned in July.[2] After some delay his resignation was accepted by the governor and a successor who could take the required oath was nominated. General Sickles then accepted the resignation and appointed the governor's nominee.[3]

But it was not only the state courts that were liable to military interference, though they alone were powerless to resist it. In June, 1867, the first Circuit Court of the United States held in the South since the commencement of the war was opened in Raleigh with Chief Justice Chase presiding. Since the close of the war the justices had declined to hold court in the South on account of military occupation with its attendant cessation of civil authority. Chief Justice Chase in opening the court, said that military authority was still exercised, but that it was not in its power as formerly to control judicial process, state or national, and it could " only prevent illegal violence to person and property and facilitate the restoration of every State to equal rights in the Union.

[1] For instance, the provost court at Fayetteville was composed of comparatively uneducated laborers.

[2] *Executive Correspondence*, Worth, vol. i, p. 524.

[3] Alexander Little.

This military authority does not extend in any respect to the courts of the United States."[1]   A different view from this was held by the military commander. Under an execution issued by order of the court, the marshal attempted to sell property in Wilmington to satisfy a debt owed to a creditor outside the State. The post commander, Colonel Frank, stopped the execution, and his action was sustained by General Sickles. The matter was then, through the Attorney-General, referred to the President, who sustained the marshal and consequently the court. General Sickles' order was suspended, so far as it applied to the proceedings of the federal courts, and this left the unusual condition of affairs that, while a debtor was protected from creditors within his own State, foreign creditors could obtain relief. General Sickles asked for time to explain his position and action, but in the meantime steps were taken by the Attorney General to obtain an indictment against him for violation of the criminal laws in obstructing the process of a United States court. The President closed the matter by acting on the advice which the Attorney-General had given him more than two months before, and removing General Sickles from command of the second district on August 26, and assigning General E. R. S. Canby to succeed him. General Sickles defended his conduct to General Grant and closed his letter with an expression of what seems to have been the opinion held generally by the military officers. He said: "I do firmly believe that Congress, intending to secure the restoration of these States to the Union, made all other considerations subsidiary to the accomplishment of this end. I do not believe that processes of the courts of the United States

[1] *Annual Cyclopædia*, 1867, p. 547.

should override the orders Congress has empowered me to make for the execution of its measures."[1]

On the whole, the administration of General Sickles may be said to have been popular in the State so far as any military administration could have been so. It certainly was so with the conservative element which opposed many of his acts as unconstitutional, but was friendly to him on account of his evident desire for the betterment of economic conditions. His constant appeal to the state officers for advice was also liked by the people, and they appreciated his testimony in the State's favor, given on several occasions in public and private.[2] He believed in general amnesty, regarding it as necessary to successful reconstruction, and favored the removal of all disabilities, as he thought that very few who were fit to hold office were enfranchised.[3] These same things made him unpopular with the radical leaders[4] whom he ignored utterly in carrying on the process of reconstruction, and who consequently looked upon him with distrust.

[1] *Annual Cyclopædia*, 1867, p. 548.

[2] When President Johnson visited Raleigh in the summer of 1867, General Sickles, in his speech, said: "Confident that it is gratifying to the Chief Magistrate and the Cabinet ministers present, to witness the admirable bearing of the people of this capital, it is my duty to testify to the President that what he has seen to-day in the capital, prevails everywhere over the broad surface of your noble State."—*Wilmington Journal*, June 7, 1867.

[3] Letter to Senator Trumbull, July, 1867.

[4] The radical convention, which met in Raleigh in September, 1867, passed resolutions of respect for General Sheridan, who had lately been removed from command of a district, but made no mention of General Sickles.

### 3. MILITARY GOVERNMENT UNDER GENERAL CANBY.[1]

The assumption of command by General Canby brought no marked change from the policy of his predecessor. All orders of the latter were declared in force soon after General Canby reached South Carolina.[2] In time, however, certain modifications were made.

The first new order issued from the military headquarters was one giving notice to all persons who, through absence from the State or other cause, had failed to give their parole, to do so within thirty days.[3] The jury order of General Sickles was then modified by making the right to vote the only qualification.[4] In other internal affairs there was the same interference. Authority was given for the suspension of the payment of taxes under certain conditions; provision was made for compelling citizens by military authority to work the roads and build bridges;[5] and, by proclamation, an official interpretation was given to certain laws of the State.[6] The refusal of clerks to issue marriage licenses, in cases where the parties were of different races, was declared a violation of United States law, which furnished ample remedy and redress to the injured parties.[7] "General Order No. 10" was modified and a change made in the date to correspond with the secession of North Carolina, May 20, 1861, being substituted for December 19, 1860.[8]

---

[1] The orders issued during Gen. Canby's administration are to be found in *Sen. Ex. Docs.*, no. 341, 40 Cong., 2 sess. Reference will only be made to the number of the order and the page.

[2] *General Orders*, no. 85, p. 60.

[3] *Ibid.*, no. 86, p. 60.            [4] *Ibid.*, no. 89, p. 61.

[5] *Ibid.*, no. 95, p. 62.            [6] *Ibid.*, no. 134, p. 75.

[7] *Sentinel*, April 11, 1868. A letter of General Miles, dated November 10, 1867, was quoted in full.

[8] *General Orders*, no. 164.

The important work of registration was carried on under General Canby. Finally, on October 18, he declared registration completed, and issued the order for an election to be held November 19 and 20. The usual regulations for the conduct of an election were made. Sheriffs and other peace officers were ordered to be in attendance; soldiers were forbidden to approach the polls except as qualified voters; all saloons were ordered to be closed, and members of the boards of registration, who were also candidates for the convention, were forbidden to serve as judges of election in their respective counties. The "iron-clad" oath was required, which excluded most native whites from service as election officials.[1]

In the latter part of October, the decisions of the general board of rules and regulations in regard to grounds of challenge were revised.[2] The circular shows the interpretation of General Canby as to disqualification for registration. The decision of General Sickles that, in case entering the service of the Confederacy or giving aid and comfort to its adherents had been involuntary, no disqualification existed, had already been published. Under the interpretation of General Canby the holding of only certain specified offices prior to the war constituted a disqualification. Among them were the following: sheriff, county clerk, member of the legislature, justice of the peace, school commissioner, tax collector, constable, postmaster, and marshal. But no disqualification was caused by having held any of the following positions: deputy sheriff, deputy marshal, assistant

---

[1] It is impossible to discover how far this rule was carried out. Accusations were made that it was disregarded.

[2] Circular, p. 69.

postmaster, clerk of the state Senate, keeper of a light-house, or notary public.[1]

As to the question of what constituted aid to the Confederacy, it was held, among other things, that investment in Confederate bonds, collecting supplies for the Confederacy, making speeches in support of the war, and holding a mail contract or any civil or military office were acts that carried disqualification. But making charitable contributions or being a candidate for office did not constitute aid and comfort in the disqualifying sense. Hiring out horses to the Confederacy was disloyalty, but hiring to Confederate soldiers was not.

The result of the registration was as follows:[2]

| | |
|---|---:|
| Whites | 106,721 |
| Blacks | 72,932 |
| Total | 179,653 |

Nineteen counties[3] had negro majorities, and in several others the white majority was less than a hundred. No definite idea can be formed of the number disqualified on account of disabilities imposed by the reconstruction acts. The registration of 1868, when the disabilities did not have the effect of disfranchisement, showed a gain of 17,220. But many who were qualified did not register in 1867 and did so in 1868.[4]

[1] These are only a few of the cases cited.

[2] This is the revised total. The first result was, whites, 106,060; blacks, 71,657.

[3] Bertie, Caswell, Chowan, Craven, Edgecombe, Franklin, Granville, Greene, Halifax, Hertford, Jones, Lenoir, New Hanover, Northampton, Pasquotank, Perquimans, Pitt, Richmond, and Warren had negro majorities.

[4] Gen. Canby, in 1867, estimated that 11,686 whites and 493 blacks were disfranchised by the act of Congress. Also that in 1867, there were 7,791 whites and 2,796 blacks qualified who did not apply for registration. The estimate was made without any evidence to support it and is utterly valueless.

Many accusations of fraud in the registration were made, but there was no disturbance of any kind during the whole period. It is undoubtedly true that many negroes not of age were registered. But the difficulty of determining their age could not be overcome, even had it been desired, for in most instances they themselves were as ignorant of the truth as the registrars. As a general thing, a negro could register upon application, even if previously convicted of felony. There was also a tendency on the part of the registrars in many places to deny registration to those who they knew were opposed to reconstruction. But it is probable, speaking generally, that the registration was as fair as could be expected under the system employed.[1]

As regards the qualification of the new electorate for the exercise of the franchise, the primary fact naturally was the dense ignorance among the negroes. Many of them, moreover, were vicious and idle, but probably not in so great a proportion as during the years immediately following. Certainly they were not so vicious. From the nature of things, also, they were able to bear a very small part of the burdens of citizenship and paid a very small part of the taxes.[2]

[1] The above was written after discussion of the matter with participants in the election from different parts of the State, of different political belief, and of both races.

[2] The *Wilmington Journal* of November 17, 1867, had an interesting comparison of the number of negroes registered with those listed for poll tax. Only 33,000 were listed as compared with 72,932 registered. Probably one-third of those registered were over forty-five years of age and, consequently, exempt from the payment of poll tax. This left 14,771 who bore no part of the expenses of government. In Cherokee and Edgecombe counties, employers listed the negroes, with the result that Cherokee showed more listed than registered, and Edgecombe, after deduction of the estimated one-third exempt from the listed, showed the two classes equal.

Only a small number of removals from office were made by General Canby. But his appointments in some instances were criticised, and justly. For example, in Jones County the sheriff was removed, and a Northern man, who had only lately become a resident, appointed. No official bond was required.[1] Seventeen magistrates were also displaced. In Craven and Pitt the old sheriffs were removed and replaced by carpet-baggers.[2]

The civil courts had only a nominal authority, their action being subject to revision by the military authorities. In consequence, Judge Fowle resigned, being un-willing to enforce military orders that were contrary to state law. A. W. Tourgee was mentioned as his successor, and notwithstanding the fact that he had never been licensed to practice law in North Carolina, would have been appointed but for the opposition of Governor Worth. The governor recommended and secured the appointment of Colonel Clinton A. Cilley, who had formerly been in command at Salisbury, and, as agent of the Freedmen's Bureau there, had won great popularity, and having left the army, had settled there and commenced the practice of law.[3]

A direct consequence probably, of the practical overthrow of the civil courts, was an increase in crime of every sort. The latter part of 1867 showed the beginning of the lawlessness which was to culminate a few years later. The sudden elevation of the negroes to the position of voters did not have a peaceful effect on either race, and violence on the part of one was met with violence by the other.[4] The most common offence was,

[1] *Executive Correspondence*, Worth, vol. ii, p. 107.

[2] *Ibid.*, p. 507.            [3] *Ibid.*, pp. 55, 70.

[4] The reports of crime were published in the *Report of the Secretary of War* for 1867, *Ho. Ex. Docs.*, no. 1, p. 350, 40 Cong., 3 sess. They show an appalling condition of affairs, but as North Carolina and South Carolina were grouped, no separate figures for the former can be given.

naturally, larceny. The military tribunals inflicted punishment in a few instances, but the State was full of
wandering negroes who could not be identified readily.
In Orange County nine burglaries were committed
within two weeks.[1] Conditions became so bad in some
sections that General Canby authorized the formation of
a police force composed of loyal whites and blacks in the
ratio of registration. The mingling of the races was not
popular, and few counties availed themselves of the
opportunity.[2] In April, 1868, a provost court with jurisdiction over thirty-two counties was established at
Raleigh, and J. T. Deweese was made judge.

The military force in the State was very small during
the whole of 1867. In the autumn, the posts were con-
solidated into four, with headquarters at Wilmington,
Raleigh, Goldsboro, and Morganton.[3]

In general, conditions were worse in the State than
during the administration of General Sickles. More dissatisfaction was expressed with the military government

[1] *Hillsboro Recorder*, March 27, 1868.

[2] *Sentinel*, January 27, 1868. Jones, Craven, Lenoir, and Pitt counties had such organizations.

[3] The following table shows the number of troops and where they
were stationed for most of the time:

| Place. | Companies. | Officers. | Men. |
| --- | --- | --- | --- |
| Raleigh | 1 | 7 | ... |
| Fayetteville | 1 | 8 | 80 |
| Salisbury | 1 | 4 | 77 |
| Wilmington | 2 | 4 | 53 |
| New Bern | 1 | 5 | 140 |
| Charlotte | 1 | 3 | 74 |
| Morganton | 2 | 7 | 188 |
| Fort Macon | 1 | 3 | 99 |
| Goldsboro | 3 | 9 | 229 |
| Plymouth | 1 | 3 | 85 |
| Total. | 14 | 53 | 1025 |

and more was felt. The workings of the reconstruction acts became increasingly unpopular with a majority of the white people. Bitterness, too, increased, particularly after the opening of the campaign for the convention.

General Canby's name became associated in the minds of many with the conditions which prevailed during the period in which he was in command, and he was personally not so well liked as General Sickles had been. In part, this may have been due to the fact that he was of Southern birth. Another cause was the fact that he generally ignored the state administration, and also that he never came into the State from the time he assumed command until January, 1868.[1]

#### 4. STATE POLITICS AND THE ELECTION OF 1867.

As has been noted previously,[2] a plan originated with the minority members of the legislature for calling a convention of the people. This was rendered unnecessary by the passage by Congress of the supplementary reconstruction act. But the committee chosen to manage affairs had already called a meeting in Raleigh and published a list of persons they wished to attend. These were one hundred and forty in number and included the leaders of the opposition to Governor Worth in 1866. There were also a number of Northern radicals who had settled in the State and had shown a disposition to take an active part in politics. The primary meeting which issued the call was presided over by C. L. Harris. Its germ may be found in the meeting of the previous September when Alfred Dockery was nominated for governor. The meeting instructed Harris,

---

[1] *Executive Correspondence*, Worth, vol. ii, p. 53.

[2] *Cf. supra*, p. 222.

"in the interests of harmony," to see the negroes and ascertain their wishes.[1] The determination which had now been reached by the extreme radicals was expressed by Holden in a characteristic editorial. He said on March 13, "The people of this State have at length reached a point when they must act and restore the State to the Union, or incur the hazards of anarchy and civil war. The Union people of this State especially have borne as much and as long as they intend to bear. All honest, thoughtful, decent citizens will either unite with them in the work of restoration or retire and remain quiet. *Traitors must* take back seats and keep silent. The loyal people, thanks to Congress, are now about to take charge of public affairs. The issue is Union or Disunion. He who is not for the Union deserves to have his property confiscated and to suffer death by the law."[2] A week later he threatened that if the "rebel" leaders took any part in opposition to reconstruction, they would "*pull down on their own heads that final and irrevocable ruin which they so richly deserve.* Is Governor Graham pardoned? Is Governor Vance pardoned? Congress may sweep away all pardons. There are some it *will* sweep away."

Although the original purpose of the convention was made unnecessary by the act of Congress, the call was continued and the meeting was held on March 27. A large number of delegates, white and black, were present, representing fifty-six counties.

When the question of organization came up, R. P. Dick suggested that the meeting should proceed to the organization of the Republican party in North Carolina.

---

[1] Harris had been, a short time before, probably the most determined opponent of the admission of negro testimony.

[2] *Standard*, March 13, 1867.

This had been the well-known intention of many of the delegates, and excited no surprise. Daniel R. Goodloe, the only native North Carolinian present who had a record clear of any adherence to the Confederacy or to secession, and who had been a Republican since the organization of the party, opposed this on the ground that it would prevent the coöperation of many desirable persons, if a name should be adopted which had previously been so odious to the Southern people generally, "and," he added, "to the great majority of your convention." B. S. Hedrick also opposed it, and suggested that "The Union Party" should be the name adopted. Both of these opposed any permanent organization at the time. But the sentiment of the convention was overwhelmingly in favor of identification with the Republican party, and the name was adopted.

In a spectacular way the colored delegates were given a prominent place in the convention. The proceedings were opened with prayer by a colored minister, and upon organization, the president was escorted to the chair by a white delegate on one side and a colored delegate on the other. The negroes made a great many speeches, but took little part in the debates. Most of the white speakers expressed delight at the advancement of the negroes to the right of suffrage. The *New York Tribune* said that the convention showed that the "loyal" white people were willing to "unitè with the colored men on terms of absolute equality." [1] Whether this was true or not, it cannot be denied that such seemed to be the case.

Resolutions were adopted by the convention declaring the full agreement of the delegates with Republican doc-

[1] Quoted in *Standard*, April 10, 1867.

trine, and arrangements were made for a state organization.[1]

As was to be expected, the convention received its
full share of abuse. Its members were given titles that
were hardly relished by them, such as " Holdenites " and
" Holden miscegenationists." The claim of the newly-
organized party to a monopoly of loyalty seemed worse
than absurd to the Conservatives, and the leaders of the
party were all distrusted by their opponents on account
of their former records. Nor was the name of the party
more popular in North Carolina than in the other States.
In this expressed dislike of the Republican party, the
former Whigs were leaders. The Democrats, who had
formerly been most bitterly hostile to the party, were not
at all prominent in political affairs just now. As has
been seen, the state administration was in the hands of
former Whigs who had opposed secession until the call
for troops, and some, like Jonathan Worth and Josiah
Turner, until the passage of the secession ordinance.
Those who had originally favored secession were in almost every instance in political retirement. With most
of them this retirement was voluntary. They were fully
conscious of defeat and ready to accept the decision and
final settlement of the questions involved in the late
struggle, and they did not care at this time to take any
active part in politics. Most of them were convinced
that things were in general out of joint, and their most
acute sensation was one of regret at the failure of the
Confederate cause. To arouse them from this condition
of mind, a change of conditions was necessary. This was
accomplished by the enforcement of the reconstruction
acts. In 1865 and later, the Democratic party seemed

*Standard*, April 3, 1867.

dead forever in North Carolina, but the organization of
the Republican party in the State under the leadership of
W. W. Holden, R. P. Dick, and Thomas Settle, three
former Democrats, and the first-mentioned the father of
the secession movement in North Carolina, began its resuscitation.

The first manifestations of feeling were directed against
the men composing the Republican party. There was
no organized opposition as yet, and there was no prospect of any opposition of importance to the reconstruction acts.[1]   Holden, naturally, was the favored object of
attack, particularly of the *Sentinel*. To the attacks of this
paper, Holden responded, " Every line of his [Pell's]
paper containing treasonable sentiment is equal to an
acre of land."

The organization of the Republican party was carried
on in every county. A feature of it was the revival of
secret political societies. The Heroes of America and
the Union League were largely extended in membership,
the latter being particularly valuable to the party in the
organization of the negroes. It, more than anything
else, made the efforts to divide the negro vote an utter
failure. Such an attempt was made in Raleigh by the
calling of a colored mass meeting, at which Governor
Worth and several other Conservatives were asked to
speak. But apparently it made no impression upon the
negroes. As a matter of fact there was no general dis-

---

[1] The *Sentinel* of April 27, 1867, expressed very well the feeling of a
great many: "Again we urge our readiness to unite our people upon
the one simple platform of the Congress. We argue that only those
shall vote in North Carolina whom the Congress says shall vote. We
agree that only those shall hold office whom the Congress says shall
hold office. We agree that those disabilities shall exist as long as the
Congress says they shall, but no longer. This is the law. Is this not
Republican? Is this not Radical enough?

position evident among the Conservatives to form any alliance with the negroes.

Another means employed to assist in organizing the party was a succession of visits to the State by leaders of the national Republican party. Senator Wilson and Hon. W. D. Kelley were among those who spoke at different places in the State.

The failure of General Sickles to abolish the existing state government was a source of constant annoyance to the radical leaders. Consequently, when Congress met in July, a committee from the State was sent to Washington, headed by James H. Harris, who had become the political leader of the freedmen, to petition that the existing state administration might be removed, and also that Holden might be relieved from his disabilities.[1] But their efforts were unsuccessful.

As the summer advanced a division in sentiment appeared among the Republicans. The radical element had a decided leaning towards confiscation, and were, in general, inclined to be proscriptive. Holden favored a test oath which would disfranchise many of the opponents of the Republican party.[2] This kind of thing was persistently urged upon the colored people. Daniel R. Goodloe, who had begun the publication of a newspaper in Raleigh,[3] was foremost in opposition to this policy. His advice was always towards moderation. He said, "Listen to no man who whispers the word confiscation in your ears or disfranchisement, or injury in any form to your law-abiding white neighbors." He warned them that the result of confiscation would be general ruin to black and white alike, and advised them to be suspicious

[1] *Philadelphia Press*, July 11, 1867; *Standard*, July 24, 1867.
[2] *Standard*, March 20, 1867.
[3] *The Union Register.*

of anyone leading them by promises of the kind. "Ask them," said he, "how long they have been champions of your rights. In ninety-nine cases out of a hundred you will find that such men would have sold you to the sugar and cotton planters of the far South at any time before you were set free."[1]

The question came up more definitely at the Republican state convention which was held in September in Raleigh.[2] Over seventy counties were represented, the negro delegates predominating. In fact the convention was largely controlled by the negroes led by the Northern men present. This was shown by the debate on the election of a permanent president, General Abbott was nominated, and the nomination was opposed by General Laflin, himself a Northern man, who stated that it was bad policy to put Northern men in the important positions. General Abbott's organization, however, was too strong for the opposition and he was chosen, the colored delegates deciding, after a consultation among themselves, in his favor, and, as a peace offering to the native whites, electing Holden chairman of the state executive committee. Alfred Dockery had been led to believe that he would be chosen to preside and had come prepared, but, to his great disgust, was never mentioned during the discussion in connection with the position. The resolutions passed at the March convention were chosen as a platform. Additional resolutions were then introduced opposing confiscation and favoring unlimited suffrage and the removal of disabilities from all "loyal" men. The resolution regarding confiscation

[1] Letter to Republican meeting, July 17, 1867. *Register*, July 30, 1867.

The account of the convention is gathered from the *Standard*, September 11, 1867, and the *Register*, September 6, and 13, 1867.

brought on a sharp debate. The majority of the colored men present[1] and quite a number of the whites were too favorable to the idea of confiscation to go on record against it, and a substitute for the resolution, expressing willingness to abide by the action of Congress in the matter, was adopted. The other resolution was then tabled. There was evidently a strong disinclination on the part of those in control to advise a removal of disabilities, even of those who were acting with the Republican party. In fact there were a number of Northerners present who felt that their chances of political success would be greatly lessened if there should be any general removal of disabilities. Their political ambition explains the failure to pass any resolution for the relief of the "loyal." Hatred of political opponents caused great bitterness of expression. One delegate,[2] in reply to a conciliatory speech made by James H. Harris, said, "They should be taught that treason should be made odious. Their children ought to be forced to say, 'My father was disfranchised on the ground of endeavoring to destroy the best government that ever the sun of high Heaven looked down upon.'" John T. Deweese, an Indiana carpet-bagger, who had had an extended career of disgrace in the army, made a violent attack upon the President for which he was dismissed from the service.

[1] A. H. Galloway, a negro delegate from New Hanover, opposed confiscation, but desired owners of large estates taxed a dollar an acre, in order that the land might be sold by the sheriffs and an opportunity given the negroes to buy land.

[2] W. F. Henderson. He was indicted a few weeks later for stealing a horse or mule. Goodloe, in commenting upon this, said: "A revolutionary period like the present is particularly favorable to that sort of patriotism which Dr. Johnson declared to be the resort of a scoundrel." *Register*, Oct. 11, 1867. The indictment failed, but was destined to serve a purpose for his opponents later.

He was soon appointed commissioner in bankruptcy. He made bankruptcy so attractive, by promising that the United States government would collect for the bankrupt all bad debts, that many went into it and paid the exorbitant fees which he demanded. Many then considered themselves discharged, only to find later that Deweese had appropriated the fees to his own use and that they had to pay them a second time. [1]

The whole tone of the members of the convention was proscriptive. Men like Goodloe, who desired harmony in the State, dissented very vigorously from the sentiments expressed, and pointed out that little sympathy could be expected from those who had not yet joined the party. As a matter of fact the leaders of the party did not desire the former political leaders of the State to join the party, knowing that it would interfere with their own plans. Goodloe declared that the action of the convention would utterly alienate the races from each other, and indicated the sentiment of the convention and its supporters to be " that white men had no rights which black men are bound to respect." [2] The ratification meetings, which followed all over the State, emphatically opposed this tendency of the convention, and Holden saw that he and his followers had been too hasty, and employed a good deal of space in several issues of his paper in attempting to prove that there was no desire on his part for confiscation. [3] But he soon returned to his threatening attitude, and in speaking of the possibility of a conservative majority in the convention, he said that dire penalties would follow it, and closed with the

[1] *Sentinel*, May 28, 1870.
[2] *Register*, October 18, 1867.
[3] *Standard*, September 19, 1867, *passim*.

following statement: "The man who gets in the way
in this crisis of restoring the Union according to the
will of the nation should not only lose the last acre of
land he has, but he deserves death by the halter."[1] General Abbott, in a speech at Wilkesboro, said, "Twenty
years from today, I would rather be a negro than a
white man in North Carolina."

A plan of centralized organization was adopted by the
convention. Goodloe declared that this was intended to
control the vote of the negroes in the interest of schem-
ing whites—"to parcel out the offices among the Ring
men"—and refused to acknowledge it as binding.[2] He
then called for a new organization of the party. declaring
the other "a preposterous abortion."[3] Holden immediately "read him out" of the party and Goodloe retorted
with considerable force, expressing a doubt as to the
former's power in the matter.[4] Finally the executive
committee met and passed a set of resolutions denying
any desire for confiscation. In the meantime, an address
to the people was prepared by John Pool, setting forth the
conservative Republican doctrine. With this view men
of the type of R. P. Dick and Charles R. Thomas agreed.[5]

As may be supposed, these disagreements in the new
party were watched with delight by its opponents, and a

---

[1] *Standard*, September 21, 1867.

[2] *Register*, September 13, 1867.     [3] *Ibid.*, September 24, 1867.

[4] Goodloe said: "Seriously we would respectfully suggest to Mr.
Holden the propriety of his getting inside the Republican party, before
he attempts to read out of it men who were of it and with it when it
was founded. If he were not a disfranchised rebel, he would be but a
probationer of less than six months standing; and his efforts to put us
out, who, in our humble way, assisted in organizing one of the first
Republican organizations in the United States, may seem to some people immodest, not to say impudent."—*Register*, September 20, 1867.

[5] *Register*, October 1 and 22, 1867.

feeble, half-hearted attempt was made by some of them to weaken them further by dividing the negro vote. This was largely the work of the *Sentinel*, which was still in favor of voting for a convention. But this action was unpopular and the position of the Conservatives was finally taken—to make the fight on the question of negro suffrage, declaring their unqualified opposition to it and denying the constitutionality of the whole reconstruction policy of Congress. This decision was largely due to the advice of William A. Graham.

A call for a state Conservative convention was issued by the *Sentinel,* and later by over one hundred citizens of Wake County, and in the latter part of September it met in Raleigh. The meeting did nothing beyond passing resolutions denouncing the action and proscriptive tendency of the Republican convention. Many of the Conservatives, including Governor Worth, were opposed to any organization. The fact is, they were so utterly discouraged and disorganized that it seemed impossible to reach any settled policy. Governor Worth had issued an address to the people urging them to register and vote, but no advice had been given as to how they should vote. Another Conservative meeting was called, and several prominent men were invited to attend and speak. William A. Graham wrote a letter to this meeting, in which, after expressing his unqualified opposition to any recognition of the right of the negroes to vote, he advised the Conservatives to vote against a convention.[1] B. F. Moore, although denying the constitutionality of the reconstruction acts, wrote the meeting that he would take no part in it as he favored a convention. No definite action was taken by the meeting on the question of negro suffrage, but the position of the Conservatives was

[1] *Sentinel*, October 16, 1867.

settled from this time on. The *Sentinel* still persisted that it did not favor a white man's party, but in this respect its influence was gone.

As will be remembered, the supplementary reconstruction act required that a majority of those registered had to take part in the election to make it valid. Despairing of a majority of the vote cast, the Conservatives in several of the Southern States now devised a plan for accomplishing the defeat of the convention. All Conservatives were urged to register and vote for delegates for a convention, but to cast no vote on the question of holding a convention. But General Canby defeated this project by an order to the effect that no votes for delegates should be counted unless accompanied by a vote on the convention question.[1] Conservative candidates were nominated in almost every county, but their canvass was listless.

The election was held November 19 and 20. The result was as follows:

Registered voters................................ 179,653
Votes cast....................................... 125,967
For convention................................... 93,006
Against convention............................... 32,961
Not voting ...................................... 53,686

Only two counties, Orange and Currituck, had a majority opposed to a convention. The vote for a convention showed not only a majority of the votes cast, but also a majority of the registered voters. Those who failed to vote were for the most part white, very few of the negroes failing to exercise the privilege.[2]

[1] *Wilmington Journal*, November 15, 1867.

[2] General Canby, by means of an estimate, proved to his own satisfaction that 11,210 registered negroes failed to vote. Apart from any question of the accuracy, in general, of estimates made by proportion, it is a known fact that the figures could not be correct.

By the failure of the Conservative voters to exercise their right, the Republicans obtained an enormous majority in the convention. No explanation can be given of this failure to vote beyond the widespread feeling that it was useless to resist Congress, and that, consequently, it would be without profit to gain a majority in the convention.

Numerous accusations of fraud were made by the Conservatives, but, as there was no hope of redress, were not pressed. That fraud existed is known, but to what extent is impossible to ascertain.[1] In one instance at least, and probably in more, a candidate for the convention was also an election official.[2]

The day of the election the *Sentinel* took the position that a white man's party was necessary, and with this declaration as a platform, the Conservatives rallied for the remainder of the period of Reconstruction.

[1] The writer has been informed by a Republican, prominent at the time, that fraud was practiced generally. In Rockingham County the polling places were changed on the Saturday night preceding the election, and no public notice was given. In this way many white voters were prevented from voting.—*Sentinel*, November 23, 1867.

[2] Gen. Byron Laflin in Pitt County.

# CHAPTER SIX

## The Convention of 1868 and its Work

### I. THE CONVENTION OF 1868

At the call of General Canby the convention met in Raleigh on January 14, 1868. The Republicans had a majority of ninety-four, the Conservatives having elected only thirteen delegates. Of the one hundred and seven Republicans, at least eighteen were " carpetbaggers " and fifteen were negroes. Many of the " carpetbaggers," or " squatters," as they were called in North Carolina, had formerly been officers in the Union army. The more prominent of them were General Joseph C. Abbott, a native of New Hampshire and formerly an editor and lawyer; Lieutenant Albion W. Tourgee, a native of Ohio, a graduate of Rochester University, and a former officer of the 105th Ohio volunteers; General Byron Laflin, a native of Massachusetts, formerly colonel of the 34th New York Infantry, and Major H. L. Grant, of the 6th Connecticut volunteers,[1] and a native of Rhode Island. Of the other carpetbaggers, David Heaton had been a special agent of the treasury department and had settled in New Bern; S. S. Ashley was a native of Massachusetts and a minister, little else being known of his past history;[2] John R. French was a native of New Hampshire

---

[1] He was a paymaster in the volunteer army in the late war with Spain and was for a number of years clerk of the United States court for the eastern district of North Carolina.

[2] The *Sentinel* constantly asserted that Ashley was of negro blood, and quoted as proof an account in the *New York Observer* of the proceedings of the American Missionary Association, which so classed him. *Sentinel*, May 28, 1868.

who had been a newspaper editor and twice a member of the Ohio House of Representatives. He had come to North Carolina as a direct tax commissioner.[1]

Of the white native North Carolinians in the convention, none had been previously of any prominence in the State, few being known at all outside their own counties. W. B. Rodman had been known as an able lawyer and as an earnest advocate of secession. He, with Calvin J. Cowles and J. M. Turner, was disfranchised under the reconstruction acts, but the fact that they were Radicals prevented any action's being taken to unseat them.

Several of the colored delegates were, comparatively speaking, men of considerable ability. James H. Harris was an orator of great power and had a fair education. With J. W. Hood and A. H. Galloway, he shared the leadership of the colored members.[2]

None of the Conservatives were men of political prominence. The two who at once took the most prominent part in the debates of the convention were Captain Plato Durham and Major John W. Graham, both Confederate soldiers and men of education.[3]

Temporary organization was effected the first day. The next day permanent organization was completed by the election of officers. Calvin J. Cowles was chosen president.

---

[1] The other " squatters " were Edwin Legg, W. A. Mann, D. J. Rich, A. W. Fisher, W. H. S. Sweet, F. F. French, J. H. Renfrow, D. D. Colgrove, Henry Chilson, J. W. Andrews, and Edward Fullings. The four first mentioned had been Union soldiers.

[2] The other colored members were Wilson Carey, John Hyman, J. H. Williamson, Henry Eppes, J. J. Hays, H. C. Cherry, P. D. Robbins, Bryant Lee, C. D. Pierson, Cuffee Mayo, Samuel Highsmith, and J. W. Peterson.

[3] The latter, who was a son of William A. Graham, had been, before the war, a tutor in the University of North Carolina.

The fact of his disabilities was ignored at the time, but later in the session a committee was appointed to examine and make a report in regard to the validity of his signature, as he was not a registered voter. The committee presented an elaborate report, which declared that the general commanding was the judge of the qualifications and election of members.[1]  The convention had already decided that Cowles should occupy the chair for the rest of the session, regardless of the finding of the committee.[2]  The convention was thus inconsistent, for it summarily declared unseated two Conservative members whom General Canby had declared elected, and neither of them was summoned before the committee before the resolution declaring their seats vacant was introduced.[3]  The election of Cowles caused general surprise in the State, as it was supposed that General Abbott and Heaton both desired the position and that one of them would be elected. Each was ambitious, but probably each concluded that more reputation and influence could be gained on the floor of the convention than as its presiding officer. Cowles was a sincere man of unimpeachable honesty, of only fair ability, and of no political experience. He was entirely favorable to Reconstruction and, accepting the carpetbaggers as leaders, was thoroughly under their influence. Their support, combined with the fact that he was a close connection of Holden's by marriage, procured his election.

An effort was made immediately after organization to secure the passage of a resolution declaring that the convention would not consider any legislative proposition until a constitution had been adopted. This met with little ap-

---

[1] *Journal*, p. 400.

[2] *Journal*, p. 372.

[3] These were Williams, of Sampson, and Marler.—*Journal*, p. 314.

proval and was referred to a committee and there suppressed.

On the third day, action was taken in regard to criticism of the convention by the newspapers and their derisive comments upon it. The day the convention met the *Sentinel* had voiced the sentiment of the majority of the white people of the State, saying, in part:

THE CONVENTION (SO CALLED)

The pillars of the Capitol should be·hung in mourning to-day for the murdered sovereignty of North Carolina. In the hall where have been collected, in days gone by, the wisdom, the patriotism, the virtue of the State, there assembles this morning a body convened by an order of ·Congress, in violation of the Constitution of the United States, and in utter disregard of the constitution of North Carolina, a body which, in no sense as a whole, represents the true people of the State, which has not been elected according to our laws nor chosen by those to whom those laws have committed the right of suffrage. In the seats which have been filled by some of the best and truest sons of North Carolina will be found a number of negroes, a still larger number of men who have no interests or sentiments in common with our people but who were left in our midst by the receding tide of war, and yet others who have proven false to their mother and leagued with her enemies.

The other Conservative papers at once took up the nickname " So Called " and it was used during the whole session whenever the convention was mentioned. In addition, the *Sentinel,* in reporting the proceedings of the body, designated the colored members by placing " negro " after their names. This caused much indignation in the convention,[1] and Abbott offered a resolution excluding from the hall of

---

[1] J. W. Hood, a negro delegate, in protesting against the language of the *Sentinel,* said that there was not a negro in the convention.

the convention the reporters of papers which treated the convention or its members with disrespect. After a heated debate, the resolution was passed, several of the moderate Republicans present voting with the Conservatives against it. The Conservative delegates then entered a formal protest. This was objected to and consequently was not received at the time. Later, however, the president decided to allow it to be entered upon the journal. By the resolution it was left to the president to decide what reporters should be excluded. For some time no one was refused admittance, but finally the reporter of the *North Carolinian* was expelled from the hall for the language of his report of the proceedings, which, he avowed, was intended to be insulting, if it were possible.[1]

The Conservatives realized fully their utter helplessness, and decided to act in such a way as to make the policy of the Radicals stand out clearly. Throughout the entire session, led by Durham, Graham, and Hodnett,[2] they were a constant source of annoyance and trouble to the Republicans.

The convention, according to precedent, had very few offices within its gift, and, strange to say, created compara-

---

[1] *Journal*, p. 97. The language was as follows: " The performance began at the usual time." The word " negro " was, also, prefixed to the names of the colored delegates. Throughout the rest of the session of the convention the paper's accounts of the proceedings were after the following type:

" *Manager Cowles' Museum!*

" *Wonderful Performances in Natural History!!*

" The Cowles Museum contains Baboons, Monkeys, Mules, Tourgee, and other Jackasses. Also McDonald, Eppes, Congleton, Mayo, and ' other horned cattle ' too tedious to mention." *North Carolinian*, Feb. 11, 1868.

[2] Philip Hodnett was elected as an independent candidate and was supposed to be a moderate Republican, but he soon became disgusted with the radicals and acted throughout with the Conservatives.

tively few.[1] The most useless, probably, was that of sergeant-at-arms. This was created to satisfy the claim of Colonel I. A. Peck, a former Union soldier, who had been very active in the organization of the Republican party in the State. A reporter was also elected to make a place for another faithful party-worker.[2] The idea of official reports of the debates also appealed to some of the delegates.[3]

The convention, by comparison with all previous public assemblies in North Carolina, was exceedingly expensive and extravagant. The *per diem* of members was set at $8, with twenty cents mileage each way. This was a compromise between the views of General Abbott, who wished it to be $10, and quite a number of others who, considering the condition of the state finances, wished something very low. Attempts were made by several members at different times to have a limit set to the number of days for which remuneration should be received. Tourgee wished the *per diem* reduced to $4 after thirty days. A resolution providing that, after March 12, no member should receive any pay, was characterized as discourteous.[4] Every proposition of the kind was voted down, almost without debate. The

[1] So far as can be ascertained by the writer, the following is the list of the employees of the convention: 1 reporter at $8 per day; 1 secretary at $8; 1 assistant secretary at $4; 1 engrossing clerk at $6; 5 clerks at $4 each; 2 doorkeepers at $2 each; 1 sergeant-at-arms at $8; and 3 servants at $2 each. Ashley, early in the session, introduced a resolution providing that the term " servitors " should be substituted for employees as more respectful. This was evidently designed to win favor with the negroes.

[2] Joseph W. Holden, the junior editor of the *Standard* and the son of W. W. Holden, was chosen. He was already the reporter of the debates for the *Standard*. The reports were never published in book form.

[3] Wilson Carey, a colored delegate, said he favored the publication of the debates, as he intended to " expatiate " to the convention and wanted his words recorded in the " archives of gravity."

[4] *Standard*, March 3, 1868.

compensation of the president was fixed at $12 per day, with the same mileage as the other members. At the close of the session he was directed to remain at Raleigh and sign warrants, receiving for his services $6 per day while so employed. Absence on the part of the delegates was frequent, and a resolution providing that no member should receive pay for the days he was absent met with prompt rejection. Many members left before the end of the session, and, with the consent of the convention, drew their pay to the time of adjournment.[1]

Fraud, too, was evident in the mileage accounts. For instance, the member from Harnett County, who could not have lived at the most more than fifty miles from Raleigh, and who actually lived only about thirty miles away, charged mileage for 262 miles each way.[2] J. W. Hood, a colored delegate from Cumberland, who lived sixty miles away, charged for the same distance. There were numerous cases of this kind, but the majority had no conscience in the matter, and although a resolution was passed directing the sheriffs of all the counties to publish the names, residences and correct mileage of all the members, it was never enforced. Fraud was common in the purchase of supplies also. Prices far above those of the market were charged and paid, particularly for wood and stationery.[3]

[1] *Journal,* p. 451.

[2] *Auditor's Report,* 1868, p. 62. *Sentinel,* March 28, April 1, 1868. The *Sentinel* said that he had probably gone to the Cape Fear boat, which was further away than Raleigh, and then had come by way of Wilmington. Other interesting charges were made as follows: Carey, the delegate from Caswell, charged for one hundred and fifty miles each way; Eppes and Hayes of Halifax, for two hundred and twenty-three each way. *Sentinel,* March 27, 1868.

[3] J. T. Deweese, a register in bankruptcy, and D. J. Pruyn, another carpetbagger, furnished wood at $6 per cord, when the market price was $4.75. The Conservatives made such an outcry at this that $1 per cord was deducted from their next account. *Journal,* p. 425.

Little regard was had for the necessity of completing their work. For a considerable time only one session was held each day. Later two were usually held. When the Republican state convention met in Raleigh, the convention met each day only for roll call, that pay might be drawn, and then adjourned that the members might take part in the proceedings of the Republican meeting.

The question of the payment of the members and officers of the convention came up soon after the convention met. At once a loan of $10,000 was authorized, in order that mileage might be paid.[1] An ordinance was then passed directing the state treasurer to pay the *per diem* of the members from the funds in his possession. But Treasurer Battle refused to recognize the convention and declined to pay the members, claiming that he was under bond to use the funds in his hands for the purposes for which they had been collected, and that the convention would have no legal status until its work was accomplished and a new state government was established. As additional ground for his refusal, he quoted the act of Congress of March 23, 1867, which directed the convention to provide for its expenses by levying a tax.[2] The matter was referred to General Canby who replied that the treasurer was correct in his decision, but informed the convention that as soon as they should have levied a tax for the purpose, he would order the treasurer to pay the members from the funds on hand.[3] A tax was accordingly levied, and the treasurer, thus protected, cashed the warrants of the convention. The tax

---

[1] *Journal*, p. 83. The Conservative press said that when it was announced that the mileage would be paid at one of the banks in the city, there was such a rush for it that it was impossible to keep a quorum present in the convention. *Sentinel*, February 6, 1868.

[2] *Journal*, p. 80.

[3] *Journal*, p. 125.

was one-twentieth of one per cent on all real and personal property, and consequently bore not at all upon the leaders of the majority, and, in fact, very little, comparatively, upon the majority of the Republican party. In the meantime various other plans had been suggested for raising money. One of the carpetbaggers introduced an ordinance providing for the negotiation of a loan of $500 for contingent expenses.[1] This was adopted.[2] A negro delegate introduced a resolution asking Congress for a loan of $3,000,-000.[3] Resolutions of this kind were frequent during the whole session.

The expenses of the convention for *per diem* and mileage amounted to $86,356.89. Printing and stationery increased this by about $5,000. In the matter of expense, North Carolina, compared with most of the other Southern States, escaped very easily. But the expenses far exceeded those of any other convention in North Carolina.[4]

Comparatively little opportunity for corruption existed, but charges were introduced that bribery had been used to obtain certain railroad legislation [5] and a committee of inquiry was asked for. President Cowles appointed on the committee Plato Durham, who had introduced the resolu-

---

[1] *Journal*, p. 132.          [2] *Ibid.*, p. 143.          [3] *Ibid.*, p. 142.

[4] The expenses of the state conventions of North Carolina, beginning with that of 1835, and exclusive of printing, which was of little cost in the case of all of them, were as follows:

| Date. | No. Sessions. | Days. | Cost. | Per Diem. | Mileage. |
|---|---|---|---|---|---|
| 1835 | 1 | 38 | $8,330.00 | $1.50 | 5 cts. |
| 1861 | 4 | 108 | 56,469.02 | 3.00 | 5 " |
| 1865 | 2 | 43 | 30,514.00 | 4.00 | 10 " |
| 1868 | 1 | 55 | 86,356.89 | 8.00 | 20 " |
| 1875 | 1 | 31 | 15,596.98 | 4.00 | 10 " |

[5] The matter referred to was the endorsement by the convention of certain bonds of the Wilmington, Charlotte, and Rutherford Railroad. *Ordinances*, p. 43.

tion, S. S. Ashley, and James H. Harris,[1] who was one of the members at whom the resolution was aimed. The two first mentioned were not on speaking terms with each other in consequence of a difficulty they had had shortly before on the floor of the convention, and Durham had never recognized any of the colored delegates. It was evident that the intention of the president was to prevent any inquiry from being made. The next day Harris retaliated by a resolution providing for an investigation as to whether Plato Durham, " the delegate (so called) from Cleveland," had not obtained his election by fraud.[2] Neither committee succeeded in discovering anything, and both were soon discharged.[3]

Notwithstanding the fact that the main purpose, supposedly, of the convention was to frame a constitution, no great eagerness was manifested to begin the work. Committees were appointed to report the various articles, but it was quite a long time before they reported. The carpetbaggers controlled the committees, capturing the chairmanship of ten of the nineteen standing committees and of most of the special committees. They were thus given an opportunity to put their constitutional theories into definite form. The result of this was that there were many differences from the former constitution of the State. Individually or collectively the carpetbaggers controlled the convention absolutely.

An ordinance was early introduced providing for some relief to the people by means of a stay law.[4] After it was ascertained from General Canby that he would enforce such an ordinance by military order, one was passed providing that civil proceedings founded on causes of action

[1] *Journal*, pp. 171, 178.
[3] *Ibid.*, pp. 426, 473.
[2] *Ibid.*, p. 178.
[4] *Ibid.*, p. 32.

prior to May, 1865, should be suspended until January 1, 1869, or until the new constitution should go into effect.[1] General Canby, at the request of the convention,[2] made this ordinance operative at once.[3] The debate on the ordinance led to a discussion of the condition of the State, and there was at once noticeable, in quite a number of the delegates, a decided sentiment in favor of repudiating the entire state debt. The most earnest advocates of this were A. W. Tourgee and his colleague from Guilford, G. W. Welker. This appeared more fully in the debate on the section of the Bill of Rights, guaranteeing the public debt of the State. Tourgee declared that the new State of North Carolina, which they were constructing, was under no obligation to pay the debts of the old State and that it would be ruinous to do so. He said, " He would be a fool who would emigrate to North Carolina if the new State is to be saddled with the debts of the old." This view was not shared by the majority, and the section was adopted. Abbott characterized Tourgee's doctrine as infamous, and Galloway, Harris, and Hood, of the colored delegates, also expressed their horror at his proposition.[4] It was suggested several times that the convention should forbid the collection of all private debts incurred in aid of " rebellion ", and as one delegate expressed it,[5] " give the citizens the same right as the State." [6] Later an ordinance was passed directing the next General Assembly to provide for the payment in cash of the interest falling due after January, 1869, on the state bonds dated after January 1, 1866. All the coupons due at the time of

---

[1] *Ordinances*, p. 45.

[2] *Ibid.*, p. 125.

[3] *General Orders*, no. 57. *Sentinel*, April 16, 1868.

[4] *Sentinel*, February 17, 1868.

[5] S. W. Watts.                    [6] *Sentinel*, February 17, 1868.

the passage of the ordinance were ordered to be funded in a new issue of bonds.[1] This was opposed by the Conservatives, who declared that it was for the benefit of Northern men who held the bonds and that the lobbyists had secured its passage.[2]

Numbers of innovations were proposed and adopted through the influence of the Northern members. Their main argument was usually that the proposed provision was in some New England or other Northern constitution. Every effort was made to reconstruct the State on such a basis, and the only matter of surprise is that the resulting constitution was not more foreign and extreme in its character. The main reason seems to have been the rivalry among the three carpetbag leaders Abbott, Heaton, and Tourgee. In their efforts to strengthen their respective positions, they yielded in many things to the natives of the State. But as it was, there was a very radical difference in the new constitution from its predecessor.

One of the changes which was most condemned by the opposition, and even by many Republican lawyers in the convention, was the abolition of the distinction between actions at law and suits in equity. This has since been acknowledge to have been on the whole a wise change.[3] Provision was also made for a commission to prepare rules

[1] *Ordinances*, pp. 84-85.

[2] There was quite a body of lobbyists, the most prominent of whom was General Milton S. Littlefield, a native of New York, and formerly colonel of a colored regiment. He was said to have been lately concerned in an extensive lumber steal in Pennsylvania and had come South for new and better opportunities. He became very prominent in 1869, both in North Carolina and Florida, from his connection with the bond frauds in both States.

[3] It is, however, admitted that, as a result of the change, there has been a development of a lack of accuracy and care in the lawyers as compared with those under the old system.

of procedure and practice in accordance with this change, and also to codify the laws. Victor C. Barringer, A. W. Tourgee, and W. B. Rodman were appointed as commissioners for a term of three years with salaries of $200 per month.[1] Tourgee had been licensed to practice law in Ohio; and, largely for his benefit, an ordinance had been passed a short time before providing that all persons who had been admitted to the bar in other States could be admitted in North Carolina without examination, upon the production of evidence of a good moral character and the payment of the required fees.[2] Later the judiciary committee was instructed to report an ordinance which would allow all citizens of the State who were of good character to practice upon payment of the necessary fees.[3]

Another change in regard to the courts was even more criticised, and with more justice. The election of judges was taken from the General Assembly and put in the hands of the people, and the term of office was changed from life to eight years. The number of Superior Court judges was increased to twelve. This was a necessary increase, for the existing courts were over-crowded, and emancipation had largely increased the work of the courts. The Conservatives opposed the increase as a useless extravagance and as designed to furnish places for Republican lawyers who were ambitious to be on the bench. Judging from the number of aspirants, it is not improbable that the change was welcome to many of the members of the bar.

Naturally a question which arose early in the debate on

---

[1] *Ordinances*, p. 79. For at least fifteen years after the adoption of the constitution, the courts were full of cases brought to secure interpretation of the instrument.

[2] *Ordinances*, p. 109.

[3] *Ibid.*, p. 123.

the constitution was that of political disabilities. Two features of the subject were considered. Regarding the disabilities imposed by the Fourteenth Amendment, a committee was appointed to prepare a list of those persons whom the convention should recommend to Congress as suitable objects for relief. After a time the names of about six hundred persons, most if not all of whom were acting with the Republicans, were presented and a violent debate followed, Durham leading the opposition and Tourgee defending the report. The former went on record, characterizing it as " a fraud upon the people of North Carolina and so intended to be." [1] Several of the Republicans favored a general removal of disabilities, but the majority were strongly opposed to such a thing, and all efforts at amendment of the resolution introduced by the committee failing, it was adopted.[2]

The question of the qualifications for voting and holding office in the State then came up. The majority of a committee, appointed to consider the subject, reported a proposed article of the constitution providing for an unqualified manhood suffrage.[3] It also provided that all persons who denied the existence of a Supreme Being, or who had been convicted of a felony or of treason, should be disqualified from holding office under the state government.[4] Three minority reports were submitted. The first, signed by two native Republicans,[5] provided for the disqualification for suffrage of all those who had ever attempted to

---

[1] He also said: "The secretary may take my words down. I do not care for the secretary or the convention either." *Journal,* p. 411.

[2] Laflin, Legg, and Rice, of the "carpet bag" contingent, favored a general removal of all disabilities. *Journal,* p. 413.

[3] Conviction of a felony did not operate as a disqualification for the suffrage.

[4] *Journal,* p. 232.          [5] Candler and Congleton.

prevent the exercise of the right of suffrage by any means, and of all those disqualified for holding office by the proposed Fourteenth Amendment, the removal by Congress of these disabilities operating to remove the disability imposed by the state constitution. It also provided an oath to be taken before registration.[1] The two Conservatives on the committee submitted the second minority report. This stated that the right of suffrage was not inherent, and that, as the great mass of the negroes were not prepared for the exercise of the privilege, there was no reason why it should be extended to them. Denying the constitutional power of Congress to prescribe who should vote in North Carolina, and declaring that the whole scheme of reconstruction was for the advancement of party purposes by " Africanizing " and " Radicalizing " the South to offset the loss of electoral votes elsewhere, the signers of the report recommended that North Carolina should refuse to alter her constitution under dictation by Congress—to " confide the power of making laws to those who have no property to protect, and to bestow the right to levy taxes upon those who have no taxes to pay." [2] The third report, submitted by a carpet-bagger, agreed with the majority report, except that it recommended that the classes debarred from holding office by the Fourteenth Amendment should also be debarred by the State until the legal removal of disabilities.[3]

[1] *Journal*, p. 234. The oath was as follows: " I do solemnly swear, (or affirm) that I will support and maintain the Constitution of the United States and the Constitution of the State of North Carolina; that I will never countenance or aid in the secession of the State from the United States; that I accept the political and civil equality of all men; and that I will faithfully obey the laws of the United States and encourage others so to do. So help me God."

[2] *Journal*, p. 235.

[3] He probably meant removal by the State; otherwise the provision was useless on account of the Fourteenth Amendment.

The debate on the question opened with a great deal of heat, and, with some interruptions, lasted for three weeks. There was no doubt of course as to negro suffrage; universal suffrage was not so certain. There were known to be many who favored some limitation so far as the Conservatives were concerned; Holden was favorable to some plan of this kind.[1] During the debate several propositions were made. One delegate favored an article which would prevent those then laboring under disabilities from ever voting;[2] another favored disfranchising all those who should vote against the constitution adopted by the convention;[3] while still a third desired that power should be given the county boards of registration, the members of which in all cases should be required to take the " iron-clad " oath, to disfranchise any person who aided or used his influence for the Confederacy, or who had thrown any obstacles in the way of reconstruction.[4] A seemingly favorite proposition was one to require an oath which should express a change of opinion from the past and the promise of good conduct for the future.[5] The Conservatives gave notice at the be-

[1] *Standard*, February 3, 1868.

[2] *Sentinel*, February 22, 1868.

[3] *Sentinel*, February 22, 1868. This member, E. W. Jones, was probably, the most bitter and proscriptive of all the members.

[4] *Standard*, January 24, 1868.

[5] An oath suggested by General Abbott is a fair type of those proposed. It is as follows: " I do solemnly swear, (or affirm) that I am truly and devotedly attached to the Union of all the States and opposed to any dissolution of the same; that I entertain no political sympathy with the instigators and leaders of the rebellion, or with the enemies of the Union, nor approbation of their principles or purposes; that I will, neither by word or act, encourage or countenance a spirit of sedition or disaffection towards the government of the United States, or the laws thereof, and that I will sustain and defend the Union of these States and will discourage and resist all efforts to destroy or impair the same. So help me God."

ginning of the debate that any imposition of disabilities as
regarded the right of suffrage would result in the necessity
of permanent military occupation of the State by the United
States,[1] as any government that might be established under
such a constitution would fall the day that troops were
withdrawn. Immediately, and apparently as a threat, the
amnesty act which had been passed by the General Assembly in 1866 was repealed.[2] The majority report was then
adopted without change.

The other chief matter of party conflict was the question
of the division of the races. Early in the debates on the
constitution, the Conservatives commenced to introduce
resolutions or amendments designed to put the Republicans
on record on the subject. The first of these was a series of
resolutions which, after expressing the desire of the people
of the State to be restored to constitutional relations with
the federal government, declared that the reconstruction
acts were unwise, unjust, and oppressive; that the white and
black races were distinct by nature, and efforts to abolish
such distinctions were crimes against nature; that the government had been instituted by the whites and should be
controlled by them, and finally appealed to the masses of the
Northern people for relief, " from the degradation now
heaped upon them." The white Republicans were not
ready to vote for this or against it, and consequently postponed it indefinitely.[3] Another attempt of the kind was
made by the Conservatives in a proposed amendment to the

---

[1] See speech of John W. Graham in the *Sentinel,* February 25, 1868.
He reminded the Republicans that the very men whose punishment they
were then considering, had opposed a test oath in 1862. The test oath
proposed in 1862, it will be remembered, was defeated largely through
the efforts and eloquence of his father, William A. Graham.

[2] *Ordinances,* p. 68. *Cf. supra,* p. 127.

[3] *Journal,* pp. 32, 35.

report of the committee on the Executive Department providing that no person of African descent should be eligible to any executive office. One of the negro members had already introduced an amendment to the effect that either the governor or lieutenant-governor should always be a negro.[1] The latter was withdrawn later,[2] and the former, needless to say, was overwhelmingly defeated.[3] A proposition made by Plato Durham[4] that the qualification for governor and lieutenant-governor should be the ability to read and write met with the same fate. In the case of the militia and public schools the convention refused to require separation of the races.[5] A proposed section of the Bill of Rights prohibiting the intermarriage of the races was promptly tabled,[6] and all marriages that had taken place under military authority, including several cases of marriage between whites and blacks, were validated.[7] But the same day a resolution was introduced by a colored member and passed, declaring it the sense of the convention that the intermarriage of the races should be discountenanced, and that separate schools should be established.[8] And finally, a proposed section, which provided that no white child should ever be apprenticed to a negro master and that no negro guardian should ever be appointed for a white ward, was also rejected.[9]

The constitution was finally drafted and adopted by the convention. The Conservatives on the final vote all voted

---

[1] This was probably the work of some Conservative sympathizer.

[2] *Sentinel*, January 28, 1868.

[3] *Journal*, p. 162.          [4] *Ibid.*, p. 158.

[5] *Ibid.*, pp. 175, 287, 343. Graham introduced a resolution providing for separate commands in the militia, and also that no white man should ever be required to obey a negro officer.

[6] *Journal*, p. 216.          [7] *Ordinances*, p. 86.

[8] *Journal*, p. 473.          [9] *Ibid.*, p. 483.

against its adoption, and consequently none of them signed it.[1]

The convention, while forming a constitution, was also engaged in other matters. The State was divided into congressional districts, with few changes from the former division. This led to a sharp debate among those who had aspirations for seats in Congress.[2] Fourteen divorces were granted by the convention, and the Conservatives were thus furnished with further ground for attack. Several of the Republican members also opposed this action of the convention.[3] A resolution was passed thanking the House of Representatives of the United States for the impeachment of President Johnson.[4] Just before adjournment a resolution was passed directing the next General Assembly to devise some plan, if practicable, to locate every citizen upon a freehold.[5] In this connection one delegate wanted a loan of $10,000,000 negotiated " to provide homes for the homeless and for agricultural purposes." [6] This, he declared, was chiefly to be used for the negroes in payment for their long labor without reward, their faithful service during the war, and their devotion to the Republican party.

Most of the daily sessions of the convention were very stormy. The Conservatives were few in number, but aided by the press, they seemed able to provoke their opponents to anger at will. Nor were the relations of the Republicans

---

[1] Durham moved that the Capitol bell be tolled while the signatures of the delegates were being affixed.

[2] *Sentinel*, February 21, 1868.

[3] One Republican delegate, in protest, introduced an ordinance which provided that all men in North Carolina were thereby divorced and at liberty to marry again.

[4] *Ordinances*, p. 126.

[5] *Ordinances*, p. 129.

[6] *Journal*, p. 119.

among themselves always the best, and disputes arose several times when the chair was powerless to restore order.[1]

Towards the middle of the session Holden recommended that the " gag law " should be strictly enforced, as regarded the Conservative members, by means of calling the previous question.[2] Possibly this, along with the hope of damaging his political prospects, caused a Conservative member to introduce a resolution providing for an inquiry into Holden's complicity in the murder of President Lincoln, through his editorials in the *Standard* calculated to inspire an assassin.[3] The reading of the resolution was not finished before objection was made to its reception, and it was returned to the member who introduced it, as was his protest, the next day, against the action of the convention.[4]

After providing for submitting the proposed constitution to the people and for holding an election for state officers, the General Assembly, and members of Congress at the same time, under the direction of the military authorities, the convention adjourned on March 17. This adjournment was *sine die,* unless the convention should be called into session by the president before January 1, 1869. It had been in session fifty-five days, and, in addition to the constitution, had adopted fifty-seven ordinances and fifty-six resolutions.

After the signing of the constitution, on the day before adjournment, the convention took a recess, which was spent

[1] Tourgee, on one occasion, engaged in an altercation with the president and was, at his order, arrested for disorderly conduct. He appealed to the convention and, by its vote, was released.

[2] *Standard*, February 8, 1868.

[3] *Ibid.*, June 5, 1861. " Who will plot for the heads of Abe Lincoln and General Scott?" Holden, in 1868, denied the authorship of the editorial.

[4] *Sentinel*, March 5 and 6, 1868.

in singing and horseplay.  The next morning the same thing was done, and General Milton S. Littlefield was invited to address the convention and sang " John Brown," the delegates joining in the chorus.  Other songs sung were "Hang Jeff. Davis," " Yankee Doodle," and a number of negro melodies.  Any departure from the dignity thought worthy of a legislative body had been previously unknown in North Carolina, and the amazement and disgust it caused were increased by the choice of songs.  The *Sentinel* the next day headed its account of the proceedings as follows:

THE CONSTITUTIONAL CONVENTION (SO CALLED)

The Disgraceful Closing Scenes!  Corn Field Dance and
Ethiopian Minstrelsy!!  Ham Radicalism
in its Glory!!!

Amidst this came to an end the " Mongrel Convention," characterized by the *Standard* as " one of the ablest, most dignified and most patriotic bodies that ever assembled in the State." [1]

2. CONSTITUTIONAL CHANGES

The new constitution as submitted to the people differed radically from the former one.  Apart from the fact that the general plan of government was of the type of the American state governments, it was practically an overthrowing of the institutions of the State.  Much that was utterly foreign to the customs and ideas of the people was introduced, and to the minds of many the best features of the old constitution were omitted or amended beyond recognition.[2]

---

[1] *Standard*, February 21, 1868.

[2] The original constitution was adopted December, 1776.  It was amended by the convention of 1835, and the property qualification for voting for state senators was abolished in 1857.

In the Bill of Rights, the original of which had been
adopted in 1776, there was less change than in any other
part of the fundamental law.  But quite a number of provisions were inserted.  The chief of these were as follows:
all men were declared equal; the right of secession was
denied, and the paramount allegiance of all citizens to the
United States was affirmed; the public debt of the State
was declared valid, and the war debt was repudiated; slavery was prohibited; the suspension of the writ of *habeas
corpus* was forbidden; the people were declared entitled to
the privilege of education; [1] the legislative, executive, and
judicial departments of government were declared forever
separate and distinct; the freedom of the press was guaranteed, as in the former Bill of Rights, but individuals
were held responsible for abuse of this freedom; the quartering of soldiers upon citizens in time of peace was forbidden; it was provided that the courts should always be
open, and in criminal cases greater protection was guaranteed defendants than in the original instrument, though
not more than was enjoyed under the laws of the State and
the usage of the courts; and finally it was declared that all
rights and powers not delegated by the constitution should
be retained by the people.

In the Legislative Department greater changes were
made.  The name of the lower house of the General Assembly was changed from the House of Commons to the
House of Representatives.  The property qualifications for
members of both houses were abolished,[2] and they were

[1] This was provided elsewhere in the Constitution of 1776.  See
Sec. 40.

[2] Previous to this, a senator had to have been possessed, for one year
before his election, in the county from which he was elected, of 300
acres of land in fee.  A member of the Commons had to have been
possessed, for six months before election, of 100 acres of land in fee
or for life.

obliged to take an oath of allegiance to the United States before taking their seats. Senators were required to be at least thirty years of age. The elective Council of State was abolished and replaced by one composed of the executive officers of the State.

In the Executive Department three new offices were created: lieutenant-governor, superintendent of public works, and auditor. The latter replaced the office of comptroller which had been created by act of the General Assembly.[1] The election of these officers, with that of the other state officers, which had formerly been in the hands of the General Assembly, was put into the hands of the people. The property qualification for governor was abolished,[2] and his term of office, together with that of the other state officers, was increased from two to four years. Only two years' previous residence in the State, instead of five, was required for the governor. He was given power to commute sentences in addition to the pardoning power. All nominations of the governor had to be confirmed by the Senate. Provision was made for a bureau of statistics, agriculture, and immigration.

In the Judicial Department, the most complete change was made. All distinctions between actions at law and suits in equity and the forms of such actions were abolished. Only one form of action, the civil suit, could be brought in the State. Feigned issues were abolished, and it was provided that the fact at issue should be tried by order of court before a jury. The county courts were abolished and a large part of their powers and duties were given to the clerks of the Superior Courts. The number of the Supreme

---

[1] *Revised Statutes* 1854, chap. 23.

[2] Previous to this a freehold in lands or tenements of $1,000 was required.

Court justices was increased from three to five, and that of the Superior Court judges from eight to twelve. Their election and also that of the solicitors was taken from the General Assembly and given to the people. The term of office of judges was changed from life or good behavior and made eight years. The election of clerks, sheriffs, and coroners was taken from the county courts and put in the hands of the people.

Regarding taxation, the constitution provided that the proceeds of the capitation tax should be applied to education and the support of the poor. Provision was made for the payment of the interest on the public debt and for the creation, after 1880, of a sinking fund for the payment of the principal. The General Assembly was prohibited from incurring any indebtedness until the bonds of the State should be at par, except to supply a casual deficiency or to suppress insurrection, unless there should be inserted in the same bill a provision for the levying of a special tax to pay the interest annually. The General Assembly was also forbidden to lend the credit of the State, except to railroads which were in the process of construction at the time of the ratification of the constitution or to those in which the State had a financial interest, unless the question was submitted to the direct vote of the people. It was also provided that every act levying a tax should state its object and the proceeds could be applied to no other purpose.

The constitution provided for universal suffrage. No one could register without taking an oath to support the Constitution of the United States, and every officer had to take an oath of allegiance to the United States. All persons who denied the being of Almighty God, who had been convicted of treason, perjury, or any other infamous crime since becoming citizens of the United States, or who had been convicted of corruption or malpractice in office and had not been legally restored to the rights of citizenship, were disqualified for holding office. Taking any part in a duel also disqualified for holding any office under the State.

County government was put in the hands of five commissioners in each county elected by the people to exercise a general supervision and control of county affairs. It was also provided that the people of each county should elect a treasurer and a register of deeds. The commissioners were directed to divide the counties into townships, and the people of each township were biennially to elect two justices of the peace. No counties or other municipal corporations could contract a debt without the consent of a majority of the voters, and all the counties were forbidden to pay any debt contracted to aid in rebellion.

The General Assembly was directed to provide a general system of public schools, and the executive officers of the State were formed into a board of education to succeed to all the powers and duties of the Literary Board. The State University was declared to be forever inseparable from the public school system, and the General Assembly was directed to establish, in connection with the University, departments of agriculture, mechanics, mining, and normal instruction.

Provision was made for a homestead exemption of $500, and it was provided that the real and personal property of a married woman should remain her separate estate and property, and in no way liable for the debts of her husband. These provisions were not new to the State, both having been incorporated in the law in 1866.

Punishments for crime were provided as follows: death, imprisonment, with or without hard labor, fines, removal from office, and disqualification to hold any office under the State. Four crimes were punishable by death: murder.

arson, burglary, and rape.[1]  Provision was made for a
penitentiary, and the General Assembly was directed to provide for the care of orphans, idiots, inebriates, deaf mutes,
and the insane, and authorized to provide houses of refuge
and correction for the punishment and instruction of certain classes of criminals, whenever it might seem necessary.

These were the more important changes.  There were
others of less interest and importance, but they are far too
numerous to mention.  A comparison of the two constitutions shows a very wide difference, and brings out very
clearly the part played by the Northern members of the
convention.

### 3. POLITICS AND ELECTION OF 1868

Early in January, the Conservative executive committee
called a State convention of " The Constitutional Union
Party," as they styled it.  It met on February 6, about fifty
counties being represented.  The majority of the delegates
were former Whigs, but a large number of Democrats were
present.  The convention is particularly notable as marking
the first re-appearance in politics of many who had been
prominent before and during the war.  Ex-Governor Graham was made chairman, and among the other officers and
delegates, were ex-Governors Vance, Bragg, and Manly;
Judges Manly, Merrimon, and Fowle; and Weldon N. Edwards, W. L. Steele, R. Y. McAden, Marcus Erwin, A. T.
Davidson, R. H. Smith, and W. N. H. Smith.  A state organization was perfected and a series of resolutions, outlining the policy of the party, adopted.  These resolutions

---

[1] Several of the carpetbaggers opposed the death penalty for rape
as being too severe, and because certain Northern States did not have
it.  Heaton agreed with the native delegates, who favored it, and
made a strong speech in its defence.

declared devotion to the United States Constitution; protested against the enforcement of the reconstruction acts as unconstitutional; declared the great political issue in the State to be negro suffrage and equality, if not supremacy, and registered their unqualified opposition to it; declared the determination of the party to protect the negroes in their civil rights and to allow such privileges as were not inconsistent with the welfare of both races; demanded early relief for the impoverished people of the State; expressed gratitude to the President for his efforts to restore the Union; declared the United States Supreme Court, and not Congress, the legitimate expounder of the Constitution; and, expressing their distrust of " the organization controlling Congress," the convention "waived all former party feeling and prejudice " and invited the people of the State to coöperate with the Democratic party, at the same time electing delegates to the Democratic national convention. Enthusiastic speeches were made by various delegates, among them Vance, who urged activity and fearlessness of the result of opposition to the radicals,[1] saying, " When free speech, a free press and a free ballot are restored, the wrath and indignation of an outraged people will damn them forever. It will be better for them that a mill stone were hanged about their necks and that they were drowned in the depths of the sea." [2] Nominations for state officers were left with the executive committee. This met later in the month and nominated a full state ticket.[3] Vance was

[1] Holden had warned the Conservatives that every person who took part in the meeting would be kept forever under disabilities.

[2] *Sentinel*, February 20, 1868.

[3] The Democratic nominations were as follows: Governor, Z. B. Vance, later, Thos. S. Ashe; Lieutenant-Governor, Edward D. Hall; Secretary of State, Robt. W. Best; Treasurer, K. P. Battle; Auditor, S. W. Burgin; Superintendent of Public Instruction, Braxton Craven;

nominated for governor, but declined, and Thomas S. Ashe was chosen. The latter was a Democrat and had been, before the war, several times a member of the General Assembly. He had been a member of the Confederate Congress and had also been elected to the Confederate Senate, but never took his seat. He was, of course, under disabilities. In the other nominations, the old Whig influence was evident, and with but few exceptions the nominees had formerly belonged to that party.

The Republican convention met on the same day as the Conservative. As was expected, W. W. Holden was nominated for governor in spite of all efforts to defeat him.[1] The carpetbaggers captured the nominations for secretary of state and superintendent of public instruction. Later, too, A. W. Tourgee was nominated for judge of the Superior Court, after being defeated for a congressional nomination.[2] The nominations of both parties for judges coin-

---

Superintendent of Public Works, S. F. Patterson; Attorney General, Sion H. Rogers; Supreme Court Justices, R. M. Pearson, W. H. Battle, E. G. Reade, M. E. Manly, and A. S. Merrimon; Superior Court Judges, D. A. Barnes, E. J. Warren, Geo. V. Strong, W. S. Devane, R. P. Buxton, R. B. Gilliam, Thos. Ruffin, Jr., F. E. Shober, W. M. Shipp, Anderson Mitchell, J. L. Bailey, and A. T. Davidson.

[1] B. S. Hedrick introduced a resolution declaring that the convention would nominate no person laboring under disabilities. The convention refused to receive it.

[2] The Republican ticket, as it finally appeared, was as follows: Governor, W. W. Holden; Lieutenant-Governor, Tod R. Caldwell; Secretary of State, H. J. Menninger; Treasurer, D. A. Jenkins; Auditor, Henderson Adams; Superintendent of Public Instruction, S. S. Ashley; Superintendent of Public Works, C. L. Harris; Attorney General, W. M. Coleman; Justices of the Supreme Court, R. M. Pearson, W. B. Rodman, R. P. Dick, Thomas Settle, and E. G. Reade; Judges of the Superior Court, C. C. Pool, E. W. Jones, C. R. Thomas, D. L. Russell, Jr., R. P. Buxton, S. W. Watts, A. W. Tourgee, G. W. Logan, Anderson Mitchell, and R. H. Cannon.

cided in several instances.[1] The convention before adjournment passed, by a large majority, a resolution introduced by one of the carpetbaggers " That it is the sense of this convention that rebels should not be enfranchised indiscriminately."

When the congressional nominations were made the carpetbaggers were more prominent. David Heaton, J. R. French, and J. T. Deweese were nominated. The last was not the first choice of his district, for James H. Harris was nominated, but, through the influence of Deweese, withdrew and was replaced by the latter.[2] The other four nominations were given to natives.[3] B. S. Hedrick ran as an independent candidate against Deweese.

The canvass was prosecuted with great activity, and apparently with great hopes of success by both parties. The Union League and the Heroes of America were again brought into service. Holden was at this time president of the former, and James H. Harris was vice-president. W. F. Henderson was at the head of the latter organization. Each issued addresses to their members urging them to continued efforts.[4] The Republicans fought the campaign

[1] The nomination of Judge Pearson by the Republicans very nearly prevented his selection by the Conservatives, but he gave private assurance that he was a Conservative and was nominated. The Republicans nominated Judge Warren for a different district from that in which he lived and where he had been nominated by the Conservatives. He refused to accept.

[2] A leader in the Republican party at that time assures the writer that, to his personal knowledge, Deweese paid Harris $1,000 to withdraw.

[3] The congressional nominations were as follows: 1st district, Republican, J. R. French, Democrat, Henry A. Gilliam; 2d, David Heaton, Thomas S. Kenan; 3d, O. H. Dockery, T. C. Fuller; 4th, J. T. Deweese, S. T. Williams; 5th, I. G. Lash, D. F. Caldwell; 6th, C. J. Cowles, Nathaniel Boyden; 7th, A. H. Jones, B. S. Gaither.

[4] *Standard*, February 5, 1868.

O

largely on matters relating to the war which would tend to excite bitter feeling. Vance's proclamations against deserters and his speeches favoring the support of the war were re-published and commented on. A special effort was made to reach the old non-slaveholding class, and, by arousing class prejudice, to excite them against the Conservatives. Among the most active of the Republican speakers was General Littlefield who was thus extending his influence with a view to future financial benefit therefrom. Every effort to influence public sentiment in the North was made, an interesting example occurring when Sergeant Bates of the Union army passed through the State. He was engaged in carrying the United States flag through every late Confederate state in order to show the falsity of the rumors concerning the state of feeling in the South. Holden sent Colonel T. B. Keogh, a carpetbagger from Wisconsin, to offer him $10,000 to abandon his journey and report in the North that he was forced to do so on account of the hostility of feeling in the State which made his life unsafe.[1]

The Conservatives made their fight on the question of ratifying the constitution, which they opposed on many grounds. They argued that it made the negro a political equal and that it was part of an attempt to bring about social equality by its failure to require the separation of the races in the schools and in the militia and by the opening of the University to negroes. They objected to the apportionment of representation among the various counties as being so arranged as to increase the importance of the negro vote. Property, they held, had no representation, and higher taxes were made necessary without any increased benefit to the people. The provision for the election of judges by the people was particularly criticised with refer-

[1] *Sentinel*, April 12, 1871.

ence to the fact that candidates for the Supreme Bench were making a political canvass and entering into general political discussions. The lack of any test of qualification for office was another feature much urged as a reason for the rejection of the constitution. They received an unexpected ally in Daniel R. Goodloe, so far as concerned opposition to Holden and the rest of the Republican ticket. When the nominations were made, he said that Holden's name was " a synonym for whatever is harsh, proscriptive and hateful to nine-tenths of the white people of the State," and declined to support him.[1] Goodloe's paper, the *Register*, while advocating the ratification of the constitution, fought almost the entire Republican ticket. H. H. Helper, who was associated with him, began the publication of a campaign sheet called " *The Holden Record*," in which he gave selections from the *Standard* which were calculated to show the inconsistency and general unfitness of Holden for the office of governor. He also advocated the election of Goodloe as governor.

On account of the great changes in the constitution, the Republicans lost the support of many who might have been counted upon to act with them. B. F. Moore, who had thought the reconstruction acts unconstitutional, but who had been in favor of a convention as the best means of reaching some settlement of disputed questions and because he thought that the constitution needed some amendment, opposed the constitution on account of its radical nature and declined to act with the Republican party.[2] This was the case with many others.

---

[1] *Sentinel*, February 29, 1868.

[2] B. F. Moore, in a letter to his daughter, dated March 28, 1868, said: " It is, in my view, with some exceptions, a wretched basis to secure liberty or property. The legislative authority rests upon ignorance without a single check, except Senatorial age, against legislative plun-

Another political element which to a slight extent played a part in the campaign was the mysterious Ku Klux Klan. Many statements in regard to its extent were made by the *Standard,* but it does not appear to have reached the greater part of the State, and had so far assumed very little importance. Nor did it commit any violence. According to the *Standard,* the Klan in Warren County indulged in a grim joke as a threat to the negroes. Night after night, in their fantastic costume, they dug graves along the roads which led into Warrenton. But there was no noticeable effect upon the vote in the county, where there was a large negro majority. In Raleigh and Wilmington placards were posted all about the streets. Those in the former place were as follows:

K. K. K.

Attention! First Hour! In the Mist!
At the Flash! Come. Come. Come!!!
Retribution is impatient! The grave yawns!
The sceptre bones rattle!
Let the doomed quake!

*It is commanded.*
2nd G. C. OF BL. HOST.

The character of the Republican candidates was attacked and attention drawn, often with justice, to their unfitness to represent the people properly, or to perform the duties of the positions to which they aspired. The most striking illustration of the case which the Conservatives were able to make against the Republicans was as follows: New Hanover County had three delegates to the convention, Gen-

der by exorbitant taxation. * * * The Radical party proposes to fill our Congressional representation with those men recently introduced from other quarters of the United States, and to impose them on us through the instrumentality and league of the ignorance of the State."

eral Joseph C. Abbott, A. H. Galloway, and S. S. Ashley. The Republican candidates for the legislature were the two first-mentioned, L. G. Estes, a carpetbagger, and G. W. Price, a negro. Ashley was candidate for the position of superintendent of public instruction. Of all these none had ever listed or paid any taxes. The assessed value of the real estate in Wilmington at the time was $3,200,000. Of this the white people owned more than thirty-nine fortieths, and were in a minority of over seven hundred. The white Republicans, about one hundred and fifty in number, who controlled the majority vote, owned, altogether, about $150,000. This was an extreme case, but it shows the possibilities of the conditions existent at the time. Others of the carpetbaggers who were not taxpayers were Tourgee, Heaton, Deweese, and J. R. French. The great majority of the whites were disgusted with the experiment of the negro in politics, and many of the Republicans felt almost as keenly as the Conservatives the irritating condition of affairs.[1]

As was to be expected, the campaign was exceedingly bitter on both sides. Personal encounters were of frequent occurrence among the candidates, and the most violent personal abuse was common. Holden was hanged in effigy in several places, including the Capitol Square in Raleigh.

The convention had provided for the submission of the question of ratification of the constitution to the voters qualified under the reconstruction acts. The state officers were to be chosen by the voters qualified under the new constitution, which meant manhood suffrage. But the voting

[1] The following is illustrative of the workings of the reconstruction acts: "During reconstruction in North Carolina, three ex-governors, a former justice of the Supreme Court, several ex-Congressmen, and a number of other distinguished men were at a dinner together. The only person present who could vote or hold office was the negro who waited on the table." *Sentinel*, June 9, 1868.

on ratification of the constitution and the election of state and county officers took place at the same time, and, by order of General Canby, on the same ballot. By this piece of entirely unjustifiable partisan politics, which was entirely characteristic of Reconstruction methods and morals, all who had been disfranchised by the reconstruction acts were prevented from voting, and the validity of the acts of the legislature thus elected is therefore open to question. A new registration had been made, and the number registered was increased considerably. The figures were:

| | |
|---|---:|
| Whites | 117,428 |
| Blacks | 79,444 |
| **Total** | **196,872** |

The election was held on April 21, 22, and 23, and resulted in a complete Republican victory. The vote on the ratification of the constitution was—

| | |
|---|---:|
| For Constitution | 93,084 |
| Against Constitution | 74,015 |
| Not voting | 29,773 |

The vote for governor was,[1]

| | |
|---|---:|
| Holden | 92,235 |
| Ashe | 73,594 |

The Conservatives elected only one member of Congress, one judge, of those whom the Republicans had not endorsed, and one solicitor. Of the eighty-nine counties, the Republicans carried fifty-eight. It was conceded that the Republicans polled almost their full strength. Thus it is seen that a large number of Conservatives, qualified to vote, failed to do so. This was, in part, the result of the general belief that, if the Conservatives were successful, Congress

---

[1] The figures are taken from *N. C. Legislative Docs.*, 1868-9.

would set aside the election, or refuse to remove the disabilities of those Conservatives who were elected to office. And doubtless, such would have been the case.

Fraud was common all over the State. By an amendatory act of Congress, passed March 11, 1868, voting upon affidavit instead of registration, was authorized, and ten days was set as the period of required prior residence. This gave room for illegal voting, and, consequently, many voted in different counties on different days.[1]

The Conservatives now directed their energies towards organization for the coming national election, hoping that victory might result, and that the new government might be overthrown. Holden and the Republican leaders, on the other hand, entered into communication with the Republican leaders in Congress, hoping to hasten the final steps of reconstruction. The State had carried out nearly all of its part of the process; and it remained for Congress to take final action and restore the State to its place in the Union.

As has been seen,[2] the convention placed itself on record in regard to the impeachment of the President. Holden, also, had taken strong ground for it, stating that " the salvation of the South depends on the conviction of Andrew Johnson." [3] He now, in the hope of securing the immediate admission of the representatives from the State, telegraphed various Northern papers, urging the displacement of the President, and stating that war would begin again in North Carolina if the President should be acquitted before the State was admitted to representation in Congress and the

[1] Daniel R. Goodloe wrote Charles Sumner protesting against the election as a bare-faced fraud.

[2] *Cf. supra*, p. 271.

[3] *Standard*, April 15, 1868.

new state government was installed.   One of the telegrams was, in part, as follows:

> Prompt action on the part of Congress, in relation to the administration of North Carolina, will be our only hope to avert a terrible civil war again, in the event that the usurper in the White House shall be acquitted.   In the name of humanity, liberty, and justice, can it be possible that Andrew Johnson will be acquitted?
>
> W. W. HOLDEN.[1]

### 4. THE COMPLETION OF RECONSTRUCTION

Although the constitution had been ratified and officers elected under it, the approval of Congress had not been given to it, nor had consent been given to put the new government into operation.   In addition, a majority of the newly-elected state and county officers and of the members of the legislature were under disabilities.   Besides the disabilities which were based upon the proposed Fourteenth Amendment, there was also the requirement that all state officers installed prior to the formal resoration of the State should take the " iron-clad " oath.   General Canby announced this with the publication of the election returns. This caused consternation among the " loyal," and Congress was looked to for relief.   But Congress for a considerable time failed to act.   Finally an act was passed which, after declaring the constitutions of six Southern States, includ-

---

[1] Quoted in *Sentinel*, May 20, 1868.   John Pool on May 9, 1868, wrote Holden, urging him not to give way to any kindly feeling towards secessionists, and closed his letter as follows: " I could not quietly submit to be again placed under the government of secessionists.   They ought to understand that the Union men would resort to force and violence before they would be again tyrannized over by men whose morality was not shocked by robbery, whose humanity was not aroused by either murder or the most atrocious cruelty, and whose insane hatred can now be neither opposed nor limited."

ing North Carolina, republican in form, provided the representatives from them should be admitted, whenever the proposed Fourteenth Amendment had been ratified by their legislatures. Their admission was also upon the condition that the constitution of none of them should ever be so amended or changed as to deprive of the right to vote in the State any citizen or class of citizens of the United States, who were entitled to vote under the constitution then recognized, except as a punishment for crimes then felonious at common law, of which they had been duly convicted.[1] This bill was vetoed by the President, on the ground that his approval of it would imply approval of the reconstruction acts. It was then passed over his veto and became a law. This was construed by General Canby to remove the necessity for the taking of the test oath by the new administration, and he so notified the governor-elect, and later issued an order to that effect.[2]

The same day that the bill admitting representatives from North Carolina became a law, the disabilities of nearly seven hundred persons, the majority of whom had been recommended by the convention, were removed. Fifty-three of the carpetbaggers also sent in a petition for the removal of disabilities. With very few exceptions, the lists contained only the names of Republicans.[3] This enabled the state government to be organized. By the act admitting representatives, the governor-elect was authorized to summon the legislature to meet, and on June 25, before it became a law by passage over the President's veto, Governor-elect Holden issued a proclamation summoning the General

---

[1] Act of June 25, 1868.

[2] *Sentinel*, June 27, 1868.

[3] The convention refused to recommend B. F. Moore, among others. His name, however, was added while the list was before Congress.

Assembly to meet on July 1.[1]   On June 29, General Canby instructed the chief-justice-elect to take the oaths of office before a United States commissioner, and then to administer them to his associates and to the state officers.   Chief Justice Pearson notified Governor Worth that he would administer the oaths to the governor on July 1.   The same day, Governor Worth was removed from office by a military order from General Canby.   The oaths were administered to Governor Holden the next day, and Governor Worth surrendered the office with the following protest:

STATE OF NORTH CAROLINA,<br>
EXECUTIVE DEPARTMENT,<br>
RALEIGH, July 1, 1868.

GOV. W. W. HOLDEN, *Raleigh, N. C.*

SIR:—Yesterday morning I was verbally notified by Chief Justice Pearson that, in obedience to a telegram from General Canby, he would, to-day at ten o'clock A. M., administer to you the oaths required preliminary to your entering upon the discharge of the duties of Civil Governor of the State, and that, thereupon, you would demand my office.

I intimated to the Judge my opinion that such proceeding was premature, even under the reconstruction legislation of Congress, and that I should probably decline to surrender the office to you.   At sundown yesterday evening, I received from Colonel Williams, Commandant of this Military Post, an extract from General Orders, No. 12, of General Canby, as follows:

" HEADQUARTERS SECOND MILITARY DISTRICT,<br>
CHARLESTON, S. C., June 30, 1868.

GENERAL ORDERS, No. 12.

(*Extract.*)

To facilitate the organization of the new State government,

---

[1] *Standard,* June 17, 1868.   Byron Laflin wrote Holden from Washington on June 15, saying that this was the advice of General Rawlins and a number of Republican senators.

the following appointments are made: To be Governor of North Carolina, W. W. Holden, Governor-elect, vice Jonathan Worth, removed. To be Lieutenant-Governor of North Carolina, Tod R. Caldwell. Original vacancy. To take effect July 1st on the meeting of the General Assembly of North Carolina."

I do not recognize the validity of the late election, under which you and those co-operating with you claim to be invested with the civil government of the State.

You have no evidence of your election, save the certificate of a major-general of the United States Army. I regard all of you as in effect appointees of the military power of the United States, and not as deriving your powers from the consent of those you claim to govern.

Knowing, however, that you are backed by military force here, which I could not resist, if I would, I do not deem it necessary to offer a futile opposition, but vacate the office without the ceremony of actual eviction, offering no further opposition than this my protest.

I would submit to actual expulsion in order to bring before the Supreme Court of the United States the question as to the constitutionality of the legislation under which you claim to be the rightful governor of the State, if the past action of that tribunal furnished any hope of a speedy trial.

I surrender the office to you under what I deem military duress, without stopping, as the occasion would well justify, to comment upon the singular coincidence that the present State government is surrendered as without legality to him whose own official sanction, but three years ago, proclaimed it valid.

I am, very respectfully,

JONATHAN WORTH,
*Governor of North Carolina.*[1]

Governor Holden delivered his inaugural address on

---

[1] *Executive Correspondence*, Worth, vol. ii, p. 17. Gov. Worth continued to reside in Raleigh until his death, in September, 1869.

July 4 to an enormous audience, composed, for the most part, of negroes. He reviewed the new constitution, and declared that the government established under it must be administered, in every department, by the friends of reconstruction. He defended the carpetbaggers, stating what was a fact, that most of the leaders in the history of the State had also been born elsewhere. He declared his opposition to mixed schools and urged a development of public education for both races. He promised the colored voters that the ballot would never be taken from them, and threatened confiscation, if an attempt should be made to do so. Speaking of negro suffrage, he said: " The repugnance to it, which exists among many of our people, will gradually subside when they shall be convinced by actual experience that none of the evils they anticipated have resulted from it." As a whole, the address gave a better promise for the future than was expected, and far better than was fulfilled.

In the meantime, the legislature met and, on July 2, ratified the Fourteenth Amendment.[1] General Canby was notified of the fact, and immediately ordered military interference with civil functions to cease. On July 6, three of the members of Congress from North Carolina were sworn in, and within a few days, two more were admitted. Two were unable to take the "iron-clad " oath,[2] and were compelled to wait until the adoption of the substitute for the benefit of those from whom disabilities had been removed.[3] On July 11, a proclamation by President Johnson announced that North Carolina had fulfilled the requirements of Congress. In the meantime, John Pool and J. C. Abbott had

---

[1] The vote on the ratification of the Fourteenth Amendment was: Senate, 34 yeas, 2 nays. House, 82 yeas, 19 nays.

[2] Nathaniel Boyden and O. H. Dockery.

[3] *Laws,* 40 Cong., 2 sess., chap. 139.

been elected to the Senate over William A. Graham [1] and M. E. Manly, and were sworn in on the thirteenth. By July 20, the representation of the State was complete. North Carolina was thus restored to her place in the Union and, legally, reconstruction was at an end. But from a social and economic standpoint, or from an internal political standpoint, it now began.

[1] Garrett Davis wrote Graham on July 7, and urged him to present himself at once at the bar of the Senate and demand to be sworn in on the ground of his previous election.

## CHAPTER SEVEN

### The Freedmen's Bureau [1]

#### I. ORGANIZATION

AMONG the most important factors in the work of Reconstruction was the Freedmen's Bureau. Created for the purpose of caring for the homeless, destitute, and suffering of the negro race, regarded by many as the wards of the nation, it became by judicious manipulation the most active radical political agency in the South, and because of that fact it has often failed to receive due credit for the good which it actually accomplished.

No sooner had the Union troops gained control of Southern territory than the problem of the Negro became one of great importance. Leaving their homes by thousands, the Negroes thronged to the camps and thus became dependent upon the troops, not only for protection against re-enslavement, but also for food and clothing. It was not in accord with Northern sentiment that they should be returned to their owners, and it was manifestly impossible to turn them adrift, not only on account of the cruelty of the action, but because they refused to be left. In several of the States, provision was made for their support and employment by the so-called Department of Negro Affairs which was conducted by military officers and which was supported by the proceeds of captured and confiscated property and by voluntary contributions from the North.[2] In North Carolina

---

[1] Reprinted from the *South Atlantic Quarterly*, Jan. and April, 1909.

[2] Garner, *Reconstruction in Mississippi*, pp. 249-253. Fleming, *Civil War and Reconstruction in Alabama*, pp. 421-424.

a multitude of Negroes came under control of the army in 1862 when New Bern was taken by the Union forces. The number increased constantly throughout the war and the problem of caring for them assumed a serious aspect. In 1865, when Sherman's columns entered the State, a swarm of negroes from South Carolina followed them, augmented from day to day by numerous recruits from North Carolina. When the army reached Fayetteville about 8,000 were in attendance. Most of these were sent from there to Wilmington, where a great number had already congregated.[1] When, in the summer of 1865, General Schofield assumed command in the State, he issued a series of regulations for the guidance of freedmen. This action, like the policy of military commanders elsewhere in the South, was not regarded as sufficient for the solution of the problem, as indeed it was not.

In the meantime, other agencies for the relief of the freedmen had been actively at work. Under the act of March 3, 1863,[2] the Secretary of the Treasury had been authorized to appoint special agents to collect captured and abandoned property in the insurrectionary States. These agents, to some extent, took hold of the question of the freedmen at once, but by the act of July 2, 1864,[3] they were directed to provide for the welfare of the former slaves, and Secretary Fessenden issued a series of regulations relating to freedmen. These regulations provided for supervision by the general agent of matters relating to the freedmen and for the establishment of freedmen's home colonies and labor colonies, the assignment of land to them, and the establishment of schools.[4] The plan went into

---

[1] *Off. Rec.*, no. 100, pp. 39, 80.

[2] *Statutes at Large*, xii, p. 820.    [3] *Ibid.*, xiii, p. 375.

[4] *Report of the Secretary of the Treasury*, 1864, pp. 294-324.

operation almost immediately, but it was not destined to succeed. The military authorities and the treasury agents clashed and were soon involved in misunderstanding. In many cases, too, the latter were notoriously corrupt. The regulations, however, continued in force until the establishment of the Freedmen's Bureau in 1865.[1]

Aid by the federal government, however, was not all that the freedmen had to look to for organized relief. The American Missionary Society by 1862 had missions and schools established in New Bern, among other places in the South, and its activity continued for many years.[2] Other organizations rendered valuable relief service elsewhere in the South, but did little in North Carolina.

As early as January, 1863, a bill was introduced into Congress providing for the establishment of a bureau of freedmen's affairs, but for various reasons its passage was not secured, and it was not until March 3, 1865, that Congress took definite action. On that day, a bill for the establishment of a bureau for refugees, freedmen, and abandoned lands passed Congress and, signed by President Lincoln, became a law. The act provided for the establishment of a bureau in the War Department which, under regulations prescribed by the commissioner and the President, should supervise and manage all abandoned lands and should control all matters relating to refugees and freedmen from the insurrectionary States and wherever the army was engaged. Its duration was limited to one year from the close of the war. At its head was to be a commissioner appointed by the President, and assistant commissioners might be appointed for each insurrectionary State.[3] Provision was

---

[1] Peirce, *The Freedmen's Bureau*, p. 25.    [2] *Ibid.*, p. 26.

[3] The commissioner was to receive a salary of $3,000, and give bond in the sum of $50,000. The assistant commissioners were to receive $2,500, and give bond in the sum of $20,000.

made for clerks, and it was provided that army officers
might be assigned to duty under the act. Supplies for the
relief of the refugees and freedmen were to be issued by
the War Department, and the commissioner might set apart
confiscated or abandoned lands for the use of the freedmen.
Of these lands, not more than forty acres might be leased
to any male citizen, whether refugee or freedman, and he
was to be protected in its enjoyment for three years. For
the important office of commissioner, President Lincoln,
before his death, chose General Oliver O. Howard, and he
was appointed by President Johnson, who knew the wish of
his predecessor. General Howard was an honest, kindly
gentleman, much given to acting upon theories based upon
insufficient knowledge, and deeply interested in the progress
and welfare of the freedmen. Lacking as he was in practical knowledge and easily deceived, his administration was,
in many respects, a failure through no fault of his own.

For the position of assistant commissioner in North
Carolina, General Howard selected Colonel Eliphalet Whittlesey, of Maine, a cultured gentleman, formerly a professor in Bowdoin College. The assistant commissioner
was given supervision over abandoned land and over all
matters relating to refugees and freedmen. The wants of
the needy were to be supplied and the freedom of the negroes guaranteed. Other matters coming within his province were the family relations of the freedmen, the settlement of differences and difficulties between the negroes and
the whites, assistance to the negroes in securing land, and
the removal of prejudice on the part of old masters. This
last duty shows very clearly the attitude of the bureau.
Stress was also laid upon instruction of the freedmen as
to their new duties and responsibilities. The assistant com-

missioner was subject to military rules, but wide jurisdiction was given him in matters of detail.[1]

On July 1, Colonel Whittlesey entered upon his duties and at once issued an address inviting the co-operation of both races. On July 15, he issued a second circular organizing the bureau in the State.[2] The State was divided into four districts and superintendents appointed as follows:

| DISTRICT | HEADQUARTERS | SUPERINTENDENT |
|---|---|---|
| Eastern | New Bern | Captain Horace James |
| Central | Raleigh | Lieut. Dexter E. Clapp |
| Western | Greensboro | Major Smith |
| Southern | Wilmington | Captain Robert B. Beath |
| | | Major Chas. J. Wickersham.[3] |

Colonel Whittlesey's first intention was to make each county a sub-district, and in pursuance of this plan he wrote a note to every member of the convention of 1865, then in session, asking for recommendations of suitable men in each county as agents. Not a delegate replied.[4] He was, however, opposed to any but military officers acting as agents, and, as there was a lack of these, he had to change his plan, and in consequence two to eight counties were embraced in each sub-district. The eastern district had eight sub-districts; the central, nine; the western, six; and the southern, four. During the first year there were thirty-three assistant superintendents, but the largest number at any one time was twenty. Three times the organization

[1] Peirce, *The Freedmen's Bureau*, pp. 50-52.

[2] The following were appointed to duty at headquarters: Major Charles J. Wickersham, assistant adjutant general; Lieutenant Fred H. Beecher, acting assistant adjutant general; Capt. Thomas P. Johnston, assistant quartermaster; Capt. George C. Almy, commissary of subsistence; Surgeon Lewis D. Harlan, medical officer.

[3] Major Wickersham succeeded Captain Beath almost immediately.

[4] *Ho. Ex. Docs.*, no. 27, 39 Cong., 1 sess., p. 14.

was almost broken up by the mustering-out of regiments.[1]
In 1867, the State was divided into ten sub-districts, aver-
aging eight counties each. Whenever possible, a military
officer was assigned to each section of three counties, but
this was not often practicable. Later the sub-divisions were
again reduced to four: Goldsboro, Raleigh, Wilmington,
and Morganton. In his instructions to the officers of the
bureau, Colonel Whittlesey stated the following objects:
(1) to aid the destitute, without encouraging dependence;
(2) to protect the freedmen from injustice; (3) to assist
freedmen in obtaining employment at fair wages; and (4)
to encourage education.[2] In the main, Colonel Whittlesey's
instructions were marked by moderation and good sense.
In his address, however, he could not refrain from the following characteristic advice to the white people of the
State: " The school house, the spelling book, and the Bible
will be found better preservers of peace and good order
than the revolver and bowie knife." But he warned the
officers that complaints would be greatly exaggerated and
that prudence was necessary to avoid injustice to both races.
To the freedmen, he said that they were given new rights,
but with these rights went new duties and responsibilities
which must be fulfilled. He further warned them that they
must be honest, patient, and law-abiding and assured them,
in such a case, of the friendship of all good men. On August 15, he advised them to enter into contracts for labor,
assuring them of the falsity of all rumors that they were to
be given land by the United States government. This
" forty acres and a mule " myth, which had been begun and
fostered by subordinate officers of the bureau and by Northern people in the South, he denounced as " an attempt of

[1] *Ho. Ex. Docs.*, no. 70, 39 Cong., 1 sess., pp. 386, 387.
[2] *Ibid.*, pp. 3-4.

rebel politicians to fire the Southern heart.[1]  The myth was spread and generally accepted by the negroes until 1866 and was a great hindrance to any improvement in labor conditions.

In May, 1866, Colonel Whittlesey, in consequence of the report of Generals Steedman and Fullerton, was displaced and was succeeded by General Thomas H. Ruger, then in command of the department.  In June the latter was assigned to other duties and was succeeded by General John C. Robinson.  Upon the departure of the latter, early in 1867, Colonel James V. Bomford acted as assistant commissioner until April, when General Nelson A. Miles assumed the office, which he filled until the termination of the bureau's activity, January 1, 1869.

During the whole period of the existence of the bureau, there was constant changing of subordinate officials, with a consequent loss of efficiency through the inexperience and ignorance of those who continued the work scarcely begun by their predecessors.

### 2. RELIEF WORK, LABOR, AND THE ADMINISTRATION OF JUSTICE

Of all the activities of the bureau, the most important was the relief of the destitute.  It is in regard to this matter, also, that it deserves most praise and least blame.  And yet, it was in connection with this that the greatest corruption appeared.  The gravest charges, however, as will appear, were not of corruption, but of inefficiency, ignorance, and intense prejudice.

The first problems that had to be settled were how to feed the starving and to clothe the naked.  Reference has already been made to the flocking of the freedmen to the towns, where hundreds, if not thousands, declining to work even

[1] *Ho. Ex. Docs.*, no. 70, 39 Cong., 1 sess., pp. 2-4.

when opportunity was afforded, were without any means of support, and were on the verge of starvation. There were also many refugees who were destitute and to these the bureau gave much needed assistance. Rations were issued by the bureau, and to some clothing and medicine were furnished.[1] It is unquestionable that much suffering and destitution were thus relieved. But it is equally true that, in spite of many efforts on the part of the higher bureau officials to prevent it, advantage was taken of this relief by the undeserving and that, in the case of freedmen, it was an encouragement to idleness and a serious hindrance to an early settlement of the labor problem. Dishonest bureau officials also used the system to build up individual influence among the negroes, and for these reasons it gained for the bureau in time the dislike and opposition of the white population. Negroes often came many miles to draw rations and then exchanged them for luxuries, which were consumed at once.[2] So great became the complaint that in August, 1866, General Howard ordered that the issuing of rations should be discontinued except to the sick in hospitals and to orphan asylums.[3] This greatly reduced the amount expended by the bureau and may have, to some extent, improved labor conditions. But in the winter and

---

[1] A ration was as follows: pork or bacon, 10 ounces in lieu of fresh beef; fresh beef, 16 ounces; flour and soft bread, 16 ounces, twice a week; hard bread, 12 ounces, in lieu of flour or soft bread; corn meal. 16 ounces, five times a week; beans, peas, or hominy, 10 pounds to 100 rations; sugar, 8 pounds to 100 rations; vinegar, 2 quarts to 100 rations; candles, 8 pounds to 100 rations; soap, 2 pounds to 100 rations; salt, 2 pounds to 100 rations; pepper, 2 ounces to 100 rations. Women and children were also allowed rye coffee at 10 pounds per 100 rations, or tea at 15 pounds per 100 rations. *Ho. Ex. Docs.*, no. 11, 39 Cong., 1 sess., p. 47.

[2] *Ho. Ex. Docs.*, no. 70, 39 Cong., 1 sess., p. 387.

[3] *Ho. Ex. Docs.*, no. 1, 39 Cong., 2 sess., p. 712.

spring of 1867, owing to the severe winter and the failure of crops the previous season, there was much suffering, and the order, already carried out only in a modified form, was supplanted by a special resolution of Congress, setting aside a relief fund. Of this, during May, June, and July, $32,480 was spent in North Carolina, and 10,185 persons were assisted.[1] Besides this, in the period from June 1, 1865, to September 1, 1868, when the issue of rations was of most importance, there were issued in North Carolina 1,895,-065½ rations, valued at $473,766.50.[2] No report was ever published in relation to clothing and other supplies furnished by the bureau, but allusions to the matter show that a large amount was expended in this way.

Closely related to this relief of the destitute was the treatment of the sick, and, as has been seen, a medical department was established at once. Eight hospitals in all were established, located at Wilmington, Raleigh, Beaufort, New Bern, Roanoke Island, Salisbury, Greensboro, and Morganton, with a united capacity of six hundred patients. Dispensaries were established in 1865 at Raleigh, New Bern, and Wilmington, and later others were added. Regimental surgeons were assigned to duty in the hospitals and dispensaries, but, on account of the lack of such officers, there were never more than four in any one year of the bureau's existence, and, consequently, contract surgeons were employed, the highest number in any one year being

---

[1] *Ho. Ex. Docs.*, no. 1, 40 Cong., 2 sess., p. 641.

[2] The statistics by years in relation to the issue of rations are as follows:

| Period | To Refugees. | To Freedmen. | Total. |
|---|---|---|---|
| June 1, 1865 to Sept. 1, 1866 | 6,716 | 1,419,978½ | 1,426,394½ |
| To Sept. 1, 1867 | 55,129 | 311,799 | 366,928 |
| To Sept. 1, 1868 | 235 | 101,508 | 101,743 |
| Total for period | 62,080 | 1,833,285½ | 1,895,365½ |

fourteen. Attendants in the hospitals were employed by the bureau, the highest number at any one time being forty-five, in 1867. Much benefit came from the work of the medical department and it deserves the highest praise for its efficiency. In the period from the organization of the bureau until July 1, 1869, 40,186 freedmen and 157 refugees were treated. Of these, 4,588 freedmen and 21 refugees died, a percentage of .114 and .135 respectively. The percentage of deaths among the colored patients in 1865 was .49, falling to .03 in 1868, but rising to .42 in 1869, when practically all the patients were incurably diseased.[1]

[1] The following tables give the details of the medical establishment in North Carolina:

| Period. | Hospitals. | Capacity. | Dispensaries. | Asylums. |
|---|---|---|---|---|
| Oct. 1, 1865 | 3 | 140 | — | 3 |
| Oct. 1, 1866 | 8 | 600 | 3 | — |
| July 1, 1867 | 6 | 447 | 1 | — |
| July 1, 1868 | 1 | 75 | 6 | — |
| July 1, 1869 | 1 | 75 | 6 | — |

In 1866 negroes were admitted to the State hospital for the insane.

MEDICAL STAFF.

| Period. | Army Surgeons. | Contract Surgeons. | Attendants. Male. | Female. |
|---|---|---|---|---|
| Oct. 1, 1865 | 1 | 5 | 9 | 13 |
| Oct. 1, 1866 | 4 | 14 | 16 | 18 |
| July 1, 1867 | 2 | 12 | 26 | 19 |
| July 1, 1868 | 2 | 10 | 17 | 19 |
| July 1, 1869 | 1 | 4 | — | 6 |

PATIENTS TREATED AND DIED.

| Period. | Freedmen. Treated. | Died. | Per Cent. | Refugees. Treated. | Died. | Per Cent. |
|---|---|---|---|---|---|---|
| Oct. 30, 1865 | 5,686 | 2,752 | .49 | 157 | 21 | .135 |
| Sept. 1, 1866 | 15,767 | 1,176 | .069 | — | — | — |
| July 1, 1867 | 7,662 | 292 | .036 | — | — | — |
| July 1, 1868 | 8,699 | 268 | .03 | — | — | — |
| July 1, 1869 | 2,372 | 100 | .422 | — | — | — |

But the bureau was created not only to care for those incapacitated for labor; its purpose was also to furnish an opportunity for labor to those who could support themselves. This was done in two ways: (1) by settling the freedmen upon confiscated and abandoned land, and (2) by exercising supervision of the contracts made for labor on the part of the freedmen. The land contemplated by the act of Congress was in the hands of the Treasury Department, but was soon turned over to the bureau. Much of it had already been leased out by the treasury agents, and no attempt was made by the bureau to interfere in such cases, but plans were made to dispose of it to freedmen and loyal refugees at the expiration of the terms of lease. President Johnson, however, took the sound view that a pardon restored property rights, and, to General Howard's great disappointment, he ordered the restoration of the property of all such pardoned persons.[1] Consequently the restoration of the land commenced at once. The bureau had possession in North Carolina of 98,568 acres and 420 pieces of town property. By January, 1866, 50,029 acres and 287 pieces of town property had been restored and most of the remainder was restored within the next two years.[2] The bureau officials were guilty of overbearing and improper conduct in a number of instances in the seizure of property. In Wilmington, the city library room in the city hall was seized and occupied for nearly a year, in spite of numerous protests by the citizens and the city authorities.[3] And a still more flagrant case occurred in New Bern, where

[1] General Howard in his *Autobiography*, vol. ii, chap. xlix, has much to say of what he calls the injustice of the President's action.

[2] The figures given are approximately correct, according to the reports of the assistant commissioner. So much carelessness appears, and so many contradictions, that they cannot be entirely accurate.

[3] *Wilmington Journal*, Oct. 2, 1866.

Capt. Horace James,[1] of the bureau, seized the house and lot of Dr. Samuel Marten. Later on Captain Rosekrans succeeded James and, the house having seven rooms, opened a boarding house. Dr. Marten applied for the restoration of his property, but was refused on the ground of a previous difficulty he had had with Captain James. The complaint was forwarded by Governor Worth to Colonel Whittlesey, who refused to surrender the house, stating that it was needed by the bureau.[2] It was later restored by General Howard upon the recommendation of General F. D. Sewall.[3] Such conduct was well calculated to render the public blind to much of the good that the bureau was actually accomplishing.

In some cases the negroes were settled upon private property, and, in spite of all efforts on the part of the owners to dislodge them, possession was secured for a long period.[4] On Roanoke Island the government had divided the seized land into one acre lots, and the negroes were so well satisfied with government support that, in November, 1866, 1,700 were still there in spite of the efforts of the bureau to dislodge them; and the district superintendent recommended the restoration of the land to its owners, that they might compel the freedmen to move.[5] In one or two instances farms were established for dependent paupers, as at Goldsboro in 1866.[6]

Even more far-reaching in its effects upon the State as a

[1] James, according to his own account, had been General Howard's first choice for assistant commissioner.

[2] *Executive Correspondence*, Worth, vol. i, pp. 57, 61.

[3] *Ho. Ex. Docs.*, no. 120, 39 Cong., 1 sess., p. 35.

[4] Bryan *v.* Spivey, 109 N. C., 57.

[5] *Sen. Docs.*, no. 6, 39 Cong., 2 sess., p. 111.

[6] *Ho. Ex. Docs.*, no. 120, 39 Cong., 1 sess., p. 4.

whole than the relief of the destitute, was the relationship existing between labor and the bureau. Soon after the bureau commenced its operations, General Howard issued instructions to his subordinates outlining the general policy of the bureau in this regard. Agents were to be appointed in each sub-district to look after labor matters, with the special duty of approving contracts and settling the rate of wages. In regard to certain things, such as the freedom of choosing employers, the abolition of any form of compulsory, unpaid labor, the abolition of the overseer system, and the prevention of any acts of oppression, the rules were general and inflexible, but his instructions otherwise were merely advisory, to be modified as local conditions might demand. Written contracts were recommended as safer and less likely to cause misunderstanding. To facilitate the work of furnishing employment, Colonel Whittlesey entered into an arrangement with L. P. Olds & Co., a firm of land agents, by which an intelligence office was maintained in almost every county in the State. The agents at once began supervising the making of contracts, and by March 31, 1866, 717 had been witnessed and approved, and over 6,000 negroes had been given employment.[1] The rate of wages varied, but the average was between $8 and $10 per month.[2] The witnessing of contracts, however, was far from making labor conditions satisfactory. Even Colonel Whittlesey, always inclined to regard the freedmen with a more partial eye than he did the Southern whites, was obliged to confess, as early as the fall of 1865, that it was extremely difficult to make the negroes keep their contracts.[3] In their unsettled and excited condition, a long period of

---

[1] No figures are available as to the whole number of contracts witnessed.

[2] *Ho. Ex. Docs.*, no. 70, 39 Cong., 2 sess., p. 391.

[3] *Ho. Reports*, no. 30, 39 Cong., 1 sess., p. 191.

work seemed too irksome, in fact, a return to slavery, and the tendency to idleness was increased by the issue of supplies by the bureau and the ease with which they were obtained. Even when they consented to make contracts, it was in most cases for a short period and, whenever possible, for wages rather than for a share of the crop. This was natural, but, in the practical working out of the plan, most disastrous. In most cases no sooner was a payment of wages made than the laborers, regardless of whether the period of employment had expired or not, abandoned work and proceeded to spend their earnings in riotous living. The bureau was powerless to remedy this; though in most instances that came before him, Colonel Whittlesey did all in his power to assist employers so treated. The same, however, could not be said of most of his subordinates. Another apparently popular plan of the negroes was to refuse to work just when the crops needed most attention. In many cases of this sort, employers were forced by the bureau to fulfil the terms of the contract, regardless of the failure of the other parties. This injustice rankled and was the cause of many of the cases of cruelty which were reported by the bureau in such horror. It was hard for the planters to accustom themselves to a condition of affairs in which a negro could refuse to work, often in a defiant and insolent way, and not be punished for it; and so it is not a remarkable fact that they at times took matters in their own hands. Nor is it to be denied that there were cases of great cruelty and oppression. But these were the exception rather than the rule. The bureau officials, partial to a degree in favor of the negroes, said that four-fifths of the white people were ready to treat the negro with fairness;[1] and it is a fact that many

---

[1] *Ho. Reports*, no. 30, 39 Cong., 1 sess., p. 191.

of the remainder would have been so inclined had it not been for the bureau. As time went by, hostility was injected into the relation between the races, and labor conditions remained in a most unsettled condition for many years. That they were finally settled after a fashion was in no sense due to the exertions of the bureau, but to the education which experience gave both races, and to the natural laws which govern labor. The bureau officials kept the freedmen stirred up and the charge was frequently made that many of the agents made a regular practice of levying contributions from employers by means of threats of taking away their laborers.[1]

To enforce fulfilment of contracts and to protect the freedmen from injustice, the bureau was given judicial powers. The jurisdiction of the bureau courts extended wherever civil courts were interrupted, where negro testimony was not allowed, or where punishment differed for members of the two races, in all cases in which a negro was a party.[2] When the punishment exceeded one month's imprisonment or one hundred dollars fine, the case went to a military commission.[3] In such cases as went to the civil courts, bureau officers were directed to appear as counsel for the freedmen.

For some time after the establishment of the bureau, its courts acted without interruption, but when the provisional state courts established by Provisional Governor Holden began their work, complaint was made of the exercise of jurisdiction by the bureau. Governor Holden and General Ruger, who was in command of the department, made an agreement as to the jurisdiction of the civil and military

---

[1] This charge was wide-spread, but the author has never been able to substantiate it.

[2] *Ho. Ex. Docs.*, no. 11, 39 Cong., 1 sess., p. 45.

[3] *Ibid.*, no. 120, 39 Cong., 1 sess., pp. 10-11.

courts, which was satisfactory for a time, but was not generally observed by the bureau courts.[1]

As soon as Governor Worth came into office, he made efforts to secure full jurisdiction for the civil courts. The laws of the State, after March 10, 1866, made little discrimination between the races, and it was thought that no valid objection could be made to leaving the entire administration of justice to the state courts. In the case of but one crime was the punishment different for black and white,[2] and negro testimony was admitted in all cases where a negro was concerned. In all other cases it was admissible by consent. This difference, however, was sufficient to prevent the bureau from surrendering full jurisdiction, especially as it was provided in the law that negro testimony should not be admitted until state courts were given their full jurisdiction. Jurisdiction in all cases of crimes committed by freedmen, however, was transferred at once.[3] In April, 1866, Colonel Whittlesey attempted to interfere with the whipping of a negro convicted of larceny by writing to Judge Fowle that, as white men were in most cases tried by military commissions, a discrimination against the negroes was the result. Judge Fowle with much point replied that under the law the penalty was the same for black and white and that, if military interference with the courts resulted in injustice, a remedy was easily to be found in leaving the cases to the civil courts.[4]

[1] *Executive Correspondence*, Provisional Governor, pp. 177-9. The agreement was that cases concerning white persons only should be tried by the civil courts, while all those cases concerning negroes should be left to military courts. But the civil courts were given power to order the arrest of negroes and bind them for trial.

[2] An assault with intent to commit rape by a negro upon a white woman was made a capital offence.

[3] *Ho. Ex. Docs.*, no. 120, 39 Cong., 1 sess., p. 5.

[4] *Standard*, April 25, 1866.

In July, the convention removed all distinctions which existed so far as justice was concerned, and, on the thirteenth, General Robinson, who had succeeded Colonel Whittlesey as assistant commissioner, directed the bureau agents to transfer all cases to the proper civil courts except such as related to wages due under contracts witnessed by bureau officials, which, for the sake of promptness, should be adjudicated as before.[1] Other claims went to the civil courts, but bureau officials were ordered to attend courts and see that justice was observed. They were also directed to take jurisdiction in such cases as the civil courts neglected. General Robinson stated later that he had no cause to regret his action, as in nearly every instance the courts were fair and impartial. This opinion was also expressed by General Sewall.[2] This was particularly true in regard to the superior courts.[3] Jurisdiction in the reserved cases was retained until the completion of reconstruction in 1868, when it was surrendered to the regular courts. To facilitate the transition, Governor Holden commissioned all the bureau agents as magistrates.[4]

No accurate figures are preserved regarding the judicial work of the bureau, but an idea of the immensity of it can be gained from a statement of Colonel Whittlesey in May, 1866, that ten thousand cases of difficulty between blacks and whites had already been settled.[5] General Miles wrote General Howard in 1867 that in one office six hundred cases

---

[1] A short time before this Governor Worth had been engaged in a very heated correspondence with General Robinson, who he thought was making a deliberate effort to bring the administration of justice in the State into disrepute.

[2] *Ho. Ex. Docs.*, no. 120, 39 Cong., 1 sess., p. 35.

[3] *Sen. Docs.*, no. 6, 39 Cong., 2 sess., pp. 101-2.

[4] *Ho. Ex. Docs.*, no. 1, 40 Cong., 3 sess., p. 1038.

[5] *Ibid.*, no. 123, 39 Cong., 1 sess., p. 21.

and in another four hundred were settled within a period of four months.[1]

As to the character of the justice administered by the bureau there is but little doubt. Probably in many cases it prevented injustice; certainly in more it perpetrated injustice. The testimony of a negro, regardless of his character and often of his knowledge of the matter involved, was usually accepted as more reliable than that of white persons of the highest character and the fullest knowledge of the case.[2] And yet ignorance and prejudice were more responsible for the conduct of the officials than bad intentions. But in many cases the power of the bureau was used by its officials for the purpose of humiliating white citizens and thereby giving the negroes a most vivid and popular manifestation of that power. That the influence of the

[1] *Standard*, December 31, 1867.

[2] An instance of this may be seen in the following case: W. R. Pool, of Wake, in 1867, had a cotton gin burned and fifteen of his hogs stolen. Some of these were killed near by and the blood and tracks were traced to the house of a freedman named Hinton, where a quantity of fresh pork was found concealed in a bed. He was indicted and at once complained to the bureau. The following letter was the result:

" BUREAU OF FREEDMEN, REFUGEES AND ABANDONED LAND,
OFFICE OF AGENT SUB-DISTRICT OF RALEIGH,
RALEIGH, N. C., Dec. 4, 1867.

W. R. Pool:—Albert Hinton complains that you charge him with stealing meat. Mr. Pool, things have come to a strange pass if a colored man cannot buy meat from a wagon in the road without incurring the charge of stealing. You had better look further than this man's house. Perhaps your olfactories will enable you to get on the right scent. You might come to market and seize every piece of meat you find on the stand, on the same principle on which you charge him of stealing. You will call at this office and explain this matter. These men shall be protected in what is just. Yours respectfully,

H. C. VOGELL,
Agt. B. R. F. & A. L."

This letter is to be found in the *Sentinel*, Dec. 19, 1867.

bureau courts upon the negroes was bad is testified to by many competent and qualified to judge. Nor was its influence good upon the white people, for it tended to bring about a condition of utter insubordination and contempt for all courts.[1]

[1] A. S. Merrimon to Jonathan Worth, Aug. 9, 1867. *Executive Correspondence*, Worth, i, p. 555.

The following extract from a letter of Major H. C. Lawrence to William A. Graham, dated Feb. 14, 1866 shows such a clear perception of conditions by a Northern Republican and a former agent of the Bureau that it seems well to quote it.

" Whilst there was and could be, no law but military law, or rather authority, the Bureau was a necessity to some extent. But to continue it after the States shall have given the blacks their civil rights seems to me the very reverse of sound policy, considered simply with reference to that. It will engender hatred towards the blacks on the part of the whites, as a favored class to whom extra legal protection is given by the Federal Government—hatred towards the Government itself, which, by this system, pronounces the people regardless of justice, and brands courts and bar and juries, in advance, as ready perjurers. It substitutes for men learned in the law and soon to administer it, for trial by jury and the right of appeal, the decision of men who, in many cases, if not most, will know nothing of law; who will often be prejudiced, and some corrupt. It will incite in the blacks, to some extent, a sense of independence of the local laws, sanction their distrust of them, the courts, and people, and certainly cannot tend to educate them in the duties of citizens. Instead of allaying, it will beget jealousy and ill-will between the races to a greater degree than now exists, and finally produce the very evils it is intended to guard against. And how such a system can be exercised, except as a temporary military necessity in a conquered country, I cannot conceive. It is liable to all our old objections to the " fugitive slave law ", and, unlike that, will be an ever-present, ever-acting evil; and its provisions are very incomplete for the end proposed, unless it is assumed that military authority is to remain paramount. * * * * * But if a State should establish such a judicial system, I think the Federal Government might well be called upon to enforce its guaranty of a republican form of government to the people of that State. I think it would be a less outrage upon the principles of self-government and upon the Constitution to treat the South as conquered territory and govern it by our territorial system, than to do what is proposed to be done."

Another activity of the bureau was the apprenticing of orphan negro children and watching the county courts to see that no such children were illegally bound out. Under the act of March 10, 1866, former masters were given the preference in securing apprentices, and this was held by the bureau to be a discrimination, working injustice to the negro and smacking too strongly of slavery. Consequently it was overruled at once. Colonel Whittlesey thought the whole system of apprenticeship wrong, because it resembled slavery.[1] In this matter the bureau undoubtedly rendered a good service, for it checked a disposition on the part of many to hold colored children in a state of subjection. All persons to whom colored children were bound were required to give a bond for the fulfilment of the contract, which required education of the apprentice to the extent of reading, writing, and arithmetic.[2] The theory of the bureau in regard to apprentice cases was based upon sound principles, but in its practical application it was at times severe upon both races. Arbitrary methods marked this sphere of bureau activity as they did all others. Opposition developed in the State, and Governor Worth even appealed to General Howard against General Robinson's action in certain cases but without effect.[3] The system continued until the State was reconstructed.

Closely connected with the relief work of the bureau, though not a part of it, was the Freedmen's Savings and Trust Company, a banking institution, chartered by Congress and intended to encourage habits of thrift among the negroes. Three branches were established in North Carolina, at New Bern, Raleigh, and Wilmington, respectively. The conduct of the company was characterized by care-

[1] *Sen. Docs.*, no. 27, 39 Cong., 1 sess., p. 16.

[2] *Ibid.*, no. 6, 39 Cong., 2 sess., p. 112.

[3] *Executive Correspondence*, Worth, i, p. 306.

lessness, extravagance, and fraud, and it soon failed. In time the depositors received a part of their money, but a large part was gone forever. The following table shows the total deposits in the North Carolina branches and what was repaid:

| BRANCH. | DEPOSIT. | REPAID. |
|---------|----------|---------|
| New Bern | $18,473.67 | $11,950.16 |
| Raleigh | 16,423.36 | 10,920.23 |
| Wilmington | 22,149.27 | 14,608.57 |
| Total | $57,046.30 | $37,478.96 |

The experience of the negroes with this institution bred a deep distrust of banks, which has not to this day been entirely removed. A more serious injury was the discouragement of habits of saving which resulted from this first experience.

### 3. EDUCATION

Probably in the mind of the commissioner of the Freedmen's Bureau, the most important duty intrusted to that organization was the education of the freedmen. Work in this field had been commenced in New Bern in 1862 by Vincent Colyer, of Massachusetts, and had been extended later by various religious denominations and benevolent associations. When the bureau undertook the relief of the destitute, these organizations devoted practically their whole attention to education.[1]

The act for the establishment of the bureau made no provision for negro education, and, therefore, for the first year it did little in the way of educational work. Some assist-

---

[1] The following were the most important of these organizations: The New England Freedmen's Relief Association, New York National Freedmen's Relief Association, American Missionary Association, Friends' Freedmen's Aid Association, Freedmen's Commission, the Protestant Episcopal Church, and the Presbyterian General Assembly.

ance, however, was given to the charitable organizations just mentioned. Colonel Whittlesey in his address had held out to the freedmen a promise of education, and on July 15, he gave assurance that schools and teachers would be protected by the bureau, and he directed all officials to exercise supervision of the schools.[1] A short time later, Rev. F. A. Fiske, a native of Massachusetts, was made superintendent of education, and preparations were made for a vigorous educational campaign. Buildings were assigned by the bureau for the use of the schools, but the enforced surrender of the property of pardoned owners made this assistance of a temporary nature only. But by the provisions of the second bureau act, authority was given for increased educational activity, and the commissioner was empowered to supply buildings and furnish protection for the schools. More important still, a considerable sum was appropriated for educational work, and this was increased by later acts.[2]

In North Carolina the number of schools receiving assistance fluctuated, but a steady increase is to be noticed from year to year. On October 1, 1865, there were 63 such schools in operation with 85 teachers and 5,624 scholars. On July 1, 1869, there were 431 schools with 439 teachers and 20,227 scholars.[3] The majority of the teachers were white,

---

[1] *Ho. Ex. Docs.*, no. 70, 39 Cong., 1 sess., p. 4.

[2] *Statutes at Large*, xiv, 173, 434.

[3] The following table shows the increase from time to time:

| TIME | SCHOOLS | TEACHERS | PUPILS |
|---|---|---|---|
| October 1, 1865 | 63 | 85 | 5,624 |
| January 1, 1866 | 88 | 119 | 8,506 |
| April 1, 1866 | 119 | 154 | 11,314 |
| October 1, 1866 | 62 | 68 | 3,493 |
| March 1, 1867 | 156 | 173 | 11,102 |
| October 1, 1867 | 158 | 158 | 7,897 |
| April 1, 1868 | 336 | 339 | 16,435 |
| July 1, 1869 | 431 | 439 | 20,227 |

and nearly all of them, both white and colored, were from the North. Transportation to and from the North was furnished by the bureau for a time in order to encourage teachers to come South, but the supply was limited and the need of institutions for the training of colored teachers was soon recognized, and substantial aid was given such institutions at St. Augustine's School in Raleigh and Biddle Memorial Institute in Charlotte.[1]

As might be expected no figures are available as to the amount spent by the bureau for educational work in North Carolina, but the following facts may throw some light upon the subject. From January to June, 1867, the bureau spent $5,525.85.[2] In 1869 and 1870, about $35,000 was spent yearly.[3] The expenditure in 1869 was $1,700 monthly for support alone.[4] Here, as in other departments of the bureau, existed opportunity for fraud, which, in consequence, was by no means unknown.[5] By this time the public school system of the State, as re-established by the convention of 1868, had gone into operation. Public and private schools included, there were in the State 347 schools for colored people, employing 372 teachers and having in attendance 23,419 pupils.[6]

All concerned with educational work among the negroes bore testimony to the eagerness with which they sought knowledge, and high hopes were entertained of the result.[7]

---

[1] Now Biddle University. Both these institutions are still in existence and are doing a useful work among the negroes.

[2] *Ho. Ex. Docs.*, no. 1, 42 Cong., 2 sess., p. 653.

[3] *N. C. Leg. Docs.*, 1870-71, no. 6, p. 315.

[4] *Report of Superintendent of Public Instruction* for 1869-70, p. 26.

[5] *N. C. Leg. Docs.*, 1870-71, no. 6, p. 269.

[6] *Ibid.*, p. 280.

[7] The following is a typical account of school work among the

Such an eagerness was to be expected, for the freedmen, naturally imitative, were striving for everything which seemed an attribute of freedom, and the teachers never lost an opportunity of telling them of the new life which education, as they said, would open up to them. No thought apparently was given to the real conditions to be faced, and, to the average freedman, a smattering of education meant freedom from all toil thenceforth. The trouble with the whole plan was the one which has hampered progress ever since. It opened no new field for the activities of the negro, and, in far too many instances, entirely unfitted him for the sphere for which his circumstances as well as his nature and capabilities best prepared him. At best the education given was, as might be expected, of a merely superficial kind and would have been insufficient under the most favorable circumstances. Upon the negro it was in most cases productive of little if any good.

Much complaint was made of opposition to negro education on the part of the native whites. This was in great part due to the bureau and to the teachers in the schools. From the beginning there was opposition among the lower

negroes, pathetic in its utter misunderstanding on the part of both teacher and taught of the realities which had to be faced:

" The benefits of education are opened to old and young, and it is no infrequent occurrence to witness, in the same rooms and pursuing the same studies, the child and the parent—youth and gray hairs, all eagerly grasping for that which obtained, they are intellectually regenerated and are then prepared to enter the new career of life so long a sealed path to them.

"As an evidence of the great interest manifested for acquiring knowledge, an instance, probably never before equalled in the history of education, is to be found in one of the schools of this State, where side by side sit representatives of four generations in a direct line, viz.: a child six years old, her mother, grandmother, and great-grandmother, the latter over seventy-five years of age. All commenced their alphabet together, and now each can read the Bible fluently."

element and a general disbelief among all classes that much good would result from the attempt to educate the freedmen, but among the influential and thinking people of the State there was no hostility, and it was favored by them rather than otherwise, provided that they were not taxed to pay for it. It was the fault of the bureau that this class was not actively enlisted in the cause of colored education. It was also constantly charged, and with truth, that the negro school houses were often burned by white people, but it was not generally recognized that the true explanation of these demonstrations of hostility was that they were directed not against the schools, but against the Union League, which, in many cases, used the school houses for meetings. The school house thus became the center of political activity among the negroes, to say nothing of its being also the source of much violence and crime.

But the explanation of the hostility which later developed towards colored education, as carried on under the auspices of the bureau, is easily to be found. With a due appreciation of the courage, devotion, and often the self-sacrifice of the teachers from the North, one is still forced to the conclusion that, as a class, they lacked moderation, tact, knowledge of the real condition and needs of the negro, and, in far too many cases, that most priceless possession, common sense. They were free in their criticism of the South and frank in expression of their dislike for Southern people. They were indiscreet in public speeches and persistently sought to antagonize the negroes against the white people of the South. They interfered with labor, particularly by influencing house servants so as to create discontent with their surroundings, and with this, they encouraged, directly or indirectly, insolence to employers. They lived often on terms of absolute equality with the negroes and complained that they were not received socially. Finally, in some instances, they were of bad character.[1] These things were nearly all matters within their own discretion. They were not crimes, but simply mistakes fatal to any manifestation of sympathy on the part of the majority of the white people of the State. They are stated, not as accusations, but only by way of explanation of the feeling towards bureau education. And so was lost the valuable ally that the white people of the State would have proved.

After all, however, the main objection to the school work was not this phase of it, but the growing dislike for the bureau, the distrust of its methods, the coming of the negro into politics, and the apparent effect of the so-called education upon him. In the face of all these things it is not remarkable that bitter prejudice should have been aroused among the white people. In addition, there was a strong feeling that the North, having freed the slaves and deprived the South of the power to settle the future relations of the two races, was thereby charged with their education. Consequently by 1868, the prevailing attitude was one of indifference, varied in many cases by violent hostility.

The statement is constantly made that the bureau began the public school system in the South. Whatever it did in other States, and it is by no means clear that any are indebted to it to any great extent,[2] this was not the case in North Carolina and any statement of the kind displays only ignorance on the part of the author.[3] No direct in-

---

[1] *Ho. Ex. Docs.*, no. 120, 39 Cong., 1 sess., p. 37. This statement is made upon the additional authority of information from many persons of entire reliability.

[2] Peirce, *The Freedmen's Bureau*, pp. 85-86.

[3] General Howard in his *Autobiography*, p. 338, asserts: " It is a wonderful thing to recall that North Carolina had never had before that time a free school system even for white pupils, and there was then no publication in the State devoted to popular education. The

fluence of the bureau affected the provision for public education in the constitution of 1868. The former constitution also contained a provision for schools and, had the bureau never existed, it would still be found there. The State had long been committed to public education.

In a final estimate of the educational work of the bureau, great praise must be given for the zeal and activity with which it was carried on. The great defects of the system were, as elsewhere in the bureau, largely the result of ignorance and inefficiency. Owing to this it is doubtful if the negroes received directly from the bureau much permanent benefit. Certainly, so far as concerned the attitude of the white people of the State towards negro education, it was productive of direct injury from which recovery was very slow, if indeed it has ever come.

## 4. GENERAL CHARACTER AND INFLUENCE OF THE BUREAU

No more difficult task can confront the historical investigator than an attempt to form a just estimate of the work, character, and general influence of the Freedmen's Bureau. Possibly no agency of Reconstruction excited more prejudice among the white people of the South regardless of political opinions; probably none more justly deserved criticism and condemnation. That it accomplished much good is undeniable, but that it was of unmixed benefit, or probably even that it accomplished more for the benefit than for the injury of either race, is a delusion, carefully fostered by its own officers and to be found only in the minds of an

death of slavery unfolded the wings of knowledge for both black and white to brighten all the future of the 'Old North State.' "

From 1840 to 1865 North Carolina had a system of common schools in operation, with Calvin H. Wiley, after 1852, as Superintendent of Public Instruction, and about $255,000 was expended yearly for their support. In 1860, there were 2,854 schools, 2,164 licensed teachers, and 135,479 pupils.

over-credulous portion of the public mainly in one section of the country and that the one knowing least about actual conditions in the South.

A summary of its work in North Carolina will show its best and its worst features. As has been seen, four objects were stated by Colonel Whittlesey when he took charge, (1) the relief of the destitute, (2) protection of the freedmen, (3) assistance of the freedmen in obtaining employment, and (4) education. Regarding the first, it is found that great relief was furnished by the bureau during its operations and that hundreds and probably thousands were thus kept from suffering and starvation. And yet it is clear that it encouraged dependence on the part of freedmen, was a cause of considerable confusion in labor matters upon which the prosperity of both races rested, and gave opportunity for extravagance and fraud on the part of the agents. In this connection mention must be made of the scandal in bureau affairs in the State in 1866.

In the spring of that year, in response to orders from the President, General James B. Steedman and General J. S. Fullerton made a tour of the South for the purpose of investigating the work and administration of the bureau. Their report in relation to bureau affairs in North Carolina was a most severe indictment of many of its officials, including Colonel Whittlesey.[1] They reported that feeling in the State against the bureau was most intense and general and was probably due to the misconduct of its officers, many of whom were working plantations, running sawmills, and, with all the advantages which their position gave them, in many other ways coming into direct business competition with citizens employing colored labor. Complaint was also made of the arbitrary methods of the officials and of their

---

[1] The report is to be found in the *Sentinel* of May 3, 1866.

ignorance and disregard of local laws and customs. Colonel Whittlesey was accused of making a false report to them in regard to the matters referred to, and also of being engaged in farming in Pitt County. Similar charges were made against Captain F. A. Seeley, superintendent of the eastern district. Captain Isaac Rosekrans was accused of theft, as was G. O. Glavis, an army chaplain and superintendent of the central district. Charges of cruelty and extortion were made against one Fitz, assistant superintendent of the Trent River settlement, opposite New Bern. The charge was made that Captain Horace James, formerly superintendent of the eastern district, with an employee, had killed a negro convict without any action's being taken against them. Other officials were charged with various offences. Major Clinton A. Cilley, superintendent of the western district, was mentioned as a bright exception and was highly commended.[1] Vehement denials were made by those accused, and it was later clearly shown that the examination had been very hasty and inadequate and that many errors had been made.[2] It is also true that the inspectors had been sent for the purpose of gathering damaging evidence against the bureau to use as proof of the charges President Johnson had made in his veto of the second bureau act, and that, on this account, their report must be taken with a grain of salt. But it is also evident that far too much of it was true.[3]

[1] Major Cilley was a Democrat and not at all popular with his colleagues of the bureau.

[2] *Ho. Ex. Docs.*, no. 123, 39 Cong., 1 sess.

[3] The following is an extract from the report, which gives an idea of the methods of some of the bureau officials:

"In one of our interviews with the freedmen at New Bern, some of them who were employed in the commissary department of the bureau, stated that rations in bulk had been taken from the supply warehouse

General Howard at once declared that the connection of bureau officials with industry was beneficial and that he had encouraged it. He further made the astonishing statement that every accusation against the bureau or against its officials was false.[1] Opinion in the State was divided on the question of the connection of bureau officials with agriculture, but, among other papers, the *Sentinel* took the ground that nothing could be said against it. But, on May 21, General Howard prohibited bureau officials from engaging in business. General F. D. Sewall was also sent by General Howard to inspect and report on the condition and work of the bureau in the State. His report shows utter carelessness on the part of the officials, but he praised the institution in no uncertain terms, more than seems deserved from his own statements of fact, which were as biased in favor of the bureau as those of Generals Steedman and Fullerton had been against it.[2]

at unusual hours, before the doors were opened for the transaction of business, and hauled off in carts and wagons, and that on one occasion they had followed a cart containing four barrels of pork, to see if it went to the freedmen's ration-house. They ascertained that it did not. We investigated the case. Captain Rosekrans stated that he knew nothing about it. His brother, a citizen, whom he has employed to act as commissary sergeant, stated that the four barrels alluded to were ordered by himself to be taken from the store-house to the building from which rations are issued to the freedmen, but *that the driver of the cart had made a mistake and took the pork to the wrong place*, a provision store kept by Mr. P. Merlin, and immediately upon discovering the mistake he had it rectified and the pork returned to the store-house. Afterwards we called upon Mr. Merlin, who stated that at about the time Mr. Rosekrans said that the pork had been sent by mistake to his store, he *borrowed* four barrels of pork from Captain Rosekrans, *which he had not yet returned.* He also stated that Captain Rosekrans on that day, and *after his examination before us*, called at his store and requested him to return the four barrels of pork immediately." *Ho. Ex. Docs.*, no. 120, 39 Cong., 1 sess., p. 68.

[1] Howard to Rev. George Whipple, *Standard*, May 23, 1866.

[2] *Ho. Ex. Docs.*, no. 120, 39 Cong., 1 sess., pp. 31-39.

Colonel Whittlesey at first said that he had no time to answer such charges, but both time and opportunity were given him, for the President on May 16 directed the arrest and trial by court martial of all the accused, including such citizens as were in business partnerships with bureau officials. Few were convicted,[1] but suspicion of the bureau remained, and with cause.[2] General Howard was directed by the court martial to censure Colonel Whittlesey, but said the direction to censure was sufficient, and, refusing to obey the order, recalled him at once to Washington where he gave him duties at bureau headquarters. No stain whatever attaches to Colonel Whittlesey's name, and, during his whole administration, he acted as fairly and impartially as his bias for the negro would allow him.

In the matter of protection of the freedmen, the bureau rendered a substantial service to the cause of justice to the negro, but here again another side, not so favorable, appears. Injustice to the white people was common, and a false idea of freedom and of their position was instilled into the minds of the freedmen to their later detriment.

Little can be said in criticism of the bureau's assistance to the freedmen in securing employment, except that it encouraged dependence and that, through its operations, the negroes were led to distrust the Southern whites.[3] If the

[1] The author has been unable to discover the result of all these trials. Glavis was convicted on several counts and was dismissed from the service. *Nation,* December 20, 1866.

[2] George O. Sanderson, of Massachusetts, for two years superintendent of the colony at Roanoke Island, testified before the Reconstruction Committee that many agents in North Carolina were corrupt. At Roanoke Island, he said, a regular trade was carried on in Government supplies. *Ho. Reports,* no. 30, 39 Cong., 1 sess., pp. 179-180.

[3] On October 12, 1865, when General Howard visited Raleigh, a public meeting was held. Among the speakers, two in particular condemned the bureau as a bad influence in labor matters. These were

charge before mentioned in this connection is true, the case is presented in a much worse light.

Finally, in its educational activities, the bureau was of considerable assistance in encouraging negro education, but, even in this regard, it held out false hopes to the negroes, gave encouragement to false educational ideals which have not yet been entirely replaced by sound ones, and through fanaticism and lack of tact made many enemies for negro education in general.

Apart from the direct objects of the bureau, it was active in a way that created the most intense hostility on the part of the white people. As early as September, 1865, its agents were busying themselves in a political way and preparing for the organization of the freedmen. This activity increased as time passed, and in 1867, the bureau agents were among the most active in extending the organization of the Union League and in arousing the negroes to political activity. An example of bureau methods was seen in Raleigh in 1867, when Dr. H. C. Vogell, a surgeon and bureau agent, issued a circular to the colored people advising them to deal with certain merchants, presumably those favoring the reconstruction policy then in operation.[1] Opinions may and do vary as to the correct view of the reconstruction measures, but there can be but one opinion of such an action as this. Political activity, particularly of the sort that strove to array race against race, was not the true policy, or even a defensible one, for the bureau. When it had come to this, it had outlived its usefulness and it was a good thing for black and white when it ceased to exist.[2]

Edwin G. Reade, president of the convention of 1865, and Alfred Dockery, a member of the same body, both inclining already to the Republican party and both later to become radicals. *Standard*, Oct. 13, 1865.

[1] *Western Democrat*, November 12, 1867.

[2] Major H. C. Lawrence, a bureau agent, in his testimony before the Reconstruction Committee, said that the bureau was no longer needed.

That the faults of the bureau were in the main due to the character of its officials is proved by the fact that, where the agents were men of character and ability, the bureau was an influence for good. This was true in a marked degree in Raleigh, Charlotte, Tarboro, Goldsboro, and Salisbury.[1] But these were exceptional cases, and in general the officers were to be distinguished for ignorance and inefficiency.

Prejudice,[2] often with a reasonable basis, existed towards the bureau from the autumn of 1865, and, though at a later period than that its services were often requested,[3] by January 1, 1869, it had become utterly hateful to the great majority of the white people of the State, who witnessed its demise without regret and with no respect for the departed.

[1] Colonel J. V. Bomford in Raleigh, Captain John C. Barnett in Charlotte, Captain Teal in Goldsboro, and Major Clinton A. Cilley in Salisbury, were popular with both blacks and whites, and there was but little friction between the races while they were in charge.

[2] As an example of the attitude of the press the following extract from the *New Bern Commercial* of May, 1866, is quoted:

"The Freedmen's Bureau is an institution of doubtful utility and needs all proper investigation. It most certainly has a very bad reputation generally, whether deserved or not, and, if half that is reported of it be true, the sooner it is locked and laid aside, the better."

[3] In a number of instances the assistance of the bureau was asked by the state or county governments for the suppression of violence on the part of the negroes.

# CHAPTER EIGHT

## THE UNION LEAGUE [1]

THE Union League was instituted in the North in 1862, when the cause of the Union was at its lowest ebb, with a view to organizing and strengthening loyal sentiment. The idea was popular and the society spread rapidly over the North, the local organizations being connected by a loose federation. Much credit is given the organization for political effect when it was most needed. When the need disappeared, the various branches disbanded or tended to become social clubs composed of members of the same political affiliations.

The society came to North Carolina with the Union armies and from time to time new members were admitted from the Union men in the State. A few negroes were also initiated. But no systematic attempt was made to extend it widely until 1866 when it became evident that Congress would control Reconstruction in the interest of the Republican party, and that negro suffrage was inevitable. The agents of the Freedmen's Bureau had been actively at work among the negroes with a view to using them politically if the opportunity should present itself, and had extended their influence very widely among the newly-emancipated. They had, at the same time, done all in their power to alienate them from the native white population. In the process, they had learned much of the characteristics of the negroes and had become aware of their general insta-

[1] Reprinted from the *Sewanee Review* of Oct., 1912.

bility.  It was therefore clearly apparent that there was a
necessity of taking further steps to control them; to bind
them to the interest of the ambitious Northern politicians
by something which would appeal to their pride and their
emotions, and would at the same time organize them.  The
Union League furnished an ideal instrument through the
effect of its ritual upon the ignorant and emotional negro
and through the discipline of its organization.  It was for
this reason the chosen instrument of the carpet-baggers to
carry on the work so well begun by the Freedmen's Bureau,
and it thus became the second handmaid of Radicalism in
the reconstruction of the State.  Introduced by carpetbaggers, it was, for the entire period of its existence in
North Carolina, controlled by them, chiefly for their own
aggrandizement, and for that reason alone would have
won the undying hatred of the native white population.  In
its development, however, it gave additional and abundant
evidence of its entire unworthiness, and its very name has
remained a symbol of all that was evil in Reconstruction.

During the latter part of 1866 and the early months of
1867, a campaign of extension was entered upon.  This
was entirely in the hands of the aliens, for, while nearly
every native white Republican joined to prove his "loyalty"
and new-found devotion to the Union, the more respectable
element soon became disgusted, and those who had joined
from selfish motives soon found that whatever hopes they
might have cherished of gaining advancement through the
power of the organization were limited by the wishes and
aspirations of the carpetbaggers who regarded the organization as a personal asset and employed it accordingly.  It
often suited them to allow the election of natives to important positions, but frequently the natives got only what
was left.  Even when the position was thus secured, more
frequently than not, there was recognition of the fact that

it was due to the grace of the aliens, and in consequence, their influence was preponderant in the conduct of the office. In the western part of the State, the League never became so important a factor because of the small negro population, the large number of native white Republicans, and also because here were to be found few of the carpetbaggers. Western Republicans joined the League, but it was never popular, and the part of its history that is of importance is confined chiefly to the central and eastern parts of the State.

The work of extension proceeded rapidly and by April, 1867, the State was well organized,[1] and by August of the same year, practically every negro who would vote at the approaching election was an enthusiastic member of the League. Some few declined to join, preferring to be guided by their former owners in their entrance to political life. This species of ingratitude, not to say treason, for so it was regarded by the carpetbaggers, was seen to be a very dangerous menace to the political solidarity of the race, and the colored members of the League were not only encouraged but ordered to deal with such unruly members of the race in a way that would convince them of the wisdom of yielding to Northern guidance and of acceptance of the planned hostility to the whites. The treatment accorded the dissenters was usually effective and a very small proportion of the negroes dared remain out of accord with the majority of their color. Those who did were subjected to every type of violence and intimidation. In Wilmington, a negro was severely whipped by order of the League.[2] In Edgecombe, there was a similar case. In Franklin county, in 1868, the League sent a deputation to attack a reputable white farmer who had advised a servant, who had come to

[1] *Conway Report.*

[2] *Sentinel,* July 20, 1868.

him for counsel, not to join.[1]   Instances of this sort might
be multiplied indefinitely for they occurred all over the
State.   Notices containing threats were posted,[2] and political addresses abounded in suggestions of violence.[3]   Strict

[1] *Sentinel,* Aug. 21, 1868.

[2] An example of this is seen in the following notice which was
posted on the door of a Conservative negro in Hillsboro:

### "NOTICE FOR THOMAS GREEN.

"A d—n Concurvitive . . . , we understand you ware out with Concurvitive lys, but d—n your time if you don't look out you will catch
h—l shure.  We herd you come very near catching it in Sharlot and if
you don't mind you will catch it in Hills Boro shure enough and that
Right.  If your d—n Concervitive friends can protect you, you had
better stick near to them in that hour for great will be your Desterny.
This is the last of Our example.  The next time will tell you your
will on good behavior.
"Postscript.  You mind me of the sun of Esaw and who sold his
birth Right for one mossel of meat and so now you have sold your
wife and children and yourself for a drink of Liquers and have come
to be a Conservitive boot licker.
"Thom, I would not give a d—n for your Back in a few days; you
Conservitive . . . ."  *Sentinel,* April 10, 1868.

[3] The following is a characteristic example:

"Nov. 4, 1867.

*"Genlman of Cole Rain, Bertie County.*
"Voters of Weston Districts will Bare in mind that the (2) Dela-
gats now is Orthorised for the frend of all collars, and that contains
Black and White Genlmans.  Want you all To Du the Best for them
that you can for this Country is in such mens hands like them and I
know that you all Have sum under-standing as Well as me.  And if
you have not for Gods Sacke go to sum Person that you know will
Correct you.  if you Du not we are Hunted fer Ever.  But you all
know That your self and farther were genlmans—how can you vote for
a man whar hav had your labor all your Days and thar ar not meny
That will give you and mee justice.  how can a collard man vote any
other way only fur a cullard man at this time, and after the Constitution then we Will send any Person that we Pleas White or cullard.
But for this time try and make the Best step that you can.  if thar
should Bee any cullard Person that wants to vote A Democratic vote,

orders were given members by their leaders not to attend
Conservative meetings.[1]  To assist in controlling the men,
a league was established for negro women who bound themselves
not to marry or otherwise associate with men who
were not members of the League.[2]  Thus, though boasting
of the liberality of their ideas, and condemning the tendency
of the South to resent differences of opinion in matters
political, the carpetbaggers, from the beginning, not only
discouraged but prevented any possibility of the negroes'
exercising any independence in the enjoyment of the franchise.
That, of course, was not the purpose of Reconstruction
and they cannot be very severely condemned, when
their character is remembered, for refraining at the beginning
from overturning a policy intended mainly to secure
party supremacy.  Such a thing was scarcely to be expected
from their kind, and therefore the chief condemnation
must be directed against the policy itself and against
the bare-faced hypocrisy which accompanied its execution.
The plan looked simply to a complete and unyielding organization
which should force the negroes to register;
arouse them to a high pitch of enthusiasm for the Republican
party and a corresponding degree of hostility against
the Conservatives, and for that matter, in many cases,
against all the white natives; lead them to the polls in an unbroken
phalanx which should secure Republican supremacy
in the State and assist in preserving it in the nation; and in
the process, put into positions of honor, trust, and profit

---

frail him untill he Knows Northing. if you Du that Will Bee just
like thay served them in Veriginia & if thar shud Bee a man of such
a Carractar make him shure fur a while.
                    Thes are able Dellagats
                                MR. PARKER D. ROBBINS.
                                BRIANT GEE."

[1] *Sentinel,* April 17, 1868.              [2] *Ibid.,* April 25, 1868.

(with due emphasis upon the latter), the patriotic would-be statesmen who had dominated the organization from the beginning. Never was a political plan carried out with greater temporary success, for never were the members of a political organization so unfitted through ignorance for the privilege of suffrage, and therefore, unmoved by argument, they were as easily handled as so many sheep. It is no exaggeration to say that out of the Union League to a great extent grew the Solid South. The native white people from it conceived a dread of Republican supremacy which became inseparably connected in their minds with negro domination, and learned from it a lesson in political organization which has not yet been forgotten.

The results of the League organization are thus seen somewhat clearly, as well as the purposes of those conducting it. But it is very evident from a study of its constitution and ritual that its career in the South was a perversion of the intent of its founders, and that nothing was further from their minds than the violence and crime with which its name is inseparably connected. It is therefore very difficult for one who knows the organization only through these documents to understand the positive detestation in which its memory is held. That is the result of its later development, due in large part to the bad character of the white leaders, and the license into which liberty soon developed with the negroes. It is true that only in scattered cases is there proof that the League in council resolved upon the commission of crimes, though there are more instances of this than are usually known. But it is a fact established beyond question that the members of the organization very frequently acted together in crime and that the meetings were the occasion for violent and incendiary speeches intended and calculated to arouse the negroes against the whites at whatever cost, and that in them all sorts of rash and extreme statements and violent threats were made.[1] It is not wonderful then that the ignorant and emotional negroes should go away with the firm belief that the gospel of "kill and burn," which was so constantly preached by their leaders, was indeed a command with final authority behind it. This was emphasized by the character of the literature sent out by the national organization. Much of this was incendiary; all of it was intended to arouse hostility against political opponents.[2]

The element of secrecy in the League was a powerful factor in making it irresistibly attractive to the negro. The ceremony of initiation was skilfully devised to heighten this feeling. Professor Fleming aptly expresses it in saying, "It made him feel fearfully good from his head to his heels."[3] The meetings were always held at night, not only to secure full attendance, but because their effect was thereby greatly increased. The night, too, was the time that the negroes regarded as particularly their own. The chief delight of the freedmen was to be found in the initiations. In outline they were as follows: The council assembled in the hall, usually a school house or church,[4] and the assistant vice-president went to an ante-room where he addressed the candidates, describing the purposes of the order as the pre-

---

[1] A young man in Raleigh who was noted for his power of mimicry went disguised night after night to the League meetings. His testimony was conclusive as to the character of those he visited. Information constantly leaked in other ways as well. But the author has been unable to persuade any member of the League to say anything good or bad about the organization.

[2] The most widely distributed of these documents was a "loyal catechism," prepared for the use of the negroes.

[3] Fleming, *Civil War and Reconstruction in Alabama*, p. 559.

[4] This explains the burning of so many schools and churches by the white people. The number, however, for North Carolina was vastly exaggerated.

servation of liberty, the perpetuation of the Union, the maintainance of the supremacy of the laws and the Constitution, the securing of ascendency of American institutions, the protection of loyal men, particularly of members of the League, the elevation and education of labor and laboring men, and the giving of instruction in citizenship. The candidates then declared their attachment to the principles of the Declaration of Independence and their allegiance to the United States, pledging themselves to resist all attempts to overthrow it, to obey all rules and orders of the League, and to keep inviolate all its secrets. The neophytes were then led into the council room where there was an altar, draped with the United States flag, with the Bible, the Declaration of Independence, and the Constitution resting open upon it. Other emblems placed in prominent positions were a censer of incense, sword, gavel, ballot-box, sickle, shuttle, anvil, and other emblems of industry. " Hail Columbia " and " The Star Spangled Banner " were then sung, and the president made a prescribed address which was entirely beyond the comprehension of the freedmen. A prayer for the loyal people of the United States [1] and the members of the League followed, after which the " fire of liberty " was lighted on the altar and the neophytes placed their hands upon the flag and took the oath of allegiance to the United States, one to support only " reliable Union men and supporters of the government " for any office, and furthermore pledged themselves, if elected to any office, to carry out the objects and principles of the League. Secrecy and protection to brother leaguers were also sworn. The entire series of oaths having been re-affirmed, they were then given the " Freedmen's Pledge," to defend and

---

[1] This was based upon the prayer for Congress in the Book of Common Prayer.

perpetuate freedom, and then, with all, including the members of the council grouped about the altar, the president made a charge containing the explanation of the more important symbols. The signs [1] having been given, the ceremony ended.

The organization in the South was very complete and consisted of a national council [2] and one council for each State and territory with subordinate councils in each. The constitution of the national council was very elaborate but was never of any great importance as the work of the League was distinctly of a local nature. The state council was composed of representatives from the subordinate councils and had general supervision and direction of the League within the State. The officers were president, vice-presidents, recording and corresponding secretaries, and treasurer, with an executive committee composed of members from each judicial district. Meetings were held annually unless called more frequently. Subordinate councils were established by the president through a deputy for each county and certain deputies for the State at large. All "loyal" citizens of eighteen years of age or over were eligible. New members were elected by a three-fourths vote of those present. The officers of a local council were

[1] To pass as a member when questioned, give "Four L's" as follows: Right hand raised to Heaven, thumb and third finger touching their ends over the palm, pronounce "Liberty." Bringing the hand down over the shoulder, pronounce "Lincoln." Dropping the hand open at side, pronounce "Loyal." With hand and fingers downward in the chest, the thumb thrust into the vest or waistband across the body, pronounce "League."

[2] North Carolina regularly sent representatives to the national council. In 1867, James H. Harris was Grand Marshal and John L. Hays and David Heaton were members of the executive committee. In 1870, General M. S. Littlefield presided over the meeting which was held at Long Branch.

president, vice-president, treasurer, secretary, marshal, herald, sentinel, and chaplain.

So far as can be discovered, Albion W. Tourgee, who in 1866, organized the League in Guilford, Alamance, and the adjoining counties, was the first president of the state council.[1] He was succeeded by William W. Holden, who held the office until he became governor. Upon his resignation, General M. S. Littlefield became president, but the negroes generally were never told of the change and continued to regard Governor Holden as their head as long as the League lasted. In the same way, they regarded the *Standard* as the governor's mouthpiece and so the organ of the League. Consequently all the violent demands and threats of that paper were regarded as authoritative utterances by such of the negro members as it reached. All of this was no doubt the intention of the leaders, who knew that the governor's name and official position would lend importance to the League and, hence, to themselves. His constant pardoning of members of the order, guilty and convicted of crime, strengthened this belief, which was not entirely confined to negroes, for white men applied to him for charters as late as May, 1869,[2] and Jordan Potter, of Granville, who succeeded James H. Harris as vice-president of the state council, said publicly and constantly that Governor Holden was still president in 1870.[3] Governor Holden authorized the *Standard* to state that he had resigned and this was probably the truth, but he constantly alluded to the fact that he had at his call and absolute disposal eighty thousand men,[4] and there is no doubt that his power over the League re-

---

[1] *Senate Report*, no. 1, pp. 147, 269, 42 Cong., 1 sess.

[2] Whittemore to Holden, *Executive Correspondence.*

[3] *Sentinel*, Feb. 18, 1870.

[4] *Senate Report*, no. 1, p. 22, 42 Cong., 2 sess.

mained as strong as though he were its head. Therefore, he was in a great measure held responsible for its acts and, inasmuch as he could control its activities, justly so. Even many of the Republicans believed that he had influenced the League to nominate persons for office whom he could control for unworthy purposes.[1] This was, however, scarcely just.

There are no accurate sources of information as to the membership of the League in North Carolina. It is safe to say that it had over ninety per cent of the negro voters and some who were younger. In the west, it had at first a large white membership. On August 1, 1867, Buncombe county had nineteen councils and 1,800 members.[2] Rutherford had 1,200 members;[3] and Burke, Lincoln, and Cleveland were all well organized; and for a time, the League was strong in a number of other western counties. Governor Holden's estimate for the whole State has been mentioned. In 1869, the *Standard* placed the total membership at 70,-000,[4] and this was no overestimate, though it must be remembered that by now most of the white members had withdrawn and the League was practically dead in the west.

Soon after the organization of the League, a step was taken which was calculated to arouse the sharpest hostility among the white natives. In 1867, arms were procured and many local councils were converted into military companies which were drilled constantly. They speedily became a menace to the peace and good order of their respective communities. Often, these drills took place on the public roads

[1] An example of this feeling is to be seen in the testimony of Judge George W. Brooks before the Senate "Outrage" Committee. *Senate Report,* no. 1, p. 282, 42 Cong., 1 sess.

[2] *Standard,* Sept. 14, 1867.

[3] *Senate Report,* no. 1, p. 130, 42 Cong., 1 sess.

[4] Issue of August 26, 1869.

and, at such times, armed sentinels were posted on both sides to turn back anyone who might come up.[1] Lawlessness of this sort, which was entirely without remedy by legal means, greatly increased the public hostility already felt. Public parades were early among the activities of the councils and were of great assistance in adding to membership, for never before had the negroes been given the opportunity to take part in demonstrations of the kind and they appealed irresistibly to their nature. The processions in many cases now became of a military character and the freedmen were entirely captivated. The effect upon the mass of the white population can readily be conceived. In any event, trouble was to have been expected and when the fact is added that a procession of armed negroes was always seeking trouble, it is no matter for wonder that they often found it and that mild riots frequently resulted. It speaks well for the self-restraint of the average citizen of the State that nothing worse happened, especially in such cases as when an entire council in Raleigh in 1868 marched under arms to register. Fear of what the future held in store increased and was soon justified, for as the League became conscious of its strength, it began to take matters into its own hands. It became increasingly difficult and dangerous to arrest a member, and, once arrested, more difficult to hold him. In Chatham County on two different occasions the League opened the jail and released its members who were imprisoned, and in many places, prisoners were taken from the arresting officer. When, in spite of the activity, in their behalf,[2] which was rather usual on the part of the judges, conviction was secured, there was al-

---

[1] *Sentinel*, Aug. 19, 1869. This statement has been confirmed to the author by the testimony of personal witnesses.

[2] Judge Tourgee, Judge Thomas, and Judge Watts were all accused of this tendency.

most the certainty of a pardon from Governor Holden. In December, 1869, at Wilson court, in the case of two members of the League who were indicted for whipping a negro for voting the Conservative ticket, Judge Thomas refused to admit any evidence to show that the League had ordered the whipping, and sentenced them, when convicted, to thirty and sixty days' imprisonment respectively. They were immediately pardoned by the governor. In one western case, the convicts were pardoned before they reached Raleigh.[1] The Leaguers as well as the Conservatives soon came to believe that the governor had promised immunity from punishment.

The most common of the graver outrages committed by the negroes was barn-burning. The full seriousness of this offence can be justly estimated only when the economic condition of the people is realized. The loss of a barn, more frequently than not, meant complete ruin and was often accompanied by the menace of absolute want of food. In almost every county in the State, there were cases of the sort, and there is a mass of evidence which proves conclusively that in many instances it had been decided upon in a meeting of the League, and in many more, that it had been done by the members under the influence of the teachings they received in the councils. Often, naturally, it was the result of some private grudge. The counties that suffered most were Orange, Caswell, Granville, Chatham, Edgecombe, Wake, Jones, and Gaston. In the last-mentioned county, there were twenty-eight cases in one week.[2] Edgecombe in two months in 1869 lost two churches, several cotton gins, a cotton factory, and a number of barns and dwellings. Most of these could be traced to negro in-

---

[1] *Senate Report*, no. 1, p. 315, 42 Cong., 1 sess.

[2] *Ibid.*, p. 365, 42 Cong., 1 sess. Shotwell MS.

cendiaries.[1] Granville County lost by incendiaries during 1869 about one hundred thousand dollars. In Orange, there were many scattered cases during 1868 and 1869. In the latter year, three barns were burned at one time in sight of each other.[2] The perpetrators, two negroes named Morrow, were hanged by the Ku Klux for this offence combined with threats they had made against women in the community. The Chatham and Wake barn-burners, who were particularly active, said that the burning had been ordered by Governor Holden.[3] This was of course not true, but it gives an insight into League methods.

It is not to be supposed that the members of the League confined themselves to politics and the burning of property. More profitable employment was popular. Ever since emancipation, theft by the freedmen had increased, but this was caused only by the nature and needs of the negro. The propensity was now organized by the League, and live stock became increasingly unsafe in the neighborhood of the meeting place of a council, and movable property of all sorts was stolen to such an extent that the burden became almost unendurable.[4] It is not in any degree likely

---

[1] *Tarboro Southerner*, Nov. 18, 1869.

[2] *Senate Report*, no. 1, p. 191, 42 Cong., 1 sess.

[3] *Sentinel*, Dec. 23, 1870. *Senate Report*, no. 1, pt. 2, p. 41, 42 Cong., 1 sess.

[4] In the beginning the white people of the State had none of the hatred of the Union League which developed later. It was regarded as a cause of the general demoralization of the negro as a laborer, and as a contributing cause to the increase of theft by the colored population, but responsibility for more serious offences was not placed upon it. The following extract from a collection of semi-humorous essays written about this time will illustrate this:

" The order was subdivided into neighborhood organizations, and the heads of these were white men, while their vertebral force was recruited from the voting population above described, the chief being as completely *en rapport* with the African brother as if he had been in

that the League as an organization often voted, counseled, or gave formal approval to such actions. It is certain, however, that its very existence, the character of its leaders, and the sort of emotional stimulation given the negroes at the meetings were responsible for much of the theft as well as the injury to property which so distinguished the period. And before a great while, the League got the credit for every violation of the law, even though committed by white men who were not members.

Acts of personal violence by members upon white people were by no means unknown, but in general, the organization worked in secret. It seldom gave warnings such as were later employed by the Ku Klux, and rarely intimated the source of any violence committed. Much of its activity was deliberately inspired by its leaders; more, probably, was sheer unprovoked deviltry, the responsibility for which belongs nevertheless to the leaders who had begun the movement. In Anson County, the members of the League entered into an agreement for murder and robbery.[1] In Edgecombe, there was a similar agreement.[2] Murder was committed by armed bands of negroes a number of times, notably of Colonel John H. Nethercutt and his wife in

truth his congener and not simply dependent upon him for patronage. Their *locus in quo* was nowhere and everywhere—each city and town numbering its lodges and sub-lodges, and the diffusion thereof, throughout the agricultural districts, being in the somewhat extravagant ratio of one to the square mile. Their object was plunder. Their raids, directed against the 'white trash,' contemplated everything that might be classed under the term commissaries, and ranged from a pig-pen to a well-grown tuber. The goods and chattels of the unreconstructed were, by Act of Congress, their lawful prey, and if their foraging expeditions were conducted by moonlight it was from constitutional reasons and not from any well-grounded fear of resistance on the part of the intimidated whites."

[1] *Wadesboro Argus*, June 2, 1868.

[2] *Sentinel*, May 13, 1867.

Jones in 1867; of the entire Foscue family in Jones in 1869; of Mr. Green in Jones in 1869; and of Willis Briley in Pitt in 1869. These two counties each had many councils of the League which had almost entirely corrupted the negro population. If not directly responsible, their influence undoubtedly brought about the condition of affairs which made such happenings possible. Of protection by the courts there was practically none, even in the rare cases where individuals were detected. At first, some attempt was made by white Conservatives to check the growth and activity of the organization by refusal of employment to all its members. But it soon became evident that this meant refusal to employ colored labor at all, and the time came when the employing class became suppliants, so sharply was the need of laborers felt. Throughout its existence, the League exerted in one way or another an evil influence upon labor,[1] and this was not the least important count in the indictment brought against it in the State. Add the alarming fact that life and property almost totally lost security in the larger portion of the State, and wonder ceases that respect for the courts and the law began to disappear, and that counter-organization followed, equally beyond the law, but intended to preserve public order. A retaliation so violent, and a retribution so swift came that in a very short time after the appearance of the Ku Klux, the activities of the League became beautifully less, and it vanished altogether by the end of 1870.

[1] *Senate Report,* no. 1, p. 207, 42 Cong., 1 sess.

# CHAPTER NINE

## THE REPUBLICAN RÉGIME

### I. INAUGURATION OF THE HOLDEN ADMINISTRATION

GOVERNOR HOLDEN in his inaugural address laid down the doctrine that no part in government should be played by those who had opposed Reconstruction. He then advocated and threatened the use of force by the state administration. These two ideas, with his defence of the carpet-baggers, were prophetic of the character of his administration, for it was bitterly partisan throughout, force was employed to uphold it, and it was entirely controlled by carpet-baggers. With the one exception of John Pool, who was, throughout his administration, his evil genius, no one had any such influence upon him as was exerted by the corrupt gang of aliens who infested the State and surrounded him. All played upon his ambition, and there lay his most fatal weakness. Into their hands he committed his future, believing that high national honors were soon to be his, and the result was not only disastrous to himself, but well-nigh ruinous to the State.

The first matter to receive the attention of the governor was, as was to be expected, the filling of such offices as lay within his gift. At first there were only justices of the peace to be chosen and the governor busied himself with the appointments, keeping clearly in mind their political value, and taking care that the negroes obtained their full share of these cheap honors. The office of magistrate in

North Carolina had always been one of honor and importance. It now became a by-word and a reproach. Governor Holden's appointments were notoriously poor and, in the main, the white men appointed were not much more fitted to discharge the duties of the office than were the negroes. Hundreds of them could not read or write and prisoners often had to make out the papers to which the justice laboriously affixed his mark.[1] Much of the later trouble in the administration of justice was due to these ignorant and often corrupt appointees of the governor.

The towns next won the governor's attention and, without any authority, he commenced the appointment of mayors and commissioners for the various towns of the State. The municipal officers of Raleigh refused to yield

---

[1] The following are two examples of the learning of magistrates appointed by Governor Holden:

" Isaac saSSer j P.                                                  AuGest
                                                         the 29 1868
I sertevfy that w p hittleley compelams that saide Wiles Grant has not wyork the Rod a Cordinly to law ant i hav yarned him a IsaaC
                                                         SaSSer j. p."

                                        " Brunswick countey
                                          Nov. 18th, 1868.
You Henry Kelly, special Constable, are hereby commanded in the name of the State personally to appear before me on the 28th day of November, 1868 at Fair Oaks Plantation, the person of Fred Shaw in a plea of debt of $6.58 due by him to Mrs. Clara Rosalfy.
    Herein fail not.
    Given under my hand and seal.              E. M. Rosalfy,
                                             *Justice of the Peace."*

A very interesting story is told of one of the new magistrates in Pitt county who went to town to take the oath of office. He told the clerk that he wished to qualify. The clerk asked him what he meant, and upon his replying that he wished to be sworn in, said: " Yes, you can be sworn in, but all h—l could not qualify you." King, *Sketches of Pitt County.* A constable in the same county, being unable to procure a firearm, carried a grubbing-hoe as his official weapon.

to the new administration which was headed by the governor's brother-in-law. The governor then telegraphed to General Canby for a military force to seat his appointees.[1] The next day he wired for the necessary force to oust the sheriff of New Hanover who also declined to recognize an appointee of the governor.[2] General Canby declined to act in the Raleigh matter, stating it as his belief that the governor's action was illegal,[3] but the new sheriff of New Hanover was installed by military force.[4] The sheriffs of Granville, Randolph, and other counties refused to yield and in every case military force was employed.[5] The towns still held out and finally the legislature came to the governor's relief and vacated all the offices.[6] This gave him a free hand and he gradually filled most of the town offices. The Orange County officials refused to yield and the attorney general carried the case to the Superior Court and Judge Tourgee decided against him. The governor also appointed new state proxies for the various railroads in which the State had stock and reorganization followed. New boards of directors for the state institutions were then appointed and all came under the control of Republicans. The most notorious of these latter changes was the one which removed Dr. Fisher from the position of superintendent of the insane asylum and replaced him by Dr. Eugene Grissom, of Granville County, who had been active in politics since the war and had been a radical member of the convention of 1868. His politics constituted his sole title to the place.

When these pressing matters were disposed of, the gov-

---

[1] *Executive Correspondence*, Holden, i, p. 20.

[2] *Ibid.*, p. 21.      [3] *Ibid.*, p. 23.

[4] *Ibid.*, p. 26.      [5]*Ibid.*, pp. 22-29.

[6] *Laws,* 1868, chaps. ii. iv.

ernor took up the organization of the militia which at his suggestion had been authorized by the legislature. He appointed as adjutant-general, Abial W. Fisher, a carpetbagger from Bladen County, who had been a member of the late convention. F. G. Martindale, of Martin County, another carpetbagger, was made major-general of the eastern division: J. Q. A. Bryan, " the Red Fox of Wilkes," who had been during the war a Union ranger, was placed in command of the western division; and Willie D. Jones,[1] of Wake County, a favorite of the governor, was chosen for the middle division.[2] Byron Laflin, a carpetbagger from Pitt, Robert M. Douglas, of Rockingham, lately of Illinois, William A. Moore, of Chowan, another carpetbagger, and William S. Pearson, of Burke, were appointed aides with the rank of colonel. On September 1, eighty-nine colonels, one from each county, were appointed.

The question of arming the force still had to be settled and, as there were many objections to submitting the question to the legislature, chief of which was the publicity involved, the governor sent Adjutant-General Fisher to the North to do what he could in the way of securing a loan from some radical state administration. On October 16, Fisher wrote the governor that he had succeeded in obtain-

---

[1] The following comment of the *Sentinel* upon this appointment gives a view of the earlier career of Jones: " We suggest a uniform for Maj. Gen. Willie D., viz. A chapeau made of paper, upon which shall be inscribed ' Negroes should not be allowed to testify in the courts '; a swallow-tailed coat, with a strip pinned *a posteriori*, and emblazoned with the device, ' I voted against the Howard Amendment '; spurs sixteen inches long; fourteen pistols and the sword which he used in the ' rebel ' service, girded around his waist. The *tout ensemble* will be complete, and military glory will be at its climax." Issue of Aug. 29, 1868.

[2] *Standard*, Sept. 2, 1868.

ing a thousand Springfield rifles from Vermont. Governor Page had approved his plan and a veiled resolution would be put through the legislature authorizing the transfer, and no one would be the wiser. From the debate on the militia bill, the State became aware that something of the sort was on foot, and the *Sentinel,* commenting on the arrival of a case of arms in Wilmington, said, " In God's name, and in the name of peace, we beseech these Northern governors to keep their arms and not to send them to North Carolina."

All during the fall, the militia was employed in various counties and was shown to be entirely worthless except as a means of distributing the loaves and fishes to the hungry adherents of Radicalism. The " North Carolina State Militia " (N. C. S. M.) was entitled by opponents of the administration, the " Negro, Carpet-bag, Scalawag, Militia," and the title endured.[1]

During this period, ten companies of negro federal troops were concentrated in Goldsboro and a reign of terror followed during which depredations of all sorts were committed and the conduct of the troops was so violent that it was unsafe for women to leave their homes.[2] The example was not a good one for the militia which was not by nature inclined to lawful methods.

The other executive officers of the State were occupied in the meantime in coming to a realization of the full financial and political importance of their offices. The legislature gave abundant opportunity for extravagance and the officers for the most part lived up to their opportunities from the beginning.

From the outset, no branch of the state administration

[1] *Sentinel,* August 29, 1868.
[2] *Ibid.,* Sept. 12, 1868.

was the object of more caustic criticism than the judiciary. The habits of the chief justice were well known when he received the endorsement of both parties, so little was said of him at first. But E. W. Jones, Superior Court judge for the second district, early brought shame to the bench. Starting to Raleigh for the inauguration of the new government, he made a triumphal progress of continued drunkenness and indecency. He was a public spectacle in Wilmington, and in Raleigh, he remained intoxicated during his entire stay. On several occasions he was guilty of deliberate exposure of his person upon the streets and was finally arrested as a nuisance. Early in the session of the legislature, James Sinclair introduced a resolution calling for an investigation of his conduct with a view to impeachment, but the House by a vote of 51 to 31 declined to act on the ground stated by A. S. Seymour and General Abbott, both carpetbaggers, that they had nothing to do with public morals and that drunkenness was not an impeachable offence.[1]  Judge Starbuck declined to serve, and the governor appointed John M. Cloud, of Surry, who was honest but entirely lacking in qualifications for the position.[2] Judge Tourgee still had his eye set upon a seat in Congress, and divided his time between holding courts to which he was always late and which he always adjourned early, canvassing for the Republican nomination for Congress in the fifth district, and, in company with Judge Rodman and Victor Barringer, transferring the New York Code to North Carolina and drawing for the work $200 per month in addition to his salary as judge. All of the Supreme Court judges and most of those on the Superior bench

---

[1] *Sentinel,* July 11, 1868. *Journal,* p. 38.

[2] In 1865, Judge Cloud threatened to cowhide a neighbor if he should let his (Cloud's) negroes know that they were free.

busied themselves in politics during the summer, and Chief Justice Pearson went so far as to issue a campaign letter in the interest of Grant's candidacy. Here the Conservatives abandoned him and heaped upon him their strongest condemnation. The *Standard* and the Republicans generally claimed the judges as strong partisans, and candor compels the statement that there was little in their conduct to disprove the claim, and the respect for the courts, which had always been a characteristic of the people of the State, dwindled rapidly.

It was not a favorable outlook for North Carolina, though the real evils of Reconstruction were scarcely dreamed of. The leaders of the dominant party were holding back until the presidential election should be won, when they would be safe from unfriendly interference by the national government. To that time they looked forward with more eagerness than any slave had ever hoped for freedom and with more longing than any weary Hebrew had ever felt for the Promised Land.

## 2. THE LEGISLATURE OF 1868

The General Assembly which met on July 3, 1868, was of the type to be expected after a consideration of the chaos in the State. The ignorance and prejudice of the majority of the Republicans made them easy prey for the corrupt minority of the party which at once assumed leadership in the body. Venality was profitable and many who did not belong in such company were betrayed into joining in the spoliation of the State.

The party division of the General Assembly was as follows:

|  | Senate. | House. | Joint Ballot. |
|---|---|---|---|
| Republicans | 38 | 80 | 118 |
| Conservatives | 12 | 40 | 52 |

Of the Republicans in the Senate, seven were carpet-baggers and three were negroes.[1] In the House, more than twenty of the Republicans were carpetbaggers and sixteen were negroes.[2] Most of the negroes and some of the whites were illiterate. The Conservatives were much stronger than they had been in the convention, both in numbers and ability, but even then they were in a hopeless minority and at first it seemed that they would only be able to put their opponents on record and make no mark in legislation. During the whole of the first session, the attendance was poor, never reaching above forty in the Senate and one hundred in the House.

The qualification of the members was attended with the usual disputes as to the right to a seat, and resulted in the refusal of the Republicans to qualify nine Conservatives in the Senate and ten in the House on the ground that they were under disabilities imposed by the proposed Fourteenth Amendment. A committee was appointed later to consider the question and gravely reported that although the proposed amendment was not a part of the Constitution, it had been ratified by North Carolina and should therefore be construed to exclude all such persons from the legislature.[3] Some of those at first excluded were later admitted upon proof that they were not banned. A number of the Republicans were equally banned, but all proposals for investiga-

---

[1] The carpetbaggers were Colgrove, Cook, Davis, Hayes, Legg, Martindale, W. A. Moore, Rich, and Sweet. The negroes were Eppes, Galloway, and Hyman.

[2] The carpetbaggers that the author has been able to identify were Abbott, Ames, Estes, Laflin, Peck, Renfrow, Seymour, Stevens, Stilley, Foster and Downing. The negroes were Cherry, Cawthorn, Falkner, Harris of Wake, Hayes, Hutchings, Leary, Mayo, Morris, Price, Robbins, Sweat, Sykes, Crawford, Williamson, and Carey.

[3] *Journal*, p. 40.

tion of their cases were voted down. The partisan intent of the framers of the Fourteenth Amendment was thus speedily carried out in North Carolina. A proposal was early made to petition Congress to remove the disabilities of all persons elected to any office, but this was opposed so bitterly by the carpetbaggers as well as by extreme radicals that it was defeated.[1] The matter was brought up again and again by E. W. Pou and Sinclair, both of whom worked unceasingly to secure the passage of such a resolution, but the carpetbagger influence was too great. Abbott insisted that it would " debauch " the politics of the State.[2] The *Standard* also strongly opposed removal of disabilities from others than Republicans.[3] The Republican caucus finally adopted a resolution instructing the senators and members of Congress to vote against all removals except upon the recommendation of the secretary of the Republican executive committee.[4] In the meantime, the seats of the excluded Conservatives were declared vacant and some, who had been allowed to qualify, were unseated. In the Senate, Bedford Brown, of Caswell, was unseated, after a contest, by John W. Stephens, and a new election ordered. In the House, Wilson Carey, of Caswell, the negro well-known for his " archives of gravity " speech in the convention, took the place of William Long, the sitting member. The debates upon the subject of the cases were very bitter, particularly as the majority showed no inclination to listen to argument.

Organization was completed at once as the Republicans were well disciplined. In the House, Joseph W. Holden

[1] *Sentinel,* July 4, 1868. *Journal,* p. 16.

[2] *Sentinel,* July 11, 1868.

[3] *Standard,* June 24, July 15, 1868.

[4] *Sentinel,* July 25, 1868.

was chosen speaker over Plato Durham. This was the result of an agreement between Governor Holden and General Abbott, the latter giving his support in exchange for the Holden influence in behalf of his own candidacy for the United States Senate. The early days of the session were largely spent in playing politics. A committee was appointed to consider the question of granting aid to the destitute and to those who did not have sufficient means to finish planting their crops. On July 25, all municipal offices in the State that had been filled by the former state government were declared vacant and the governor was empowered to fill them.[1] The governor was then given similar powers with regard to county commissioners.[2] Later on, the House discussed at length a proposed law to punish those who had committed offences under the authority of the Confederate government. Governor Holden saw unlimited political possibilities in such a law and sought to have it passed, but it was referred to the judiciary committee and, upon its recommendation, postponed indefinitely.[3]

The position of legislator did not prove as profitable as desired by some of the members and, in spite of the fact that they were furnished with comforts and luxuries hitherto unknown to them, they desired more. Many propositions for small benefits were made, the most interesting of which was contained in a resolution introduced by J. H. Renfrow, a carpetbagger, to furnish free postage to all members. Some difficulty was encountered in deciding what should be the compensation of the members, but it was finally settled at $7 *per diem* and twenty cents mileage. This was, strange to say, less than the committee recom-

[1] *Laws*, 1868, chap. ii.          [2] *Ibid.*, chap. iv.
[3] *Sentinel*, Aug. 20, 1868.

mended and the decision was a blow to many of the members, one of whom voiced the sentiments of his kind by saying that they wanted something worth while to compensate them for the persecution they had to endure and the fear that they would never be allowed to come back.[1] It was not long, however, before many discovered that in that legislature other compensation than *per diem* could readily be obtained for service of a certain sort.

Among the gratuities at the disposal of all, were the refreshments dispensed by what was popularly known as "the third house." Throughout the session, a bar abundantly supplied with wines, liquors, and cigars was conducted in the west wing of the Capitol. It was installed by General Littlefield and his associates who were making plans for extensive financial operations based upon the credit of the State. The later success of those plans, thanks to the coöperation of the legislature, makes it entirely correct to say that the expenses of the bar were paid by the State though without legal warrant. Mere words cannot adequately express the disgust and hatred felt by the respectable people of the State, outside of the legislature, for this open shame in the Capitol. There is, however, no doubt that many Conservative members daily enjoyed the hospitality of the "third house," though without surrendering any right to condemn it in public.

At the beginning, the Conservatives did not hope to exert any influence in legislation, even in the way of opposition. As in the convention, they sought chiefly to place their opponents on record, particularly in regard to the race question which they already saw would be of first importance in the future politics of the State. This was done by the introduction of a resolution in the Senate which declared

[1] *Wilmington Journal*, July 28, 1868.

that racial differences were recognized and that therefore intermarriage between the races should be forbidden and that in the schools and militia there should be separation. This was contemptuously refused. Later on, somewhat similar resolutions, introduced by Shoffner, were adopted by the Senate. The resolution directed against the intermarriage of the races received more opposition than any, three negroes and four carpetbaggers voting against it.[1] Plato Durham, with the training he had received in the convention, was the Conservative leader in the House, and was ably seconded in the Senate by William M. Robbins. The latter attempted in vain to secure the passage of a resolution declaring that North Carolina did not consider itself bound by the Omnibus Bill which had admitted it to representation in Congress. This was intended as a warning to the Republicans and to the world of the view of the Conservatives.

But little constructive work was done during the session. The financial legislation will be discussed later in detail and that occupied but little time, as light was not desired by those promoting it. Much of the time was spent in useless discussion of matters of small moment and but few laws of interest or importance were passed. The board of education was directed to prescribe and report to the next session a code of laws for the establishment and regulation of a new system of public schools.[2] Criminal courts were established for Wilmington and New Bern with exclusive jurisdiction and the old county criminal courts were abolished, but no provision was made for the transfer of the cases brought in the latter.[3] Acts providing for the regis-

---

[1] *Sentinel*, Aug. 26, 1868. *Senate Journal*, p. 238.

[2] *Resolution* 10, *Laws*, 1868.

[3] *Laws*, 1868, chap. xii.

tration of voters, giving the right to vote anywhere in the
county on certificate, and forbidding any challenge of a
registered person on election day, were passed.[1] A new
law in relation to punishments was adopted and murder
and rape became the only capital offences. Corporal punishment was abolished.[2] A joint committee of the two
houses, with the superintendent of public works, was directed to select and purchase a site for the penitentiary and
to put the convicts to work upon the buildings. To pay the
expenses of the purchase and work, the treasurer was authorized to sell six per cent bonds to an amount not to
exceed $200,000.[3] The duties of certain county officers
were prescribed.[4] The ordinance of the convention admitting lawyers from other States to practice before the
Supreme Court was amended so as to include the Superior
Court.[5] An act to punish bribery and coercion in elections made it unlawful to bribe, to attempt to influence a
voter by threats of discharge from employment, or to discharge because of any vote cast.[6] The danger of such extreme legislation was shown, but without effect. A law punishing conspiracy and rebellion was passed which classed
as such an offence any opposition to the enforcement of a
law or aid and comfort to those opposing it.[7]

One of the most interesting and significant acts of the
legislature was the passage of a resolution affirming the
validity and constitutionality of the state government. It
was based upon President Johnson's contemptuous reference to Governor Holden as " the man who writes himself
governor of North Carolina "—which the Republicans held

[1] *Laws*, 1868, chaps. xlix-l.
[2] *Ibid.*, chap. xliv.
[3] *Ibid.*, chap. lxi.
[4] *Ibid.*, chaps. xx, xxxv.
[5] *Ibid.*, chap. xxxvi.
[6] *Ibid.*, chap. lxii.
[7] *Ibid.*, chap. lx.

to be an incitement to insurrection; upon Governor Worth's letter of protest to Governor Holden, when he surrendered his office as governor to the latter; upon the Democratic national platform of 1868, which declared the whole process of Reconstruction unconstitutional; upon Frank P. Blair's Brodhead letter; and upon the North Carolina Conservative platform of 1868, which was of like tenor with the other documents mentioned. These were declared calculated to produce civil war, and in order to restore confidence, the state government was declared valid in every respect.[1] The resolution was introduced by L. G. Estes and shows the fear of the Republicans that the administration might be overturned. It also bears testimony to the deep-seated determination of the Conservatives not to recognize the validity of the acts of the state government.

The most important act passed was that providing for the organization of the militia. The motives which underlay it have already been discussed. On July 17, the governor sent a message to the legislature urging the organization of a militia and police force, making the entirely false charge that without it the officers recently appointed by him could not be installed. Calling attention to the fact that many people in the State did not recognize the existing government as lawful, he announced it as his policy to overawe them by a display of force, and reiterated the intention expressed in his inaugural of appointing to official position in the State only such persons as were friendly to his administration.[2] On the same day, G. W. Welker introduced in the Senate a militia bill which was passed. But the House hesitated to agree, and finally, after a fierce filibuster by the Conservatives, adopted a substitute intro-

---

[1] *Resolution* 35, *Laws*, 1868.
[2] *Legislative Documents*, 1868-1869, no. 7.

duced by Seymour.[1] The question was then taken up by the Republican caucus and later F. G. Martindale's substitute, based on the action of the caucus and drawn by John Pool, was adopted in both houses.[2] In neither house did it receive the undivided support of the Republican members. Pou and Sinclair in the House were among its bitterest opponents and lost no opportunity of attacking it. The latter denied its constitutionality and, claiming that it served notice to the world that government by the Republican party in North Carolina was a failure, said that it stamped Reconstruction as revolutionary, contrary to the will of the people, and only to be supported by force. He expressed the belief that the bill was designed to cause trouble at the polls and to give the executive too much power both in directing the militia and over the treasury. After a prophecy of riot and disorder, he read a letter from B. F. Moore containing an unanswerable argument against the constitutionality of the bill. It closed as follows: " I cannot omit to declare it my most solemn opinion, that, if passed into law, it will spread terror over the State and produce much more bloodshed than it will ever prevent, and open and aggravate wounds now nearly closed." [3] In the Senate, R. I. Wynne, of Franklin, was its chief Republican opponent. The Conservatives, it is needless to say, opposed the bill unanimously. W. L. Love in the Senate attempted to secure the adoption of an amendment forbidding the placing of white persons under negro officers, but the proposition was defeated.[4] After the final passage of the bill, twenty-nine members of the House, including Sinclair, en-

---

[1] *House Journal*, pp. 133-149.

[2] *Senate Journal*, p. 181; *House Journal*, p. 183.

[3] *Sentinel*, Aug. 8, 1868.

[4] *Senate Journal*, p. 175.

tered a protest against it as unconstitutional, inexpedient, and calculated to cause civil war.[1]

The provisions of the bill were as follows: Every person liable to military duty had to serve unless excused by a physician or relieved by the annual payment of two dollars. All power of appointment was in the hands of the governor who was authorized to accept and organize not more than six regiments of infantry, apportioned throughout the State and divided into three divisions, east, west, and middle, each to be the department of a major-general. He was also empowered to accept three regiments of cavalry and one battery of artillery. The total enrollment of the militia could not exceed fifty for each member of the House of Representatives, or 6,000 in all, unless the governor deemed that number inadequate, in which case he could raise more. Provision was made for the separation of the races in different companies. Every member had to be an elector in the State. At the request of any five justices of a county, the governor was empowered to direct the colonel commanding there to detail a force to preserve the peace and enforce the law. The force was under the command of the governor and could be sent by him to any part of the State. In addition, any officer of the militia could call out the force at the written request of any judge, justice of the peace, sheriff, deputy sheriff, county or town constable, or county commissioner. He could also call it out whenever he deemed it necessary to preserve the peace. The governor was directed to appoint an adjutant-general to organize the force.[2]

It will be seen that the act was admirably adapted for the establishment of a military despotism. It was mainly intended for that purpose. It looked to the establishment of

---

[1] *House Journal*, p. 155.          [2] *Laws*, 1868, chap. xxii.

a standing army which was in violation of the state constitution and the Constitution of the United States, and in
addition, a recent act of Congress had expressly forbidden
the establishment of a militia system in the lately seceded
States.[1] But Governor Holden and his allies were too well
aware that their position was insecure; that unless extraordinary measures were resorted to, the first election would
put an end to their tenure of power. That terrorism and
fraud would in time react upon them seems not to have occurred to the native leaders of the dominant party, and the
most important and influential of the leaders—the carpetbaggers—did not care. When such a reckoning should
come, most of them hoped to be living in comfortable retirement somewhere north of Mason and Dixon's line and
beyond the reach of a just retribution.

The debates in the legislature showed that the membership, with a few exceptions, was far below the average in
ability. Prejudice and party feeling were rampant on both
sides and the majority treated the minority with utter contempt, usually denying them the privilege of debate, and
even going so far as to print the bills, which had been decided upon by the Republican caucus, before they were introduced.[2] The sessions were perhaps more orderly than
those of the convention, but occasionally there were angry
scenes in which the lie was passed with frequency. Abusive
language was not uncommon. Sinclair became unpopular
with his Republican colleagues because of his opposition
to several measures, particularly the militia bill, and was in
constant open quarrel with them, particularly with F. W.
Foster, the carpetbagger representative from Bladen.[3] As

---

[1] *Laws of the United States*, chap. clxx, 39 Cong., 2 sess.

[2] *Wilmington Journal*, Aug. 14, 1868.

[3] Sinclair related with great gusto a story of Foster's activities at the

in the convention, the accounts of the proceedings as given in the Conservative papers excited anger and the reporter of the *Sentinel* was excluded from the House for putting "negro" after the names of the colored members. Twenty-one members entered a formal protest against this action.[1]

The reputation for extravagance, set by the convention, was continued. The session lasted forty-seven days and the expenses of the legislature alone were more than $80,000. It is impossible to give any accurate figures as to the incidental outlay.

Adjournment was the occasion for the presentation of a gold watch to the speaker of the House. L. G. Estes, with true carpetbag thrift, collected the money for it from the members, bought the watch, but neglected to pay for it.[2] The closing scenes were marked by the same horseplay and boisterousness which had accompanied the adjournment of the convention. Morris and Carey, two of the negro members occupied the chair in succession and the other negro members were called upon for speeches. Dancing, singing, and obscene stories occupied the last hours of the session, and with the adjournment, the decent element of the State drew a breath of relief.

### 3. THE PRESIDENTIAL CAMPAIGN OF 1868

The Conservatives were naturally greatly disheartened by their overwhelming defeat in the state election, but, as

close of the war. As an undertaker in Wilmington, he received an order from a gentleman in the North to disinter his son who had died in service in Wilmington as the result of the amputation of his left leg. Foster could not find the body and, being a thrifty soul, selected another, cut off a leg, and shipped it North. By mistake he cut off the right leg and in this way the substitution was discovered. *Sentinel,* July 29, 1868.

[1] *House Journal,* pp. 46-47.

[2] *Sentinel,* Aug. 3, 1868.

there had been no real expectation of victory, there was no surprise. There was, however, still hope of an overthrow of Congressional Reconstruction through Democratic success in the approaching presidential election, and to that consummation, all directed their best energies. A full delegation attended the national Democratic convention at New York and commenced the break which resulted in the nomination of Seymour. The nominations were entirely acceptable to the party, and the emphasis laid in the platform on the unconstitutionality of Reconstruction won immediate favor. Not less attractive to them was Blair's letter to Colonel Brodhead with its threat of the complete overthrow of the system.

The Republicans were not less pleased with the choice of Grant and Colfax. As a matter of fact, any nomination, even though it had been of His Satanic Majesty, would have been entirely acceptable, so entirely and unthinkingly were the members of the party committed in their allegiance.

The Conservative leaders had good hopes of carrying the State and at once called a state convention for the purpose of perfecting their organization. In the meantime, Democratic and Conservative mass meetings were held all over the State and great enthusiasm was excited.

Just at this time, Chief Justice Pearson published in the *Standard* an address to the Conservative party, urging their support of Grant and the Republican party on the ground that Democratic success would mean civil war. He denied entirely any belief in the constitutionality of the Reconstruction acts, but, declaring them extra-constitutional, he said that a subjugated people had no right to protest, particularly as the presidential plan of restoration was equally unconstitutional. He stated that two other members of the Supreme Court, unnamed, agreed with him in his analysis of the situation and of the law.  The letter provoked much criticism from the Conservatives who said with truth that North Carolina had not been accustomed to political activity on the part of its judges.  The *Standard* immediately claimed that all of the Supreme Court and most of the Superior Court judges were active Republican partisans and said that Judge Pearson's letter was the best campaign document that had appeared.  Fifty thousand copies of it were distributed by the Republican executive committee.

The Conservative convention was called for August 13, and delegates from every part of the State poured into Raleigh.  The delegations from the east, headed by the one from New Hanover, arrived the night before and were received by the Conservative club of the city.  The negroes made a demonstration against the procession and only the forbearance of the crowd and the efforts of A. H. Galloway prevented a riot.[1]

The convention met the next day with an attendance of more than one thousand.  It remained in session for two days.  R. H. Cowan, of Wilmington, was elected president.  Addresses were made by Josiah Turner, R. H. Cowan, William M. Robbins, William A. Graham, James C. Dobbin, E. G. Haywood, and others, all of whom devoted most of their attention to the situation in the State.  Nominations were made for electors for the State at large,[2] and a resident central committee was chosen.[3]  The platform endorsed the national Democratic nominations and

---

[1] *Sentinel*, Aug. 15, 1868.

[2] These were James W. Osborne and Joseph J. Davis.

[3] The resident central committee was composed of M. A. Bledsoe, R. C. Badger, Seaton Gales, Bryan Grimes, E. G. Haywood, D. G. Fowle, and A. S. Merrimon.  The state executive committee was as follows: Charles Latham, W. G. Morisy, J. A. Engelhard, James S. Amis, A. M. Scales, R. M. Oates, and A. C. Avery.

platform, declared the acceptance by the party of the war and its legitimate results, condemned Reconstruction, the election of carpetbaggers and other men without fitness for their positions, and the extravagance and the proscriptive tendencies of the Republican party, denounced the militia bill as unconstitutional and intended as a party measure, and finally, called upon the Conservatives of the State to rally to the cause of good government.[1]

In connection with the convention appears an interesting example of Radical policy. W. A. Smith, the president of the North Carolina Railroad, refused to give any reduced rates for the occasion and his example was followed by the other roads. A little later, for the Republican convention, the rate was reduced more than one-half. Another interesting sidelight upon Republican sentiment is to be found in the *Standard's* editorial greeting to the convention. "We tell you, decrepid, back-broken, old rebels, that your days are numbered. We are willing that you should gasp a little, and, therefore, look on your feeble efforts to rise from your backs with pity and compassion. But attempt to rise higher than your knees, or to assume any other attitude than that of prayer, and you will be thrust back to the earth, never to rise again." [2]

On August 17, there was a state meeting of the Union League in Raleigh for the purpose of reorganization. General Littlefield was elected grand president and H. J. Menninger, grand secretary. Throughout the campaign, the activity of the League continued and as always it was a most effective instrument for rousing the negroes and keeping them in line. John T. Deweese performed a valuable service for it by sending out all of its documents under his

---

[1] *Sentinel*, Aug. 15, 1868.
[2] Issue of Aug. 15, 1868.

congressional frank.[1]   As has been mentioned, the white
members of the League had by this time become disgusted
with the negro and carpetbagger domination of the society and were rapidly leaving it.  The leaders of the party
saw the necessity of taking some action and on August 26,
W. F. Henderson issued an address to the Heroes of
America,[2] and once more, and for the last time, the " Red
Strings " appeared in North Carolina politics.

When the General Assembly adjourned, eighty-eight of
the Republican members signed an address to the people,
written by John Pool and Judge Reade.[3]  No more incendiary document has ever been published in the State than
this address.   It was directed against the Conservative
party which was accused of threatening war, of duplicity
and bad faith, of having rejected both President Johnson's
plan of restoration and the Howard Amendment, and of
disturbing the peace by threats and intimidation, with negro
suffrage as a pretext, but in reality with hostility to the
United States as a basis.   The chief proofs of this character of the party which were recited were the same happenings which had been enumerated as reasons for passing
the resolutions affirming the validity of the state government.  The address was full of threats and was calculated
and intended to inflame the negroes and alarm the Conservatives.   It was a deliberate step in the policy of terror
adopted by the Republican party in North Carolina.  The
following is a characteristic extract which excited much
attention and condemnation:

---

[1] *Sentinel,* Sept. 30, 1868.  He was later indicted for this.

[2] The address appeared in the *Standard,* August 26, 1868, and was
evidently prepared by someone else as he was almost illiterate.

[3] Their connection with the address was not made public, but the fact
was given to the writer by a leader in the Republican party.

Did it never occur to you, ye gentlemen of property, education, and character—to you, ye men, and especially ye women, who never received anything from these colored people but services, kindness, and protection—did it never occur to you that these same people who are so very bad, will not be willing to sleep in the cold when your houses are denied them, merely because they will not vote as you do; that they may not be willing to starve, while they are willing to work for bread? Did it never occur to you that revenge which is sweet to you, may be sweet to them? Hear us, if nothing else you will hear, did it never occur to you that if you kill their children with hunger they will kill your children with fear? Did it never occur to you that if you good people maliciously determine that they shall have no shelter, they may determine that you shall have no shelter?

And now, be it remembered that in the late election there were more than twenty thousand majority of the freemen of North Carolina who voted in opposition to the democratic party. Will it be safe for the landholders, householders, and meatholders to attempt to kick into disgrace and starve to death twenty thousand majority of the freemen of this State?

The Republican convention met in Raleigh on September 16. A tremendous crowd attended, the majority being negroes, and the Capitol was full of them, eating, drinking, singing, fighting, and, when night came, sleeping there. The call for the meeting contained the main features of the program, and provided for a great mass meeting and, to the utter horror of conservative citizens, irrespective of party, who were full of reverence for the judiciary, it was announced that Judges Reade, Dick, Rodman, and Settle, of the Supreme Court, and Judge Tourgee, of the Superior Court, would take prominent parts in the demonstration, Judge Reade being president, Judges Dick, Rodman, and Settle vice-presidents, and Judge Tourgee grand marshal of the day as well as chairman of the committee on railroad transportation.[1] The press was not chary of hostile comment, and the Supreme Court judges were soon made to recognize the light in which their conduct was viewed, and when the meeting was held, none of them were present. But Judge Tourgee, although an able man and one who in time became an exceedingly strong judge, was throughout his public career in North Carolina, entirely shameless and without any sense of propriety, and he not only acted as chief marshal at the Raleigh meeting, but served on the Republican state executive committee, and, with his eye still on the nomination for Congress, made stump speeches throughout his district even from the bench.[2]

There was little business before the Republican convention other than the ratification of the national ticket and platform. The time of the meeting was given up to speeches from the leaders present and the reading of letters from prominent Republicans elsewhere, including George S. Boutwell, John W. Forney, and William C. Wickham. Governor Hawley, of Connecticut, was the guest of the day and made an address, as did also Governor Holden, Attorney General Coleman, Joseph W. Holden, and A. H. Galloway. The governor said in part, " Meanwhile see to it, on your own acount, and on account of those gallant dead who sleep in graves all over this land, fallen in defense of your rights and of mine; by your regard for unborn posterity, while we regard the rights of rebels so long as they demean themselves as they should—see to it that in no event does any rebel get a single ' bite ' at a public office." The speech of J. W. Holden, as reported, was very violent. A part of it follows: " I do not address you as Joseph W. Holden, but in the name and spirit of an inspired

[1] *Sentinel,* Aug. 19, 1868.

[2] *Ibid.,* Sept. 19, 1868.

prophet. Go to the polls, armed with guns, pistols, and bludgeons and vote. Implore the God of turpentine to shower down torches or flames upon the dwellings of the rebels." [1]

Both parties nominated candidates for Congress in every district.[2] Nathaniel Boyden, after serving faithfully as a Democratic member of Congress, came home and announced that he would support Grant. He was at once nominated by the Republicans and the Conservatives nominated a new candidate. But the Republicans were in serious difficulties in two districts. In the first, C. L. Cobb, the sitting member, received the regular nomination and John R. French, a carpetbagger, led a bolt in his own interest. In the fifth, W. F. Henderson secured the nomination of the convention, and Judge Tourgee, after denouncing Henderson as a liar and thief and being himself described by the latter as " an escaped Ohio convict," [3] with the aid of Judge Dick, organized a bolting convention which gave him the nomination. A heated campaign followed, marked by bitter personal abuse, culminating in a personal encounter.[4] Henderson then withdrew in favor of I. G. Lash, the sitting member, and Tourgee soon followed suit. In the fourth, Deweese was confronted by the renewed candidacy of

[1] Holden absolutely denied saying anything of the sort, and there is no doubt that he did not intend to do so.

[2] The candidates were as follows: 1st district, Republican, C. L. Cobb, John R. French; Democrat, D. A. Barnes. 2d, David Heaton; T. S. Kenan. 3d, O. H. Dockery; A. A. McKay. 4th, J. T. Deweese; S. H. Rogers. 5th, I. G. Lash, W. F. Henderson, and A. W. Tourgee; Livingston Brown. 6th, Nathaniel Boyden; F. E. Shober. 7th, A. H. Jones; Plato Durham.

[3] This charge, which was entirely without foundation, was constantly made against Tourgee during his entire stay in North Carolina.

[4] *Sentinel,* Oct. 21, 1868.

James H. Harris who depended upon his color for his strength. His claim was finally settled by the payment by Deweese to him of two thousand dollars. John A. Hyman, another negro of influence, had to be paid five hundred dollars before he would consent to support Deweese.[1]

The *Standard* was very bitter throughout the campaign, but particularly so during the early part. The paper was nominally owned by N. Paige & Co., but was really the property of General Littlefield, who bought it from Governor Holden for $40,000, but did not wish the fact to be known. On September 2, the following editorial appeared:

### RETALIATION.

Something must be done. The law of self-preservation must necessarily be obeyed. Something must be done at all hazards; but the more quietly and peaceably it can be done, so much the better. The question then is, Can there be any remedy under the forms of law? We think so, unquestionably. Of course it is not to be supposed that men and women and children will starve to death while corn is still standing in the fields and while hogs and cattle are not kept under lock and key! But these are matters of minor importance and are to be expected, however much the necessity may be deplored. What we mean is, that there is one efficient remedy for this wholesale crusade of oppression carried on against the colored race to starve him into voting against his choice. The remedy is this: Whenever the Republicans have control of a county, let a meeting of the commissioners be called at once. Let them make out a list of all the colored stonemasons, bricklayers, plasterers, painters, and carpenters. Then let them select a site of sufficient dimensions for a village of from five to fifteen hundred colored paupers, as the case may be. The work itself will give employment to a considerable number of

[1] Letter of Deweese to *Cleveland Leader* copied in *Charlotte Democrat*, Aug. 28, 1876.

persons, and some time will be required to complete it. Then let the county paupers be moved in and be provided with houses and food at the expense of those who have made them paupers. Let the tax be so laid as to affect only the large land-holders. Not one in twenty owns any land at all, and the large land-holders are much rarer. This tax will fall lightly upon the great mass of the people, while the oppressive land-holder will be compelled to throw his broad acres upon the market to raise money to pay the taxes. And in addition to this, let the legislature deprive these exacting tyrants of the benefit of the stay law and compel them to pay their debts, to pass their lands under the sheriff's hammer and give the poor a chance to buy land.

On September 19, the following appeared:

### WORK.

But whatever else you work, don't forget to work among the women. The Confederacy wouldn't have lasted a year if it hadn't been for them. One good rebel woman is worth a dozen rebel men. Go after the women, then. They will make their husbands and their lovers shout for Grant and Colfax until they are hoarse, if you will manage to replace some of the diamond rings and laces Frank Blair stole from them when he was here. And don't hesitate to throw your arms around their necks now and then, when their husbands are not around, and give them a good ——. They all like it, and the Yankeer you are the better it takes. Our experience with female rebs is, that with all their sins they have a vast amount of human nature, and only want to have it appreciated to be the most loving creatures imaginable. Scalawags and carpet-baggers! Don't fail, therefore, as you canvass the State, to look after the women. You are all good-looking and they know it, but with native modesty, like sweet New England girls, they like to be approached first. Don't be afraid of their eyes—they glare like young leopards by daylight, but under the moon no blue, death-stricken fawn is half so tender or half so deep.

Don't read Judge Pearson's letter to them, but give them Byron and Shelley in volumes, and you will have them in your arms, if not in your party, in less than a week.[1]

The paper had hardly reached the public before organization commenced among certain of the citizens of Raleigh and but for the fact that information was given to Paige in some way which enabled him to leave before night, he would have been lynched. Feeling ran high and in consequence N. Paige & Co. had to give up the nominal control of the paper, and J. B. Neathery & Co. took it and, as before, the real control was in the hands of General Littlefield, probably acting under the advice of Governor Holden as to general policy. The feeling aroused by the article continued very bitter and while it had little if any effect upon the pending election, it was not forgotten and aroused considerable public sentiment against the Republican party and the administration. The *Sentinel* placed it at the head of its editorial columns where it remained for a long time. It may well be questioned why the editorial of a newspaper owned and edited by carpetbaggers should arouse indignation against the state administration, but it must be remembered that the *Standard* was the organ of the governor and bore the stamp of his general approval at least.

---

[1] The *National Intelligencer* had the following comment on the editorial:

" The wives and daughters of the people thus marked out for the insulting advances of Radical emissaries, it will be remembered, are the wives and daughters of the same men who, for four years, resisted the entire power of the Federal Government, and were able to put three hundred thousand men in the field. They fought, as we believe, in an entirely mistaken cause. Whether they will be able to make as good a contest in defence of the honor of their wives, daughters, and sisters thus marked out as the prey of the spoiler and the libertine, is a question which Wall Street and its speculators would do well to consider."

The Conservatives devoted much of their attention to the extravagance of the state administration and implored all thinking people to assist in ridding the State of the burden of Radical misrule. Not yet, however, had the people come to know the party, and many of those who were opposed to the state administration, were favorable to the election of Grant. The apathy of the voters was unusual and the congressional campaign really excited more interest than the presidential contest.

Governor Holden was determined not to take any chances of losing the election, and throughout the fall he busied himself with the campaign to the exclusion of nearly everything else. In September, he appealed to General Meade to authorize General Miles to station troops as he [the governor] might wish " to inspire a salutary terror " among the disaffected.[1] General Meade at once refused to do anything of the kind,[2] so the governor was compelled to fall back upon the resources of the administration which were the militia and the Union League, Governor Holden's twin allies in his policy of terror. In order to provide a basis for his military activity, he pretended to discover, or thought he discovered, that arms in large quantities were being imported into the State by the Conservatives for use at the election, and on October 12, he issued a proclamation, stating the supposed fact and admonishing the people to be orderly.[3] The *Standard* coöperated with him and urged the Republicans to arm themselves and drill in preparation for the third of November.[4] Much delight had been felt by the Republicans when the proposition was made

[1] *Executive Correspondence*, Holden, i, p. 44.
[2] *Ibid.*, p. 47.
[3] *Western Democrat*, Oct. 20, 1868.
[4] Issue of Sept. 30, 1868 *et seq.*

in Congress to furnish Southern governors with arms. All the North Carolina delegation favored it except Dockery and Boyden, the latter acting at the time with the Conservatives, but prepared to join the Republican party.[1] Both of them denounced the plan in the strongest terms,[2] and declared that there was no need of them in North Carolina. But the carpetbaggers put their usual policy into operation, and the press and the halls of Congress were full of the clamor of carefully manufactured recitals of " rebel outrages." Only by national aid, it was insisted, could " loyal " men be protected. Pressure was brought to bear on the governor and he ordered the organization of the " detailed militia." The matter was brought to the attention of General Meade and shortly thereafter, Governor Holden suspended his order. The probability is that he was warned by General Meade that the organization would not be allowed. The militia, however, were sent to Halifax and Robeson counties where they did no good and not much harm. In neither county was there any threat of interference with a free election but it seemed to the governor good politics to think that danger of such a thing existed. Just before the election, General Littlefield and Attorney General Coleman went to Washington and without success besought Grant and the Secretary of War to send troops to North Carolina to quell this threatened uprising of the Conservatives, or, as they phrased it, the " rebels." Two interesting examples of political activity came to

---

[1] Boyden said on the floor of the House: " Great God! We cannot afford to fight each other. . . . I warn the House that if arms are sent there, we will be ruined; we cannot live there. If we need anything in the way of arms, in God's name send an army of the United States there, but do not arm neighbor against neighbor." *Sentinel*, Aug. 8, 1868.

[2] *Globe*, Appendix, p. 472, 40 Cong., 2 sess.

light during the campaign. In New Bern, in October, a Union League circular, containing instructions, was found on the streets and published. It urged tri-weekly meetings of the League with as much excitement of the negroes as possible. They were to be drilled constantly and told that if the Democrats won the election, they would all be sold back into slavery. Farms and mules should be promised to all who voted for Grant, with the additional promise that, if he was elected, most of the offices should go to negroes. All methods were to be employed to poison their minds against the native white people, and if riots followed, no harm would be done. If needed to rouse them, some cabins should be burned and the deed attributed to the Conservatives.[1] The other was a circular, signed by S. Schenck, which was sent out. purporting to come from the national Republican headquarters, directing those to whom it was sent to urge the League and the Republicans generally to enroll in the militia, but to give assurance to the white men that they would not be called into service. It further stated that, if Grant was elected, the negro vote would not be needed again and the next Congress would inaugurate a system of colonization for the race. The Republicans denied responsibility for the circular and accused the Conservatives of having prepared it for circulation; and the latter asserted that the Republicans were employing it to conciliate such of the white Republicans as would not " swallow " the negro. It does not appear who was responsible for it.

A few days before the election, General Miles issued a general order forbidding officers and soldiers of the army from fraternizing with political parties. To the citizens of

[1] New Bern *Journal of Commerce*, Oct. 27, 1868; *Sentinel*, Oct. 31, 1868.

the State, he said that the campaign had been conducted with creditable quiet, and he expressed the hope that this would be the case until the end. " The record of North Carolina is yet unmarred by acts of lawlessness . . . and the present exercise of moderation and wisdom will hereafter be the source of much satisfaction to her citizens." [1]  In company with many of the officers and soldiers in his command, he promptly, and in violation of the laws of the State, registered and voted.[2]

The election, except for one disturbance, was very quiet throughout the State. Troops were stationed in a number of places and the one outbreak occurred at Asheville. A riot, commenced by negroes, resulted as usual in their dispersal by the white people and in the killing of one negro. The coroner's jury found the civil authorities guilty of neglect in not guarding against such an occurrence.[3]  All over the State the negroes voted illegally and the authorities made no efforts to prevent them.

The result of the election was a sweeping victory for the Republicans. Grant carried the State by a majority of 12,890, the vote standing as follows:

Grant ............................. 96,449
Seymour ........................... 83,559

Five of the Republican candidates for Congress were elected, the Conservatives electing F. E. Shober and Plato Durham. But in the case of the latter, the secretary of state held up the returns for about three months and, after reporting to the governor the election of Durham,[4] with the governor's knowledge, altered the returns and gave

[1] General Order no. 10, Oct. 31, 1868.

[2] Sentinel, Nov. 3, 1868.          [3] Ibid., Nov. 18, 1868.

[4] Report of the Secretary of State, 1869, p. 20.

A. H. Jones the certificate of election.[1] John Pool had already written the governor that if possible Jones must be given the certificate. C. L. Cobb was successful over the Conservative candidate and J. R. French. Nathaniel Boyden unsuccessfuly contested Shober's election and the latter, although he was under no disability other than his inability to take the " iron-clad " oath, had to wait until the law was altered to take his seat.[2]

The result of the election gave a free hand to the plunderers, who waited eagerly to begin their real work, and the State lay open to their hands.

### 4. THE LEGISLATURE OF 1868-1869

The legislature met in adjourned session in November. The governor in his message congratulated the General Assembly on the re-establishment of the state credit on a firm basis. Speaking of the state debt, and estimating the value of the property in the State as $200,000,000, he advised the levy of an *ad valorem* tax of one per cent to raise the necessary revenue. He recommended internal improvements, the encouragement of immigration, public education with separate schools for the two races, the repeal of all stay laws, and the thorough organization of the militia. The recommendation as to taxation was the most remarkable feature of the message. The estimate of the value of the property was far too high and the state constitution forbade the legislature to tax property more than at the rate of two-thirds of one per cent, both for state and county purposes.[3]

[1] *Raleigh Era*, Sept., 1872, quoted in *Wilmington Journal*, Sept. 13, 1872.

[2] *Globe*, pp. 245-248, 42 Cong., 2 sess.

[3] The *New York Express*, in commenting upon the message, said: " It is difficult to tell which is most to be pitied,—the people of the State or its finances."

The legislature went to work very slowly. Three newly-elected senators, Oates, Purdie, and Avery, were declared banned by the Fourteenth Amendment and refused seats. Avery's seat was at once declared vacant,[1] while Oates was allowed a month's time to get his disabilities removed. At the same time, a resolution in the House, looking to an investigation into the question of what members were banned, was voted down.[2] The Senate, a few days later, passed a similar resolution,[3] but nothing was done under it. John W. Stephens took the seat made vacant by the exclusion of Bedford Brown at the previous session. Among the other new members was one carpetbagger, G. Z. French. Jasper Etheridge and A. J. Jones, two of the new members, were both banned but since they were Republicans were not troubled. The changes made in this way made the political complexion of the two houses as follows:

|  | Senate | House | Joint Ballot |
|---|---|---|---|
| Republicans | 41 | 82 | 123 |
| Conservatives | 9 | 38 | 47 |
| Republican majority | 32 | 44 | 76 |

There was the same laxity in attendance which had been seen in the previous session. Renfrow, of Halifax, was a mail agent on the Raleigh and Gaston railroad; Stevens, one of the carpetbaggers, was very much occupied in looking after a boarding-house and a fish market which he had

[1] *Sen. Jour.*, Nov. 20, 1868. Avery had been a county solicitor before the war and had never taken the oath of allegiance to the United States. Judge Brooks, Chief Justice Pearson, and two Superior Court judges had already given opinions that county solicitors were not banned. Later the Supreme Court decided that they were, the chief justice dissenting.

[2] *Ho. Jour.*, Nov. 19, 1868.

[3] *Sen. Jour.*, p. 17.

established; Lieutenant-Governor Caldwell left his seat to go to Burke County and take the stump in the campaign for a successor to Avery; Etheridge was absent at his fishery; and Estes and a number of others held positions in the internal revenue service. Others failed to attend because it suited their convenience, and it was estimated that at least fifty members were absent daily.

At the opening of the session, it was proposed by a Conservative member that the *per diem* of the members should be reduced to four dollars and the mileage to ten cents. The Republicans ridiculed this and postponed indefinitely the consideration of the motion.[1] In the Senate, Shoffner, a Republican, offered a resolution for the appointment of a committee to examine members on oath as to mileage accounts. This was greeted with a howl by the carpetbaggers and some of the others who felt themselves not only insulted by the proposition but also threatened with financial injury.[2] One member, so it was stated on the floor, had already drawn for fifteen hundred miles and his was not a solitary case. In this connection, the cost of the session in *per diem* and mileage, is interesting. The session lasted one hundred and fifteen days and cost $195,529.10. Printing[3] for the session amounted to $23,893.08, and contingent expenses and the like made the total cost upwards of quarter of a million dollars. The members, however, were not satisfied and motions were made to pay those who remained in Raleigh during the Christmas recess $3 per day. In April, just before the session closed, G. Z. French made the same proposition for the summer recess. The only remark-

---

[1] *Standard,* Nov. 23, 1868.

[2] *Sentinel,* Nov. 25, 1868.

[3] Everything possible was printed even when the motion to print failed. Bills agreed upon in the Republican caucus were often printed before they were introduced.

able thing about these attempts is that they were not successful.  Truly might Josiah Turner, who assumed control of
the *Sentinel* in December, say, " Yes, we have a new North
Carolina and every true son of the State hangs his head in
humiliation and sorrow as he looks upon the evidences of
the metamorphosis.  In the gubernatorial chair, a man rejected and flouted, over and over again, by the people of
old North Carolina and owing his accidental elevation
(which commands ·no respect while obedience is yielded),
to an unscrupulous reversal of all his former principles!
In the judiciary, mountebanks, ignoramuses, and men who
bedraggle the ermine in the mud and mire of politics!  In
the offices of State, mercenary squatters and incompetents!
In the Legislative halls, where once giants sat, adventurers,
manikins, and gibbering Africans! " [1]

Rumor which had been busy with the legislature during
the recess, now became more active, and on November 30,
W. H. S. Sweet, a carpetbagger from Craven, introduced
a resolution for an investigation of the charges of bribery
and corruption in the legislature, particularly in relation to
the acts concerning the Chatham Railroad.  He stated that
he was able to prove conclusively that votes had been
bought.  A good deal of opposition was at once manifested,
but the resolution passed the Senate.  When it reached the
House, Estes, French, and Laflin, though not daring to
voice any active opposition, never lost an opportunity to
hinder its passage.  It was finally amended so as to reduce
the power of the committee, and then passed.  At once,
Pou, Ingram, and Seymour joined with the Conservatives
in supporting the original resolution and, leading the fight,
finally secured a reconsideration which resulted in its passage.  An attempt in the Senate to remove Sweet from the

---

[1] Issue of Dec. 10, 1868.

committee failed only by the vote of the lieutenant-governor which broke the tie. The *Standard* attacked Sweet very bitterly, but every other Republican paper in the State endorsed his course. The investigation resulted in little except a blow to the Conservatives. Senator Robbins had been exceedingly active in securing the investigation and, to the horror of his party, the report of the committee showed that at the preceding session he had accepted a fee of twenty dollars to assist John W. Stephens in securing his *per diem* and mileage in his contest with Bedford Brown. Robbins, at the time he took the fee, had already publicly announced his intention of voting in Stephens' favor, and he at once made a frank acknowledgment of the whole matter to the Senate. The committee reported that they were convinced that he had not acted dishonestly, but, viewed in any light, it was an unfortunate happening for the Conservatives. At his own request, he was censured by the Senate, an attempt to expel him failing by a decisive vote. The *Standard* demanded that he and Sweet should both be expelled, and an attempt was made without success to censure the latter. The charges made by Sweet were the result of information given him by a Mrs. Caverley who promised to testify, but Littlefield succeeded in getting her out of the State and rapidly followed with " Judge " Alden, a carpetbagger lobbyist who was working for him. After the committee was discharged, Littlefield returned.

Early in January, the news leaked that the location of the penitentiary had been accomplished by gross fraud upon the State, and a committee of investigation was at once raised. This met with a good deal of opposition from the more venal who openly condemned investigation of every sort. Hugh Downing, who was a member of the penitentiary committee, offered to buy the property, stating that he had an immediate chance to realize a large profit upon the transaction.   Pruyn, who with J. M. Heck had handled the deal, now came forward and offered to buy the land with certain deductions.   Both offers wese refused. The facts of the case were these.   The penitentiary committee, composed of C. L. Harris, superintendent of public works, R. W. Lassiter, J. H. Harris, J. H. Renfrow, J. A. Hyman, Hugh Downing, and W. M. Robbins, upon the representations of Heck and Pruyn and after a visit to the building site alone, Harris having visited the rest, agreed to purchase certain lands upon Deep River, not then owned by the other contracting parties.   A tract of twenty-five acres was selected for the site and eight thousand acres additional were accepted, separated from the former by about seven miles.   The owner of the latter tract was on the point of giving away about six thousand acres of it to negroes to avoid the taxes, when Heck bought it at sixty cents an acre.   The other land was purchased by him at a higher rate, one thousand acres at $3, and three hundred and fifty at something under $15.   Before the purchase, Heck agreed to sell to Pruyn for $56,000, and the latter came to an agreement with the committee, Robbins dissenting strongly, for $100,000.   No deeds passed until the whole deal was complete.   Then Harris gave Pruyn and Heck orders upon the treasurer for the bonds to the amount of $44,000 and $56,000 respectively and received deeds in return which were not warranted and in which over six thousand acres were undescribed.   None of the land was suitable, and the report of the committee to the effect that there were valuable mineral deposits there proved false.[1]

Much interest was excited by resolutions which were introduced in both houses requesting Congress to remove the disabilities of all citizens of the State.   After considerable

---

[1] *Legislative Documents,* 1868-1869, no. 7 and no. 19.

debate, in which the proscriptive tendencies of the carpet-baggers appeared very clearly, the resolutions were rejected. In the main the negroes favored removal and men like Ingram and Pou of the white Republicans were untiring in their efforts in behalf of the resolutions. How far the majority of the party were from such a point of view is best illustrated by the fact that, a little later, they seriously debated the question whether Vance's name should not be stricken from the list of incorporators of an insurance company which had applied for a charter. ,

The Fifteenth Amendment was ratified in March with large majorities in both houses, the vote being as follows:

|  | For | Against |
|---|---|---|
| Senate | 32 | 6 |
| House | 88 | 20 |

A number of Conservatives voted for it and supported it, including Hodnett, Jarvis, and Osborne.

A great deal of freak legislation was proposed and some was enacted. Notable in this was the " twenty dollar lawyer " act which admitted to the practice of law anyone who would pay the license tax mentioned and was of good moral character.[1] This later requirement was effectual only in theory. Naturally there was much opposition to it, but the argument that it was favorable to the negroes was very effective in securing its passage. A resolution was passed which, after reciting the confidence felt by the legislature in President Grant, instructed the senators and requested the members of Congress to vote for the repeal of the tenure of office act. A proposal to annex the city and county of Norfolk, Virginia, excited considerable interest and was seriously debated. A resolution was proposed which, after

[1] *Laws*, 1868-1869, chap. xlvi.

stating that doubt existed as to the length of the term of the members of the legislature, declared it to end in 1870. This did not suit the plans of those who had caused the ambiguity in the constitution and the resolution was stifled.

At the previous session, the apportionment of rooms in the Capitol to the state officers had been placed in the hands of a committee. In August, the papers and other effects of the Supreme Court were removed to the third floor of the building and put in small rooms not at all suited to the needs of the court. Adams, the auditor, and Ashley, the superintendent of public instruction, then took possession of the two rooms hitherto occupied by the court. The first meeting of the court was not due until January and it was currently rumored that its early hours would be interesting. When the court assembled, it took possession of its former quarters, had its papers brought down, and ordered Ashley to leave and remove the property of his office. Ashley ignored the order and the court appealed to the legislature for assistance. With some opposition on the part of the carpetbaggers, a resolution was passed ordering Ashley to vacate; another resolution instructed the attorney general to inquire into the legality of the action of the committee in moving the court; and the governor was requested to assign rooms to the state officers. The last resolution, as introduced, placed the location of the court in the governor's hands, but the friends of the court, realizing that he would ally himself with his colleagues, succeeded in striking out that provision. About the same time, the auditor was directed by the court to vacate the clerk's office. He ignored the order and, on February 13, was arrested by the marshal and committed to jail for contempt. The papers of the office were thrown into the corridor where they remained for some time. As the marshal, starting to jail with Adams, passed Governor Holden's office, the latter, rushing out in great excitement, exclaimed, "Supreme Court or no Supreme Court, chief justice or no chief justice, d—d if my officials shall go to jail. If they do, it shall be over the dead bodies of my militia." A crowd collected and forced the marshal with his prisoner into the office where he remained until peace was restored and the court placated in some way never made public. The debate in the legislature on the subject was angry, abounding in denunciation of the court and its action, and revealing considerable friction between the court and the legislature, but the auditor was finally given another room on the ground floor and the superintendent moved to the loft of the Capitol.

One of the most important acts of the session was the passage of a law making it a felony to go masked, painted, or disguised upon the highway with intent to terrify any citizen.[1] This was introduced by a carpetbagger and was of course directed against the Ku Klux who were beginning to attract public attention. A few days before, the governor had sent militia to Alamance County and the time was ripe for legislative action. As first presented, the bill exempted from punishment anyone who killed a person so disguised, even without provocation. In this form it passed the House, but the Senate struck out this provision which its opponents said was of such a character that the law should be entitled " An act to legalize murder."

The legislature could not be accused of a disinclination to legislate. Two hundred and eighty-two public laws and sixty-three public resolutions and almost as many of a private nature were passed. Much of this was of course the enactment of the code of civil procedure which was ground out by the code commission with the assistance of the New York Code which lawyers pronounced entirely un-

[1] *Laws*, 1868-1869, chap. cclxvii.

suitable to North Carolina law. The duties of state officers were defined,[1] and the salaries of the governor and treasurer fixed at five thousand and three thousand dollars respectively.[2] An elaborate act defining contempt of court and providing rules of procedure in contempt cases was passed.[3] This later proved an irksome limitation upon the power of some of the judges who were inclined to be thin-skinned where political criticism was concerned. A bill to define and punish bribery, introduced into the Senate the day after the exposure of Robbins' conduct in the Stephens matter, was characterized by one member as an insult to the State, but passed nevertheless. It was very stringent and provided a maximum punishment of a fine of five thousand dollars and five years' imprisonment. Members of the legislature, if convicted were thereby deprived of their seats and rendered forever incapable of holding office of honor, trust, and profit under the State.[4] Could this have been enforced, there would have been many vacancies in the body which passed the act.

One of the most creditable acts of the legislature was in relation to the swamp lands owned by the board of education. It became a matter of common knowledge that these were to be sold below their value for the benefit of certain interested parties, and immediately an act was passed making the consent of the legislature necessary to any sale of property appropriated to educational purposes.[5] An interesting light is thrown upon local economic conditions by the passage of forty-nine acts authorizing county commissioners to levy special taxes. Thirty-six of the counties concerned were in the hands of the Republicans. The reve-

---

[1] *Laws*, 1868-1869, chap. cclxx.

[2] *Ibid.*, chap. cx.                    [3] *Ibid.*, chap. clxxvii,

[4] *Ibid.*, chap. clxxvi.                [5] *Ibid.*, chap. lxxix.

nue bill, which was debated a long time, when finally passed, imposed a tax wherever possible. Like the Irishman at the fair, whenever they saw a head, they hit it. The act included an *ad valorem* tax of one-third of one per cent on real and personal property, an income tax of two and one-half per cent, an inheritance tax, progressive according to relationship, license taxes of every conceivable kind, and franchise taxes.[1]

The most important, and, from the standpoint of some of the legislators, most profitable, legislation was in relation to railroads. Sixteen acts on the subject were passed and nine of these carried provisions for state aid which would increase the state debt by fifteen million dollars. Fifty-five thousand dollars was appropriated to build two turnpikes. In none of this legislation were proper precautions taken to secure the State, and in the execution of the laws, the state officials were even more careless. By this time railroad legislation had become deservedly a scandal, and public criticism was severe. The majority of the legislators were either ignorant or reckless and far too many were entirely corrupt. Bill after bill was introduced without regard for constitutionality or policy. By the close of the session repudiation was in sight. Even such carpetbaggers as Sweet and Seymour began to protest. The former had had his eyes opened as to the motives and considerations influencing the legislation; the latter considered it chiefly from the standpoint of policy and expediency. In a speech made by him the last of January, he called attention to the fact that the convention had authorized the issue of bonds to the amount of $3,150,000, the legislature at its first session had authorized $6,700,000, and that by February, 1869, bills had been introduced which would authorize

[1] *Laws*, 1868-1869, chap. cviii.

a further increase of $17,650,000. He showed the impossibility of paying the interest and called attention to the bad policy of increasing the already serious depreciation of the state bonds by further issues. The result, he said, would be heavy taxation for one year, " taxation such as no free people ever endured," and total repudiation the next.[1]

By the close of the session the legislature was entirely discredited with all thinking people. There was little hope in anyone's mind of its doing any good and the only question was how it might be prevented from doing more harm. It had recklessly plunged the State so deep in debt that it was on the verge of avowed bankruptcy, and in doing so, it had been utterly contemptuous of constitutional restrictions.[2] It had shown itself partisan, selfish, incompetent, and corrupt. Judge Alden, before mentioned, told a New York banker that he could buy a majority of the body. George W. Swepson and M. S. Littlefield had bought for their joint use, among others, Abbott, Laflin, Estes, Foster, Hyman, Sinclair, Stevens, J. H. Harris, and Rev. Hugh Downing.[3] These facts were not clearly proved as yet, but they were suspected, and the result was fatal to the majority. At the beginning of their term they had presented a united front to the Conservatives who were ignored in debate or silenced by the call of the previous question. This condition of affairs was now soon changed. Friction among themselves increased until the majority was apparently about to break up into hostile cliques. The deportment of the members was never good and became worse as the session progressed. Abusive and profane language was com-

---

[1] *Sentinel,* January 30, 1869.

[2] Almost every bill authorizing the levy of a special county tax was in violation of the constitution. Art. II, sec. 16.

[3] The proof of this fact is to be found in the two fraud commission reports.

mon in debate and there were occasional personal encounters. Horseplay and buffoonery were usual and on the
day of adjournment for the Christmas recess, a brass band
was brought into the hall of the House and played from
time to time. At the April adjournment, a large number
of the members bought fox horns from a peddler and in
the two houses and all over the Capitol, including the
top of the dome, blew them constantly and vociferously.
A large number were drunk and the scene was disgraceful
beyond words. During the session, a circus visited Raleigh
and the doors of the two houses had to be locked and the
seregants-at-arms sent out to arrest absent members [1] in
order to secure a quorum.

The record was not one to inspire reverence for government or admiration for Reconstruction and its results.
How full of evil those results were, was, however, not yet
clearly seen.

[1] *Sentinel,* March 5 and 9, 1869.

# CHAPTER TEN

## THE REPUBLICAN RÉGIME (*Continued*)

### I. POLITICS IN 1869

THE lines of cleavage in the Republican party were not concealed from the Conservatives, but the latter received with the knowledge no promise of immediate benefit; it only seemed to indicate a cause for hope for the future. Nevertheless, no opportunity was lost to widen any breach that was visible, nor was the battle against the Radicals lessened at all when the legislature adjourned. The most influential agency in this contest was the *Sentinel,* edited by Josiah Turner with an enthusiasm for polemics that seemed little short of diabolical to his opponents. He was a man of positive genius for political warfare, sparing not and caring little where he struck. Quick-witted, ingenious in putting an opponent on the defensive and keeping him there, and at the same time ignoring a counter attack, gifted with a keen sense of humor, he saw the ridiculous side of everything and employed it as a means to an end, realizing clearly that in politics a dangerous enemy is often rendered harmless by laughter and ridicule. He had a nickname for nearly every carpetbagger and for a number of the native Republicans. The " hands," " Pilgrim " Ashley, " Windy Billy " Henderson " who stole Darr's mule " (or as he later phrased it, " who was tried and acquitted of stealing Darr's mule "), " Kildee " Lassiter, " Chicken " Stephens, "Greasy Sam " Watts, " Blow your Horn Billy " Smith, " the Governor's son Joseph," " Ipecac " Menninger, " Colonel Heck who teaches the Sunday School," "Parson" Sinclair, "Sleepy" Downing, "Ku Klux" Ingram, "Grapevine" John Ragland, and "Captain" Thomas Settle, are terms that are familiar in North Carolina even to-day. No man in the State was so bitterly hated by the Republicans and, as time went on, so intensely feared. He saw everything. Through sources of information never revealed, he learned of plans and policies that were studiously concealed from the public by their originators. He never forgot or overlooked a vital point, never lost his temper, and never forgave, but cunning as a serpent, writing with a pen that seemed dipped in gall, he relentlessly pursued what now became the chief aim of his existence, the overthrow of the Republican party in the State. No man was ever better adapted to such work, for his genius was destructive always and he naturally belonged to the opposition. He was the inspiration of the Conservative party in its deepest gloom, and to him more than to any other one man belongs the credit for the speedy overthrow of Reconstruction in North Carolina.

Among the first to writhe under his lash was Governor Holden. The first manifestation of this was an attack made upon Turner by Joseph W. Holden. In company with several of his associates, including Laflin, Sloan, and Pruyn, all carrying heavy sticks, he visited the *Sentinel* office in March. Turner was absent, but upon his return that afternoon, he was met outside the railroad station by Holden, Menninger, a brother of the secretary of state, C. L. Harris, and a number of others. Menninger accosted him and was threatening him when Turner, seeing the group advancing upon him, drew a pistol and warned them to keep away. He was at once arrested, carried to the mayor's office, and bound over to a higher court. Holden was also held to bail. The governor was present and gave bail for his son's ap-

pearance, after which he made a speech in which he said
that he had been aware of what was planned, that he approved it fully, and that he had come down for the purpose
of giving bail. The mayor, who was his son-in-law, sought
without success to silence him. Turner then suggested that
they should hold a joint debate and the governor in a rage
almost precipitated a riot. The incident was of course
turned to advantage by Turner.

One of the most important political happenings of the
year grew out of an action on the part of the bar of the
State which was not intended to have any partisan political bearing. Reference has already been made to the part
played by several judges in the presidential campaign of
1868. Nothing in Reconstruction caused such a shock to
the bar as their action which was so far removed from the
precedents set by the bench during the period prior to 1868.
B. F. Moore, the " father of the bar," was much aroused
and felt it incumbent upon himself to sound a note of warning and take such steps as would prevent the recurrence of
such conduct. He therefore drew up the following protest
which he sent over the State for signatures:

A Solemn Protest of the Bar of North Carolina Against
Judicial Interference in Political Affairs.

The undersigned, present or former members of the bar of
North Carolina, have witnessed the late public demonstration
of political partisanship by the judges of the Supreme Court
of the State with profound regret and unfeigned alarm for the
purity of the future administration of the laws of the land.

Active and open participation in the strife of political contests by any judge of the State, so far as we recollect, or tradition or history has informed us, was unknown to the people
until the late exhibitions. To say that these were wholly unexpected, and that a prediction of them by the wisest among
us would have been spurned as incredible, would not express

half of our astonishment, or the painful shock suffered by our feelings when we saw the humiliating fact accomplished.

Not only did we not anticipate it, but we thought it was impossible to be done in our day. Many of us have passed through political times almost as exciting as those of to-day; and most of us recently through one more excited; but never before have we seen the judges of the Supreme Court, singly or *en masse,* moved from that becoming propriety so indispensable to secure the respect of the people, and throwing aside the ermine, rush into the mad contest of politics under the excitement of drums and flags. From the unerring lessons of the past we are assured that a judge who openly and publicly displays his political party zeal renders himself unfit to hold the "balance of justice," and that whenever an occasion may offer to serve his fellow partisans, he will yield to the temptation, and the "wavering balance" will shake.

It is a natural weakness in man that he who warmly and publicly identifies himself with a political party will be tempted to uphold the party which upholds him, and all experience teaches us that a partisan judge cannot be safely trusted to settle the great questions of a political constitution, while he reads and studies the book of its laws under the banners of a party.

Unwilling that our silence should be construed into an indifference to the humiliating spectacle now passing around us, influenced solely by a spirit of love and veneration for the past purity, which has distinguished the administration of the law in our State, and animated by the hope that the voice of the bar of North Carolina will not be powerless to avert the pernicious example, which we have denounced, and to repress its contagious influence, we have under a sense of solemn duty subscribed and published this paper.

One hundred and eight lawyers signed it.[1] In order to

---

[1] Judge Battle, Judge Manly, and Judge Ruffin, all of whom had been members of the Supreme Court, declined from motives of delicacy to sign the protest. Judge Battle, in addition, thought it would do no good, but the others heartily approved it.

prevent a political construction from being placed upon their action, the matter was not made public until April 19, 1869, when it appeared in the *Sentinel* and other papers. It excited less comment in the press than might have been expected. It won general approval from the Conservative papers and ridicule from the Republican, but no one voiced any belief that the Supreme Court would take official notice of it. When the court met in June, to the entire surprise of the protesting lawyers, the chief justice stated that the protest was a contempt of court and directed the clerk to serve a rule upon twenty-five of the protestants, who practiced before the court, to show cause why they should not be silenced until they had purged themselves of the contempt. Those affected, who were present, were not allowed to appear in their cases. It was finally arranged that the rule should be served upon B. F. Moore, E. G. Haywood, and Thomas Bragg, and that the matter should be argued before the court a week later. Chief Justice Pearson declared in court that " as the case appeared, it was as if the bar had been lying in wait to murder the judiciary."

There was naturally great excitement not only among the lawyers, but also among the politicians. A storm of protest against the action of the court came from the Conservative press, while the Republican papers declared the protest simply an example of the dishonest political methods employed by wily politicians who had now fallen into their own net.[1]

On the appointed day, the case was called. The respondents were represented by an unusually able body of counsel, including one former Supreme Court judge, three former Superior Court judges, and a future chief justice, all of whom volunteered for the case.[2] The chief justice

---

[1] *Standard*, June 10, 1869.

[2] W. H. Battle, D. G. Fowle, D. A. Barnes, S. H. Person, and W. N. H. Smith were the lawyers alluded to.

announced that the proposed mediation of the bar would not be accepted and then called the case against Moore. His answer was declared to be the answer of all. In substance, it was: (1) He admitted signing the protest, but denied the jurisdiction of the court. (2) He claimed that the publication was neither libellous nor calculated to impair the respect due the court. (3) He admitted that the purpose of the protest was to express disapproval of the conduct of individuals on the bench, but disavowed any intention of committing a contempt, declaring that his motive was to preserve the purity which had always distinguished the administration of justice in the courts of the State. In the argument which followed, Moore's counsel held that such proceedings could not be commenced except upon affidavit; that there could be no contempt without intent; and that the court had no authority for its act, particularly since the passage by the legislature of an act defining contempt, under which the protest could not come. They also recalled the activity of the judges in the campaign.

The decision of the court was read by the chief justice on June 19. He declared that no affidavit was necessary for opening the case; that the statute, referred to in the answer, did not deprive the court of its common law jurisdiction over the behavior of its attorneys; and that the protest was libellous and of a character " to impair the respect due to the authority of the court "; but he accepted the disavowal as sufficient, and ordered the rule discharged, at the same time administering a scolding to Moore for the reference in his answer to the conduct of individuals on the bench. In the other cases, a disclaimer was accepted without further process. The opinion of the chief justice was weak and unworthy of his intellect and ability. But the court, bent on revenge, had taken an indefensible position and discovered the fact too late. The protesting attorneys came out of the case with credit and the court suffered a severe blow in reputation and in public respect.[1]  In private, many supporters of the judges condemned them for their action,[2] and the political effect of the matter was distinctly injurious to the Republican party.  The question was also raised by some of the judges later.  Judge Dick and Judge Settle refused to allow signers of the protest to appear before them in proceedings at chambers until they had answered the rule.  Thomas Ruffin, Jr., later a judge of the Supreme Court, was silenced by the former who asked him afterwards what he thought of the action.  Ruffin's reply was that the judge had behaved contemptibly.  Judge Dick

---

[1] Moore wrote to his daughter soon after the decision of the court: "While I rejoice that my course is sustained by all the virtuous and sensible, yet I weep over the degradation into which the Court has plunged itself and the liberties of freemen.  I had no purpose to degrade the Court; God knows that my only object was to purify it and elevate it.

"The conduct of individuals composing the Court was unbecoming the judges, according to my judgment, founded upon all the past examples of the enlightened men who had adorned our annals.  I saw that if such conduct should be tolerated and become common, the judiciary would sink into partizan political corruption.  I felt it my duty as the oldest member of the bar to lift my wavering voice against the pernicious example.  I did so as an act of duty.  I feel now still more sensibly that it was my duty.  I made no sacrifice in doing my duty.  The ordeal I have passed through has made me proud of my position.  I felt that I was called to account for having rebuked a great vice, for having discharged fearlessly a high and noble duty, and I was prepared to come off more than conqueror.  I feel no stain on my name.  There is none.  I am cheered by every lawyer and gentleman I have heard speak, without as well as within the State.  Every man of sense ridicules the opinion of the Court.  It is without law to sustain it, contradictory, despotic, spiteful, and malignant.  It is the common sport of every man.  I wish I could have saved the Court from the degradation into which they have fallen, but it was bent on revenge and lo! they have fallen into their own pit."

[2] Judge Watts, in speaking of the matter, said, "If any member of the bar insults me in court, I say, 'Go to jail;' if out of court, I say, 'Go to hell.'"

called him a liar and was the immediate recipient of a vigorous chastisement.

In the summer, a disagreement arose between the governor and C. L. Harris as to the right of the former to appoint a state proxy and directors for the railroads in which the State had an interest. Each hurled injunctions against the other, but the governor was successful. The quarrel was important as the first outward manifestation of the defection from Holden of the important Harris-Logan group of Republicans in Cleveland and Rutherford. Governor Holden had persuaded Harris to accept the nomination for superintendent of public works, instead of demanding the presidency of the North Carolina Railroad which had been promised him, by assuring him that he should have the entire control of the state railways. The governor now declined to fulfil the agreement, and the break came. The *Rutherford Star,* a Republican paper, began to criticise the governor and, by the end of the year, was openly hostile. In the meantime, the *Standard* threatened to read Harris out of the party. This paper was still owned by Littlefield whom, in the face of protest, the governor had shamelessly appointed state printer. It was the most devoted supporter of the administration. The *New Bern Times,* also Republican, was another exponent of hostility to the governor. This was caused by the belief that Holden was seeking to discriminate against the east in his railroad appointments and policy. This same thing won him the enmity of Alfred and Oliver H. Dockery.

Spice was added to politics in the State by the personal difficulties of the radicals, particularly of Senator Abbott. In the spring, Senator Sprague, of Rhode Island, on the floor of the Senate, called him a " puppy dog." Abbott blustered, declared that such language might be endured by cold-blooded senators from the North, but that, to a

Southern man, it was unbearable. He therefore made a public demand for an apology, which Sprague contemptuously declined to make, and Abbott subsided. A little later, he attempted to threaten into silence the editor of a New Hampshire paper who was commenting upon certain not altogether creditable incidents of Abbott's career in that State. The only result was a flood of caustic criticism. In August, Abbott wrote an editorial for the *Wilmington Post,* which he owned and controlled. The article was grossly insulting to J. A. Engelhard, the editor of the *Wilmington Journal.* He then had himself put under bond to keep the peace. Engelhard challenged him, offering to pay the bond. In reply, Abbott expressed his willingness to join in a retraction of all harsh words and in a truce for the future. This was declined by Engelhard's friends in the matter who insisted upon an unconditional apology, which Abbott then made. The incident was particularly humorous because of the fact that he had charged Engelhard with cowardice.[1] These were not all of Abbott's troubles. As talk of the Ku Klux became general, he began to address the negroes in Wilmington advising them to arm and prepare to defend themselves. He did not always confine himself to such comparatively pacific suggestions, but, by implication at least, suggested retaliation. There were no Ku Klux in Wilmington, but a number of citizens shortly thereafter went to him and warned him to desist on pain of personal punishment. He blusteringly replied that he would not be threatened. The answer to this was that the warning was not intended as a threat but only as a simple notice that, in the event of any trouble in the city with the negroes, he would instantly be put to death.[2] For the rest of

[1] *Sentinel,* Aug. 20, 1869.

[2] This information was given the author by one of the participants in the interview.

his public career, the general was the most reserved of all the carpetbaggers. He had said in August, 1868, while in the legislature, " the people must learn that we are their masters," but, during the two years of Republican rule, he learned several lessons to the contrary. In the Senate, he still spoke of Raleigh as " the capital of the province," but any influence that he might have had disappeared, and in 1870, the *Nation* said that a Conservative victory in North Carolina would be a blessing, if only for the fact that it would remove Abbott from the Senate.

Other Republican leaders were not so prudent as Abbott when personal safety was concerned. J. W. Holden and William M. Coleman fought in public, and, on another occasion, the former engaged in a public brawl somewhat to his disfigurement and entirely to his discredit. He was in bad company—that of the worst element of the carpetbaggers—and this evil influence rapidly transformed a nature that seemed to have had much in it that was attractive and caused the prostitution of an intellect far above the average.

During the summer, so it was said, the influence of the state administration was brought to bear upon the President to secure the removal of Coleman by means of some foreign appointment. He was regarded as incompetent and was thought to be an injury to the party. He was appointed consul to Stettin and, accepting, departed from the State.

Early in the year, the discussion of the state debt became general. The Republicans were put on the defensive at once and were never able to justify themselves to the public for its creation. Not only its size, but the methods by which it had been incurred and the squandering of the funds were discussed with no resulting benefit to the administration. Repudiation was openly and generally advocated and the doctrine daily found new adherents. The activity of the railroad lobby excited disgust which increased as the credit of the State sank steadily lower. The extravagance of the administration was also largely discussed by the Conservatives with considerable political effect.

The Ku Klux operations which were not very widely extended and not nearly so lawless as those of the Union League, excited the anger, fear, and hatred of the Republican leaders. The sending of militia to Alamance County, to be followed later by federal troops, had a corresponding influence upon the Conservatives. The governor planned to send troops to Hillsboro, but his friends warned him not to do so.[1] Late in the same month, he warned the people of Orange, Chatham, Lenoir, and Jones to abstain from lawlessness and threatened to declare them in insurrection. About the same time, Chief Justice Pearson wrote a letter to George Little, in which he said the entire State was in as profound peace as it had ever been. The governor's action did not at all aid the Republican party and was probably a cause of strength to the opposition. The mass of the people were fully aware of the fact that, if the governor had been more zealous in trying to prevent radical lawlessness, he would not have had as much occasion to worry over Ku Klux outrages, many of which had been carefully invented for the press with a full realization of their political value. At the same time, it seems beyond question that Governor Holden believed that the condition of affairs seriously menaced the safety and welfare of the State as well as of his party. In so far he was justified.

There were a number of elections in August to fill vacancies. The results gave no indication of political change. One of them gives a striking example of the political

---

[1] T. C. Evans to W. W. Holden, Oct. 26, 1869.

methods in vogue. Pitt County before this time had seven voting precincts. These were now reduced to five. One was one hundred yards from the Edgecombe line; the second, three miles from the Martin line; the third, three miles from the Craven line; the fourth, half a mile from the Greene line; and the fifth, in Greenville, the county seat. Some of the voters had to go nearly thirty miles to vote, while the negroes from the adjoining counties mentioned could very conveniently come to help out the Republican cause in Pitt.[1] The *Sentinel* had little comment to make upon the results of the elections, but sounded this note of warning:

THE DAY OF RECKONING WILL COME!

\*    \*    \*    \*    \*    \*

Our firm conviction is that the people will not tolerate these villainies a great while longer; the day of reckoning cometh, and it will be terrible. The carpet-bagger race will then hurry off to some other field of spoils and laugh at the calamity of their dupes and co-workers in iniquity, but the *native* culprits must answer at the bar of public opinion, and in many cases at the bar of the Court of high crimes. We tell the native scalawags that the day is not far distant when the veil that now hides their crimes from the public gaze will be withdrawn, and they will be exposed to the scorn and indignation of an outraged people.[2]

A month later, getting a clear view of the situation, it advocated a complete acceptance of Reconstruction and its results, including negro suffrage, and urged renewed efforts on the part of all citizens to secure good government.[3] This was good politics, for there was no hope of overthrowing the new order, and its acceptance was necessary before re-

[1] *Sentinel*, Oct. 6, 1869.     [2] Issue of Aug. 6, 1869.
[3] Issue of Sept. 9, 1869.

form could be secured. The time was ripe for Conservative activity, for the Republican party was in worse straits than it realized. In addition to the factions already mentioned, others were forming. The negroes were becoming dissatisfied with their share of the spoils and their leaders boldly claimed a large proportion of the public plunder. The white natives, attempting to fix upon the carpetbaggers the blame for extravagance and corruption, were so busy defending themselves that they had small time to question the " loyalty " of their opponents. The witty saying that " loyalty means stealing by statute " was rapidly coming into general acceptance and the word lost caste. The beginning of the end was seen in the autumn [1] and the session of the legislature, dreaded at first by the Conservatives because of the financial burden it entailed, was nevertheless welcomed as the opportunity of proving conclusively that the Republicans were unfit to rule.

## 2. THE LEGISLATURE OF 1869-1870

The third and last session of the " mongrel " legislature differed greatly from its predecessors. The credit of the State was gone, all resources were taxed to their limit, and there remained nothing for the corrupt to exploit; nothing to steal. The haughty and proscriptive spirit displayed by the majority had disappeared, and the hitherto despised minority began to assume importance as the majority of a rapidly approaching to-morrow which would bring a reckoning. In consequence, unity departed from the Republicans, and, during most of the session, the Conservative minority drove before them the badly-demoralized majority.

The governor's message was of little importance except in respect to three things. He recommended the payment

---

[1] *New York Herald*, Oct. 27, 1869.

of the interest on the debt, declaring that the State had received the money from the bonds, but advised against any further increase of the debt. He advised an appeal to Congress for a general amnesty bill, not because he thought amnesty was deserved, but because it would relieve friction. Most important of all, was a request to the legislature to increase his power in the use of the militia. Governor Holden evidently desired to appear to his political opponents equipped with an olive branch and a sword.

There was some slight change in the membership of the legislature, caused by death or resignation, but the political complexion remained the same. One more negro was in the House, succeeding Estes who had resigned.[1]

Immediately after the session began, bills to carry out the governor's suggestions were introduced. A resolution favoring general amnesty passed both houses by good majorities.[2] One introduced by Seymour endorsing the validity of the debt, opposing any increase, and condemning repudiation, failed to pass. The debate indicated clearly that most of the members did not expect the bonds to be paid. Later, a bill was passed, intended to restore the credit of the State by requiring strict account by the various railroad presidents for the bonds received from the State, with the return to the treasury of all that were still unsold, as well as of the unexpended money received for those already sold. The bill also provided that no bonds should be sold for less than sixty cents on the dollar.[3] The Conservatives exerted a large influence in the debates on this bill.

The third recommendation of the governor resulted in a

[1] J. S. W. Eagles of New Hanover.
[2] *Resolutions*, 1869–1870, p. 333.
[3] *Laws*, 1869–1870, chap. xxxviii.

bill " for the better protection of life and property," introduced in December by Senator Shoffner, of Alamance, and
thereafter known by his name.  The author of it, however,
was John Pool and rumor had it that Shoffner was paid a
considerable sum of money for consenting to father it.
The act empowered the governor, whenever, in his judgment, the civil authorities in any county were unable to
protect its citizens, to declare the county in a state of insurrection and to call into active service the militia of the
State for its suppression.  The judges and solicitors were
given power to remove to another county the trial of any
person indicted in any county for murder, conspiracy, or
going masked, painted, or disguised.  All expenses incident
to either action were to be borne by the county concerned,
the privilege being given to the county to tax the costs upon
any persons convicted.[1]  The bill was vehemently opposed
by the Conservatives who declared it unnecessary and denounced it as unconstitutional and intended simply to give
the governor unlimited miltary power to use for political
purposes.[2]  It passed all three readings in the Senate on the
day of introduction by a strict party vote and was sent to
the House where it came up on the following day, but many
Republicans were absent, and the Conservatives succeeded
in preventing a quorum from voting on the third reading,
and the bill went over until after the Christmas recess.
During this time, the *Sentinel* strove to arouse public sentiment against the bill to such an extent as to insure its failure, but the Republicans were determined to force it
through, and, after a bitter debate, passed it with a number
of the party voting against it, for Republican sentiment
was not at all united on it.  W. T. Gunter, of Chatham, an
intense Republican, led the fight on it in the House and even

[1] *Laws*, 1869-1870, chap. xxvii.        [2] *Sentinel*, Dec. 18, 1869.

Deweese wrote many letters from Washington in opposition to its passage. Seymour, who was its chief defender, acknowledged that it was wrong in principle but declared that the times demanded it. In private conversation, he made no secret of the fact that it was passed as the only hope of holding the State Republican.[1] The chief defence of the Republicans was that the bill did not authorize the suspension of the writ of *habeas corpus.*

The most interesting feature of the session was the amount of time spent in discussion of investigation of the widespread charges of fraud, and in making such investigations, at least three-fourths of the time of the session being consumed in this way. The session had scarcely commenced before bills providing for various inquiries were introduced. The one that attracted most immediate attention provided for an investigation of the Western North Carolina Railroad. A. J. Jones, a railroad president himself, who had already stolen a large amount of bonds, was vehement in his opposition and denunciation of the resolution.[2] It failed, but others followed, were passed, then reconsidered and defeated only to be replaced by others. All the influence of the administration was brought to bear against any investigation, and the carpet-baggers fought every suggestion of such a thing, declaring the very proposition an insult. The *Standard* pronounced any such resolution " a stab at the Republican party," and called upon the party to form a solid phalanx and act without regard to a " snarling minority." Speaking of Republicans who voted with Conservatives, it said, " Let them be refused the confidence of Republicans or admittance to the councils of the party. Let them be treated as Judases, who seek to betray

[1] *Report* of the Senate Ku Klux Committee, p. 224.
[2] *Sentinel*, Nov. 20, 1869.

those who have trusted them. Let Republicans act with Republicans and not with enemies." [1] The last editorial was caused by the action of the House in going into the commitee of the whole and summoning the treasurer before it. Immediately, Littlefield left Raleigh. Nothing came of the investigation so conducted. The Republicans voted down every genuine effort to secure the truth, and, when the committee of the whole met, showed the same disposition, demanding that the Conservative members should conduct the investigation, but declining to assist or to sustain them. The superintendent of public works was summoned and showed a complete ignorance of the condition of the various railroads in which the State was interested. The treasurer was summoned a second time and with the governor's approval declined to appear. [2] The sittings of the commitee continued until close to the end of the session, amounting to little because of the determination of the Republicans to protect certain persons. In March, Littlefield finally appeared, but Sinclair, Seymour, French, Downing, and James H. Harris combined and were able to exert enough influence to prevent his being seriously troubled. [3] Governor Holden and W. A. Smith, the president of the North Carolina Railroad, got Swepson out of town on a special train at midnight to avoid appearance.

In January, the Senate authorized a committee of investigation, and Lieutenant-Governor Caldwell appointed Thomas Bragg, S. F. Phillips, and W. L. Scott, who conducted an investigation as exhaustive as the time allowed them permitted. The testimony taken by them showed to some extent the condition of affairs, but no action was taken. The situation became increasingly embarrassing

---

[1] Issues of Nov. 20, 1869, and Nov. 29, 1869.

[2] *Sentinel*, Dec. 15, 1869.     [3] *Ibid.*, Mar. 8, 1870.

for the Republicans, for the Conservatives were pressing investigation at every point, and it was bad policy to oppose
such plans openly, and still worse to allow investigation to
continue. One element never ceased opposition and the
*Standard* became its mouthpiece. The *Sentinel*, referring
to this, said, " Rave on, ye Radical plunderers; but your
days of iniquity and fraud and corruption are fast coming
to an end. The people, insulted and robbed, will not much
longer suffer you to pursue your foul practices and elude
public justice." [1] A little later, it addressed the following
to the legislature:

Did you never read, Hands, that " there is a time when
great States rush to ruin "? That time is now upon this State.
North Carolina is now no more like the North Carolina of
former days than Chicken Stephens is like Bartlett Yancey,
or Cuffee Mayo is like Judge Gilliam. The North Carolina
served, loved, and honored by Gaston, Nash, Badger, Swain,
and Ruffin is the same North Carolina no more. She is now
the " hog trough " of the Union where Littlefield, Deweese,
Laflin, Tourgee, Heaton, Ashley, Brewer, and Abbott, and
such swine, come to wallow with native hogs like Holden,
Victor, and Greasy Sam.[2]

In spite of the entreaties of the *Standard* and the carpetbaggers, the legislature passed a number of resolutions
under Conservative pressure. The treasurer was requested
to inform the legislature as to the whereabouts of the bonds
issued to Pruyn and Heck for the penitentiary site, and of
those issued to the Chatham Railroad, which had been declared unconstitutional. He was also asked for reports on the
sums paid to the code commissioners and clerks of the legislature, on the number of bonds issued, and on the expenses

[1] Issue of Feb. 9, 1870.
[2] The reference is to Judge Watts. Issue of Feb. 19, 1870.

of the state government. The auditor was asked to report the amount and items of contingent expenses, the amounts spent on the Capitol Square and for ice. Committees were appointed on these and a number of other matters, including the state printing. Finally, Littlefield and his coterie determined to check the movement and, on the night of March 1, 1870, a large number of Republican members of the legislature were entertained by Littlefield at an oyster supper at which liquor was unlimited. A large number were soon drunk and party spirit having been roused to a high degree, nineteen senators agreed to vote for abolishing the fraud commission, and this was done the next day.[1]

In the meantime, something more than investigation had been accomplished, though against the real desire of the majority. The Senate passed a resolution instructing the treasurer not to pay any interest on the special tax bonds until further action by the legislature. This is interesting as an expression of sentiment on the subject. The office of state printer was abolished to dispose of Littlefield and re-established a few days later with the power of appointment vested in the legislature. Most important of all was the repeal of all appropriations of bonds in aid of railroads,[2] which was accomplished after a bitter debate. At this point, the *Standard* repudiated the legislature in the following words:

Its every act now directly injures the State. Under pretense of benefiting the people, bills are passed which are antagonistic to the interests of the people.

It has ruined the credit of the State. It has forced dishonor upon a people whose good name none have dared till now to traduce.

[1] *Sentinel*, March 4, 5, 1870. *Report* of the Bragg Fraud Commission.

[2] *Laws*, 1869–1870, chap. lxxi.

It has, led by men who care for nothing save their unworthy selves, passed laws which will render its name infamous forever, forever.[1]

A pretty piece of rascality came to light after the close of the session, though it never became known generally. O. S. Hayes, a carpetbagger, introduced a bill requiring foreign insurance companies to deposit with the state treasurer a sum in gold equal to one-half the amount of their policies in force in the State. This was passed and ratified and was then taken from the office of the secretary of state and not included in the published laws. Soon after adjournment, Barry Brothers, of Wilmington, who represented the Liverpool, London & Globe Insurance Company, were notified that such an act had been passed and that if they would pay a proper amount, it would never be heard of again. They at once inquired of the secretary of state if such a law had been passed, but he did not reply. A visit by an agent secured the statement that there was no record of such a law. Once more a demand was made for money coupled with the statement that the Republican executive committee was in urgent need of funds for the coming campaign. Barry Brothers and Silas N. Martin, the Republican mayor of Wilmington, then laid the case before Governor Holden. Immediately a letter came from the secretary of state saying that the bill had been stolen, and referring them to Foster, of Bladen, another carpetbagger, as a person who knew all about it. Martin and Barry pressed the matter, the former declaring it would ruin the party, and Governor Holden, who seemed entirely indifferent, said, " Dishonesty and corruption on the part of a few cannot injure the Republican party. The party as a party is not to blame." Martin replied that the party was justly

[1] Issue of Feb. 22, 1870.

blamed. " With our credit completely annihilated, our taxes large, our progress slow, it becomes us to root out all dishonest men. If we do not, our fate is beyond doubt." [1]

Not long after the legislature assembled, the question of the length of its term again arose. The point of the matter was this. One provision of the constitution declared that the term of the legislature chosen in April, 1868, should " terminate as if they had been elected at the first ensuing regular election." A later provision made the term two years and ordered the first election to be held on the first Thursday in August, 1870. With this ambiguity as a basis, a considerable group shamelessly attempted to prolong the life of the legislature to 1872. The intention was evident and Plato Durham, in order to draw public attention to the matter, introduced a resolution declaring that the term ended in 1870. The matter was finally referred to the Supreme Court which had, of course, nothing to do with the matter. But Chief Justice Pearson was known to have been favorable to the four-year term,[2] and it was probably thought that he would carry the court with him. Governor Holden was believed to have favored it at first but to have changed his mind upon discovering that a majority of the existing body favored Judge Settle as Abbott's successor in the Senate. The *Standard* also opposed the plan for somewhat the same reason. In the midst of the discussion, Judge Tourgee volunteered the information that he, Sweet, and Heaton had agreed in the convention that the first legislature would be unpopular, and that, for the sake of the party, they had inserted the clause mentioned in order

[1] Barry to Holden, April 11, 1870; Martin to Holden, April 11, 1870, April 20, 1870; Barry to Martin, April 20, 1870. These letters are to be found in the Holden papers in the executive office in Raleigh.

[2] *Memoir of W. W. Holden*, p. 159.

that the body might hold over.[1] Sweet and Heaton at once denounced Tourgee as a liar so far as his charges concerned themselves.[2] Much discussion was provoked and the *Sentinel* wittily said that the Radicals " were trying to persuade Cuffee Mayo that biennial meant once in four years and four months." When the matter was referred to the Supreme Court, Judges Pearson and Dick declared in favor of the two-year term and the other three judges declined to discuss the question. The matter was put off until the suspicion became general that the majority would fail to order an election. Finally, when that course was seen to be dangerous, the election was ordered.

But little legislation of importance was secured. A proposition for a constitutional convention was voted down. Forty-eight counties were allowed to levy special taxes and seven to issue bonds. As usual, most of them were under Republican control.

In March, J. W. Holden resigned the speakership to assume editorial control of the *Standard* for the coming campaign, and was succeeded by W. A. Moore, of Washington. The legislature adjourned on March 28, having been in session ninety-seven days. The expenses of the session were heavy, $74,176.20 being spent for *per diem* and mileage and $19,156.43 for printing. The cost of the other items, such as stationery, was large, but is not definitely known. Several attempts were made by members of both parties to secure the reduction of the *per diem*, but the suggestion was received with scorn and mockery.[3]

Adjournment was accompanied by wild demonstrations

---

[1] *Wilmington Journal*, Dec. 4, 1869, Dec. 31, 1869, Jan. 21, 1870.

[2] *Sentinel*, Jan. 15, 1870.

[3] Blythe, a Republican, introduced such a bill which, after being amended so as to apply to him alone, was passed. *Sentinel*, Jan. 13, 1870.

on the part of the Republican members and by quiet rejoicing on the part of the opposition. The *Sentinel* said:

"Sound the loud timbrel o'er Carolina's dark sea!" [1]

Yesterday exactly at 12 o'clock, M., that body which convened in this city in special session, on the first day of July, 1868, and has been in session, off and on, nearly ever since, by courtesy called the General Assembly of North Carolina, having done all the mischief that presented itself to their perceptive faculties, adjourned, *sine die.* [2]

### 3. CHARACTER OF ADMINISTRATION

The two leading characteristics of the administration of public affairs during the Republican régime were extravagance, combined with corruption, and incompetence. The former appeared in every department of government, for the poverty-stricken condition of the people was ignored and those in office sought to fatten at public expense. The salaries of the state officers were higher than ever before and their number was greatly increased. [3]

In addition, every department was allowed almost un-

---

[1] Referring to Laflin's song at the close of the convention of 1868.
[2] Issue of March 29, 1870.
[3] The following is the table of salaries:

| | |
|---|---:|
| Governor | $5,000 |
| Secretary of State | 2,500 |
| Treasurer | 3,000 |
| Auditor | 2,500 |
| Superintendent of Public Works | 2,500 |
| Superintendent of Public Instruction | 2,500 |
| Attorney General | 1,500 |
| Five Supreme Court Judges | 12,500 |
| Twelve Superior Court Judges | 30,000 |
| Adjutant-General | 1,200 |
| Total | $63,200 |

limited clerical assistance.[1] The state officers were authorized to purchase all necessary furniture and supplies. In
consequence, every department had more clerks than it
could keep occupied and every office was rather elabor-
ately refurnished. The expenses in the gross were very large,
for everything was purchased at the highest price and usually from someone with whom the administration was
closely connected. The number of cuspidors used in the Capitol must have ben enormous to judge from the amounts
paid for them. New carpets were purchased at a cost of
$3,750, and shades put in all the windows. The latter were
very expensive, running as high as $24 per pair. While the
taxpayers were pinched by poverty, the public officials lived
in a luxury to which not one had been accustomed. The
ice bill for the four summer months of 1869 amounted to
over $600, and over forty-five thousand pounds were con-
sumed. The contingent expenses which had always been
low, rose amazingly and covered much graft.[2] For the

[1] The following is the table of clerks and salaries under the law:

| Department. | Number of clerks. | Total salaries. |
|---|---|---|
| Executive | 3 | $2,700 |
| State | 4 | 3,700 |
| Treasury | 3 | 3,700 |
| Auditor | 3 | 3,600 |
| Adjutant-General | 1 | 1,080 |
| Public Works | 2 | 1,900 |
| Public Instruction | 3 | 3,400 |
| Capitol | 4 | 2,030 |
| Total | 23 | $22,110 |

[2] Table of contingent expenses:

| | |
|---|---|
| 1866 | $29,997.93 |
| 1867 | 29,876.05 |
| 1868 | 35,345.94 |
| 1869 | 76,506.64 |
| 1870 | 57,884.82 |

years 1869 and 1870, they amounted to $134,391.46, and
of this, about $70,000 was expended on the Capitol Square
for which a force of hands was kept constantly on the pay
roll. Large numbers of fancy trees and shrubs were purchased, none of which survived. Over five thousand dollars was employed in subsidizing Republican newspapers by
paying for the publication of laws and proclamations. The
expenses of the departments were increased by much travel-
ing, most of it useless. The attorney general had no clerks,
but the State, during two years, paid $5,400 in counsel fees.
Interestingly enough, the attorney-general himself received
$500 of this.

Other costly features of the government were the militia,
which cost the State $76,607.61, and the detective service,
which cost $4,179.59. Stationery during the two years
cost $37,718.83. Some of this was sold and the secretary
of state, who had charge of the purchase and issuance of
it, was accused of fraud. He escaped by blaming one of
the doorkeepers of the legislature.[1] Menninger was, however, corrupt and profited greatly from his office, coming
out of it quite well off, although he was bankrupt when he
took it. Another expense of the government which proved
profitable to some was the purchase of wood. It was obtained from D. J. Pruyn, the carpetbagger with whom
Deweese had been in partnership, who always received
twenty-five per cent above the market price.

Government had always been economically administered
in North Carolina and it had become traditional. If the
high cost of government had procured a correspondingly
high quality of administration, it would not have been altogether a bad thing, but never before or since was the State
so hopelessly misgoverned by its officials from township

---

[1] *Sentinel*, Feb. 17, 1869.

constables to chief executive. The governor was much more interested in party politics and personal advancement than in good government and was surrounded by incompetent sycophants and highly-skilled plunderers. For party reasons he was ready to overlook any lack of honesty, as was shown by his selection of Laflin for state proxy in the North Carolina Railroad in spite of the protests of Swepson, himself openly dishonest, and by his forcing the election of Littlefield and Swepson as railroad presidents and approving the election of Sloan and Jones. He was fully aware of the character and record of all and, in the case of Swepson, Sloan, and Jones, he had definite proof in their cotton transaction in 1865 of their entire unworthiness for public position. He never, so far as can be discovered, profited to the extent of a penny from the frauds committed by them and others, but he attempted to shield them and must be held at least partially responsible for their acts. A strong man and a good one in his place could have held back the plunderers and crowned his name with honor, but with his eyes open, he chose the worse part.[1]

The other state officers were incompetent or worse. Dr. Menninger, as has been noted, was utterly corrupt,[2] and, at the close of his term, after he had gone North, Governor Caldwell had to threaten him with criminal indictment for misappropriation of funds. D. A. Jenkins seems to have been personally honest so far as the funds in his hands were concerned, but, like all the administration, he was perfectly aware of the wholesale stealing that was going on.

---

[1] Daniel L. Russell in his testimony before the Senate committee on the Ku Klux said that the frauds were largely due to Holden's imbecility and incapacity. Page 183.

[2] There is evidence to show that his house was largely furnished at the expense of the State. An instance of this is to be found in the *Report* of the Shipp Fraud Commission, p. 534.

Henderson Adams, the auditor, was a nonentity. C. L. Harris, the superintendent of public works, was personally honest but was a " practical " politician and very partisan. When he protested against a proposed fraud, his colleagues read him out of the party. Ashley was corrupt. On every side there was nepotism. The governor made his son director of two railroads, his brother a director of one, one son-in-law attorney general and another mayor of Raleigh. Josiah Turner, commenting on this in the *Sentinel,* said, " But if any provide not for his own, and especially for those of his own house, he hath denied the faith and is worse than an infidel." Ashley had a near relative in his office and secured a professorship at the University for his brother-in-law. In respect to this latter achievement, he was rivalled by Judge Settle and John Pool.[1] Adams and Menninger each had brothers as clerks and Jenkins had his son in his office.

In the judicial branch, conditions were somewhat better as regards morals and worse as regards ability. The Supreme Court was a very able body with the grave fault that it was actively in politics. Of the justices, Reade was the worst offender, though he was very successful in concealing it. The condition of the Superior Court bench was pitiful indeed. E. W. Jones was not only an habitual drunkard but was brazenly immoral and entirely incompetent. George W. Logan seems to have been honest on the bench, but was entirely " innocent of law " in addition to being incompetent from lack of ability. He never lost sight of politics. Tourgee was without character, partisan, and undignified, but had more than usual ability, and, being very studious, became a most capable judge in all cases where

[1] Few families benefited by Reconstruction as much as the Pools. Six offices were held by them.

politics could not enter.[1] In other cases he was likely to lose all sense of propriety. Judge Henry was of only average ability and while charges that he was habitually intoxicated were constantly made, there is no proof of their correctness. Judge Cloud and Judge Cannon were honest but unlearned country lawyers who could never have reached the bench except in Reconstruction. Judge Buxton was exceedingly able but somewhat inclined to dabble in politics. Judge Watts was ignorant and corrupt, being hand in glove with the corrupt carpetbaggers, and, having received from Littlefield five thousand dollars when the latter was presented by the grand jury of Wake, Watts adjourned the court at once in order to prevent the solicitor from drawing a bill. He was a bitter partisan and was very active in politics, taking the stump in every campaign, or rather making one of the bench. C. C. Pool and Charles R. Thomas were both of average ability. Almost all the judges were careless and nearly every court was delayed by the tardy arrival of the judge. Tourgee was also in the habit of adjourning court early and, on one occasion, he left Orange court before the grand jury closed its session. That body then, at the instigation of Josiah Turner, presented him. An interesting contrast of the idea of law of the Superior Court judges with that held by the higher court is to be seen in the reversal of their decisions in seventy of the one hundred and fourteen cases heard on appeal by the latter court at January term, 1870.

In the counties conditions varied. In the black counties, they were terrific; in many white counties in the hands of the Republicans, there seems to have been honest and cap-

---

[1] A number of able lawyers, who were his political opponents, have assured the writer that Tourgee was the ablest judge that they had ever practiced under.

able administration. Nor were all the Democratic counties fortunate in government. But there was a marked tendency in the Republican counties to an extravagance not warranted by the abilities of the people. The county commissioners were wasteful at first and, in many counties, incompetent and corrupt. A notable example was in Wake County where the board was in session for one hundred and fifty days during the first year of the new system. Two members who lived in Raleigh charged mileage for one hundred and fifty-four miles, and a third, who had a home in the country but who lived in the city, of which he was postmaster, charged for 4,268 miles.[1] The chairman of the board in Craven County stole $1,260 from the school fund.[2] The most common offenders among the county officers were the sheriffs, and their opportunity for rascality was naturally great. Wake and New Hanover both had carpetbaggers in the office and both suffered from their defalcation in large sums. Because of its financial importance, the position attracted carpet-baggers more than any other county office, and there were a number of them in the State. Pitt County was ridden with carpetbaggers, having aliens for senator, representative, sheriff, deputy sheriff, tax collector, treasurer, chairman of the board of county commissioners, a justice of the peace, and the deputy register of deeds who did all the work of the office. This seems to be the record for the State, though Craven labored under a very heavy burden of the same sort. Many of the Republican county officers could not give bond and it was the practice of Abbott, Deweese, and other carpetbaggers to go on their bonds so as to enable them to qualify. It was good politics and even the governor soon followed their example.

Probably the highest average of ignorance, inability, and

[1] *Sentinel*, Sept. 29, 1869.          [2] *Ibid.*, Sept. 13, 1870.

inefficiency was to be found among the magistrates. One negro magistrate in Wilmington had a prisoner, who was accused of murder, carried to the body of the victim to see if the blood would flow.[1] Another New Hanover justice, appointed by Holden, was a convicted felon, who was nevertheless allowed to qualify and serve. So far as can be discovered, no negro magistrate was competent to fill the position and the same may be said of many of the white ones.[2]

In the federal service, conditions were little if any better. From those appointed, one could not be blamed for arriving

[1] Raleigh *News*, June 18, 1875.

[2] The following are interesting examples of official papers issued by three of the county officials:

" Notis.

" Wil be sole next tusdy was a week at John Engh's sicks mills on Rolly rode won hoss 4 yerr ole. Won cow and cafe. Won silver spune. Won sow with pigs by me.

G. Imbles,<br>Constable."

" Mr. Robbard Ivy, I hearby Notify you to Come over to Tryal saturday morning 10 oClock to my house if you donte the plaintiff Will tak Jugrnent Against yo.       ISaac Wooten, J. P.

Caesar
By Cear Caesar Wooten."

" State of North Carolina,
" guilford County.

" to ina lawful officer to execute forthwith whereas information has this Day been made to me one of the Justices of the Said Centy on oath of Andrew pelekten that on the 19 of December, 1868 and in said County one Henry Coe her set forth the efence of and against the State and against the peace and dignity of the State. this is therefore to Comand you to arest the said henry Coe and have Henry Coe before me or Sum other Justices of the said County to anser the foresaid Complaint and bee further dwelt according to law herein fail not and have you ther this warnt given under mi hand and Seeal this 22d Day December, 1868.       Frederick Smith, J. P.

" Nnten H. parker you are debitised to attend to this warnt. I hereby Debetize N. H. parker to arest and return this warnt.

Frederick Smith, J. P."

at the conclusion that an evil character was the highest recommendation. Many of them made good use of their time. L. G. Estes, collector of internal revenue, was convicted of malfeasance and judgment for $30,000 entered against his bondsmen, of whom Abbott was one.[1] H. E. Stilley, a carpetbagger and an embezzler, later was appointed collector of the first district. The assessor of internal revenue was a carpetbagger who traveled over the State accompanied by a negro woman of ill-fame, and A. H. Galloway declined to allow him to come to his house.[2] The same illiteracy and incompetency were to be found among the federal office holders that has been noticed in the state and county service.[3] Well might H. H. Helper write Secretary Boutwell of the federal officials, " They are for the most part pestiferous ulcers feeding upon the body politic."

[1] The defaulting collectors according to the newspapers were:

| District. | Collector. | Amount. |
|---|---|---|
| 1 | W. C. Laflin | $1,621.36 |
| 2 | L. G. Estes | 74,774.67 |
| 3 | C. W. Woolen | 56,816.26 |
| 4 | John Read | 56,948.66 |
| 5 | W. H. Thompson | 50,327.79 |
| 5 | John Crane | 166,290.09 |
| 6 | John B. Weaver | 59,125.47 |

Total ........................................ $465,904.30

The author has never been able to verify these figures.

[2] H. H. Helper to Secretary Boutwell, March 23, 1871.

[3] The following is an example of an official document issued by a revenue official:

Lincolnton November the 2 day, 1871.

This is to surtifi That —— was Rain By Mea Beefore the U. S. comishner R. P. Vest at the coat Hous in Lincoton of Bein Berlongin to the in viserl Emphire and was Dischargd of the vilatin of the Acct of congress charged in the With in Warrant, This 2 day of November, 1871.    Thos. W. Womble,

D P Marshal.

One of the most common charges against the governor was his free use of the pardoning power, particularly in behalf of his party. Compared with the usage of to-day in the State, it was not a startling exercise of executive clemency, but for that time, it was far more frequent than was usual. During his term of two years, Holden pardoned one hundred and seventy-five persons, some of whom were undoubtedly deserving.[1]

The evil characteristics of the Republican administration have been indicated sufficiently clearly to show one of the chief causes of the uprising of the people at their first opportunity. To one familiar with the character of the people of North Carolina, no other result would seem possible, and, while it was assured by other contributing causes than bad government, this alone would have been sufficient.

### 4. SOCIAL AND ECONOMIC CONDITIONS, 1868-1870

The congressional policy of Reconstruction, designed primarily to work a political revolution, also brought about a social and economic one. It is true that the war had done

---

[1] The following table shows the pardons by year and the offences for which the persons had been convicted:

| Offence. | 1868 | 1869 | 1870 | |
|---|---|---|---|---|
| Larceny | 20 | 32 | 20 | |
| Assault | 5 | 24 | 5 | |
| Houseburning | 1 | .. | .. | |
| Murder | 9 | 5 | 8 | |
| Burglary | 1 | 3 | .. | |
| Affray | 4 | .. | .. | |
| Riot | 1 | .. | 1 | |
| Horsestealing | 1 | .. | .. | |
| Manslaughter | .. | 3 | 2 | |
| Attempt at rape | .. | 3 | 1 | |
| Robbery | .. | 1 | 1 | |
| Miscellaneous | .. | 15 | 9 | |
| Totals | 42 | 86 | 47 | 175 |

this to some extent, but there were evidences of an approaching adjustment in 1865 and 1866 which was prevented by the establishment of the military government. The effect of the whole system was to postpone for some time a settlement of the relations of the two races upon any basis that was acceptable to the white people. The negroes were separated from them in politics and in religion and a strong effort was made for political reasons, and with some success, to persuade the negroes that they had no interest in the prosperity of the white people. In consequence, labor conditions were unsettled during the whole period and, combined with this, sufficient in itself to cause economic distress, there were bad seasons for several years. Short crops and the burden of taxes, which were largely paid by the land-holding class, made the industry of agriculture languish and, since then the key to the whole economic situation of the State was to be found in agriculture, the industrial development which has been so phenomenal having then scarcely begun, the situation could not have been much worse.

Other elements contributed to the distress of the State. Crime increased and public morals degenerated. Theft became so common that it was a menace to prosperity. Live stock was stolen until in some communities the raising of sheep and hogs was abandoned. Farm products of all sorts were taken to such an extent that the profits of a farm were often thereby swept away. This was partly due to the natural propensities of the negroes, intensified by their necessities, but they were also encouraged in it by white thieves who dealt largely in farm products purchased at night in small quantities with no questions asked. This evil assumed such proportions that the legislature of 1871 passed a law forbidding the purchase of such commodities after dark. That want was common among the negroes is

well known, but it is not a matter of such common knowledge that among the white people there were many who
scarcely knew from day to day from whence the next day's
support would come and this in spite of the fact that every
effort was made to find work that could be done. The war,
which swept away so much property, in many cases did not
leave the capability of making a living. That so many succeeded in acquiring that capacity argued well for the stock
and bore good promise of future performances in the economic and industrial upbuilding of the commonwealth. It
is interesting to see how helpless emancipation left both
classes who were freed by it. The one which was really
most benefited was the slower to realize it, but when once
it saw the truth, ceased to bewail the lost shackles which had
bound it to the institution of slavery and made haste to lend
its aid in the process of dignifying labor. It was without
doubt a bitter experience but that it was productive of good
results is proved beyond all question by the facts of to-day.
The negroes, on the other hand, were stimulated into an
outburst of ecstasy at relief from the metaphorical chains
of bondage, and, regarding liberty as inseparable from idleness, proceeded to put it to the test. It must be said for
most of them, however, that, when undisturbed by political
agitators or outside influences, their behavior was good.
They, too, had a bitter lesson, but were prevented from
learning it thoroughly by the syren voices of the carpetbaggers who assured them of the gratification of every desire when once they obtained the franchise and lifted their
alien friends to profitable office. It took many years of
experience before the mass of them discovered that their
race had been employed as a step to help white men into
office and that their activity in politics had won the dis-
pleasure of those who paid wages for labor and to whom,
instinctively and in spite of slander and falsehood, they

turned when in trouble. In the meantime, the morals of the race had degenerated, the opportunity of political instruction, and, of greater importance, political division, had passed, and the white man's party would have none of them.

From the presence of the negro in politics grew one of the greatest evils for which Reconstruction was responsible, namely, the inevitable blunting of the political moral sense of the white people. North Carolina, unprogressive as it was, had always a highly-developed political sense and an equally high standard of political morality. The greatest shock of Reconstruction was the revelation of the depths to which politics could sink. But during these two years of Radical misrule, when the ideals of the community were shattered, when an ignorant, inferior, and lately enslaved race, controlled by selfish and corrupt aliens, held the balance of power and, by combination with a small minority of the native whites, administered the government, then the practical necessities of the case overcame scrupulous notions of political morality, and a determination to rule by any methods possible possessed the mass of the white people and held them during the three following decades. That they were right is not to be doubted in the face of the facts, but it must nevertheless continue to be a cause of regret that such a thing was necessary to secure good government.

How far political and social conditions affected the economic interests of the State can not of course be determined. That there was a close relation existing must of course be true. Wages were low, but probably would have been so under any government the State might have had. They fluctuated little during the period. Money was scarce and the usual plan in the country was to rent land to " croppers " on shares which varied in proportion to what the owner supplied. The plan was uncertain in its results but probably not so much so as was the hiring of hands with regular wages, for, in the latter case, there was little or no redress for an employer when his hands deserted him. When wages were paid, they were about as appear in the following table where they are contrasted with earlier rates.

| Year. | Men. | Women. | Boys. |
|---|---|---|---|
| 1860 .............. $110 | | $49 | $50 |
| 1867 .............. 104 | | 45 | 47 |
| 1868–1870 ......... 89 | | 41 | 39 |

The usual wages for servants in town were $120 for men and $60 for women.

The period saw a steady decline in the value of most of its agricultural products though its live stock rose slowly in number. The following tables are illustrative:

| Year. | Corn. | Wheat. | Rye. | Oats. | Barley. |
|---|---|---|---|---|---|
| 1867 ..... | $18,692,960 | $7,205,650 | $548,450 | $2,226,560 | $4,500 |
| 1868 ..... | 18,225,480 | 5,942,000 | 501,810 | 2,261,350 | 3,875 |
| 1869 ..... | 17,400,000 | 5,921,100 | 460,000 | 2,275,000 | 3,500 |
| 1870 ..... | 17,550,000 | 5,103,780 | 388,000 | 1,567,500 | 1,220 |

| | Buckwheat. | Potatoes. | Tobacco. | Hay. |
|---|---|---|---|---|
| 1867 ..... | $19,580 | $519,560 | $6,956,676 | $2,158,740 |
| 1868 ..... | 19,090 | 745,820 | 6,849,672 | 2,790,000 |
| 1869 ..... | 12,070 | 540,000 | 4,589,500 | 1,937,600 |
| 1870 ..... | 10,324 | 519,400 | 4,230,000 | 1,938,430 |

| Total. | |
|---|---|
| 1867 ............................................. | $38,332,710 |
| 1868 ............................................. | 37,339,097 |
| 1869 ............................................. | 33,138,770 |
| 1870 ............................................. | 31,308,654 |

The statement of property values for the same period is still more interesting, though the assessments were probably somewhat low.

| Year. | Land. | Town lots. | Live stock. | Other personalty |
|---|---|---|---|---|
| 1867 .... | $87,993,293 | $9,654,973 | Not available. | Not available. |
| 1868 ..... | 82,204,267 | 7,386,019 | $20,052,456 | Not available. |
| 1869 ..... | 69,990,991 | 9,566,353 | 18,377,591 | $27,536,688 |
| 1870 ..... | 68,240,609 | 12,900,901 | 17,424,231 | 22,344,478 |

Upon this property, taxes increased with a leap when the reconstructed government was established. The following table will show the figures:

| Year. | Poll. | Income.[1] | State tax.[1] | Special Taxes.[1] |
|---|---|---|---|---|
| 1866 ... | $1. | $1.  to $3.50 | .10 | ... |
| 1867 ... | .50 | .50 to 1. | .10 | .50[2] |
| 1868 ... | .50 | .50 to 1. | .10 | .05[3] |
| 1869 ... | 1.05 | 2.50 | .35 | .59[4] |
| 1870 ... | 1.10 | 1.50 | .20 | .1666 |

The chief burden of this taxation fell upon the Conservatives not only because a majority of the white people belonged to that party, but also because they possessed the greater part of the wealth of the State. In addition, in many Republican counties, property was assessed so as to bring about that result. This continued long after the Conservatives obtained control of the state government.

The result of these conditions was to force upon the market much of the land, particularly of large holders, which ceased to be profitable. A great deal was sold for taxes and still more to get rid of it. The prices were pitifully small. In 1869, twenty-three plantations containing 7,872 acres were sold for taxes in Wake County and brought only $7,718.[5] In 1871, twenty-five thousand acres

[1] This is the tax on $100.

[2] This tax was levied on personal property consisting of luxuries and jewelry.

[3] Tax levied for the convention of 1868.

[4] Special taxes authorized to pay interest on railroad bonds.

[5] *Sentinel*, May 3, 1869.

and one hundred and thirty-three Wilmington town lots
were sold for taxes in New Hanover and brought $3,-
019.66.[1]

In an industrial and commercial way, the State was moving ahead but slowly. In 1870, the industrial situation contrasted with that of 1860 was as follows:

| Year. | No. estab-lishments. | Hands. | Capital. | Wages. | Value of products. |
|---|---|---|---|---|---|
| 1860......... | 3689 | 14,217 | $7,456,860 | $2,383,456 | $9,111,050 |
| 1870......... | 3642 | 13,622 | 8,140,473 | 2,195,711 | 19,021,327 |

The manufacture of cotton was beginning and the manufacture of tobacco was already of great importance. In
the latter industry, the negroes found employment in large
numbers and had a practical monopoly of certain branches
of it.

During the whole period, there were only six banks in
the State, all of them national, having a combined capital
of less than one million dollars. A number of small firms
did a private banking business, however, without charter.

Because politics was of such absorbing interest, newspapers flourished more than was to be expected. In 1870,
there were fifty-two in the State, excluding six religious
publications, and thirty-six of these were political. Twenty-
six were Conservative, seven, Republican, and three, independent. Eight of the total number were dailies. Of the
Republican papers, five were edited by carpetbaggers.

The growth of religious organizations was normal except
for the increase due to the establishment of negro churches
of the various denominations in almost every community.
By 1870, the separation of the races in religious affairs was
as complete as it was in things political.

In daily life and in business alike, uncertainty was the

[1] *Sentinel*, June 3, 1871.

chief characteristic of the attitude of the people. No one knew what to expect of the future and it became increasingly difficult to plan for it. Conditions grew steadily worse and, when partial political redemption came in 1870, there were not a few who believed that economic salvation was impossible. The overwhelming debt threw a gloom upon business and injured personal credit as well as that of the State. Thousands went North or West to begin life again and their number would have been greatly increased had means to go been more easily obtained. It was a gloomy population that inhabited North Carolina, and, viewed from any standpoint, the economic outlook for the future was dark.

# CHAPTER ELEVEN

## RAILROAD LEGISLATION AND THE FRAUDS

THE policy of internal improvement by state aid had been begun by North Carolina many years before the war. Practically all the bonded debt had been incurred in aiding in the construction of railways and other channels of communication. Much had been accomplished for the benefit of the State by the roads thus built and there were many who honestly believed that further steps in the same direction would result in the increased prosperity of all the people, as a result of which, in 1866, and 1867, in spite of the economic and financial depression in the State, the public debt was increased by $3,015,000 in aid of railways. The experience of the war had proved very conclusively the need of improved transportation facilities, and those who advocated state aid therefore looked to the new government to continue it. Unfortunately, a gang of plunderers fixed upon the same policy as the one best adapted to their plan of looting the State, and for a time they used honest men who were without suspicion of their sinister designs, not only as tools to accomplish their evil purpose, but also to shield the character of their operations from public observation.

Practically all of the new railroad legislation was enacted by the convention of 1868 and the legislature at its special session of 1868 and its regular session of 1868-1869. On January 1, 1868, the public debt of the State was as follows:

| | |
|---|---|
| Contracted prior to May 20, 1861 ............ | $8,510,000 |
| Contracted between 1865 and 1868 ............ | 5,214,900 |
| Total ............................ | $13,724,900 |

On this debt was due interest amounting to nearly $2,-000,000. In addition, the State during the war had issued bonds to the amount of $1,128,000, under the authority of acts passed before the war in aid of internal improvements. On this there was about $150,000 due in interest. This was not recognized by the convention of 1865 though not specifically repudiated.

On January 1, 1868, the bonds of the State were selling at 70. On July 1, they had risen to 75 but fell again almost immediately and fluctuated until October when they fell to 65. In December the old bonds were 62½ and the new, 59½.

The work of increasing the debt was begun by the convention which was attended by a quiet but influential lobby. Bonds of the Wilmington, Charlotte, and Rutherford Railroad to the amount of one million were endorsed,[1] in spite of considerable opposition. A little later, the Northwestern North Carolina Railroad, planned to extend from Greensboro and Lexington to Salem and thence to some point on the northwestern boundary of the State, was chartered and authority given the state treasurer to loan the company fifty thousand dollars for every section of five miles between Greensboro and Salem, as soon as the grading should be completed, the loan to be secured by a mortgage on the entire road.[2] The next move was the passage of an ordinance directing an exchange of state bonds to the amount of $1,200,000 for an equal number of the bonds of the Chatham Railroad,[3] and the same day a loan of $150,000

---

[1] *Ordinances*, chap. iii.         [2] *Ordinances*, chap. xvii.
[3] *Ordinances*, chap. xix.

in bonds to the Williamston and Tarboro Railroad, secured by a mortgage upon the road, was authorized.[1] By a later ordinance, the Western Railroad was directed to return the bonds of the Wilmington, Charlotte, and Rutherford Railroad to the amount of half a million dollars which sum had been paid to it by the State, and receive in return the same amount of state bonds.[2] Still later the first legislature was directed to fund the interest on the valid debt of the State in bonds and to provide for paying in cash the interest falling due on January 1, 1869, and thereafter.[3] In addition to this assistance to the railroads, the convention gave to the Chatham Railroad all the State's interest in the Cape Fear and Deep River Navigation Company between Gulf Dam on the Deep and Northing Dam on the Cape Fear.[4] Practically all of this legislation was accomplished by the use of money, and accusations to this effect were made on the floor of the convention.[5]

By the terms of the constitution, until the bonds of the State should reach par, the legislature was forbidden to contract any new debt except to supply a casual deficit or to suppress invasion or insurrection, unless in the same bill it should levy a special tax to pay the interest. It was also forbidden to give or lend the credit of the State to any person, association, or corporation, except for the completion of such railroads as were unfinished at the time of the adoption of the constitution, or in which the State had a direct pecuniary interest, unless the subject was first submitted to a vote of the people and ratified by them.[6]

---

[1] *Ordinances*, chap. xx.      [2] *Ordinances*, chap. xxx.

[3] *Ordinances*, chap. xliv.      [4] *Ordinances*, chap. xxxiv.

[5] Shipp Fraud Commission *Report*, p. 527. Hereafter, this will be referred to by the name of the chairman alone.

[6] *Constitution*, art. v, sec. 5.

When the legislature met in special session in July, 1868, the work begun by the convention was continued, for there was small thought of constitutional restrictions, and by this time a well-organized lobby was crying loudly for the prosperity which could only come through the building of railroads and the issue of state bonds for the purpose. At the head of the lobby was General M. S. Littlefield with an able body of allies, chief of whom were John T. Deweese and George W. Swepson, the latter being the paymaster of the " Ring." Beginning at this session, he allowed members of the legislature to cash their *per diem* at the Raleigh National Bank, of which he was a director, without charging them any discount. The " third house " aided greatly in the work of the lobby, and Littlefield's readiness to make loans to needy statesmen with no expectation of their being repaid, made him the idol of the carpet-baggers and corrupt scalawags, while his Radicalism commended him to Republicans who were not tainted with dishonesty. His charm of manner and *bonhomie* made his company acceptable to many Conservatives who at first did not question his motives or character. In the legislature, Byron Laflin was the chief member of the Ring, and as chairman of the committee on internal improvement, was able to render great service to the cause. The Ring not only put through its own schemes, but in a short time undertook to market bond legislation at the rate of ten per cent of the bonds received. Only through its aid could such legislation be secured and it was thus able to make its own terms. During the period the following sums were paid by Swepson to members of the legislature and other persons in public position:

| | |
|---|---:|
| A. W. Tourgee | $3,702.55 |
| Joseph W. Holden | 950.00 |
| John T. Deweese | 16,000.00 |
| John T. Deweese and R. J. Wynne | 200.00 |
| John A. Hyman | 2,100.00 |
| Byron Laflin | 785.00 |
| James H. Harris | 7,500.00 |
| Andrew Jackson Jones | 10,000.00 |
| James Sinclair | 3,500.00 |
| George Z. French | 500.00 |
| G. Z. French and L. G. Estes | 20,913.74 |
| J. H. Davis | 1,000.00 |
| Henry Eppes | 95.00 |
| Hugh Downing | 4,000.00 |
| L. G. Estes | 13,000.00 |
| Joseph C. Abbott | 20,000.00 |
| T. Foster | 25,000.00 |
| G. P. Peck | 4,500.00 |
| Total | $133,746.29 |

Swepson also paid Littlefield in cash $66,103.46, most of
which was used for the corruption fund.[1] Four of the
items are known. A. W. Stevens received $1,200, J. W.
Stephens, $100, J. T. Harris, $75, and J. H. Harris, $100.[2]
How much more was paid is not known. The expenses of
the bar in the Capitol were met by a note of Littlefield's
which he later refused to pay.

Very little was done by the legislature at the special session because of the approaching national election which
carried with it the possibility of the complete overthrow of
Reconstruction. There was a disposition on the part of
the plunderers to avoid offending public sentiment as much
as possible and to wait until the regular session, which
would begin after the election was past. But quietly the
treasurer was authorized to issue to the Chatham Railroad,
in exchange for bonds of the company, state bonds to the

[1] Shipp, pp. 316–17.          [2] Shipp, p. 515.

amount of two million dollars.[1] Against the passage of
this bill, twelve senators, including a number of Republicans, protested, on the ground that with this issue the State
became responsible for $3,200,000 for a road not more than
one hundred and fifty miles long, which could not possibly
confer a corresponding advantage upon the State. In addition, they argued that the act was unconstitutional since
no special tax was levied to pay the interest, and because
the question was not submitted to the people. In the House,
strong opposition developed, led by E. W. Pou, a Republican member, who throughout the term of the legislature
was the inveterate foe of all dishonesty and corruption.

A similar act was passed authorizing the Williamston
and Tarboro Railroad to receive bonds to the amount of
three hundred thousand dollars.[2] The Western North
Carolina Railroad was divided into two parts, the eastern
division from Salisbury to the French Broad River, and the
western from there to the Tennessee line. Its authorized
capital stock was increased to twelve million dollars, the
State being pledged to subscribe for two-thirds of it.[3] The
charter of the Northwestern North Carolina Railroad was
amended so that the State became responsible for ten thousand dollars per mile of the road from Salem to Mount
Airy as soon as it was graded, and one hundred thousand
dollars additional stock was subscribed.[4] Finally, in obedience to the instructions of the convention, an act to fund
the interest due on the state debt was passed.[5]

These appropriations were not made without much protest and criticism. Conservative members of the legislature
on the floor of the two houses gave warning that the bonds

[1] *Private Laws*, 1868, chap. xiv.     [2] *Ibid.*, chap. xv.
[3] *Ibid.*, chap. xxiv.     [4] *Ibid.*, chap. xxviii.
[5] *Laws*, 1868, chap. xxxii.

were invalid and would not be paid. The *Sentinel,* while favoring several of the appropriations, in and out of season implored greater care in passing such laws, and even the conservative Charlotte *Democrat* said: [1]

The impression prevails among the people that a considerable amount of the appropriations are going unfairly into the pockets of a set of speculators and sharpers whose influence induces the Legislature to make them; therefore, no one need be surprised if a disposition to favor repudiation is engendered by extravagance and burdensome taxation.

The time may come when the people of this State will not be willing to be taxed to pay $100 in gold to the man who holds a bond that cost him only $50 or $70 in paper money, or that cost him nothing at all, except a little scheming about Raleigh and the Halls of Legislation.

These objections all had their effect, and in the autumn the rumor spread that the interest on the bonds due in January would not be paid. In September, Governor Holden sent out a public letter stating that all the interest would be paid on time. This was done for the October interest by the sale of the State's dividend from the North Carolina Railroad, which was paid in bonds of the road to the amount of $180,000. These were sold to G. W. Swepson and A. J. Jones at a price far below par, and were soon after sold at a large advance by them. Swepson knew some time before the public that the interest was to be paid and speculated in state bonds, clearing a large sum. Of this he paid Treasurer Jenkins six hundred dollars.[2]

In the meantime, the Chatham Railroad and the Williamston and Tarboro Railroad had received their bonds. Both roads gave mortgages which, under the existing

[1] Quoted in *Sentinel,* Aug. 26, 1868.
[2] Shipp, p. 354.

United States internal revenue laws, required stamps to the amount of one-tenth of one per cent. The attorney general decided that no stamps were needed, and the treasurer issued the bonds, although the act required that the mortgages should first be registered with the secretary of state who, for his part, declined to register them for the lack of stamps. The most remarkable feature of the whole case was the fact that the Chatham mortgage included lands undescribed, which were not at the time in the possession of the company.

Of the Chatham bonds, 1,502 were sold at prices ranging from 54 to 63, including one hundred sold to Littlefield, for his draft at sixty days without endorsement, at 60 when the market price was 65, for his services in getting the bill passed.[1] Forty-eight were hypothecated by J. F. Pickrell, of New York, for iron, leaving 1,650 in the hands of the company. The total amount received was $906,196.74, and over $600,000 was spent upon the road.

The Williamston and Tarboro Railroad sold thirty-eight of its bonds for twenty-five thousand dollars and held the rest. About this time, the question of the validity of the bonds was raised, and the New York Stock Board excluded the new state bonds from the Exchange.

This was the situation when the legislature met in November, free from any fear of interference. What was going to be done was well recognized, and John Pool wrote Governor Holden a most caustic letter, in which he said the reputation of the State was already greatly injured by the frauds known to have been committed which were already notorious, and urged him to use his influence to prevent any repetition of them. The Ring was better organized than ever, and a flood of railroad bills was introduced

[2] Bragg Fraud Commission *Report*, p. 127. This report will hereafter be referred to by the name of the chairman.

within a few weeks authorizing an increase of about twenty million dollars in the debt.

This was accompanied by much protest, but so thoroughly organized were the forces of plunder that they were able to command at all times a majority in each house. Outside the legislature, however, there was much feeling, intensified by the rumors that had been current regarding the methods by which the legislation of the previous session had been secured, and the continuance of those methods in the existing session. Consequently, late in December an act was passed, which, after reciting that doubts existed as to the validity of the bonds issued for certain railroads, reenacted the acts of the preceding session in relation to the Williamston and Tarboro and Western North Carolina railroads, and after providing that upon the surrender of the bonds already received, the treasurer should issue new ones to the same amount, levied a special tax of one-thirtieth of one per cent to pay the interest on the bonds of the former and one-twentieth of one per cent for the interest on those of the latter. To the Chatham Railroad, which was permitted to extend its line, the treasurer was directed to issue bonds to the amount of two million dollars upon the surrender of a like amount of those already received, and a special tax of one-twentieth of one per cent was levied to pay the interest.[1] For this act, Swepson paid Littlefield, acting for the Ring, personally or on his order as mentioned above, more than $240,000 in cash and a large number of bonds.[2] Seven members of the House, representing both parties, entered a protest against the passage of the act, on the ground that it was unconstitutional in several respects and did not properly safeguard the interests of the State.[3]

[1] *Laws*, 1868–1869, chap. vii.       [2] Shipp, p. 203.
[3] *Sentinel*, Dec. 21, 1869.

On December 29, A. J. Galloway, of Wayne, as a tax-payer, applied to Judge Watts for an injunction to restrain the treasurer from issuing the bonds to the Chatham Railroad, on the ground that the act authorizing them was unconstitutional. The injunction was granted and the case heard on January 4, when the injunction was dissolved and the case carried to the Supreme Court on appeal, where the contention of the plaintiff was sustained and the act declared unconstitutional because it had not been submitted to the people, and the bonds therefore void.[1]

The unsold bonds of the Williamston and Tarboro Railroad, two hundred and sixty-two in number, were exchanged for new ones, which were then sold for $135,-948.47 which was expended upon the road.

Under the same act, four million dollars in bonds was issued to the western division of the Western North Carolina Railroad and a little later the charter of the road was amended so as to allow the capital stock of the western division to be increased to ten million dollars and that of the eastern division to six and one-half millions, the State being still pledged to take two-thirds of the stock as soon as five per cent of the rest was paid in. Of the amount appropriated to the eastern division, eighty thousand dollars was to be spent in the construction of a branch line to some lime beds in Catawba County, said to be owned in part by Dr. J. J. Mott, the president of the road. An injunction was at once obtained against the use of the bonds under the latter clause. The former acts in relation to the road were declared valid and the special tax was increased to one-eighth of one per cent.[2] Under the authority of these acts, bonds were issued to G. W. Swepson for the

---

[1] Galloway *v.* Jenkins, 64 N. C., 147.
[2] *Laws*, 1868–1869, chap. xx.

western division to the amount of $6,367,000 and to Dr. Mott for the eastern division to the amount of $613,000. The western division held a meeting of the stockholders at Morganton for the purpose of raising the additional stock required by the first act, and only about three hundred thousand dollars was subscribed. Thereupon, Littlefield, Swepson, R. M. Henry, who was known to be insolvent, and S. McD. Tate, a former president of the road, made up the rest. Littlefield took a large part of it, and also took the contract for building the whole road, a step necessary to securing the bonds. Later, in a similar way, the second subscription of stock was made by taking Littlefield's check for five per cent of $1,100,000, although he had never paid his first subscription. The law required the president of the road to certify to the governor that the stock had been subscribed and the required amount paid in, but so far as can be discovered Swepson never certified for the second subscription. Nevertheless, Governor Holden ordered the bonds issued to him.

The bonds received by Swepson were then used in various ways. Ninety were lent to Hooper, Harris and Company of New York; twenty to the North Carolina Home Insurance Company; some were deposited as margins for Laflin, Martindale, W. A. Moore, and Judge Rodman, who were all speculating in state bonds; [1] and a large number were sold to pay for obtaining control of the Florida Central and Jacksonville, Pensacola, and Mobile railroads, upon which he and Littlefield had designs. [2] Both became prominent in that State to its great injury. General J. C. Abbott and General Thomas L. Clingman were their agents in part

[1] These speculations proved disastrous for Swepson, who lost on account of Laflin, $76,000, Martindale, $26,000, and Moore, $28,000.

[2] An account of their work in Florida is to be found in Wallace, *Carpetbag Rule in Florida.*

of the work there.   The sum of $1,287,036.03 was spent in this way.[1]  In the process, 6,263 of the bonds were disposed of.   In his account, Swepson was unable to locate 1,278 bonds, but later said that they had been disposed of as the others.   The highest price received was 62⅜ and the lowest 43, the average being 53¾.   The number sold was 3,132 and 1,924 were hypothecated.   Soutter and Company, of New York, the financial agents of the State, handled most of them.   Very little was spent upon the road.   Both Swepson and Littlefield, who succeeded him in 1869 as president, intended to build the road by bonding it, and it is likely that they had in mind the plan of securing the bonds and getting possession of the road.   Littlefield was made state proxy by Governor Holden, who regarded the state interest in the railroads only as a political asset of the Republican party, and used it as such.   The governor was directly responsible for the election of both of them and indirectly for the choice of William Sloan and Andrew J. Jones for the Wilmington, Charlotte, and Rutherford and Western railroads.   Through the state vote, a bonded indebtedness of $1,400,000 was incurred with the provision that, whenever the interest was not paid on time, the mortgage might be foreclosed.   The road was scarcely paying running expenses and the annual interest upon the bonds was $112,000. The bonds were hypothecated for $240,000, on which the interest was seventeen per cent, and were later sold at an average of 25½.   Sibley and Clews sued in the United States Circuit Court in 1872, and in November the mortgage was foreclosed.

Of the six hundred and thirteen bonds received by the eastern division, one hundred and seventy were sold, ninety-three hypothecated with Henry Clews and Company, and

[1] Shipp, p. 290.

fifty hypothecated with Soutter and Company. The highest price received was 45½ and some sold as low as 23. The amount received from sales and hypothecation was $166,580, all of which was spent upon the road.

By the next act, the capital stock of the Wilmington, Charlotte, and Rutherford was increased to seven million dollars, and the treasurer was given authority to make a subscription for the State of four millions in bonds, a tax of one-eighth of one per cent being levied to pay the interest.[1] L. G. Estes paid Deweese $2,500 to be divided between Laflin and himself for the former's vote and influence in behalf of this bill. The amount was repaid to Estes by Soutter and Company whose agent he probably was. It was proposed to divide the road and give the western division alone six million dollars, but the plan was defeated. R. H. Cowan was president of the road, but it was arranged that he should be forced out and William Sloan put in his place, and this was soon accomplished. Before that time, however, Cowan received 1,000 bonds, of which 970 were sold for $436,988.84 and 30 deposited with Soutter and Company to be held for the road. All the money received was spent in paying the various expenses of the road. The thirty bonds mentioned were later paid by Soutter and Company to D. G. Fowle, E. G. Haywood, and Samuel Person, the lawyers who were engaged for the rehearing of the University Railroad case presently to be described.[2] Dr. Sloan became president in July, 1869, and received 2,000 bonds. Of these, 1,700 were hypothecated with J. F. Pickrell and 300 deposited with him. The loan made by Pickrell was $391,026.62, and in ten months, by means of commissions and interest, it was made to grow to $481,100.65.[3]

---

[1] *Laws*, 1868–1869, chap. xxvii.

[2] Shipp, p. 402.  [3] *Ibid.*, Shipp, p. 18.

About this time, Sloan sold Pickrell a half interest in an unworked and undeveloped sulphur mine for $25,000. The bonds were sold at 17½ and from the amount received there was a deduction of seven and three-fourths per cent of the face value for commissions. Sloan also hypothecated company bonds to the amount of $600,000 with Pickrell for a loan of $272,000. They were sold at 46¾ and practically none of the money received was spent upon the road.

Another act incorporated the University Railroad Company, authorized three hundred thousand dollars in construction bonds, and levied a tax of one-one-hundredth of one per cent to pay the interest.[1] The directors of the road were to be appointed by the governor and were instructed to organize at once. The appointments were promptly made[2] and Henry C. Thompson, of Orange, was elected president. In the meantime Governor Holden had consulted the attorney-general, who pronounced the act unconstitutional.[3] The directors at once applied for a mandamus against the governor and treasurer to force the issue of the bonds. This was refused and the case carried to the Supreme Court on appeal. It was argued there, and, while the entire court concurred in declaring the act unconstitutional, there was division among the judges as to how far the decision extended. Chief Justice Pearson thought all the special tax bonds unconstitutional, and, at the request of his colleagues, prepared an opinion as a basis of discussion. He read the opinion to William Johnston, president of the Atlantic, Tennessee, and Ohio Railroad, a former law pupil of his, who told Swepson of it and also mentioned the matter to K. P. Battle. Battle telegraphed the informa-

---

[1] *Laws*, 1868–1869, chap. xxii.

[2] The directors were J. W. Holden, T. M. Argo, H. C. Thompson, Solomon Pool, and E. A. Wood.

[3] *Executive Correspondence*, Holden, i, p. 139.

tion to his friend T. H. Porter, a member of the firm of
Soutter and Company, who had asked that he be kept advised of the status of the case. Most of the judges seem
to have discussed the matter rather freely.[1]  The news
spread in New York, and Judge Person, the attorney of
the Wilmington, Charlotte, and Rutherford Railroad, who
was in New York, telegraphed a request for a rehearing
which was granted by the court. With him, as counsel for
the roads which had received special tax bonds, were associated D. G. Fowle and E. G. Haywood. The expenses of
the rehearing as charged by Soutter and Company were divided between the western division of the Western North
Carolina Railroad and the Wilmington, Charlotte, and
Rutherford Railroad, the former paying sixty bonds and
$21,250 in cash, and the latter thirty bonds and $8,259 in
cash. Of this, seventy-five bonds and $20,500 in cash were
paid to the counsel. What became of the rest is not
known. Dr. J. J. Mott and A. J. Jones agreed for their
roads to pay a proper proportion, but never did so. The
decision of the court, handed down on July 21, declared
the act unconstitutional because there was no grantee, no
power was given the legislature to contract the debt, and
the tax was not in a proper proportion. Judge Pearson's
opinion was strongly against the validity of the special tax
bonds.

Many accusations were made against the Supreme Court
at the time, but there is no evidence to show improper conduct on the part of any particular member of it. Swepson,
on one occasion, tapped his pocket and said that he had
there another decision which had been prepared by the
court and that it had cost him a large sum of money to

[1] Shipp, pp. 460 *et seq.*
[2] University R. R. Co., *v.* Holden, 63 N. C., 410.

prevent its being rendered, but his word carries little weight.[1] The following telegram, sent him two days before the case was first argued, casts an unpleasant light upon the general situation of affairs:

RALEIGH, N. C., JUNE 24, 1869.

GEORGE W. SWEPSON,
    Baltimore, Md.

The case will be tried, but the opinion of the Court reserved until your return; this is all I can effect.

W. W. HOLDEN.[2]

A few days after the passage of the University Railroad act, the charter of the Western Railroad was amended and the state treasurer was directed to exchange five hundred thousand dollars in bonds for an equal amount of stock in the road, to issue an equal amount in exchange for the bonds of the Wilmington, Charlotte, and Rutherford Railroad, which had been paid to the former road by the State, and, for the purpose of extending the road to Wilkes County, to make an additional stock subscription of five hundred thousand dollars, making a total authorized issue of $1,500,000. To pay the interest, two special taxes were levied, one of one-eightieth of one per cent and one of one-fourth of one per cent. The act provided for the retention by the treasurer of one hundred and eighty of the bonds as security for the payment by the road, during the first two years, of ninety thousand dollars for interest, both of which sums were to be repaid at the expiration of that time.[3] Under the provisions of this act, A. J. Jones, the president of the road, received 1,320 bonds. Fifty-five of

---

[1] Shipp, p. 307.

[2] An autograph copy of this telegram is in the Holden papers in the Executive Correspondence at Raleigh.

[3] *Laws*, 1868–1869, chap. xxviii.

these were sold by New York biokers for $24,255, and, from that amount, seven and five-eighths of one per cent of the face value of the bonds was charged as commissions, so that the company only received $20,893.13. The rest of the bonds were deposited with certain brokers in New York, by whom, under instructions from Jones, part were hypothecated in an attempt to raise money to buy bonds on margin to bull the market. A pool was formed for this purpose by Swepson, Littlefield, Sloan, Jones, and a number of bondholders, including T. P. Branch, a Richmond broker, S. McD. Tate, T. W. Dewey, and R. Y. McAden. Treasurer Jenkins and Governor Holden were present in New York when it was formed and were frequently consulted by the members. At the same time it was decided by the railroad presidents that Henry Clews and Company should succeed Soutter and Company as the financial agents of the State. To this, Governor Holden consented and the change was made. Soutter and Company had been paid a thousand dollars a year as compensation for their services.[1]

The interest on the debt due in January and April, 1869, had not been paid and the bondholders began to complain loudly. Governor Holden was overwhelmed with correspondence from the North, where practically all the bonds were held, demanding payment, and it was clear that there was no chance for the bonds to rise in price unless something was done to satisfy the holders of those already sold. Swepson and Jones now agreed to advance the money to pay the interest on the special tax bonds, and Jenkins advertised that the April and October interest would be paid,[2] and Governor Holden wrote an open letter to Clews and Company in which he said that the State would pay all its

---

[1] Shipp, p. 552.  [2] *Ibid.*

debts, especially the special tax bonds.[1]  The railroad stock
owned by the board of education was now sold at a very
low rate, and the proceeds, $150,000, along with the money
received from the land scrip, $125,000, were invested in
special tax bonds.  The bonds rose slightly, Black Friday
came, and the pool was broken with a loss of between three
and four hundred thousand dollars.  According to the
agreement, $280,000 of this was to be borne by Swepson,
Sloan, Jones, and Littlefield, in addition to their share of
the rest.  Jones paid his share, Swepson paid for himself
and Littlefield, and Sloan declined to pay anything at all.

Jones never accounted to his road for the bonds, but it
was known that a large number were sold at a very low rate,
the money going no one knows where, and a large number
were gambled away by Jones in New York.  On one occasion, he sat in a gambling room there, with a pile of bonds
on a chair beside him, which he cashed in for chips, one
by one, losing in a very short time sixty of them.[2]  This
method of disposition was prolonged for several weeks
with results that can readily be conjectured.  Some of the
bonds fell into the hands of the notorious Josie Mansfield,
and the rumor was general that they circulated largely
among the *demi-monde*.

Four other railroad acts were passed on the same day as
that for the Western road.  The first provided that, whenever fifty thousand dollars should be subscribed to the stock
of the Oxford Branch of the Raleigh and Gaston Railroad, the treasurer should subscribe to a further amount
of two million dollars, payment to be made in bonds with
the usual amount retained as security for the payment of
interest.  To pay the interest, a special tax of one-twen-

[1] *Sentinel*, Nov. 2, 1869.
[2] Statement of a bystander to the author.

tieth of one per cent was levied.[1] No bonds were ever issued under this act, which was clearly unconstitutional. The second act authorized the extension of the Williamston and Tarboro Railroad to Plymouth, Washington, and Wilmington, and from Edenton to Suffolk, Virginia, and provided that when two hundred thousand dollars additional stock should be subscribed, the State should subscribe to the amount of $2,700,000. A special tax of one-sixteenth of one per cent was levied to pay the interest.[2] The usual amount was to be retained to pay interest. No bonds were issued under this act.

The next road to benefit was the Atlantic, Tennessee, and Ohio Railroad, the charter of which was amended so that it was aided to the extent of two million dollars in exchange for bonds of the company to the same amount. A special tax of one-twentieth of one per cent was levied for interest.[3] Sloan and Laflin both opposed the bill and were paid $20,000 apiece to withdraw their opposition to it and consent to its passage. In June, John T. Deweese, after being refused by several lawyers to whom he had applied, employed E. G. Haywood to secure an injunction forbidding the treasurer to issue the bonds authorized by the act. As Deweese was not a taxpayer, he secured Robert C. Kehoe as the nominal plaintiff, though the latter had no interest in the matter, Deweese and probably W. F. Askew and Littlefield being the real parties in the matter. Application for an injunction was then made to Judge Watts, who declined to grant it without giving the matter further consideration, but the next day issued the injunction. Deweese said five thousand dollars was paid Watts to induce him to grant it and there is abundant evidence, including

---

[1] *Laws*, 1868–1869, chap. xxix.    [2] *Ibid.*, 1868–1869, chap. xxx.
[3] *Ibid.*, 1868–1869, chap. xxxi.

that of Watts himself, to show that he received from Deweese five bonds of this issue. The judge maintained that
it was simply a personal loan from Deweese. The whole
purpose of the suit was to force the company to compromise by delivering a part of the bonds to the Ring. William Johnson had promised Littlefield the usual ten per
cent for the passage of the bill, but the latter fled the State
to avoid appearing before the Sweet investigating committee, and no bonds were paid him.[1]   Deweese had already threatened to bring suit if he was not paid five thousand dollars.[2]   The officers of the company saw through
the thing and R. Y. McAden, who was financial agent of
the road, employed Littlefield to secure the compromise.
The latter, acting through Tim Lee, the carpet-bag sheriff
of Wake, secured this for seventy-seven bonds and charged
for his own services eighty-six, ten of which he gave to
Lee and the rest sold in New York.[3]   Of the seventy-seven
received by Deweese, five were given to Judge Watts,[4] four
to Kehoe, ten to Askew, and sixteen to Fowle and Badger,
who assisted Haywood as counsel for Deweese. Deweese
and Haywood seem to have divided the rest.[5]   Fowle and
Badger became convinced, after the compromise, that the
whole suit had been instituted for the purpose of blackmail,
and returned the bonds they received to the company.[6]

The company received from the treasurer 1,760 bonds
of which one hundred and sixty-three, as mentioned, were
paid to Littlefield. The others were then deposited in New
York with Clews and Company and Soutter and Company
to secure the money advanced to the State to pay interest.
They were later released and, the price of North Carolina

[1] Shipp, pp. 208–09.          [2] Bragg, p. 151.
[3] *Ibid.*, p. 178.                 [4] *Ibid.*, p. 162; Shipp, p. 464.
[5] *Ibid.*, p. 466.                 [6] *Ibid.*, p. 158.

bonds being now below 30, were never sold and were later returned to the State.

The last of the acts passed on the fatal third of February was in aid of the Northwestern Railroad to which the treasurer was directed to loan bonds to the amount of $20,000 per mile for each division of the road as soon as five per cent of a stock subscription of $150,000 for one and $100,000 for the other should be paid in and a mortgage of the entire road delivered to the State. A tax of one-twentieth of one per cent was levied to pay interest and three hundred and sixty bonds were ordered retained as security for the payment of $180,000, as in the case of the other roads.[1] Edward Belo, the president of the road, received 1,080 bonds and, considering the market price too low, made no attempt to sell them and later returned them to the State.[2]

Two other railroad acts were passed during the session. One chartered the Eastern and Western Railroad, the directors to be appointed by the governor, authorized the construction of the road through the counties of Granville, Person, Caswell, Rockingham, Stokes, and Surry, appropriated two million dollars in bonds to pay for it, and levied a tax of one-twentieth of one per cent to pay the interest.[3] The other chartered the Edenton and Suffolk Railroad, the directors to be appointed by the governor, authorized the issue of eight hundred and fifty thousand dollars in bonds to pay for it, and levied a special tax of one-fortieth of one per cent to pay interest.[4] Both these acts were clearly unconstitutional and were so pronounced by the attorney general to whom the governor referred them

---

[1] *Laws*, 1868-1869, chap. xxxii.  
[3] *Laws*, 1868-1869, chap. xcii.  
[4] *Ibid.*, 1868-1869, chap. cxxxviii.  

[2] Bragg, pp. 122-23.

before he appointed directors.[1]   Consequently no organization was ever made and, of course, no bonds were issued under them.

These acts ended the work of the Ring in securing legislation.   By this time the whole State knew what was being done and the people were greatly roused.   By the end of the summer of 1869, talk of repudiation was general and when the legislature met in the autumn no further legislation was possible and, as has already been seen, the presidents of the various roads were directed to return all unsold bonds to the treasurer and to account for the rest.   A little later all the acts in aid of railroads were repealed.

The following tables give the available information in a condensed form:

| Road. | Amount authorized. | Issued. | Returned. |
|---|---|---|---|
| Chatham .... ................ | $3,200,000 | $3,200,000 | $1,650,000 |
| Western N. C., W. D. ...... | 6,387,000 | 6,367,000 | None. |
| Western N. C., E. D......... | 613,000 | 613,000 | None. |
| Williamston & Tarboro ...... | 300,000 | 300,000 | None. |
| W. & T. (Branch line) ..... | 2,700,000 | None. | None. |
| University .................. | 300,000 | None. | None. |
| Northwestern ............... | 2,000,000 | 1,080,000 | 1,080,000 |
| Western .................... | 1,500,000 | 1,320,000 | None. |
| Atlantic, Tennessee, & Ohio.. | 2,000,000 | 1,760,000 | 1,615,000 |
| Wilmington, Charlotte, & Rutherford ............... | 4,000,000 | 3,000,000 | None. |
| Oxford Branch .............. | 2,000,000 | None. | None. |
| Eastern & Western .......... | 2,000,000 | None. | None. |
| Edenton & Suffolk........... | 850,000 | None. | None. |
| Total ............ | $27,850,000 | $17,640,000 | $4,345,000 |

[1] *Executive Correspondence*, Holden, i, pp. 133, 139.

| Road. | Special tax levied. | Tax on $100. | Bonds left outstanding. |
|---|---|---|---|
| Chatham ················ | $\frac{1}{20}$ of 1% | .05 | $1,550,000 |
| Western North Carolina, both divisions·········· | $\frac{1}{8}$ of 1% | .125 | 6,980,000 |
| W. & T. ················ | $\frac{1}{30}$ of 1% | .0333 | 300,000 |
| W. & T. (Branch line) ·· | $\frac{1}{16}$ of 1% | .0625 | None. |
| Univ. ··················· | $\frac{1}{100}$ of 1% | .01 | None. |
| Northwestern ············ | $\frac{1}{20}$ of 1% | .05 | None. |
| Western ················ | $\frac{3}{80}$ of 1% | .0375 | 1,320,000 |
| A. T. & O.·············· | $\frac{1}{20}$ of 1% | .05 | 163,000 |
| W. C. & R. ············· | $\frac{1}{8}$ of 1% | .125 | 3,000,000 |
| Oxford ·················· | $\frac{1}{20}$ of 1% | .05 | None. |
| E. & W. ················ | $\frac{1}{20}$ of 1% | .05 | None. |
| E. & S. ················ | $\frac{1}{40}$ of 1% | .025 | None. |
| Total ········ | $\frac{2}{3}$+of 1% or .6683 | | $13,313,000 |

### TABLE.

Prices of State Bonds in 1869.

| | Highest. | | Lowest. | |
|---|---|---|---|---|
| | Old. | New. | Old. | New. |
| January ······ | 66 | 73 | 62 | 59⅜ |
| February ····· | 64¼ | 61½ | 62 | 58½ |
| March ······· | 64 | 59¾ | 60¾ | 56½ |
| April ········ | 63½ | 56⅞ | 60¼ | 53 |
| May ········· | 63¼ | 56¼ | 57 | 54½ |
| June ········· | 60¾ | 56⅞ | 58 | 50¾ |
| July·········· | 59½ | 53 | 50½ | 44½ |
| August······· | 58½ | 56 | 49⅛ | 49 |
| September ··· | 56¾ | 48 | 50½ | 46 |
| October······ | 52½ | 40⅝ | 47 | 37½ |
| November ··· | 48 | 38½ | 40 | 29 |
| December···· | 43½ | 33⅛ | 41¾ | 28¼ |
| | | 1870. | | |
| January ······ | 43 | 29 | 40 | 24⅛ |
| February ····· | 48 | 26½ | 40½ | 23 |
| March ······· | 47¾ | 23⅞ | 45 | 22½ |
| April········· | 47 | 22⅜ | 46½ | 21 |
| May ········· | Not listed. | | Not listed. | |

From the dishonest officials, little was ever recovered. Littlefield, after leaving the State, went to Florida, where, resting under the protection of the various governors of that State, he defied requisition papers. All refused to surrender him upon the demands of Governor Caldwell who never rested in his efforts to capture him.[1] Once Littlefield had to surrender to the sheriff of Leon County on a charge of bribery to avoid being sent to North Carolina, and, on another occasion, Governor Caldwell sent a member of the legislature to abduct him if necessary, and he was almost captured. The legislature offered a reward of five thousand dollars for him and two attempts were made by Floridians to win it. In both, Littlefield succeeded in escaping. With Swepson, he was indicted in Buncombe County in 1870, and requisitions were made upon the governors of New York and New Jersey for them.[2] Swepson was arrested in Raleigh in 1871 upon a bench warrant issued by Chief Justice Pearson upon the governor's affidavit, and held to appear at Buncombe court, but was never punished. He and Littlefield, the latter being in London, at different times made partial settlements with the Western North Carolina Railroad represented by N. W. Woodfin, but the road received only a very small part of what was due it. Swepson's account with the State, skilfully handled by his lawyers, Merrimon and Ransom, steadily grew less, until it seemed wise to accept and make an immediate settlement.

William Sloan and John F. Pickrell were indicted in New Hanover for a conspiracy to defraud the Wilmington, Charlotte, and Rutherford Railroad, and the former was criminally indicted for not accounting. He was found guilty in the latter case, but the Supreme Court reversed

---

[1] *Executive Correspondence*, Caldwell, pp. 34-35, 146.

[2] *Ibid.*, p. 30.

the decision on a technicality, and he escaped.[1] A. J. Jones was convicted of not accounting and appealed to the Supreme Court, which, as in the Sloan case, reversed the decision.[2] He was also criminally indicted in Moore County, convicted, and sentenced to ten years in the penitentiary. He appealed in this case and died before the case was heard.

A number of attempts were made to force the payment of the interest upon the special tax bonds. L. P. Bayne and Company sued for a mandamus against Jenkins to compel him to pay the interest which the legislature had forbidden, but the Supreme Court on appeal dismissed the case. Later, another case was brought in the federal courts with the same result. No attempt was made to pay interest and the matter rested for several years. The holders of the bonds, issued before the war, to aid in the construction of the North Carolina Railroad, by suit in the federal court secured the sequestration of the stock of the road held by the State, and thus obtained payment and security for the principal. For the rest, the State, having received little or no benefit from the railroads, was left with the burden of the bonds dishonestly issued and corruptly spent, a debt which was in addition invalid, without reference to the methods employed to create it, because of the fatal defect in the election of the body by which it was contracted.

[1] State *v.* Sloan, 67 N. C., 357.  [2] State *v.* Jones, 67 N. C., 211.

# CHAPTER TWELVE

## THE KU KLUX MOVEMENT

### I. PURPOSES

THE Ku Klux movement, which appeared in almost every Southern State during the decade following the war, grew naturally out of the chaos in society which was caused by the ordinary results of the war and, more especially, by Reconstruction. The old order with its security and stability had disappeared and the people of the South were confronted with problems which required immediate solution. Not the least pressing and important of these was that of the relation of the races, with its important bearing upon the labor question. The first attempt towards a settlement of this furnished one of the chief pretexts of the radicals in entering upon their policy and the adoption of the congressional plan apparently destroyed any possibility of the control of the lower race except by force. The force of law, the power of the government, were in the hands of aliens or their tools, and conditions grew rapidly more unsettled until the statement of the committee on Reconstruction that the governments of the Southern States " afford no adequate protection for life or property, but countenance and encourage lawlessness and crime," false when it was made in 1866, became entirely true. Liberty with the negroes rapidly degenerated into license and, banded together in secret leagues which to radical officers served as a valid political cloak for all offences, instigated to violence by unprincipled adventurers who had been lifted into

452

political power by the negro vote, alienated from their former friends by slander, they unconsciously set about the destruction of civilization in the South. Crime and violence of every sort ran unchecked until a large part of the South became a veritable hell through misrule which approximated to anarchy. Called into existence by this state of affairs, the Ku Klux lifted the South from its slough of despond by the application of illegal force which overthrew Reconstruction and ultimately restored political power to the white race. In the process, it furnished protection to the oppressed, but, degenerating from its high purpose and estate, as might have been expected from its nature and organization, it was often violent and sometimes oppressive, and in the end, fell into the control of reckless spirits who used it for private vengeance rather than public punishment. But when this evil day came, its purpose was in a fair way of accomplishment. The women of the South once more could leave their doors without the accompaniment of a deadly terror. Property became fairly safe again. Heart had been put into the despairing whites and a revolution had been wrought through its operations, or, to be more exact, the results of a revolution had been overthrown and a form of government, wickedly, illegally, and unconstitutionally imposed upon the people, had come into the hands of the class best fitted to administer government, and the supremacy of the white race and of Anglo-Saxon institutions was secure.

The inherent evils of the movement are plain, but it is an old adage that desperate diseases require desperate remedies. Certain it is that no open revolt could ever have accomplished so much of good as did the secret operations of the so-called Klan, and few to-day would deny that there was necessity for some remedy for the conditions then existent. The justification for the movement even then some-

times seems difficult, but when all the elements are considered, the conclusion seems inevitable that if there be such
a thing as the sacred right of revolution, then the Ku Klux
movement as planned and carried out at first was justifiable.
No free people ever labored under more galling oppression
or more grievous misrule, and, in the absence of any effective legal remedy, the principle of *salus populi* would
seem to apply.    At any rate, it is clear that the movement
was primarily designed for protection and its influence
upon politics was purely incidental.   The evidence is overwhelming in support of the theory that the chief purpose
of the Ku Klux was to oppose the Union League and check
its operations.[1]   The unfortunate thing is that such an extreme and, under ordinary circumstances, indefensible
policy should have been necessary.   Like practically every
other evil of Reconstruction, its effects survive and are too
often manifested in Southern life and thought.   The responsibility for it must ultimately rest upon those who
planned and put into effect for partisan purposes the congressional plan of Reconstruction.

## 2. ORGANIZATION AND MEMBERSHIP

In North Carolina, the Ku Klux movement was directed
by three separate organizations, all of which were included
under the generic term, and all of which were alike in outward seeming and, to a very slightly less extent, inward
character.   These, in the generally accepted but very doubtful order of establishment in the State, were The White
Brotherhood, The Constitutional Union Guard, and The
Invisible Empire.   The exact, or, for that matter, approxi-
mate time that they appeared cannot be ascertained.   The
White Brotherhood seems to have come late in 1867 or early

---

[1] A striking example of this is to be found in the testimony of H. W.
Guion before the joint committee on the Ku Klux.   See pp. 246-83.

in 1868. Its origin is unknown but it seems to have had no vital connection with the original Tennessee Ku Klux. Its purpose was primarily the protection of the homes and families of its members and of all Confederate soldiers, and its entrance upon an aggressive political campaign was a departure from its original intent so grave in its nature that one " camp " at least, the one at Hillsboro, disbanded because the large majority of its members were opposed to the active aggressions of some of the members who acted without the consent of the camp. The organization was spread very widely and finally became in fact, though not in name, a part of the Invisible Empire.

The ritual of the White Brotherhood was not very elaborate.[1] Under its laws each person initiated had to receive the unanimous vote of the camp. The camps were under the direction of a captain and all the captains in a county were responsible to the county chief. The oath which summed up the purposes of the order was as follows:

You solemnly swear in the presence of Almighty God that you will never reveal the name of the person who initiated you; that you will never reveal what is now about to come to your knowledge; and that you are not now a member of the Red String Order, Union League, Heroes of America, Grand Army of the Republic, or any other organization whose aim and intention is to destroy the rights of the South, or of the States, or of the people, or to elevate the negro to political equality with yourself; and that you are opposed to such principles: So help you God.

You further swear before Almighty God that you will be true to the principles of this brotherhood and the members thereof; and that you will never reveal any of the secrets,

---

[1] No copy so far as is known was ever printed, but enough of its secret work appears in the reports of the various investigations to form a definite conclusion as to its nature.

orders, acts, or edicts, and that you will never make known to any person, not a known member of this brotherhood, that you are a member yourself, or who are members; and that you will never assist in initiating, or allow to be initiated, if you can prevent it, any one belonging to the Red String Order, Union League, Heroes of America, Grand Army of the Republic, or any one holding radical views or opinions; and should any member of this brotherhood, or their families, be in danger, you will inform them of their danger, and, if necessary, you will go to their assistance; and that you will oppose all radicals and negroes in all of their political designs; and that should any radical or negro impose on, abuse, or injure any member of this brotherhood, you will assist in punishing him in any manner the camp may direct.

You further swear that you will obey all calls and summonses of the chief of your camp or brotherhood, should it be in your power so to do.

Given upon this, your obligation, that you will never give the word of distress unless you are in great need of assistance; and should you hear it given by any brother, you will go to his or their assistance; and should any member reveal any of the secrets, acts, orders, or edicts of the brotherhood, you will assist in punishing him in any way the camp may direct or approve of: So help you God.[1]

The sign of recognition was to slide the hand down the lapel of the coat as if looking for a pin and the answer was the same motion on the other side of the coat, and the sign of distress was the word, " Shiloh," or two claps of the hands.[2] There was also a grip [3] and a code. The latter was simple, being as follows:

[1] *Senate Report*, no. 1, p. xiv, 42 Cong., 1 sess. This will be indicated hereafter in this chapter by the title *Senate Ku Klux Report*.

[2] *Senate Ku Klux Report*, p. 265.

[3] *Ibid.*, p. 7. It was given by pressing the forefinger upon the back of the hand and was returned by pressing the thumb and forefinger upon the middle finger between the second joint and the hand.

A B C D E *etc.*

K L M N O *etc.*

signs of meeting were given by symbols, a day meeting being indicated by intersecting lines with figures, and a night meeting by a half moon with figures, as

$\frac{4 \mid 3}{9}$  4 × 3 = 12th at 9 o'clock A. M.

$4)\frac{3}{9}$  4 × 3 = 12th at 9 o'clock P. M.

When at meetings or on a raid, disguises were worn, made often by women who had been initiated, and answering generally to the following description:

It is a large loose gown, covering the whole person quite closely, buttoned close around and reaching from the head clear down to the floor, covering the feet and dragging on the ground. It is made of bleached linen, starched and ironed, and in the night by moonlight it glitters and rattles. Then there is a hood with holes cut in for eyes, and a nose, six or eight inches long, made of cotton cloth, stuffed with cotton, and lapped with red braid half an inch wide. The eyes are lined with the braid, and the eyebrows are made of the same. The cloth is lined with red flannel. Then there is a long tongue, sticking out about six inches, made of red flannel also, and so fixed that it can be moved about by the man's tongue. Then in the mouth are large teeth that are very frightful. Then under the tongue is a leather bag placed inside, so that when the man calls for water he pours it inside the bag and not into his mouth at all. The head dress has three horns on top, made of cotton, about a foot long; these were also lapped with red braid.[1]

But little has been made public regarding the Constitutional Union Guard. It is known, however, that it was organized in the North in 1868 with an entirely political

[1] *Senate Ku Klux Report*, p. 9.

purpose. Its aim was to secure the election of Seymour and Blair, and when it was brought South, its initiates were told that it had a membership in the North and West of over a million.[1]   It is scarcely likely that this had any basis in fact and there is certainly no proof of any.   It continued to exist, side by side or blended with the other orders, until the movement had spent its force.   Its reputed state head was Edward Graham Haywood, of Raleigh, but there is no proof that he had connection with it and considerable reason to believe that he had none.

The Constitutional Union Guard was organized into " klans," each under the orders of a south commander, assisted by a west commander, a north commander, and an east commander, ranking in the order named.   Other officers were conductor, outside guard, inside guard, secretary, and treasurer.   The south commander of the oldest klan was the commanding officer of the county.   The sign of recognition consisted in crossing the right hand over the heart, which closely resembled the sign of the White Brotherhood.   The sign of distress was given by passing both hands clasped over the head backward and forward, spreading out the thumbs.   The word of distress was " Ahoy."[2]   The disguises of the members were nearly always black and had tall pointed caps without the horns which adorned those of the White Brotherhood.   Practically nothing is known of the ritual except that it was printed.

The Invisible Empire was the original of the Ku Klux orders, being founded in Pulaski, Tennessee, in 1865.   In its origin, it had no special purpose other than a social one, but its possibilities were soon seen and it spread with incon-

---

[1] It is very likely that the story that President Johnson was at the head of the Ku Klux grew out of the origin of this organization.

[2] *Holden Impeachment Trial*, p. 1973.

ceivable rapidity. General Nathan B. Forrest became its head, or Grand Wizard, and did much to control its activities and to spread its organization. It was first brought to North Carolina by an emissary of General Forrest who visited many counties in the State and began the work of organization by initiating some chosen person in each. The date of this visit is not known, some persons placing it in 1867 and some in 1868. In 1870, General Forrest himself visited Greensboro but there is no evidence that his visit had any connection with the Ku Klux. As he had officially disbanded the order in 1869, it is probable that it had not.

The constitution and ritual of the Invisible Empire were the most elaborate of those of any of the orders.[1] At the head of the order was the Grand Wizard; over each State, a Grand Dragon; over such districts as might be set up, a Grand Titan; and over each county, a Grand Giant, who in North Carolina was usually called Grand Mogul; and over each den or local organization, a Grand Cyclops, with numerous subordinate officers associated with each. On paper, there was provision for a very complete and effective organization, but it was never perfected because, from the very nature of the order, its officers could not control it. Its ritual shows clearly that it could not have been other than political, whatever may have been the purposes and intentions of its leaders. After denying that he had ever been a member of the Radical Republican party, the Loyal

[1] Two prescripts of the Ku Klux Klan were printed; the original early in 1867, and the Revised and Amended Prescript, probably in 1868. Of the former only one copy is known to be in existence and is in the possession of Professor Walter L. Fleming. Of the latter there are three, one in the Library of Columbia University, one in the Library of the University of North Carolina, and one in the possession of Mr. J. L. Pearcy. Both editions are reprinted in Fleming's edition of Lester and Wilson: *Ku Klux Klan.*

League, and the Grand Army of the Republic, and that he
had fought against the South in the war, and after affirming his opposition to the organizations mentioned, to negro
equality, social and political, and expressing his belief in
constitutional liberty, a free white government, and the in-
alienable right of self-preservation of the people against
the exercise of arbitrary power, the initiate took the following oath.

I, —— ——, before the Great Immaculate Judge of Heaven
and earth, and upon the Holy Evangelist of Almighty God,
do, of my own free will and accord, subscribe to the following
sacred, binding obligation:

I. I am on the side of justice and humanity, and constitutional liberty as bequeathed to us by our forefathers in its
original purity.

II. I reject and oppose the principles of the radical party.

III. I pledge aid to a brother of the Ku Klux Klan in sickness, distress, or pecuniary embarrassments; females, friends,
widows, and their households shall be the special object of
my care and protection.

IV. Should I ever divulge, or cause to be divulged, any of
the secrets of this order, or any of the foregoing obligations,
I must meet with the fearful punishment of death and traitor's
doom, which is death, death, death, at the hands of the
brethren.[1]

There were several signs of recognition. One was given
by stroking the side of the head above the right ear with
the ends of the fingers of the right hand and the answer
was given in the same way, the left hand being used. Another was picking the right lapel of the coat with the right
hand and in the answer the left hand was used. This, it
will be seen, was about the same sign as that employed by

---

[1] *House Report*, no. 22, pt. 2, p. 399, 42 Cong., 2 sess. This will
hereafter in this chapter be called *Joint Report*.

the other two orders. A third was given by standing at attention with the right hand in the side pocket of the trousers with the thumb left outside, the left hand being used in the same way for a reply. The grip was given by locking the little fingers and pressing the wrist with the forefinger. " Avalanche " was the word of distress and the hailing sign in the dark was " I S.A.Y," the answer being " N.O.T.H.I.N.G." [1] The costumes varied with the locality but were usually more decorated than those of the other two orders. But a man who belonged to all three, as was often the case, usually had but one disguise. Red suits were seen frequently and on one raid in Orange County all wore them.[2]

At the head of the Invisible Empire in North Carolina was Colonel William L. Saunders, of Chapel Hill, who, although he directed it, and, through it to an extent, the other two orders, for the membership was often, and the leaders nearly always, identical, never took the oath of membership and hence was, strictly speaking, not a member.[3] There are few more convincing tributes of confidence than this and well did he deserve it. Summoned in 1871 to appear before the joint committee on " affairs in the insurrectionary States," he declined in spite of threats and the attempts of the committee to punish him for contempt, to answer any question which in any way related to the Ku Klux, and in the end, escaped any punishment.[4] Below him in rank were the chiefs of the various counties, but few of whom, apparently, were in any communication with him.

---

[1] *Joint Report*, p. 399.

[2] *Senate Ku Klux Report*, p. 44.

[3] Colonel Joseph Webb in a letter to the author, dated December, 1903.

[4] *Joint Report*, pp. 354-61.

It is impossible at this time to distinguish in most of the county organizations between the three orders. The same is true of their leaders. Often the same person was county chief of more than one and sometimes of all three. So far as can be discovered, the leaders were as follows: Orange: Colonel Joseph Webb and later F. N. Strudwick; Alamance: White Brotherhood and Invisible Empire, Jacob A. Long; Constitutional Union Guard, James A. J. Patterson;[1] Mecklenburg: Hamilton C. Jones; Lincoln: Dr. Ephraim Brevard; Gaston: Dr. Joseph Graham and later Calvin E. Grier; Burke: A. C. Avery; Cleveland: Lee M. McAfee; Rutherford: Ladson Mills and R. A. Shotwell in succession; Franklin: Joseph J. Davis; Caswell: John G. Lee; Lenoir: Jesse C. Kennedy; Guilford: Major Steiner and Macon Apple.

Beneath these were the local "dens," "camps," or "klans," as the case might be. In Alamance, there were ten camps of the White Brotherhood each under its chief.[2] There were five klans of the Constitutional Union Guard.[3] The organization in other counties during the period is not known, but in 1870, Rutherford had five local organizations; Polk, two; Cleveland, six; McDowell, two; and Burke, three.[4]

[1] *Holden Impeachment Trial*, pp. 2249-50.

[2] These were: 1, Jacob A. Long, who was also county chief; 2, Jasper N. Wood; 3, John T. Trolinger; 4, Albert Murray; 5, George Anthony; 6, David Mebane; 7, William Stockard; 8, John Durham; 9, James Bradsher; 10, Job Faucette. Impeachment Trial, p. 2250.

[3] The leaders of these were: 1, James A. J. Patterson; 2, Eli Euless and John T. Fogleman; 3, Jasper N. Wood; 4, Jacob A. Long; 5, George Anthony.

[4] Shotwell Manuscript. At one time or another the following were local chiefs: Rutherford: William Webster, J. R. DePriest, Fayette Eaves, Elias Hambrick, who was a Republican, Madison McBrayer, William Edgington, John Witherow, and Mack Deck; Cleveland: Joseph Walker, Matt McBrier; Polk: Aden Rucker.

The discipline of the movement was good at first. Nearly all the manifestations of its power were carefully planned, executed with silence and dispatch, almost always by camps from other counties, and not mentioned by the members. At first designed for protection, it acted only as a regulating influence and, as a result of its operations, a large part of the population of the State had lifted from it a burden of terror. Crime of all sorts grew rapidly less, and so by illegal methods the observance of law was maintained. But as the organizations became more political in character, the membership increased and, the mass of the members realizing their power, discipline relaxed until finally there was none. Punishment became more frequent until the very nature of the movement was radically changed. The Ku Klux continued to be a terror to evil-doers, but it was also a terrible menace to the personal quiet of its active political opponents. When the tendencies of the movement were seen, the orders were officially disbanded, but they were beyond the control of their leaders [1] and, the best element in the main having withdrawn, the name of Ku Klux by the summer of 1870 had come to be associated with much of unjustifiable violence, of injustice, and of wrong. It became the cloak for the private vengeance of those who were unworthy, and in many instances, of those who had never been connected with it. In Alamance, there was a raid by negroes dressed as Ku Klux, all of whom were captured and convicted. Randolph Shotwell in his autobiog-

---

[1] The Invisible Empire was disbanded by General Forrest in 1869, but it is not likely that the order was obeyed in many parts of North Carolina, if indeed it ever reached the State. The White Brotherhood and Invisible Empire in Alamance were disbanded in the same year by the chiefs of the local camps, upon the advice of Jacob A. Long. The Constitutional Union Guard in Alamance was disbanded in 1870. In almost all the counties, efforts were made by the original leaders, with small success, to check the activities of the orders.

raphy speaks of the difficulty experienced by genuine Ku Klux in Rutherford on account of the activity of independent imitators who sought only the gratification of private wishes. This was the heritage that was to be expected and, while the worthy original members of the orders had no part in it, they were in part responsible and no estimate of the movement is correct or adequate which does not include in its calculations the work of this bastard offspring of the Klan. Through its activity, the defenders of the movement were alienated, its very originators became its enemies, and an efficient public sentiment was aroused which greatly assisted in putting an end to its existence.

It is not likely that the full extent of the organizations will ever be known, either as regards membership or territory covered. Few if any of the members knew themselves. Forty thousand was a very usual estimate but there is nothing to prove the correctness of the figures. Certainly no such number were ever active in the State. Many were doubtless initiated who, for various reasons, were never called upon to do anything. In some of the counties which had an organization, the leaders never found any occasion to use it. Estimates of the number of members in certain counties are interesting even though not entirely reliable. The following table gives some of these.

| County | Number. |
|---|---|
| Alamance | 600–700 |
| Orange | 1800 [1] |
| Guilford | 800 |
| Lenoir | 100 |
| Cleveland | 800–1000 |
| Rutherford | 500 |

The territorial extent of the movement is exceedingly in-

[1] This was probably exaggerated, though Orange was probably better organized than any other county.

teresting. It was essentially a movement of the Piedmont region of the State and was never very successful in spreading in the eastern counties where there was a large negro population. The only counties with negro majorities in which the Ku Klux appeared were Caswell, Lenoir, Jones, Franklin, and Wayne, and only in Caswell were they active. The counties in which the orders displayed any activity fall into two groups, a central and a western one. In the former, were Alamance and Orange, where Daniel R. Goodloe said the movement was hereditary and closely akin to the Regulation, Caswell, Chatham, Cumberland, Duplin, Harnett, Lenoir, Jones, Moore, Person, Franklin, Wayne, Guilford, Rockingham, and Stokes. In the latter, were Burke, Catawba, Cleveland, Gaston, Lincoln, Mecklenburg, Polk, McDowell, Rowan, and Rutherford. Orange and Alamance formed the storm centre of the central group and Cleveland and Rutherford of the western. So far as outward manifestation is proof, the movement was of comparatively little importance elsewhere. But it is not to be doubted that it was in a quiet way very important, both protectively and politically, in many counties where it did not attract any public attention. In the latter respect it was an organization which kept its members aroused. Its chief work in the State and in the South, in addition to the protection it furnished, was in restoring heart and courage to the white people who at first seemed overwhelmed by the immensity of their misfortunes. In this way it was the active agent which secured political redemption. The western group of counties was largely influenced by South Carolina and was practically unconnected with the central group. In fact the chief activities in the west commenced only as the movement ceased further eastward. In the west the organization was far less complete and the discipline less effective. Its punitive measures were far less productive of public benefit and, in its period of greatest activity, the movement had little to recommend it.

### 3. ACTIVITIES OF THE ORDERS

The activities of the Ku Klux organizations may be classified under two heads: punitive, or those of a regulating nature; and political. From the fact that the orders were organized for the protection of the white people through the process of spreading a salutary terror among the evil-doers of the various communities where they operated, their history as regulators of public conduct is far more extended and probably more important than their political activity which was always a secondary consideration. Reference has already been made to the appearance of the Ku Klux in Warren County during the campaign of 1868. At that time there was no violence of any sort committed. The fact that the organization never appeared again in that section of the State might lead to the belief that it never really existed there and that the one manifestation of its presence was really the work of practical jokers; but it was probably genuine Ku Klux activity, though, when the orders commenced their real work later, it was a much more serious affair.

During the presidential campaign of 1868, the Republicans spoke in vague terms of Ku Klux outrages in various parts of the State. Governor Holden even wrote the sheriff of Granville in October that some had occurred in that county,[1] but no evidence that such was the case was found. But there is abundant evidence that the Klan was at work in other sections of the State, although no violence occurred that was worthy of special mention until the next year when a different condition of affairs presented itself. In a num-

[1] *Standard*, Oct. 21, 1868.

ber of counties, severe punishment was inflicted upon evil-doers, for the orders at once constituted themselves active censors of public morals and manners. The localities chiefly affected were Alamance, Orange, Caswell, Jones, Lenoir, and Chatham counties.

In Alamance, the organization was widespread and there was a very general sentiment among the people in favor of the movement. Only one raid was ever made by the White Brotherhood or Invisible Empire with the official sanction of the county chief. The town of Graham, which was a quiet little village, suddenly arrived at the dignity of a night police force consisting of three negroes who were instructed to stop all persons (and this in its enforcement meant Conservatives) who came on the streets after nine o'clock, and ascertain their business. This naturally excited much anger in the town, and Jacob A. Long ordered thirty men in disguise, without arms, to ride through the town with the purpose of frightening the police. Thirty-one men came in, all armed, and when fired upon by Wyatt Outlaw and Henry Holt, two negroes, the former the head of the Union League in the county, they returned the fire to the extent that each one emptied his pistol. Long saw at once the impossibility of controlling the orders and refused to give his consent to any other demonstration. Later he called a meeting of the local chiefs and they disbanded the White Brotherhood and Invisible Empire. His belief was justified by facts; the movement was beyond the control of any man, whatever his authority; and without regard to the laws of the orders, a period of great activity on the part of the individual members followed. An attempt was made to whip Henry Holt, but he eluded his pursuers. Caswell Holt, another negro who had grossly insulted a young girl in the country by exposing his person in her presence, was severely whipped in January, 1869. He suspected several persons who were arrested and carried before a Republican magistrate, but all were cleared.[1] About a year later he was visited by the Ku Klux who fired into his house wounding him severely.[2] The second visit was probably due to his loud and frequent threats against the Ku Klux.

Probably the most interesting example of Ku Klux punishment in the State was a case, the details and even the fact of which have never before been published. In the country lived the widow of a Confederate soldier with one daughter, a young girl of about sixteen years of age. All of their former slaves left except a boy who had always been a house servant. He told the girl one day that he was going to marry her, that he was free and as good as she. Upon her ordering him to be silent, he told her that if she ever mentioned what he had said, he would kill her mother, and that she might as well remember that he was going to marry her. The girl was young and simple and, terribly alarmed for her mother's safety, remained silent but steadily lost health and spirits. Finally at church, her uncle, who lived in another section of the county, remarked upon her loss of health and she told him the story of what had occurred. He took her to his home, and that night with six other members of the Ku Klux went to see the negro, who never appeared again. The matter never attracted any public attention since the negroes were so constantly moving about that a sudden disappearance of one without a family excited no comment.

In the autumn of 1869, the Ku Klux whipped Alonzo Corliss, a Northern man who was teaching a negro school at Company Shops. He had been president of the Union League and shortly before this had insisted upon the ne-

[1] *Senate Ku Klux Report*, p. 343.　　　[2] *Ibid.*, p. 345.

groes' going to church and sitting among the white people.[1]
In addition to whipping him, they shaved one side of his
head and painted one side of his face black.[2] He had four
men arrested and examined before a Republican magistrate but could produce no evidence against them. He was
a cripple and many Ku Klux were angry at what had been
done to him, but shortly thereafter, a flag was set up in the
road near his school, trimmed with crape, and a coffin
stamped upon it with the following inscription: " Corliss
and the negroes. Let the guilty beware. Don't touch.
Hell." [3]

During the year a large number of persons in the county
were whipped, nearly all for some particular offence or for
their general mode of life, and none so far as can be discovered for political reasons. Many negroes were whipped
for the purpose of intimidation, eighteen of them in one
section in one night. In one case, a child was trampled
and died from its injuries.[4] In another case, a negro woman
used an axe with such effect that one of the visitors carries
its mark across his face to-day. A coffin was placed at the
door of a white Republican, who had been talking loudly
against the Klan, with the inscription across its head, "Hold
your tongue, or this will be your home," and down its
length, "Alive to-day, but dead to-morrow. K. K. K." [5]
Negroes and whites were visited and made to grasp skel-
eton hands or bring buckets of water for the thirsty spirit
who " had not had a drink of water since he was killed at
Shiloh." One old man, Benjamin Cable, burst into the
office of the clerk of the court, the day after such an experience, crying, " God, Albright, the Ku Klux don't hurt any-

[1] *Senate Ku Klux Report*, p. 254.     [2] *Ibid.*, p. 145.
[3] *Ibid.*, p. 149.     [4] *Ibid.*, p. 33.
[5] *Impeachment Trial*, p. 1502.

body but they scare a man 'most to death. They made me bring six buckets of water and then I said, ' Go to the spring.' "

In 1870, still more severe measures were taken. T. M. Shoffner, who had introduced the bill " for the better protection of life and property," lived in Alamance and his death was voted by the Orange Ku Klux who prepared to kill him and send his body to Governor Holden.[1] The news reached Alamance upon the day chosen for his assassination. James E. Boyd told Dr. John A. Moore, " They are going to suspend Shoffner's writ of *habeas corpus* to-night," and remarked that he was going to leave the county for the night.[2] The latter at once rode to the appointed place to stop the proposed murder and turned back the visitors. In the meantime, Eli Euless, the head of a klan of the Constitutional Union Guard, carried Shoffner to Greensboro.[3] Shoffner was naturally terribly alarmed and soon after moved to Indiana.

Wyatt Outlaw, as has been noted, fired upon the Ku Klux at their first public appearance in the county. He was a blatant negro who as head of the League was reported by the negroes to have said, " Put fire to mills, barns, and houses," and his death was determined upon by certain members of one of the orders. A party of them rode into Graham on the night of February 26, 1870, and, seizing Outlaw in his home, carried him to a tree in the courthouse square and there hanged him, leaving upon his breast the inscription, " Bewar, ye guilty, both black and white." As the raiders went home, a semi-idiotic negro named William Puryear saw some of them and reported the fact. He disappeared that night and was found some weeks later in a neighboring pond.[4] All attempts to discover the perpe-

---

[1] *Impeachment Trial*, pp. 1975-76.    [2] *Ibid.*, p. 1526.
[3] *Ibid.*, p. 1976.    [4] *Senate Ku Klux Report*, p. 35.

trators of these two murders were unavailing. Public sentiment in the county strongly condemned the hanging of Outlaw, but many believed that the Ku Klux had nothing to do with Puryear's death.

With these acts, the operations in Alamance came to an end.

In Orange, the Ku Klux were probably less active but their punishments were more severe, though whipping and milder punishments were not unknown. Five persons, all negroes, were put to death during the year 1869, none for any political reason.

Late in July, three barns in sight of each other were burned on the same night and at the same time. The owner of one of them, with complete ruin staring him in the face, lost his mind and committed suicide the next day.[1] A few days later, the county jail was opened and two negroes accused of another barn-burning taken out. One was released, but the other was shot and died of his wounds two weeks later.[2] Suspicion, in the meantime, fell upon two negroes, Dan and Jeff Morrow, who had burned the barns, and on August 7, they were hanged on a tree by a public road in the southern part of the county and left with the inscription, " All barn burners and women insulters, we Kuklux hang by the neck until they are dead, dead, dead. K. K. K."

Later in the year, Wright Woods, a negro who had threatened rape, was found hanged with a paper on his foot on which was written, " If the law will not protect virtue, the rope will." [3] Later still, Cyrus Guy was hanged for the

---

[1] A member of the League, who had been whipped a few days before this happening and was in a communicative frame of mind, said that the burning had been inspired by the governor who had said the negro must rule. *Sentinel*, July 27, 1869.

[2] *Senate Ku Klux Report*, pp. 41–47; 190–201.

[3] *Sentinel*, Sept. 28, 1869.

same offence. Public sentiment in Orange was somewhat more divided than in Alamance, and Thomas Ruffin, W. A. Graham, John Norwood, W. H. Battle, and others were outspoken in their opposition to the movement. But with the mass of the white people, it was very popular and, considering the protection it had given, naturally so.

The acts of the Klan in Orange at first excited more attention in the State than those of any other county, and Governor Holden decided to send troops to Hillsboro, but changed his mind after receiving good advice from there. On November 3, the *Standard,* declaring that it was speaking for the governor, threatened a proclamation that the county was in insurrection. A week later, it closed an editorial on the subject of the Ku Klux with the following sentence: " They will be dealt with as traitors by both the State and general governments, even if there has to be a gibbet for every tree in the forests of Orange."

Jones County was early notable for several acts for which the Ku Klux received the credit. Lawlessness was very prevalent in the county and members of the League had murdered a large number of persons. Three carpetbaggers who had won the hatred of the mass of the white people by their activity among the negroes were D. D. Colgrove, a member of the convention, his brother O. R. Colgrove, and one Shepperd, who enjoyed the title of colonel. O. R. Colgrove had served a term in the New York penitentiary before he became a captain in the Union army. General Canby had appointed him sheriff of the county and, although he could not give bond, kept him in the position which he succeeded in retaining under the new dispensation. He had the reputation of being a bad and dangerous man.[1] Shepperd was from Pennsylvania and, after serving in the

[1] *Senate Ku Klux Report*, pp. 98, 373.

federal army, remained in North Carolina where he became a county commissioner and colonel of militia.[1]  Notices were posted warning him and Colgrove to leave, but both disregarded them.  In May, Colgrove and a negro who was driving with him were shot and killed.  No one was ever implicated in the murder, although the responsibility of the Ku Klux was quite clearly proved.[2]  On August 16, Shepperd, who was running a saw mill, was shot and killed by some unknown person across the river and, while no clue was ever found, public opinion settled upon the Ku Klux as responsible.

Chatham County had the reputation of great Ku Klux activity, but in time, it was clearly proved that many of the supposed Ku Klux outrages were in reality the work of the Union League.  The Ku Klux organization in the county was, however, quite widespread and at times perniciously active.

Caswell County suffered bitterly at the hands of the League, which was under the guidance of John W. Stephens, who was one of the governor's detectives, a man of bad reputation and of evil political life.  In organizing the League, he had advised violence and, finally, at a meeting at the home of his brother-in-law, one Jones, gave to each of the twenty negroes present a box of matches, still a rarity among them, and told each one to burn a barn.  Not all followed his instructions, but nine barns were burned in one night.  Some time afterwards, a white man in the neighborhood overheard two of his negro hands mention Jones as connected with the burning, and that night, Jones was taken from his home and given an opportunity to tell what he knew.  He refused at first, but when the hickory

[1] *Standard*, Aug. 19, 1869.
[2] *Senate Ku Klux Report*, p. 242.

sprouts began to strike his bare back, he confessed the whole thing. The Ku Klux were well organized and Stephens' death was resolved upon. In March, 1870, a large Conservative meeting was held in Yanceyville. Stephens was present taking notes upon a speech of Judge Kerr when he was requested to come down stairs for a few moments. In company with the person making the request, he walked down stairs, through the corridor which was crowded with people listing taxes, and went into an unoccupied office. Instantly, seven men seized him, and his companion departed closing the door after him, leaving Stephens tightly held. After three seven-shot revolvers had been taken from him, he was bound, gagged, and laid upon a pile of wood in the corner. One man, left to keep guard, stretched out on the hearth in order that the negroes who thronged the square on which the windows opened might not see him, and the other six left and walked down the corridor to Judge Kerr's office, which was unoccupied during its owner's speech upstairs. The original plan had been to keep Stephens until night and then to hang him in the square, but the danger of discovery was so great that it was now decided not to delay at all. Walking back through the crowd, they re-entered the room and cut his throat, at the same time drawing a rope tightly about his neck, and stabbed him to the heart, after which they left. The provocation was undoubtedly great, but few can deny the horror of the punishment. His body was not discovered until the next day and, while the Ku Klux were at once suspected, no evidence could be secured. Many people, including a large number of Republicans, thought that he had been killed by members of his own party, since he was known to have many enemies in its ranks, and this opinion gained strength when it became known that a short time before Governor Holden had said to a delegation of negroes, who had gone to discuss with him the condition of affairs in Caswell and to complain of the violence of Stephens in speech and act, " We must get rid of Stephens," meaning of course as a party leader. No one accused the governor of complicity or of evil intention, but many thought that his words had been misunderstood by the negroes and that the death of Stephens was the result.

With the exception of this striking example of its power and secrecy, the activity of the Ku Klux organization in Caswell was very slight. Two or three negroes were whipped for stealing, some were warned,[1] and that was about all. There, as elsewhere, its influence upon the negroes was beneficial to the public.

In the other counties of the central group, the activity of the Klan amounted to little, so far as the public was aware. Undoubtedly many of the doings of the organizations never became publicly known, while, on the other hand, they received the credit for much with which they had no connection. The *Standard* published the confession of Daniel Graham, a supposed reformed member, in which he accused some of the best men in Cumberland County of various horrible crimes, but upon investigation, he proved to be a murderer and one-time outlaw, so his testimony was not accepted by the public. Shortly before this time, a horrible murder had occurred in the county, but the victim happened to be a Conservative and members of the Union League were suspected of being the perpetrators of the crime, so the governor apparently gave himself little concern about it. In Robeson County, the Lowry Gang were committing all sorts of depredations but, as they were all Republicans and supposed to be Red Strings, they were not molested by Gov-

---

[1] A negro magistrate received the following warning in the spring of 1870: " Mr. Cook beware. Take care of your head or we shall have it before you leave the county for we are Kuklux and sworn."

ernor Holden or by his successor, Governor Caldwell. In the Northern press, they were first said to be Ku Klux and later, when more was learned of them, that their acts were in retaliation for Ku Klux outrages. As a matter of fact, their lawlessness antedated the Ku Klux organization.

These are the most notable examples of the work of the Klan. A study of all available sources of information concerning the organization brings conviction that only in a very small degree was it political in purpose. In effect it was a very powerful political influence.

No correct estimate can be made of the number and character of the visitations made by the Ku Klux. The following table, which includes the western counties to be discussed later, was prepared from the entirely unreliable documents and testimony found in the two reports of congressional investigating committees and in that of the impeachment trial:

| | White. | | | | | | | Colored. | | | | | | | | |
|---|---|---|---|---|---|---|---|---|---|---|---|---|---|---|---|---|
| | Whipped. | Shot. | Wounded. | Property Destroyed. | Miscellaneous. | Warned. | Killed. | Whipped. | Hanged. | Shot. | Wounded. | Property Destroyed. | Miscellaneous. | Warned. | Killed. | Total. |
| Alamance | 22 | .. | .. | 2 | 1 | 3 | .. | 54 | 1 | 1 | .. | .... | 2 | 1 | 3 | 90 |
| Buncombe | 1 | .. | .. | ... | .. | .. | . | .... | .. | .. | .. | .... | .. | .. | .. | 1 |
| Caswell | 2 | .. | .. | .. | .. | .. | 1 | 6 | .. | 1 | .. | 1 | .. | .. | 1 | 12 |
| Chatham | 5 | .. | .. | .... | .. | .. | .. | 6 | .. | .. | .. | .... | .. | .. | .. | 11 |
| Catawba | 10 | .. | .. | 1 | .. | .. | .. | 12 | .. | .. | .. | ... | .. | .. | .. | 23 |
| Cumberland | 1 | .. | .. | .... | .. | .. | .. | .... | .. | .. | .. | .... | .. | .. | .. | 1 |
| Cleveland | 13 | .. | 1 | .... | .. | .. | .. | 4 | .. | .. | 1 | .... | .. | .. | .. | 19 |
| Guilford | 1 | .. | .. | .... | .. | .. | .. | 2 | .. | .. | .. | .... | .. | .. | .. | 3 |
| Harnett | .. | .. | .. | .... | .. | .. | .. | 1 | .. | .. | .. | .... | .. | .. | .. | 1 |
| Jones | .. | 2 | .. | .... | .. | .. | .. | 1 | .. | 1 | .. | .... | .. | 1 | .. | 5 |
| Lenoir | .. | .. | .. | .... | .. | .. | .. | 1 | .. | 1 | 1 | .... | .. | .. | 2 | 5 |
| Lincoln | 5 | .. | .. | .... | .. | .. | .. | 18 | .. | 6 | .. | 1 | .. | .. | .. | 30 |
| Moore | 1 | .. | .. | .... | 2 | .. | .. | 5 | .. | .. | .. | .... | .. | .. | .. | 8 |
| Madison | .. | .. | .. | .... | .. | .. | .. | 1 | .. | .. | .. | .... | .. | .. | .. | 1 |
| Orange | .. | .. | .. | .... | .. | .. | .. | 4 | 4 | 1 | 2 | .... | .. | .. | .. | 11 |
| Randolph | .. | .. | .. | .... | .. | .. | .. | 2 | .. | .. | .. | .... | .. | .. | .. | 2 |
| Rutherford | 10 | .. | .. | 1 | .. | . | .. | 15 | .. | .. | .. | .... | .. | .. | .. | 26 |
| Stokes | .. | .. | .. | .... | .. | .. | .. | 1 | .. | 1 | .. | .... | .. | .. | .. | 2 |
| Wake | .. | .. | .. | .... | .. | .. | .. | 7 | .. | .. | .. | .... | .. | .. | .. | 7 |
| Yancey | 1 | .. | .. | .... | .. | .. | .. | 1 | .. | .. | .. | .... | .. | .. | .. | 2 |
| Total | 72 | 2 | 1 | 4 | 3 | 3 | 1 | 141 | 5 | 12 | 4 | 2 | 2 | 2 | 6 | 260 |

Comment upon the work of the Klan was not lacking at the time. The Republican papers were full of editorial denunciation of the perpetrators of the real and imaginary outrages which crowded their columns. A few Conservative papers, including the Charlotte *Democrat,* condemned the organization and its acts. The *Sentinel* either ignored them or used them as a text to preach against the Union League. The usual Conservative attitude is to be seen in the following editorial from the *Wilmington Journal:*

The crimes committed in the earlier months after the war,

and which aroused the people in some portions of the State to organize for mutual protection, were almost universally committed by members of the Loyal League. . . . . We have known the time when the arrest of a Loyal Leaguer in Wilmington, regardless of the offence which he had committed, was attended with difficulty and danger.

The same condition of things existed throughout the State, and in some counties the crimes were more frequent and flagrant. This state of affairs resulted from the direct teachings of the Leagues or from a belief that such conduct would not be punished and that the offenders would find protection from the civil or military departments of the government. None of them were punished and this immunity caused a rapid increase in the number and boldness of crimes.

It was in this crisis that counter organizations were formed for mutual protection. Some may have been bound together by oaths, but many had no other rallying cry than self-protection—the first great law of nature. We do not here propose to go into an argument as to how far the citizen may go for protection when the law is inadequate, or its administrators unwilling to furnish it. We know what they will do under such circumstances, and what human nature justifies them in. Their organizations were intended only, as we honestly believe, for protection. If, in some instances, they have taken the law into their own hands, it has always been to punish some offender of the League who had made himself amenable to the law, but had not been punished. We are no defenders of such conduct. Men who violate the law should be adequately punished—the majesty of the law should be vindicated at all hazards. But we can see how citizens, law-abiding citizens, may be led into the committal of acts which they would scorn to do had they not lost confidence in the will or ability of their duly constituted authorities to afford them protection; who did not believe that a band of political criminals in their midst were afforded protection by the officers themselves.

If the Governor will disband his Loyal Leagues, all counter

organizations will be broken up. If all criminals are dealt with without favor, citizens will not be tempted to take the law into their own hands. If our civil officers will act so as to deserve the confidence of the people, the old regard and veneration for the law will return. And when it does, Loyal Leagueism and its offspring, Ku Kluxism, will be buried in a common grave.[1]

In spite of the hysterical press notices which would indicate the contrary, there was never a time when the Ku Klux were disturbers of general public peace and order. In fact, for a time, at least, after their appearance, there was improvement in this respect. The courts were undisturbed and the officers of the law went unhindered about their duties. Wrong-doers and radical politicians, names then too often synonymous, trembled, a small class of timid whites became alarmed, and panic, not soon allayed, spread among the negroes,[2] but the mass of the white people remained undisturbed and unafraid. Reference has already been made to Chief Justice Pearson's statement that North Carolina in 1869 had as much law and order as it had ever had,[3] and while the facts of the case would scarcely bear out his belief, it would be even more incorrect to say that there were anarchy and widespread violence.

The Ku Klux movement ended in central North Carolina in the summer of 1870. In the western counties, it reached its climax during the following six months. Conditions in several counties, particularly Rutherford and Cleveland, were bad, and the Invisible Empire there had degenerated

---

[1] *Wilmington Journal*, quoted in *Sentinel*, Nov. 6, 1869.

[2] The writer remembers distinctly in his boyhood in Orange County, more than a decade after the events narrated, when the sound of more than two horsemen passing along the country roads together was sufficient to make many negroes spend the rest of the night in the woods.

[3] *Tarboro Southerner*, July 22, 1869.

until it bore little or no resemblance to the organization elsewhere. In Rutherford a number of Republicans had joined
it in order to protect blockade stills.[1] One of these was for
a time county chief. Additional proof that it was not a
party organization is to be found in the whipping of three
Conservatives in Cleveland.[2] But it was violent, unrestrained by its nominal leaders, and greatly influenced to
its detriment by the South Carolina counties just across the
line. It had clearly outlived any usefulness it may have
had and deserved the downfall which soon came.

Three notable cases of its work occurred in Rutherford
in 1871. The one of most importance had little real connection with the Ku Klux, since it was the result of what
was in the nature of a neighborhood feud. Aaron Biggarstaff, an old man who had been a Union sympathizer during
the war and a Republican afterwards, was one of a number
of men who fired into the house of his half-brother. Shortly
thereafter,[3] a band of disguised men visited him and assaulted him most brutally, hanging him and leaving him for
dead. He was cut down and having recognized a number
of the party present at this " Home Raid " as it was called,
had them arrested on bench warrants issued by Judge
Logan. There was not sufficient evidence to hold them, so
Judge Logan put them under heavy bond, and they were
then arrested on a United States warrant, and Biggarstaff
and his daughter were summoned as witnesses. While on
their way to the hearing, they encamped for the night and
the " Grassy Branch Raid " occurred in which both Biggarstaff and his daughter were assaulted, the former receiving
very serious injuries. The case was not tried in the District Court at Marion, but was postponed until the meeting
of the Circuit Court in Raleigh in September.

[1] *Joint Report*, pp. 222, 234, 532–33, 552, 572.      [2] *Ibid.*, p. 330.
[3] April 8, 1871.

The other two cases, occurring on the same night, were of genuine Ku Klux origin. James M. Justice, a lawyer and member of the legislature, who had been very active in politics and in the hearings before Judge Logan, growing out of the Biggarstaff raids, was visited. His house was broken open and he was struck several times and, partially unconscious, was dragged out and carried some distance away. He was then lectured in regard to his politics, threatened, forced to promise to keep quiet and abstain from politics, after which he was released.[1] Justice thought he recognized a number of his assailants and they were at once arrested and held for trial.

The same night, the office of the *Rutherford Star,* a Republican paper, edited by J. B. Carpenter, clerk of the court of the county, and Robert Logan, a son of the judge, was wrecked, the press broken, the cases cut to pieces, and the type pied.[2]

In Cleveland County there is much general evidence of the activity of the Klan but there were no cases of special note.

In none of these counties did the organization operate after 1871, for the passage of the enforcement acts speedily brought it to an end, a consummation worthy of praise and one likely under any circumstances to have been accomplished by the growing sentiment of the people in relation to it.

---

[1] *Joint Report,* pp. 115–31.          [2] *Ibid.*, pp. 126–27, 176–77.

# CHAPTER THIRTEEN

## The Reign of Terror

### I. SUPPRESSION OF THE KU KLUX

REPUBLICAN opposition to the Ku Klux was to be expected from the very nature of the case. The operations of the orders were mainly directed against members of that party and, even when they were not, the very existence of the secret organizations of self-constituted regulators indicated a condition of affairs which the party had no reason to be proud of. In addition, from the very beginning, the organizations were regarded by Republican leaders, at least, as political in nature. Less important members of the party agreed to this in public, but many of them in their hearts probably had a guilty consciousness that the offences for which they feared the visitation of the dreaded night-riders were not at all political; that, in fact, their Republicanism was the least of their sins. In some communities that had suffered greatly at the hands of the negroes, the Republicans were secretly grateful to the Klan, and, in the days of its degeneracy, a considerable number of them joined it, in order that, under the shelter of its disguise and its fellowship, they might violate the laws of the land, particularly those in reference to the manufacture and sale of whiskey. But this of course was not loyal Republicanism. Hatred of the Ku Klux speedily became a cardinal doctrine of the party and it was regarded as good party policy to magnify the violence of its acts as much as possible, connecting it at the same time with the opposition party, and thereby to attract as much attention as possible in the North. Right faithfully most of the "loyal" carried out this obligation, taking due care, however, not to get their names connected with the ingeniously manufactured product which appeared in the press under the heading, "Southern Ku Klux Outrages."

As has been mentioned, the governor, just before the election of 1868, issued a proclamation warning the people against disorder.[1] Though the Ku Klux was known to exist in the State, this was issued chiefly for political effect. During the next session of the legislature, Governor Holden sent a company of militia under the command of a Raleigh saloon keeper, to Alamance County where Caswell Holt had been whipped. Nothing was accomplished in Alamance, but the expedition did much to secure the immediate passage of the law which made going masked, painted, or disguised a misdemeanor, and made any act of trespass, force, or violence, committed while so disguised, a felony. On April 16, 1869, Governor Holden issued a proclamation publishing the law and expressing his determination to see that it was enforced.[2] The same legislature authorized the governor to employ a force of detectives to assist in arresting fugitives from justice. Governor Holden construed the law to empower him to employ detectives as he saw fit and he at once planned a secret campaign against disturbers of the peace who wore Ku Klux costumes. He delegated his powers to Adjutant General Fisher who appointed more than twenty detectives, including two members of the House, one of the Senate, himself, and two other carpetbaggers. Their activity was largely directed towards increasing expenses and, with one exception, they accom-

[1] Holden, *Third Annual Message*, Appendix, p. 1.
[2] *Ibid.*, Appendix, p. 6.

o

plished nothing. One of the detectives was William Huskey, of Chapel Hill, who, clothed with new authority, began to open letters in the post office until he was suspected. He expressed a strong wish to join the Ku Klux, but could find no one who would assist him in obtaining his desire. Finally, he was invited to join, and, late at night, was carried to the town pump, tied to a neighboring tree, and given sixty lashes on his bare back with a buggy trace. This, he was informed, was the initiation into the first degree; the next one would be conferred the following night. From that day to this, the would-be member of the Ku Klux has never appeared in Chapel Hill. Governor Holden then asked for and secured federal troops for the town.

In the meantime, the activity of the Klan presented a difficult problem to the governor and other officers of the law. Judge Thomas, upon the application of one of the detectives, issued bench warrants for certain persons in Greene and Lenoir counties, who were arrested and given a preliminary examination, after which he bound them over to the Superior Court.[1] This ended the operations of the Klan in the counties named. Judge Settle twice issued bench warrants and conducted examinations, but discovered nothing.[2] Judge Tourgee announced loudly on the train that he was on his way " to give Orange county h—l," but further than changing his quarters every night to avoid unpleasant visitors, he did nothing, though for once he held court for the entire term. The solicitor of his district, J. R. Bulla, was a very timid man who was of no assistance to the judge in obtaining evidence. In Rockingham, in a charge to the grand jury, Tourgee advised retaliation as a means of

[1] *Senate Ku Klux Report*, pp. 92-100.
[2] *Ibid.*, pp. 84-92.

putting an end to the disorder. It was such judges as he that gave the Klan a reason for existence. In Alamance, in 1871, he issued bench warrants for a large number of persons for the murder of Outlaw, in spite of the fact that there was no evidence against them. Jacob A. Long, the county chief, was one of these, and Tourgee attempted to bribe him with immunity and immediate release provided he would implicate the higher officers of the orders. His offer was peremptorily refused and, the solicitor refusing to draw the bill of indictment, Tourgee drew it himself. The grand jury refused to act upon it, and Long was released. A company of militia was sent to Jones County during the summer of 1869, and, beyond proving themselves a menace to law and order, did nothing worthy of note. Disorders of a grave sort occurring in Chatham, Thomas B. Long was appointed an aid to the governor and sent there and to Orange to see the people and talk over the situation with them in the hope of composing the troubles.[1] It was an unfortunate appointment and did no good. In the meantime, the governor had issued another proclamation, warning the people of Lenoir, Jones, Orange, and Chatham that if the disorders did not cease, he would proclaim those counties in a state of insurrection and exert the whole power of the State to enforce the law.[2]

When the legislature met in the autumn of 1869, the governor urged the passage of a law which would give him greater power and, as a result, the law " for the better protection of life and property " was passed in January, 1870, which gave him power to declare a county in a state of insurrection. Shortly thereafter, Wyatt Outlaw was hanged and, on March 7, 1870, the governor issued a proclamation

---

[1] *Standard*, Oct. 30, 1869.

[2] Holden, *Third Annual Message*, Appendix, p. 7.

declaring Alamance in insurrection.[1] But he sent no troops there and took no steps to carry out the most admirable and commendable sentiments expressed in his message. Had the governor's acts been in accordance with his words, there could be no criticism of him in this connection.

Affairs in Orange had been in some respects worse than in any other county. There were in Hillsboro a large number of influential citizens, Conservatives in politics, who were opposed upon principle to the existence of such an organization as the Ku Klux, and who saw the impending danger. A group of these gentlemen approached Dr. Pride Jones, who was a man of much influence in the county,[2] and persuaded him to apply to Governor Holden for a commission with a view to disbanding the organization in the county.[3] The governor at once appointed him a captain on his staff, and N. A. Ramsey received a similar appointment for Chatham. Both accomplished much good. The truth is that the force of the movement was spent and the majority of the members, in Orange at least, were tired of it and ready to sever their connection with the orders, if there was any security that conditions would improve and that they would not be punished. For this reason, Dr. Jones suggested to the governor that it would be well to authorize him to give assurance of this and also that the League should be put upon the same footing as the Ku Klux. The governor replied that he had no power to proclaim amnesty,[4] but disavowed any intention of wreaking

[1] Holden, *Third Annual Message*, Appendix, p. 10.

[2] Dr. Jones had been a member of the White Brotherhood, but had withdrawn in company with a number of others when its protective character was lost sight of by a number of aggressive members. This information was given the author by his father, who, with Dr. Jones, called the meeting for the purpose of disbanding.

[3] Holden, *Third Annual Message*, Appendix, pp. 41–47.

[4] Governor Holden did have the power of amnesty but may not have known it. It is certain that he had no desire to employ it.

vengeance. By implication, he defended the League, but declared that the time had passed for secret political societies. A little later, Dr. Jones wrote him that Orange was quiet.[1]

A few days after this, the governor notified the President of his action in relation to Alamance, and asked for federal troops. He suggested that Congress authorize the President to suspend the writ of *habeas corpus* in order that criminals might be arrested and, after trial by military tribunals, shot.[2] He also notified the Senators and members of Congress from North Carolina of his action, making similar suggestions to them. He did not rest with this, but three days later sent the following telegram:

> STATE OF NORTH CAROLINA,
> EXECUTIVE DEPARTMENT,
> RALEIGH, MARCH 17, 1870.
>
> *Hon. J. C. Abbott, U. S. Senator.*
> Washington, D. C.
>
> What is being done to protect good citizens in Alamance County? We have federal troops, but we want power to act. Is it possible the Government will abandon its loyal people to be whipped and hanged? The *habeas corpus* should be at once suspended. Will write you to-morrow.
>
> W. W. HOLDEN, *Governor.*

Caswell County had been troubled by very little disturbance, but reports of disorder reached the governor, who wrote Thomas A. Donoho, a prominent citizen, and appealed to him to use his influence to restore quiet. Donoho replied that the reports were exaggerated and that the county as a whole was in good condition. He placed the blame for most of the trouble on John W. Stephens, and

[1] *Executive Correspondence*, Holden, i, p. 350.

[2] Governor Holden enclosed copies of the various North Carolina laws which served as models for the later Ku Klux legislation of Congress.

suggested the employment of some moderate " gentleman of character " to do the same work that Dr. Jones had done in Orange. Stephens was one of the governor's detectives and was devoting a large part of his time to incendiary politics. On May 21, he was murdered, and investigation failed to reveal the offenders. Wilson Carey fled in terror and the governor wired Pool and Abbott that he had been driven out of Caswell and that Congress should act.[1] On June 6, the governor issued a proclamation reciting eleven outrages supposed to have been committed by the Klan, offering a reward of five hundred dollars for the arrest of any person connected in any way with the crimes, and enjoining all officers to bring the offenders to justice.

The campaign for the August elections was now in progress. The governor was deeply interested in the result and the prospects were dark. He was in constant consultation with his chosen advisers, who were in favor of putting the condition of affairs in the State to practical political advantage, and accordingly, in pursuance of a plan devised by Pool, on July 8, he proclaimed Caswell County in a state of insurrection. The final results of his action will be discussed later.

## 2. POLITICS IN 1870

The campaign of 1870 was formally begun by the Conservative members of the legislature who, at the time of adjournment, issued an address to the people of the State, in which, after accepting Reconstruction as final, condemning the record of the Republican party for the preceding two years, denouncing the governor for his Alamance proclamation,[2] and expressing their condemnation of the crimes

---

[1] *Executive Correspondence*, Holden, i, p. 369.

[2] The following extract is taken from the address: "There is and has been no armed resistance—no uprising of the people—no outbreaks to

committed by the League and the Ku Klux, they called upon the people to observe the law and preserve order, and urged the support of the Conservative party at the approaching elections. A state executive committee was appointed, and organization was thus begun.

There was every reason for hope on the part of the Conservatives. Not only was it generally evident that the people of the State were weary of the Republican administration and legislature, but the very leaders of the radicals were hopeless of success. This was made evident by the fact that frequent attempts were made by some of them to bring about a new alignment of parties. One plan was intended to secure a combination of native white Republicans, backed by such a part of the negroes as they could control, with the old Whigs. The carpetbaggers were to be rigorously excluded from the organization and were to be made scapegoats for the sins of the Republican party. Such Conservatives as would not submit were to be ignored. The old Whigs, however, could not be induced. Josiah Turner was approached upon the subject and his editorial comment was that it was " a plan devised solely on account of the political necessities of Holden, Settle, Reade, and Co." It is almost beyond doubt that the governor was ready to make terms. He inclined very much at this time to some such plan, but could not find a friend in the opposition, and, having made his bed, had perforce to lie in it. Nor was

disturb or hinder the full administration of the civil law. We assert that there is not a county in the State in which any sheriff or other peace officer may not go unattended, and with perfect safety, and execute any process upon any citizen of the State. It is true that murders and other outrages have been committed, but they have not been confined to any locality or any one political party; ard when Governor Holden represented to the President and to Congress that these acts are evidences of disloyalty, he is guilty of a wilful libel upon a people whose rights he has sworn to protect."

the party united, for in the west the Harris-Logan faction was still heartily opposed to the administration and was not slow to attack it. The *Rutherford Star,* edited by Judge Logan's son, said, " Shall W. W. Holden, or the honest Republicans of North Carolina rule the State?" The influential Dockery clan, sincere Republicans though they were, were shocked at the way the state government was conducted and were almost as open in their hostility. The most serious menace to party success, however, was the breach in the rank and file, who were disgusted with the negroes and alarmed at their violence, and who, overwhelmed with taxes, were showing no uncertain signs of a wavering of allegiance that might at any time develop into revolt. The relations existing between the factions of the party were clearly displayed when the *Standard* repudiated the legislature. And finally all over the State rose mutterings against the aliens who were chiefly responsible for its ruin. The more brazen of the carpet-baggers, seeing the state of affairs, made no secret of their belief that their day was nearing its end. Byron Laflin took the bus at the hotel the day the legislature adjourned, and, when a bystander asked, " You are coming back, General?" replied with a leer, " Is there anything to come back for?" [1] The rats were deserting the sinking ship.

The exposure of new rascality on the part of Republican officials at the beginning of the campaign was also a heavy burden for the party. Deweese was, by a resolution declaring him unworthy to hold a seat in Congress, forced to resign. His offence was selling a cadetship for five hundred dollars. He made no attempt to defend himself other than by the statement that he was not expelled for selling the cadetship but for underselling the market. He accused A.

[1] *Wilmington Journal,* June 28, 1870.

H. Jones of offering one to George W. Swepson for one thousand dollars, but this was vehemently denied by Jones.[1] Deweese did not come back to the State, but removed to Cleveland, Ohio, where he had invested his tidy savings in a city block. Here he lived in affluence and was heard of no more until 1876, when, his newly-honest soul revolting at the corruption in the Republican party, he appeared as the champion of Tilden and political morality, and assisted the cause by shamelessly unfolding the tale of his own villainy and that of his associates during his stay in North Carolina. Still another blow was the revelation of the dishonesty of federal and local officials. The Raleigh *News* in July [2] published a list of seven defaulting revenue collectors whose stealings amounted to $465,904.30. It was known at this time that a number of the sheriffs were defaulters, some of them in large sums, and the mileage accounts of the commissioners in many counties as well as their *per diem* became a public scandal.

The *Sentinel* was the most active and effective agency in the State in the publication of Republican wrong-doing, and its editorial page, conducted with more than customary spirit and ingenuity, was one of the most powerful influences in the campaign, though many of the Conservatives began to declare Turner too violent. He discovered early that Governor Holden meditated a policy of intimidation, and he first called attention to the fact that the trusted agent of the governor, who visited President Grant to secure his assistance in the campaign, was General Littlefield. Judge Settle had already visited Washington and, by his account of conditions in the State, prepared the way. The selection by the governor of Littlefield, the leader of the

---

[1] *Sentinel*, April 26, 1870; *Standard*, April 29, 1870.

[2] Issue of July 15, 1870.

spoilsmen, for such a mission excited a hostility against Holden that was not confined to Conservatives.

On the Conservative side, the chief burden that had to be carried was the Ku Klux. But this was not so heavy as might be supposed. In spite of all the violence for which, justly or unjustly, it received the credit, its service to the people was recognized by the masses, who had never regarded it in the same light as the political leaders had. In the next place, the very denunciation of it by the Republicans, combined with their highly-colored accounts of its real and supposed outrages, tended to intimidate the negroes politically far more than the Ku Klux had ever done, and thousands of negroes who had never been molested by the Ku Klux determined to have nothing to do with politics, in this campaign at least. The truth is that many of the negroes, chiefly those in the country, were beginning to discover the falsity of political promises and had come to believe that politics as conducted by the carpetbaggers and other whites had little of good for them. Disappointed in the past by their failure to receive " forty acres and a mule," they were taking steps to acquire those coveted possessions by hard work.

In addition to the regular congressional elections, there were special elections in two districts to fill the vacancies caused by the resignation of Deweese and the death of Heaton. Both parties nominated different candidates for the unexpired term and the new term. There were thus nine candidates from each party in the field.[1]   In the first

[1] The candidates by district were, 1, Republican, C. L. Cobb. Conservative, Timothy Morgan; 2, 41st Cong., Joseph Dixon, C. J. O'Hara; 42d Cong., Charles R. Thomas, L. W. Humphrey; 3, O. H. Dockery, A. M. Waddell; 4, 41st Cong., M. Hawkins, R. B. Gilliam; 42d Cong., J. H. Harris (colored), S. H. Rogers; 5, W. L. Scott, J. M. Leach; 6, F. H. Sprague, F. E. Shober; 7, A. H. Jones, J. C. Harper.

district, Timothy Morgan, a Republican of liberal views, ran as an independent candidate and was endorsed by the Conservatives. Judge Thomas, who was the Republican candidate in the second district, conducted his campaign without leaving the bench and was much criticized by the Conservatives in consequence. The precedent set by him, however, is not without later Democratic followers. In the seventh district, Plato Durham was nominated, but withdrew. James H. Harris obtained the Republican nomination in the fourth district and remained the candidate throughout the campaign, possibly because no one was willing to do what Deweese had done and pay him liberally for the nomination, and possibly because no one had a Swepson to advance the money. More probably he was convinced that it was time for men of his color to be given a chance. This was certainly the case so far as concerned the nominations for the legislature, a very large number of negroes being successful in securing the endorsement of their party. Arguments that such a course would injure the party had no effect, for they were determined to obtain fuller recognition than had hitherto been accorded them.

The chief interest in the campaign, apart from carrying the legislature, lay in the contest for attorney general. The Democrats nominated William M. Shipp, a man of ability and good record. The Republicans held a convention in Raleigh in May which was the scene of a sharp factional contest. Senator Abbott was very anxious to be president, as was John Pool. Governor Holden was very bitter against the former as a carpetbagger, and because he himself had designs on the seat in the Senate which Abbott was trying to retain. He was also anxious that his administration should receive the endorsement of the convention and that his son-in-law, L. P. Olds, should be nominated for attorney general. Pool kept very quiet and, thus winning the governor's support, was elected president. The carpet-baggers were angered and Pool then used them to prevent the desired endorsement and nomination.[1] It was out of the question, from the standpoint of party policy, to nominate Olds. He was of poor ability and his appointment by his father-in-law had been very unpopular. Samuel F. Phillips had been agreed upon and, receiving the nomination on the first ballot, appeared in the convention and, declaring himself a Republican, accepted. The whole thing had been carefully planned and he had an elaborate speech prepared in which he said, " The constitution framed by the state convention of 1868 will live in history as one of the grandest and most beautiful instruments of the character ever formed. The spirit of magnanimity alone which pervades it will render it imperishable." He denied the charges of extravagance and corruption and endorsed the financial policy of the party without reservation.[2] Few political acts ever gave such a severe shock to North Carolina as this defection of Phillips. It was known that he was not entirely in accord with his party and that he had voted for Grant in 1868, but no one had ever dreamed of his forming this alliance and at such a time. To the majority of the people, it seemed simply that he had sold himself for office, and his reputation, which was an enviable one, suffered a blow from which it never recovered. His more intimate friends maintained that he had entered the Republican party in the hope of " putting on brakes ", but his later extreme radicalism, particularly as chairman of the Republican executive committee, does not lend much weight to this argument.

From the beginning, the campaign was conducted with great activity by the Conservatives, who carried on political

[1] *Sentinel*, June 16, 1870.    [2] *Standard*, May 13, 1870.

" protracted meetings " in every section of the State. In their minds, there was a clear assurance of victory, and against this feeling the Republicans could not prevail. The *Standard* strove to fasten the blame for the extravagance and corruption of the legislature upon them.[1] It tried in every way to arouse discord between the Whigs and Democrats in the opposition, calling attention to the prominence of the former.[2] It was stated at the time that about eighty per cent of the nominees for county office were old Whigs. Five of the men nominated for Congress had been Whigs, as had been Shipp. At the same time, it belittled the friction among the Republicans.[3] The burden fell upon the *Standard* because of its location and former influence and because there were now in the State only seven Republican papers, two of which were hostile to the governor. He made the fatal mistake of entering the campaign through his son, who was editor of the *Standard,* for the opinion that he was using his high office for selfish ends was already prevalent,[4] and a bitterness was excited which in many quarters was intense. An extreme example of this is to be seen in the following editorial from the *Tarboro Southerner,* after the plans of the governor were known : " In the days of old, when a ruler of the people prostituted his position to wicked purposes of oppression, and so basely betrayed his public trust as the Governor of North Carolina has so frequently done for partisan purposes, the swords of patriots leaped from their scabbards, the knife of the assassin felt, uneasily but surely, for the heart of the ruffian ruler. . . . While we do not advise and could not

[1] A good example of this is to be seen in the issue of Feb. 18, 1870.

[2] Issue of June 25, 1870.

[3] Issue of May 2, 1870.

[4] The correspondent of the *New York Tribune* soon discovered this fact, as his letters of that summer show.

countenance anything not warranted by law, we are at a loss to say what should be done with such a Governor." [1] Not any less bitter were the threats of the *Standard*.

But the Conservatives were not to be intimidated or disheartened. Theirs was the cause of righteousness and everywhere there was shown a determination to win and thus put an end to the horrible conditions which had existed in the State during the whole period of Republican supremacy. This determination expressed itself in a confidence and a unity which revealed to the radicals their own weakness and should have proved to the governor the truth of a remark made to him by a relative early in the year, " The white people of this State are like caged lions. When once they realize their strength, they will beat you by thirty thousand votes." But he was unconvinced.

### 3. THE KIRK-HOLDEN WAR

Governor Holden now faced certain defeat unless new measures could be taken to win the election. The inspiration for such measures was soon furnished by his evil genius, John Pool. Acting upon his advice, the governor determined to raise a force of state troops and put into full effect the policy of terror which he had constantly threatened but from which he had shrunk through timidity and from motives of policy. He realized clearly that the effects of failure might be very disastrous, but he seems never to have comprehended the certainty of failure and the extent of the impending disaster. He thought the spirit of the people was broken to a far greater degree than was possible, and he had expressed this feeling a little earlier by saying of the people of the State, " They remind me of a terrapin lying flat on his back with his shell cracked; all he can do is to wiggle his tail." Not for one instant did he

[1] Issue of June 10, 1870.

comprehend the immensity of their just wrath against him and his administration, and thus guided by the villains who were his trusted advisers and impelled by a gnawing ambition, he went forward to his ruin.

On June 2, Pool wrote Governor Holden that he would be in Raleigh on June 7, and that it was most important that some action should be taken at once. The day after he arrived, a meeting was held in the governor's office at which were present, on Holden's invitation, in addition to Pool and himself, James H. Harris, Isaac J. Young, W. D. Jones, W. J. Clarke, W. F. Henderson, Richard C. Badger, A. W. Fisher, S. F. Carrow, Henderson Adams, D. A. Jenkins, and J. W. Hood. There was much discussion of what should be done and Holden stated that in his opinion the militia was not worthy of confidence and that United States troops were no good for their use. Pool thereupon suggested the organization of a force of two regiments of regular troops and their use in arresting various persons in the State. Badger opposed this vehemently, but Holden was entirely in Pool's hands and Badger finally yielded upon the latter's insistence that it was the proper course to pursue, particularly when Governor Clayton's action in Arkansas [1] would serve as a precedent. The question then arose as to the effect of the issue of a writ of *habeas corpus* for the persons arrested and Badger suggested that it should be refused. Pool's idea was that it should be obeyed and then followed by immediate re-arrest on some other charge. This plan, he said, was favored by President Grant. It was then decided to use a military commission to try and to punish those arrested by the troops, but Badger finally succeeded in persuading them to send a judicial officer with the force.

[1] Governor Powell Clayton was at this time using state militia to great partisan advantage.

Pool now made a characteristic suggestion that a friend of his, one McLindsay, a pirate,[1] should be employed, who, if any of those arrested gave trouble, would kill or lose them. Holden looked to Badger for a decision and the latter denounced the suggestion as villainous to the last degree. Pool attempted to pass the whole thing off as a joke, and, turning to Holden, told him that it was necessary for him to do something as he was called a failure in Washington; that President Grant had said so.[2]

With the plan thus outlined, it only remained to put it into effective execution. Holden seems to have had some misgivings, but, as he told Oliver H. Dockery later, " Pool suggested it and I am ready to follow where Pool leads and the election must be carried anyhow." [3]    Dockery was bitterly opposed to the scheme as wrong and entirely unnecessary, and when he entered upon his campaign for re-election to Congress he denounced the plan freely and consistently, thereby winning the hostility of Holden and his carpetbag adjutant general, A. W. Fisher, both of whom hoped for his defeat.[4]

In accordance with the plan, Governor Holden, on the day of the conference, wrote to W. W. Rollins, at Marshall, to report to him for service and to enlist forty-five or fifty stout and loyal mountaineers to be placed on a footing with soldiers in the regular army.[5]    At the same time, William J. Clarke, who was to command the other regiment, was sent to Washington to secure an outfit for the force. On June 18, he wrote the governor that on the day before he had seen the President, who had granted his request.    Gen-

---

[1] McLindsay later denied publicly the character assigned him by Pool.

[2] *Sentinel*, April 8, 1871.    Testimony before Senate Committee.

[3] *Sentinel*, July 30, 1870, and private information to the author.

[4] Fisher to Holden, July 2, 1870.

[5] *Executive Correspondence*, Holden, vol. i, p. 378.

eral Sherman sent word that Holden would have to sign a bond to pay for the supplies, but that in effect it would " be payable at the day of judgment." Grant had also spoken of sending four companies to the State and Clarke urged the governor to apply for them. He closed his letter as follows: " Heaven seems to smile on us and I trust that the undertaking will end as auspiciously as it has begun." [1]

Major Rollins, who was in Washington when Holden's call reached him, was wisely unable to take command and recommended George W. Kirk who was also in Washington. Kirk was thirty-three years of age and lived in Washington County, Tennessee. He was a native of that State and, except for a few months spent in North Carolina in 1866, had always lived there. He had been in the United States service during the war as colonel of the Third North Carolina United States Volunteers and was notorious for his desperate and brutal character.[2] Holden at once wired Rollins to send Kirk to Raleigh, and, on June 20,[3] the latter reached there, accompanied by George B. Bergen, of New Jersey, a kindred spirit, who now entered North Carolina for the first time.[4] Holden laid the plan before Kirk, who consented to serve, and the governor himself wrote the following call of which he had five hundred copies printed for Kirk's use: [5]

[1] Clarke to Holden, June 18, 1870.

[2] *Senate Report* no. 1, 42 Cong., 1 sess., p. 5 *et seq.* Hereafter in this chapter this volume will be referred to as *Senate Report*, simply.

[3] Kirk himself said June 21, but a letter to Holden from him shows that to have been an error.

[4] *Senate Report*, p. 150 *et seq.*

[5] The evidence in the impeachment trial proved that Holden had written the call, but the printer said that Kirk had brought it to the office in April. There is no other evidence to show that Kirk was in Raleigh at that time, and it is not possible that such was the case. *Impeachment Trial*, pp. 282, 283. This book will hereafter be referred to as *Impeachment*.

RALLY UNION MEN
IN DEFENCE OF YOUR STATE!
RALLY SOLDIERS OF THE OLD
N. CAROLINA 2D AND 3D FEDERAL TROOPS!
RALLY TO THE STANDARD OF YOUR OLD COMMANDER!

Your old commander has been commissioned to raise at once a regiment of State troops, to aid in enforcing the laws, and in putting down disloyal midnight assassins.

The blood of your murdered countrymen, inhumanly butchered for opinion's sake, cries from the ground for vengeance.

The horrible murders and other atrocities committed by rebel K. K. K. and "southern chivalry", on grayhaired men and helpless women, call in thunder tones on all loyal men to rally in defence of their State. The uplifted hand of justice

N. CAROLINA 2D AND 3D FEDERAL TROOPS!

must overtake these outlaws.

1,000 RECRUITS

are wanted immediately, to serve six months unless sooner discharged. These troops will receive the same pay, clothing, and rations as United States regulars. Recruits will be received at Asheville, Marshall, and Burnsville, North Carolina.

For further information address or call on me at Asheville, N. C.                                    GEORGE W. KIRK,
Colonel 2d Regiment State Troops.

Kirk left Raleigh and, on June 22, wrote Holden from Burnsville that he was leaving for the Greasy Cove of East Tennessee but would post no handbills outside the State and none would know of his presence there. From there he would slip back with the men he had enlisted through the mountain passes to Asheville and Marshall.[1] This letter would seem to settle forever the question of Governor Holden's knowledge of the nature of Kirk's force.

---

[1] Kirk to Holden, June 22, 1870. This letter has never been published.

By this time, the handbills were scattered throughout the western part of the State to the horror and alarm of all the inhabitants save political extremists and those of like character with Kirk. Immediately the governor was flooded with letters from prominent Republicans urging him not to carry out his plan; reminding him that Kirk was not a citizen of the State; that he was known to be of bad character and a man who allowed his passions to control his reason; that he was generally detested; and that the plan would do great harm and would result in the entire overthrow of the Republican party at the coming election.[1] On June 27, a petition came from Asheville signed by a large number of persons there, including Judge Cannon, Judge Henry, Solicitor V. S. Lusk, and the clerk and the sheriff of Buncombe County, urging the governor not to raise troops or use Kirk, and protesting against his circular.[2] Judge Henry went further and in his charge to the grand jury at the spring term of Buncombe court, denounced the governor for organizing the force and declared that there was no need for it.[3] Other Republicans known to oppose the governor's course were W. P. Bynum, D. A. Jenkins, and H. J. Menninger.

Some, of course, approved, but few had much to say. J. W. Bowman asked and secured the appointment of H. C. Yates as major under Kirk, urging that the entire programme be carried out and the election won.[4] Dr. J. J. Mott, the president of the eastern division of the Western North Carolina Railroad, wrote Holden early in July not to withdraw Kirk as he was the best appointment that could have been made. " Let him alone except to assist and en-

---

[1] Unpublished Executive Correspondence not included in letter books.
[2] Unpublished Executive Correspondence and *Sentinel*, April 4, 1871.
[3] *Sentinel*, July 5, 1870.
[4] Bowman to Holden, June 28, 1870.

courage him.  And by the Eternal God, I say deluge the
State in blood from one end to the other rather than our
people should suffer again the treatment of the last six
months." [1]

In the meantime, of course, the whole State had learned
of the plan.  On June 15, the *Standard* had announced the
intended organization of state troops and the next day had
stated that they would deal with the Ku Klux in a summary manner.  At the same time, the tone of the paper
changed and became more confident.  In answer to the attacks of the Conservative press upon Kirk, it said, " Let the
weight of a finger be laid upon him.  The loyal men who
fought under him during the war will avenge his death."
As early as June 11, it contained threats that, if necessary,
the leading Democrats in the State would be killed. [2]  On
June 16, with the statement that it spoke by the governor's
authority, it warned the editors of the *Roanoke News,* who
were very hostile to him, that soldiers might be sent for

---

[1] J. J. Mott to Holden, July 2, 1870.

[2] The editorial was as follows: " We are authorized by the Governor
of the State to announce that these outrages must come to an end.
His purpose is fixed to punish these assassins, and to protect the people in their houses, and in the freest expression of their political opinions.  He intends to demand and to *have* indemnity for the past and
security for the future.  In doing this he will strike the so-called highest
as soon as he will the poorest and humblest; as well the leading man
who encourages or winks at these outrages as the depraved devil in
human shape who plays Ku Klux whether on foot or horseback.  The
Governor will do this, and there are threats that he will be assassinated
for so doing.  Let them try it.  The Governor does not fear these
fiends in human shape.  If he is even personally menaced, his friends
will resent it and punish the man or the men who may do it; if he is
slain or even wounded, it is already determined that leading Democrats
and Conservatives, who might be named, will be put to death.  The
Governor's mind is made up.  He will allow these outrages to proceed
no further, and he will promptly arrest and punish any man who may
preach sedition, or who may counsel resistance to State or Federal
authority."

them if they advised any resistance to law or any step to subvert established authority, and that, if they resisted, they would be shot.

Immediately after the conference in Raleigh, Pool had gone back to Washington to carry on a campaign of misrepresentation in order to build up public sentiment in the North in favor of the proposed scheme.[1] To quote him: " We intend to use the military in the election and must get these statements [of supposed outrages] disseminated through the North." [2] He told a reporter of the *Washington Chronicle* that, to carry the State, it was necessary to use troops, and he wanted lists of North Carolina outrages published regularly to rouse the North.[3] A part of the North Carolina delegation in Congress visited President Grant on June 17, and he assured them that he was behind the movement.[4] It was common talk with Pool and Abbott at this time that William A. Graham was to be arrested for complicity in the Ku Klux outrages.[5] On June 28, the former advised Governor Holden to come on to see the President,[6] and the governor left for Washington the same day. On July 30, he and Pool had an interview with Grant who, according to Holden, agreed to stand behind him and said, " Let those men resist you, Governor, and I will move with all my power against them." [7] Whether this be true or not, Governor Holden came away with entire confidence that he would be sustained by the President in all that he might do. He also determined to institute a military com-

---

[1] Cincinnati *Gazette*, July 23, 1870.

[2] New York *Tribune*, June 22, 1870.

[3] Appendix, *Globe*, p. 232, 42 Cong., 1 sess.

[4] Washington *Chronicle*, June 20, 1870.

[5] *Sentinel*, July 14, 1870.

[6] Pool to Holden, June 28, 1870.

[7] *Standard*, July 22, 1870.

mission to try the arrested persons. This suggestion may
have come from Pool; it is not at all unlikely that it came
from President Grant himself. It was at least in entire
accord with his methods.

On July 6, Kirk and a part of his force left Morganton. His entire force consisted of nine companies [1] with a
total of 670 men, 399 of whom were under age, and 64,
over forty. Over 200 were from other States, most of
them from Tennessee, but some from Virginia and South
Carolina. All the field officers were from outside the State.[2]
Enlisted in the force, and in violation of the laws, were a
number of negroes. The progress of the force was marked
by the most extreme rowdyism and disorder, for the troops
were always utterly undisciplined. At Newton they left
the train and forced the bystanders to do their bidding at
the pistol's mouth, meanwhile, in like manner, preventing
the engineer from starting the train.[3] All along the route
and at every stop they fired pistols, cursed the citizens, and
showed their lawless character. When they reached Salisbury, they made threats of burning the town and, pretend-
ing that they had been fired upon from the hotel, they ran
to the windows of the dining-room and made a demonstration against women and children with muskets, bayonets,
and pistols.[4] At Salisbury, Kirk received orders to carry
his command to Company Shops (now Burlington), and
he reached there that day. He then hastened to Raleigh for
a conference with the governor, who gave him instructions and furnished him with a list of persons to be arrested.

All this time, Governor Holden was being congratulated

---

[1] *Senate Report*, p. 11.

[2] *Impeachment*, p. 2306.

[3] J. F. Murrell to Holden, July 8, 1870.

[4] W. F. Henderson to Holden, July 9, 1870. *Senate Report*, p. 67.
*Sentinel*, July 13, 1870.

by the vile brood of sycophants that surrounded him, and was made to believe that he had performed the greatest act of his life and one that would greatly advance him in reputation. W. F. Henderson, who was one of his trusted advisers, wrote him that the Kirk movement was necessary for the success of the party and for his [Holden's] future advancement.[1] Whatever excuses were made later for the movement, it is clearly evident that at this time Holden's sympathizers, as well as his opponents, regarded it as undertaken for party benefit pure and simple. Nor has any evidence been discovered which attacks seriously the correctness of their estimate.

On July 15, Colonel Stephen A. Douglas,[2] the governor's aid and the acting adjutant general, went to Company Shops and mustered the force into the service of the State, using the United States articles with merely the substitution of the words " North Carolina " for " United States." [3]

The next step to be taken was to provide for the trial of the prisoners. The military commission, as finally constituted by the governor, consisted of the officers of Kirk's regiment and Major General Willie D. Jones, Brigadier General C. S. Moring, Brigadier General W. R. Albright, Colonel H. M. Ray, Major L. W. Hardin, and Captain R. W. Hancock, all of whom were of ability less than mediocre, and partisan to a degree. In addition, most if not all of them were entirely subservient to Governor Holden in all things and were chosen for that reason.[4] Bergen was

[1] W. F. Henderson to Holden, July 18, 1870.

[2] A son of Stephen A. Douglas of Illinois.

[3] *Impeachment*, p. 2306.

[4] William A. Graham in his speech in the impeachment trial had this to say of them:

"These, Mr. Chief Justice and senators, are the sages who are to supersede the judges and juries appointed by law for the trial of citizens

ordered to serve on the commission but was possessed of sufficient foresight to decline.[1] Dr. Mott was urged by the governor to serve, but he also was cautious.[2] Holden's first plan was for the commission to assemble on July 25, so that sentence could be executed just before the election, but he later set the time for the second week in August.

On July 17, he ordered about twenty men sent to Cleveland County " to keep an eye on Plato Durham ". Later, he ordered Kirk to send as many home to vote as possible. The company raised in Gaston County was to remain there, as their votes were needed and they could " control Gaston, Lincoln, and Catawba ".[3]

At first, the Conservatives had viewed the threatening situation with disgust, but with more fear of an outbreak on the part of the citizens than of violence by Kirk's men. The movement was regarded as a scheme to carry the election by threats rather than by actual violence, for the full plan was of course not known to the public. The state executive committee of the Conservative party, on July 7, issued a powerful yet calm and dignified address to the people of the State, condemning the action of the governor but urging patience and moderation. In it is to be seen a recognition of some of the underlying purpose of the movement. It said in part, " It is very generally believed, and there is much ground for such belief as we have reason to

accused of crime; and their trial is to be conducted, not according to the doctrines of the bill of rights, of Coke, Foster, or Blackstone, but by the laws and usages of war as expressed by Turenne or Vauban, McComb or Halleck—authors who have doubtless been profoundly studied by these *improvised* heroes, some of whom were offered here as witnesses."

[1] *Senate Report*, p. 153.      [2] J. J. Mott to Holden, July 15, 1870.

[3] *Impeachment*, p. 2318. These letters were in Holden's own hand and were left by Kirk in Alamance. They were not copied in the official letter book.

know, that this armed movement has been set on foot by preconcert and arrangement just before an important general election in the State, for the purpose of controlling it by intimidation or defeating it entirely, by provoking the people to a violent conflict with the armed men referred to, and then proclaiming the whole State in insurrection." [1] Ex-Governor Reid, from his retirement, issued an appeal to the people to the same effect.[2] In a political way the movement was of great importance, though with different results from those intended. The Conservatives, already active, were given new life and spirit. Instead of terrorizing them as intended, it aroused such hostility that, more than ever, the Republicans were put on the defensive. In addition to the burden they already carried, which would in all probability have defeated them, they now had that of supporting the administration in this new policy, and many refused to do anything of the sort, and, badly split as they already were, their demoralization became worse and their defeat became a foregone conclusion.

On July 15, Bergen arrested at Graham, James S. Scott, a merchant, James E. Boyd, the Conservative candidate for the House, and Adolphus G. Moore, and refused to give them any reason for their detention other than that it was by order of Kirk who was acting under instructions from Governor Holden. They were carried before Kirk who declined to admit them to bail. Later Bergen informed them that they were to be tried by a court martial.[3]

On the sixteenth, a petition for a writ of *habeas corpus* in behalf of Moore was presented to Chief Justice Pearson in Raleigh by an eminent body of counsel.[4] Judge Pearson

---

[1] *Annual Cyclopaedia*, 1870; *Sentinel*, July 7, 1870.

[2] *Sentinel*, July 29, 1870.  [3] *Impeachment*, p. 602.

[4] William A. Graham, Thomas Bragg, Augustus S. Merrimon, E. S. Parker, and William H. Battle and Sons.

at once granted the writ returnable to him in Raleigh. The writ was served upon Kirk the next day as, in response to orders from Holden, he was proceeding to Yanceyville with a large part of his force. He listened to the reading of the writ, looked at the signature, and replied that he could take no notice of such papers; that they had " played out." He directed the server of the process to take it back and reply that a court had been appointed to try the prisoners, and that he would not surrender them except upon the governor's order.[1]  Application was then made for a writ of attachment against Kirk and for a precept to some sheriff to bring the petitioner before the chief justice, employing a *posse comitatus* if necessary. Richard C. Badger was present and suggested that the governor might wish to be heard. Chief Justice Pearson accordingly wrote him enclosing copies of the writs, for by this time, the other prisoners had also sued out writs, and adjourned the case until the next day. When the hearing began on the nineteenth, Badger, acting as counsel for the governor, read the following letter:

Executive Office,
Raleigh, July 19, 1870.

*To the Hon. Richmond M. Pearson,*
    *Chief Justice of North Carolina.*

*Sir:* Your communication of yesterday concerning the arrests made by Col. Geo. W. Kirk, together with the enclosed is received.

I respectfully reply:—That Col. Geo. W. Kirk made the arrests and now detains the prisoners named by my order. He was instructed firmly but respectfully to decline to deliver the prisoners. No one goes before me in respect for the civil law, or for those whose duty it is to enforce it, but the condition of Alamance County, and some other parts of the State,

---

[1] Battle, *Habeas Corpus Cases*, p. 8.

has been and is such that, though reluctant to use the strong powers vested in me by law, I have been forced to declare them in a state of insurrection.

For months past there has been maturing in these localities, under the guidance of bad and disloyal men, a dangerous secret insurrection. I have invoked public opinion to aid me in suppressing this treason! I have issued proclamation after proclamation to the people of the State to break up these unlawful combinations! I have brought to bear every civil power to restore peace and order, but all in vain! The Constitution and the laws of the United States and of this State are set at naught; the civil courts are no longer a protection to life, liberty, and property; assassination and outrage go unpunished, and the civil magistrates are intimidated and are afraid to perform their functions.

To the majority of the people of these sections the approach of night is like the entrance into the valley of the shadow of death; the men dare not sleep beneath their roofs at night, but abandoning their wives and little ones, wander in the woods until day.

Thus civil government was crumbling around me. I determined to nip this new treason in the bud.

By virtue of the power vested in me by the Constitution and laws, and by that inherent right of self-preservation which belongs to all governments, I have proclaimed the county of Alamance in a state of insurrection. Col. Geo. W. Kirk is commanding the military forces in that county, made the arrests referred to in the writ of *habeas corpus,* and now detains the prisoners by my order.

At this time I am satisfied that the public interests require that these military prisoners shall not be delivered up to the civil power.

I devoutly hope that the time may be short when a restoration of peace and order may release Alamance County from the presence of military force and the enforcement of military law. When that time shall arrive I shall promptly restore the civil power. W. W. HOLDEN, *Governor.*

The enclosures mentioned were his five proclamations against the Ku Klux. The chief justice, after the letter had been read, laid down four lines of argument for the counsel. (1) Did Kirk have a reasonable excuse for refusing to make return? (2) Did the facts show an insurrection of such an extent as to suspend the writ? (3) If the writ was not suspended, would not an attachment produce civil war, and was not the act of 1868-1869 providing for an attachment on failure to make proper return of a writ of *habeas corpus* in effect subservient to the militia clause of the constitution? (4) If so, should the writ be directed to the governor?

The counsel for the petitioners [1] then addressed the court arguing that the governor's letter should not be noticed, and Badger, for the governor, argued that the latter had power by law to declare a county in insurrection and that the constitution empowered him to declare martial law and that therefore the writ was suspended.

On July 23, the chief justice delivered his opinion in the case, which was in accord with the views of Governor Holden. He accepted the argument of R. C. Badger as to the power of the governor, but denied that the writ had been suspended. He therefore acknowledged the right of the petitioners to a writ of attachment, but refused to address it to any sheriff as it would plunge the State into civil war. He denied any power to call out a *posse comitatus* because the counties concerned were in insurrection and insurgents could not be called into the service of the State. No one else could serve in those counties, and in addition, the citizens, being militia, could not be called out into conflict with the governor who was the commander-in-chief. Only moral power, he said, was possessed by the judiciary; the

---

[1] B. F. Moore had by this time been added to those mentioned above.

physical power was entirely in the hands of the executive.
He closed his opinion as follows:

The writ will be directed to the Marshal of the Supreme
Court, with instructions to exhibit it, and a copy of this opinion to His Excellency the Governor. If he orders the petitioner to be delivered to the Marshal, well; if not, following
the example of Chief Justice Taney, in Merriman's case, Annual Cyclopedia, for the year 1861, page 555, I have discharged
my duty; the power of the Judiciary is exhausted and the
responsibility must rest on the Executive.          PEARSON.

The chief justice in his opinion was very critical of the
counsel for the petitioners because of their display of feeling, and said that their language, though more courtly, was
fully as strong as that employed by Kirk. All had used
the expression, " Let justice be done though the heavens
fall." Judge Pearson said, " Justice must be done, or the
power of the judiciary be exhausted, but I would forfeit
all claim to prudence tempered with firmness, should I,
without absolute necessity, add fuel to the flame and plunge
the country into civil war, provided my duty can be fully
discharged without that awful consequence. Wisdom dic-
tates, if justice can be done, ' let heaven stand.' "

This was in striking contrast to his utterance in 1863,
when he was making use of every legal technicality to discharge Confederate soldiers from the service. Said he,
" Will it be said that this denial of justice is necessary for
the good of the public to prevent desertion? God forbid.
*Fiat justitia ruat coelum*, let justice be done without regard
to consequences."

On the same day, Judge Pearson issued writs for all the
other prisoners held by Kirk. Governor Holden, on July
26, replied as follows:

EXECUTIVE DEPARTMENT,
RALEIGH, JULY 26, 1870.

*To the Hon. R. M. Pearson,*
   *Chief Justice of the Supreme Court of N. C.*

*Sir:*—I have had the honor to receive, by the hands of the Marshal of the Supreme Court, a copy of your opinion in the matter of A. G. Moore; and the Marshal has informed me of the writ in his hands for the body of said Moore, now in the custody of my subordinate officer, Col. George W. Kirk.

I have declared the counties of Alamance and Caswell in a state of insurrection, and have taken military possession of them. This your Honor admits I had the power to do "under the Constitution and laws." And not only this, " but to do *all* things necessary to suppress the insurrection," including the power to " arrest all *suspected* persons " in the above-mentioned counties.

Your Honor has thought proper also to declare that the citizens of the counties of Alamance and Caswell are *insurgents,* as a result of the Constitutional and lawful action of the Executive, and that therefore, you will not issue the writ for the production of the body of Moore to any of the men of the said counties; that " the *posse comitatus* must come from the county where the writ is to be executed," and that any other means would be illegal.

I have official and reliable information that in the counties above-named, during the last twelve months, not less than one hundred persons, " in the peace of God and the State," have been taken from their homes and scourged, mainly if not entirely on account of their political opinions; that eight murders have been committed, including that of a State Senator, on the same account; that another State Senator has been compelled, from fear for his life, to make his escape to a distant State. I have reason to believe that the governments of the said counties have been mainly if not entirely in the hands of men who belong to the Ku Klux Klan, whose members have perpetrated the atrocities referred to; and that the county governments have not merely omitted to ferret out and bring to justice those of this Klan who have thus violated the law, but that they have actually shielded them from arrest and punishment.[1] The State judicial power in the said counties, though in the hands of energetic, learned, and upright men, has not been able to bring criminals to justice:[2] indeed, it is my opinion, based on facts that have come to my knowledge, that the life of the Judge whose duty it is to ride the circuit to which the said counties belong, has not been safe, on account of the hatred entertained towards him by the Klan referred to, because of his wish and purpose to bring said criminals to justice. For be it known to your Honor that there is a widespread and formidable secret organization in this State, partly political and partly social in its objects; that this organization is known, first, as " *The Constitutional Union Guard,"*—secondly, as " *The White Brotherhood,"*—thirdly, as " *The Invisible Empire* "—that the members of this organization are united by oaths which ignore or repudiate the ordinary oaths or obligations that rest upon all other citizens to respect the laws and uphold the government; that these oaths inculcate hatred by the white against the colored people of the State; that the members of this Klan are irreconcilably hostile to the great principle of political and civil equality, on which the government of this State has been reconstructed; that these Klans meet in secret, in disguise, with arms, in uniform of a certain kind intended to conceal their persons and their horses, and to terrify those whom they assault or among whom they move; that they hold their camps in secret places, and decree judgment against their peaceable fellow-citizens, from mere intimidation to scourgings, mutilations

---

[1] Few official communications in the history of North Carolina contain so large a proportion of falsehood as is to be found in this letter, particularly in the portion to this point. The statements were untrue and Governor Holden knew them to be so.

[2] But for the fact that he would have been guilty of party disloyalty, the governor might truthfully have said that they had made no very strenuous efforts to do so.

and murder, and that certain persons of the Klan are deputed to execute these judgments; that when the members of this Klan are arrested for violations of law, it is most difficult to obtain bills of indictment against them, and still more difficult to convict them, first, because some of the members or their sympathizers are almost always on the grand and petit juries, and secondly, because witnesses who are members or sympathizers unblushingly commit perjury to screen their confederates and associates in crime; that this Klan, thus constituted and having in view the objects referred to, is very powerful in at least twenty-five counties of the State, and has had absolute control for the last twelve months of the counties of Alamance and Caswell.

Under these circumstances I would have been recreant to duty and faithless to my oath, if I had not exercised the power in the several counties which your Honor has been pleased to say I have exercised constitutionally and lawfully; especially as, since October, 1868, I have repeatedly, by proclamation and by letters, invoked public opinion to repress these evils, and warned criminals and offenders against the laws of the fate that must in the end overtake them, if, under the auspices of the Klan referred to, they should persist in their course.

I beg to assure your Honor that no one subscribes more thoroughly than I do to the great principles of *habeas corpus* and trial by jury. Except in extreme cases, in which beyond all question "the safety of the State is the supreme law," these privileges of *habeas corpus* and trial by jury should be maintained.

I have already declared that, in my judgment, your Honor and all the other civil and judicial authorities are unable *at this time* to deal with the insurgents. The civil and the military are alike constitutional powers—the civil to protect life and property when it can, and the military only when the former has failed. As the Chief Executive, I seek to restore, not to subvert, the judicial power. Your Honor has done your duty, and in perfect harmony with you I seek to do mine.

It is not I nor the military power that has supplanted the

civil authority; that has been done by the insurrection in the counties referred to. I do not see how I can restore the civil authority until I "suppress the insurrection," which your Honor declares I have the power to do; and I do not see how I can surrender the insurgents to the civil authority until that authority is restored. It would be a mockery in me to declare that the civil authority was unable to protect the citizens against the insurgents, and then turn the insurgents over to the civil authority. My oath to support the Constitution makes it imperative on me to "suppress the insurrection" and restore the civil authority in the counties referred to, and this I must do. In doing this I renew to your Honor, expressions of my profound respect for the civil authority, and my earnest wish that this authority may soon be restored to every county and neighborhood in the State.

I have the honor to be, with great respect,

Your obedient servant,

W. W. HOLDEN, *Governor.*

This letter was read on the twenty-seventh, and the counsel for the petitioners at once sought an attachment against the governor or one against Kirk and asked that instructions be given the marshal to bring the prisoners before Judge Pearson. On the twenty-eighth, the chief justice denied all three motions and the case rested. Judge Mitchell about this time issued the writ and it was served upon Kirk who tore it up.[1] So far as furnishing a remedy was concerned, the judiciary was indeed exhausted. Had Judge Pearson taken other ground, there would have been little difficulty in enforcing the writ. Several thousand citizens, so it is said, had volunteered for service on the *posse comitatus* and Kirk's force would have been overwhelmed.

In the meantime, Kirk had transferred a large part of his force to Yanceyville, where on the eighteenth, he oc-

---

[1] *Sentinel*, July 23, 1870.

cupied the court-house. On the same day, another detachment of his men took possession of Alamance court-house
at Graham. As soon as he was settled at Yanceyville, he
proceeded to terrorize the town. Here and in Alamance,
his men, entirely undisciplined, plundered and robbed
without let or hindrance. It was their custom also to un-
dress and bathe in full sight of the town, and it soon became
unsafe for women to appear upon the streets for fear of
insult.

On the day of his arrival, he arrested a number of prominent citizens of the county, including John Kerr, Samuel P.
Hill, Frank A. Wiley, Jesse C. Griffith, the sheriff, and
Felix Roan. Several of these were accused of complicity in
the murder of Stephens, but against a large number, including John Kerr, there was no charge whatever. John
Pool later said that Kerr was arrested for an imprudent
speech he had lately made in Roxboro, and it is likely that
such was the case.[1] Some of these men remained under arrest, enduring close confinement and exposed to the brutality of the troops, for five weeks. When a hearing finally
came, no evidence at all was presented against them.

On July 26, the same group of counsel that had appeared
for the other petitioners, applied to the chief justice for
writs in behalf of these new prisoners. George Williamson, who attempted to serve the writ on Kirk, was not allowed to see him and was finally driven away from the
camp by a squad of men under Major Yates.[2] Judge Pearson upheld Kirk on the ground that Williamson was a citizen of Caswell and therefore an insurgent. The writ was
then served by the marshal only to have the return refused.[3]
As before, Judge Pearson refused to grant an attachment,

---

[1] *Senate Report*, p. 403.

[2] Battle, *Habeas Corpus Cases*, p. 50.          [3] *Ibid.*, p. 55.

stating that he had discussed the cases with the other justices of the Supreme Court and that they all concurred
with him.[1]

When Kirk carried James E. Boyd to Yanceyville, W.
R. Albright, of Alamance, went to Raleigh at Boyd's suggestion and told Holden that Boyd would tell all he knew
about the Ku Klux. The result of the conference was that
Kirk carried Boyd to Raleigh where he had a number of
interviews with the governor. On the seventeenth, Holden
wrote Kirk that Boyd was going to confess; and on the
nineteenth, Boyd was released upon his own bond in the
sum of $50,000, and accepting a fee of $250 as counsel,
agreed to work up evidence against the Ku Klux and make
a public confession. He returned to Alamance and published a card the next day denying that he had made any
revelation to the governor and stating that he had no knowledge to reveal.[2] He then devoted his energies, according
to his own account, to securing evidence.[3] On July 30, the
*Standard* contained a confession of membership in the Ku
Klux signed by Boyd and fifteen others whom he had induced to join him.[4] Tremendous excitement followed and
several hundred young men hastily left the State for the
Southwest, many of them never to return. Immediately
upon the publication of his card, Boyd withdrew from the
canvass.

His public confession revealed practically nothing that
was of value to the administration. Its chief value was its
effect upon the public mind. He was twice judicially ex-

[1] Battle, *Habeas Corpus Cases*, p. 59.

[2] *Impeachment*, pp. 1616–1620. [3] Boyd to Holden, August 1, 1870.

[4] The signers of the confession were Clement C. Curtis, James E.
Boyd, Robert Hanner, John R. Stockard, Jacob Michael, J. N. H.
Clendenin, Henry Albright, James H. Foust, D. D. Teague, A. J.
Patterson, J. A. J. Patterson, John G. Albright, Christ. C. Curtis, S.
A. Curtis, W. S. Bradshaw, and Jasper N. Wood.

amined in North Carolina [1] and suffered badly at the hands of the lawyers who cross-examined him. His testimony makes highly interesting and enlightening reading.[2] He was also examined by the Senate " outrage " committee in 1871, and in the minority report, signed by Senators Blair and Bayard, was harshly condemned.[3] Both Blair and Bayard later on the floor of the Senate [4] expressed their highly uncomplimentary opinion of him, one, it is needless to say, common to many in North Carolina at the time, and not wholly unknown to-day.

Returning now to the time preceding the events just related, on July 19, Colonel W. J. Clarke, with two companies of negro troops from New Bern, arrived in Raleigh and encamped there. Governor Holden was becoming alarmed for his own safety and desired protection. A few days later (July 26), three companies of United States troops, sent by the President in accordance with his promise to the governor, also came to Raleigh. A few days later, the governor was furnished with five thousand ball cartridges from Fort Monroe. Holden was becoming excited and this was clearly reflected in the *Standard,* which on July 18, warned all editors and other persons not to rant about arbitrary power, and on the twenty-third, said that Josiah Turner, who was bitterly denouncing the governor, must beware.

In Alamance, Kirk and his force had arrested eighty-two men, who were confined and treated with great brutality and cruelty. Lucien Murray had a noose put about his neck and was suspended until he was unconscious. He was later threatened with death if he would not confess to some knowledge of Outlaw's death. Upon further denial of any

[1] See proof.    [2] *Impeachment*, pp. 1580–1687.   *Sentinel*, Sept. 2, 1870.
[3] *Senate Report*, pt. 2, p. 8.
[4] *Globe*, Appendix, pp. 17–18, 211, 42 Cong., 1 sess.   Since 1900 Boyd has been federal judge of the Western District of North Carolina.

knowledge, he was called " a damned liar." ¹ William Patton was drawn up by a noose until he fainted, was called a " God damned liar," and was finally tied up for an entire night. He was later forced to sign a paper denying any ill-treatment.² George S. Rogers was hung by the neck for some time.³ Jeremiah Albright was arrested at the house of Miss Barbara Bason who begged the men not to hang him. The officer in command replied, " God damn you, I ought to hang you for having such a God damned set of scoundrels in your house and I have a damned good notion to burn your house." ⁴

In Caswell, the prisoners were treated with the same brutality. Captain George B. Rodney, an army officer stationed there included in his report the following statement: " The condition of affairs in Yanceyville is beginning to be serious, the North Carolina State troops under Colonel Kirk being nothing more than an armed mob, and the more generally exasperated at the present condition. I have fears of an outbreak. Colonel Kirk is endeavoring to create a disturbance between the people, or my men, and his troops, in order to justify his recent conduct. His men roam around the country, and pillage and insult the people with impunity, and some threaten to attack my men. . . . The militia threaten to burn the town of Yanceyville when they leave, and unless there is a strong force of United States troops there when they are disbanded, nothing will prevent them."

As in Alamance, many persons were arrested in a brutal fashion. W. B. Bowe, when he was taken, was the object of epithets that are unprintable. Kirk himself would rush in on occasions and curse the prisoners most viciously. At

---

¹ *Impeachment*, p. 660 *et seq.*       ² *Ibid.*, p. 672 *et seq.*

³ *Ibid.*, p. 701 *et seq.*       ⁴ *Ibid.*, p. 716 *et seq.*

times, the soldiers fired at them,[1] and blows were not infrequent. At Yanceyville, the rumor came that a rescue was to be attempted and Kirk prepared to shoot down the prisoners.[2] On another occasion, his men threatened to shoot up the town or to burn it.[3] Their occupation of Caswell court house greatly injured it, and with Holden's approval they excluded the county officers from the building.[4] The recital of happenings such as these could be continued indefinitely, but enough has been told to indicate the character of the " State Troops." Well did they deserve the title of " Kirk's Lambs " which was of course at once applied.

During the period of excitement over the situation, Bedford Brown [5] went to Washington to try to persuade the President to interfere. In reply, Grant assured him that, if Holden was resisted, he would employ the United States army to uphold him.[6] That portion of the army which was in the State, though not taking any part in the struggle, had discovered the truth of the situation and were in entire sympathy with the citizens by whom they were hailed as friends and protectors.[7]

In the North, much attention was attracted, and while a few extreme papers defended Governor Holden, most of their comment was bitterly critical.[8]    Public opinion, as re-

---

[1] *Impeachment*, p. 796.        [2] *Ibid.*, p. 820.

[3] *Ibid.*, p. 750.        [4] *Ibid.*, p. 745.

[5] William A. Graham and Matt W. Ransom were to accompany him, but for some reason failed to do so.

[6] *Sentinel*, September 9, 1870.

[7] *Senate Report*, pp. liv–xciv.

[8] Several examples follow: The Washington *Star*, a Republican paper, quoted in the *Sentinel* of August 1, 1870, after bitterly denouncing Governor Holden's course, said: " It is the fault of just such men as Holden that North Carolina is not soundly Republican to-day, if she is not.    In

vealed in the press, was overwhelmingly against the governor.

The election was held quietly on August 4, and resulted in a sweeping Conservative victory. Shipp was elected by a majority of 4,221 in a total vote of 171,075. His vote showed a gain of 3,902 over that of Seymour in 1868,

no State of the South was there so large a Union element during the war and in no State was the work of reconstruction entered upon under more favorable auspices. As for Holden, he is simply a demagogue, trickster, and political desperado. A blatant secessionist when secession was uppermost, he is just the style of a man now to persecute with rabid vindictiveness not only his secession neighbors, but all Republicans who oppose his oppressive reign.''

The *New York Times* on August 2, 1870, said editorially: "The troubles in North Carolina have assumed a phase which renders an interpretation of their real character comparatively easy. At an earlier stage they suggested a contest between the local Executive and the enemies of law in limited portions of the State. They now exhibit the Governor as the enemy of law, and as the arbitrary, unrestrained, military ruler of a State in which civil authority should be supreme. * * * The population of North Carolina are not wholly unknown and they are known not to be either thieves or assassins, or the aiders and abettors of robbery and murder. * * * Governor Holden has chosen another course and one so flagrantly wrong that it is impossible to respect his motives, and at the same time credit him with a judgment befitting his position. We must conclude either that he is playing the part of a reckless partisan, and without regard to decency or right is preparing to control the State election,—or, that yielding to bad advisers, he forgets his duty to the people whose servant he is, to the State whose interest and honor he has sworn to protect, and to the law whose majesty is superior to even his pretensions.''

On August 15, the *Times* said: "The tone of Governor Holden's organ, the Raleigh *Standard*, is simply infamous. If its purpose were to provoke civil war, it could not be conducted differently. . . . The Republican Party cannot too soon or too emphatically repudiate both the man and his doings.''

The New York *World*, quoted in the *Sentinel* of July 29, said, "The imbecility of the judiciary of North Carolina is, if possible, a shade more disgraceful to the present administration of affairs in that commonwealth than the insolent rapacity of its Executive.''

while Phillips received 12,795 fewer votes than Grant. The total Conservative gain was therefore 16,697. Twenty-five counties showed Republican gains over 1868. Five regular Conservative candidates for Congress were elected,[1] as well as one of the Conservative candidates to fill out an unexpired term.[2] The legislature was overwhelmingly Conservative, the Senate with a two-thirds majority. The day of the carpetbagger and the scalawag was over and the first step was taken in the overthrow of Reconstruction.

The day after the election, and while the result was still in doubt and while Holden thought the Republicans had won, he ordered the arrest of Josiah Turner. Turner had been a thorn in the side of all the Republicans but had attacked no one else with the same severity which marked his editorials on the subject of the governor. Holden apparently now determined to get his revenge. Undoubtedly, too, he believed that Turner was a Ku Klux. All during June and July, the threats of the *Standard* against him had grown more and more definite and increasingly bitter, and finally, the accusation, constantly made by the governor, that Turner was " the King of the Ku Klux " was repeated in its columns. Late in July, Turner's house near Hillsboro was fired upon several times and he left Raleigh to go home and protect his family. Governor Holden then wrote to him offering protection, hoping thereby to silence him. Turner replied editorially on July 18 with a bitter attack upon the governor, refusing at the same time to accept protection from one who, he said, was responsible for the whole condition of affairs. He was unwearying in his

---

[1] Alfred M. Waddell, Sion H. Rogers, James M. Leach, Francis E. Shober, and James C. Harper.

[2] Robert B. Gilliam.

efforts to arouse sentiment against the administration in this way and by laying the whole situation before the public. He also made the entirely correct statement of the fact, not then generally known, that the use of Kirk and his force was the result of a conspiracy.[1] He wished for nothing more than to be arrested in Orange County which had not been declared in insurrection, and that fact probably had some influence upon his remaining there. On July 28, referring to the threat of the *Standard* that he would be arrested, he said editorially:

The devil incarnate who signed the ordinance of secession and called for the head of Abe Lincoln before Booth took it off, cannot and shall not threaten through his son our arrest and hanging in the jail yard without our throwing back defiance in his teeth.

This wicked rascal who, through his Railroad Presidents has wronged, robbed, despoiled, and plundered the people, shall be told of it. Grant and his grand army of the Potomac cannot silence us nor shut the complaining mouths of the hundred thousand taxpayers of the State who are groaning under the burden, oppression, and insult that have been heaped upon them.

On August 2, he wired the following editorial to the *Sentinel*:

### LIES LIKE A THIEF

The governor has been lying on us for twelve months; his profligate son and organ lies on us to-day by calling us a Ku Klux. If we are, why don't the pumpkin-faced rascal arrest us? We defy and dare him to arrest.

On August 3, the following was at the head of the *Sentinel's* editorial column:

---

[1] *Sentinel*, July 26 and 27, 1870.

TO GOVERNOR HOLDEN

Gov. Holden: — You say you will handle me in due time. You white-livered miscreant, do it now. You dared me to resist you; I dare you to arrest me. I am here to protect my family; the jacobins of your club, after shooting powder in the face of Mrs. Turner, threw a five-pound rock in her window, which struck near one of my children. Your ignorant jacobins are incited to this by your lying charges against me that I am King of the Ku Klux. You villain, come and arrest a man, and order your secret clubs not to molest women and children.

Yours with contempt and defiance — *habeas corpus* or no *habeas corpus,*                                          JOSIAH TURNER, JR.

Late in the evening of the fourth, or early in the morning of the fifth, Governor Holden telegraphed the order for the arrest of Turner.[1] On the fifth, he was arrested in Hillsboro by a detachment of Kirk's men and carried to Company Shops, from which place he was taken to Yanceyville, confined in the room in which Stephens was killed, and refused all comforts even such as soap and towels. Part of the time he was locked in a cell with a negro under sentence of death and was not even given a seat of any sort. The

---

[1] In his answer to the articles of impeachment, Holden denied that he had ordered the arrest of Turner in Orange County. An inside view of the matter is interesting. Colonel C. L. Harris, who was superintendent of public works in 1870, told the author in 1906 that he heard on the morning of August 5 that the order had been given and, although he and Holden had not spoken for a year, he went at once to the latter's office to be greeted with the question, "What in h—l are you doing here?" Harris replied, "Governor Holden, is it true that you have ordered Turner's arrest?" Holden then said, "It is none of your d—d business, but I have ordered it." Harris said, "Governor, for God's sake, for your own sake, for the sake of the Republican party, don't do it. It will rniu everything." The interview was then closed by the governor's ordering Harris to leave the office.

cell was full of vermin and was altogether loathsome.[1]
There is scarcely doubt that Holden hoped by the arrest and
bad treatment of Turner to provoke the people to a collision
with Kirk's men and thereby find some justification before
the world for his policy. Even Bergen believed that such
was his object. The *Standard,* however, said that Turner
had been arrested as King of the Ku Klux and because he
had attempted in his paper to cover up the murder of
Stephens and Outlaw and had incited his followers to resist the authority of the government.[2]

Upon their failure to obtain relief from the state courts,
the counsel for the prisoners determined to apply to Judge
Brooks of the United States District Court. Judge George
W. Brooks had been an old line Whig before the war and
during the conflict had been a strong and avowed Union
man. He had been appointed judge in 1865, on Holden's
recommendation, prior to which he had served in the convention of 1865. A petition was accordingly prepared
which stated among other things the failure to obtain relief
from the state judiciary. Judge Brooks gave the matter
very careful consideration and finally decided that he had

---

[1] On the walls of the room where Turner was confined appear the following lines written by him while a prisoner:

"Armed violence with lawless might around and hallowed by the
name of right.

Josiah Turner, Jr., Prisoner.  July, 1870."
"The love of liberty with life is given, and life itself the inferior gift
of Heaven.

Josiah Turner, Jr., Prisoner.  July, 1870."

[2] Turner was not the only citizen of North Carolina outside the so-
called insurrectionary counties who was in danger. Kirk ordered his
men to shoot A. C. Avery on sight, and later he sent a detachment to
Hillsboro to arrest Jacob A. Long, who was studying law there. Long
was quick enough to realize his danger and shrewdly induced a detective,
employed by Kirk, to reveal the plan and so was able to escape by the
same train that brought Kirk's men to Hillsboro.

jurisdiction, but intimated that it was not necessary to allude to the state courts. That portion of the petition was accordingly stricken out, and on August 6, Judge Brooks issued the writ for all the prisoners held by Kirk including Turner, who, however, a little later instructed William A. Graham not to apply for one in his case.

The news of Judge Brooks' action came like a thunderbolt to the governor and his coterie. On the seventh, Holden telegraphed President Grant as follows:

> STATE OF NORTH CAROLINA,
> EXECUTIVE DEPARTMENT,
> RALEIGH, AUGUST 7TH, 1870.

*To the President of the United States:*

*Sir:* The chief justice of the supreme court of this state, sustained by his associate justices, has decided that I have a right to declare counties in a state of insurrection, and to arrest and hold all suspected persons in such counties. This I have done.

But the district judge, Brooks, relying on the fourteenth amendment and the act of Congress of 1867, page 385, chapter 28, has issued a writ of *habeas corpus*, commanding the officer Kirk to produce before him the bodies of certain prisoners detained by my order.

I deny his right thus to interfere with the local laws in murder cases. I hold these persons under our state laws, and under the decision of our supreme court judges who have jurisdiction of the whole matter, and it is not known to Judge Brooks in what manner or by what tribunal the prisoners will be examined and tried.

The officer will be directed to reply to the writ that he holds the prisoners under my order, and that he refuses to obey the writ. If the marshal shall then call on the *posse comitatus* there may be conflict, but if he should call first on the federal troops it will be for you to say whether the troops shall be used to take prisoners out of my hands.

It is my purpose to detain the prisoners, unless the army of the United States, under your orders, shall demand them.

An early answer is respectfully requested.

W. W. HOLDEN, *Governor.*

The next day Secretary Belknap transmitted an opinion‚ of Attorney General Akerman advising the state authorities to yield.[1] Before this was received, the *Standard* expressed the attitude of the state administration in the following editorial:

We learn that Judge Brooks, the District judge who was in this city yesterday, has issued a writ of *habeas corpus* against Colonel Kirk, commanding him to produce the bodies of certain prisoners held in Yanceyville. *What has Judge Brooks to do with murder cases in North Carolina?* Governor Holden is sustained by the Supreme Court of the State. By what authority does Judge Brooks disregard the action of a State Court?

Is Judge Brooks ready to involve the people of North Carolina in civil war? Does he suppose Governor Holden will recede before *him?*

\* \* \* \* \* \*

The Governor will *not* recede until the federal army is used against him; and the federal army *will not* be used against him. We are on the eve of civil war, and when it begins all the blood and all the horrors of it will be on the skirts of Judge Brooks.

The *Standard* was hysterical by the time the news came that the President had deserted the governor. Proof of this is to be seen in another quotation:

The great Republican party of North Carolina has been defeated, and this result was as unexpected by its foes as by its

[1] *Impeachment*, p. 214.

friends. Loyal men are bound once more in chains, and this is done throug'.i fear.

Yes, this is the cause. Not the Democrats, the Whigs, the Conservatives — but the CONSTITUTIONAL UNION GUARD, the WHITE BROTHERHOOD, and the INVISIBLE EMPIRE have gained the victory. Their weapons have not been arguments or eloquence; but the SCOURGE, the KNIFE, and the ROPE have been the instruments with which they have gained their triumph.

\*    \*    \*    \*    \*    \*

At such a time as this every man asks himself what will the Executive do now. Will he disband the State troops and leave us to the tender mercies of these murderers? No, NO, HE WILL NOT. There is but one power to which he will bow his head and before which he will disperse his troops—THE UNITED STATES OF AMERICA, and *that power* is his *friend.*

Every effort was being made meanwhile to induce the belief in the North that the action of the governor had been taken in an effort to remedy a situation in which the Ku Klux had overcome the civil power. The press reports were full of imaginary outrages. The most remarkably mendacious of these was traced directly to Governor Holden.[1] But in this the party leaders saw a lone chance for salvation and it was used to the fullest extent, but with small success.

[1] In the *New York Tribune* appeared a letter from Judge Tourgee to Senator Abbott reciting the fact that the Ku Klux had committed fourteen arsons, had opened four or five thousand houses in the State, and had committed thirteen murders in his district alone. Judge Tourgee at once wrote correcting the letter, stating that he had said *four* arsons, four or five *hundred* houses, and that the murders were for the whole State. The *Tribune* stated that the letter had been received from Governor Holden in the form in which it had appeared. Abbott at once furnished proof that it had not been altered when he gave it to the governor. The latter issued a statement in which he contradicted himself pitifully and he was scored unmercifully by the *Tribune. Tribune,* August 3, 1870, September 21, 1870. *Sentinel,* September 24, 1870.

When it became evident that he could obtain no help from the President against Judge Brooks, Governor Holden called Kirk to Raleigh and, after conferring with him, sent a letter by special messenger to Judge Pearson announcing that he had ordered Kirk to obey the writ. The chief justice at once returned to Raleigh, writing Holden that he would receive the prisoners but declining to accept any responsibility for the governor's action.

When the court opened on August 18, Kirk was present with a number of the prisoners. The counsel for the petitioners then withdrew their application on the ground that Judge Brooks had already issued the writ, returnable that day in Salisbury. The attorney general, L. P. Olds, then applied for bench warrants for a number of the prisoners [1] on the charge of complicity in the murder of Stephens and Outlaw. All of these were later discharged, most of them without any attempt to bring evidence against them. [2] Three prisoners [3] were held to bail but, after an extended examination in which a great mass of testimony was taken, and which was held largely to save the face of the governor and the chief justice, they were discharged for the lack of any evidence against them.

In the meantime, Judge Brooks held proceedings at chambers in Salisbury. Kirk appeared with some of his prisoners and was granted a day longer to make his return, and the next day made return for all with the statement that they had been arrested by order of Governor Holden. All were dismissed upon motion of counsel, the counsel for the governor who were present objecting, although they were unable to produce any evidence against the prisoners. In

[1] A. G. Moore, J. T. Mitchell, Joseph R. Fowler, S. P. Hill, F. A. Wiley, Felix Roan, and L. M. Totten.

[2] Battle, *Habeas Corpus Cases*, pp. 59–66.

[3] F. A. Wiley, J. T. Mitchell, and Felix Roan.

regard to this action there were two points of view in the State which are well reflected in the following quotations:

The writ of *Habeas Corpus*, instead of being "played out," *has become a living, potent, health-giving principle, which still survives amidst the usurpations of an executive despot and the tame subserviency of a partisan Chief Justice.*[1]

JUDGE BROOKS

The world, we think, cannot fail to join us in the most perfect surprise at the extraordinary action of the above-named gentleman in regard to the *habeas corpus* cases at Salisbury. WITHOUT HEARING ONE WORD OF TESTIMONY, WITHOUT WAITING ONE MOMENT FOR CONSIDERATION OR INVESTIGATION, HE TURNS LOOSE UPON THE STATE A BODY OF MEN CHARGED WITH CRIMES WHICH WOULD PUT TO BLUSH THE DARKEST PAGE OF CRIMINAL HISTORY. Was this usual? Was it fair? Was it right?[2]

Motions were then made for an attachment against Kirk and a peace warrant against Bergen. Both motions were adjourned to be heard in Raleigh. There on August 18, after argument by counsel,[3] Judge Brooks rendered a powerful opinion in which, though it contained by implication sharp criticism of the governor and chief justice, he refused to grant the motion. Later, however, he issued a bench warrant against Bergen. Judge Brooks based his action in issuing the writ upon the Fourteenth Amendment and the act of Congress of February 5, 1867, which gave federal judges power to grant the writ of *habeas corpus* in all cases where any person might be restrained of liberty in violation

---

[1] *Tarboro Southerner*, September 1, 1870.

[2] *Standard*, August 20, 1870.

[3] Attorney General Olds denied the jurisdiction of the court and Judge Brooks threatened him with contempt proceedings.

of the Constitution, or any treaty or law of the United States.[1]

On September 1, Turner applied to Justices Dick and Settle for a bench warrant against William W. Holden, Kirk, Bergen, Hunnicutt,[2] and Alex Ruffin.[3] They promptly refused it in the case of the governor, and allowed it for the others except within the borders of Alamance and Caswell counties. As all of Kirk's force was in those two counties, the warrant was of little effect. In succession, Turner then applied to Justices Reade [4] and Rodman and to Judges Watts, Thomas, Tourgee, Cloud, Henry, and Jones, all of whom refused the application so far as the governor was concerned. Turner then carried the matter to Orange Superior Court where the grand jury found a true bill against Holden for assault and battery and a capias was sent to the carpetbag sheriff of Wake who very naturally refused to serve it. This ended the matter for the time. Suits were brought against Kirk in the federal court by many others but he was allowed by the marshal to remain with his men. Bergen, in the meanwhile, was in jail.

On August 25, Judge Mitchell issued an injunction against D. A. Jenkins, the state treasurer, and A. D. Jenkins, paymaster, forbidding the payment of the state troops.[5] Thereupon the governor removed A. D. Jenkins and ap-

---

[1] *Laws of the United States*, chap. xxviii, 39 Cong., 2 sess.

[2] One of Kirk's officers who had arrested Turner.

[3] A colored member of Kirk's force.

[4] Judge Reade replied as follows to the application: "I am of the opinion that the application within does not justify the issuing of a bench warrant; and if it were sufficient in other respects, no reason is given for passing over the local authorities."

[5] The injunction was issued upon the petition of R. M. Allison of Iredell County.

pointed John B. Neathery who paid them.[1]  On September 21, they were mustered out and the majority fled to the mountains, preserving their organization in fear of the just anger of an injured people, but still marking their route by violence and outrage.

On August 29, Governor Holden appealed to Judge Bond of the United States Circuit Court to come to Raleigh and hear the cases against Kirk and Bergen.  Kirk was arrested by the marshal in Alamance and carried to Raleigh by him, thus escaping arrest on a state warrant.  Judge Bond, who had been appointed by President Grant because he was thought to be well suited, from the administration standpoint, to try Ku Klux cases, consented and came to Raleigh. He heard the argument in the case of Bergen and reserved his decision.  Early in October, he wrote the order for Bergen's release, but waited until the Circuit Court met at Raleigh in November, and on the twenty-fourth secretly released Bergen, and several days later handed down an opinion overruling Judge Brooks' action in the case.[2]  Sheriff Lee, of Wake, in spite of the fact that he held state criminal and civil processes against him, allowed him to depart unmolested.[3]  Bergen went to Danville where he was recognized and, after being run down by bloodhounds, was arrested for stealing a pistol from F. A. Wiley, of Caswell. He was, however, released and went to Washington to receive soon after at the hands of a grateful President the appointment as consul to Pernambuco.  The nomination was not confirmed and Grant was finally forced to withdraw it.

---

[1] The cost of the militia was $74,267.70 distributed as follows:

| | |
|---|---:|
| Rations | $14,409.61 |
| Transportation | 10,775.60 |
| Pay | 49,182.49 |

[2] Battle, *Habeas Corpus Cases*, p. 141.

[3] *Senate Report*, p. 168.

A week after Bergen's release, Judge Bond released Kirk who was under parole to the marshal and, Sheriff Lee assenting in spite of the papers in his pocket, he left Raleigh and, first on horseback, and later by carriage, made his way across country to the Virginia line, thus escaping the punishment which awaited him. He too was the object of tender Republican solicitude and became an officer of the police force of the government buildings in Washington.

In the meantime, on November 10, Governor Holden issued a proclamation declaring the insurrection in Alamance and Caswell at an end and congratulating the people upon the good order existing in the State.

The Kirk-Holden War had ended.

# CHAPTER FOURTEEN

## THE REFORM LEGISLATURE OF 1870-1871

### I. ORGANIZATION AND MEMBERSHIP

THE new legislature met on November 21. In the Senate, Lieutenant Governor Caldwell presided and in his opening address, after admitting that much had been done by the preceding legislature that merited condemnation, urged wise and careful legislation, the preservation of individual rights, and a searching investigation of the charges of fraud against those who had held in their keeping the interests of the State. In the House, Thomas J. Jarvis, of Tyrrell, was chosen speaker over T. L. Hargrove, of Granville. He had been one of the leading Conservatives in the preceding legislature and in that way had won his preferment. Hargrove was a new member.

The membership of the legislature by parties according to certificate was as follows:

|                | Senate. | House. | Joint Ballot. |
|----------------|---------|--------|---------------|
| Conservatives ........ | 33 | 72 | 105 |
| Republicans .......... | 17 | 45 | 62 |
| Independents ......... | .. | 3 | 3 |

In the Senate, there was some objection to the seating of R. W. Lassiter, W. A. Smith, and L. C. Barnett, all three Republicans, but the majority, remembering their condemnation of the arbitrary methods of the Republicans two years before, preferred to allow them to take their seats and let investigation follow. They were accordingly qualified, after which contests were begun against Lassiter and Barnett by W. A. Bradsher and L. C. Edwards. These

534

cases were referred to a committee which sent a commissioner to Granville and Person to take testimony. The report was in favor of Barnett, in spite of a technicality which might have been construed as invalidating his election, but it recommended the seating of Edwards who had received a majority of the votes. The report was adopted in January. In the meantime, Wilson Carey, of Caswell, and W. A. Smith, of Alamance, had been unseated on the ground that, those counties having been declared in a state of insurrection and having been, at the time of the election, occupied by troops, there could not have been a free election. There was much criticism of the failure to unseat John A. Gilmer who was elected from the same district as Smith, but the facts of the case were that the former was elected with or without the vote of Alamance, while the latter was defeated unless the vote of Alamance was counted. His Conservative opponent declined to contest, so a new election was ordered and James A. Graham, a Conservative, was chosen. Livingston Brown, another Conservative, was elected in Caswell.

In the House, similar action was taken in regard to Alamance and Caswell, and the new elections resulted in Conservative victories. The election officers in Madison County had counted the vote cast by Kirk's men while stationed in Alamance and Caswell and, on this ground, W. W. Rollins, the Republican incumbent, was unseated and his opponent declared elected. A contest from Hertford resulted in the unseating of the Conservative incumbent and the seating of the Republican candidate, W. D. Newsom, a negro, and another contest by a Conservative from Wayne County failed; so it is seen that the decisions in election cases were not entirely partisan.[1] There was an attempt to dispose of

[1] The author has examined the testimony and other papers in all these cases and they prove conclusively the justice of the reports.

A. W. Fisher by appointing a committee to see if he was a citizen of Bladen, but it was unable to find any evidence upon which to base proceedings against him.

These proceedings in the two houses made their political standing as follows:

|  | Senate. | House. | Joint Ballot. |
|---|---|---|---|
| Conservatives | 36 | 75 | 111 |
| Republicans | 14 | 42 | 56 |
| Independents | .. | 3 | 3 |

Among the Republican Senators, were three negroes,[1] and two carpetbaggers.[2] In the House, there were nineteen negroes [3] and two carpetbaggers.[4]

One of the most striking facts about the membership of the legislature was the number of young men. Seventy of them were under thirty years of age, and there were very few old men, the majority of the remainder being under forty. Only a comparatively small number had seen legislative service, but those who had experience proved themselves able leaders, and the majority displayed throughout the existence of the body an unusual degree of unity, and manifested so clearly a determination to secure genuine reform that they assured the uninterrupted ascendency of their party in the legislature for the next generation, and, with one interval of four years, until the present day. The Conservative leaders in the Senate were E. J. Warren, of Beaufort, who was chosen president *pro tem.*, John W. Graham, William M. Robbins, H. C. Jones, A. C. Cowles, and

[1] Henry Eppes, J. A. Hyman, and G. W. Price.

[2] Lehman and Moore.

[3] J. R. Bryant, E. R. Dudley, W. Bunn, W. Cawthorne, S. Ellison, R. Falkner, R. Fletcher, R. M. Johnson, G. L. Mabson, W. Morgan, W. D. Newsom, J. R. Page, W. H. Reavis, P. D. Robbins, C. Smith, T. A. Sykes, R. Tucker, G. Willis, and J. Williamson.

[4] A. W. Fisher and G. Z. French.

W. L. Love.   On the Republican side were C. H. Brogden, L. P. Olds, and R. F. Lehman.   In the House, Jarvis, T. D. Sparrow, W. P. Welch and, for a time, F. N. Strudwick, were the leading Conservative members, while S. F. Phillips, who had been elected to fill a vacancy, G. Z. French, A. W. Fisher, and J. M. Justice were the most prominent Republicans.   J. H. Williamson, a colored member, was the ablest representative of his race and often took a prominent part in the debates.

In every way, the body was superior to its predecessor. In ability, the contrast was sharp and in morals and a sense of public responsibility, there could be no comparison, so much was its personnel in advance of that of the first Reconstruction legislature.

## 2. THE IMPEACHMENT AND TRIAL OF GOVERNOR HOLDEN

The result of the election was scarcely known to the public before the *Tarboro Southerner*, followed by a few other newspapers, voiced a widespread demand for the impeachment of the governor.[1]   The *Sentinel* had little to say on the subject at first, but agreed in the demand, and later insisted that Judge Pearson should also be impeached as his guilt was equally great.   Comparatively little was said about the matter in the press, but that little was enough to excite in Governor Holden the liveliest anxiety.   The anger against him in the State was clearly apparent and the election had brought complete disorganization and demoralization to the Republican party.   A plan to divide the Conservative ranks by a revival of jealousy between those of former Democratic and Whig affiliations failed because

[1] Issue of Aug. 11, 1870.   The editorial was in part as follows: " He is the vilest man that ever polluted a public office and his crimes are now crying in trumpet tones against him.   Impeach the Traitor, the Apostate, and the Renegade, and drive him into the infamous oblivion which is so justly his due."

premature. Too lately had they faced a common foe and a common danger for the alliance to be easily broken. On the other hand, the great cause of division among the Republicans was Holden himself who was hated by many of the party and particularly by the influential Dockery family. The course of the *Standard* after the election, and in fact, during the whole of the recent trouble had not helped either Holden or the party. It abandoned all efforts to give the truth to the public and sought by appealing to the worst passions to gain advantage for the party and more particularly for the governor. All during the *habeas corpus* proceedings it vilified Judge Brooks, denounced William A. Graham, Thomas Bragg, B. F. Moore, and William H. Battle as " Ku Klux lawyers " [1] and charged them with the responsibility for the Ku Klux. It was fighting a losing game, however, and on September 17, it suspended publication, William A. Smith, the owner, saying in disgust, "What in h—l is the good of running a Republican paper when none of the party can read? " But on the twenty-sixth, publication was resumed with S. S. Ashley, the superintendent of public instruction, as the *sub rosa* editor.

Coincident with the demand for the impeachment of Holden, came the discussion of a constitutional convention to rid the constitution of its most serious defects. A large part of the press and most of the Conservative leaders were in favor of it and the question was argued all over the State. The advocates of the convention opposed any change in the rights of the negro and in the homestead provision, but laid stress upon the necessity of reducing the number of officers and taking steps to settle the question of the state debt. They estimated the cost of the convention at $25,000, and argued that the money saved by the changes would pay

---

[1] *Standard*, Aug. 20, 1870, *et seq.*

for it. The Republicans, particularly the carpet-baggers, who felt a proprietary interest in the existing constitution, estimated that the lowest cost would be $200,000. As a matter of fact, the Republicans were viewing with horror the threatened destruction of their power and were using every possible means to defeat the policy of the Conservatives. The most potent arguments against a convention were expense and the possibility that it might result in interference by Congress and a fresh Reconstruction. The Republicans also accused the Conservatives of plotting the entire overthrow of the existing system. The following is a characteristic expression of this:

> The plans of the Conservatives, as thus far shadowed forth, we have already hinted at. They propose
> To call a Convention;
> To impeach the Governor;
> To remove the present eminent and able State officials;
> To revolutionize the common school system;
> To abolish the homestead law;
> To nullify the Fourteenth Amendment;
> To nullify the Fifteenth Amendment;
> To nullify the Reconstruction acts;
> To inaugurate the Invisible Empire.[1]

Judge R. B. Gilliam, who had been elected to succeed Deweese in the 41st Congress, died in October, and a heated contest followed, in which John Manning, of Chatham, defeated Joseph W. Holden. Governor Holden's prestige would have been helped by his son's election and no efforts were spared to win it, but they were in vain.

As the time approached for the meeting of the legislature, discussion of impeachment was revived. The *Sentinel*, voicing undoubtedly the sentiment of a majority in the

---

[1] *Standard*, October 11, 1870.

State, again demanded the punishment of the chief justice
as well as of the governor.  The General Assembly met on
November 21, and on the next day, a memorial of A. G.
Moore, of Alamance, asking the impeachment of both, was
presented.  This was followed by a flood of similar petitions.  Both the governor and the chief justice were
alarmed.  The former made use of his annual message as
a defence and in it discussed the whole question of his
action and attempted to justify it.  He also annexed to his
message certain selected documents which he thought would
help his case.  The chief justice took more unusual steps
in his own behalf.  On November 25, he sent a memorial
to the Senate in vindication of his conduct.  This was being
read to the Senate when objection was made and it was
withdrawn.[1]  This remarkable attempt to induce the Senate to prejudge his case thus failed.  Governor Holden, in
the meantime, made it known that he would favor the removal of Vance's disabilities, and offered Senator Murphy
a place upon the board of public charities, apparently in the
hope that they might be influenced in his behalf.[2]  Vance
was opposed to impeachment, why, no one seemed to know.
Of it, he said afterwards, " It was the longest hunt after
the poorest hide I ever saw."  It still seemed advisable to
the governor and his friends to appear unafraid, and on
November 19, the *Standard,* which still represented Governor Holden's opinions, after threatening the Democratic
party, said, " We have heard enough on this subject.  We
want acts after to-day.  In the name of the people of North
Carolina, who elected the governor and chief justice, we
demand a trial at the bar of the Senate.  Innocent or guilty,
the matter has reached that point from which there is only
one course to pursue and that is—give these men a trial—

[1] *Senate Journal,* 1870–71, November 25, 1870.
[2] *Sentinel,* November 29, 1870.

clear them if innocent and convict them if guilty. If the Democratic party will not try these men, then we denounce the party as being more corrupt and dishonest than has been charged against the Republican party."

In the meantime, the idea of impeachment had not been dropped. The Democratic caucus of the House decided upon it, and on December 9, Frederick N. Strudwick, of Orange, who had been a prominent member of the Ku Klux, introduced the resolution of impeachment which was at once referred to the judiciary committee. Chief Justice Pearson expected to be impeached and had already employed Thomas C. Fuller to defend him.[1] He would have been impeached but for the influence of the bar of the State. For many years he had conducted a private law school and had endeared himself personally to a majority of the bar. His great abilities were also recognized. Hence any proposition to impeach him was always defeated by his friends and he thus escaped a fate he richly deserved. Other elements, as well, entered into the matter. Many members of the legislature thought it impolitic and unwise to make too clean a sweep, and thinking Holden the chief offender and a more dangerous man, preferred his impeachment to that of Pearson.

On December 14, the judiciary committee, after reporting the facts of the previous summer, offered the following resolution which was adopted by a vote of sixty to forty-six:[2]

[1] With the concurrence of the other justices, Chief Justice Pearson presented an elaborate defence of his action to the Supreme Court at the January Term, 1871. It is to be found in 65 *North Carolina Reports.*

[2] Nine Conservatives voted against impeachment. They were J. S. Anderson, J. T. Brown, B. L. Bryan, T. D. Darden, Jona Harris, J. Clinard, B. K. Dickey, and E. B. Lyon. Cawthorne, a negro member from Warren and a Republican, voted for the resolution.

"That William W. Holden, Governor of the State of North Carolina, be impeached of high crimes and misdemeanors in office."

On the next day, the House appointed F. N. Strudwick, W. P. Welch, and Thomas Sparrow a committee to appear at the bar of the Senate, and, in the name of the House, impeach Governor Holden of high crimes; and the same day, they appeared before the Senate, and Welch impeached him in the following words:

*Mr. President and Senators:* We would display the most callous indifference—the most remarkable and unnatural absence of sensibility if, in appearing at the bar of the Senate of North Carolina, in obedience to the commands of the Representatives of the people, charged, as we are, with the performance of so solemn a duty, that of the impeachment of the Governor of a great Commonwealth, were we not oppressed with the awful responsibilities of the situation; but sustained by a consciousness of right, and calling to the aid of our inexperience the experience of one of England's purest patriots and most distinguished statesmen, we proceed with more confidence than we would otherwise have.

Permit us, Mr. President and Senators, to adopt almost the very language used by him under circumstances somewhat similar, and to ask: "What is it we want here to a great act of national justice?" "Do we want a cause?" "You have the cause of an oppressed people." "Do you want a criminal?" "Where was there so much iniquity ever laid to the charge of any one?" Senators, "it is a prosecutor you want?" "You have before you the Representatives of the people of North Carolina." "Do you want a tribunal?" Where will you find one superior to this? Therefore it is that, ordered by the Representatives of the people of this Commonwealth, we impeach William W. Holden, Governor of the State of North Carolina, "of high crimes and misdemeanors in office."

We "impeach him in the name of the Representatives of North Carolina whose national character he has dishonored."

We "impeach him in the name of all the people of North Carolina whose laws, rights, and liberties he has subverted."

We "impeach him in the name and by the virtue of those eternal laws of justice which he has violated."

We impeach him in the name of human nature itself which he has cruelly outraged, injured, and oppressed; and in the name of the Representatives of the people do demand that the Senate organize a high court of impeachment and take order that William W. Holden appear at its bar to answer the particular charges which the House of Representatives will in due time exhibit, and that the Senate do make such other and further orders in the premises as may seem to them best calculated to bring this trial to a just and speedy conclusion; and in conclusion, the House of Representatives, through us, most heartily prays that God, the God of Eternal Justice, may protect the right.

On the nineteenth, the House appointed Thomas Sparrow, George H. Gregory, W. P. Welch, Thomas D. Johnston, C. W. Broadfoot, James G. Scott, and John W. Dunham as a board of managers. Welch and Johnston declined to accept and were replaced by R. P. Waring and Lee M. McAfee. F. N. Strudwick, who might have been expected on the board, was not chosen because of his connection with the Ku Klux, in order that all appearance of the impeachment's being a " Ku Klux prosecution " might be avoided.[1] The House empowered the managers to employ counsel to assist them, and William A. Graham, Thomas Bragg, and Augustus S. Merrimon were chosen for the purpose.[2]

[1] Strudwick was much disappointed and deeply offended by this action.

[2] B. F. Moore was sought as counsel by both sides, but declined to serve. He was, however, heartily in favor of impeachment. He wrote his daughter at the time, " Holden's impeachment is demanded by a sense of public virtue and due regard to the honor of the State. He is an exceedingly corrupt man and ought to be placed before the people as a public example of a tyrant condemned and punished."

Throughout the campaign and after the election, the Conservatives had constantly assured the negroes that no harm to them was intended, but the Republicans had at the same time assured them that not only would they be deprived of the suffrage, but that slavery would be restored.[1] Consequently, there was much uneasiness among the negroes generally and on December 19, the colored members of the legislature, seventeen in number, issued an address to the colored people of the State. In figures drawn from the Old Testament, they compared the Conservative majority in the legislature to Haman, Holden to Mordecai, and themselves to the persecuted Jews, and called upon their race to take action to avert the evils which threatened them. Said they:

The only offense of Governor Holden, and that which has brought down the wrath of the dominant party upon him, is that he thwarted the designs of a band of assassins who had prepared to sacrifice this State in the blood of the poor people on the night before the last election on account of their political sentiments and to prevent them from voting. Because he dispersed this murderous host organized by the so-called Conservative party, they propose to destroy him. First propose to suspend him, then to go through with a mock trial before the Senate as they have already done before the House, where a true bill has been found without taking testimony.

After impeachment his enemies will not be satisfied until he is hanged, unless happily their own gallows should overtake them. When Governor Holden is disposed of, those whom he protected will be the next victims. For the blood of one man will not satisfy their thirst. They are mad because Reconstruction measures have triumphed and we are permitted to represent you in this body. They are mad because we refuse to bow the knee to them.

[1] Referring to the fact that a Republican had voted for impeachment, a negro member of the legislature said, "The governor has been bit by his own dogs."

In consideration of these supposed facts, they recommended that Friday, January 13, 1871, be set aside as a day of fasting and prayer to God in behalf of the governor.[1]

Soon after his impeachment, Governor Holden was converted and was publicly baptized. Little public notice of this was taken in the State from a feeling of delicacy, but the Northern press had much to say on the subject in a very caustic vein.[2]

On December 19, the House adopted eight articles of impeachment. In brief, they were as follows:

Article 1. Raising unlawful armed bodies of troops and causelessly declaring the county of Alamance in a state of insurrection, and afterwards unlawfully arresting eighty-two citizens of the county and unlawfully detaining them, when there was no insurrection and when the civil officers of the law were in the full exercise of all their functions.

Article 2. The same as to Caswell county with the arrest of eighteen citizens.

Article 3. Unlawfully arresting, in the county of Orange, Josiah Turner, Jr., and imprisoning him.

Article 4. Unlawfully arresting and detaining in the county of Caswell, John Kerr and three other citizens.

Article 5. Refusing to obey the writ of *habeas corpus* in the case of Adolphus G. Moore.

---

[1] *Sentinel*, Dec. 30, 1870. There is strong ground for the belief that the governor himself suggested this move.

[2] The New York *Herald* of December 20, 1870, said, "Governor Holden goes to impeachment as if he were going to be hanged. On Friday he professed religion and to-day he is to be baptized." The *Nation* of December 22, 1870, said, "No record of any similar preparation for impeachment is, we believe, to be found in the books, and the effect of it will be watched by jurists with deep interest." The New York *World* said, "That nasty tenderness which fondles the poor, dear murderer, and says the ravisher has been only too acutely moved by emotion capable of making him a grandsire in Israel if you let him go, is at work to defend Governor Holden of North Carolina."

Article 6. Refusing to obey the writ of *habeas corpus* in the case of John Kerr and eighteen other citizens of Caswell county.

Article 7. Unlawfully recruiting a large body of troops from the State of North Carolina and the State of Tennessee and placing in command of them one Kirk and other desperate and lawless men from the State of Tennessee; unlawfully arresting and imprisoning John Kerr and many others; hanging by the neck William Patton, Lucien H. Murray, and others; thrusting into a loathsome dungeon Josiah Turner, Jr., and F. A. Wiley, and without lawful authority making his warrant upon David A. Jenkins, Treasurer of the State, for $70,000 or more, to pay the said unlawful troops.

Article 8. Inciting and procuring the State Treasurer to disregard the injunction to restrain him from paying the sum of $80,000 or more out of the public treasury for the unlawful purpose of paying his unlawful troops.[1]

The next day the board of managers, accompanied by the whole House went to the Senate and presented the articles. Whereupon Lieutenant Governor Caldwell vacated his seat with a farewell speech to enter upon the duties of governor in accordance with the constitutional provision.[2] The Senate by a vote of twenty-four to eighteen appointed a committee to notify the chief justice, who, on the twenty-third, appeared and, after stating that he did not deem it necessary to take an oath and after swearing in the senators as a court of impeachment, announced that the court was organized.[3] A summons was at once served upon Governor Holden who, through his counsel, Richard C. Badger, asked for thirty days to prepare an answer and to employ counsel. This was granted and the managers were given

[1] This summary is taken from the *Sentinel* of March 22, 1871.

[2] *Constitution of North Carolina*, Article III, sec. 12.

[3] *Impeachment*, pp. 18–21.

six days to reply, and the date of the trial was set for January 30, 1871.[1]

On January 23, Governor Holden, through his counsel, R. C. Badger, J. M. McCorkle, Nathaniel Boyden, William N. H. Smith, and Edward Conigland,[2] submitted his answer to the articles of impeachment. To the first article, was presented an elaborate answer containing a copy of Governor Worth's protest, which was claimed to be indicative of the state's attitude towards the reconstructed government. Out of the protest, according to the answer, grew the later opposition to Holden's administration. The growth of the Ku Klux, the passage of a law against them, the governor's proclamation against them, and those declaring Alamance and Caswell counties in insurrection were then recited. It was denied that the persons arrested had been ill-treated, and constitutional authority was claimed for all the governor's acts. To the second article, was opposed the claim that all the persons were arrested upon probable cause. To the third article, it was denied that the arrest of Josiah Turner had been ordered elsewhere than in Alamance or Caswell, but it was admitted that orders had been given for his detention after arrest. The fourth article was answered as the first and second. In answer to the fifth, the suspension of the writ of *habeas corpus* was admitted, but the governor claimed that it was his intention to hold the prisoners only until they could with safety to the State be surrendered to the civil authorities, and he

---

[1] *Impeachment*, pp. 22, 23.

[2] This was a brilliant array of talent. Two were later on the Supreme Bench of the State, one as chief justice, and all were of exceptional ability. Holden tried to secure Vance as counsel, but without success. He also made an effort to add Benjamin F. Butler, but the latter declined to serve. Why anyone who could realize the value of Vance in such a case should have sought to prejudice his case by the employment of Butler is inexplicable.

claimed constitutional and legal justification. The sixth
article was answered similarly to the others. The answer
to the seventh denied that the troops had been raised in
Tennessee, but claimed that as within the governor's power.
He denied that portion of the article relating to his drawing
the money from the treasury. To the eighth article was submitted a denial and a demand for proof.

The next day the replication of the managers was presented. It consisted of a general denial of the governor's
answer.[1]

On January 30, the managers asked leave to amend the
eighth article and, after some objection by counsel for the
governor, it was granted. But as this made a change necessary in the answer to that article, time was granted for that
purpose. When the Senate re-convened, L. C. Edwards, of
Granville, appeared and when he was called forward to be
sworn, his right to sit on the trial was challenged by the
counsel for the respondent. A long argument followed, but
the chief justice decided that Senator Edwards was entitled
to be sworn in as a member of the court.[2] On the same
day the final oath was taken by the Senate, and on the next
day, the trial began.

In no State up to this time had a governor been impeached,
and the case presented many points where a need of precedents was felt. Both sides relied extensively upon the
reports of the impeachment trial of President Johnson, each
interestingly enough from the other's previous viewpoint.

On February 2, Thomas Sparrow opened the case for the
managers, outlining the charges as contained in the articles
and stating more definitely what the managers intended to
prove. The examination of witnesses for the managers
then began and lasted until February 18, during which time

[1] *Impeachment*, p. 57.                    [2] *Ibid.*, p. 100.

fifty-seven witnesses were heard. The evidence all went to prove beyond doubt the main contentions upon which impeachment was based. The undisturbed exercise of jurisdiction by the courts in Alamance and Caswell was proved by many, and the statements of the articles as to the use of the troops, their illegal character, and the responsibility of the governor in their employment and payment were substantiated. The evidence also indicated that the governor had ordered Turner's arrest, but the defence had secured the removal of all the records of the telegraph office just before the trial, and they could not be used.[1]

A number of interesting questions as to the admission of evidence arose during the trial. On the ninth day, during the cross-examination of one of the witnesses, the counsel for the respondent asked him if he knew of the existence in Alamance of the Ku Klux, White Brotherhood, or Constitutional Union Guard. The managers at once objected and an extensive argument, lasting three days, followed, in which Graham, Bragg, and Merrimon for the managers and Conigland, Boyden, and Smith for the respondent addressed the court, the former maintaining that, as the question at issue was the fact of the existence of an insurrection in Alamance, before any evidence was admitted upon the subject, it was necessary to show some overt act of resistance to government, and no evidence on the subject of riots and murder could have any bearing. No combination or conspiracy, unless directed against the government, bore any relation to the fact at issue. The counsel for the governor argued that the secret societies existed for the purpose of resisting the government in the enforcement of the law and were, therefore, treasonable. In addition, they argued that the act of January 29, 1870, gave the governor discretionary

[1] *Impeachment*, pp. 918-32.

power in declaring a county to be in a state of insurrection, and therefore it was only necessary to show that the governor acted with good faith to secure his acquittal. This latter argument met with great opposition from the managers, who insisted that the act was unconstitutional and that the governor, under the constitution, could never be irresponsible. Both sides took advantage of the argument to wander from the direct point at issue.[1] The chief justice decided that the evidence was admissible as tending to disprove the allegations of falsehood, corruption, and wickedness on the part of the governor.[2]

Later in the trial, the counsel for the respondent objected to an attempt on the part of the managers to show the bad character of the persons who were victims of the Ku Klux by way of proving that the Ku Klux outrages were not of a political nature. The chief justice decided that the testimony was admissible.[3] On another occasion, counsel for the respondent objected to the admission of newspaper articles as proof in reference to the governor's knowledge of the treatment of the prisoners. Again the chief justice decided in favor of admission. In almost every case of dispute, the decision of the chief justice upon appeal was accepted by the court.

On February 9, the House of Representatives adopted a ninth article of impeachment, charging the governor of conspiracy with George W. Swepson to defraud the State by the wrongful issue of bonds to the western division of the Western North Carolina Railroad. It was adopted by a vote of 74 to 9 and disappears from view, neither the journal nor the press ever mentioning it again. Why it was never presented cannot be ascertained.

---

[1] *Impeachment*, pp. 302–474.          [2] *Ibid* , pp. 475–77.

[3] *Ibid.*, p. 508.

On February 23, Edward Conigland opened for the respondent. He was an orator of great power, full of fire and energy, and thoroughly Celtic in temperament. He had long been regarded as one of the ablest members of the bar of the State and his opening speech was awaited with great interest. With an impressive warning of the danger of prejudice in the prosecution of political offences, he called the attention of the Senate to the action of Fessenden and his Republican associates in the trial of President Johnson, and urged them to follow the example thus set. Alluding to the intense feeling in the State he characterized the action of the House in employing counsel to assist the managers as political persecution to which the mass of the people were opposed. He also criticized the House for its failure to spend a long time in investigation of the charges against the governor. This was clever argument but not of great weight in view of the general knowledge of the governor's part in the events of the preceding summer. He turned from his argument to declare that there was no purpose on the part of the respondent to cast any reflection upon the memory of Governor Worth. This was done to allay the criticism which had arisen after the filing of the governor's answer. Conigland then declared the purpose of the defence to prove the existence of secret associations in Alamance and Caswell, having a common purpose to subvert the laws by threats, intimidation, acts of outrage, and murder; that they had committed many outrages in those counties, including six or seven murders; and that they exercised such an extensive control within those counties that witnesses could not be induced to testify or grand juries to present, in consequence of which the ordinary administration of the laws had become inadequate to protect life, liberty, property, and the public peace. This, he claimed, would be sufficient for the defence. He denied that the constitution by insurrection meant only open resistance to the government, and insisted that under no rule of justice could the governor be held responsible for the execution of an unconstitutional statute. His denunciation of secret political societies was perhaps the best part of his speech and without doubt struck a responsive chord in most of his hearers. He closed with an eloquent appeal for fairness.[1]

The defence then commenced to offer testimony. One hundred and thirteen witnesses were examined, many of whom were colored. The evidence showed clearly the existence of the secret societies and their illegal activity, but the defence was unable to prove any purpose to resist the government or the processes of the courts. The managers objected to the introduction of Governor Worth's protest, but, after considerable argument, the chief justice decided against them, and the Senate accepted his ruling. The managers also objected to the introduction of Governor Holden's inaugural address, and the chief justice decided that it was not admissible. Another argument took place when the letter to Dr. Pride Jones was offered in evidence. Judge Pearson ruled in its favor and, upon appeal to the Senate, was sustained.[2]

The two most interesting witnesses among those examined during the entire trial were Josiah Turner for the managers and James E. Boyd for the respondent. Turner was still being lionized for his share in the events of the summer and was in his element upon the stand. He gave a vivid account of the treatment he had received and, when questioned as to his relations with and feeling towards the governor, spoke so freely and frankly that Governor Holden, who had been present at the trial to that time, left and did not return.[3] Boyd's notoriety during the campaign was

---

[1] *Impeachment*, pp. 1039-1089.    [2] *Ibid.*, p. 1158.
[3] Holden went to Washington, where he soon became the editor of the *Chronicle*.

largely the reason for the interest felt in his testimony. Upon cross-examination, he suffered severely in spite of much turning and twisting on his part.  The counsel for the governor attempted to prevent questions as to his activity as counsel for the governor in prosecuting the Ku Klux, on the ground that he could not be forced to reveal what had passed between his client and himself.  But it was brought out clearly by the managers that his fee was paid from the treasury and that the relation was, therefore, public and not personal.  The chief justice decided that the questions were permissible.[1]  Boyd, since his exposure of the Ku Klux and during his testimony had posed as one who had opposed the Ku Klux from the time he had found out its real nature, which was just after he joined it.  But he was forced to admit that he had made the suggestion to his " camp " that it should enter politics and that the proposition was voted down.[2]

The testimony for the respondent was closed on March 14, the thirty-seventh day of the trial.  The case had been conducted thus far without any indications of partisanship. The position of the chief justice had been particularly trying, and he had apparently filled it with great honor to himself and without any leaning to either side.  But, according to two of the governor's counsel, he advised them as to procedure and points of law throughout the trial, and thus added additional shame to his record in the whole matter.[3] The cross-examination of the witnesses was conducted by Badger and Merrimon for their respective sides and both displayed unusual ability.

William A. Graham spoke first for the managers.  He

---

[1] *Impeachment*, p. 1633.          [2] *Ibid.*, p. 1641.

[3] Boyden and Badger were the counsel alluded to.  They informed Holden of the facts in the case after the trial.

made no attempt at oratory but with great power he defended the employment of counsel by the managers, on the ground that members of the legislature could not spare the time for the preparation of such a case. He also took occasion to dissent from the view that Congress would interfere with the State on account of the conviction of the governor. He then proceeded to an elaborate review of the testimony which he summed up in a masterly and logical way, and demanded a verdict for the people.[1]

On March 16, the Senate adjourned on account of the illness of Nathaniel Boyden, who had intended to speak on that day. He spoke on the following day, devoting a large part of his speech to discussion of the various legal authorities and to an argument on the impossibility of holding the governor responsible for his execution of an unconstitutional law.[2]

W. N. H. Smith followed and closed for the respondent. He laid stress on the alleged absence of evil intent and denied that a conviction could be obtained without proof of this. He then sought to show the right and duty of the governor to call out and use military force, provided an exigency existed which made it seem necessary, and that the proclamation declaring the insurrection had been rightfully issued and under the requirements of the law, and that the force employed was regularly organized and officered according to law. He also sought, illogically it would seem to a layman, to justify the refusal to obey the writ of *habeas corpus,* acknowledging at the same time that the privilege of the writ could not be legally suspended.[3] By many, this speech was regarded as the ablest delivered during the trial.

Thomas Bragg closed the case for the managers. He

[1] *Impeachment*, pp. 2270-2311.    [2] *Ibid.*, pp. 2317-2366.
[3] *Ibid.*, pp. 2367-2438.

called attention to the appeals for acquittal which had been made to the senators on the ground of policy and condemned the intimations of unfairness made by counsel for the respondent. Said he:

Senators, I have not the least doubt whatever that notwithstanding all this, you will do as you have done heretofore— render a fair and just verdict as you have given the accused a fair and impartial trial. If he is not guilty under the articles which have been preferred against him, in the name of God let him go free; but if he be guilty,—in the name of all that is right and just, pronounce him so, without regard to consequences.

Senators, this is no party trial, no trial in which the political foes of the accused seek to obtain over him a political victory, and punish him for political purposes. It is a trial in which the principles of civil and constitutional liberty, handed down to us by our forefathers, are involved, and the question whether those great principles are to be maintained or whether hereafter they are to be regarded as mere mockery.

He denied that in an impeachment for malfeasance in office there was any necessity for showing corruption or malice. The nature of the act rather than the intent was the main question. Taking up the charges contained in each article, he summed up with great power the evidence proving them and demanded conviction.

An order was at once adopted for a vote on the articles on the following day with a week's time allowed for senators to file opinions. Tremendous interest had been displayed throughout the trial, and the galleries were crowded all the time. Governor Holden, as has been mentioned, was present during the first part of the trial. At times, the evidence was such as to affect him powerfully and he would sigh, groan, and shudder. Before the close of the trial he went to Washington where the " outrage committee " of the

Senate was in session and where he occupied himself with arousing sentiment against the State. He was entirely confident at first, so it is said, that he would be acquitted, but as the trial proceeded, he lost hope. Every attempt was made by his friends to secure an acquittal, and talk of a compromise was everywhere, the Republicans asserting that the withdrawal of the articles would mean the removal of Vance's disabilities. Such talk showed small knowledge of the temper of the people of the State.

On March 22, the vote was taken. Only one senator, Flythe, of Northampton, a Republican, was absent. Each article was read and the roll-call followed. The governor was convicted on all the articles except the first two. The vote was as follows:

| Article. | Guilty. | | | Not Guilty. | | |
|---|---|---|---|---|---|---|
|  | Dem. | Rep. | Total. | Dem. | Rep. | Total. |
| 1 | 30 | 0 | 30 | 6[1] | 13 | 19 |
| 2 | 32 | 0 | 32 | 4[2] | 13 | 17 |
| 3 | 36 | 1[3] | 37 | 0 | 12 | 12 |
| 4 | 33 | 0 | 33 | 3[4] | 13 | 16 |
| 5 | 36 | 4[5] | 40 | 0 | 9 | 9 |
| 6 | 36 | 5[6] | 41 | 0 | 8 | 9 |
| 7 | 36 | 0 | 36 | 0 | 13 | 13 |
| 8 | 36 | 0 | 36 | 0 | 13 | 13 |

The chief justice announced the result, and Sparrow then rose and said,

*Mr. Chief Justice and Senators:*
It having been announced by the chair that the defendant

[1] Cook, Cowles, Flemming, Gilmer, Norment, and Speed.
[2] Cook, Cowles, Flemming, and Norment.
[3] Moore.
[4] Cook, Cowles, and Flemming.
[5] Hawkins, Lehman, McCotter, and Moore.
[6] Barnett, Hawkins, Lehman, McCotter, and Moore.

has been convicted on six of the eight articles of impeachment preferred against him, the managers, speaking through me as their chairman, and in the name of the House of Representatives, and of all the people of North Carolina, demand that the court proceed to judgment against the respondent in this his conviction.

Senator John W. Graham, of Orange, offered the following resolution which was adopted by a party vote: [1]

THE STATE OF NORTH CAROLINA.
### THE SENATE OF NORTH CAROLINA.
MARCH 22, 1871.
*The State vs. William W. Holden.*

Whereas, The house of representatives of the State of North Carolina did, on the 26th day of December, 1870, exhibit to the senate articles of impeachment against William W. Holden, governor of North Carolina, and the said senate, after a full hearing and impartial trial has, by the votes of two-thirds of the members present, this day determined that the said William W. Holden is guilty as charged in the 3d, 4th, 5th, 6th, 7th, and 8th of said articles:

Now therefore, it is adjudged by the senate of North Carolina sitting as a court of impeachment, at their chamber in the city of Raleigh, that the said William W. Holden be removed from the office of governor and be disqualified to hold any office of honor, trust, or profit under the state of North Carolina.

The rights of the people of North Carolina had been vindicated, and a part of their grievous injuries had been avenged. Not soon again was the State to be at the mercy of the ambition and partisan hate of a few reckless men. Not soon again would a public officer disregard the law and

---

[1] Senator Moore, a Republican, announced that he voted against it only on account of the disqualifying clause.

the constitution to the injury of the whole people. The second step in the overthrow of Reconstruction was complete.

### 3. LEGISLATIVE ACTIVITIES

The legislature assembled with a clearly defined intention of speedily undoing as much as possible of the work of Reconstruction, in so far as it affected the prosperity and comfort of the people. Important among the reforms planned was the inauguration of the régime of economy. In connection with this, it was hoped that some settlement of the debt might soon be made, but many of the members wanted delay in this and finally prevailed, chiefly because there was no possible solution other than in repudiation. A committee was appointed to ascertain what the debt amounted to, but further than this nothing was done. Governor Holden in his message advised the scaling of the debt, though he denied that he favored such a policy, declaring that the people would not consent to be taxed two and a half million dollars annually, which was his estimate of the amount necessary to pay the interest and carry on the state government. The wish of the people, he said, should be supreme. The best indication of the temper of the legislature in regard to a portion of the debt is to be found in an act directing the treasurer to use the special tax fund to pay the ordinary expenses of government.[1] In connection with the bonds, a commission to investigate the charges of fraud, consisting of William M. Shipp, J. G. Martin, and J. B. Batchelor, was appointed and made a long investigation, which furnished most of the material relating to North Carolina financial history during the period. One cannot but feel, however, that the investigation might have been made more exhaustive with profit

---

[1] *Laws*, 1870–1871, chap. xix.

to history, though the results would doubtless have been disastrous to certain members of the Conservative party.[1]

In pursuance of the program of economy, the salaries of the state officers and the number of employees were greatly reduced. The salaries of the superintendent of public works and the adjutant-general, for instance, were reduced to $300, and their offices practically destroyed. It was proposed to do the same for the superintendent of public instruction, but wiser counsel prevailed and the salary was only reduced to $1,500. On salaries alone there was an annual saving of $13,520. The *per diem* of the members of the legislature was reduced to five dollars. A majority of the Conservatives wanted it placed at four dollars, but the rest, aided by the Republicans, placed it at the former figure. The office of state printer was abolished and the disposition of the printing put in the hands of a committee, and the code commission was forbidden to make any contracts for printing. The fees of county officers were greatly reduced and a large saving effected in that way.[2] The special city courts for Wilmington and New Bern were abolished and the old special county courts restored.

On the second day of the session, the repeal of the Shoffner act was proposed. This was the first bill introduced in the House. Its mover was F. N. Strudwick, of Orange, and the Republicans at once denounced it as Ku Klux legislation. It passed, however, with but little opposition.[3] A partial offset to this in the minds of many was the passage of an act forbidding the existence of secret political societies. The law was very stringent and even forbade drilling

---

[1] M. S. Robins and Judge George Howard were elected to the commission, but declined to serve.

[2] *Laws*, 1870–1871, chap. cxxxix.

[3] The vote was: Senate, 32–7; House, 79–23.

except by the militia or military schools.[1]   Approval of this act was very general in the press.   The Raleigh *Telegram,* commenting upon it, said, " The leagues of the Republicans and the klans of the Conservatives have already damaged the material interests of North Carolina beyond computation, and their influence will be felt for years to come.   The impeachment trial, now progressing in the State Capital, originated in the organization of these two opposing associations, and over one-half the lawlessness of the State can be traced to their closed doors.   It behooves the good men of both parties to repudiate and condemn them.   Laws should be passed prohibiting them.   They bode no good to a people.   They are a nuisance and an utter abomination and, if continued, will undermine our liberties and subvert the government." [2]

Other laws with the same general purpose were ones defining contempt more clearly and limiting the power of the judges; [3] allowing challenge at the polls and requiring residence in the township as a prerequisite for voting; [4] requiring voters in municipal elections to be electors and to have resided ninety days in the corporation and ten days in the ward; [5] holding judges strictly liable for refusal or failure to grant and have executed the writ of *habeas corpus*; [6] making burglary and arson capital crimes; [7] requiring under heavy penalties the presidents of railroads in which the State had an interest to account to their successors; [8] providing severe punishment for defaulting railroad officials; [9]

---

[1] *Laws*, 1870–1871, chap. cxxxiii.   The vote was: Senate, 42–1; House, 85–14.   The opposition came entirely from Republicans.

[2] Issue of Feb. 10, 1871.

[3] *Laws*, 1870–1871, chap. ccxvi.          [4] *Ibid.*, chap. cxii.

[5] *Ibid.*, chap. xxiv.                              [6] *Ibid.*, chap. ccxxi.

[7] *Ibid.*, chap. ccxxii.                          [8] *Ibid.*, chap. lxxii.

[9] *Ibid.*, chap. ciii.

making the definition of bribery broader;[1] and taking from the governor the power to appoint state proxies and state directors and giving it to the president of the Senate and the speaker of the House.[2]

In connection with this last-mentioned act, it may be well to digress for a moment and show its results. The power of appointment was exercised by the president of the Senate and speaker of the House, who appointed full boards for the various state institutions and directors for the state railways. In a number of cases, the old boards declined to yield, and suits were brought to determine the matter. In all of them the Supreme Court decided in favor of the old boards on the ground that the legislature could not deprive the governor of any of his constitutional powers.[3]

Resolutions were passed directing the governor to furnish the names and salaries of the detectives, and to take all necessary steps to secure the arrest of Swepson and Littlefield. A committee to investigate the conduct of John Pool in relation to the Kirk-Holden war was appointed, the preamble of the resolution being a bitter censure of Pool's recent career. The report of the committee, based chiefly upon the testimony of R. C. Badger, was never acted upon, but, showing Pool's responsibility, produced the political effect desired.[4]

From the beginning of the session, public demands for the impeachment of different officials were frequent, but the leaders were not anxious to make too clean a sweep, even if the punishment was deserved. Probably for this reason Judge Watts was not impeached, though a committee was appointed to investigate his conduct. As has been seen,

[1] *Laws*, 1870-1871, chap. ccxxxii.  [2] *Ibid.*, chap. cclxxxii.
[3] Clark *v.* Stanly, 66 N. C., 59.
[4] *Sentinel*, April 8, 1871.

Chief Justice Pearson was saved by his old students. But there was no question that Judge Jones would be impeached and he only hastened matters when he forced his case upon the attention of the legislature by making a brutal assault, while intoxicated, upon a negro strumpet who was in his room. She promptly had him indicted, and a committee of investigation, which was at once appointed, found that his whole life and conduct had been such as to make him an outcast from the society of decent men. He was promptly impeached, thirteen intense Republicans voting against the resolution; five articles of impeachment, charging him with so many cases of public drunkenness, were drawn up; and a board of managers appointed, headed by S. F. Phillips, the Republican leader in the House. The Senate had organized as a court of impeachment, when a number of leading Republicans, including Chief Justice Pearson and Judge Rodman, induced Jones to resign. Governor Caldwell, in shining contrast to another contemporary chief executive, declined to accept the resignation, since impeachment proceedings had already commenced, and referred the matter to the House, which immediately withdrew the articles, and the court of impeachment adjourned. But for the expense, Jones would have been tried as a public example. To succeed him, Governor Caldwell appointed W. A. Moore, the speaker of the preceding House. About the same time, Judge Settle was appointed minister to Peru, and Nathaniel Boyden succeeded him on the Supreme bench.

The term of Senator Abbott was to expire in March, 1871, and one of the first things before the legislature was the selection of his successor. M. W. Ransom, W. A. Graham, E. J. Warren, Thomas Bragg, A. S. Merrimon, and Z. B. Vance were all mentioned for the place. The chief objection to Vance was the fact that he was laboring under disabilities, but he was confident that they would be removed, and demanded the election. His chief competitor was Ransom, and only the great popularity of Vance secured for him the caucus nomination, and that only after twenty-seven ballots and by a majority of two. On November 30, he was elected over Abbott by a vote of 95 to 43, and shortly thereafter a resolution was passed requesting Congress to remove his disabilities, the same request being made a little later for S. H. Rogers and A. M. Waddell, who had been elected to Congress. Still later, a petition was made for general amnesty. Vance had said repeatedly that he would resign if he was not relieved. During the closing session of the 41st Congress he was not relieved and Senator Abbott succeeded in getting protests against any action sent in by meetings of negroes in Wilmington, and at the opening of the next Congress, claimed the seat on the ground that Vance's election was void, since he was banned, and that therefore, since he himself had received the next largest number of votes, he was entitled to the seat. His claim was one of great impudence, for he was not only not the choice of the State, but his own party voted for him only because he had no chance of election. Otherwise Settle or Phillips, each of whom had his eyes upon the Senate, would have displaced Abbott. As time passed and Vance was not rendered eligible, opposition to him came to the surface. Finally, in March, a negro member introduced a resolution requesting his resignation. This was referred and ignored, but a week later, a Conservative member introduced a similar resolution which was debated at length in the caucus. There Cowles read a letter [1] from John Pool, expressing his certain belief that Vance would soon be relieved, and the resolution was defeated. In the meantime, there was quite a widespread demand in the press for his

---

[1] This letter and a full account of the caucus are to be found in *Sen. Mis. Docs.*, no. 47, p. 346, 42 Cong., 2 sess.

resignation and on March 20, he sent a letter to the Raleigh *Telegram* in which he said that his pledge to resign had been made only to his friends. A bill for his relief had already passed the Senate, but it never came up in the House. A number of Democratic senators asked him to resign, but he refused, though some important Republican measures passed which might have been defeated by one more Democratic vote. The party suffered from the situation, and Vance made many enemies.

The matter of constitutional reform had been a burning one since the last meeting of the legislature and naturally came up for discussion early in the session. Bills on the subject were introduced into both houses, and in December, the Senate committee on constitutional reform reported one favorably which, after reciting the need of amendment of the constitution, directed the governor to issue a proclamation submitting to the people, on April 13, the question of a convention, and providing for the election of delegates at the same time. Under the terms of the act, the convention was to be restricted by being forbidden to touch the homestead and personal property exemption clauses, to deprive colored persons of their rights, to compensate former owners of slaves, to recognize the war debt, to restore corporal punishment, to abolish the public schools, to require an educational or property qualification for voting, to change the ratio between the poll and property taxes, to pass any ordinances of a legislative nature, except for a settlement of the public debt, to change in any way the mechanics' and laborers' lien, and the clauses declaring that there was no right of secession and that the paramount allegiance of every citizen is due the United States. All amendments had to be ratified by the people. When the bill came up for its final reading in the Senate, Lieutenant Governor Caldwell stated that he believed a two-thirds majority necessary, and asked the opinion of the Senate on the question. The Senate voted 28 to 12 that an extraordinary majority was not required, whereupon Caldwell vacated the chair, and the bill passed 28 to 15. A month later, the bill passed the House 65 to 46. The question was a pretty one, for the constitution provided that the legislature could not call a convention except by a two-thirds vote in each house. No other method was mentioned. On the other hand, the original constitution of North Carolina had not provided any method and the convention of 1835 had been called by the vote of the people after the question had been submitted to them by the legislature. It had been a generally accepted doctrine in the State that the right of the people to call a convention could not be taken away, and the best lawyers in the State upheld the position of the legislature.[1]

A few days after the passage of the bill, one hundred and four Conservative members of the legislature issued a statement urging the people to vote a convention and mentioning, as the changes most necessary to reform, a return to the old system of county government, a reduction of the number of officers, and some settlement of the public debt other than by taxation. In the meantime, Governor Caldwell, who had succeeded Holden, asked the opinion of the Supreme Court on the question. Changing their ideas of judicial propriety to suit the occasion, all of the justices except Reade replied and declared the act of the legislature unconstitutional. The governor then called together a number of party leaders and, after consulting them, notified the legislature that he would not issue the proclamation. He, too, had changed, for, in the legislature of 1850, he had voted to submit the question of a convention to the people

[1] For an exceptionally strong defence of the legislature, see B. F. Moore's testimony, *Senate Ku Klux Report*, p. 211.

by a mere majority.[1] His message was followed by a sharp burst of anger from the Conservatives in the legislature and from the Conservative press. A resolution of censure of the governor and the four justices was passed, and a little later, a new convention bill, which ignored the governor and directed the sheriffs to hold the election, was also passed.[2] The election was set for August and the campaign began at once. The legislature adjourned in April, after a session of ninety-seven days, and a majority of the members hastened to enter the contest.

Both parties were exceedingly active, the Republicans retaining their old organization with S. F. Phillips as chairman in place of Holden, and the Conservatives forming a special committee headed by Thomas Bragg. Phillips wrote the Republican address, which, after declaring the law unconstitutional, defended the constitution of 1868, and warned the people that tampering with it would be dangerous and certain to bring immediate federal interference.[3] In 1866, he had taken the ground that the people could by ratification validate a constitution drawn up by an unconstitutional body. The Conservative address emphasized the need of reform and defended the method of calling the convention.[4]

Many Republicans in the legislature were personally in favor of a convention but did not dare to vote in opposition to the party leaders. As the campaign progressed, others expressed themselves favorably on the question. E. W. Pou favored a change if only for the reason that the existing constitution was not the work of the people of North

---

[1] *Journal*, p. 300.

[2] *Laws*, 1870–1871, chap. ccxi. The vote was: Senate, 34–12; House 51–40.

[3] *Sentinel*, June 23, 1871.

[4] *Ibid.*, May 18, 1871.

Carolina.[1] Nathaniel Boyden also wanted a change. The Conservative leaders, almost without exception, favored the movement and the press was overwhelmingly favorable, but as the press was overwhelmingly Conservative, that was to be expected.[2] Against the convention, the Republicans threw all the weight of their influence. Judge Dick took the stump, as did most of the other politicians connected with the administration.[3] Attorney General Akerman came down from Washington and joined in the campaign, warning the people, that if a convention was called, Congress and the President would withdraw their recognition from the State. The *Standard,* claiming to have definite information upon the subject, gave the same warning. The Conservatives continued to appeal to reason with perfectly sound arguments on the need of reform, and the necessity of economy, but the Republicans beat the bushes with threats of a new Reconstruction and warnings that the homestead would be lost, the colored people deprived of their new rights, and the State bankrupted by the expense. Federal officials threatened violators of the revenue laws and those suspected of membership in the Ku Klux. Needless to say, the latter arguments were most effective.

When the results of the election became known, the Conservatives, to their great dismay, found that they had lost and that the convention was defeated. The election figures were:

| | |
|---|---|
| For Convention | 86,007 |
| Against Convention | 95,252 |
| Voting Population | 237,800 |
| Registered | 196,568 |
| Not Voting | 15,309 |
| Not Registered | 41,232 |
| Majority against Convention | 9,245 |

[1] *Sentinel*, June 3, 1871.

[2] There were thirty-six political papers in the State. Twenty-seven Conservative papers favored a convention, seven Republican and two so-called independent papers opposed it.

[3] *Greensboro Patriot*, July 6, 1871.

Forty-one counties gave majorities for and forty-nine against the call. The vote for delegates gave the Conservatives sixty-one and the Republicans fifty-nine. The aggregate vote for Conservative candidates was 84,300 against 74,510 for their opponents. Here was to be found almost the only grain of comfort for the Conservatives, in that it was apparent that a majority of the voters preferred Conservative candidates.

The failure of the convention made the second session of the legislature an important one. In October, the Conservative executive committee published an address urging amendment by legislative action and suggesting certain important changes, chief of which were those providing for the abolition of certain offices, the reduction of salaries, the removal of the University from the control of the board of education, and the striking out of the clause making the public debt inviolable.[1] The address also advised full affiliation with the national Democratic party.

On the first day of the session, a bill providing for these and other amendments was introduced and referred to a joint committee which later reported a bill which passed both houses by the three-fifths majority required by the constitution. The Republicans voted almost solidly against it.[2] It provided for striking out the provisions relating to the state debt, the township system, the state census, the code commission, the superintendent of public works, and for the reduction of the number of Superior and Supreme Court judges, for a biennial election of members of the legislature and biennial sessions with compensation of three hundred dollars for the entire term and ten cents mileage, for placing county government in the hands of the legisla-

[1] *Sentinel*, Oct. 30, 1871.

[2] Three Republican members of the House voted for the bill.

ture, and for a prohibition of holding a plurality of offices. The suggestions mentioned above were also included.

One of the most interesting matters which came before the legislature was the case of Judge Logan. He was violently unpopular in his district, partly because of his political activity which was, however, unusually well concealed, but more on account of his lack of qualifications for his position. In April, 1871, he exhibited great cowardice, or pretended to do so for political effect, and refused to hold court at Shelby.[1] His letter, giving a highly-colored account of conditions in the State, was published in Washington and shortly thereafter, David Schenck, of Lincoln, a prominent lawyer, wrote a letter to Senator Blair in which he used the following language concerning Logan: " He is an ignorant, corrupt, vile man whom no one respects and for whom the whole bar have a sovereign contempt." This was also published, and Judge Logan promptly disbarred Schenck for contempt, only to have his action reversed by the Supreme Court.[2]

In the meantime, a petition declaring Logan's utter incompetency, had been drawn up by the bar of his district and signed by thirty-one lawyers, including the only two Republicans there, exclusive of the solicitor, who was favorable to the movement, but declined to sign the petition from motives of delicacy. This was presented and referred to a committee which declared him disqualified through ignorance and an inefficiency which amounted in effect to a denial of justice to his district. The testimony of the witnesses, among whom were Rufus Barringer, W. H. Bailey, and Judge Boyden, all Republicans, made it clear that he was unfit. The matter was again referred and a

---

[1] For a full account of this matter see *infra*, pp. 575-6.

[2] *Ex parte* Schenck, 65 N. C., 353.

resolution of impeachment was later introduced, and defeated after considerable debate, which showed that the chief grounds of opposition were the expense attendant upon a trial and the fact that it would be regarded outside the State as a Ku Klux prosecution, since others guilty of as serious offences were allowed to escape.

Quite a number of important laws were passed at this session. A genuine attempt was made to bring about a settlement of the debt, and an act was finally passed which provided for the exchange of the corporation stocks held by the State for the bonds by which they had been acquired, except in the case of the special tax bonds and where the stock was specifically pledged.[1] The question of the public debt was regarded by many as of primary importance. A bill providing for a compromise on all except the special tax bonds and those which had already been declared void passed the House, but failed in the Senate. A bill for flat repudiation also failed. The views of the members on the subject were very widely at variance many believing in repudiation; a very few in paying the whole debt. A popular suggestion was to pay the amount the State had received and repudiate the rest, the usual estimate of what had been received being half a million dollars. Other important legislation was a new school law, which strengthened the system greatly,[2] and a re-apportionment of representation in both houses with some slight change in favor of the Conservative party. The bill distributing senatorial representation was frankly a gerrymander but made little change and was no more extreme than the apportionment made by the convention of 1868, which it replaced. The only important change in the congressional districts was the removal of Warren County from the fourth to the second, which made of the latter a " black " district.

---

[1] *Laws*, 1871–1872, chap. xciii.    [2] *Ibid.*, chap. clxxxix.

During the year, no steps had been taken in Congress towards the removal of Vance's disabilities. Much feeling was excited in certain quarters by his retaining the senatorship when all hope of his being seated had disappeared from everyone else, particularly when an additional Democratic vote would count in the legislation then before Congress. A resolution asking for his resignation was introduced in the House but was never allowed to come to a vote. Finally, just before the close of the session, he resigned, and M. W. Ransom was elected. Then only did the Senate committee report adversely to Abbott's claim to a seat. A minority report was presented by Senators Rice and Carpenter, but the majority report was adopted and Ransom seated, John Pool and nine others voting for Abbott. Towards the close of that session of Congress, Vance's disabilities were finally removed.

# CHAPTER FIFTEEN

## THE CLOSING YEARS OF RECONSTRUCTION

### I. THE KU KLUX PROSECUTIONS

ON December 16, 1870, the United States Senate passed a resolution requesting the President to furnish it with information regarding the organization of disloyal persons in North Carolina. In reply, President Grant, early in January, 1871, sent a mass of documentary material dating back to 1865, relating to disorder in the South, and a few days later, sent a letter from Governor Holden, dated January 1, transmitting various documents relating to the Ku Klux, and also sent numerous letters and reports from army officers stationed in the State, most of which were contradictory of the governor's claims. The message and papers were referred to a committee of five,[1] which organized on January 21, and a few days later began the taking of testimony, J. W. Holden being the first witness examined, followed by George W. Kirk and James E. Boyd, all of whom were already there for the purpose. The committee continued its sittings until March, and during that time, examined fifty-three witnesses, thirty-three of whom were Republicans and twenty, Conservatives. Abbott and Pool furnished the committee with the names of persons to be called as witnesses and, assisted by J. W. Holden, prompted the Republican members with questions.

[1] The members of the committee were Senators Scott, Chandler, Wilson, Rice, and Nye.

A large part of the testimony was hearsay, but from it, or rather with it, the majority succeeded in producing a report which declared the existence of the Ku Klux organization, composed of Democrats with a political purpose which it carried out by violence, at the same time protecting its members from punishment by secrecy and perjury, and that the authorities of the State were unable to secure to its citizens life, liberty, and the pursuit of happiness. The minority were able to frame a very strong dissenting report, in which they denounced the investigation as a conspiracy to restore Republican rule in North Carolina where it had so signally failed. They were, of course, unable to deny the existence of the Ku Klux organization, but declared it a natural result of Reconstruction. Both reports are good examples of partisan documents.[1]

On March 23, the President sent another message to Congress in which he said:

A condition of affairs now exists in some of the States of the Union rendering life and property insecure, and the carrying of the mails and the collection of the revenue dangerous. The proof that such a condition of affairs exists in some localities is now before the Senate. That the power to correct these evils is beyond the control of State authorities, I do not doubt. That the power of the Executive of the United States, acting within the limits of existing laws, is sufficient for present emergencies, is not clear.

He therefore recommended suitable legislation, and in pursuance of his recommendation, an act to enforce the provisions of the Fourteenth Amendment became a law on April 20. This act, in which, as Professor Burgess says, " Congress simply threw to the winds the constitutional

[1] The reports, with the testimony, form a volume of 588 pages. See *Senate Report*, no. 1, 42 Cong., 1 sess.

distribution of powers between the States and the United States Government in respect to civil liberty, crime and punishment," ignored the fact that the Fourteenth Amendment gave Congress power only against state action, and provided for the arrest, trial, and punishment of individuals by the federal courts, and made all persons depriving another of rights under the Constitution liable to the party injured in heavy damages. It prescribed penalties for conspiring against the United States or for the hindrance of any of its laws. Penalties were imposed for going upon the highways in disguise with the intent to hinder anyone in the exercise of rights guaranteed by the Constitution. The President was authorized to take such measures as he might deem best to suppress the trouble, and was given power, when the civil authority was powerless to perform its functions, to proclaim any portion of a State or the entire State in a condition of insurrection and to suspend the writ of *habeas corpus.*

Before the passage of this act, a joint committee was appointed and began a prolonged investigation designed to furnish campaign material for the Republican party.[1] The results of the investigation were reported to the next session of Congress in thirteen volumes.[2] Of it, Mr. William Garrott Brown says, " From these volumes, he who lives long enough to read it all, may learn much that is true, but not important; much that is important, if true; and somewhat that is both true and important." Nineteen witnesses

---

[1] The members of the committee on the part of the Senate were Scott, Rice, Chandler, Bayard, Pratt, Blair, and Pool; on the part of the House, Poland, Maynard, Schofield, Farnsworth, Coburn, Lansing, Cox, Stephenson, Van Trump, Beck, Butler, Hanks, Waddell, and Robinson. Blair, Beck, Bayard, Cox, Van Trump, Waddell, Robinson, and Hanks were Democrats.

[2] *Ho. Report*, no. 22, 42 Cong., 2 sess. This will hereafter be called *Joint Report.*

were examined for North Carolina, of whom nine were Republicans, including three carpetbaggers and two negroes. The most notable witness was William L. Saunders, head of the Invisible Empire, who appeared before the committee and declined to answer any question relating to the Ku Klux. He was bullied and threatened, but stood steadfast and quietly defiant until the end, when he was dismissed without any action's being taken against him,[1] though his case was referred to the Senate for action. In strong contrast, was the testimony of David Schenck who, after avoiding appearance as a witness, suddenly developed a great eagerness to appear and unbosom himself of all that he knew in connection with the organization.[2] Most of the testimony taken had to do with affairs in Cleveland and Rutherford which have already been described.

When the news of the Justice raid reached Judge Logan, he saw an opportunity to use it for political profit. For some time, he had displayed uneasiness and fear of interference by the Klan and had sent a representative in the person of Victor C. Barringer to President Grant to ask for the protection of federal troops. The answer had naturally been that any request for such aid must come from the governor. Logan now wrote to Governor Caldwell asking what he should do, stating that he had no confidence in the county officials of his district or in the militia, and expressing a desire for " blue coats." [3] When the Biggarstaff trouble arose, he at once notified the governor who asked for and obtained troops from the President.[4] Logan then found and complained of a new grievance in the fact

---

[1] *Joint Report*, pp. 354-362. Waddell: *Life and Character of W. L. Saunders*.

[2] *Joint Report*, pp. 362–414.

[3] *Executive Correspondence*, Caldwell, p. 36.

[4] *Ibid.*, pp. 81, 84.

that the officers would not call upon him socially. Now when the Justice raid occurred, he wrote the governor a report of it in which he said that he could not hold the Cleveland court because of the danger to himself, and sending the letter to Raleigh, although he knew that the governor was in Morganton a few miles away, he directed the messenger to carry it on to Washington where it arrived at the psychological moment—just before the vote on the amnesty bill, which was probably defeated by the publication of the letter.

When the news reached Shelby that the judge would not hold the court, the citizens of the town and county held a meeting and sent the sheriff with an escort to protect the judge, who, however, declined to come, although the solicitor, W. P. Bynum, urged him to do so, assuring him that there was no danger.

When the account of conditions in the West reached Governor Caldwell, he at once summoned a meeting of leading Conservatives and Republicans, and a special court was decided upon. Chief Justice Pearson urged that the best way to settle the trouble was to make Logan resign. The special court was never held. A little later a large number of influential Conservatives joined in an appeal to the people to put down lawlessness of every sort and to cooperate with the officers of the law in bringing offenders to justice. In the meantime, Judge Cloud and the attorney general went to Rutherford to look into conditions there.[1]

By this time, Judge Logan's fears had apparently vanished, and he was busily engaged in issuing bench warrants for every person whose name was brought before him. A large number were arrested and brought to Rutherfordton, where they were confined without trial or bail. The town

---

[1] *Executive Correspondence*, Caldwell, p. 93.

was under military control with all the roads leading into it picketed to prevent any rescue of the prisoners. During the next two months, there was great activity on the part of the United States deputy marshals throughout the west. Over one hundred men were arrested, a large number of them without warrant, a number of them imprisoned without hearing or bail, and the rest examined before the United States commissioner, Nathan Scoggins, a recent Republican acquisition and a man of evil life and character who was later removed from office for accepting bribes. The officer most active in the arrests was Joseph G. Hester, another person of ill fame who was later still more notorious for his activities in Alabama. Both had been Ku Klux.[1] Every possible indignity was heaped upon the prisoners, who were denied every comfort and almost starved while confined in filthy prisons. Twenty-two were kept in jail and seventy-one bound over to court. The Circuit Court in June refused to try the cases and adjourned to September, the jury having been discharged in order that one better suited to the purpose might be obtained. S. F. Phillips, who had been appointed assistant district attorney, instructed the marshal to select for the new one only such men as would be inclined to convict the prisoners, and in consequence the jury was made up of partisan Republicans. Two of the grand jury were illiterate negroes. The character of the trial jury may be inferred from the fact that some of the jurors repeatedly offered to sell an acquittal to Randolph Shotwell.[2]

The Circuit Court of the United States met in the Senate

---

[1] J. G. Hester had been on the "Sumter" during the war and had there been guilty of murder. For a time he had commanded a blockade runner and was intense in his hatred of the North and the Republicans. From the close of the war, he was in real-estate business in North Carolina until he became one of Holden's private detectives.

[2] Shotwell Manuscript in possession of the author.

○

chamber in Raleigh in September with Judge Hugh L. Bond presiding. Only three cases were tried, those being for the Justice and the two Biggarstaff raids. Forty persons were indicted for participation in these. The indictments in the case of eight were dropped, eleven were acquitted, and twenty-seven convicted. The trials were marked by great partisan activity. The government was represented by D. H. Starbuck, assisted by V. S. Lusk and S. F. Phillips. For the defence, a number of leading lawyers volunteered, including Thomas Bragg, D. G. Fowle, Plato Durham, and T. C. Fuller. Plato Durham was under indictment himself, but there was not any evidence against him, so the case was continued. Judge Bond's behavior was doubtful for a judge who cared to appear unbiased, but he was lacking in any sense of decency and, throughout the trials, was in close touch with the prosecution and assumed in court the position of prosecutor. This was of course what he had been chosen for, but its effect was unfortunate. During the trials Governor Caldwell was very active, conducting an informal examination of the witnesses in the hope of implicating some leading Conservatives, particularly Josiah Turner. The chief efforts of the prosecution were directed to securing the conviction of Randolph Shotwell who, as an editor in Asheville and in Rutherfordton, had been a source of much discomfort to the Republicans. When it is remembered that criticism of the Republican party was announced by S. F. Phillips in the trial to be an attack upon the United States government,[1] it can readily be seen that to secure Shotwell's removal from political life was in the eyes of the prosecution an act of the highest patriotism and altogether proper for " loyal " men. Shotwell was county chief of the Ku Klux in Rutherford County, having assumed the position

---

[1] *Wilmington Journal*, Sept. 26, 1871; Oct. 5, 1871.

at the request of a number of leading men in the hope of checking the movement. He had never been on a raid or ordered one and had sought to prevent the raid on Justice and on the *Star* office, but had been utterly unable to control the men, many of them entirely unknown to him, who were bent upon carrying out their plan. Most of his witnesses were out of the State and he knew that any others he might summon would at once be made parties defendant in the same case. Many of those who were tried upon the same indictment were seen by him then for the first time. Relying upon his innocence, he stood his trial without much fear of conviction. The false evidence against him had been carefully prepared, and, upon it, he was convicted and sentenced to a fine of five thousand dollars and six years' imprisonment in Albany. As soon as sentence was passed upon him, he was tied with ropes in the presence of the court and carried in that condition through the streets of Raleigh, not because there was any fear of his escape, but simply to humiliate him and for the effect it would have upon the public. When he was on his way to Albany, C. L. Cobb came down from Washington to travel with him on the boat and, in behalf of the President, offered him immediate pardon if he would implicate some of the leading Conservatives in the State. The offer was indignantly rejected. Soon after he reached Albany, Gerrit Smith visited him at the request of President Grant and made a similar proposal which was also declined. Shotwell was not the sort of man to betray a trust and, though deserted in his adversity by many who should from any consideration of honor have stood by him, he kept silence and endured the horrors of his imprisonment until he was finally pardoned.

At the close of the trials, a number of Conservative lawyers wrote Judge Bond asking for a continuance of the other cases until the next year, pledging themselves to the dissolution of the Ku Klux and the restoration of order. He declined to grant their request and at once gave out the letter to be used in the Northern press as evidence that the leading Conservatives were involved in the Ku Klux movement.[1]

In the meantime, the operations of the deputy marshals, more lawless still by far than those of the Ku Klux and more dangerous to the spirit of free institutions, continued without cessation.   Arrest without warrant, imprisonment without a hearing and with bail denied, were characteristic of their activities.   D. S. Ramsour, a student at Wake Forest College, was arrested while attending a meeting of his literary society and dragged out forcibly, not because the time was particularly suitable, but because the officers had waited, knowing that it would attract attention and increase fear.   Josiah Turner, who was an attorney at law, advised several persons, arrested without warrant and without cause, to indict the marshal.   He was at once arrested on a charge of obstructing the officers of the law in the discharge of their duties, and, through the efforts of Republican politicians, notably S. F. Phillips, his trial was refused for several years.   Dr. Brinton Smith, a Northern clergyman who was at the head of a negro school in Raleigh, was indicted for conspiracy under the Ku Klux Act because he told one of his students who was under age that he was not entitled to vote.   The case was dismissed a year later without trial. Against many Ku Klux in the west were indictments for violation of the internal revenue laws.   These were dismissed if a promise was made to give evidence against the Ku Klux.   W. F. Henderson, the assessor of internal revenue, offered freedom to anyone who would give evidence implicating J. M. Leach, who in 1870, had defeated him for

[1] *Charlotte Democrat*, Oct. 10, 1871.

Congress.[1] Hundreds of persons were imprisoned at one time or another, many of whom were treated with great cruelty, and all the safeguards of liberty disappeared. The federal courts became instruments of oppression and wrong and have never since been popular in the State. The chief purpose of it all was political, although the officers reaped a rich harvest from fees and from the bribes which they did not refuse, provided always that they were large enough. In pursuance of the plan, when the fears of the public had been sufficiently aroused, there came the promise of immunity on condition of support of the Republican ticket at the next election. At the spring term of the federal court in Raleigh in 1872, over fourteen hundred persons were indicted under the Ku Klux Act, of whom only six were tried. Between that time and the election, the activity of the officers continued. As soon as the campaign was over, the arrests stopped, and in February, 1873, the United States marshal ordered the suspension of the processes. During 1873, all the prisoners in Albany were pardoned. The Ku Klux organization had long since disappeared never to reappear, but the Republicans made its existence an issue in many campaigns thereafter and skilfully attempted to intimidate by threats of renewed federal activity.

## 2. THE ELECTIONS OF 1872 [2]

Both parties looked forward with deep interest to the campaign of the summer of 1872, which bade fair to be the most exciting in the history of the State. State issues of the utmost importance were to be settled, the Republicans were seeking desperately to recover the ground lost in 1870, and the Conservatives were striving not only to maintain their advantage, but also to win the executive department

[1] *Greensboro Patriot*, Nov. 30, 1871.
[2] Reprinted from *South Atlantic Quarterly* of April, 1912.

and to gain such a majority in the legislature as would enable them to remedy the glaring defects of the constitution of 1868. Nor was this all. For the first time in its history, the State had an election that was of national importance and interest, since it would take place in August and, preceding all others, would be regarded as an index of the state of feeling in the country, and would influence the result in November.

The campaign was commenced in March by the Republicans, who held county meetings which were almost without exception controlled by federal office-holders. Late in March, Daniel R. Goodloe and H. H. Helper issued a call for Liberal Republican conventions to meet in each county and congressional district, and also for a state convention to be held in May. Helper, shortly before this, had been engaged in an acrimonious controversy with John Pool over the latter's recommendation of an embezzler to be special mail agent for North Carolina. This led to Helper's giving information to Secretary Boutwell and the press as to the conditions existent in the internal revenue service in the State. He was promptly removed from his position as postmaster of Salisbury, and, with strong public condemnation of the whole national administration from President Grant down, he now, joined by Goodloe, who for some years had felt decidedly out of place in the Republican party, recanted and joined the Liberal movement. The truth of Helper's charges was clearly recognized by many of the party who evinced an honest desire to secure reform. The Raleigh *Era,* now the organ of the Republican party, said, " The party has been too long weighted down by a set of men of tainted reputation and known criminal acts who are generally believed to have attached themselves to it for the purpose of plunder." [1]    But the influence of the corrupt

---

[1] Quoted in Raleigh *News*, May 15, 1872.

element, with its hold upon the negro vote and its reliance upon the support of many honest but bitterly prejudiced partisans, was too strong, and there was little hc)e for permanent reform in their part of state politics and none at all in the federal service where corruption was limited only by the boundaries of the United States.

In the Republican party, the contestants in the race for the gubernatorial nomination were Governor Caldwell, Judge Settle, Oliver H. Dockery, and George W. Logan. The last two were, however, negligible in the contest, the chief interest being in the candidacy of Settle and Caldwell. The former was sustained by the Holden wing of the party and depended also on influence from Washington, but Governor Caldwell had much greater strength in the State. The chief question to be decided, therefore, was how great an influence could be exerted from Washington.

The state convention met in Raleigh on April 17, with representation from seventy-eight counties. James H. Harris, of Wake, was made temporary chairman,[1] and made a speech upon taking the chair in which he thanked the convention for the honor paid him as the representative of 80,000 negro voters, and declared that the time had come when the black man demanded and must have perfect social equality for himself and his wife and children " on your cars, on your steam-boats, and at the tables and in the parlors of your hotels." [2]   After much confusion and speeches by all four candidates and one by John Pool, Samuel F. Phillips was elected permanent president. Late in the afternoon, the first ballot was taken, and Governor Caldwell received the nomination with a majority of nine votes. If

---

[1] This was done at the instance of Samuel F. Phillips.

[2] *Sentinel*, April 25, 1872. The negroes of Wilmington had shortly before adopted resolutions demanding to be more than hewers of wood and drawers of water.

he had failed to secure the nomination on the first ballot, he would probably have lost strength steadily thereafter.

When the nominations for the other offices were reached, eight men were presented for the lieutenant governorship.[1] Curtis H. Brogden was chosen on the second ballot. Tazewell L. Hargrove was unanimously nominated for attorney general. Ten names were brought forward for secretary of state, two of them of negroes, and W. H. Howerton was chosen. D. A. Jenkins was renominated for treasurer over S. H. Wiley. John Reilly, a carpetbagger, was nominated for auditor. Silas Burns, another carpetbagger, was named for superintendent of public works, and James Reid, a retired minister of over seventy years of age, for superintendent of public instruction. The latter nomination was the work of John Pool who wished to defeat Alexander McIver, the other candidate, and a very suitable man, because he favored a reorganization of the University which would have deprived Solomon Pool of his honorary position of president.

A platform was adopted endorsing the administration of Grant and Caldwell, and making certain demands, chief of which were the removal of internal revenue taxes, particularly on spirits, a general amnesty bill, protection of the civil and political rights of all citizens, and national aid to education. The so-called Ku Klux legislation was warmly endorsed and more demanded. The proposed constitutional amendments were condemned as a forced issue, but the convention refused to go on record in opposition to all of them. Resolutions requesting the seating of Abbott in the United States Senate and endorsing ex-Governor Holden were passed, and the convention adjourned.

[1] R. L. Patterson, Curtis H. Brogden, C. L. Harris, G. W. Price, a New Hanover negro; John B. Respass, Joseph W. Holden, A. S. Seymour, a carpetbagger; and Tazewell L. Hargrove.

In the Conservative ranks there was considerable interest as to the candidate for governor. The leaders wanted Vance, but Vance declined to run and was not to be moved by any of the pleadings of his friends. Augustus S. Merrimon was then selected, but he was equally unwilling and at first refused to make the race. The leaders finally assured him that it was absolutely necessary for the party that he should be the candidate and that, if he was defeated, he should be elected to the United States Senate. This was a fairly safe promise as the legislature was almost certain to be Conservative. He then consented to accept the nomination.

The Democratic convention met in Greensboro on May 1, with delegates from eighty-five counties. Thomas C. Fuller was made temporary chairman and John Kerr, president, Speeches were made at the opening by Thomas L. Clingman, John Kerr, and Z. B. Vance, all endorsing the Cincinnati platform and candidates. A. S. Merrimon, J. M. Leach, and D. M. Barringer were placed in nomination for governor. Josiah Turner and W. M. Shipp were also named but withdrew at once. Merrimon was nominated on the first ballot, and the entire ticket was then filled, all the nominations but one being by acclamation.[1] A platform was adopted calling for reform, condemning secret political societies, the Ku Klux acts, internal revenue taxes with politically active officials, the recent action of the Republicans in endorsing Abbott and Holden and in calling for national aid to education. Civil service reform and the proposed amendments to the state constitution were endorsed. After the organization was perfected and plans

---

[1] The other nominations were: Secretary of State, John A. Womack; Treasurer, John W. Graham; Attorney General, W. M. Shipp; Auditor, C. Leventhorpe; Superintendent of Public Works, J. Separk; and Superintendent of Public Instruction, Nereus Mendenhall.

made for a vigorous campaign, the convention adjourned. A very noticeable thing in this convention, and in the nominations all over the State, was the avoidance of candidates who labored under disabilities. The experience with Vance had not failed to teach the party a lesson, and no chances were taken. Another noticeable thing was the prominence of old Whigs among the Conservative candidates for office. Every candidate for Congress, for instance, had been a Whig prior to the war. For this reason, a distinction was often made between the names Conservative and Democrat.

Judge Settle, early in the year, resigned his position as minister to Peru and returned home. The position was at once offered to Holden, but he did not care for it and declined. Judge Settle was permanent president of the national Republican convention which met at Philadelphia, and thus far he is the only Southern Republican who ever held that position. His choice was probably due to President Grant who held him in high personal esteem. Judge Dick was soon after made judge of the western district and Settle succeeded him on the supreme bench.

The campaign began in earnest as soon as the Republican convention adjourned. Caldwell took the stump and, when the Conservative nominations were made, Merrimon joined him. The joint debate did not continue long, for the governor found himself no match for Merrimon as a campaigner and declined to continue with him. The two spoke on the same day at Pittsboro, and Caldwell promptly accused Merrimon of having been the author of the various railroad bills which Swepson had had passed in the interest of his nefarious schemes. Merrimon was forced to acknowledge the truth of the charge, but defended himself by the statement that he had drawn them simply as a lawyer under the direction of his client. The advantage that Caldwell might well have gained from this injurious admission was at once destroyed by Merrimon's readiness in the *tu quoque* argument when he showed Caldwell's part in securing their passage. The joint debate was then abandoned, and the governor visited many places in the State and, though continuing his attacks upon his opponent, devoted most of his attention to a discussion of the part the Conservatives had played in bringing on the war, condemning their conduct of it, and interspersing in his speeches the usual Ku Klux campaign material. His campaign was frankly an appeal to prejudice, and he relied largely upon the solid negro vote and the influence which would be exerted for him by federal officers. Merrimon's campaign was on a higher plane. His speeches were scathing indictments of the Republican administration of the affairs of the State, and contained but few personalities.

In the meantime, the congressional candidates had also been nominated,[1] and the contest became increasingly interesting. The Liberal Republican organization gave its support to the Conservative candidates, nearly all of whom had accepted Greeley, but some with manifest restiveness under the burden. This feeling was very strong with many Conservatives in the State. Vance, for instance, said it was " eating crow " with a vengeance. The whole truth of the matter is that it was almost an impossiblity to arouse any enthusiasm in North Carolina for Greeley among those who had disliked him, to use a mild term, for long years, and the pledge of support by political leaders carried with it no certainty of activity among the rank and file of the voters.

[1] The candidates were as follows: 1st district, Republican, C. L. Cobb, Conservative, D. M. Carter; 2d, Charles R. Thomas, W. H. Kitchin; 3d, Neill McKay, A. M. Waddell; 4th, W. A. Smith, S. H. Rogers; 5th, Thomas Settle, J. M. Leach; 6th, O. H. Dockery, Thomas S. Ashe; 7th, D. M. Furches, W. M. Robbins; 8th, W. G. Candler, R. B. Vance.

From the beginning of July, both parties, with outside assistance, maintained a determined fight which lasted until the election. Among those who came to the support of Merrimon was Colonel A. K. McClure, of Pennsylvania, who had seen something of Republican misrule in the State in 1869, and who said, upon mature reflection, that the state administration " was surrounded by the most corrupt and reckless gang of men I have ever met, although I have had every opportunity to test the qualities of the carpet-bag rulers of the Carolinas and Virginia." [1]   In this campaign, he waxed eloquent on the subject. Others who came in advocacy of Merrimon were Carl Schurz, one of the origi-nators of the Liberal Republican movement, ex-Senator Miller, of Georgia, Senator Tipton, of Nebraska, and Gov-ernor Walker, of Virginia. In behalf of Caldwell, came ex-Governor Harriman, of New Hampshire, Secretary Boutwell, Secretary Delano, Senator Henry Wilson, the Republican candidate for Vice-President, and many of lesser note. Senator Wilson declined to meet any of the Conservative speakers in joint debate, and Secretary Bout-well, in his Greensboro speech, protested against " shaking hands across the bloody chasm." [2]   Unlimited funds were promised if needed, and large sums were furnished. John Pool had a large amount at his disposal, and Abbott at one time received for distribution $25,000. Patronage was em-ployed also, a characteristic example being the appointment of C. L. Harris, J. C. L. Harris, and John A. Hyman, the latter a negro who had been defeated for the congressional nomination in the second district by the strenuous efforts of his white Republican allies, as assistant assessors of internal revenue with duties that were political only.

[1] This quotation is taken from a letter to the author, dated Oct. 29, 1907.

[2] *Greensboro Patriot*, July 24, 1872.

The most potent ally of the Republicans, however, was the United States Department of Justice, ably assisted, it is true, by the Treasury Department. Probably there was never in any other State such wholesale political activity and interference by federal officials, with the full approval of the administration, as marked this campaign in North Carolina. Twelve hundred and eight persons had been indicted by February, under the Ku Klux acts,[1] and by the time of election this number had been nearly doubled. An army of revenue officials were appointed for service during the campaign, and their activity was tremendous. Assessor Perry made no secret of the fact that the service was entirely turned over to politics, and the plan was most effectual. United States commissioners issued blank warrants to deputy marshals who used them for election purposes or for blackmail.[2] Just before the election three thousand persons were under arrest by the federal authorities, and most of them were promised that the cases against them would be dropped if their influence should be used for the Republican candidates. An indication of what was going on is to be seen in a comparison of the expenses of the federal courts prior to 1872 and during that year. Before 1872, $5,000, covered all expenses other than salaries. In that year, Marshall Carrow obtained from the treasury $250,000.[3] Bribery and intimidation were chiefly employed in the west where illicit distilling and the Ku Klux gave pretexts.[4] In the east, reliance was placed on the heavy negro vote.

[1] *Sentinel*, February 5, 1872.

[2] *Ibid.*, Feb. 1, 1872.

[3] Raleigh *News*, quoting *Washington Patriot*.

[4] David A. Jenkins, the state treasurer, offered to testify as to the outrages of revenue officials in Gaston county. *Charlotte Democrat*, Oct. 8, 1872.

No one in the State was more interested in the result of the election than John Pool.  Reference has been made to the campaign fund placed at his disposal.  With this as a basis, he established headquarters at Raleigh and directed his campaign against Merrimon, whom he feared, whether elected or not.  He published a pamphlet against him which resulted in a libel suit by Merrimon at the close of the campaign.  But Pool's influence was manifestly waning.

The election was held on August 1, amid intense interest on the part of the whole country.  Fraud was evident in many parts of the State on election day, although most of that sort of thing had already been done.  Over two hundred negroes were fraudulently registered in one township in Halifax County.[1]  Nine hundred negroes were sent from Washington City to Norfolk and thence distributed throughout the State to vote.  Six hundred of these were in the employment of the board of public works and were shipped South on the "Vanderbilt" on July 27, and brought back on August 4.[2]  Negroes were also brought in from South Carolina, Virginia, and Tennessee.  The following table of excess of the vote cast above the voting strength in some of the Republican strongholds is enlightening.  The two counties last named went Democratic:

| | |
|---|---:|
| Bladen | 46 |
| Cumberland | 321 |
| Duplin | 526 |
| Swain | 183 |
| Franklin | 265 |
| Halifax | 852 |
| Nash | 496 |
| Northampton | 184 |
| Robeson | 171 |
| Sampson | 145 |

[1] *News*, July 30, 1872.          [2] *Ibid.*, Aug. 28, 1872.

The first returns that came in indicated a Democratic victory, and there was great rejoicing in the party. Events proved that it was ill-timed, for the returns from many of the Republican counties were held back, and, when they came in, Caldwell's vote was materially increased. At the end of a week, his election on the face of the returns was assured. The cry of fraud which had gone up on election day was now redoubled, and there was a widespread popular demand that Merrimon should contest the election. The Greeley papers in the North, charging fraud, also insisted upon this.[1] Merrimon was willing to contest if the proofs of fraud were convincing, but only on that condition, and he left the decision of the question to the Conservative state executive committee.[2] On October 20, the Conservative and Liberal Republican executive committees met in joint session to decide the matter and came to the conclusion that it was best not to contest. The official vote stood as follows:

Caldwell.......................................... 98,132
Merrimon ......................................... 96,234
Caldwell's majority .............................. 1,898

Merrimon carried fifty-four counties, but the heavy adverse majorities in several of the black counties defeated him.

No doubt can be entertained that, if the campaign and election had been fairly conducted, the result would have been a complete Conservative victory. As it was, the legislature was won.

With the close of the state campaign, the Conservatives lost heart, and the result in November soon became a fore-

[1] The *New York Herald*, the *New York World*, the *New York Tribune*, and the *Washington Patriot* all have much interesting material bearing on this election. All of them made charges of fraud.

[2] Letter to S. A. Ashe in *Carolina Messenger*, Sept. 19, 1872.

gone conclusion. Dislike of Greeley, dormant at first, was revived and soon became apparent. Where there was not active dislike, there was apathy, and this marked the two closing months of the campaign. A number of leading Republicans came to the support of Greeley, among them being Lewis Hanes and R. M. Henry. There was also an interesting and quite considerable negro Liberal organization,[1] but no serious inroads were made on Republican strength. The nomination of Charles O'Conor by the " Straight-Out Democrats," in spite of vigorous efforts on the part of the Republicans to promote it, injured the Democratic party scarcely at all. Plato Durham was the only Democrat of prominence who joined in the movement, and there is good reason to believe that his part in it was the result of an agreement which bore testimony to his self-sacrifice.[2]

There was no need of fraud in November, for the indifference of the " stay-at-home " Democrats accomplished for the Republicans all that they could have desired. Grant carried the State by a majority of 24,675, the total vote being 164,863. His total vote, 94,769, showed a loss of only 3,363 from Caldwell's vote, while Greeley with a total of 70,094 votes lost 26,140 from Merrimon's total. Grant carried fifty-five counties as contrasted with forty-one carried by Caldwell. The figures are convincing proof of how widespread was the dissatisfaction with Greeley and how small the hope of victory. Several political changes were made during the election. The distinction between Conservatives and Democrats became more marked. Little fric-

[1] One Cross, a Greeley negro in Raleigh, was assaulted by negroes because of his politics. One of his assailants was prosecuted under the Ku Klux act and convicted. *News*, July 24, 1872;

[2] There is much ground for the belief that Durham was told by certain prominent officials that if he would support O'Conor and later act with the Republicans, all the Ku Klux prosecutions in his county would be dropped.

tion was so far apparent, but it was clearly seen it would soon develop. In the Republican party there was an evident tendency on the part of the natives to ignore the carpetbaggers, and, so far as possible, to keep all the offices to themselves, but the plan thus far was accompanied by little success by reason of the strong hold which the strangers had upon the negro vote.

Although the result of the year was in reality favorable to the Conservatives, since they retained the legislature, from the party standpoint it lacked completeness, and it was accompanied by many bitter disappointments.

### 3. THE LEGISLATURE OF 1872-1874

The legislature of 1872 differed little from its predecessor in the character of its membership. The most interesting facts concerning it were its youth and legislative inexperience. A very large number had been in the Confederate army. Fifty-four were farmers and forty-five lawyers.[1] The political affiliation of the members was as follows:

|  | Senate. | House. | Joint Ballot. |
|---|---|---|---|
| Conservatives | 32 | 66 | 98 |
| Republicans | 18 | 54 | 72 |

Of the Republicans, four in the Senate[2] and twelve in the House[3] were negroes. Two carpetbaggers were in the Senate.[4] There was one contest in which the Conservative

---

[1] The other occupations of the members were distributed as follows: merchants, 19; physicians, 12; ministers, 7; manufacturers, 5; teachers, 4; revenue officials, 4; scattering, 20.

[2] J. H. Harris, J. A. Hyman, G. L. Mabson, and Eppes.

[3] Abbott, Dudley, W. P. Mabson, Bunn, Williamson, Hughes, McLaurin, Lloyd, Fletcher, Ellison, King, and Paschall.

[4] A. S. Seymour and H. E. Stilley.

was seated but later displaced by his Republican opponent. G. L. Mabson, a negro member of the Senate, was found to be a resident of Beaufort instead of Edgecombe, the county he represented, and was expelled during the second session.

Much interest was aroused by the contest for Pool's seat in the Senate. Merrimon had been promised the election by certain leaders as a reward for running against Caldwell, but Vance was a candidate and by making a persistent campaign had succeeded in pledging a majority of the Conservatives before the legislature met. For that reason, many Conservatives thought the vote of the caucus should not be binding and a number refused to regard it. The Republicans sought desperately to re-elect Pool, promising that if he was returned, there would be general amnesty proclaimed for the Ku Klux by the federal government, and that liberal appropriations would be made for internal improvements in the State, including four million dollars for the Western North Carolina Railroad. In addition, threats were made of the arrest of members of the legislature, as in the recent case in Alabama,[1] if he were not chosen.[2]

When the election of senator came, seven Conservatives in the Senate,[3] disregarding the action of the caucus, voted for A. S. Merrimon. In the House, eleven members[4] did likewise. Of these eighteen, none from the Senate and only three from the House were returned to the next legislature. By their action, Vance lacked seven votes of an election on the first ballot. Six days' voting made no change except that Vance lost strength slightly and Merrimon's

[1] Fleming: *Civil War and Reconstruction in Alabama*, pp. 755–56.

[2] Raleigh *News*, Nov. 21, 1872.

[3] Avera, Cowles, Humphrey, Love, Merrimon, Powell, and Welch.

[4] Anderson of Clay, Bryson of Swain, Dickey, Hanner, Haynes, Hinnant, Joyner, Marler, Moring, Waugh, and Whitmire.

vote rose to thirty-one. On November 30, Vance withdrew
" in the interest of harmony " and Merrimon followed suit.
On the following ballot sixty-five persons received votes,
Pool's vote falling to fifty-nine and Merrimon coming second with nine. The Conservative caucus met and again
nominated Vance and, on the next day, the Republicans
abandoned Pool, and, voting solidly for Merrimon, who
was still supported by most of the bolting Conservatives,
elected him. The Conservatives were very angry and much
hard feeling was stirred up.[1] The Republicans were correspondingly elated, Pool declaring it a Republican victory,
and sedulously endeavored to alienate the Conservatives
from Merrimon by creating the impression that he had been
bought. They stated that he would act with the Republican party in the Senate, that a bargain to that effect had
been made before he received a Republican vote; but his
course there soon dispelled any illusions they may have had
in regard to his intentions.

One of the most important matters before the legislature
was the bill for amending the constitution, passed by the
preceding legislature. This came up and was divided into
separate bills, eight of which were adopted.[2] Those passed
provided for striking out the clause requiring the legislature to levy a tax to pay interest on the public debt, for
omitting the census, for abolishing the code commission and
the office of superintendent of public works, for placing the
trustees of the University under the legislature, for extending the three hundred dollars exemption to all property, for
making federal and state officers ineligible to the legislature, and for biennial sessions of the legislature.

[1] *Laws*, 1872–1873, chaps. lxxxi–lxxxviii.

[2] The best accounts of the contest are to be found in the Raleigh
*News* for January, 1873.

Probably one of the most interesting measures before the legislature was one extending amnesty to any person who had committed any crime except rape, deliberate and wilful murder, arson, or burglary, while a member of the Heroes of America, Loyal Union League, Red Strings, Constitutional Union Guard, White Brotherhood, Invisible Empire, Ku Klux Klan, North Carolina State Troops, North Carolina Militia, Jay Hawkers, or any other association, whether secret, political, or otherwise, in obedience to the commands and decrees of such organization, provided the offence was committed prior to September 1, 1871.[1] This passed the Senate by a vote of 25 to 15, a number of the Conservatives voting against it. The vote in the House was strictly a party one, 57 to 50.

Several resolutions of interest were passed, including one requesting Congress to remove the disabilities of thirteen persons named and all other citizens of the State who were still laboring under them.[2] This was introduced by R. C. Badger, the Republican leader in the legislature, and promptly passed both houses. Shortly after the introduction of this, he proposed a resolution for the removal from W. W. Holden of the disqualification to hold office of honor, trust, or profit under the State. This was postponed indefinitely in the House by a party vote,[3] and a similar resolution in the Senate failed to pass its second reading by a party vote.[4]

The condition of the penitentiary was investigated for the second time since the Conservative victory, and the report of the committee showed that the institution was still

---

[1] *Laws*, 1872–1873, chap. clxxxi.

[2] Those named were W. A. Graham, Lawrence S. Baker, W. N. H. Smith, Burton Craige, David Coleman, James G. Martin, D. H. Hill, George Davis, W. H. McRae, and John T. Williams.

[3] *Journal*, p. 287.        [4] *Ibid.*, p. 431.

badly managed. The committee attempted to put the blame for this on the governor who had refused to recognize the Conservative board of directors and, declining to sign their warrants, had prevented them from buying proper and sufficient food. This accusation was in the main clearly political.

A noticeable thing about this legislature was the marked increase of good feeling between the two parties. J. L. Robinson was chosen speaker over R. C. Badger and each voted for the other. During the sixty-nine days of the session, there was scarcely any extreme partisan feeling displayed. This, of course, does not include the manifestation of feeling between the friends of Vance and Merrimon, for that was in the nature of a family quarrel.

The legislature submitted the constitutional amendments to the people and adjourned to meet in November, 1873. The ratification election was held in August and resulted in the ratification of all by good majorities.

When the second session opened, Governor Caldwell in his message urged the members to complete their work before the day for counting the vote on the amendments, as on that date, he thought, the existence of the legislature would terminate. He also expressed grave doubts as to the validity of the amendments, assigning, however, no reason for his opinion. The legislature appointed a committee which, after consultation with the attorney general, reported that the amendment did not affect the existing session, so the governor's opinion was ignored and the work of the session began in the usual way.

The proceedings were of little interest, as no important general law was enacted, and most of the time was consumed in private or local legislation. The usual general laws were passed, an election was ordered to fill the vacancy in the office of superintendent of public instruction and in two judgeships, and a resolution was passed requesting

Congress to refund the cotton tax collected in the State during the four years following the war.  The Senate passed a bill providing for scaling the debt, but later recalled it from the House and never acted further upon it.  The House also passed two bills upon the subject which were never considered in the Senate.  All these propositions ignored the special tax bonds.

A resolution protesting against the proposed civil rights bill passed both houses, a large number of Republicans voting for it.[1]  A resolution for the impeachment of Judge Watts was presented to the House, but the committee reported that, on account of the impossibility of conviction, because of the fact that so many important witnesses were outside the State, it was inexpedient to impeach.

The session lasted sixty days only, and, as has been hinted, was remarkable chiefly for what it did not do.

### 4. POLITICS IN 1874

The course of the Conservatives while in control of the legislature had commended itself to the people of the State. Expenses had been largely reduced, taxes were lower, and the State generally was far more prosperous.  The fears of many of the people that the party would be violent, reckless, and proscriptive had not been realized, and the party entered upon the campaign of 1874 in better shape than it had ever been.  Its record justified the claim it had made and it had proved itself fit to rule.  The Republicans had, on the contrary, nothing to point to with pride, and were still split into factions of which the dominant one was composed of federal office-holders who had their hands upon the organization and who have never since surrendered it.

Of the three great influences which caused the "tidal wave" of 1874, namely, the exposure of fraud and corrup-

[1] *Sentinel*, Jan. 18, 1874.

tion in the national government, including the "salary grab," the Southern policy of the administration, and the proposed civil rights bill, only the last-mentioned powerfully influenced the result in North Carolina. The State was entirely accustomed to the connection of the Republican party with corruption, knowing it, in fact, only in that connection; the entire delegation in Congress, save Shober, who did not vote, had supported the "salary grab;" and the attitude of the administration towards the South was no new thing. The civil rights bill, however, was a menace that was apparent to all and it was not favored by a majority of the white Republicans, to say nothing of the Conservatives, or, as they now began to call themselves, Democrats. This proposed legislation was, therefore, the chief connecting link between North Carolina and the new movement in national politics. It played a very large part in the campaign and, more than anything else, broke the last hold of the Republican party upon the State. A temporary reaction came a year later, but lasted only a short time.

The election of a superintendent of public instruction to succeed McIver was the only contest which could test the strength of the parties as a whole in the State, but in addition to the congressional elections, nine judges, twelve solicitors, and a legislature were to be chosen. The Democrats were particularly anxious to win the legislature, as they hoped to call a constitutional convention, and the Republicans, hoping to defeat such a move, were exceedingly active.

The Conservative-Democratic executive committee selected as the candidate for superintendent, Stephen D. Pool, a young man who since the war had been an editor. He was a cousin of John Pool but was one of the few members of the family who did not join the Republican party. The

Republicans nominated Thomas R. Purnell, a recent convert to the faith. For the judgeships, both parties nominated full tickets.[1]  In the second and eighth districts, there was doubt as to whether the terms of W. A. Moore and J. M. Cloud would expire, and a number of Republicans tried to prevent the party from nominating candidates, but the fear that they might thereby lose two offices was effective, and, ignoring the incumbents, they chose two other candidates.[2]  A. S. Seymour was the regular Republican candidate in the third district, and W. J. Clarke ran as an independent against him.  The Democrats secretly nominated Henry F. A. Grainger, announcing his name only on election day.  In the seventh district, John Kerr received the Democratic nomination and Tourgee, the Republican.  But the latter was certain of defeat and still hankered after a seat in Congress, so the Republicans looked about for some Democrat to support.  Judge Kerr had been one of the judges under the old constitution and owed his nomination to that fact, combined with the treatment he had received at the hands of Kirk and his men.  Many Democrats were opposed to him, and finally, Thomas Ruffin, a son of the former chief justice, who was himself later a justice of the Supreme Court, announced himself an independent candidate.  Tourgee at once withdrew, and the Republicans endorsed Ruffin.  In the ninth district, there was strong Republican opposition to Logan, Republican lawyers like Barringer and Bynum wanting him dropped, and, as the dis-

[1] They were as follows: 1st district, Democrat, M. L. Eure, Republican, J. W. Albertson; 2, T. J. Jarvis, Louis Hilliard; 3, H. F. A. Grainger, A. S. Seymour, W. J. Clarke, independent Republican; 4, A. A. McKay, D. L. Russell; 5, B. Fuller, R. P. Buxton; 7, John Kerr, A. W. Tourgee, who withdrew in favor of Thomas Ruffin, independent Democrat; 8, T. J. Wilson, W. H. Bailey; 9, David Schenck, G. W. Logan.

[2] *Wilmington Post*, Feb. 18, 1874.

trict had a Democratic majority of about twelve hundred, some independent Democrat endorsed. Bynum said publicly, " I am resolved not again to cast a ballot for a grossly incompetent judge whose blunders may involve the reputation, the property, and the life of every citizen in the district." But Judge Logan would not listen to argument and, having influence enough to secure the nomination, insisted upon being the candidate.

The congressional campaign was accompanied by the usual contests within the parties. In the first district, C. L. Cobb was regularly nominated by the Republicans, and Edward Ransom, who had been acting with the party in an independent fashion, came out against him and so divided his strength as to defeat him. Charles R. Thomas was anxious for a renomination, but John A. Hyman thought the time had come for one of his race to have a share of the larger rewards, and the district, being of a dark complexion, agreed with him, to the discomfiture of Thomas, who began to see what negro suffrage might mean. Garland H. White ran against Hyman, but did not succeed in dividing the Republican vote, and Hyman was successful over him and the Democratic candidate. James E. Boyd and Tourgee both wanted the nomination in the fifth district, as did several others of lesser light. After seventy ballots, W. F. Henderson was chosen for sacrifice. Tourgee soon after reached the conclusion that Reconstruction was " an ignominious failure," an opinion he held for some years until a pension agency made him see a brighter side.[1]

[1] The congressional candidates were: 1st district, Democratic, J. J. Yeates, Republican, C. L. Cobb and Edward Ransom; 2, G. W. Blount, J. A. Hyman and G. H. White; 3, A. M. Waddell, Neill McKay; 4, J. J. Davis, J. H. Headen; 5, A. M. Scales, W. F. Henderson; 6, Thomas S. Ashe, Nat. McLean; 7, W. M. Robbins, C. L. Cook; 8, R. B. Vance, Plato Durham.

The campaign was hotly contested. Several interesting features are worthy of mention. One was the activity of the negroes. Hyman's nomination has been noticed already. More negro candidates appeared than at any time before and greatly added to the strength of the Democrats, for not many native white Republicans wanted negroes in office. In Craven, the county ticket was composed of five negroes, four carpetbaggers, and three white natives. New Hanover had a solid negro ticket,[1] and the white Republicans revolted and chose white candidates. They came together towards the end of the campaign, but the negroes retained most of the places on the ticket and, the condition continuing, contributed to Democratic success.

Another factor in the campaign was the friction among the white Republicans caused by personal control of party machinery. In Wake County, W. W. Holden, who had been made postmaster of Raleigh in 1873, was industriously engaged in building up a machine. The leader of the opposing faction was Timothy Lee, the carpetbagger sheriff, who was now about thirty thousand dollars short in his accounts.[2] The two groups could not be reconciled and, though they submitted to an arbitration of their differences, in which Lee won, the Holden faction held off and Wake went Democratic for the first time since Reconstruction began.

As in previous campaigns, the influence of the former Whigs was paramount in the Conservative-Democratic party. Both the senators, the nominee for superintendent, six of the candidates for Congress and five of those for judge had been Whigs. The Republicans, as usual, tried to make capital of this but without much success.

[1] *Charlotte Observer*, June 12, 1874.
[2] *Ibid.*, Sept. 9, Dec. 23, 1874.

The arguments of the campaign differed little from those of previous contests. The Ku Klux figured largely in Republican speeches for a time, but their enthusiasm for the subject waned when the fact appeared that Purnell had been a member. The federal service was again enlisted and the expenses of the western judicial district reached $139,-000 for the year, of which $52,600 were marshal's fees. But the Republicans were losing ground and, towards the end, their campaign was listless.

Governor Caldwell died in Hillsboro in July and was succeeded by Lieutenant Governor Brogden. The cause of the governor's death was uric acid poisoning, and the negroes, hearing this, spread the report that he had been poisoned by the Democrats.

The result of the election was a clean sweep for the Democrats. The legislature at last had a two-thirds Democratic majority. Pool was elected with a majority of over fourteen thousand; M. L. Eure, A. A. McKay, John Kerr, T. J. Wilson, and David Schenck were elected judges; Hyman was the sole successful Republican candidate for Congress; and nine Democratic solicitors were chosen.

An interesting situation developed soon after the election. As soon as the result was known, Judge Moore wrote Governor Brogden asking him not to commission Hilliard as judge, as the act providing for his election was unconstitutional. He warned the governor that he was prepared to go to extremes in resistance and that he would continue to act as judge until the Supreme Court decided against him. Governor Brogden replied that he had already commissioned Hilliard and said that he greatly regretted to see such a scramble for office.[1] When Hertford court opened, both claimants were present and a contest

---

[1] *Executive Correspondence*, Brogden, pp. 13-14.

ensued, Moore succeeding in retaining his seat. The attorney general then took the case to the higher court. In the meantime, Judge Cloud, who had fully believed that his term expired in 1874, and who had been confirmed in that opinion by Attorney General Olds, decided that, if there was any doubt, he might as well get the benefit of it and concluded to hold on. T. J. Wilson, the newly-elected judge at his first court, instructed the sheriff to remove Judge Cloud bodily from the bench, which he did by force. Cloud then served a writ of *quo warranto* upon Wilson, and Judge Kerr decided in favor of the latter, but the Supreme Court declared that under the constitution, Cloud's term did not expire until 1878, and that Wilson was therefore not legally elected.[1] The other case above referred to followed this immediately and the decision was the same.[2]

### 5. THE LEGISLATURE OF 1874

The legislature convened in November with its membership politically divided as follows:

|  | Senate. | House. | Joint Ballot. |
|---|---|---|---|
| Democrats | 38 | 93 | 131 |
| Republicans | 12 | 27 | 39 |

For the first time since 1867, there were no carpetbaggers in either house, but the member of the House from Warren died during the session, and J. W. Thorne, a carpetbagger, took his place. He was, however, not suffered to remain long. Four Republican senators [3] and thirteen members of the House [4] were negroes.

---

[1] Cloud *v*. Wilson, 72 N. C., 155.

[2] Hargrove *v*. Hilliard, 72 N. C., 169.

[3] R. Tucker, W. P. Mabson, John Bryant, and J. M. Paschall.

[4] Wilson Carey, Willis Bunn, Alfred Lloyd, J. R. Goode, J. A. White, John Newell, W. H. Crews, H. T. Hughes, W. H. Moore, H. Brewington, E. H. Hill, J. A. Jones, and R. Elliott.

The elections of presiding officers in the two houses resulted in the choice of R. F. Armfield as president of the Senate and J. L. Robinson as speaker of the House.

The chief interest in the session was in the bill calling a convention of the people. Concerning the need of one, few Democrats differed, but there was a wide diversity of opinion as to the expediency of calling one. Senator Ransom, after consulting with party leaders in Washington, advised strongly against it, and many were doubtful, fearing federal interference. But an imposing list of local leaders favored it. W. A. Graham and B. F. Moore published strong letters advising it and nearly every prominent member of the party supported the movement,[1] with only D. G. Fowle and William Eaton, in addition to Ransom, opposing it. The Democratic executive committee by an almost unanimous vote recommended it, and in January, 1875, a general party conference was held in Raleigh to discuss the question in the hope of clarifying the situation. The most important Democratic newspapers, namely, the *Wilmington Journal,* the Raleigh *News,* and the *Sentinel,* all were zealous in the cause. But still it was very doubtful if the bill could be passed. In January, President Grant was asked if he would interfere, and, in reply, assured a member of the House that he would not.[2] A little later, a resolution was adopted by both houses pledging constitutional reform. This helped a little, but the day was really carried by the work of W. L. Saunders as editor of the *Wilmington Journal.* With Josiah Turner, he divided the honor of bringing about the redemption of the State, and

---

[1] The list included George Davis, Robert Strange, Z. B. Vance, George Howard, M. E. Manly, Edward Conigland, E. J. Warren, G. N. Folk, W. A. Wright, O. P. Meares, R. S. French, J. L. Holmes, W. L. Saunders, and Montfort McGehee.

[2] *Wilmington Journal,* Feb. 5, 1875.

his work, in sharp contrast to that of Turner, was constructive to a high degree. He fought the battle in this case and won, for in March the Democratic caucus voted in favor of a convention.[1]  The bill passed the Senate a few days later by the required majority, in spite of the fact that a large number of Democrats were instructed against it. It then passed the House. In neither house were the parties entirely solid.[2]

The convention was restricted by the act in two ways. The oath required for the members upon organization and the act itself prohibited any interference with the homestead provision, the laborers' and mechanics' lien, the rights of married women, the ratio between poll and property taxes, any provision for compensation for slaves, for paying the war debt, for restoring imprisonment for debt, for educational or property qualifications for voting, and for vacating any office before its term expired. It was also forbidden to pass any ordinance of a legislative nature except for submitting its work to the people for ratification.

Quite a ripple of interest was started by the action of two Republican members of the House who, upon the passage of the civil rights bill by Congress, issued a statement withdrawing from the Republican party, and introduced a resolution calling upon all white men to do likewise.

Soon after J. W. Thorne took his seat, a committee was appointed to investigate charges that he was ineligible on account of infidelity. It appeared that he had shortly before published a pamphlet which was, from the standpoint of North Carolina, anything but orthodox, in that it denied the complete authority of the Bible. The committee recom-

---

[1] The caucus vote was 68 to 13.

[2] In the Senate, Cantwell, a Republican, voted for the bill and Marler, a Democrat, against it. In the House, Mendenhall, a Democrat, voted against it and Candler, Glenn, and Foote, Republicans, for it.

mended his expulsion. In the debate that followed, it appeared further that Thorne was a member of a religious society, and his defence was very able and clever, but he was expelled. Had he been a Democrat or even a native Republican, it is not likely that such action would have been taken and it seems that grave injustice was done. Twelve members joined in a strong protest against the decision. A new election was ordered and Thorne was triumphantly re-elected, but never took his seat.

A resolution to remove the disabilities of W. W. Holden was introduced in the House, and after two unfavorable reports, was indefinitely postponed.[1]

A large part of the time of the session was spent in the discussion of a proposition to recognize the debt due on account of the land scrip fund, which had been invested by the Republican board of education in worthless bonds, by giving the University a certificate of indebtedness for the amount and paying the interest. The opposition to the measure, which proved to be considerable, was chiefly based upon arguments that the University stood for aristocracy. But after many very long and exciting debates, and after the bill had failed once, it was passed.

Next to the convention bill, a bill to settle the state debt was easily the most important matter before the legislature. This was to be accomplished by scaling the valid bonds and repudiating the special tax bonds. After long debates, this was passed.

Other acts of importance were those providing for the establishment of an insane asylum for white people at Mor-

[1] A similar resolution was introduced into nearly every legislature until Governor Holden's death, but was never passed. Once it was certain of passage if Governor Holden would write a request for it coupled with the statement that, while he had acted with good intentions, he realized that he had been wrong. He declined to do this and died without being relieved.

ganton and one for the colored people at Wilmington.[1]  A
new charter was given Wilmington by which the city was
divided into three wards, two white and one colored.  This
was passed over the violent protest of Mabson, who threatened armed resistance and advised the negroes of Tarboro
to take the same course if the charter of that town was
altered.[2]  Later an attempt was made to secure an injunction from Judge Bond of the United States Circuit Court
to prevent its going into effect, but he declined to grant it.

With the passage of the convention bill the Democrats
began to see the end of the long struggle for supremacy and
for reform.  So confident were they of complete victory
that they relaxed their vigilance with rather disastrous results.  The adjournment of the legislature was the signal
for the campaign to commence, and in it the Republicans,
quietly, but none the less effectively, proved that the party
in North Carolina was neither dead nor sleeping.

[1] This was never established, and a few years later the state hospital
for colored insane was built at Goldsboro.

[2] *Wilmington Journal*, Feb. 26, 1875.

# CHAPTER SIXTEEN

## EDUCATION IN RECONSTRUCTION

### I. THE PUBLIC SCHOOLS

ONE of the chief purposes of the Northern settlers in North Carolina, if their words can be taken as evidence, was to establish an effective system of common schools based upon the New England plan. They ignored entirely the system which had already been established and which was temporarily inactive, and made their demand for the creation of schools for all one of the main defences of the policy of Reconstruction. There is little doubt that much of this sentiment was real, but, obscured by the greed which characterized the activities of the aliens, it did little for the cause of education in the State. From the beginning, their plans were threatened by the hostility which was aroused by the determination of many of them to prevent the separation of the races, their ignorance of the people of North Carolina and of the conditions existent in the State, and the economic and financial prostration which prevented the expenditure of the necessary funds to maintain the system.

At the beginning of the war, Calvin H. Wiley, the superintendent of schools, was fearful that the school fund of over two million dollars would be used for other purposes. But the governor and Council of State entered into an agreement with him to assist in keeping it intact. In the first legislature, propositions were made to take it, but a violent contest resulted in the preservation of the fund, the securities of which were not later in doubt. Nor were the securities changed, for, in spite of the pressure to invest in Confederate bonds, the fund remained invested mainly in bank stock which seemed more secure. But the banks were ruined at the close of the war by the loss of Confederate securities and the repudiation of the state war debt, so the result was much the same. The other investments were more secure and had a par value of about one million dollars, but the sum finally saved from the wreck amounted to scarcely more than a third of this.

A law was passed allowing the county courts to stop the levy of taxes for schools, but few took advantage of it, and in the majority of the counties, the schools were continued in the face of obstacles that might well have daunted spirits far from timid. If one man may be given the credit for such a thing, that man was Superintendent Wiley. His faith in the schools never faltered and his activity never lessened, even when his salary through depreciation sank almost to nothing. He remained in his position until 1865, when Governor Holden refused to recognize him officially and would not allow him to report to the convention.[1] When the convention met, his office was declared vacant. Against his earnest protest, the schools were later suspended and no one was chosen to succeed him.

In the convention of 1868, the report of the committee on education was adopted by a strict party vote, and amendments providing for the separation of the races in the University and in the schools were voted down. The carpetbaggers were planning mixed schools and the decision of the question was left for each county. The general control of the system was vested in the board of education consisting of the state officers.

---

[1] *Record of the Provisional Governor*, p. 70.

S. S. Ashley, who was elected superintendent, was, as has been seen, a carpetbagger from Massachusetts. He was not lacking in ability, but only in character and in a suitable temperament for his position. He was full of prejudices which made him narrow and regardless of the wishes of the people among whom he had elected to live. This was clearly apparent from his course in the convention. He favored mixed schools, and, like all of his kind, was far more interested in the welfare of the negroes than in anything else except himself. If the charge that he was of negro descent be true, this feeling was not at all unnatural. There is no convincing evidence of his having been as corrupt as some of his colleagues, but he was hand in glove with them, supporting their every act, and he was regarded as one of the most unpleasant carpetbaggers in the State. The " Pilgrim," as he was dubbed by Turner in the *Sentinel,* was full of energy, and entered upon his duties with more enthusiasm than judgment.

The board of education met soon after the new government was put in operation, but devoted most of its attention to the University. The legislature by resolution ordered the board to prepare and report by November a plan for the schools, and it did so, but the legislature took no steps in the matter until April, 1869, when an act was passed authorizing the superintendent and the board to organize a system of schools. One hundred thousand dollars was appropriated to assist in the work, and it was provided that seventy-five per cent of the poll tax levied by the counties should be used in their support. The question of mixed schools came up again, but the influence of the carpetbaggers was strong enough to prevent their prohibition.[1] By November, 1869, a school census was taken, county ex-

[1] *Standard,* April 2, 3, 1869.

aminers appointed, and the county commissioners ordered
to assume the duty of superintendence. J. W. Hood, one
of the colored members of the convention, was appointed
agent of the board of education and, notwithstanding the
fact that neither the law nor the constitution made provision
for such an office, assistant superintendent of public instruction for work in the colored schools. His report
showed that educational work was being done among his
race by the five following agencies:

|  | Schools. | Teachers. | Pupils. |
|---|---|---|---|
| American Missionary Asso- ciation and Freedmen's Union | 19 | 68 | 2840 |
| Friends' Society | 29 | 40 | 2425 |
| Episcopal Commission | 6 | 11 | 600 |
| Presbyterian Church | 16 | 21 | 1100 |
| Private Schools | 82 | 84 | 4861 |
| Total | 152 | 224 | 11,826 |

The number of schools was later increased to 257 and the
enrollment to 15,647.[1]

The lack of funds for putting the new system into operation was a very serious handicap. The income of the literary fund from all sources was reduced to thirty-three
thousand dollars and the assets of the fund were soon invested in special tax bonds which never paid any interest
and in time were repudiated. The stock of the fund in the
Cape Fear and Deep River Navigation Company was sold
in a very suspicious manner at a very low rate to T. S.
Lutterloh.

In 1870, the system went into operation. The report of
the superintendent for the year showed the total income to
have been $152,281.82, the State appropriation having

[1] *Report of the Superintendent of Public Instruction for 1869.*

never been paid. Of the sum mentioned, $42,862.40 was paid to teachers.

No accurate figures can be obtained as to the number of schools, teachers, or pupils. Ashley never troubled himself with small details and a large part of his report was contradictory and avowedly guesswork. According to his estimate, seventy-four counties had schools and the total number was 1,415. He placed the number of pupils at 49,000, of whom 25,000 were colored. His report showed fewer houses than in the preceding year. Eight schools with about 1,500 pupils were aided by the Peabody Fund. Two of these schools, located in Wilmington, deserve special mention. In January, 1867, the Soldiers' Memorial Society of Boston and the American Unitarian Association sent Miss Amy M. Bradley to Wilmington to open a school for negroes. She was a woman of far more than ordinary gifts, possessed of unbounded faith and energy and of the priceless gift of tact. Realizing at once that more good could be accomplished by the training of white teachers, she established two grammar schools, and later, through the generosity of Mrs. Hemenway, of Boston, a normal school was built, which is now the city high school. Out of this work, grew the city system now in existence. Many of Miss Bradley's pupils became enthusiastic teachers and her influence still lives.

Assistant Superintendent Hood's report was far more enlightening, although he did not distinguish between public and private schools. According to him, there were 347 colored schools, 372 teachers, and 23,419 pupils in attendance. By far the best work among the colored people was done by the schools conducted under the supervision of the associations before mentioned.

The financial condition of the schools did not improve. The State by the close of 1870 owed them $87,291.75. The

securities other than bonds brought no interest and the outlook was dark.   The board of education still held the
swamp lands, and in 1869, D. P. Bibles, a carpet-bagger
who was supposed to be acting in combination with General Daniel E. Sickles,[1] offered to buy all the lands in Hyde,
Tyrrell, and Washington counties, amounting to about three
hundred thousand acres, for thirty thousand dollars.   He
had already sold them in New York for ninety thousand
dollars.   The board was closing the sale, though the details
of the matter were well known to them, when the legislature passed an act prohibiting any sale made without its
consent.   The deal thus fell through for the time being,
but later another offer was made by Bibles who was now
associated with Samuel T. Carrow, the United States marshal.   They offered to pay fifty thousand dollars for the
lands, and the board was very anxious to close the matter,
particularly as several members were financially interested.
The proposal was submitted to the legislature in 1870 and
its consent was given to the sale upon certain conditions,
chief of which was that one hundred actual settlers should
be resident upon the lands before the deed was made.   The
purchasers soon announced to the board that this requirement had been fulfilled, and the deed was about to be made
when C. L. Harris was approached by several carpetbaggers who informed him of the existence of the " ring "
which would profit by the sale.   It included two members
of the board of education.   He at once began to oppose the
sale in spite of the threats, promises, and entreaties of those
interested.   He relied upon the support of the governor in
his position, but the latter declined to listen to his exposition
of the conspiracy.   The breach between them, already wide,
now increased until all relations ceased.   Harris was not

[1] H. E. Stilley to W. W. Holden, July 26, 1869.

summoned to the meetings of the Council of State, and he and the governor did not speak. His threat to expose the matter prevented the sale at that time and brought forth from Ashley in his last report the following bit of sarcasm:

The Board entered into this contract with great deliberation and caution. Notwithstanding by a large vote of both houses of the General Assembly the sale was authorized, and notwithstanding it was urged upon the Board as a desirable and profitable transaction by persons not interested but thoroughly acquainted with the lands, still the Board refused to act until certain further conditions were assented to by the other contracting party—conditions which rendered it certain that neither the Board or the State could in any event suffer loss.

The result has justified the action of the Board. And now, without the loss of an inch of ground, or one cent of money, the Board holds its own, and the State can still rejoice in the possession of some three hundred thousand acres, more or less, of unclaimed, untaxable, unprofitable, wild waste of swamp, over which the moor fowl wings his flight, unscared, and through whose jungles the serpent and the bear make leisurely their way.

The sale was made, however, after the legislature adjourned, and Ashley must have been cognizant of the fact at the time he wrote his report. The terms of the sale were far from favorable to the State, a long period being granted the purchasers in which to make payment and no adequate protection being furnished the State against the loss of the lands.

The following year saw no improvement in the condition of the schools. The Conservative legislature took all control of the funds out of the hands of the board of education [1] and reduced the salary of the superintendent to fifteen

---

[1] *Laws*, 1870–1871, chap. cclxxix.

hundred dollars with no allowance for expenses or clerk hire.[1]  On September 30, 1871, Ashley resigned and accepted an appointment to Straight University in New Orleans, an institution for negroes, where he found an atmosphere far more suitable and congenial to him than that of North Carolina, though possibly the financial opportunities were not so good.  Before leaving, he had served for a time as editor of the *Standard* assisted by Martling, his relative, whom he had located in the faculty of the University, but who was finding the financial support given him there scarcely sufficient for his needs or expectations.

To succeed Ashley, Governor Caldwell appointed Alexander McIver, professor of mathematics at the University. McIver was a sincere and honest man who was keenly anxious to build up the schools, but was unable to accomplish much for lack of support.  He was defeated for the Republican nomination in 1872 for reasons already mentioned, but Reid, who was elected, died before taking office and consequently before McIver retired.  There was strong pressure brought to bear on Governor Caldwell to make a political appointment, Judge Settle, for example, pressing the choice of G. W. Welker,[2] but the governor offered the place to Kemp P. Battle who accepted.  McIver declined to surrender his office on the ground that no successor had qualified and that there was therefore no vacancy.  He was sustained in this position by the Supreme Court and retained the place until the next election.

Conditions improved somewhat during this period.  The legislature of 1872 levied for the support of the schools a special tax of eight and one-third cents on the hundred dollars, a special poll tax of twenty-five cents, and, as before,

[1] *Laws*, 1870–1871, chap. lxxxi.
[2] Thomas Settle to T. R. Caldwell, Dec. 31, 1872.

gave seventy-five per cent of the state and county poll tax to them. By 1874, the total revenue for school purposes had grown to $412,070.60 and the schools had increased until the figures were as follows:

|  | White | Colored | Total |
|---|---|---|---|
| Number of schools ..... | 2,820 | 1,200 | 4,020 |
| Number of teachers .... | 2,108[1] | 767[1] | 2,875 |
| Number of pupils........ | 119,083 | 55,000 | 174,083 |
| Number of school age.. | 234,846 | 123,088 | 357,934 |

The average length of the school term was, however, about ten weeks and the proportion of persons of school age who were not in school was so large that the case seemed almost hopeless. But there were visible signs of a reviving interest in education. The State Education Association roused public interest and the movement for the establishment of normal schools did even more in this direction. The Peabody Fund was of immense assistance through its financial aid to a number of schools in the State and also in stimulating interest. Its grants to schools for the entire period follow:

| | |
|---|---|
| 1868............... | $2,700 |
| 1869............... | 6,350 |
| 1870 ............... | 7,650 |
| 1871 ............... | 8,950 |
| 1872............... | 8,250 |
| 1873............... | 9,750 |
| 1874............... | 14,300 |
| 1875............... | 16,900 |
| 1876............... | 8,050 |

In 1874, the Conservatives nominated Stephen D. Pool for superintendent. The wiser plan would have been to put the office forever out of politics by the nomination of Mc-

[1] The difference between the number of schools and teachers is explained by the fact that many teachers taught different schools at different times.

Iver, who was a far more suitable man, but such a thing was scarcely to be expected, political considerations being paramount and party feeling naturally very bitter. Pool was elected and entered upon his duties January 1, 1875. He served until July, 1876, when, to the intense horror, anger, and disgust of his party which had made official corruption the chief count of its indictment against the Republicans, he employed a considerable amount of money appropriated to North Carolina from the Peabody Fund in buying a house and lot in Raleigh. He was at once forced by the party leaders to resign and Governor Brogden appointed his cousin, John Pool, to succeed him. This action was naturally heartily condemned by the Conservatives who felt that Pool was without the pale. The *Sentinel* commenting upon the appointment, said, " The life history of John Pool is written in the prostitution of splendid talents to the base achievements of a selfish demagogue and deceitful political charlatan. A more unfit or unworthy public educator could not be found in the person of any equally able and capable man in the State." Pool served until the inauguration of John C. Scarborough who was elected in 1876.

The cause of education in North Carolina suffered greatly from the connection of the public school system with politics. The fear of mixed schools made the people dislike the system and, even when that possibility was removed by the amendment of the constitution, the effects were felt for a long time. The real poverty of the State immediately after the war and during Reconstruction had even a more lasting effect upon the people. Always averse to taxation and extravagance, their fear of both was intensified in the reaction from Reconstruction, and any proposition for large expenditure was violently unpopular. This is not the least part of the heritage of evil from Reconstruction. The people did not soon form the habit of spending public money even for a public purpose, and the schools, comparatively speaking, showed little improvement during the two decades following the close of Reconstruction.

## 2. THE UNIVERSITY

During the entire period of the war, the University of North Carolina never closed its doors. Year by year, its student body decreased until there remained only a mere handful, all disabled by service or too young to go to the front. With the students went the younger members of the faculty, but the older professors, led by President Swain, continued at their posts, determined that the exercises of the institution, begun in 1795, should not be suspended.[1]

With the return of peace, it was hoped that students would return and that the University might soon reach its former prosperity. There were, however, two great obstacles to this consummation. The most important was the appalling economic prostration of the State and the South;[2] the other was the financial condition of the University itself. The debts were more than one hundred thousand dollars, not including arrears of salaries. To pay this sum there were two thousand shares of worthless bank stock, twenty-five thousand dollars in Confederate securities, and some

---

[1] The contribution of the University to the Confederate service was remarkable. Of its matriculates between 1830 and 1867, numbering 2592, it is known that 1100 or 42.4 per cent entered the army. Of those entering between 1851 and 1861, 1331 in number, 800 or 60.1 per cent were in service. The death list was more than three hundred. The University contributed one lieutenant general, one major general, thirteen brigadier generals, fifty colonels, twenty-eight lieutenant colonels, forty majors, forty-six adjutants, seventy-one surgeons, two hundred and fifty-four captains, one hundred and fifty-five lieutenants, and thirty-eight non-commissioned officers.

[2] About fifty per cent of the students in 1860 were from states other than North Carolina.

small amounts otherwise invested.   The debt was later scaled to twenty-seven thousand dollars and the University pledged as security for payment its property at Chapel Hill and its lands in Buncombe County.[1]   The legislature in 1866 appropriated seven thousand dollars for running expenses, and this was of considerable temporary assistance.

Early in 1867, President Swain secured from the General Assembly the transfer of the land scrip granted by Congress under the Morrill Act of 1862 for the support of an agricultural and mechanical college.   Certain conditions were imposed which were agreed to.   North Carolina was entitled under the act to thirty thousand acres and President Swain at once went to Washington to secure it.   President Johnson ordered the transfer made and the trustees decided to sell the scrip at the market price, and in August, made an agreement of sale with a Detroit firm at fifty cents an acre, ten thousand dollars to be paid at once and the remainder when Congress should recognize the State.   The trustees decided to apply a small part of the purchase money to running expenses and this was done without reference to the legislature, which was prevented from meeting by military order.

In the spring of 1866, the student ball managers selected as honorary managers, President Davis, General William R. Cox, General John C. Breckinridge, General Robert D. Johnson, General Robert E. Lee, and ex-Governor Vance. This action was taken without consulting the wishes of the faculty or of the gentlemen selected.   The faculty was panic-stricken and laid the matter before the trustees who decided that the election was improper.   The effect of the thing in the North as well as in the State was feared, and, as events proved, this feeling had a good foundation, for

---

This mortgage was later declared void by the Circuit Court of the United States.

the radical press was unsparing in harsh criticism of the " rebel sentiment " which was said to dominate the institution, the *Standard* going so far as to threaten punishment in the future.

In 1867, President Johnson, Secretary Seward, Postmaster General Randall, and General Sickles were present at commencement. The President had received the degree of LL.D. the year before, and it was now conferred on Secretary Seward.

During 1867, two professors resigned and it became evident that failure was near. Governor Worth called the trustees into special session in August and urged that efficient measures be taken to preserve the institution. It was clearly apparent that President Swain had outgrown his usefulness. He was growing old, was very deaf, and was not equipped for meeting the new conditions which now had to be faced. He had naturally no realization of these facts, but on July 23, wrote Governor Worth, " I am ready to give place to any one who can assume my position under more favorable auspices, at the earliest period at which the board may be pleased to designate a successor." [1] It never occurred to him, however, that his offer would be accepted. The meeting was held and was attended by the leading trustees. Kemp P. Battle, in consultation with Professor Charles Phillips, had determined to secure the remodeling of the institution and, in pursuance of the plan, Dr. Phillips obtained the resignations of all the faculty, including the president. These were accepted by the trustees with the request that they hold over until their successors should be chosen, and a committee was appointed to devise a plan of reorganization. An elaborate report was made in December and adopted, with the provision that it should go into effect in 1868.

[1] Hamilton, ed., *Correspondence of Jonathan Worth*, p. 1010.

In the meantime, the new constitution had been adopted, and by its provisions, the existing board of trustees, which had been elected by the General Assembly, was replaced by one chosen by the board of education, consisting of the state officers, who were *ex officio* trustees. In consequence of this, the outgoing board at their last meeting re-elected the president and faculty and abandoned the new scheme of reorganization.

The new system of control which went into effect in July, 1868, was purely political and was designed to be so. The governor was chairman of the board of trustees and also of the executive committee, which consisted of the board of education and three trustees chosen by the trustees. This political character was apparent when the new board of trustees was finally elected. The constitution required that they should be selected, one from each county, but this was not followed because of the desire of the board of education to place upon the board of trustees certain prominent Republicans, chiefly carpetbaggers. Of the new board, eighteen were alumni, but only five members had previously served on the board.[1] Almost every member was a partisan Republican, and the executive committee was dominated by Governor Holden. It was a matter of common knowledge, long before the meeting of the board, that a clean sweep would be made of the old faculty and that a " loyal," that is to say partisan Republican, University would be established. The change was received with deep anger and distress by the friends of the old University, who were not slow to express their feelings and to contrast the governor of 1868, bent upon making the University Republican, with the editor of the *Standard,* who in 1856, led the hue and

[1] Neill McKay, Thomas Settle, John Pool, M. McGehee, and W. W. Holden.

cry against Professor Hedrick whose only crime had been a quiet desire to vote for Fremont.

The first meeting of the trustees was held in July. President Swain was notified of the meeting and was present, certain of his retention as president. Ex-Governor Manly, who had been for many years secretary of the board, was also present by invitation and read his report. The next day, in Swain's absence, his resignation and those of his colleagues, which had been presented to the old board in 1867, were accepted and their later re-election ignored. In August, Swain sent a protest to Governor Holden, in which he insisted that the board had no power of removal save for " misbehavior, inability, or neglect of duty." No charges of the sort had been made against him, and in addition, he urged, the constitution recognized the president and made him *ex officio* a member of the executive committee. No attention was paid to his protest, and a week later he was thrown from his buggy and fatally injured.

To serve on the executive committee, the trustees chose Thomas Settle, William B. Rodman, and J. F. Taylor. R. W. Lassiter was elected secretary and treasurer. Upon motion of W. F. Henderson,[1] a committee was appointed to prepare a plan for the continuance of the institution. The executive committee was given full power to put into operation a " thorough and efficient organization of the University upon the proper and liberal basis contemplated by the constitution," to elect a president, devise a system of government, and to resume exercises. The one limitation placed upon them was that no one should be elected to the faculty who had not " an established national reputation as a scholar and educator." Many trustees, notably Chief

---

[1] There is something tragically comic in the activity of Henderson in the "rebuilding" of the University, for he was uneducated, almost illiterate, and not of a type that had any interest in education.

Justice Pearson, were opposed to the great power of the executive committee.

The first step in the reorganization of the institution was the offer of the presidency to L. P. Olds, a son-in-law of the governor. He declined, and during the delay that followed, a son of C. L. Harris, the superintendent of public works, was appointed superintendent to care for the buildings and grounds. The trustees met again in November and voted down a proposition for co-education and one, championed by Judge Rodman and Judge Tourgee, for provisional appointments to the faculty. A proposal that the state treasurer should serve as treasurer of the board and the superintendent of public instruction, as secretary met the same fate. After this meeting the charge was made by the *Sentinel* [1] that Rodman, Ashley, and J. F. Taylor had introduced a resolution providing for the admission of negroes, and this story spread all over the State and is heard to-day. The minutes mention no such proceedings, and there is scarcely any doubt that the rumor was false. A considerable number of Republicans, most of them carpetbaggers, strongly favored such a plan, and it was even proposed in the legislature. Just prior to this meeting of the trustees, Sinclair proposed to pay the trustees the same *per diem* and mileage as the members of the legislature. [2] This fortunately failed to pass or the State would have been cursed with another such body as the legislature in almost constant session so long as the funds held out.

One open and active candidate for the presidency appeared in the person of Rev. W. H. Doherty, a carpetbagger who had been an army chaplain. He submitted a voluminous report to the board containing a plan of reor-

[1] Issue of Nov. 23, 1868.
[2] *Ho. Journal*, pp. 23, 25.   *Sentinel*, Nov. 21, 1868.

ganization, but ideas on educational subjects were not looked for by the executive committee, and, lacking family influence, he was not considered. The executive committee met on January 2, 1869, and elected Rev. Solomon Pool president. He was a brother of John Pool, a graduate of the University who had served as tutor and as adjunct professor. He had left in 1867 to accept a position in the internal revenue service. Not only did he lack national reputation, but he was unknown to the State. He was, however, a man of some ability. He owed his election to his brother's influence and to a public statement which he had made some time before, that the University " should be thoroughly loyalized. Better close it than have it a nursery of treason to foster and perpetuate the feelings of disloyalty. Let the present Board of Trustees be superseded by a loyal Board and the University will be a blessing instead of a curse."

The selection of professors was made on a somewhat similar plan. As professor of mathematics, they chose Alexander McIver, a graduate of the University and a member of the faculty of Davidson College. He was able, active, and entirely honest, but owed his election chiefly to the fact that he had practically been forced from his position at Davidson on account of politics. Fisk P. Brewer, a graduate of Yale and a man of undoubted scholarship, was elected professor of Greek.[1] He was at the time at the head of a negro school in Raleigh. He injured himself very much in public estimation by boarding in a negro family for some time after his arrival in Chapel Hill. David S. Patrick, a nephew of Judge Settle, also a graduate of the University, was chosen professor of Latin. He was without qualifications or reputation. James M. Martling, of Missouri, a brother-in-law of Ashley, was elected pro-

[1] Brewer was a brother of Justice Brewer of the United States Supreme Court.

fessor of belles-lettres. He also lacked reputation or any other qualifications. George Dixon, an Englishman, was made professor of agriculture. What influence led to his appointment cannot be discovered.

The University, so organized and officered, was doomed to failure from the outset. It opened for students March 3, 1869, and a very small number attended. Practically all of them were from Republican families or from the village of Chapel Hill. Without reference to political considerations, there was not much offered by the institution that anyone wanted, and all who could afford it, whether Conservatives or Republicans, sent their sons elsewhere. The attendance during the first year was thirty-five, twenty-five of whom were in the preparatory department. The second year the number rose to fifty-three, twenty of whom were preparatory pupils. By this time, it was apparent that the end was approaching. There was no money, a proposed appropriation of twelve thousand dollars having been defeated in the legislature, and salaries, small as they were, were paid but slowly. President Pool took up his work as a revenue officer, for which he was far better adapted, and the faculty began to leave. The Republicans declared the result was caused by a Conservative conspiracy, and while there was nothing of the sort, the old friends of the institution made no secret of their hostility towards the new administration and of their determination not to recognize it or support it in any way. The University as constituted was a fraud and a farce and deserved to die. The administration made a great show for a time, and the prosperity of the institution, the soundness of its scholarship, and the breadth and liberality of its culture were all enlarged upon, but the facts were all against the statements.

The property of the University was badly cared for, the buildings and library in particular being abused. In 1870, the end came and the doors were closed. Governor Holden advised that the property should be rented, but no one applied for it. The student body having disappeared, there was nothing for the faculty to do, and it was reduced to the president and three professors who still held on. Pool gave practically all his time to his duties in the revenue service and, when urged to resign by a friend in Chapel Hill, replied, " I would not resign for fifty thousand dollars."

Finally, at a faculty meeting in 1871, when Pool was absent, McIver introduced a resolution to the effect that no member of the faculty desired to be in the way of the resuscitation of the institution and that it was clear that they did not have the confidence of the public. Patrick voted with him and Brewer opposed the resolution. Martling was in Raleigh assisting Ashley in editing the *Standard* or he would doubtless have voted with Brewer. Shortly afterwards, McIver succeeded Ashley as superintendent of public instruction, and in 1872, advocated the complete reorganization of the University. By this time, Martling had gone, and Brewer had received some minor foreign appointment. He held this for several years, but returned to the United States later and became a professor in the still more unfortunate University of South Carolina in the closing years of Reconstruction. Interest in reorganization was general among the alumni, but the lack of means and the Republican board of education presented obstacles that seemed insuperable.

In 1873, the board of education called a state educational convention which met in Raleigh in July. Judge William H. Battle was chairman and in his address made a strong plea for the University. Robert Bingham also spoke in its behalf, and the committee on the subject brought in a report which called for immediate revival. This was adopted as was a resolution expressing the feeling of the convention that the institution should be entirely removed from political or sectarian control or interference. The passage of this latter resolution was brought about by the demand made by two ministers present that their respective denominations should be represented on the faculty. There was to be seen in the discussion the germ of the denominational opposition to the University which was to develop later.

During the session of the legislature in the spring of 1872, after that body had shown itself favorably inclined towards the public schools, the question of the University was brought to the personal attention of the members. There was a strong disposition to revive it upon a non-partisan basis, but the chief difficulty was the attitude of Solomon Pool who did not wish to surrender the title of president. The trustees adopted a resolution asking the assistance of the alumni [1] and, in response, fifty-five of them met in Raleigh and expressed their entire willingness to aid if the institution was taken out of politics. A quorum of the trustees conferred upon the matter and instructed McIver to send to each member of the board an account of what had been done and to request them to resign. At first there was a very favorable response and resignations came in rapidly. Then the Pool influence was brought to bear upon the threatening situation. John Pool wrote McIver that he disapproved of the whole plan and sent out a circular letter to the trustees, urging them in behalf of the Republican party not to resign and, if they had already done so, to recall their letters. Rev. James Reid, who was a member of the board, agreed with Pool that the institution should be kept on a partisan Republican basis, and, in grati-

---

[1] President Pool had already issued a letter to the alumni asking their assistance, but no attention had been paid to his request.

tude, Pool secured his nomination for superintendent of public instruction. Another opponent of any change in the system was R. W. Lassiter, who drew a salary of one thousand dollars for his nominal position as secretary and treasurer. Reid had been instrumental in preventing a reduction of his salary and thereby won Lassiter's gratitude.[1] In consequence of these facts, the plan for revival slumbered until the legislature of 1872 met and adopted the amendment to the constitution proposed by the preceding legislature, by which the appointment of trustees was placed in the hands of the legislature. This was ratified by the people in 1873 and a new board of trustees was chosen, which met in February, 1874, and organized with William A. Graham as chairman and Kemp P. Battle as secretary and treasurer. Governor Caldwell was asked to preside, but he denied the validity of the constitutional amendment and refused to recognize the new board. A committee was at once appointed to take charge of the property of the University. McIver notified the governor of his intention to turn over to it the seal and records, and Caldwell replied that he denied the right of the legislature to elect trustees and warned McIver not to yield to them. McIver urged the governor to give in, but Caldwell was determined to fight the matter out and would not listen. The chief cause of his opposition was ill-temper, but the assigned reason was that the legislature of 1871 had passed sixteen amendments in one bill, and the legislature of 1874 had accepted only eight of them and had submitted them to the people in as many separate bills. A demand upon Pool for the keys met with a decided refusal. A friendly suit was then brought against McIver and was decided in favor of the trustees.[1] About

---

[1] Alexander McIver to the *Sentinel*, April 23, 1872.

[2] University *v*. McIver, 72 N. C., 76.

this time the mortgage upon the University property which had been foreclosed was declared void and the institution was thus left unincumbered.

The new board of trustees met in the spring of 1875, and, having adopted a plan of reorganization, elected a faculty, three of whom had served in the former one. Dr. Charles Phillips was elected chairman, and the doors of the institution were opened in the autumn with much ceremony. The next year, Kemp P. Battle was chosen president and the University began slowly to climb back to health and strength that it might enter with its full powers upon a career of greater usefulness, free from any taint of politics, in the service of all the people.

# CHAPTER SEVENTEEN

## THE OVERTHROW OF RECONSTRUCTION

### I. THE CONVENTION OF 1875

SCARCELY had the legislature of 1874 adjourned when the press and people of the State commenced a discussion of the convention question. From the beginning, the Republicans had high hopes of electing a majority of the members and, on account of the division of sentiment among the Democrats as to the wisdom of calling a convention, their hopes seemed not unfounded.

On June 1, the Democratic executive committee [1] issued an address to the people on the subject. The history of the existing constitution was reviewed and stress was laid on its origin in a military despotism, and on its lack of suitability to the needs of the State. The plurality of judges in two districts, the slow administration of justice in many counties, and the question of the penitentiary were mentioned as examples of its defects. The address showed that proper restrictions had been placed upon the convention by the General Assembly and that the people need have no fear that they would be deprived of any protection guaranteed by the existing constitution. Republicans who were disgusted with the scandals of the national administration and who were opposed to the civil rights bill were invited to

---

[1] The committee was composed of William R. Cox, chairman, R. H. Battle, C. M. Busbee, R. B. Haywood, J. J. Davis, W. H. Jones, S. A. Ashe, W. N. H. Smith, and O. P. Meares.

631

coöperate with the Democrats in the work of reform, and assurance was given that the Republican party, still controlled and guided by carpetbaggers, would do nothing for them.[1]

The Republicans devoted most of their time to condemnation of the legislature for calling a convention and to painting lurid pictures of what the Democrats would do if they secured a majority. The party, however, was divided upon the question, and a number of prominent members were frankly in favor of a convention, notable examples being Marcus Erwin and Charles R. Thomas, the latter refusing to accept the party nomination for delegate from Craven.[2] The final policy of the party was summed up in a pledge made by a majority of its candidates to adjourn as soon as the convention was organized. Here again was to be found dissent, for Chief Justice Pearson said publicly that such an action would be utterly wrong, and Judge Rodman, who declined to accept the Republican nomination for delegate but ran as an independent, urged that the convention should make certain needed reforms. Judge Buxton was also a candidate, but as a Republican and an exceedingly partisan one. Judge Watts, strange to say, was not a candidate, but took the stump and made a number of bitter speeches, many of them while holding court.

Every effort was made to frighten the people into giving a Republican majority. The press gave daily assurance that, if the Democrats controlled the convention, it would levy a tax to pay for the slaves;[3] that townships would be abolished and county courts restored;[4] that Jefferson Davis

[1] *Sentinel*, June 3, 1875.

[2] *Carolina Messenger*, July 1, 1875.

[3] Raleigh *Constitution*, Aug. 5, 1875.

[4] Raleigh *Era*, June 24, 1875.

would be made president of the University with a salary of
ten thousand dollars; that the public schools would be abolished;[1] and even that there was grave danger of secession.[2]
The Raleigh *Constitution*[3] summarized the chief arguments
against the convention as follows:

Convention means Revolution.
Convention means the Whipping Post and Pillory.
Convention means Imprisonment for Debt.
Convention means War.
Convention means Apprentice laws, which is one of the
worst features of Slavery.
Convention means Ruin.
Convention means poll-tax qualification for voting.

The negro question was soon injected into the campaign.
Page, a negro candidate in Chowan, in one of his speeches,
said, " If we get control of that convention, we will give
the white folks h—l, d—n 'em. No distinction of color
shall be known in anything. If a negro woman wants to
marry a white man, or a negro man a white woman, no law
shall prevent it."[4] The increasing claims of the negroes
had attracted notice, and in several districts of the State, it
seemed likely that every federal office would be filled by a
negro. Just before the election, the Charlotte *Democrat*
said, " White men of North Carolina, are you ready for
mixed schools, for negro Judges, for negro Representatives,
for negro Senators? Are you ready to forget that while
you guarantee to the negro all his political and legal rights,
this is a white man's government, framed by the wisdom
of the white men, and secured by the blood of the white

[1] *Constitution*, Aug. 3, 1875.
[2] *Era*, May 20, 1875.
[3] Issue of July 30, 1875.
[4] *Sentinel*, July 27, 1875.

race? If you are ready for such tremendous changes, stay away from the polls on the day of election. If you are not ready for all these, come up, every man of you, and vote for the men of your race." [1]

It was very difficult to rouse much enthusiasm in the campaign, particularly among the Democrats, who felt certain of success and were, therefore, inclined to be apathetic. The Republicans were not intensely aroused, but in the party was hope and at this time almost every member of the party could be relied on as certain to go to the polls, a factor which was very uncertain among the Democrats. But the leaders on both sides struggled valiantly and a steady campaign was maintained until the election.

Election day came and went quietly. The result was in doubt for two days, at the end of which the Democrats claimed a majority in the convention. Two days later they conceded that the Republicans would have a majority of at least two. The blow was a hard one, for the most conservative Democratic estimate had given the party a majority of ten. A few days later, however, more returns came in and the Democrats claimed a majority of one, while the Republicans, on the strength of the election of several independent candidates, asserted that the victory was theirs. In Robeson County, there was a contest. On the day of election, W. R. Cox, the Democratic chairman, had telegraphed there, "As you love the State, hold Robeson." There indeed was the pivotal point and both sides claimed the victory. McEachern and Sinclair, the Democratic candidates, received the certificate, but Norment and McNeill, the Republican candidates, sued for a mandamus and filed a complaint in the courts. The case was argued before Judge Settle at chambers on the first of September and he

---

[1] Issue of Aug. 2, 1875.

ruled himself without jurisdiction and the matter was left for the decision of the convention. The organization of the convention was seen to be of great consequence, for control would belong to whichever party might be strongest at the beginning. Therefore, every influence was brought to bear by each side, with entire success, to have its full strength on hand when the session began.

Returning to the election, the vote is exceedingly interesting. By districts it was as follows:[1]

| District. | Democratic candidates. | Republican candidates. |
|---|---|---|
| 1 | 13,607 | 12,064 |
| 2 | 11,074 | 20,917 |
| 3 | 13,765 | 14,195 |
| 4 | 14,136 | 15,133 |
| 5 | 9,904 | 10,521 |
| 6 | 12,016 | 10,950 |
| 7 | 10,274 | 3,311 |
| 8 | 10,261 | 8,100 |
| Total | 95,037 | 95,191. |

It is thus seen that more Republican votes were cast than Democratic. Only the fact that they were grouped in fewer counties saved the Democrats from defeat. As it was, they had no margin that entitled them to boast.

The race issue was quite sharply drawn in several parts of the State, and Franklin County, for example, had only nine white Republican voters. Apathy and over-confidence, however, on the part of the Democrats in general came near throwing the State into the hands of the Republicans. The negro vote was practically solid and the charge was made, apparently with some truth, that negroes were imported into Mecklenburg County from South Carolina. As

[1] *Wilmington Journal*, Sept. 15, 1875.

a result of the campaign, Democratic policy entered upon a new era which is best described in the following editorial extract: [1]

This paper in the future is in favor of drawing the line between the white and black, regardless of the consequences. Let the line be drawn. Are you in favor of the white man's government? This will be the only question in the future.

Let the watchword be hereafter—Stick to your color! It is useless to attempt to reason with ignorant negroes. The election clearly demonstrates that fact.

William A. Graham, who was one of the delegates from Orange, died soon after his election, and Governor Brogden issued the writ for another election, fixing its date ten days after the day appointed for the meeting of the convention. The Democrats at once charged the governor with partisanship in thus delaying the election but it soon appeared that he was obeying the law and most of his critics made the *amende honorable.*

On September 5, the convention met and was called to order by Judge Settle of the Supreme Court.[2] The convention was composed of fifty-eight regular Democrats, fifty-eight regular Republicans, and three independents. The death of William A. Graham deprived the Democrats of one vote that they needed greatly and no one was able to say what would be the result of the meeting. The members were not of any unusual ability, but quite a large number had had legislative experience, thirty-two being mem-

---

[1] *Albemarle Register,* quoted in *Sentinel,* August 13, 1875.

[2] Judge Settle stated that he did this at the request of the justices of the Supreme Court and of the secretary of state, the latter being the only person mentioned in the act providing for the convention and being unwilling to assume the responsibility of organization when so much was in doubt.

bers of the existing legislature. One member had been in the convention of 1861,[1] three had served in the convention of 1865,[2] and six in the convention of 1868.[3] Six were negroes.[4]

Immediately after the convention was called to order, A. W. Tourgee offered the following protest against the required oath, signed by twenty-five Republican delegates:

We, the undersigned delegates to this convention, protest against the validity of the oath prescribed in the act of the General Assembly calling this convention as being beyond the power of any legislature to impose, contrary to the political history, usages, and precedents heretofore acknowledged and acted upon by both political parties in this State, subversive of the rights and derogatory to the dignity of the people of the State.[5]

When the delegates came forward to be sworn, objections were raised in the case of those from Robeson. Judge Settle then directed McEachern and Sinclair to stand aside, whereupon objections were made to the qualification of six others, five of whom were Republicans,[6] and all were made to stand aside. At the close of the roll call, all were sworn in and the question of validity of election left to the future action of the convention.

The first test of party strength came in the election of a president. Oliver H. Dockery was nominated by the Republicans and ex-Governor Reid, amidst great applause

[1] Ex-Governor David S. Reid.

[2] R. P. Buxton, William Barrow, and W. T. Faircloth.

[3] A. W. Tourgee, Wilson Carey, J. Q. A. Bryan, Plato Durham, G. Z. French, and R. W. King.

[4] J. H. Smythe, Wilson Carey, W. P. Mabson, E. J. O'Hara, J. R. Page, and J. O. Crosby.

[5] *Journal*, p. 3.

[6] Joseph Dobson, a Democrat, and R. C. Badger, J. M. Bateman, T. J. Dula, J. Q. A. Bryan, and B. F. Jones, Republicans.

by the Democrats, nominated Dr. Edward Ransom, of Tyrrell, one of the independents who had formerly been a Republican but had recently shown signs of inclining towards the Democratic party. He promptly declined the nomination amid Republican applause. The ballot was then taken and Ransom received fifty-nine votes, one less than the number required for election, and Dockery fifty-eight. A second ballot made no change, and the convention adjourned. On the following day, eleven ballots were taken without an election. The Democratic strength never varied but Dockery's vote dropped as low as forty-eight. Finally, on the fourteenth ballot, Ransom said, " This balloting has gone on long enough. I have not sought this position; I do not desire it. I have cast my vote twice to defeat myself. The people seem to demand that this body be organized. I have made every effort to procure a compromise; I now cast my vote for Edward Ransom, the delegate from Tyrrell County, let the consequences be what they may." This vote broke the deadlock, and the final result was Ransom, sixty; Dockery, fifty-eight; Durham, one. An interesting happening during the progress of the balloting was a speech by Dixon, a Republican member, in which he said. pointing to the negroes who crowded the galleries and lobbies, " It is very close; this may last forever. These are all our friends; why should we not select a president? " [1] There was an immediate uproar among the negroes and it was feared that there was a plan of violence, but if there was such a thing, it met with no success, for quiet was restored in a few moments.

Immediately after the officers were elected, Tourgee moved that the convention adjourn *sine die*. The motion was defeated 59 to 57. This attempt to carry out the party

[1] *Carolina Messenger*, Sept. 16, 1875.

pledge was renewed without success twelve times during the session.

On the day of organization, R. C. Badger introduced a resolution providing for the relief of William W. Holden from the disabilities imposed by the court of impeachment. It was placed upon the calendar and caused a great deal of debate at intervals during the session. The committee to which it was referred took the ground that the resolution was legislative in character and consequently beyond the power of the convention. A. C. Avery offered a substitute providing that no person convicted upon an impeachment should be pardoned except by a bill passed by a majority of the members of each house of the General Assembly and only after five years from conviction.[1] This was later withdrawn. Not all the Republicans favored removing Holden's disabilities, Rufus Barringer, of Mecklenburg, for instance, making a strong speech against it in which he said that in 1869, a Republican committee, of which he was a member, had warned Holden of the danger of his course. There was, however, in the State a considerable Democratic element in favor of removal. The Charlotte *Democrat* was the mouthpiece of this sentiment, and, in the convention, Plato Durham was the leader. But on September 24, the resolution was rejected, the vote standing 53 to 56.[2]

Several efforts were made to secure definite action in the Robeson County contest. The matter was referred to the committee on privileges and elections, which reported adversely to a resolution unseating the two Democratic members, on the ground that it was necessary for the contestants to show cause. A minority report in favor of the contestants was also presented.[3] A motion to recommit with

[1] *Sentinel*, Sept. 25, 1875.         [2] *Journal*, p. 127.
[3] *Ibid.*, p. 120.

authority to take testimony elicited considerable debate and a sharp filibuster by the Republicans.  When the vote was reached, Tourgee offered an objection to the vote of the sitting members from Robeson, and upon an adverse decision by the president, the Republican side burst into an uproar of hoots, howls, and hisses which continued for two hours.  The members crowded into the aisles, cursing and threatening, and at the same time a large number of armed negroes filled the lobbies.  It was unquestionably an attempt to terrorize the Democrats, but it failed entirely and the demonstration ceased.[1]  The election case was again referred and, the Republicans opposing all efforts to have testimony taken, no further report was made.  The convention, however, allowed the contestants *per diem* and mileage for the session [2] and nineteen members entered a protest against this action.  The convention fixed the *per diem* at $4, and the mileage at ten cents.

A resolution on the judicial department, reducing the number of Supreme Court judges from five to three, provoked a sharp debate.  The Republicans chose to regard it as an attack upon the Supreme Court, but, upon the final passage of the resolution, nineteen of them voted for it.[3]  In the debate, many caustic allusions to carpetbaggers were made, and Tourgee came forward in their defence.  He made a very heated speech and involved himself in an argument in which he was worsted.  He maintained that Columbus, the Pilgrims, and even Jesus Christ were carpetbaggers.  As in 1868, he was prominent in all the debates, but contributed little to constructive work.  Josiah Turner replied to him very effectively.  Tourgee had requested that the shades might be pulled down to shut out the sunlight.

[1] *Sentinel*, Sept. 28, 1875.          [2] *Journal*, pp. 203–04.
[3] *Ibid.*, pp. 74, 90.

Turner during his speech proceeded to show to his own satisfaction and to the discomfort of Tourgee that his parallels were not well selected. Declaring that the convention wanted light, and asking that the shades might be raised, so that the light poured into Tourgee's face, he called attention to the characteristics of the carpetbaggers and declared Judas Iscariot the original carpetbagger if he might be judged by his character and acts.

Naturally the relations of the races caused much discussion, but the various ordinances on the subject were passed by good majorities. During the debate on the prohibition of intermarriage, O'Hara, a negro delegate, offered an amendment making the cohabitation of a white person with a negro a felony. This was rejected by a vote of 46 to 59. An amendment introduced by Tourgee making sexual intercourse between the races a misdemeanor was also rejected, the vote standing 43 to 61.[1]

As was to be expected with so narrow a majority, the Democrats had to be very careful of their movements. During the first ten days of the session, no Democratic delegate left the hall even for a moment without pairing with some one of the opposite party. Matters changed somewhat a little later, but great care was observed until the session closed.

To the bitter disappointment of the State as a whole, the convention took no action in regard to the debt. Every proposition in regard to it was rejected or stifled in committee. The sentiment of the majority in the body was probably favorable to the entire repudiation of the special tax bonds, but they saw no way to do it safely and thought it best to let the whole matter rest for the time being, without, however, having any intention of ever recognizing any obligation to pay them.

[1] *Journal*, pp. 263-4.

After providing for submitting the amendments to the people, the convention adjourned on October 11, the thirty-first day of the session. The total cost of the meeting was $35,061.52.

The work of the convention was of great importance. Thirty amendments were adopted out of a much larger number proposed. Sixteen of these passed unanimously, while four were adopted by a strict party vote. They may be summarized as follows:

In the Bill of Rights, a new clause authorized the legislature to forbid the carrying of concealed weapons.[1] Another declared secret political societies dangerous to the liberties of a free people, and that they should not be tolerated.[2]

In the Legislative Department, some changes were made. The time of meeting was changed from the third Monday in November to the first Monday in January. The apportionment of each house was stricken out. The terms of the members were made to begin at the time of election and the *per diem* was fixed at $4 for a period not to exceed sixty days and the mileage was fixed at ten cents. In the event of an extra session, compensation could continue for twenty days only.

Very small changes were made in the Executive Department, the direction to the legislature to establish a department of agriculture and statistics being the most important.

Quite a number of important changes were made in the Judicial Department. The number of Supreme Court justices was reduced from five to three and of Superior Court judges from twelve to nine. All were to be chosen by the people on a general ticket for a term of eight years, but it was left within the power of the legislature to return to

---

[1] Art. I, sec. 24.                    [2] Art. I, sec. 25.

election by district and to increase the number of districts and judges. The principle of rotation of the judges was adopted. The legislature was given power to alter and distribute the judicial power among the courts inferior to the Supreme Court, and to provide for election of judges. In this way control of the justices of the peace was gained by the legislature. It was also provided that any judge might be removed from office by a two-thirds vote of both houses of the legislature for mental or physical incapacity.

Under the head of Suffrage and Eligibility to office, the residence required for voting in any county was changed from sixty to ninety days. All persons convicted of a felony or infamous crime were debarred.

Other important changes were those giving the General Assembly full power over county government, including justices of the peace, setting aside for the school fund the proceeds from all fines and forfeitures, giving authority to the state government to farm out convicts, providing that a call for a constitutional convention must be submitted to the people, while amendment by the legislature was simplified by a provision that it might be done without the concurrence of the succeeding legislature. Marriage between a white person and a negro to the third generation inclusive was prohibited, and separate schools for the races were required. It was also provided that none of the amendments adopted should have the effect of vacating any office.

The convention failed to do much that the people desired, and, while what was accomplished was important, the constitution remained defective and is so to a great extent to this day.

## 2. THE CAMPAIGN OF 1876

Both parties now turned their attention to the campaign of 1876. The press, particularly the Democratic newspapers, began to devote much space to discussions of proposed candidates and a large number were mentioned for governor, among whom were A. M. Scales, J. M. Leach, W. N. H. Smith, D. G. Fowle, George Davis, David S. Reid, John A. Gilmer, and Josiah Turner. But the eyes of the whole party turned to Vance, and there was never really any doubt that he would head the Democratic ticket. In some respects, he was a dangerous candidate, for he had been in public life for a long time and had made many enemies, particularly during the war. But, on the other hand, there was no man in the State who seemed as strong in a campaign and who held such a high place in the estimation of the people.

In March, William R. Cox, the Democratic chairman, was arrested for conspiracy under the Enforcement Act, the particular offence being his telegram sent during the campaign of the preceding summer, " As you love the State hold Robeson." If this was intended to accomplish the former result of the force legislation, namely, political intimidation, the instigators were disappointed, for the Circuit Court of the United States at once dismissed the case.

The Democratic convention met in Raleigh on April 14. Every county in the State was represented and over a thousand delegates attended. In no convention of the party since the war had there been such enthusiasm or such determined confidence of success. Seven names were presented to the convention,[1] but Vance was nominated on the first ballot, only four votes being cast against him. Thomas J. Jarvis was chosen for lieutenant governor. A very strong ticket for state officers was then nominated and a reform platform adopted. Vance's nomination was well received by the people and his solemn avowal, on being

[1] D. G. Fowle, D. S. Reid, W. R. Cox, John A. Gilmer, C. C. Clark, W. F. Martin, and Z. B. Vance.

notified of his selection, that " Before God these hands are clean," began the campaign well.

The Republican convention met in Raleigh on July 12. Every county but two was represented and here also was great enthusiasm. The membership once more included a very large number of carpetbaggers and negroes, the chief reason for this being the fact that the party machinery was in the hands of federal office-holder, where it was to continue for many years, and carpetbaggers were particularly favored by the federal government. As proof of this the following facts are interesting. Two of the internal revenue collectors, ten of the thirty-six deputy collectors, seven of the forty-seven gaugers, nine of the one hundred storekeepers, two of the four registers in bankruptcy, thirteen of the thirty United States commissioners, one marshal, the postmaster at Wilmington, the postmaster at Goldsboro, and the pension agent at Raleigh were carpetbaggers.[1] The presence of the negroes is partially to be explained by a marked race division in the party caused in part by a growing recognition among the white Republicans of what negro rule meant, and in part by a growing demand of the negroes for office for themselves since they furnished the votes.

J. W. Hood, by this time a bishop of a colored Methodist Church, was temporary chairman. S. F. Phillips, who had been solicitor general of the department of justice since 1872, came to Raleigh for the convention and was its permanent president. He also represented President Grant who took an active interest in the campaign and who had indicated his wish that Judge Settle should be nominated for governor. His second choice was R. M. Douglas. There was no need of a second choice, for the convention, controlled by federal office-holders, was entirely subservient.

---

[1] *Sentinel*, Aug. 23, 1876.

Oliver H. Dockery was also a candidate with the support of John Pool, who was bitterly hostile to Grant, and before the convention assembled, seemed to have some chance of success; but when it met, it was clearly evident that he could hope for nothing and, before the result of the first ballot was announced, he withdrew in favor of Settle, who was thus unanimously chosen.[1]    W. A. Smith was nominated for lieutenant governor over Alfred Howe, a negro from New Hanover.[2]    The sharpest contest in the convention was over the nomination for secretary of state for which there were eight candidates, including Judge Watts, who saw little chance of serving another term as judge.    J. W. Albertson, of Perquimans, was successful. The rest of the ticket was then filled.[3]    The platform consisted chiefly of denunciation of the Democratic party. Phillips appointed an executive committee with T. B. Keogh, a carpetbagger, as chairman.    Eight of the members were office-holders, most of them in the federal service, and the other four had recently been so.

Soon after the campaign opened, Josiah Turner announced himself an independent candidate for governor, and a little later, an assault was made upon Republican solidarity by the candidacy of a Charlotte negro, representing the " Equal Righters."    Neither party was at all injured.

Full electoral and congressional [4] tickets were nominated,

---

[1] The unannounced vote was Settle, 176; Dockery, 64.

[2] Howe was proposed by G. W. Price, another Wilmington negro, who was himself a candidate for some place on the ticket.

[3] The other nominations were: treasurer, William H. Wheeler; auditor, John Reilly; superintendent of public instruction, J. C. Carson; attorney-general, T. L. Hargrove.

[4] The congressional nominations were: 1st district, Democratic, J. J. Yeates, Republican, D. McLindsey; 2d, —— Green, C. H. Brogden;

the Republicans showing some partiality for federal office-holders. Hyman, the negro member of Congress, was completely discredited because of his having swindled a large number of tradesmen in Washington and Baltimore,[1] and was regarded as a heavy burden for the party to carry in the face of the marked reaction against the negroes. Governor Brogden was a candidate to succeed him and, as the district was "black," took care to secure the friendship of the negroes. O'Hara, one of their leaders, was anxious to succeed Judge Settle on the Supreme Court and the governor was in a quandary. He made no appointment, however, for some time and also delayed in filling the position of superintendent of public instruction, from which Stephen D. Pool had been forced by his party. Finally, however, he appointed John Pool to the latter office. The selection of this discredited politician, who was justly held responsible for the troubles of 1870, was naturally not popular with the Democrats, while the Republican machine saw in him only a bitter opponent.[2] William T. Faircloth was appointed to succeed Judge Settle. In the meantime, the governor was nominated for Congress, a difficult feat which was only accomplished by unseating the delegation in the district convention from Warren and seating a contesting delegation which was friendly to the governor. O'Hara was nominated for elector and as it was already apparent that the negro question would play an important part in the campaign, shrewd Republicans saw in this nomi-

---

3d, A. M. Waddell, William P. Canaday; 4th, J. J. Davis, I. J. Young; 5th, A. M. Scales, James E. Boyd; 6th, W. L. Steele, O. H. Dockery; 7th, W. M. Robbins, T. J. Dula; 8th, R. B. Vance, E. P. Hampton.

[1] *Carolina Messenger*, Aug. 17, 1876.

[2] Pool had already left the regular Republican party and, after this campaign, he directed the fortunes of some political labor association in Washington.

nation a dangerous mistake.   Before the end of the campaign, he withdrew and was replaced by a white man.

The negro question entered into the campaign at the beginning and was never absent.   In it, the Democrats found an effective reply to the " bloody shirt " arguments of the Republicans, and they made no attempt to placate the negroes.   That it was a vital issue was shown by the number of negroes nominated for office in the eastern part of the State and the control of public affairs already exerted by them there.   In Jones County a majority of the commissioners were negroes and white paupers were hired out to the lowest bidders with the result that white persons were often bound to negroes.[1]   The superintendent of the Bertie County home was a negro.   In Halifax County, the board of commissioners had been for several years in the absolute control of negroes, J. E. O'Hara serving as chairman and as county attorney.   The Republican nominees for senator, two representatives, and four commissioners were all negroes.   In Craven, all the nominees except two were negroes or carpetbaggers.   In all the black counties, the expenses of government were very large and, while the taxes increased, nearly all had large debts and county warrants were far below par.   This was partly due to the fact that county officers speculated in them and purposely kept them down.   Nor was this condition of affairs true only in the black counties, for practically every Republican county was in a similar situation.   The burden of crime in the black counties was even greater than the burden of taxation.   In every one it was on the increase, and there was a strong feeling in the State that the contest of the Democrats was not merely one of reform but even of righteousness.   Republicans were influenced and there was quite an exodus

[1] Charlotte *Democrat*, May 22, 1876; July 31, 1874.

from the party ranks. Among the more prominent men who left it were Edward Cantwell, W. H. Bailey, Charles R. Thomas, and Marcus Erwin. Two of the Grant electors of 1872 stumped the State for Tilden.

Probably never before in North Carolina, and certainly never since, were so many voters reached by campaign speakers. All the electoral and congressional candidates, the candidates for state office, and many volunteers were on the stump throughout the campaign. George Davis appeared once more and exerted a large influence, particularly in the Cape Fear section, by his powerful speeches. Naturally the chief interest of the campaign centred about the candidates for governor. They were both unusually strong men and, at first, many of Vance's friends feared that he would have a difficult time on the stump with Judge Settle. Often, the reasoning element of his supporters were disappointed in his speeches, but there could be no question of his success with the people. It was early arranged that the two should meet in joint debate, and together they canvassed the State, speaking in sixty-four counties before they separated to continue the canvass alone. In this latter part of the campaign, each made twelve speeches. Vance is said to have reached one hundred and twenty-five thousand people. Judge Settle profited by the joint debate, so far as the number of his auditors was concerned, for the name of Vance, the " War Governor," was one to conjure with in the State, and enormous crowds came to see and hear him. After Settle left him, Vance's crowds were as large as ever, but there was a decided falling off in the size of the Republican meetings.

In the joint debates, Vance fulfilled the promise of his campaign of 1864 with Holden. No words can describe the power of the man before a North Carolina audience. J. P. Caldwell's description of him is entirely true. " As a

popular orator and debater there has been in North Carolina no man who approached him. Never has the State had
a son who could so sway the multitude. His style of address was unique and never to be forgotten. I pass by the
inimitable humor which lightened up his speeches. While
to the heedless this was the distinguishing feature of
Vance's oratory, it was indeed the merest incident of his
public addresses. His arguments were ponderous, distinguished for originality of proposition and power of statement. He was a thinker, a logician, and while no thought
escaped his tongue that had not already been subjected to
the crucible of reason, no faulty argument could be advanced by an opponent and its weakness escape detection by
him. His alertness was amazing; his readiness will ever
remain a proverb in the State. He was never taken un-
awares; never found without an answer, and it a sufficient
one. He was capable of the loftiest eloquence, and adorned
with handsomest decorations whatever subject he chose
to. But amidst references to his humor, his quickness, his
aptness and eloquence, the fact should not be lost sight of
that these were but the adornments of what were masterful
intellectual performances; for he was a great intellect who
himself set no store by the arts of speech, except in so far
as they might serve to give emphasis to the grave argument
he would enforce." [1]

Judge Settle was a very magnetic man, an eloquent
speaker, and a powerful debater, but he was at a disadvantage throughout the campaign on account of Vance's personal popularity, and because a majority of the white people

---

[1] Governor Holden's mature opinion of Vance is interesting, particularly in view of his bitter public abuse of him. "And I also state un-
reservedly, having said thus much, that Zebulon Baird Vance, their
leader in all these things [North Carolina's part in the civil war], was
and is, their foremost man in all their annals, old and new. I know
whereof I speak." *Memoir of W. W. Holden*, p. 29.

of the State were intensely aroused against his party. Vance was adroit and never lost an opportunity to rout his opponent. An example of this was seen when Settle produced copies of Vance's war letters, furnished by the War Department where the letter book was kept. Vance asked to see the letters, and, displaying them, called attention to the fact that there were numerous omissions indicated in them. He said that he was denied access to his own letters, but that the United States government allowed Settle to use garbled copies against him. The sympathy of the crowd was instantly drawn to Vance. Settle's valid arguments were usually nullified by Vance's ready wit and so soon as the former began to "wave the bloody shirt," and blame Vance for the horrors of the war, the latter would retort with some question involving his opponent's official endorsement of the Kirk war. He also had ten questions with which he tormented Judge Settle. They were:

1. Was Holden's suspension of the writ of *habeas corpus* legal?
2. Which of the constitutional amendments are good?
3. How did the South get out of the Union?
4. Were the reconstruction acts constitutional?
5. Can Congress confer the right of suffrage?
6. Was the Louisiana outrage constitutional?
7. Was Judge Settle not elected to the Supreme bench by fraud?
8. Does Judge Settle approve Grant's administration?
9. Does he approve of the civil rights act?
10. Was desertion from the Confederate army right?

These questions were never answered.

Judge Settle in time became convinced that his cause was hopeless and, in consequence, he often lost his temper. On one occasion, when he was rudely interrupted, he burst out, "You Ku Klux scoundrels, you infernal fiends of hell."

Vance was always insistent upon Settle's having a fair hearing and was usually successful in obtaining it for him, but he never lost an opportunity to prod his opponent with the hope of putting him on the defensive or causing him to lose his temper.[1]   But the debate in the main was on a high plane and echoes of it can still be heard in the State.   It marked a return to the political methods of an older and better day and it was a hopeful and healthy sign that such a campaign could be conducted and, better still, that its spirit, generally speaking, should have been so admirable. At the end of it, the two competitors parted as warm friends,[2] and each had won new laurels.   The debates were powerful and instructive in spite of the constant references to each other's record.   Not only state issues were discussed but national questions were debated at length.

Among the events of interest in the campaign, was the publication in the Raleigh *News* of the account of an interview between Rev. C. T. Bailey and ex-Governor Holden, in which the former said that Governor Holden had expressed to him his belief that the death of John W. Stephens had been brought about by enemies in his own party.   Holden promptly denied ever having made such a statement, but it was used with some effect by the Democrats.   The same charge had been made at the time and this seemed confirmatory evidence.[3]   Still more spicy, were the revela-

[1] The most memorable example of this occurred in an eastern county when a number of pretty girls came up and kissed Vance who at once turned to Settle and, pointing to a group of negro women on the Republican side, said, "Judge, aren't you going to salute your fair supporters?"

[2] Settle said at the close of the campaign, "Vance is absolutely a truthful man, for in our long heated campaign all over the State he never quibbled or prevaricated."   Dowd, *Life of Vance*, p. 184.

[3] Whatever may have been the facts of the interview, the explanation of Stephens' death was of course incorrect."   Cf. *supra*, pp. 473–5.

tions of Republican methods in 1868 and 1869, made by Deweese who was living in comfortable retirement in Cleveland, Ohio, upon the proceeds of those methods. In the Cleveland papers and later in the *Sentinel*,[1] he published long letters containing considerable campaign material. But these two incidents were far less important than they would have been a short two years before. They belonged to the past, and now all eyes were turned to the future. Not that the events of the past were not used as arguments in the campaign; far from it. But there was such venality and corruption, so much oppression and wrong, to select arguments from, that simple incidents tended to decrease in importance.

The election was very quiet all over the State and there were few charges of fraud in connection with it. One interesting happening not generally known marked the day in Raleigh. Late in the afternoon, the Democratic chairman received a telegram with the information that General Kilpatrick was coming to count the vote of the State for Hayes. No information was given as to how this purpose was to be accomplished. Wild as the report was, the record of the past twelve years contained so much of political violence and illegality that the news caused some excitement. Kilpatrick got off the train outside the town limits and drove to the hotel in a closed carriage and, without registering, went to the room of Thomas B. Keogh, the Republican state chairman. The news of his arrival spread and a large crowd assembled in the street before the hotel. Wild talk commenced, the crowd grew more angry as the rumor of his mission spread, and finally made a rush into the lobby of the hotel, and, but for the presence of mind of Basil Manly, the chief of police, would probably have disgraced

---

[1] Issue of Sept. 2, 1876.

the State by wreaking summary vengeance upon General Kilpatrick for the acts committed by him when he came to the State in 1865 with Sherman's army and, to a lesser extent, for his supposed mission.

The election resulted in a complete Democratic victory. The State and national tickets were chosen, and every candidate for Congress but one was elected, Governor Brogden of course carrying his district for the Republicans. Vance received a majority of 13,009 out of a total vote of 233,521. Tilden's majority was 16,178 out of a total vote of 228,602, which exceeded that of 1872 by 25,000. All the amendments were ratified by good majorities. The legislature was overwhelmingly Democratic.

The cause of peace, order, and good government had triumphed. Righteousness, by righteous methods, had at last prevailed and Reconstruction in North Carolina was ended.

### 3. ECONOMIC AND FINANCIAL CONDITIONS, 1870-1876

If anyone in North Carolina had a lingering belief in 1870 that Conservative control of the State would mean prompt economic regeneration, it was soon dispelled. Undoubtedly there was more public confidence abroad in the land; the decline in the value of property ceased, but the state debt was still in existence; government, in spite of Conservative retrenchment and economy, was still expensive; and poverty was still general. Labor conditions for a short while promised to be even more chaotic, thanks to the campaign which had been made among the negroes to imbue them with the belief that Conservative success meant the restoration of slavery, but this fear was soon dispelled and, after being aroused again in 1872 and 1874, sank into a sleep from which it has never been entirely awakened, although the argument was employed with some effect by the Republicans in 1875 and in 1884. It was used in every campaign until the passage in 1900 of the constitutional amendment which limited the suffrage.

The prostration of the State was too serious to be cured by a mere political change, important and necessary as that change was in this case. Good government was a necessary tonic, but years of care and struggle were inevitable before full economic health could be restored. The constitution which had greatly increased the cost of government remained unamended, the people fearing that a convention might mean federal interference and in any event would be an immediate expense. Many preferred to endure the evils caused by it if only peace might prevail for a time.

The Conservatives, once in power, began a policy of rigid economy. Salaries were reduced, better terms made for supplies furnished, and, during the first year, the expense of government was reduced by more than one hundred thousand dollars.[1] Within the next few years, other reductions were made and the expenses of the state gov-

[1] The following table contains some of the items of saving:

| | |
|---|---|
| Executive | $2,100.00 |
| State | 3,656.25 |
| Auditor | 2,887.50 |
| Treasurer | 2,807.20 |
| Public Works | 3,410.15 |
| Public Instruction | 4,141.60 |
| Attorney General | 3,450.00 |
| Adjutant General | 900.00 |
| Capitol Square | 3,000.00 |
| State Library | 200.00 |
| Fuel | 1,825.00 |
| Contingencies | 21,670.04 |
| Legislature | 43,484.53 |
| Total | $93,532.27 |

ernment were substantially reduced.[1]  In spite of the rigid economy practiced by the Conservatives, their expenditures on state institutions steadily increased to the great benefit of the State.[2]

[1] The following tables give certain comparisons for the entire period:

|  | 1868–1869. | 1869–1870. | 1870–1871. |
|---|---|---|---|
| General Assembly | $269,212.92 | $161,431.70 | $117,849.17 |
| Printing | 34,682.06 | 34,503.43 | 22,292.01 |
| Contingencies | 76,606.64 | 57,884.82 | 36,274.78 |
| Ordinary | 123,444.32 | 146,880.32 | 94,866.08 |
| Impeachment | ......... | ......... | 13,098.08 |
| Militia | 1,800.00 | 74,742.70 | ......... |
| Total | $505,745.94 | $475,442.97 | $284,380.12 |

|  | 1871–1872. | 1872–1873. | 1873–1874. |
|---|---|---|---|
| General Assembly | $81,279.20 | $87,960.20 | $81,436.60 |
| Printing | 14,448.91 | 10,264.25 | 13,196.14 |
| Contingencies | 24,266.25 | 26,816.50 | 30,267.14 |
| Ordinary | 93,176.83 | 97,890.22 | 100,000.00 |
| Total | $213,171.19 | $222,931.17 | $224,899.88 |

|  | 1874–1875. | 1875–1876. |
|---|---|---|
| General Assembly | $109,234.80 | ......... |
| Printing | 14,845.45 | $9,320.12 |
| Contingencies | 22,885.29 | 18,054.62 |
| Ordinary | 146,545.63 | 90,430.18 |
| Convention | 10,709.60 | 15,596.98 |
| Total | $304,220.77 | $133,401.90 |

Total for two years and five months Republican rule, $981,188.91.

Total for six years Conservative rule, $1,383,005.03.

[2] The comparative expenses are shown in the following tables:

|  | 1869. | 1870. | 1871. | 1872. |
|---|---|---|---|---|
| University | ...... | ..... | ...... | ...... |
| Penitentiary | $21,000 | $74,000 | $113,500 | $107,956 |
| Deaf and Dumb | 37,000 | 39,218 | 48,281 | 48,750 |
| Insane | 66,267 | 64,872 | 88,826 | 87,844 |
| Total | $124,267 | $178,090 | $250,607 | $244,550 |

|  | 1873. | 1874. | 1875. | 1876. |
|---|---|---|---|---|
| University | ...... | ...... | $3,750 | $7,500 |
| Penitentiary | $97,913 | $88,000 | 104,998 | 108,166 |
| Deaf and Dumb | 50,000 | 46,125 | 48,875 | 44,500 |
| Insane | 93,211 | 50,947 | 122,406 | 174,603 |
| Total | $241,124 | $185,072 | $280,029 | $334,769 |

During the whole period there was a slow rise in values, accompanied by a fall in the rate of taxation as can be seen from the accompanying tables:

TABLE OF PROPERTY VALUES:

|  | 1871. | 1872. | 1873. | 1874. |
|---|---|---|---|---|
| Land | $69,442,946 | $70,132,370 | $76,959,193 | $74,489,707 |
| Town Lots | 12,717,117 | 13,855,078 | 16,652,131 | 16,414,319 |
| Live Stock | 17,467,685 | 17,464,685 | 18,214,692 | 14,888,740 |
| Personalty | 23,879,880 | 23,839,430 | 31,897,797 | 34,160,595 |
|  | $123,507,628 | $125,291,563 | $143,723,813 | $139,953,361 |

|  | 1875. | 1876.[1] |
|---|---|---|
| Land | $75,309,799 | $74,221,398 |
| Town Lots | 17,047,321 | 17,458,520 |
| Live Stock | 16,683,096 | 16,130,509 |
| Personalty | 43,505,807 | 40,753,781 |
|  | $152,546,023 | $148,564,208 |

TABLE OF TAX RATES.

|  | 1871. | 1872. | 1873. | 1874. | 1875. | 1876. |
|---|---|---|---|---|---|---|
| Poll | $0.90 | $1.05 | $1.05 | $0.95 | $0.95 | $0.95 |
| General Property. | .30 | .1666 | .20 | .1666 | .1466 | .1466 |
| Special | .22 | .1833 | .22 | .15 | .15 | .15 |
| Income | 1.00 | 1.00 | 1.00 | 1.00 | 2.00 | 2.00 |

As the state taxes fell, the county taxes began to loom large. The most extravagant and worst governed were the black counties. The following table shows the figures for these counties in 1873:

[1] The author has been unable to discover any reason for the falling-off of values in 1876.

|  | Tax Valuation. | County Tax. |
|---|---|---|
| Bertie | $1,709,876 | $12,124.66 |
| Caswell | 1,864,706 | 7,911.73 |
| Chowan | 977,241 | 6,332.50 |
| Craven | 2,270,678 | 36,412.83 |
| Edgecombe | 4,957,053 | 29,893.52 |
| Franklin | 2,527,391 | 19,893.34 |
| Granville | 3,590,077 | 21,893.66 |
| Greene | 1,407,145 | 12,169.10 |
| Halifax | 3,069,492 | 19,099.98 |
| Hertford | 1,280,974 | 10,736.61 |
| Jones | 758,500 | 6,812.16 |
| Lenoir | 1,553,403 | 12,750.10 |
| New Hanover | 6,010,904 | 47,422.71 |
| Northampton | 2,507,192 | 16,392.69 |
| Perquimans | 1,165,546 | 8,779.88 |
| Richmond | 1,827,285 | 19,370.71 |
| Warren | 2,236,766 | 14,436.07 |
| Total | $39,714,229 | $302,522.25 |

In all the black counties there was not only extravagance but dishonesty. Graft of every kind was general, and the public benefited but little. Edgecombe County is an example. It was a typical black county having a colored voting majority of 1,794. The county tax for 1875 was distributed as follows:

| General Fund | $15,005.92 |
|---|---|
| Poor Fund | 10,598.17 |
| School Fund | 8,773,68 |
| Total | $34,377.77 |

Against the general fund and poor fund, orders were issued as follows:

| Poor | $9,444.95 |
|---|---|
| Juries | 881.86 |
| Prosecutions | 786.93 |
| Prisoners in jail | 6,480.42 |
| Bridges | 2,664.61 |
| Miscellaneous | 6,331.17 |
| Total | $26,589.94 |

The deficit was met as might be expected from the school fund.

This condition was not confined entirely to the black counties. Every Republican county in the east was governed in the same way. Bladen paid in the period between 1868 and 1876 more than one hundred thousand dollars in county taxes. Both the sheriff and treasurer were defaulters and county orders were not worth ten cents on the dollar.

The closing years of the period saw some improvement along all lines. Life became more settled. Political animosities and those growing out of the war began to die away. The labor problem was not so great as it had been immediately after the war. The convention of 1875 accomplished a good deal in the way of reform, and good and, to North Carolina almost as important, cheap government was well established. All of these things tended to economic and social progress and improvement.

During the entire period the debt was a cause of great anxiety to the people. There was no desire to repudiate the old debt, but there was strong determination not to pay the special tax bonds. Even to pay the old debt with its accrued interest was beyond the power of the State and hence there was a strong desire to scale it. The legislature of 1874 made a proposition to the bondholders, but very few accepted it and the plan came to nothing. There was much disappointment that the convention of 1875 did not take up the question, for the belief was general that there could be no genuine prosperity until such a settlement was made. Finally the legislature of 1879 took up the matter and brought about a compromise, by which the bonds were grouped into three classes and provision was made for their exchange for new bonds.[1] Class One consisted of the bonds

[1] *Laws*, 1879, chap. xcviii.

issued prior to May 20, 1861, which were made convertible
at forty per cent. Class Two consisted of bonds issued
after the war, under authority of acts passed before the
war, and were convertible at twenty-five per cent. Class
Three was made up of bonds issued under the funding acts
of 1866 and 1868 which were convertible at fifteen per cent.
None of the interest was recognized nor were the bonds
issued during the war for internal improvements. Adequate provision was made for the payment of the interest
on the new bonds. The amount outstanding in each class
was:

| | |
|---|---:|
| Class I | $5,477,400 |
| Class II | 3,261,045 |
| Class III | 3,888,600 |
| Total | $12,627,045 |

Under the terms of the act, the privilege of exchange expired in 1883, but the time was extended by each succeeding legislature until 1909. By 1893, bonds had been exchanged as follows:

| Class. | Bonds redeemed. | Bonds issued. | Bonds left outstanding. |
|---|---|---|---|
| I | $5,159,400 | $2,063,760 | $318,000 |
| II | 2,721,345 | 680,336.25 | 539,700 |
| III | 3,525,300 | 528,795 | 363,300 |
| Total. | $11,406,045 | $3,272,891.25 | $1,221,000 |

By December 1, 1909, $154,109 additional in consolidated
bonds had been issued in exchange for old bonds.[1]

The creditors of the State generally recognized that these
terms were the best that could be obtained or even expected, and most of them accepted. Some declined, and in

[1] The classification for those later than 1893 is unavailable.

1901, Schafer Brothers, a firm of brokers in New York, who owned a large number of bonds of the second class, gave ten of them to the State of South Dakota which brought suit in the Supreme Court of the United States for their recovery. Owing to the circumstances connected with the gift of the bonds, the suit was regarded in North Carolina as an attempt to bring a test case intended as a step in securing the payment of the special tax bonds. For that reason, and because there was a general feeling that the compromise refused had been a fair one, the suit was contested. Politics entered into the question as well. The validity of the bonds was upheld by the court,[1] and, as they contained a lien upon the stock owned by the State in the North Carolina Railroad, collection was easy. That the bonds were valid is beyond all doubt, and the State was in error when, by contesting the suit, it assisted in confusing them in the popular mind with the special tax bonds.

The act of the legislature of 1879 in compromising the debt, excepted from its provisions the bonds issued to aid in the construction of the North Carolina Railroad. As a result of a suit in the United States Circuit Court, the stock of the State in this corporation had been sequestrated to pay the interest on these bonds and it was a settled fact that the stock would be liable for the payment of the principal. Therefore a committee of three, appointed to settle this debt, succeeded in reaching a compromise at about eighty per cent of the debt with interest.

The same legislature took the final step in the settlement of the debt by submitting to the people a constitutional amendment forbidding the legislature to levy or collect any tax to pay the debt incurred by the convention of 1868 or the legislatures of 1868, 1869, and 1870, except those bonds

---

[1] South Dakota *v.* North Carolina, 192 U. S., 286.

issued to fund the interest on the old debt, without first
submitting the question to the people for ratification.[1]    This
amendment was ratified by the people at the next election,
and its constitutionality has since been affirmed by the
United States Supreme Court.[2]    Since that time, a number
of attempts have been made to secure payment either by
suit or by giving the bonds to States.    For some reason,
North Carolina bonds have seemed attractive, and within
the past few years, an association with headquarters in New
York has been very active in its efforts to intimidate the
State into paying the bonds.    They have been offered to
New York, Rhode Island, Nevada, and other States, but
every attempt to bring them before the Supreme Court of
the United States has failed.    There is no likelihood of their
ever being paid.    Even if they come before the court, a
thing which is exceedingly doubtful, the facts of the case
against their validity are sufficient to secure a decision in
favor of the State.    If for no other reason, the lack of
legality in the election of the legislature authorizing their
issue would be sufficient to warrant a decision against them.
Interestingly enough, the special tax bonds were the chief
issue on the surface of the state campaign of 1910, and
there is strong likelihood that they will cause discussion
again.    But the people of the State will have to be made
anew before they will at the ballot-box register their assent
to the payment of these peculiarly hated bonds.

#### 4. GENERAL CONCLUSIONS

The crime of Reconstruction is to-day generally recognized by all who care to look facts squarely in the face.    To
a close observer of Southern conditions, the heinousness of
the offence is increased by the knowledge that the South of

---

[1] *Laws*, 1879, chap. cclxviii.

[2] Baltzer *v*. North Carolina, 161 U. S., 240.

the present time is still laboring under the burdens thereby imposed. It has made many a Southerner fail to comprehend the wonderful benefits which have really come to the South from emancipation, and it has drawn the sections apart when, with the barrier of slavery removed, they should have come together. So far as North Carolina was concerned, the partisan plan was one of greatest folly. But for Reconstruction, the State would to-day, so far as one can estimate human probabilities, be solidly Republican. This was clearly evident in 1865, when the attempted restoration of President Johnson put public affairs in the hands of former Whigs who then had no thought of joining in politics their old opponents, the Democrats. So strong was the opposition to such a thing that it was eight years before there was an avowed Democratic party in the State, the Whigs who formed and led the Conservative party having so decided a detestation for the very name. To-day, there are men in the State who regularly vote the party ticket but who will not acknowledge themselves to be Democrats. It was this element that the Republican party rejected for the solid negro vote. The latter was soon lost, for the negroes in the mass proving to be lacking in political capacity and knowledge, were driven, intimidated, bought, and sold, the playthings of politicians, until finally their very so-called right to vote became the sore spot of the body politic. Their participation in politics gave the Democratic party the preponderance of the talent and character of the population and, for many years, a safe majority of the white voters. Coming into power as a result of the disgust of the people for the infamy of the Republican administration of the government, the party remained in control of affairs because it proved itself fit to rule, and because there was no hope of decent government outside of it. From time to time it would either have been forced to a more progressive spirit, or would have lost control had the people been willing to trust the opposition. The result was that politics was embittered and freedom of political thought and action was restricted to such an extent that a condition of affairs existed that bore a striking resemblance to that of the fifties, when slavery stifled freedom of speech and thought, with the one difference that in the later case, the very preservation of good government was at stake.

No better description of the origin of the Republican party in North Carolina can be given than one written just at the close of Reconstruction by the ablest of the aliens who came to the State. Said Tourgee in 1878:

The Republican party was never indigenous to Southern soil. In truth, it has never become acclimated there, but has remained from the first an exotic. A few thousand of the white people of North Carolina accepted it in 1868, simply as the equivalent of the Unionism which has always held so dear a place in their hearts. A few hundred Adullamites accepted it as the alternative of political bankruptcy and the shibboleth of profitable power; and a few score of earnest natives accepted it with a clear perception of its basic principles, and a *bona fide* belief in their beneficence and righteousness. A few hundred carpet-baggers received it as the spontaneous product of their native States, the sentiments for which they fought and bled. The African race in bulk received it as the incarnation and sheet anchor of that liberty which they had just tested. This was the Republican party of North Carolina. Ignorance, poverty, and inexperience were its chief characteristics. That it was bitterly opposed and hated by the democracy, whose boast that it monopolized the wealth and intelligence of the State cannot be gainsayed [sic] by the most devoted radical, was, under the circumstances, the most natural thing upon earth. That this malignity should extend to the business and social relations of life, is hardly a matter of surprise. That it did much to verify the adage, "Give a dog an ill name and he will soon deserve it," cannot be questioned. That the old unionists began to drop away from it as soon as they found that republicanism meant more than unionism, was to have been expected. That the old should die, and the young should abandon a party which it required the faith and nerve of a martyr to adhere to, was a thing to have been anticipated. When its power began to wane, the Adullamites began to desert; the number of carpet-baggers became, by degrees, beautifully less; and only the few true believers, with a few more who still gambled for place and power against desperate odds, remained to man the water-logged hulk upon the leeshore, where she finally stranded and went to pieces more hopelessly than the *Metropolis* on the shoals of Currituck.[1]

The Republican party in North Carolina, however, differed from the organization in the other Southern States in that it had always a larger number of able and respectable members. There are a number of reasons for this, the chief of which are to be found in the facts that political sentiment was not nearly so solidified in North Carolina just before the war as it was in the other Southern States, and that the downfall of the party came so rapidly after Reconstruction began that many had not been driven from its ranks by the corruption of those whom it had placed in power. The corruption, having been ended by the overthrow of the party, ceased to repel, and a large number of members were thus saved to it. But the party machinery fell into the hands of federal office-holders and has been there practically ever since. Not until their grip upon it is broken, is the party likely to make serious inroads upon Democratic strength.[2]

---

[1] *The "C" Letters*, p. 24.

[2] President Taft in 1906, while he was Secretary of War, said at the Republican convention in Greensboro: " In my judgment the Republican Party in North Carolina would be much stronger as a voting party if all the Federal offices were filled by Democrats. . . . As long, how-

Their leadership has been singularly lacking in ability, but despite the fact, the party has always been able to put their opponents on their mettle and, more often than not, divide congressional representation with them. In 1894, by a fusion with the Populists, the Republicans won control of the legislature, and two years later elected a fusion state ticket, a Populist and a Republican senator, a majority of the members of Congress, and most of the judges. By wise exercise of power, they might have retained control, but the experience of the past had taught them little if anything, and it soon became apparent to the State that the net result of Republican victory was corruption, misgovernment, and control by the negroes of the eastern part of the State. An example of the doings of the legislature may be found in its action in 1895, when it refused to adjourn on Lee's and Washington's birthdays, but did adjourn in honor of Fred Douglass when the news of his death was received. This may have been a fair expression of the sentiments of the majority, but it was also, to put it in the mildest form, poor politics, and there were other acts just as insane. In 1898, upon the issue of white supremacy, the Democrats were able to win back the support of the rank and file of the Populists and elect the legislature. A constitutional amendment, restricting the suffrage by an educational qualification accompanied by a " grandfather clause " was adopted and submitted to the people and ratified in 1900. In the same year, the Democrats elected their state ticket. An educational revival followed, since the party had pledged itself to maintain an efficient system of

ever, as the Republican Party in the Southern States shall represent little save a factional chase for Federal offices in which business men and men of substance in the community have no desire to enter, . . . we may expect the present political conditions of the South to continue."

schools which would in the future protect everyone from disfranchisement regardless of color. The negro has largely ceased to be a political question, and there is in the State to-day as a consequence more political freedom than at any time since Reconstruction. As yet the Republican party, largely on account of its leadership, has apparently not drawn to itself many Democrats, but that it will do so, when the federal office-holders cease to control, is on the other hand scarcely in the field of doubt and no better thing could happen to the State.

There are two other legacies of Reconstruction that should be mentioned. The first is a constitution never suited to the needs of the State and, in spite of amendments, less so as the years go by. There are strong indications that before many years a revision of it, already begun, will be made complete. The other is a strong dislike of Northern interference in Southern affairs which has produced a States' Rights sentiment that is scarcely less intense than that invoked in defence of slavery. It is a protest against anything that might threaten a repetition of the past, when selfish politicians, backed by the federal government, for party purposes attempted to Africanize the State and deprive the people through misrule and oppression of most that life held dear.

# INDEX

## A

Abbott, I. B., 593n.

Abbott, Joseph C., agreement with Holden, 362; agent for Swepson, 431, 437-8; elected to Senate, 292-3; candidate for re-election, 352, 563, 571; in convention 1868, 253, 258, 263-4; on N. C., 212; quarrels, 395-6; mentioned, 246, 249, 255-6, 268n., 285, 348, 350n., 386, 397, 405, 408, 416, 418, 487-8, 493, 528n., 562, 572, 585, 588

Adams, Henderson, characterized, 414; quarrel with court, 382-3; mentioned, 497

Advance, the, work of, 73-4

Akerman, Amos T., 527, 567

Alamance County, Ku Klux in, 398, 462, 464-5, 467-71, 477, 483, 485, 487, 514, 549; Kirk's force in, 504, 507, 516, 518-9, 531; militia in, 483; in insurrection, 512, 533; mentioned, 508-9, 535, 545-6, 551

Albertson, J. W., 600n., 646

Albright, W. R., 508, 517

Alden, "Judge", 379, 386

Allison, R. M., 531n.

Almy, George C., 298n.

Alvord, J. W., 211n.

Ames, General Adalbert, 158n.

Ames, General J. W., 158n.

Ames, James S., 362n.

Amnesty proclamation, 108

Anderson, J. S., 541n., 594n.

Anderson, George B., 35n.

Andrews, J. W., 254n.

Anthony, George, 462

Apple, Macon, 462

Argo, Thomas M., 440n.

Armfield, R. F., 605.

Armistead, Lewis F., 35n.

Arrington, A. H., 178n.

Ashe, Samuel A., 631n.

Ashe, Thomas S., in Confederate Senate, 66; candidate for governor, 280; mentioned, 178n., 279n., 587n.

Ashe, W. S., Confederate agent, 46

Ashley, S. S., characterized, 414; in convention 1868, 253, 262; editor, 538; supt. pub. instruction, 611, 616; university trustee, 624; mentioned, 258n., 280n., 285, 382, 388, 405, 613, 615, 627

Askew, W. F., 445-6

Atlantic, Tennessee & Ohio Railroad, 445, 448-9

Avera, W. H., 594n.

Avery, A. C., 362n., 376, 462, 525n., 639

Avery, General R., 165

Avery, Waightstill W., 11, 14n., 17, 34n., 37, 49

## B

Badger, George E., in convention 1861, 27-32; letter of, 42; mentioned, 25n., 26, 405

Badger, Richard C., counsel for Holden, 508, 546-7; opposes use of troops, 497; mentioned, 362n., 446, 497-8, 510, 553, 561, 596-7, 637n., 639

Bailey, C. T., 652

Bailey, J. L., 280n.

Bailey, J. W., 86n.

Bailey, W. H., 569, 600n., 649

Bain, Hope, 179n., 211n.

Baker, Lawrence S., 35n., 596n.

Ball, Mrs. Isham, 166

Bancroft, George, 85

Barnett, John C., 326n.

Barnett, L. C., 534-5, 556n.

Barringer, D. M., at Peace Conference, 17-8; mentioned, 49, 585, 639

Barringer, Rufus, 35n., 569

669

INDEX 671